Pro .NET 1.1 Network Programming

Second Edition

CHRISTIAN NAGEL, AJIT MUNGALE, VINOD KUMAR,
NAUMAN LAGHARI, ANDREW KROWCZYK,
TIM PARKER, SRINIVASA SIVAKUMAR,
AND ALEXANDRU SERBAN

Apress®

Pro .NET 1.1 Network Programming, Second Edition

ISBN (pbk): 1-59059-345-6

Printed and bound in the United States of America 9 8 7 6 5 4 3 2 1

Lead Editor: Dominic Shakeshaft
Technical Reviewer: Alexandru Serban
Editorial Board: Steve Anglin, Dan Appleman, Ewan Buckingham, Gary Cornell, Tony Davis, Jason Gilmore, Chris Mills, Dominic Shakeshaft, Jim Sumser
Project Manager: Sofia Marchant
Copy Edit Manager: Nicole LeClerc
Copy Editors: Marilyn Smith, Ami Knox
Production Manager: Kari Brooks
Production Editor: Janet Vail
Compositor and Artist: Diana Van Winkle
Proofreader: Greg Teague
Indexer: Brenda Miller
Cover Designer: Kurt Krames
Manufacturing Manager: Tom Debolski

Distributed to the book trade in the United States by Springer-Verlag New York, LLC, 233 Spring Street, Sixth Floor, New York, NY 10013 and outside the United States by Springer-Verlag GmbH & Co. KG, Tiergartenstr. 17, 69112 Heidelberg, Germany.

In the United States: phone 1-800-SPRINGER, fax 201-348-4505, e-mail `orders@springer-ny.com`, or visit `http://www.springer-ny.com`. Outside the United States: fax +49 6221 345229, e-mail `orders@springer.de`, or visit `http://www.springer.de`.

For information on translations, please contact Apress directly at 2560 Ninth Street, Suite 219, Berkeley, CA 94710. Phone 510-549-5930, fax 510-549-5939, e-mail `info@apress.com`, or visit `http://www.apress.com`.

The source code for this book is available to readers at `http://www.apress.com` in the Downloads section. You will need to answer questions pertaining to this book in order to successfully download the code.

Contents at a Glance

Contents

About the Authors

CHRISTIAN NAGEL has about 20 years of experience as developer and software architect. He is working as an independent trainer and consultant offering courses, seminars, and coaching, based on Microsoft .NET technologies.

Christian started his computing career with PDP 11 and VAX/VMS platforms, covering a variety of languages and platforms. Since 2000 he has been working with .NET and C# developing and architecting distributed solutions. Certified as a Microsoft Certified Trainer (MCT), Microsoft Certified Solution Developer (MCSD), Microsoft Certified System Engineer (MCSE), and MSF (Microsoft Solutions Framework) Practitioner, he furthermore loves writing and enjoys a good reputation as an author of several .NET books, such as *Professional C#, Professional .NET Network Programming, C# Web Services*, and *Enterprise Services with the .NET Framework*. In his role as Microsoft Regional Director and MVP for Visual C#, he speaks at international conferences. Christian is also known as Regional Manager of INETA Europe (International .NET User Group Association), and since 2004 he has become an associate of Thinktecture, a team of experts who offer consultancy and training about .NET technologies.

You can contact Christian via his web site at `http://www.christiannagel.com`.

AJIT MUNGALE has extensive experience with Microsoft technologies and has worked with almost all languages and technologies. He also has experience with IBM products, including IBM WebSphere and MQ. He is author of a couple other books and published articles on Microsoft .NET.

ANDREW KROWCZYK is a software architect and MCSD.NET working in the Chicago area. He currently works heavily with cutting edge .NET technologies. Andrew's area of expertise includes Enterprise applications and theoretical computer science. He also works as an adjunct faculty member at Elmhurst College. He can be reached at `KROWCZYK@I-NETWAY.COM`.

VINOD KUMAR is a Microsoft MVP from Chennai, India. He has authored many books on Microsoft technologies, such as `MOBILE APPLICATION DEVELOPMENT USING .NET` and *Planning, Implementing, and Maintaining a Windows Server 2003 Active Directory Infrastructure*. He also owns a site named .NET Force (`HTTP://WWW.DOTNETFORCE.COM`). The site provides the latest information and publishes original articles on .NET technology. He can be reached at `VINOD@DOTNETFORCE.COM`.

S. SRINIVASA SIVAKUMAR works as a solution architect for Microsoft Corporation India and is an author and speaker specializing in Web and mobile solutions using .NET technologies.

About the Technical Reviewer

ALEXANDRU SERBAN is a software engineer for MMC Softlabs, building enterprise management information systems for large, geographically distributed companies.

Alexandru started his addiction to computers when he first saw video game machines. He started his programming career at the age of 9, when he bought his first Z80 processor–based computer and started learning BASIC. He then moved toward languages like Visual Basic, C, and C++. He graduated in computer science and automatic systems. Now, he specializes in network communications, and he is very enthusiastic about C# and the .NET Framework, which he strongly believes is set to revolutionize programming.

In his free time, he likes to drive and travel, in the summer to the sea, and in the winter to the mountains, where he hits the slopes with a snowboard.

Introduction

Network programming is one of the core tasks of enterprise-level development—the need for disparate computers to communicate efficiently and securely, whether within the same building, or across the world, remains fundamental to the success of many systems. With the .NET 1.1 Framework comes a new set of classes for tackling networking tasks.

These classes make common network programming tasks very easy and straightforward, as they provide a layered, extensible, and managed implementation of Internet services that can be integrated into your applications.

After reading this book, you will be a confident .NET 1.1 network programmer who understands all the underlying protocols. The current set of protocols supported by .NET 1.1 classes is limited to the transport-level protocols TCP and UDP, and the application-level protocols HTTP and SMTP. In this book, we provide not only full coverage of these classes, but also examples of implementing application-level protocols in .NET—so this book will be vital reading for anyone who needs to use a protocol that isn't currently supported by .NET 1.1, as well as for anyone who wants to get to grips with the predefined protocols.

Who Is This Book For?

You do not need any prior knowledge of network programming to read this book, because you will learn the basic and then more advanced networking concepts as you follow each chapter. You may already be familiar with network programming from another environment, of course—in which case, you will still find the pace strong enough for the book to prove valuable.

We're going to assume you have a working knowledge of C# to read the examples and code solutions we provide. Sometimes we will also present techniques that are specifically suitable to the C# language.

What Is in This Book?

We begin this book by introducing you to some of the basic concepts and protocols of networking in **Chapter 1**. Whatever your requirements from network programming—whether you plan to develop server applications running as Windows Services offering data for clients using a custom protocol, whether you want to write client applications that request data from web servers, or whether you want to create multicasting applications or applications using mailing functionality—this chapter is your first port of call.

We begin Chapter 1 with a look at the physical network, and the hardware used in network communication. We will start with an introduction to the types of networks in use today, like local area networks (LANs), wide area networks (WANs), and metropolitan area networks (MANs); and network architectures and network devices, such as network interface cards (NICs), routers, hubs, and bridges. Then, we'll take a look at the OSI seven-layer model, and how the TCP/IP protocol suite fits into the OSI layers. After that, we introduce you to the various network, Internet, and e-mail protocols, such as IP, TCP, UDP, ICMP, IGMP, FTP, HTTP, SMTP, POP3, IMAP, and NNTP. The end of this chapter explains domain names, firewalls, web proxies, and XML web services.

Chapter 2 provides you with a background for working with streams. A stream is an abstract representation of a sequence of bytes such as a file, an I/O device, or a TCP/IP socket. Through this abstraction, different devices can be accessed with the same process, and similar code can be used to read data from a file input stream as can be used to read data from a network input stream, for example. In this way, the programmer's need to worry about the actual physical mechanism of the device is removed. We take a look at streams in .NET 1.1—the `STREAM` base class for all other stream types, and work with the concrete `FILESTREAM`, `BUFFEREDSTREAM`, `MEMORYSTREAM`, `NETWORKSTREAM`, and `CRYPTOSTREAM` classes and stream manipulation. We also show you how to read from and write to binary and text files, and serialize objects into XML and binary format.

Chapter 3 starts to get you to grips with network programming in .NET 1.1, beginning with classes from the `SYSTEM.NET` namespace. We kick off with a discussion of these classes—and you'll see later on how they play a fundamental role in all the following chapters of this book. Specifically, we'll see how to work with URIs, IP addresses, and DNS lookups. We see how to handle requests and responses through the `WEBREQUEST` and `WEBRESPONSE` classes, and begin looking at authentication, authorization, and the permissions relevant to network programming.

Chapter 4 is about socket programming, and we explain to you the low-level programming that is required to perform network-related tasks. A socket is one end of a two-way communication link between two programs running on a network. We'll look at the socket support in .NET—the `SYSTEM.NET.SOCKETS.SOCKET` class, building a port scanner application, and creating both synchronous and asynchronous client-server applications.

Chapter 5 deals with the details of raw socket programming, the base for building custom network protocols. The first part of this chapter covers the basic implementation of the Internet Control Message Protocol (ICMP) and the second part the Simple Network Management Protocol (SNMP). As ICMP deals with Internet control messages, we will build two of the most used utilities in network diagnostic scenarios: `PING` and `TRACEROUTE`. Then, we will show an implementation of the SNMP protocol, used for remote network device management.

Chapter 6 is about a new addition in .NET Framework 1.1: the support for the IPv6 protocol. IPv6 is short for Internet Protocol Version 6. IPv6 is the "next generation" protocol designed by the Internet Engineering Task Force (IETF) to replace the current version Internet Protocol, IP Version 4 (IPv4). IPv6 fixes a number of problems in IPv4, such as the limited number of available IPv4 addresses. It also adds many improvements to IPv4 in areas such as routing and network auto-configuration. We will discuss the .NET and Windows operating system support for IPv6, showing how to install and configure this protocol. Then we will build an IPv6-based client-server application and a simple multicast application showing the basics of multicast network communication.

In **Chapter 7**, we begin a tour of the higher-level network classes in the .NET Framework, commencing with those for dealing with the Transmission Control Protocol (TCP). We start with a general introduction to TCP, and its architecture and data structures, before moving on to explore the `TCPCLIENT` and `TCPLISTENER` classes for working with TCP. You'll build client-server applications using the `TCPCLIENT` and `TCPLISTENER` classes, and then write a fully functional e-mail client to see the power of `TCPCLIENT`. You'll also create a multithreaded echo server, with the support of the .NET multithreading classes. We end this chapter for you with a quick look at the .NET Remoting Framework, and particularly the TCPCHANNEL transport channel provided with the .NET 1.1 Framework.

Chapter 8 is about the UDPCLIENT class, through which we implement the User Datagram Protocol (UDP). You'll learn about the fundamentals of the UDP protocol, and then see how to use the UDPCLIENT class. While TCP is a more reliable protocol than UDP, it also adds a lot of overhead. Accordingly, UDP is faster, and is well suited for multimedia transmissions such as video streams—where the precise order that packets arrive in may not be critical. In this chapter, we also discuss with you the higher-level UDP-based protocols.

Chapter 9 is about multicasting. This is the technology that made possible the transmission of a live Rolling Stones concert in 1994 over the Internet; it allows us to watch astronauts in space, or to hold meetings over the Internet, to name but a few benefits. With multicasting, a server only has to send messages once, and they will be distributed to a whole group of clients. We therefore begin Chapter 9 by comparing unicasts, broadcasts, and multicasts. You'll study the architecture of multicasting, and learn how to implement multicast sockets in .NET 1.1. You create two Windows applications in this chapter using multicasting features—one application makes it possible to chat with multiple systems, where everyone is both a sender and a receiver. The second application—in the form of a picture show—demonstrates for you how large data packets can be sent to multiple clients without using a large percentage of the network bandwidth.

Chapter 10 covers the HTTP protocol and its robust implementation exposed by .NET. The HTTP protocol's importance as an application protocol is significant, since a large share of web traffic today uses this protocol. In Chapter 10, we therefore begin with an overview of the HTTP protocol—the HTTP headers, and the format of HTTP requests and responses. You'll take a deep look at the classes in .NET for working with HTTP, and see how to read and write cookies. You'll then see how to create an HTTP server with ASP.NET support, before continuing your study of .NET Remoting and the HTTP transport channel. You'll be well set in this area after reading this chapter.

We get to e-mail in **Chapter 11**. In this chapter, we begin with a high-level overview of the various e-mail protocols and how they are accessed and used in a .NET 1.1 environment. We'll show you the fundamentals of the SMTP, POP3, IMAP, and NNTP protocols, and see how these protocols work together to send and receive e-mail messages over the Internet. We'll also take a look at sending e-mails with the .NET Framework's classes for sending e-mails via SMTP, as well as developing some grassroots protocol implementation classes for POP3 and SMTP.

In **Chapter 12**, we discuss the topic of securing network communications. The SYSTEM.SECURITY.CRYPTOGRAPHY namespace of the .NET Framework provides programmatic access to the variety of cryptographic services that we can incorporate into our applications to encrypt and decrypt data, ensure data integrity, and handle digital signatures and certificates. In this chapter, we'll therefore explore with you this namespace, but also provide you with an introduction to cryptography and all of its key concepts. This is a topic you can take much further, of course, but we open that door for you in this chapter. We'll also take a look at securing a particular chat application that we created earlier in the book.

We close the book with **Chapter 13**, where we take a look at authentication protocols. Authentication has become a major issue for any application developer who expects code to run across a network, or across the Internet. Making sure that users are who they say they are, and verifying machine identities on demand, is all part of an application's security module. In this final chapter, you'll see what the authentication protocols involved in Microsoft's networking schemes are, how they work, and how they apply to the various versions of Windows.

We will discuss protocols such as NTLM, Kerberos, and various types of Windows authentication methods such as Credentials Management, GINA, LSA, smartcard authentication, and Winlogon. At the end of the chapter, we'll show you the .NET security architecture, and provide you with an explicit implementation of the .NET Resource Security.

What You Need to Use This Book

To run the code solutions and examples in this book, you need to have a machine with the .NET 1.1 Framework installed. This means that you'll need to be running either a type of Windows server (Windows 2000 Server or above) or a Windows workstation type (Windows 2000 Professional or Windows XP). We also recommend that you use Visual Studio .NET 2003 with this book, but you can also build the sample applications using the .NET Framework 1.1 SDK.

CHAPTER 1

Networking Concepts and Protocols

In this chapter, we introduce some of the basic networking concepts and protocols. The chapter serves as a foundation to networking that will allow you to tackle programming in the rest of the book. It doesn't matter if you plan to develop server applications running as Windows Services (offering some data for clients using a custom protocol), if you write client applications that request data from web servers, or if you create multicasting or mailing applications—you should start with reading this chapter. If you don't already know what a router or a network switch is, if you aren't sure about the functionality of the seven layers in the Open Systems Interconnection (OSI) protocol model, or if you just want a refresher or an overview of the different network protocols and their uses, then this chapter is addressed to you.

We start with an introduction to the hardware used in local area networks (LANs), such as routers, hubs, and bridges. Then we take a look at the seven layers of the OSI model and their functionality, and how the Transmission Control Protocol/Internet Protocol (TCP/IP) suite fits into the OSI layers. After that, we cover the functionality of various network protocols.

In particular, we discuss the following topics:

- The physical network
- The OSI seven-layer model
- Network protocols (including basic protocols, Internet protocols, and e-mail protocols)
- Sockets
- Domain name lookups
- The Internet
- .NET Remoting
- Messaging

The Physical Network

In essence, a *network* is a ***group of computers or devices*** connected by ***communication links***. In networking terms, every computer or device (printer, router, switch, and so on) connected to the network is called a ***node***. Nodes are connected by *links*, which could be cables or wireless links (such as infrared or radio signals), and they can interact with any other node by transmitting ***messages*** over the network.

We can differentiate networks according to their size:

- A ***local area network***, or LAN, connects nodes over a limited area. This area can be as large as the site of a big company or as small as connected computers in someone's home. The most commonly used LAN technology is the Ethernet network (see next section).
- ***A wide area network, or WAN***, connects multiple LAN sites. WAN technologies that you might know of include frame relay, T1 line, Integrated Services Digital Network (ISDN), X.25, and Asynchronous Transfer Mode (ATM). In the next section, we discuss the means of connecting to a WAN.
- A ***metropolitan area network***, or MAN, is very similar to a WAN insofar as it connects multiple LANs. However, a MAN restricts the area of the network to a city or suburb. MANs use high-speed networks to connect the LANs of schools, governments, companies, and so on, by using fast connections to each site, such as fiber optics.

BACKBONE

In discussions about networks, the term "backbone" is often used. A *backbone* is a high-speed network that connects slower networks. A company can use a backbone to connect slower LAN segments. The Internet backbone is built of high-speed networks that carry WAN traffic. Your Internet service provider (ISP) connects either directly to the Internet backbone or to a larger provider that in turn connects directly to the Internet backbone.

WAN Lines

You have several options available to connect to a WAN:

- In case a specific customer requires a dedicated network capacity, you can use ***leased lines***. Such lines are usually charged at a flat rate, no matter how much traffic is sent.

  Examples of leased lines are digital data service (DDS, running at 2.4 Kbps and 56 Kbps), T1 (1.544 Mbps), and T3 (equivalent to 28 T1 lines).
- ***Switched lines*** are used by the regular telephone service. A circuit is established between the transmitter and the receiver for the duration of a call or data exchange. When the line is no longer needed, it is available for use by another customer of the network provider.

Examples of switched lines are Plain Old Telephone Service (POTS, standard analog lines that support speeds up to 56 Kbps), ISDN, and Digital Subscriber Line (DSL).

- A ***packet-switching*** *network* is where the service provider supplies switching technology to interface with the backbone network. This solution provides increased performance and shares resources between customers, so that bandwidth is available on demand.

  Protocols used for switching networks include X.25 (up to 64 Kbps), frame relay (up to 44.736 Mbps), and ATM (up to 9.953 Gbps).

Ethernet

To give you a better understanding of how physical networks work, we'll look at the most common LAN network architecture, ***Ethernet***. Ninety percent of devices attached to a LAN use Ethernet, which was developed by Xerox, Digital Equipment Corporation (DEC), and Intel. In 1980, the IEEE 802.3 CSMA/CD standard specified a 10 Mbps Ethernet.

Nowadays, Ethernet can support 100 Mbps and 1 Gbps lines. Many cabling technologies can be employed with Ethernet. There is a standard naming convention that indicates the speed of the Ethernet network and the properties of the cable technology in use. Such names start with a number indicating the maximum data transfer speed, followed by a word indicating the transmission technology supported, followed by a number indicating the maximum distance between nodes. For instance, 10Base2 denotes an Ethernet that operates at 10 Mbps using baseband transmission, with cables that have a maximum length of 200 meters. Some other common configurations are shown in Table 1-1.

Table 1-1. *Ethernet Cables*

Ethernet Standard	Speed	Typical Cable Type	Description
10Base5	10 Mbps	Coaxial copper	This was the original standard for Ethernet, a so-called thick-net cabling technology.
10BaseT	10 Mbps	Copper	10BaseT is a 10 Mbps network with twisted-pair cabling. A *twisted pair* is simply that—a pair of wires twisted around each other.
100BaseTX	100 Mbps	Copper	This is a 100 Mbps network with twisted pair cabling and full-duplex (X) capability. *Full duplex* means that data can pass in both directions simultaneously.
100BaseSX	1,000 Mbps	Multimode fiber	This is a 1,000 Mbps network with fiber optic cables. The "S" indicates the short wavelength (850 nm) of the laser.

CSMA/CD

Ethernet is a Carrier Sense Multiple Access/Collision Detect (CSMA/CD) network. Multiple devices are connected to the same network, and all have simultaneous access. When a message is sent, it is transported across the complete network as shown in Figure 1-1. The receiver is identified by its unique address, and only this node reads the message; all other nodes ignore it.

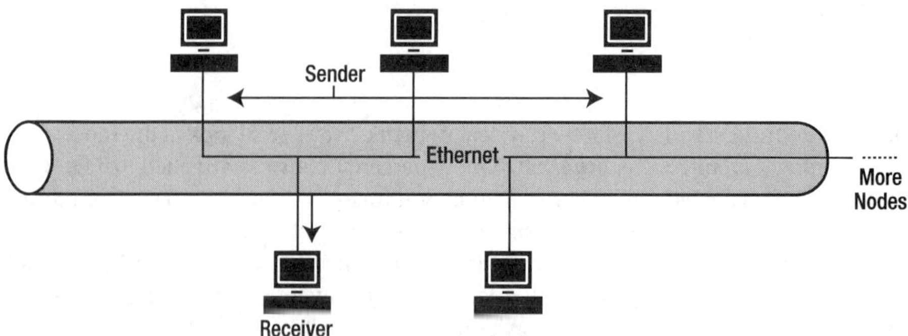

Figure 1-1. *Ethernet*

There is a potential problem: more than one node could attempt to send a message at the same time, which could result in the packets becoming corrupted. The solution used by Ethernet is that every node monitors the network and is thus aware of traffic. A node can start sending data only if no data is already being sent over the network. In short, this is the *CSMA* part of CSMA/CD.

There is still, however, the possibility that two nodes, after checking that the network is not already in use, start sending a packet at exactly the same time on the same network cable. This would cause a collision between the two packets, resulting in corrupted data. Both senders are aware of the corrupted packet because they still listen to the network while sending data and thus detect the collision. This is the *CD* in CSMA/CD. Both nodes then halt their transmissions immediately and wait a random time interval before checking the network again to see if it is free to resend the packet.

Every node on the local network uses a Media Access Control (MAC) address for unique identification. This address is defined by the network interface card (NIC). A network packet is sent across the network, but if the NIC does not identify its host as a receiver, it ignores the packet. Incidentally, if the packet has the same destination address as the node that is listening, the message is dealt with.

Other Network Architectures and Protocols

Token Ring (IEEE 802.5) is a network architecture developed by IBM. The nodes are connected in a ring, as shown in Figure 1-2. With Ethernet, any node can send a message as long as there isn't already traffic. With Token Ring, every node has guaranteed access to the network in a predefined order. A token circulates around the network ring, and only the node that holds the token can send a message. Nowadays, Ethernet is gradually replacing Token Ring networks because Token Ring is more expensive and more difficult to implement.

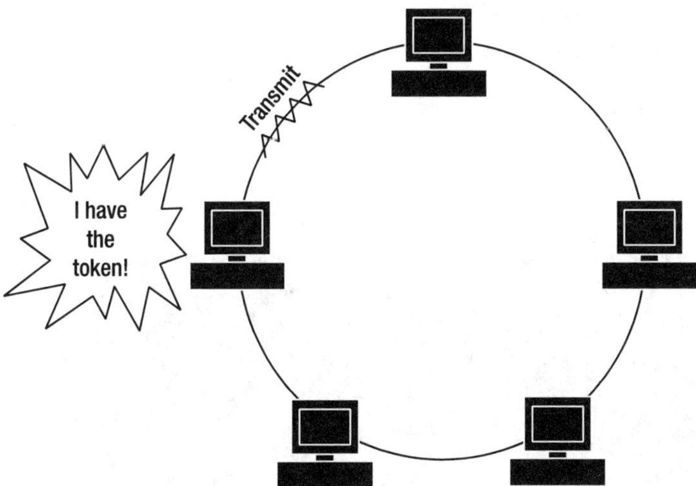

Figure 1-2. *Token Ring transmissions circulate only when a node owns the token.*

AppleTalk is a LAN protocol developed by Apple for Apple Macintosh networks that has been quite popular in schools, factories, and so on.

Asynchronous Transfer Mode (ATM) is another protocol that can be found in LANs. It supports fast network-switching and has a guaranteed quality of service (QOS), but because the cost of ATM network cards is very high, ATM is a niche player in the LAN market. ATM is used for LANs only in installations that require extremely high performance, for example, to transmit medical images such as X-rays between hospitals. In the backbone that drives WAN networks, ATM plays a more important role.

Physical Components

An important aspect of understanding the network is knowing the hardware components. In this section, we cover the major components of a LAN:

- NIC
- Hub
- Switch
- Router

Network Interface Card (NIC)

A NIC is the adapter card used to connect a device to the LAN. It allows you to send messages to and receive messages from the network. A NIC has a unique ***MAC*** address that provides a unique identification of each device.

The MAC address is a 12-byte hexadecimal number uniquely assigned to an Ethernet network card. This address can be changed dynamically by a network driver (as is the case with the DECnet system, a network developed by Digital Equipment Corporation), but usually the MAC address is not changed.

You can find the MAC address of a Windows machine using the command-line utility `ipconfig` in a DOS/CMD prompt with the `/all` switch. Figure 1-3 shows the output produced on a machine where the MAC address is 00-04-23-83-D1-BB. The first part of this number, 00-04-23, is assigned to the manufacturer of the network card; the manufacturer uses the remainder to create a unique MAC address.

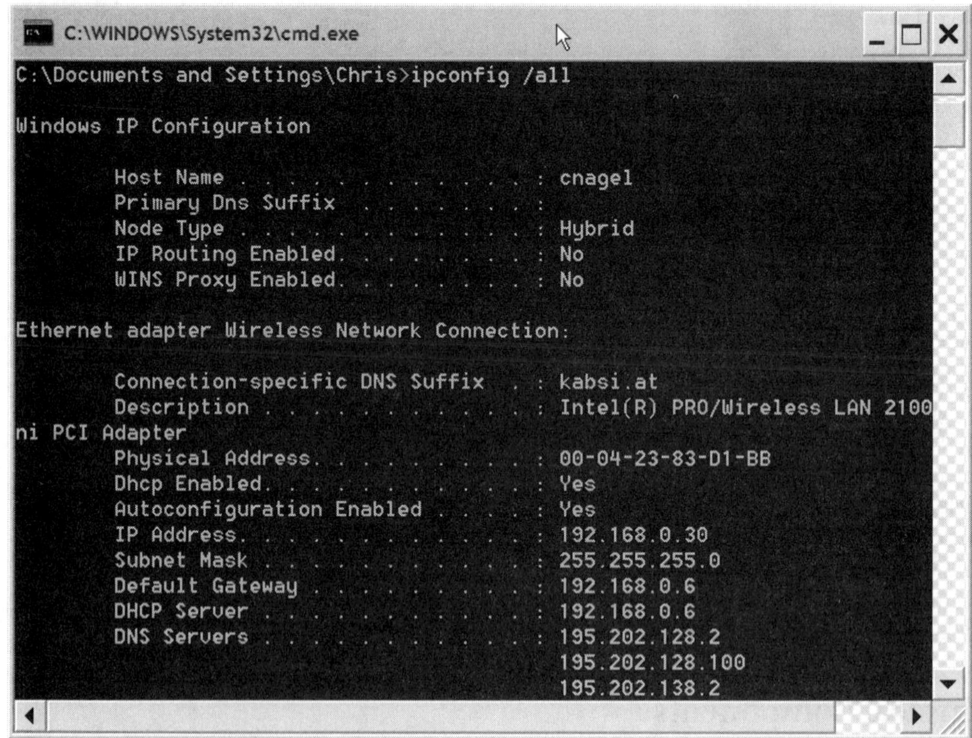

Figure 1-3. *Output of* `ipconfig` *command*

Hub

Multiple devices can easily be connected with the help of a *hub* (see Figure 1-4). A hub is a connectivity device that attaches multiple devices to a LAN. Each device typically connects via an unshielded twisted pair (UTP) cable to a port on the hub. You may have already heard about the Registered Jack-45 (RJ-45) connector. This is one of the possible port types on a hub, but a hub can also support other cable types. A hub can have from 4 to 24 ports. In a large network, multiple hubs are mounted in a cabinet and support hundreds of connections.

The hub acts as a *repeater* as it forwards every message from each port to every other port, and to the network. A hub is a fairly simple element of a network, operating at the physical network layer to retransmit data without any processing. This makes a hub easy to install and manage, as it doesn't require any special configuration.

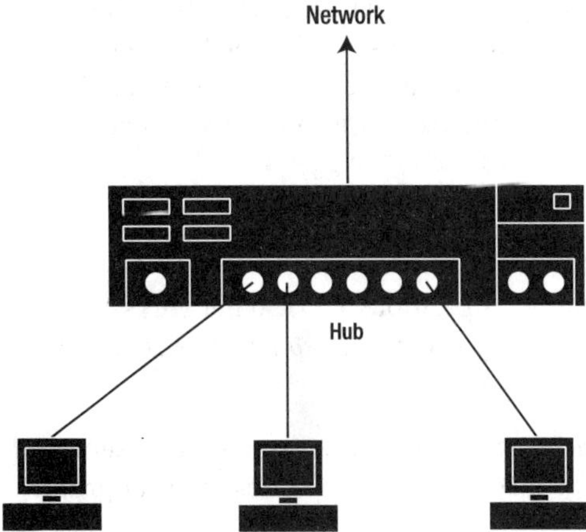

Figure 1-4. *A hub*

Switch

Switches separate networks into segments. Compared to a hub, a switch is a more intelligent device. A switch stores the MAC addresses of devices that are connected to its ports in lookup tables. These lookup tables allow the switch to filter network messages and, unlike the hub, avoid forwarding messages to every port. This eliminates possible collisions, and a better performing network can be achieved. Switching functionality is performed using hardware (through application-specific integrated circuit, or ASIC, chips).

As shown in Figure 1-5, a switch can be used to connect hubs at a site. If node A sends a message to node B, the switch doesn't forward the message to segment 2 because the switch knows that node B is on the same portion of the network as node A. However, if node A sends a message to node C, the message is forwarded from segment 1 to segment 2.

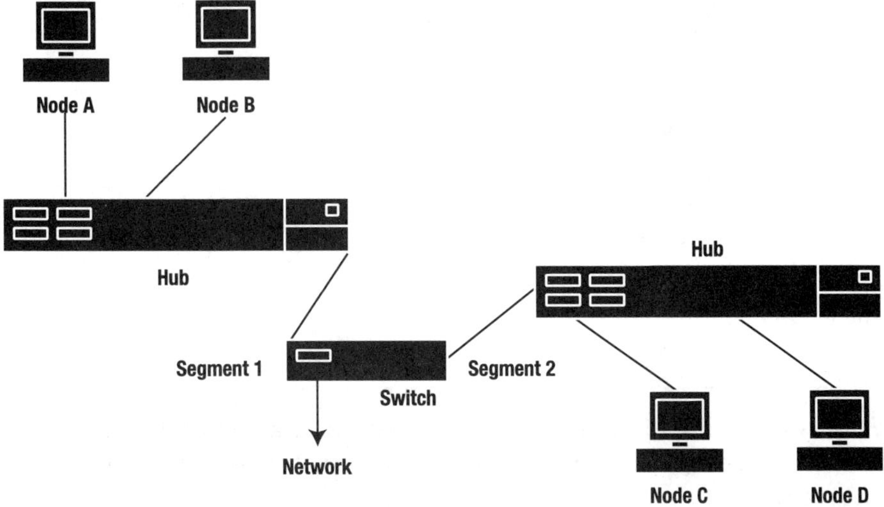

Figure 1-5. *A switch*

This sort of arrangement was popular in the early days, when hubs were much cheaper than switches, but it is less common now, as the price of switches has dropped to pretty much the same as hubs. Because of the enhanced network performance from collision reduction, new networks often use switches in place of hubs, and end users are connected directly to a switch.

Router

A *router* is an intermediary network device that connects multiple physical networks. With many hosts, it can be useful to split a LAN into separate portions, or *subnets*. The advantages of subnets are as follows:

- Performance is improved by reducing *broadcasts*, which is when a message is sent to all nodes in a network. With subnets, a message is sent only to the nodes in the appropriate subnet.
- The capability of restricting users to particular subnets offers security benefits.
- Smaller subnets are easier to manage than one large network.
- Subnets allow a single network to span several locations.

Figure 1-6 shows how routers might connect several subnets.

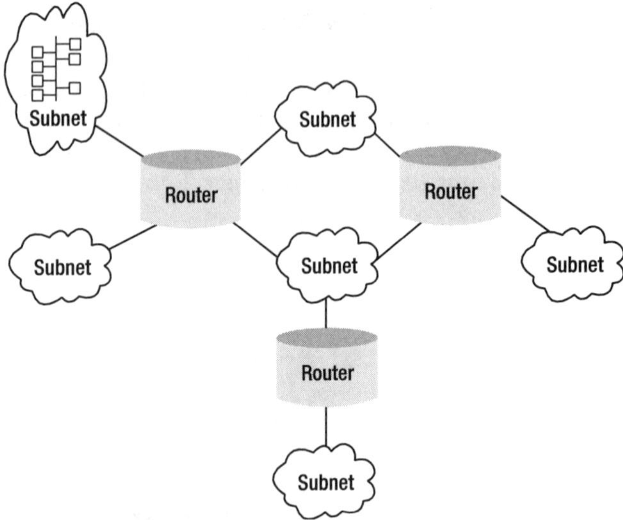

Figure 1-6. *Routers and subnets*

NOTE If you're using a router in a LAN, be aware that a router isn't as fast as a switch. The router must apply more processing to messages than a switch needs to, and consequently it takes a little more time before passing on packets.

Routers are not only used within LANs, but also have an important place in WANs where they connect different network lines. The router receives a message and forwards it to the destination using the last known best path to that destination, as illustrated in Figure 1-7.

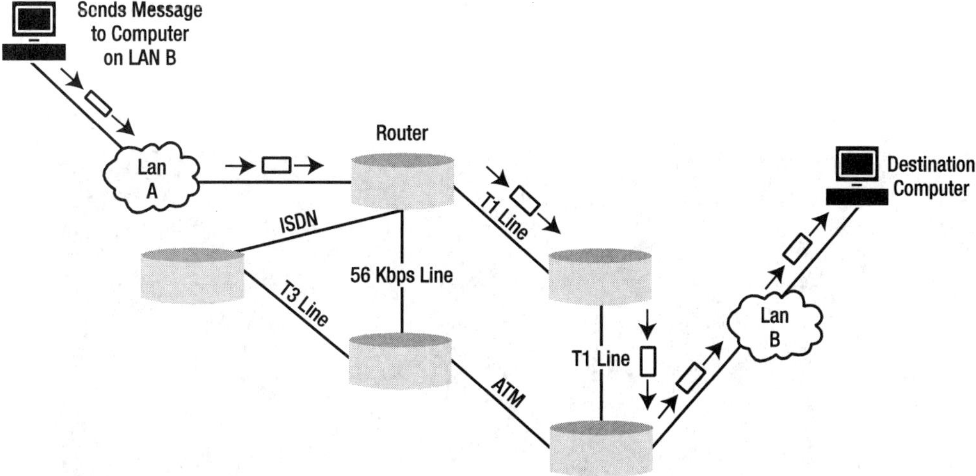

Figure 1-7. *Routers know the best path.*

A router holds a routing table that lists the ways particular networks can be reached. There will often be several different routes from one network to another, but one of these will be the best, and it is the best one that is described in the routing table. Routers communicate using routing protocols that discover other routers on the network and support the exchange of information about networks attached to each router.

The information that a router collates about the paths between networks is known as *router metrics*, and it may include information such as packet loss and transmission time. The information used to produce the metrics depends on the routing protocol:

- *Distance vector routing protocols*: Routing Information Protocol (RIP) and Interior Gateway Routing Protocol (IGRP) use a *hop count*, which indicates the number of routers that are passed through on the way to the target network. These protocols prefer paths with fewer routers, regardless of their speed and reliability.

- *Link state routing protocols*: The best path calculation of the Open Shortest Path First (OSPF) routing protocol and Border Gateway Protocol (BGP) takes into account multiple factors such as the speed, reliability, and even cost of a path.

- *Hybrid routing protocols*: Hybrid routing protocols use a combination of distance vector and link state calculation.

Finding the Route

With the TCP/IP configuration, you can set up a *default gateway*. This is the Internet Protocol (IP) address of the router port that the machine's subnet is connected to. This router is used when a host outside the subnet needs to be contacted.

You can see the local routing table on a Windows system by entering **ROUTE PRINT** at the command line. This command displays the gateways that will be used for each network connection. Figure 1-8 shows the output for a machine with an IP address (discussed in further detail in the "Internet Protocol" section of this chapter) of 192.168.0.30. If a host with the address 192.168.0.x is accessed, the local IP address 192.168.0.30 is used as a gateway—we can connect to these hosts directly. For other network destinations, the router 192.168.0.6 is used.

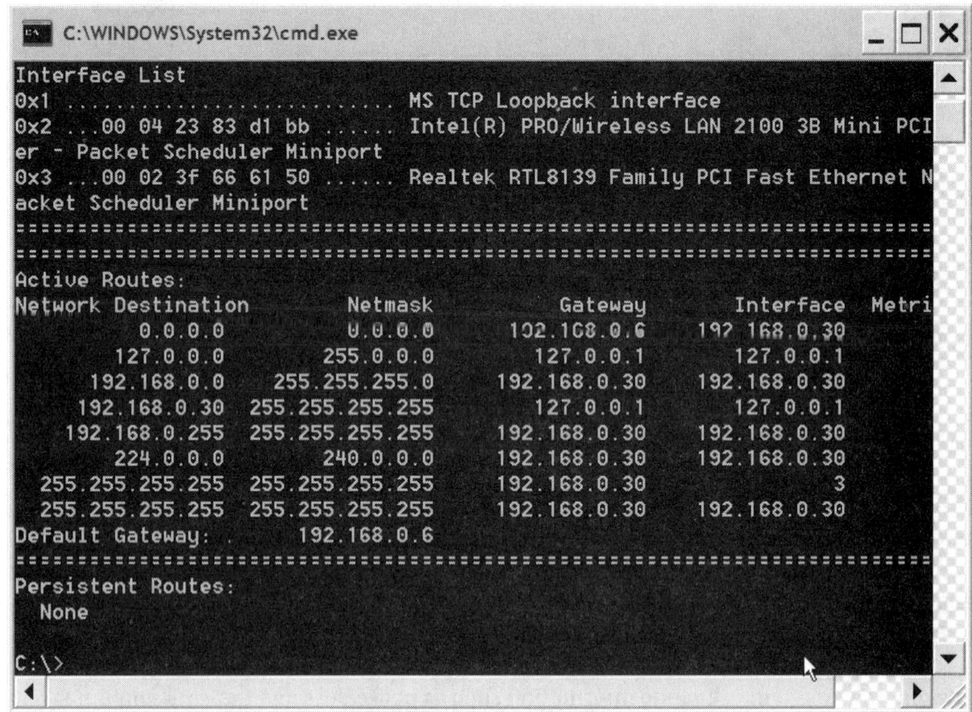

Figure 1-8. *Route output with the command ROUTE PRINT*

The `ROUTE` command has an option (`ROUTE ADD`) to specify the IP address of a router (gateway) and the network address to use with that router. This router will then be used to connect to hosts on the specified network.

Another useful command is `TRACERT`. This command allows you to examine the path used to reach a destination. Simply specify the host name or IP address after the `TRACERT` command. `TRACERT www.apress.com` in Figure 1-9 shows all routers that were used to reach the specified host. As you can see in the figure, the command also displays the time needed to reach the next hop. This command is very helpful if a host cannot be reached, which could indicate that some network in between is down or not available.

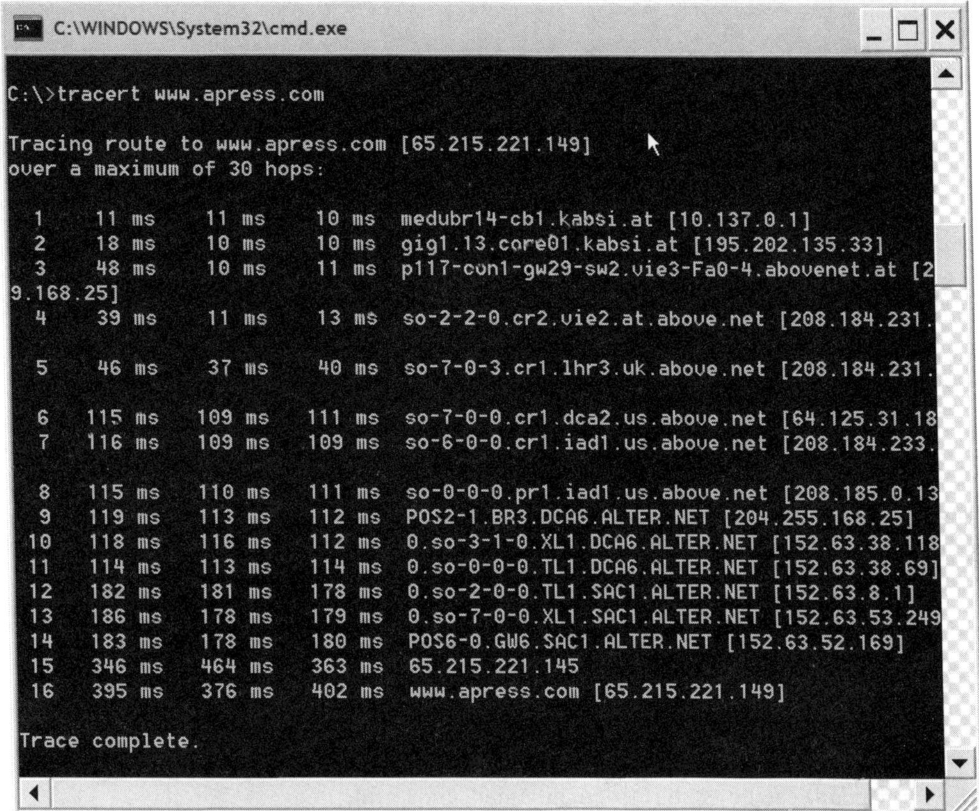

Figure 1-9. *Trace output with the TRACERT command*

The Layered OSI Model

With the OSI protocol suite, the International Organization for Standardization (ISO) defined a model that grew out of a need for international networking standards designed to facilitate the communication between different architectures of hardware and software.

Because of the complexity of this suite, not many implementations were built and put to use. TCP/IP is much simpler, and thus can now be found everywhere. However, many new ideas from OSI can be found in the next version of IP, IPv6.

While the OSI protocol suite didn't catch on, the OSI seven-layer model was very successful, and it is now used as a reference model to describe different network protocols and their functionality.

The layers of the OSI model separate the basic tasks that network protocols must accomplish and describe how network applications can communicate. Each layer has a specific purpose and is connected to the layers above and below it. The seven layers defined by OSI are shown in Figure 1-10.

7	Application
6	Presentation
5	Session
4	Transport
3	Network
2	Data Link
1	Physical

Figure 1-10. *OSI layers*

- The application layer defines a programming interface to the network for user applications.
- The ***presentation*** layer is responsible for encoding data from the application layer ready for transmission over the network, and vice versa.
- The ***session*** layer creates a virtual connection between applications, defining how connections can be established, maintained, and terminated.
- The ***transport*** layer allows reliable communication of data.
- The ***network*** layer makes it possible to access nodes in a LAN using logical addressing.
- The ***data link*** layer accesses the physical network with physical addresses. It is responsible for error correction, flow control, and hardware addressing.
- The ***physical*** layer defines network transmission media such as connectors, cables, and so on.

Figure 1-11 shows an example of communication between two machines, and how data passes down through the *protocol stack* on the sender and up through it on receipt. The D sent from the application on the first machine is shown in the figure as the box containing the letter *D*. The application layer (layer 7) adds a header to the message (called H7 in the figure) and passes the message to the presentation layer (layer 6), which adds H6 to the message before passing it to the session layer (layer 5). This continues until the message, with all its headers, arrives at the physical network (layer 1) and is transmitted to the receiver. At the receiving side, every layer performs any necessary processing and removes the relevant header, passing the message up to the next layer. At the end of all this, the receiving application accesses the original data sent by the application on the first computer.

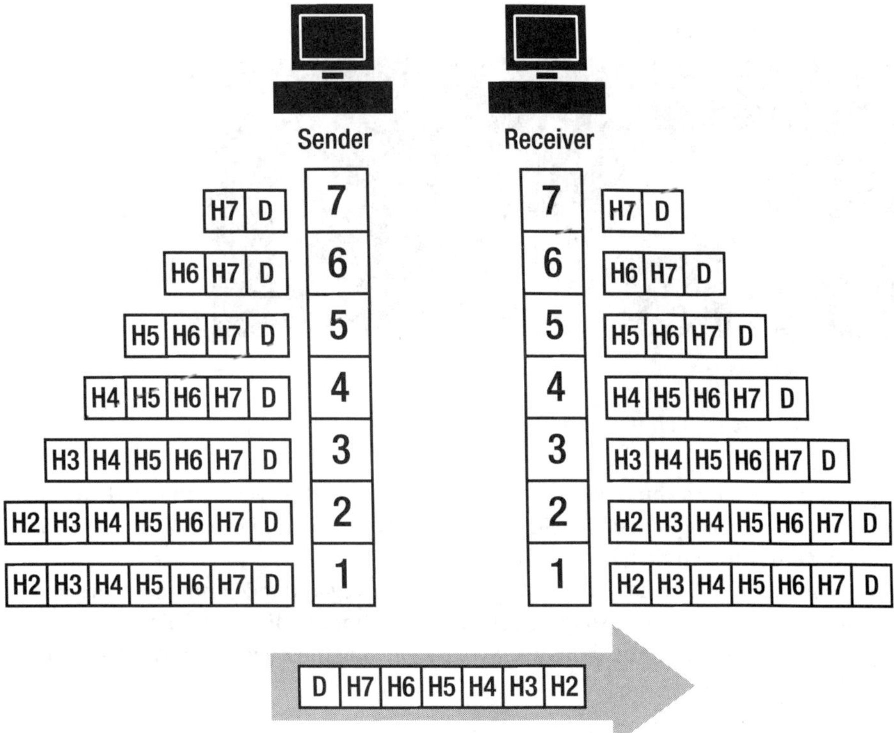

Figure 1-11. *Communication across the layers*

Now that you understand the concept of these seven layers, let's examine the functionality of each layer in more detail. We'll start at the bottom and work our way up.

Layer 1: Physical Layer

The physical layer defines the physical environment, such as cable requirements, connectors, interface specifications, hub and repeater specifications, and the like. This layer specifies exactly what physical network signal will be used to send a "1" and what will represent a "0."

Layer 2: Data Link Layer

The MAC address that we discussed earlier is a layer 2 address. Nodes on the LAN send messages to each other using IP addresses, and these must be translated to the corresponding MAC addresses by the data layer.

The *Address Resolution Protocol* (ARP) translates IP addresses to MAC addresses. A cache of known MAC addresses speeds this process, and it can be examined with the `arp` utility. `arp -a` shows MAC addresses of all recently used nodes in the ARP cache (see Figure 1-12).

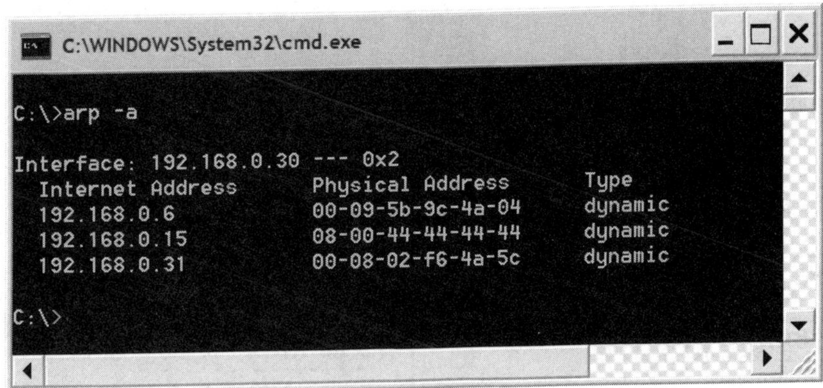

Figure 1-12. *MAC addresses shown with arp -a*

The arp utility also allows you to map IP addresses to MAC addresses so that ARP queries for MAC addresses are no longer needed. However, the mapping would break if the network card were replaced, so you should use it with care.

Other responsibilities of the data link layer include sending and receiving messages and error detection. With Ethernet, you also have collision detection, as discussed already.

A network switch operates at the data link layer by filtering messages according to their recipients' MAC addresses.

Layer 3: Network Layer

One layer above the data link layer is the network layer. Within layer 3, logical addressing is used to connect to other nodes. MAC addresses of layer 2 can be used only inside a LAN, and you have to use layer 3 addressing when accessing nodes in a WAN.

The Internet Protocol (IP) is a layer 3 protocol that uses IP addresses to identify nodes on the network.

Routers work at layer 3 to route traffic between networks.

Layer 4: Transport Layer

Whereas the network layer identifies hosts by logical addresses, the transport layer identifies an application by what is known as an *endpoint*. With the TCP protocol, an endpoint is given by a *port number* and IP address combination.

The transport layer is differentiated according to whether or not you're using *reliable* or *unreliable* communication. Reliable communication is when an error is produced if a message was sent but not received correctly, whereas unreliable communication sends a message without checking if it was received at all. In reliable communication, the transport layer is responsible for sending acknowledgments of data packets, for retransmitting messages if data was corrupted or missing, for discarding duplicate messages, and so on.

Another way network communication can be differentiated at the transport layer is as either *connection oriented* or *connectionless*:

- With connection-oriented communication, a connection must be made before messages can be sent or received.
- With a connectionless communication, setting up individual connections is not necessary, and messages are sent immediately.

TCP uses a connection-oriented communication mechanism, while User Datagram Protocol (UDP) uses a connectionless communication mechanism. Connection-oriented communication is reliable as acknowledgments are sent and retransmitted if data is not received or has become corrupted for any reason. Connectionless communication can be useful with broadcasts where messages are sent to multiple nodes. Here, message arrival is not guaranteed. If reliable messaging is needed, reliability can be enforced by a higher-level protocol on top of the connectionless mechanism.

Layer 5: Session Layer

With the OSI model, the session layer defines services for an application, such as logging into and out of an application. The session represents a virtual (logical) connection between applications. The session layer connection is independent of the underlying physical connection at the transport layer, and the virtual connection can exist for a longer time than the connection at the transport layer. Multiple transport layer connections may be required for a single session layer connection.

We can compare this functionality with functionality offered by ASP.NET session objects. The session objects exist until a session times out (usually 20 minutes), independent of the underlying TCP connection.

Layer 6: Presentation Layer

The presentation layer is used to format the data according to application requirements. Encryption, decryption, and compression typically happen in this layer.

Layer 7: Application Layer

The application layer is the highest layer of the OSI model. This layer contains applications using networking features. These applications can perform tasks such as file transfer, printing, e-mail, web browsing, and more. The example applications that we present in this book reside in this layer.

Network Protocols

The OSI layers define a model of protocol layers, their purpose, and how they work together. Let's now compare the OSI layers with a concrete implementation: the *TCP/IP protocol stack*.

The TCP/IP protocol stack is a simple form of the OSI model, which can be viewed in four layers as opposed to seven. The IP protocol corresponds to OSI layer 3; TCP and UDP are OSI layer 4 protocols. HTTP, FTP, and SMTP don't fit in one layer of the OSI model, and the tasks they accomplish encompass the session, presentation, and application layers (see Figure 1-13).

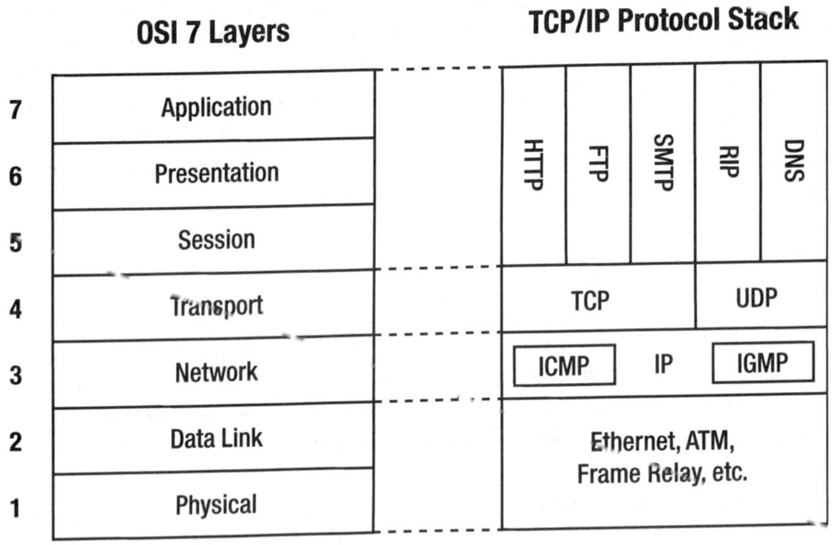

Figure 1-13. *OSI layers and the TCP/IP protocol stack*

In the following sections, we look into the functionality and purpose of the protocols of the TCP/IP suite in the following order:

- Basic protocols
- Internet protocols
- E-mail protocols
- Other protocols

Basic Protocols

As you can see, the TCP/IP protocol suite has a much simpler layered structure than the seven layers of the OSI model. The TCP and UDP protocols are transport protocols corresponding to OSI layer 4. Both protocols make use of IP, an OSI layer 3 protocol (the network layer). In addition to these three protocols are two more basic protocols in the TCP/IP suite that extend the IP protocol: ICMP and IGMP. The functionality of these protocols must be implemented in the layer housing the IP protocol, hence they are shown in that layer in Figure 1-13.

Internet Protocol (IP)

The IP protocol connects two nodes. Each node is identified by a 32-bit address, called its *IP address*. When sending a message, the IP protocol receives the message from upper-level protocols such as TCP or UDP and adds the IP header, which contains information about the destination host.

The best way to understand the IP protocol is by examining the IP header in detail. The information it contains is listed in Table 1-2.

Table 1-2. *IP Header Information*

Field	Length	Description
IP version	4 bits	The IP version that created the header. The current IP protocol version is 4.
IP header length	4 bits	The length of the header. The minimum value is 5, in units of 32 bits (4 bytes), so the minimum length is 20 bytes.
Type of service	1 byte	The service type allows a message to be set as normal or service high throughput, normal or high delay, and normal or high reliability. This is useful for datagram packets sent to the network. Several kinds of networks use this information to prioritize certain traffic. Also, network control messages have a higher precedence and reliability than normal messages.
Total length	2 bytes	These 2 bytes specify the total length of a message, header and data, in octets. The maximum size of an IP packet is 65,535 bytes, but that is impractical for most networks. The largest size that must be accepted by all hosts is 576 bytes. Large messages can be split into fragments through a process called *fragmentation*.
Identification	2 bytes	If the message is fragmented, the identification field helps to assemble the fragments of a message. If a message is split into multiple fragments, all fragments of a message have the same identification number.
Flags	3 bits	These flags indicate whether or not the message is fragmented and if the current packet is the last fragment of a message.
Fragment offset	13 bits	These 13 bits specify the offset of a fragmented message. Fragments may arrive in a different order than when sent, so the offset is necessary to rebuild the original data. The first fragment of a message has an offset of 0, and other fragments give the offset where the fragment should be appended. The offset unit is 8 bytes, so a fragment offset value of 64 means that the second fragment should be appended after 512 bytes of the first packet.
Time to live	1 byte	The *time to live* (TTL) value specifies the number of seconds a message can live before it's discarded. This value doesn't necessarily specify the number of seconds, as every router the message crosses must decrement the TTL value by 1, no matter if the handling of the message took less than 1 second. So in practice, this value gives the number of hops to live.

continues

Table 1-2. *Continued*

Field	Length	Description
Protocol	1 byte	This byte indicates the protocol used at the next level in the protocol stack for this message. The protocol numbers are defined in an online database at the Internet Assigned Numbers Authority (IANA, `http://www.iana.org/assignments/protocol-numbers`). Here are some examples: ICMP has the value 1, IGMP has the value 2, TCP has the value 6, and UDP has the value 17.
Header checksum	2 bytes	This is a checksum of the header only. Because the header changes with every message that is forwarded, the checksum changes also.
Source address	4 bytes	This field gives the 32-bit IP address of the sender.
Destination address	4 bytes	This is the 32-bit IP address where the message is to be sent.
Options	Variable	Optional fields can appear here. You can specify that a message is confidential or top secret, and there is also room for future extensions.
Padding	Variable	This field contains a variable number of zeros such that the header ends on a 32-bit boundary.

■ **NOTE** The IP protocol is defined in RFC 791. The Request for Comments (RFC) documents contain technical information about many important Internet technologies. You can find RFCs at `http://www.ietf.org/rfc.html`.

IP Addresses

Every node on a TCP/IP network can be identified by a 32-bit IP address. Usually the IP address is represented in a quad notation with four decimal values, such as 192.168.0.1. Each of these numbers represents 1 byte of the IP address, meaning that each falls in the range 0 to 255.

An IP address consists of two parts: the network part and the host part. Depending on the network class, the network part consists of the first 1, 2, or 3 bytes (see Table 1-3).

Table 1-3. *IP Address Ranges*

Class	Byte 1	Byte 2	Byte 3	Byte 4
A	Network (1–126)	Host (0–255)	Host (0–255)	Host (0–255)
B	Network (128–191)	Network (0–255)	Host (0–255)	Host (0–255)
C	Network (192–223)	Network (0–255)	Network (0–255)	Host (0–255)

The first bit of a Class A network address must be 0, so the first byte of a Class A network is in the binary range 00000001 (1) to 01111110 (126). The remaining 3 bytes serve to identify nodes on the network, allowing us to connect more than 16 million devices on a Class A network.

Note that the networks in Table 1-3 make no mention of addresses with 127 as the first byte—this is a reserved address range. The address 127.0.0.1 is always the address of the local host, and 127.0.0.0 is a local loopback. *Loopbacks* are used to test the network protocol stack on a machine without going through the NIC.

Class B networks always have the first 2 bits of the IP address set to 10, giving a range of 10000000 (128) to 10111111 (191). The second byte further identifies the network with a value of 0 to 255, leaving the remaining 2 bytes to identify nodes on the network, a total of 65,534 devices.

Class C networks are denoted by an IP address where the first 3 bits are set to 110, allowing a range of the first byte from 11000000 (192) to 11011111 (223). With this network type, only 1 byte is set aside for node identification, so only 254 devices can be connected.

■ NOTE The number of devices that can be connected to each of these different network classes with a distinct IP address is inversely proportional to the number of networks of that type available. For instance, a Class A network, allowing 16 million hosts, leaves only part of the first byte for identifying the network. The result is that there are just 126 Class A networks available worldwide. Only big companies such as AT&T, IBM, Xerox, and Hewlett-Packard have such a network address.

When a company requests an IP network from a network authority, it will usually only be allocated a Class C network. Should the company desire more hosts to be directly connected to the Internet, that company can seek an additional Class C network. Another option applies if each network host doesn't need direct Internet access, when a private IP address can be used. We discuss private IP addresses in the next section.

Class A, B, and C network addresses leave addresses that have a first byte of 224 to 255. Class D networks (224–239) are used for multicasting, as you'll see in Chapter 9, and Class E (240–255) is reserved for testing purposes.

■ NOTE IANA assigns network numbers and lists them at `http://www.iana.org/assignments/ipv4-address-space`. Nearly every country has a regional registration authority to give network numbers to requestors. The regional authority receives a network range from IANA.

Private IP Addresses

To avoid exhausting IP addresses, hosts that aren't directly connected to the Internet can use an address in the private address ranges. Private addresses aren't globally unique; they're just unique locally within the network. All network classes reserve certain ranges for use as private addresses for hosts that don't require direct two-way access to the Internet (see Table 1-4). Such hosts may well access the Internet through a gateway that doesn't forward private IP addresses.

Table 1-4. *Private IP Address Ranges*

Class	Private Address Range (Network Part of IP Address)
A	10
B	172.16–172.31
C	192.168.0–192.168.255

■NOTE Address allocation for private addresses is described in RFC 1918.

Subnets

Connecting two nodes of different networks requires a router. Twenty-four bits of a Class A IP address define the host number, while with a Class C network just 8 bits are available. A router splits the host number into a subnet number and host number. Adding additional routers will reduce broadcasts in the network, which can reduce network load. The main reason for adding routers is to improve connectivity between sites in different buildings, cities, and so on.

Let's look at a subnetting example of a Class C network with an address of 194.180.44.0. Such a network may have a subnet mask of 255.255.255.224 to filter addresses. The first 3 bytes (which consist of all 1s) are the mask for the Class C network. The last byte, 224, is the decimal value for the binary representation 11100000, so that 3 bits of the host number indicate the subnet, and the remaining 5 bits represent the host number on a particular subnet. These 3 subnet bits represent 128, 64, and 32, and thus support the subnet addresses shown in Figure 1-14.

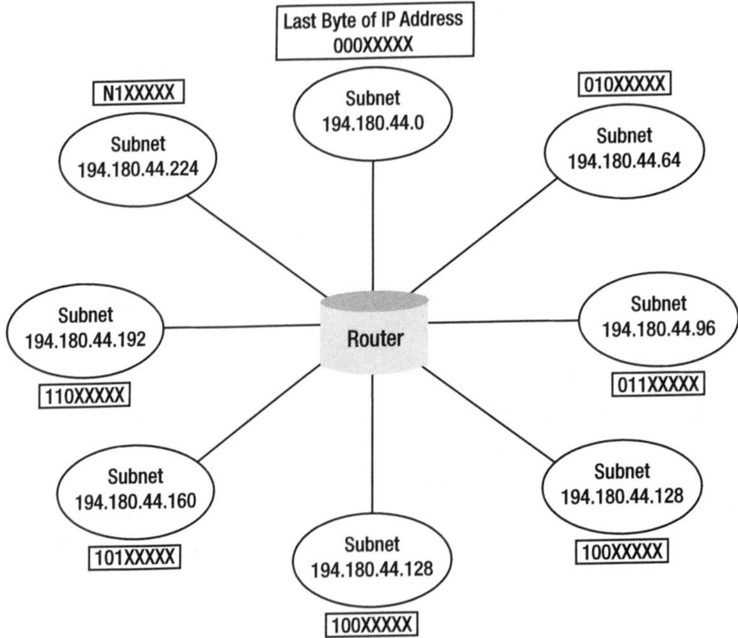

Figure 1-14. *Subnetting with a Class C network*

So the subnet 194.180.44.64 contains hosts with addresses from 194.180.44.65 to 194.180.44.94, and the subnet 194.180.44.160 contains hosts from 194.180.44.161 to 194.180.44.190.

IPv6

The predecessor of IP was developed by the U.S. Department of Defense's Defense Advanced Research Project Agency (DARPA) in the 1960s, and the TCP/IP protocol suite was not established until 1980. Because IP was based on the existing DARPA network protocols, it became version 4, now known as IPv4. At that time, the number of hosts supported by IP seemed more than adequate. Now, however, it seems everyone wants to connect their refrigerator and lawnmower to the Internet. To meet this demand, a new IP version has been under development by the Internet Engineering Task Force (IETF): IPv6. The most important change over IPv4 is the use of 128 bits to address nodes, rather than 32 bits, which should allow every Tablet PC, Pocket PC, mobile phone, TV, car, lawnmower, coffee machine, and trash can to become a full-fledged Internet host.

As well the ability to allocate an address to just about every atom in the solar system, there are a few other useful changes with IPv6:

- *Extended addressing capabilities*: Multicast routing information can be added to IPv6 addresses to define the scope of a multicast address. Also, there's now an *anycast address* to send a message to any host or group of hosts.
- *Simplified header format*: Some of the header fields of IPv4 have been removed, and others are now optional. However, the complete header length of IPv6 is longer than IPv4 because of the 128-bit addresses for source and destination.
- *Improved extensibility support*: It should be easier to add extensions to the IPv6 protocol in the future. The length restriction for options has been removed.
- *Flow labeling*: A new capability has been added for particular traffic flows. A *flow* is a sequence of packets traveling from a source to a destination. With the new protocol, applications can offer real-time audio and video capabilities over different flows. Each flow can request real-time or specific quality handling from routers it travels through.
- *Improved authentication and privacy*: To support authentication, privacy, and confidentially of data sent, IPv6 extensions have been added.

Transport Layer: Port Numbers

The IP protocol uses IP addresses to identify nodes on the network, while the transport layer (layer 4) uses endpoints to identify applications. TCP and UDP protocols use a *port number* together with an IP address to specify an application endpoint.

The server must supply a known endpoint for a client to connect to, although the port number can be created dynamically for the client.

TCP and UDP port numbers are 16 bits and can be divided into three categories:

- System (well-known) port numbers
- User (registered) port numbers
- Dynamic or private port numbers

The system port numbers are in the range 0 to 1023. System port numbers should be used only by system privileged processes. Well-known protocols have default port numbers in this range.

User port numbers fall in the range 1024 to 49151. Your server applications usually will take one of these ports, and you can also register the port number with IANA if you wish to make it known to the Internet community.

Dynamic ports are in the range 49152 to 65535. When it is not necessary to know the port number before starting an application, a port in this range would be suitable. Client applications connecting to servers might use such a port.

If you run the `netstat` utility with the `-a` option, you'll see a list of all ports currently in use and also an indication of the state of the connection—for example, if it's in listening state or if a connection has been already established (see Figure 1-15).

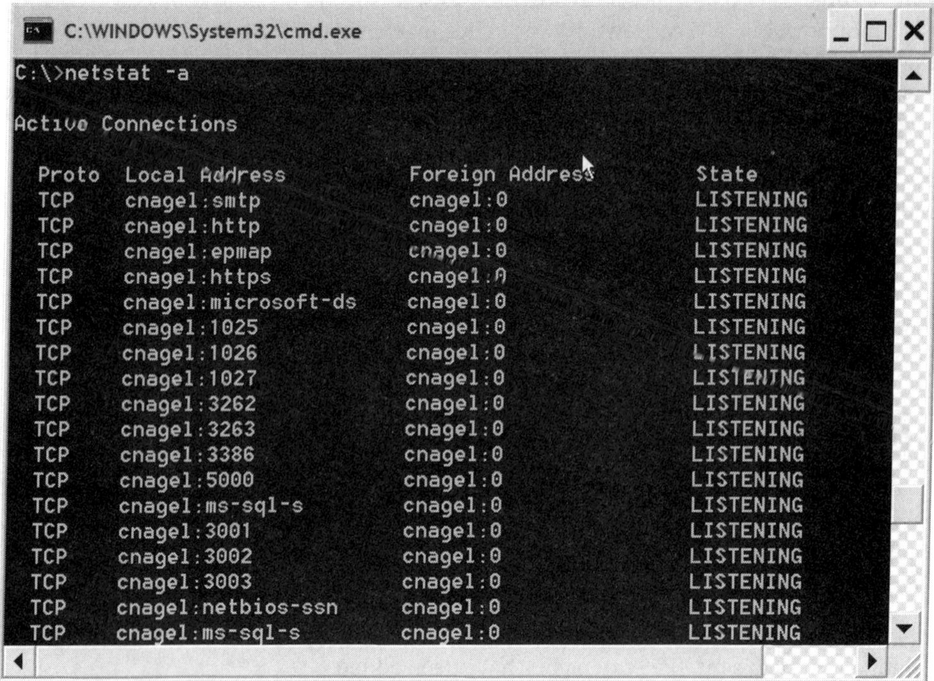

Figure 1-15. *netstat -a*

The services file in the directory `<windir>\system32\drivers\etc` lists many predefined user and system port numbers. If a port is listed in this file, the `netstat` utility will display the name of the protocol instead of the port number.

■ **NOTE** IANA assigns system and user port numbers. You can find a list of defined port numbers at `http://www.iana.org/assignments/port-numbers`.

Transmission Control Protocol (TCP)

Connection-oriented communication can use reliable communication where the layer 4 protocol sends acknowledgments of data receipts and requests retransmission if data is not received or corrupted. The TCP protocol uses such reliable communication. Some of the application protocols that use TCP are HTTP, FTP, SMTP, and Telnet.

TCP requires a connection to be opened before data can be sent. The server application must perform a *passive open* to create a connection with a known port number, where rather than making a call to the network, the server listens and waits for incoming requests. The client application must perform an *active open* by sending a synchronize sequence number (SYN) to the server application to identify the connection. The client application can use a dynamic port number as a local port. The server must send an acknowledgment (ACK) to the client together with the SYN of the server. The client in turn answers with an ACK, and the connection is established.

Now sending and receiving can start. After receiving a message, an ACK message is always returned. If the sender times out before receiving an ACK, the message is placed in the retransmit queue for sending again.

The TCP header fields are listed in Table 1-5.

Table 1-5. *TCP Headers*

Field	Length	Description
Source port	2 bytes	Port number of the source.
Destination port	2 bytes	Port number of the destination.
Sequence number	4 bytes	The sequence number is generated by the source and is used by the destination to reorder packets to create the original message and to send an acknowledgment to the source.
Acknowledgment number	4 bytes	If the ACK bit of the control field is set, this field contains the next sequence number that can be expected.
Data offset	4 bits	Details where the packet data begins.
Reserved	6 bits	Reserved for future use.
Control	6 bits	The control bits contain flags that denote if the acknowledgment (ACK) or urgent pointer (URG) field is valid, if the connection should be reset (RST), if a synchronize sequence number (SYN) is sent, and so on.
Window size	2 bytes	This field indicates the size of the receive buffer. The receiver can inform the sender of the maximum data size that can be sent using acknowledgment messages.
Checksum	2 bytes	A checksum for the header and data to determine if the packet has become corrupted.
Urgent pointer	2 bytes	This field informs the target device of urgent data.
Options	Variable	Again, option values will be specified only when relevant.
Padding	Variable	The padding field adds zeros so that the header ends on a 32-bit boundary.

The TCP protocol is complex and time consuming because of the handshaking mechanism, but this protocol takes care of guaranteeing delivery of packets, obviating the need to include that functionality in the application protocol.

■ **NOTE** The TCP protocol has a reliable delivery built in. If a message isn't sent correctly, you'll be informed by an error message.

■ **NOTE** The TCP protocol is defined in RFC 793. We cover programming with the TCP protocol in Chapter 7.

User Datagram Protocol (UDP)

In contrast with TCP, UDP is a very fast protocol, as it specifies the minimum mechanism required for data transfer. Of course, this does have some disadvantages. Messages can be received in any order, and a message that was sent first could be received last. The delivery of UDP messages is not guaranteed at all, and messages can be lost, or even two copies of the same message might be received. This latter scenario can happen when two different routes are used to send the message to the same destination.

UDP doesn't require a connection to be opened, and data can be sent as soon as it's ready. UDP doesn't send acknowledgment messages, so the data can be received or it can be lost. If reliable data transfer is needed over UDP, it must be implemented in a higher-level protocol.

So what are the advantages of UDP, and why would you want to use such an unreliable protocol? To understand the most important reason for using UDP, you have to differentiate between unicast, broadcast, and multicast communications.

A *unicast* message is sent from one node to just one other. This is also called *point-to-point communication*. The TCP protocol supports only unicast communication. If a server wants to communicate with multiple clients using TCP, each client must make a connection, as messages can be sent only to single nodes. *Broadcast* means that a message is sent to all nodes in a network. *Multicast* is something in between unicast and broadcast—messages are sent to select groups of nodes.

UDP can be used with unicast communications if fast transfer is required, such as for multimedia delivery, but the major advantages of UDP apply to broadcasts and multicasts. Usually, you won't want an acknowledgment from every node when sending a multicast or broadcast, as the server would be deluged and the network load would be too great. An example of such a broadcast is time service. A time server broadcasts a message containing the current time, and any host that wishes to do so may synchronize the time with that in the broadcasted message.

The UDP header is a lot shorter and simpler than the TCP header, as shown in Table 1-6.

■ **NOTE** UDP is a fast protocol, but delivery isn't guaranteed. If you require message ordering and delivery, you should use TCP. UDP is primarily a protocol for broadcasts and multicasts.

Table 1-6. *UDP Header*

Field	Length	Description
Source port	2 bytes	Specifying the source port is optional with UDP. If this field is used, the receiver of the message can send a reply to this port.
Destination port	2 bytes	The port number of the destination.
Length	2 bytes	The length of the message, including the header and data.
Checksum	2 bytes	A checksum for the header and data for verification.

■ NOTE UDP is defined in RFC 786. We provide information on how to program applications using UDP in Chapter 8.

Internet Control Message Protocol (ICMP)

ICMP is a control protocol used by an IP device to inform other IP devices of activity and errors in the network. Without TCP, IP is not a reliable protocol, and there are no acknowledgments, no error control for data (only a header checksum), and no retransmissions.

Errors detected may be reported with ICMP messages. The ICMP messages are used to send feedback about the status of the network. For example, a router sends an ICMP "Destination unreachable" message if a suitable entry for a network cannot be found in a routing table. A router can also send an ICMP "Redirect" message if a better path was found.

ICMP doesn't sit on top of the IP protocol as it may appear; rather, ICMP messages are sent within the IP header. Hence, the ICMP protocol must be implemented by the IP module of the network stack. These ICMP message fields are prefixed to the IP header (see Table 1-7).

Table 1-7. *ICMP Message Fields*

Field	Length	Description
Type value	1 byte	This field specifies the ICMP message type. For example, a type of 3 means that the destination is unreachable, 11 specifies that the time was exceeded, and 12 indicates that incorrect header parameters were found.
Code	1 byte	The code provides more information about the message type. If the type is destination unreachable, the code specifies whether the network (0), host (1), protocol (2), or port (3) is unreachable.
Checksum	2 bytes	A checksum of the ICMP message.
Depending on the type	4 bytes	The last 4 bytes of the ICMP header can supply additional information depending on the message type.
Regular IP header		The IP header follows the ICMP information.

Some of the types that can be sent using ICMP messages are as follows:

- *Echo and Echo Reply*: The ping command sends an ICMP Echo command to the destination device, and if all goes well an Echo Reply is sent back.
- *Destination unreachable and Redirect*: A router returns the ICMP Destination unreachable message if a target cannot be reached or a Redirect message if a better path is found to a target.
- *Time exceeded*: The time to live (TTL) value was exceeded.

ping Command

The Windows command-line utility `ping.exe` sends an ICMP Echo message to the target device specified by the host name or IP address in the `ping` command. If the device can be reached, an ICMP Echo Reply is sent back.

This command is useful for checking if a device can be reached, if there are intermediate problems (`ping -t` continues sending Echo messages until it is stopped), and how long it takes to send a message to the device.

■ **NOTE** If you can't reach a host using the `ping` command, it isn't necessarily the case that the host can't be reached by using other protocols. The ICMP Echo messages may be blocked by routers or firewalls.

Figure 1-16 shows the output produced by `ping` for a host with the IP address 65.215.221.149. By default, `ping` sends four ICMP messages to the target and waits for the Echo messages. Figure 1-16 shows that 32 bytes of data were sent, and the time until the reply was received was 244 milliseconds on average. A summary appears after the four ICMP results, where you can see that 0 percent of the packets was lost. Intermediate failures would usually lose a certain percentage of the packets.

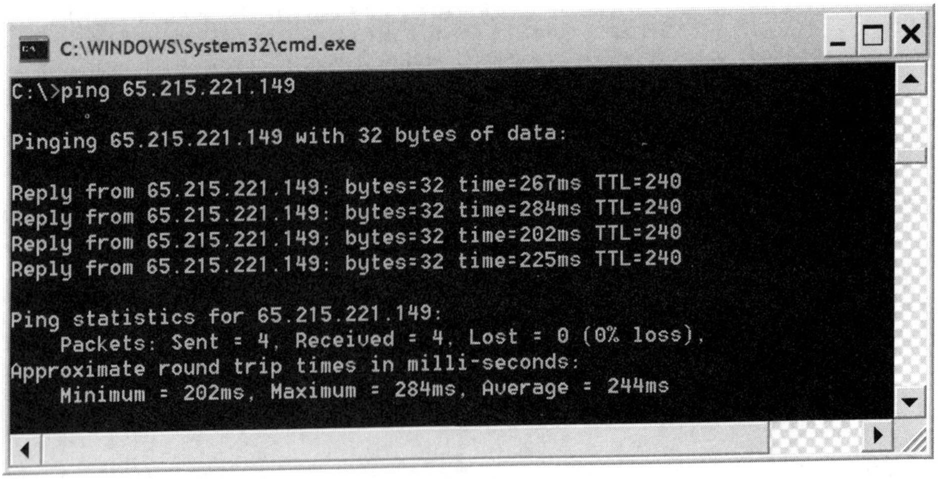

```
C:\WINDOWS\System32\cmd.exe
C:\>ping 65.215.221.149

Pinging 65.215.221.149 with 32 bytes of data:

Reply from 65.215.221.149: bytes=32 time=267ms TTL=240
Reply from 65.215.221.149: bytes=32 time=284ms TTL=240
Reply from 65.215.221.149: bytes=32 time=202ms TTL=240
Reply from 65.215.221.149: bytes=32 time=225ms TTL=240

Ping statistics for 65.215.221.149:
    Packets: Sent = 4, Received = 4, Lost = 0 (0% loss),
Approximate round trip times in milli-seconds:
    Minimum = 202ms, Maximum = 284ms, Average = 244ms
```

Figure 1-16. *ping command*

NOTE ICMP is defined in RFC 792.

Internet Group Management Protocol (IGMP)

Similar to ICMP, IGMP is an extension to the IP protocol and must be implemented by the IP module. IGMP is used by multicasting applications. When sending a broadcast message to a complete LAN, every node in the LAN analyzes the message up to the transport layer to verify if some application wants to receive messages from the port of the broadcast. If no application is listening, the message is destroyed and does not progress beyond the transport layer. This does mean that some CPU cycles are needed by every host whether or not the broadcast message is of interest.

Multicasts address this concern by sending messages only to a group of nodes rather than to every node in the LAN. The NIC can detect if the system is interested in a particular message by analyzing the broadcast MAC address without needing the assistance of the CPU.

Registering interest in a multicast message is done by sending a group membership request for a multicast address with an IGMP message. Similarly, IGMP can be used to drop a membership.

NOTE You can read more about the use of IGMP in Chapter 9, where we create .NET multicasting applications. IGMP is defined in RFC 2236.

Internet Protocols

Now that we've discussed the base protocols, we can step up to a higher level. The HTTP and FTP protocols cover layers 5–7 of the OSI model.

File Transfer Protocol (FTP)

FTP is used to copy files from and to a server, and to list files and directories on a server. It is an application-level protocol based on TCP, where FTP commands are encapsulated within the TCP data block of a TCP message.

An application model with an FTP server and client is illustrated in Figure 1-17. The client application presents a user interface and creates an FTP request according to the user's request and the FTP specification. The FTP command is sent to the server application over TCP/IP, and the FTP interpreter on the server interprets the FTP command accordingly. Depending on the FTP command, a list of files or a file from the server's file system is returned to the client in an FTP reply.

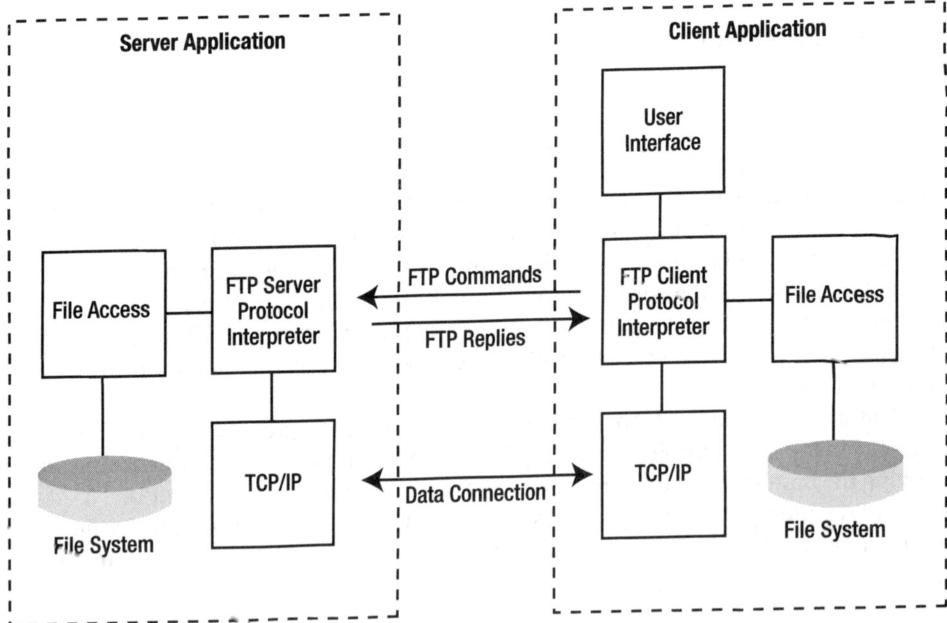

Figure 1-17. *FTP protocol*

The FTP protocol has these characteristics:

- Reliable data transfer through TCP
- Anonymous access or user authentication with a user name and password
- Files are sent as ASCII in a form supported by the target platform, or as unchanged binary data

FTP commands can be grouped into these categories:

- *Access control commands*: FTP access control commands specify the user name (USER) and password (PASS). The settings can be reset (REIN), and the connection can be ended (QUIT).
- *Transfer parameter commands*: FTP transfer can be configured with transfer parameter commands. Changing the transfer from ASCII to binary data compression and changing of ports to send data are supported by these commands.
- *FTP service commands*: Copying files from the server (RETR), copying files to the server (STOR), deleting files (DELE), renaming files (RNTO), creating directories (MKD), and asking for a list of files (LIST) are some of the FTP service commands.

■ **NOTE** FTP is defined in RFC 959.

FTP Clients

The best way to get to grips with the FTP protocol is by using the `ftp.exe` command-line utility as shown in Figure 1-18. The `ftp` program operates through the `ftp>` command prompt, allowing you to enter commands. These commands are different from the commands of the FTP protocol—you can see them all by entering **?**.

Figure 1-18 shows the command `open ftp.microsoft.com` to create a connection to the host `ftp.microsoft.com`. Setting the user name to `anonymous` indicates a guest user. The response `230` from the server indicates that a connection has been established, and the files on the server can be listed using the `dir` command. On receiving the `dir` command, the `ftp` program sends an `FTP LIST` command to the server. `cd` can be used to change directories on the server, and the `get` command copies a file to the client by sending a `RETR` command. The `ftp` utility uses the `bye` command to close the connection.

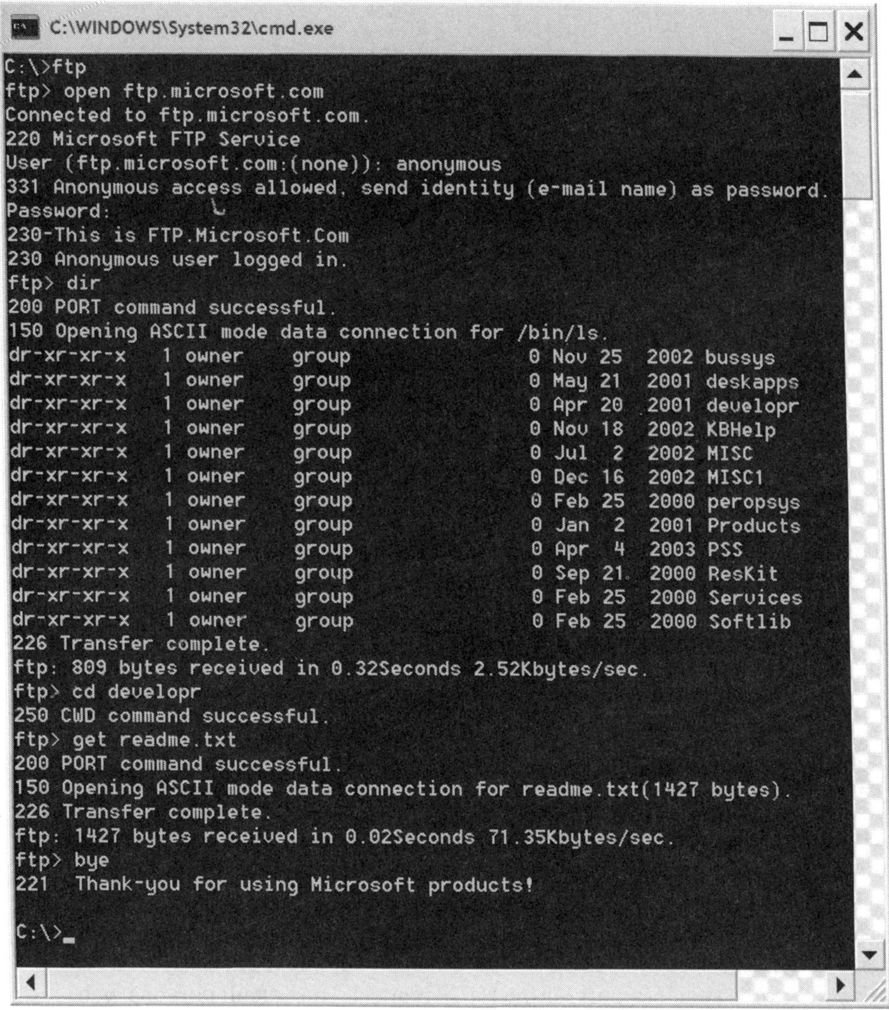

Figure 1-18. *Using ftp.exe*

Another FTP client is Microsoft Internet Explorer. Instead of using a URL such as `http://hostname`, you start the FTP client with `ftp://` as a schema identifier. This tool allows files to be copied with drag and drop (see Figure 1-19).

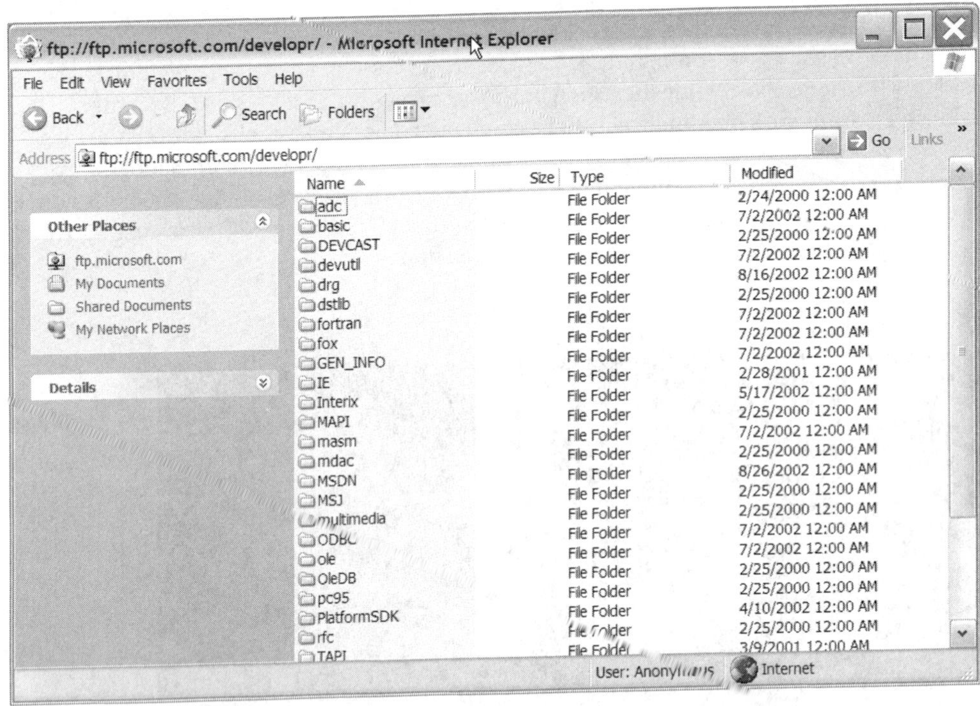

Figure 1-19. *Using Internet Explorer to access an FTP server*

Hypertext Transfer Protocol (HTTP)

HTTP is the main protocol used by web applications. Similar to the FTP protocol, HTTP is a reliable protocol that is achieved by using TCP. Like FTP, HTTP is used to transfer files across the network. Unlike FTP, it has features such as caching, identification of the client application, support for different attachments with a MIME format, and so on. These features are enabled within the HTTP header.

To demonstrate what an Internet browser is doing when it requests files from a web server, you can use the telnet application to simulate a browser (see Figure 1-20). Start the telnet application by entering **telnet** in the Run dialog box of the Start menu. You should see the `Microsoft Telnet>` prompt. Enter **set localecho** (**set local_echo** on Windows 2000) to display the entered commands locally for demonstration purposes. If you don't set this option, commands you send to the server won't be displayed by the telnet application. You can specify a log file with the `set logfile` command. Now you can connect to the web server with the `open` command. The command `open msdn.microsoft.com 80` creates a TCP connection to port 80 of the server at `msdn.microsoft.com`. The telnet application uses port 23 by default, hence you have to specify a port for the HTTP request. The default port of a web server offering HTTP services is port 80.

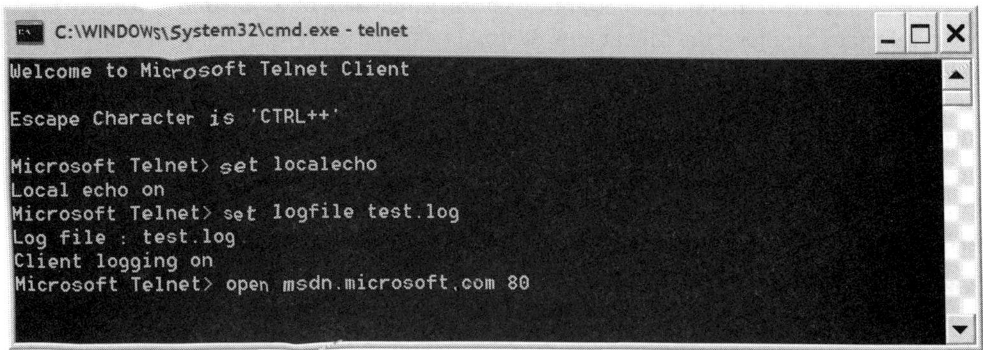

Figure 1-20. *Using telnet.exe to access a web server*

As soon as the connection is initiated, you can send an HTTP request to the web server. A simple request consists of a request line followed by two returns (two carriage return/linefeed [CR-LF] sequences). Such a request line can look like this: `GET /default.aspx HTTP/1.0`. The server returns a HTTP response that consists of the status information (in this case, `200 OK`) followed by the HTML content that is shown here. Here is an extract of the telnet logfile:

```
GET /default.aspx HTTP/1.0 Client
HTTP/1.1 200 OK
Cache-Control: public
Content-Length: 28883
Content-Type: text/html; charset=utf-8
Expires: Sat, 31 Jan 2004 11:55:26 GMT
Last-Modified: Sat, 31 Jan 2004 11:50:26 GMT
Server: Microsoft-IIS/6.0
X-AspNet-Version: 1.1.4322
P3P: CP='ALL IND DSP COR ADM CONo CUR CUSo IVAo IVDo PSA PSD TAI TELo OUR SAMo C
NT COM INT NAV ONL PHY PRE PUR UNI'
level: C7
X-Powered-By: ASP.NET
Date: Sat, 31 Jan 2004 11:50:35 GMT
Connection: close
<!DOCTYPE HTML PUBLIC "-//W3C//DTD HTML 4.0 Transitional//EN" >
<html>
<head>
        <title>MSDN Home Page</title>
...
```

As you have seen, a basic HTTP request has only a single request line. A full HTTP request, however, will consist of a request line with additional headers and data.

HTTP commands such as `GET`, `HEAD`, and `POST` can be specified in the request line. Both `GET` and `POST` request data from the server. The `GET` command includes request parameters in the URL, while the `POST` request specifies that parameters follow in the data block. The `HEAD` command means that you just want to know when the requested file was changed so you can verify that the newest version is already in the cache.

General headers, request headers, and an entity header can follow the request line. This header information allows the client to tell the server about the browser in use and any preferred languages, to send a cookie, or to request files only if they have been changed. In the telnet example, you saw some header information returned by the server: the date, server version, content length, content type, and cache control.

■NOTE Chapter 10 contains more information about the HTTP protocol and programming with the HTTP protocol. HTTP is defined in RFC 1945.

HTTPS: HTTP over Secure Sockets Layer (SSL)

If there is a requirement to exchange confidential data with a web server, HTTPS can be used. HTTPS is an extension to the HTTP protocol, and the principles discussed in the last section still apply. However, the underlying mechanism is different, as HTTPS uses Secure Sockets Layer (SSL), originally developed by Netscape. SSL sits on top of TCP and secures network communication using a public/private key principle to exchange secret symmetric keys and a symmetric key to encrypt the messages.

To support HTTPS, the web server must install a certificate so that it can be identified. The default port for HTTPS requests is 443.

■NOTE For more information on SSL, go to the following page on the Netscape website: `http://wp.netscape.com/eng/ssl3/ssl-toc.html`.

E-mail Protocols

There are quite a few protocols for use with e-mail. In this section, we provide an overview of the most important mail-related protocols. In Chapter 11, we'll delve into these protocols in more detail, and you'll learn how to create applications that use these protocols.

Simple Mail Transfer Protocol (SMTP)

SMTP is a protocol for sending and receiving e-mail messages. It can be used to send e-mail between a client and a server that both use the same transport protocol, or to send e-mail between servers that use different transport protocols. SMTP has the capability to relay messages across transport service environments. SMTP does not allow you to read messages from a mail server, however; for this activity, you should use the POP3 or IMAP protocol.

An SMTP service forms part of the Internet Information Server (IIS) installation of Windows 2000 and XP.

■NOTE The SMTP standard is defined in RFC 821. The SMTP message format is defined in RFC 822.

Post Office Protocol (POP3)

POP3 was designed for disconnected environments. In small environments, it is not practical to maintain a persistent connection with the mail server, for instance, in environments in which the connection time must be paid. With POP3, the client can access the server and retrieve the messages that the server is holding for it. When messages are retrieved by the client, they are typically deleted on the server, although this is not necessarily the case.

Windows Server 2003 includes a POP3 server.

■ NOTE POP3 is defined in RFC 1081.

Internet Message Access Protocol (IMAP)

Like POP3, IMAP is designed to access mail on a mail server. Similar to a POP3 client, an IMAP client can have an offline mode where mail can be manipulated on the local machine. Unlike a POP3 client, an IMAP client has greater capabilities when in online mode, such as retrieving just the headers or bodies of specified mail, searching for particular messages on the server, and setting flags such as the replied flag. Essentially, IMAP allows the client to manipulate a remote mailbox as if it were local.

■ NOTE IMAP is defined in RFC 1730.

Network News Transfer Protocol (NNTP)

NNTP is an application layer protocol for submitting, relaying, and retrieving messages that form part of newsgroup discussions. This protocol provides client applications with access to a news server to retrieve selected messages, and it also supports server-to-server transfer of messages.

■ NOTE NNTP is defined in RFCs 850, 977, and 1036.

Other Application Protocols

There are two other interesting application protocols that we discuss in this section: *Simple Network Management Protocol* (SNMP) and Telnet.

SNMP aims to permit management of devices on the network. There is no lack of information such as performance counts from devices; instead, there is too much information to manage it effectively. SNMP aims to manage devices effectively by using alarms that are triggered by performance problems and faults, and it allows devices to be configured.

An SNMP agent associated with a particular network device (see Figure 1-21) will have a Management Information Base (MIB) database that contains all manageable information for that device in an object-oriented manner (that is, consisting of objects, attributes, and instances). An SNMP client accesses the information in this database by sending SNMP `GET` requests. Conversely, SNMP `SET` requests are used to configure the MIB database.

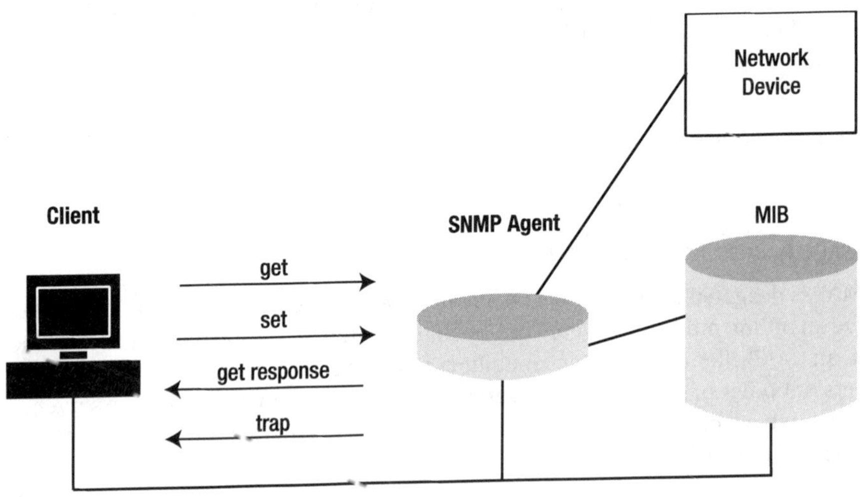

Figure 1-21. *SNMP*

In case of faults or performance problems, the SNMP agent sends trap messages to the SNMP client.

■ NOTE SNMP is defined in RFC 1157. The MIB database is defined in RFCs 1155 and 1156.

Earlier we used the telnet application to simulate a browser as it was carrying out an HTTP request. However, the telnet application is primarily intended for connecting to a telnet server using the Telnet protocol. This protocol enables you to connect to a remote system using user authentication and then invoke commands remotely from a console environment.

Sockets

The term "socket" doesn't define a protocol; it has two meanings, but neither relates to a protocol. One meaning is the socket programming API that was created initially by the University of California, Berkeley, for Berkeley Software Distribution (BSD) UNIX. BSD sockets were adapted as a programming interface for the Windows environment (and given the name WinSock). The WinSock API is wrapped in the .NET classes of the `System.Net.Sockets` namespace. Windows Sockets is a protocol independent programming interface for writing networking applications.

■ **NOTE** Chapters 4 to 9 present more information about socket programming. In later chapters where we show higher-level classes for Internet programming, sockets are used behind the scenes.

The second meaning of the term "socket" denotes an endpoint for communication between processes. In TCP/IP, an endpoint is bound to an IP address and a port number. We have to differentiate between *stream* and *datagram* socket types. A stream socket uses connection-oriented communication by using the TCP/IP protocol, whereas a datagram socket uses connectionless communication using UDP/IP. We'll talk more about sockets in Chapter 4.

Domain Names

It isn't easy to remember IP addresses with quad notation, so more human-friendly names are given to hosts on the network. Because such names must be unique, the domain name system used supports hierarchical names. Examples of such host names are `www.apress.com`, `msdn.microsoft.com`, and `kerberos.vienna.christiannagel.com`. These names don't have to have three parts, but reading from right to the left, the name starts with the top-level domain. These top-level domains are country specific (such as `.com.tw`) or generic (such as `.org`) and are defined by IANA. The name appearing directly to the left of the top-level domain is the domain name. To the left of that name, the person or organization holding the domain is responsible for maintaining uniqueness.

Table 1-8 lists the generic top-level domains. In recent years, some new top-level domain names have been added.

Table 1-8. *Generic and New Top-Level Domains*

Domain Name	Description
`.aero`	Air industry
`.biz`	Businesses
`.com`	Commercial organizations
`.coop`	Cooperative associations
`.info`	No restriction on usage
`.museum`	Museums
`.name`	Individuals
`.net`	Networks
`.org`	Nonprofit organizations
`.pro`	Professionals
`.gov`	United States government
`.edu`	Educational institutions
`.mil`	United States military
`.int`	Organizations established by international treaties between governments

■ **NOTE** You can find detailed descriptions of these generic top-level domains, and of the sponsors and registrars of the domains, at `http://www.iana.org/gtld/gtld.htm`.

In addition to the generic top-level domains, every country has a domain name. Table 1-9 shows some examples.

Table 1-9. *Sampling of Country-Specific Domains*

Domain Name	Country
`.at`	Austria
`.cc`	Cocos (Keeling) Islands
`.de`	Germany
`.fr`	France
`.tv`	Tuvalu
`.uk`	United Kingdom

■ **NOTE** You can find a complete list of the country domains at `http://www.iana.org/cctld/cctld-whois.htm`.

Whois Service

The whois service provides a means for querying a registration service to find the person or organization that registered a specific domain, their contact information, registration addresses, and so on. Such a whois service is available at `http://www.internic.net/whois.html`.

Domain Name Servers

Host names are resolved using Domain Name System (DNS) servers. These servers have a database of host names and alias names mapping names to IP addresses. DNS servers also register information for mail servers, ISDN numbers, mailbox names, and services.

In Windows, the TCP/IP settings specify which DNS server is to be used for queries, and the command `ipconfig /all` shows the DNS servers that have been set up, along with other configuration settings. When a host name is used to connect to a remote system, the DNS server is queried for the IP address. The DNS server will first check its own database and cache, and if that fails to resolve the name, the DNS server asks a DNS root server. There are several root servers (named `a.root-servers.net` through to `m.root-servers.net`) worldwide that can access DNS servers of the top-level domains. The DNS server of the top-level domain knows the DNS server for a specific subdomain and will return the IP address corresponding to a particular host name. DNS servers store information not found in their database in a cache to speed up subsequent requests.

nslookup

The `nslookup` command-line utility provides IP addresses for host names by querying the default DNS server. In the case shown in Figure 1-22, the DNS server is `signal.kabsi.at`. When this server is asked for the IP address of `www.microsoft.com`, it returns the real name of the server, `www2.microsoft.akadns.net`; eight IP addresses configured for this server; and its aliases `www.microsoft.com` and `www.microsoft.akadns.com`.

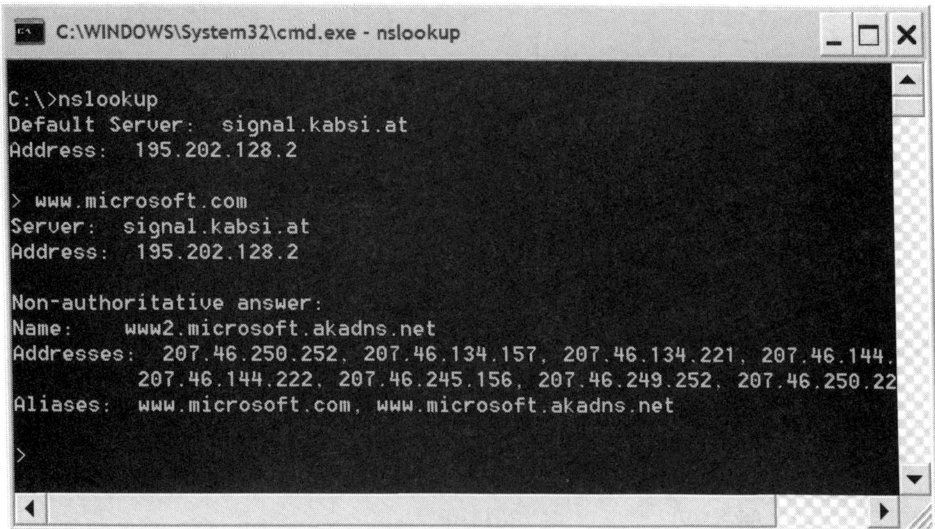

Figure 1-22. *nslookup utility*

This is a nonauthoritative answer, meaning that this server is not responsible for the domain that was queried, and it reads the information of this domain from its cache. Incidentally, this caching is the cause of many host-name lookup problems. A name server will clear its DNS cache infrequently, with the effect that different servers will hold inconsistent information. It can take whole days for a change of an address to filter through the Internet. The `nslookup` command-line utility lets you set up a different DNS server for querying, so you can compare information from different servers.

The Internet

In this chapter, we have covered many of the base technologies that underpin the Internet: hardware, protocols, and DNS. There remain some interesting topics for us to discuss:

- Intranets and extranets
- Firewalls and web proxies
- XML web services

Intranets and Extranets

An *intranet* can use TCP/IP technologies in a similar way to the Internet. The difference is, of course, that an intranet is a private network, in which all users are known. An intranet is not intended for general public access, and some—if not all—data must be secured from outside access. Securing an intranet from the Internet at large is a task carried out by firewalls (see Figure 1-23).

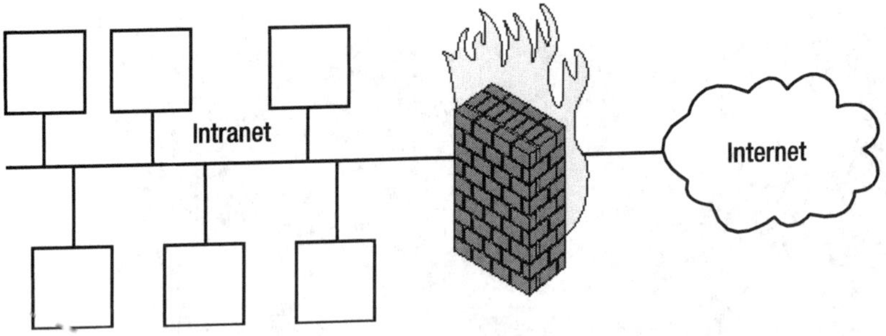

Figure 1-23. *Using a firewall to secure an intranet*

An *extranet* is a private network like an intranet, but it connects multiple intranet sites that belong to one company or partner companies over the Internet using a *tunnel* (see Figure 1-24). Creating a virtual private network (VPN) over the Internet in this way offers significant cost advantages compared to leasing private lines.

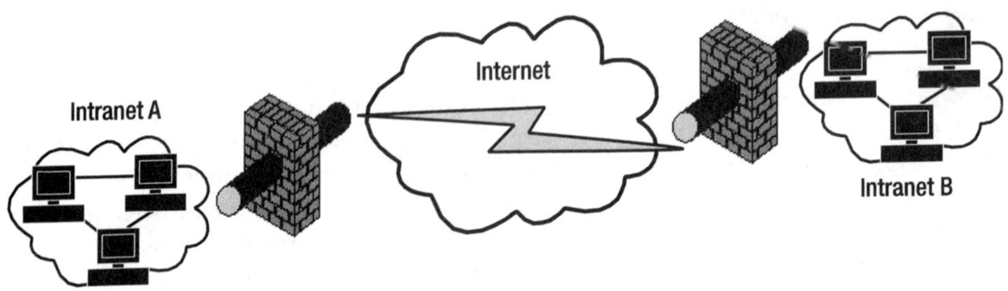

Figure 1-24. *Using a tunnel across the Internet*

Firewalls

A *firewall* secures the intranet from the mayhem and disorder that is the Internet. A firewall is also often used to secure a subnet inside a company from other subnets, to restrict access to the first subnet to only specified users and/or tasks.

To create a secure network with a firewall, this network must be configured for all incoming and outgoing traffic to pass through the firewall—naturally, there must be no alternate routes that bypass the firewall.

Firewalls can work at various layers of the OSI model. *Packet filters* check packets and filter them according to the IP addresses and port numbers of the network and transport layers. Packets from or to particular IP addresses can be granted permission to pass through the firewall, either into the network or out to the world beyond. Port numbers can be used with packet filtering to specify what services can be used on each side of the firewall. For example, a firewall can be set in a way that the Internet side (known as the *red side* in firewall terminology) may access only web servers, at certain IP addresses behind the firewall, through HTTP. Such a configuration can be seen in Figure 1-25, where a second firewall secures the internal company network that contains the mail server, file services, and user workstations. If applications running on the web server need access to data from the intranet, specific protocols and ports can be configured for the second firewall.

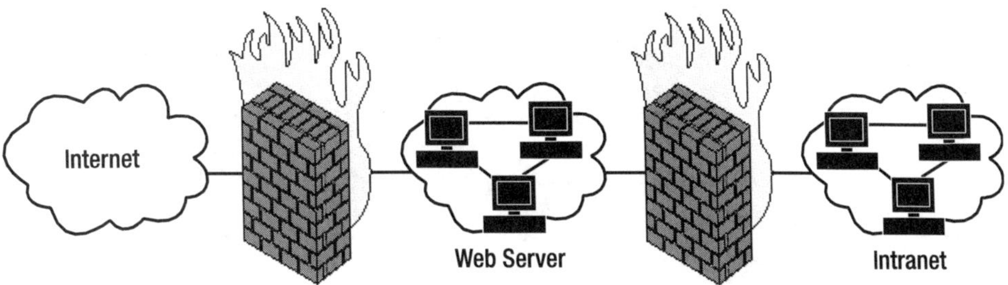

Figure 1-25. *Securing a web server and intranet*

If security filters with a port number are defined, every packet sent through the firewall must be passed up to the transport layer to be checked. A higher level of checking is possible by using *application filters*. An application filter must know about the commands of the application-level protocol, such as FTP, HTTP, or SMTP, and can permit certain files to be copied from the Internet to the intranet, but not the other way around, by allowing FTP `GET` commands, but not FTP `PUT` commands. SMTP application filters often deny mail that uses `DEBUG` commands, as SMTP `DEBUG` mail can be used to break into local networks.

Web Proxies

A *web proxy* caches web requests from clients. Internet browsers on the intranet can be configured to use a web proxy that forwards the HTTP request to the web server on the Internet. The web proxy can cache web requests so that future client requests requesting the same page are not answered by the web server, but with the cached page stored by the web proxy.

Other functions of the web proxy are to restrict access to specific websites and to log the web requests made by users.

■ **NOTE** The Microsoft Internet Security and Acceleration Server (ISA) acts both as a firewall and a web proxy to secure the network and to increase performance.

XML Web Services

An *XML web service* is an application that can be identified by a Uniform Resource Identifier (URI) and called remotely using Internet-friendly protocols such as HTTP.

At the heart of XML web services lies the Simple Object Access Protocol (SOAP). SOAP defines an XML format for calling remote methods regardless of the technologies used to implement those methods.

A typical process for invoking web services is shown in Figure 1-26.

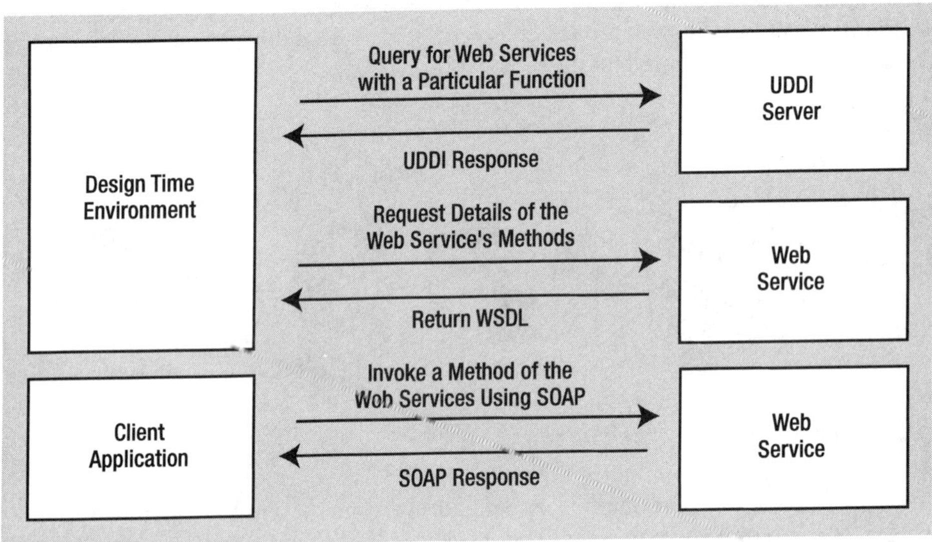

Figure 1-26. *XML web services technologies*

First, you have to find a web service that meets your requirements, which you can do by querying a Universal Description, Discovery, and Integration (UDDI) server. The UDDI server is queried by using the UDDI protocol. Publicly available web services can be registered on a UDDI server, such as `http://www.uddi.org` or `http://www.salcentral.com`, which provides search functionality. The UDDI server returns certain information about web services that match specified requirements, such as a link to a Web Services Description Language (WSDL) document that details the methods exposed by the web service in a computer-readable XML format. If a web service is not to be made publicly available, its WSDL document can be exchanged in other ways or by a private UDDI server. Microsoft offers a UDDI server that can be installed with Windows Server 2003.

The methods and parameters described by the WSDL document can be used to build SOAP requests to call the web service.

■ **NOTE** You can use ASP.NET to easily create a web service using the classes in the `System.Web.Services` namespace.

NOTE You can find the SOAP specification at `http://www.w3.org/2000/xp/Group`.

.NET Remoting

The Remote Procedure Call (RPC) protocol was the first widely recognized way to call functions across a network. RPC is a high-level protocol that does not require the client to create a message and send it to the receiving side, and to pick up the message on the server and analyze it to invoke the required function. Instead, the application programmer can invoke a function directly on the server. The RPC proxy running on the client marshals the remote method call (that is, transforms it to a network message) to send it to the server, whereas the RPC stub unmarshals the message and invokes the method.

Because RPC was function oriented, Microsoft's Distributed Component Object Model (DCOM) extended it to add object orientation.

.NET brings a new model for distributed applications and a successor to DCOM: .NET Remoting. .NET Remoting offers far greater flexibility and extensibility over DCOM.

Figure 1-27 shows an architecture overview of .NET Remoting. The remote object exposes some methods for remote calls. A *proxy* is created on the client mirroring the remote object insofar as it exposes the same public methods. The client invokes these methods on the proxy class, and the proxy uses a *formatter* to format the messages so that they can be sent across the network.

The network transport is defined by the channel. On the server, another *formatter* unformats received messages and passes them to the *dispatcher*, which calls the methods on the remote object.

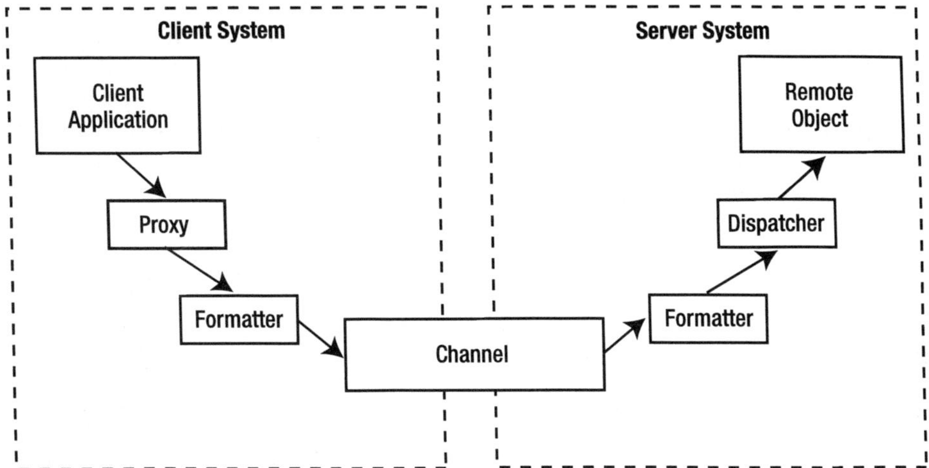

Figure 1-27. *.NET Remoting architecture*

.NET Remoting permits *interceptors*, or *sinks*, to be placed at certain points in the flow on the client or server side to add additional functionality, such as logging, duplicating calls for reliability reasons, or dynamically finding servers.

.NET Remoting supports a variety of channels and formatters. The .NET Framework v1.0 and v1.1 offer a TCP and a HTTP channel, and SOAP and binary formatters. If you choose the HTTP channel and the SOAP formatter, .NET Remoting becomes the same as XML web services. The TCP channel with binary formatters is a fast communication mechanism. If both the client and the server use .NET technologies, .NET Remoting is a fast and easy-to-use communication mechanism.

TIP You can learn more about .NET Remoting in the book *Advanced .NET Remoting* by Ingo Rammer (Apress, 2002).

Messaging

Messaging is the process of sending messages from a client to a server. All networking protocols we have covered thus far require a connected environment. No matter if you use TCP or UDP sockets, the HTTP protocol, or .NET Remoting, the client and server must be running concurrently—that is, at the same time.

With *message queuing*, the client and server can be running at different times, and the client can send messages even when the connection to the server is not available. The message will be queued and will reach the server later. Message queuing also gives you an easy way to set priorities for messages, which can be useful in a connected environment too, where you may wish to read higher priority messages first.

One scenario in which message queuing can be particularly useful is when an application is run on a portable computer not connected to the company network—for example, where the computer belongs to a salesperson at a customer's site (see Figure 1-28). Message queuing allows the application to send a message but store it in the message queue of the client until it's connected back to the network. As far as the application that sends the message is concerned, the message is sent immediately.

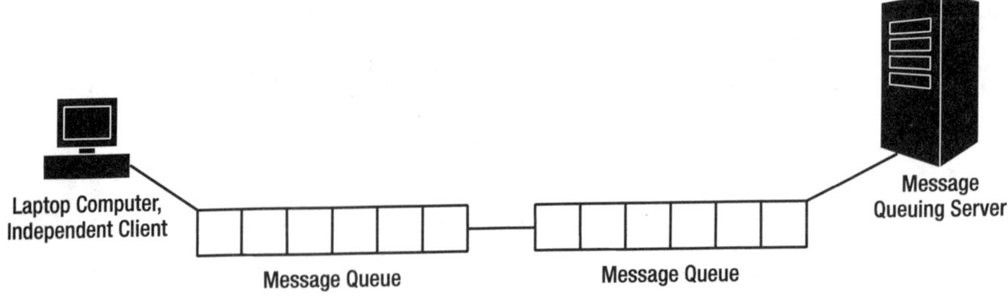

Figure 1-28. *Message queuing*

Other Ways to Access Network Objects

Lightweight Directory Access Protocol (LDAP) was designed for hierarchical object stores that hold long-lived objects. LDAP, or Active Directory, creates such stores for long-lived objects that are of interest in the enterprise, such as users, groups, computers, printers, network shares, services, or any custom object type. LDAP lets you read, write, and search for objects in the stores. Classes in the `System.DirectoryServices` namespace allow the .NET Framework to access objects in the Active Directory or other LDAP data stores.

The `System.Management` namespace offers classes to access Windows Management Instrumentation (WMI) classes. WMI enables management to be performed across the network, such as accessing hardware information, and configuring and administering services that offer WMI providers. WMI can be used to obtain information about hardware, such as free disk space, CPU utilization, performance data, and DNS server and terminal services configuration.

Internet Organizations and Standards

A whole host of standard committees are working on the development of networking specifications and standards. Table 1-10 lists the important groups in this area.

Table 1-10. *Internet Organization and Standards*

Standards Organization	Website	Technologies
International Organization for Standardization (ISO)	`http://www.iso.org`	ISO defined the OSI network. The OSI model now is commonly used.
Institute of Electrical and Electronics Engineers (IEEE)	`http://www.ieee.org`	IEEE is responsible for LAN standards and hardware specifications: Ethernet, Token Ring, MAN, wireless LAN, and broadband.
Internet Architecture Board (IAB)	`http://www.iab.org`	IAB is responsible for editorial management of RFCs, and it appoints the IETF chair.
Internet Engineering Task Force (IETF)	`http://www.ietf.org`	Internet standards and RFCs can be found on the IETF website.
Internet Assigned Numbers Authority (IANA)	`http://www.iana.org`	IANA is responsible for assigning Internet numbers such as reserved IP address ranges, port numbers, protocol numbers, and so on.
World Wide Web Consortium (W3C)	`http://www.w3.org`	W3C is active in developing Internet technologies, for example, HTTP, HTML, XML, SOAP, and so on.

Summary

This chapter covered the basics of networking, to provide an overview of important networking concepts and networking protocols. We started with a discussion of the physical network, and looked at the purpose and function of the crucial components of a network: network interface cards, hubs, routers, and switches.

Another piece of fundamental knowledge that underpins much work in networking is that of the magic OSI seven-layer model. These seven layers are, from top to bottom, application, presentation, session, transport, network, data link, and physical.

We also took a close look at the headers of the key IP, TCP, and UDP protocols, to gain an understanding of connection-oriented and connectionless communication.

We discussed the purpose of some important application protocols, namely HTTP, FTP, SMTP, and IMAP. These are only a few of the technologies found in use on the Internet and other networks.

With this knowledge of the basics, you're now ready to move on to writing some programs that perform stream manipulation in the next chapter, as this is very useful in network programming. You'll start with network programming proper in Chapter 3. These first three chapters lay the foundation that all later chapters of this book are based on.

CHAPTER 2

■ ■ ■

Streams in .NET

A *stream* is an abstract representation of a sequence of bytes such as a file, an I/O device, or a TCP/IP socket. Through this abstraction, different devices can be accessed with the same process, and similar code can be used to read data from a file input stream, as can be used to read data from a network input stream, for example. Furthermore, the programmer's need to worry about the actual physical mechanism of the device is removed.

In this chapter, we'll discuss the following topics:

- Streams in .NET
- The `Stream` class and its members
- The `FileStream` class and other `Stream`-derived classes
- Reading to and writing from binary and text files
- Serialization

Streams in .NET

The .NET Framework provides rich set of classes for performing operations on various types of streams. `Stream`, an abstract class from which all other stream-related classes are derived, is the main class.

Since a stream is an abstraction of data as a sequence of bytes, to manipulate these sequences of bytes you have to perform a basic operation such as reading, writing, or seeking. With the `Stream` class, you can perform binary I/O operations on a stream. With the `TextReader` and `TextWriter` classes, you can perform character I/O operations, whereas with the `BinaryReader` and `BinaryWriter` classes, you can perform I/O operations on primitive types

Synchronous and Asynchronous I/O

There are two kinds of operations you can perform on a stream: *synchronous* and *asynchronous*. Your choice will depend upon the requirements of your application. As you'll see in a moment, the `Stream` class provides methods for both synchronous and asynchronous operations, but first we'll discuss some of the advantages and disadvantages of each type of operation.

Synchronous I/O

By default, all operations on streams are performed synchronously—this is the simplest way to perform I/O operation. The disadvantage of synchronous I/O is that it blocks processing until the I/O operation is complete, and then the application is allowed to continue processing.

Synchronous I/O is useful for performing operations on small files, but with large files, the application may give poor performance as it blocks the execution. Synchronous I/O is not suitable for performing operations over a network where you have little control over the time required to complete the operation. Therefore, synchronous I/O is not a good choice for passing huge streams on a network with low bandwidth or speed. By threading synchronous methods, you can simulate asynchronous I/O.

Asynchronous I/O

In asynchronous I/O, other tasks can be performed while the I/O operation is being completed. When the I/O operation completes, the operating system notifies the caller. Therefore, a separate notification mechanism is required for asynchronous I/O.

This method is useful when an application needs to continue performing other tasks while processing large amounts of data from a stream, or when an application needs to work with slow devices whose rate of access would otherwise slow it down.

In asynchronous I/O, a separate thread is created for each I/O request, which can lead to an extra overhead for the operating system.

Stream Class

The `Stream` class in the `System.IO` namespace is the base class for all the other stream classes, and it provides the functionality for performing fundamental operations on streams. If you understand the functionality of the `Stream` class, then you can easily understand the other derived classes, too. The key thing to learn is how to create the different types of streams with each class. In short, all the `Stream`-derived classes represent various types of streams with common or derived methods from the `Stream` class and some extra methods for performing operations on that specific type of stream.

Figure 2-1 illustrates `Stream`, the derived classes, and various other classes provided for performing operations on stream.

Each derived class is characterized according to its underlying device or backing storage. For example, the `FileStream` class uses files as a backing storage for streams. The `NetworkStream` class does not have any backing storage, but this class is specially created for transferring streams across a network.

Table 2-1 shows some of the main classes derived from `Stream`, along with their purpose.

Now let's have a look at the `Stream` class's members.

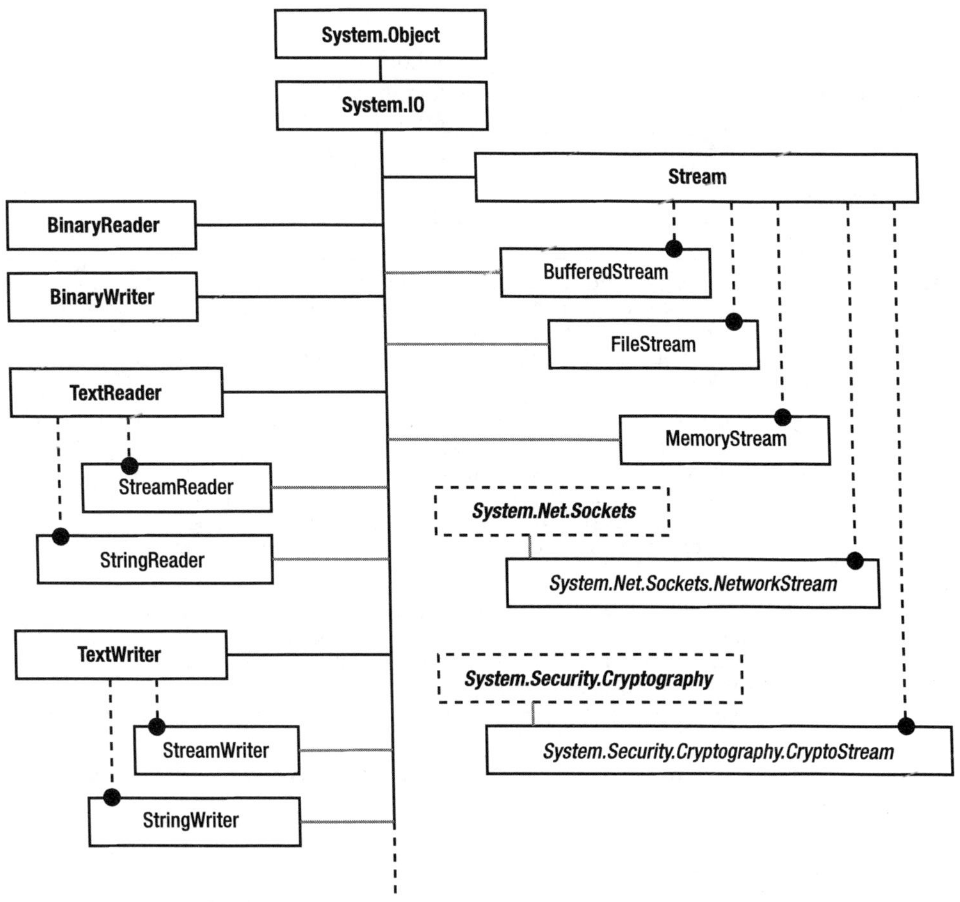

Figure 2-1. *Stream class*

Table 2-1. *Classes Derived from the Stream Class*

Class	Purpose
`FileStream`	Uses files as backing storage. This is the most widely used `Stream` class.
`BufferedStream`	Uses a buffer as backing storage. This class is used as intermediate storage for improving performance.
`MemoryStream`	Uses memory as backing storage and performs faster I/O operations when compared to other streams.
`NetworkStream`	Does not have any backing storage. This class is used with other streams for transferring data across a network.
`CryptoStream`	Used with other stream classes for performing encryption and decryption on streams.

Stream Members

We'll start with the public properties. First are three public properties, shown in Table 2-2, that tell us whether or not a stream supports a particular feature, which can be determined when the stream is created through the relevant constructor.

Table 2-2. *Stream Properties*

Property	Description
`CanRead`	This property is used to check whether or not the current stream supports reading. In general, this property is used before performing any reading operation on a stream. It returns `true` if the stream supports reading; otherwise, it returns `false`. A .`NotSupportedException` is thrown if the stream does not support reading and an attempt is made to read from it
`CanSeek`	Seeking is used to set the position within the current stream. `CanSeek` checks whether or not the current stream supports seeking. It returns `true` if the stream supports seeking; otherwise, it returns `false`. A stream's ability to seek depends on its backing storage—media such as a disk or memory will generally allow seeking, but streams without any backing store, such as network streams, will always return `false`. A `NotSupportedException` is thrown if seeking is attempted on a stream that does not support it.
`CanWrite`	This property is used before doing any write operation on the current stream to check whether or not it supports writing. This property returns `true` if the stream supports writing; otherwise, it returns `false`. Attempting to write to a stream that does not support writing throws a `NotSupportedException`.

Two further properties, shown in Table 2-3, determine the size of the stream and the current position within the stream.

Table 2-3. *More Stream Properties*

Property	Description
`Length`	This read-only property returns a `long` value representing the length of the stream in bytes. This property can be used for checking the end of the stream, for determining the size of an array of bytes.
`Position`	This property can be used to set or to get the current position within the stream. It is used for moving around within a stream. To use this property, the stream must support seeking, which can be checked using `CanSeek` property discussed in Table 2-2.

The `Stream` class has a number of methods for moving through the stream, reading from and writing to the stream, and managing the stream.

Let's look first at the Seek method for moving through the stream. Seek is used for setting the position within stream. This method provides random access to the stream and is generally used while modifying or reading specific contents of the stream. Seek takes a long value and a value from the SeekOrigin enumeration. The long value specifies the offset from reference point specified by the SeekOrigin value, which can be Begin, Current, or End, representing the beginning of the stream, the current position, or the end of the stream, respectively. (Seek is the method actually used when you set the Position property.)

The methods for reading from and writing to streams fall into two categories, and there are corresponding sets of methods for synchronous and asynchronous operations. Table 2-4 shows the synchronous methods.

Table 2-4. *Synchronous Methods for Reading from and Writing to a Stream*

Method	Description
Read ReadByte	Read and ReadByte are used for performing synchronous reading from a stream. Read reads a specified number of bytes and advances the position within the stream by the number of bytes read, whereas ReadByte reads a single byte from the stream and advances the current position within the stream by 1 byte. Note that Read returns 0 at the end of stream, and ReadByte returns -1.
Write WriteByte	These methods are used to perform synchronous writing to a stream. Write writes a sequence of bytes in a stream and advances the current position within a stream by the number of bytes written, whereas WriteByte writes a single byte at the current position within a stream, advancing the position by 1 byte.

Table 2-5 presents the asynchronous methods.

Table 2-5. *Asynchronous Methods for Reading from and Writing to a Stream*

Method	Description
BeginRead BeginWrite	BeginRead and BeginWrite are the methods through which you can perform asynchronous I/O operations. Both methods take five parameters. The first three parameters are a byte array buffer that data is read from or written to, an integer offset that indicates the starting position for reading or writing the data, and an integer count specifying the maximum number of bytes to read or write. The fourth parameter is an optional AsyncCallback delegate, which is called when the read or write operation is complete. The fifth and last parameter is a user-provided object to distinguish this particular read or write request from other requests. Both methods return an IAsyncResult interface that represents the status of an asynchronous operation.
EndRead EndWrite	These methods are used for completing asynchronous I/O operations. These methods wait for the asynchronous operations to finish.

Finally, Table 2-6 shows methods for managing a stream.

Table 2-6. *Methods for Managing a Stream*

Method	Description
`Flush`	`Flush` clears all buffers and moves information to its destination depending upon the state of the `Stream` object.
`Close`	`Close` is used to free resources such as file handlers and sockets associated with the stream. This method automatically flushes any stored data, so there is no need to call `Flush` before a `Close` method. The underlying mechanism for closing a stream is different for each stream type—in `FileStream` it releases all file resources, whereas in `NetworkStream` it closes the underlying socket. It is advisable to put a `Close` method into a `finally` block to ensure that the stream is closed regardless of any exceptions thrown.
`SetLength`	`SetLength` is used to set the length of the current stream. Note that if the specified value is less than the current length of the stream, the stream is truncated. If the specified value is greater than the current length of the stream, the stream is expanded. A stream must support both writing and seeking for `SetLength`—this can be checked with the `CanWrite` and `CanSeek` properties.

When we look at the classes derived from `Stream`, we don't discuss these methods any further unless they have meaning specific to that type of stream.

Our first `Stream` example is the `FileStream` class. Once you've seen how to implement the members we've just looked at with the `FileStream` class, it's a short stretch to understand how to apply them to the other `Stream`-derived classes.

FileStream Class

The `FileStream` class is useful for performing I/O operations on files, and as such, it's one of the most important and widely used of all the `Stream`-derived classes.

With the `FileStream` class, you can perform operations not only on files, but also on operating system file handles such as standard input and output devices. You can use this class with other derived classes to create temporary files. You can serialize objects to a binary file, for example, and then convert them back whenever required. While transferring the file across a network, you can stream the file contents using this class on the server side, and on the client side you can re-create and store the retrieved stream back into the original file format.

The `FileStream` constructor allows several ways to create a `FileStream` object, but they all involve specifying either a string for the file path or a file handle that can be used for physical devices that support streaming.

Creating a FileStream Instance with a File Path

Various methods for creating a `FileStream` instance by specifying a path to a file are described in the sections that follow. A default buffer of 8,192 bytes is allocated to the stream when it is created. This can be changed with one of the constructor overloads you'll encounter in a moment.

Specifying the File Path and Mode

By specifying a string representing the path to a file and a value from the FileMode enumeration, you can create a FileStream object. The FileMode parameter describes how to open a specified file. Table 2-7 presents its values.

Table 2-7. *FileMode Options and Descriptions*

FileMode Value	Description
Append	Opens or creates a new file for appending data to. The file cannot be used for reading, and the file pointer is set to the end of the file.
Create	Creates a new file, overwriting if the file already exists.
CreateNew	Creates a new file, throwing an exception if the file already exists.
Open	Opens an already existing file, throwing an exception if file does not exist.
OpenOrCreate	If the file specified exists, it is opened; otherwise, a new file is created.
Truncate	Opens a file and deletes its contents, setting the file pointer to the beginning of the file.

Thus, to create a FileStream object that creates a new file called C:\Networking\MyStream.txt, you would use the following:

```
// Using file path and file mode
FileStream inF = new FileStream("C:\\Networking\\MyStream.txt",
                                FileMode.CreateNew);
```

Specifying File Access

You can create an instance of FileStream by providing additional file access parameters from the FileAccess enumeration. This enumeration allows you to restrict the user to specific operations on the stream. Table 2-8 presents the FileAccess enumeration values.

Table 2-8. *FileAccess Options and Descriptions*

FileAccess Value	Description
Read	Allow read-only access to the file.
Write	Allow write-only access to the file.
ReadWrite	Allow both read and write access to the file.

You can use the CanRead and CanWrite properties discussed earlier to check the FileAccess permission given to the file. Thus, to create a FileStream object that creates a new file called C:\Networking\MyStream.txt with write-only access, you would use the following:

```
// Using file path, file mode, and file access
FileStream inF = new FileStream("C:\\Networking\\MyStream.txt",
                                FileMode.CreateNew, FileAccess.Write);
```

Specifying Sharing Permissions

With the addition of sharing permissions, you can control access to other stream objects. This is useful when a file is shared between two or more processes. The sharing permissions are determined by a value from the `FileShare` enumeration that represents various access modes. Table 2-9 presents the `FileShare` enumeration values.

Table 2-9. *FileShare Options and Descriptions*

FileShare Value	Description
`Inheritable`	The child process can inherit the file handle. This is not supported by Win32.
`None`	No process (including the current one) can access the file, thus the file cannot be shared.
`Read`	Gives read-only permission to the current process and other processes.
`Write`	Gives write-only permission to the current process and other processes.
`ReadWrite`	Grants read and write permission to the current process and other processes.

The following code shows how to create a `FileStream` instance using the `FileMode`, `FileAccess`, and `FileShare` properties:

```
// Using file path, file mode, file access, and sharing permission
// Open file for writing, other processes will get read-only access
FileStream inF = new FileStream("C:\\Networking\\MyStream.txt ",
                                FileMode.Open, FileAccess.Write, FileShare.Read);
```

Specifying Buffer Size

You can also create a `FileStream` instance by specifying the size of the buffer in addition to the parameters discussed previously. Here, we set the size of the buffer to 1,000 bytes:

```
//Using path, mode, access, sharing permission, and buffer size
FileStream outF = new FileStream(C:\\Networking\\MyStream.txt ",
                                FileMode.Open, FileAccess.Write,
                                FileShare.Read, 1000);
```

If the buffer size specified is between 0 and 8, the actual buffer is set to 8 bytes.

Specifying Synchronous or Asynchronous State

With a further Boolean value, we can specify whether to use asynchronous or synchronous I/O operations on the stream. A value of `true` indicates asynchronous.

```
//Using path, mode, access, sharing permission, buffer size, and
// specifying asynchronous operations
FileStream outF = new FileStream("C:\\Networking\\MyStream.txt",
                                FileMode.Open, FileAccess.Write,
                                FileShare.Read, 1000,true);
```

It's also possible to create a FileStream object using a file handle rather than passing a path to a file. A *file handle* is a unique identifier that the operating system assigns to a file when the file is opened or created. A file handle is represented using the IntPtr structure, which represents an integer of platform-specific length.

Creating a FileStream object with a file handle requires you to specify at least the file handle and the FileAccess value. A further overload allows you to define the ownership of the stream, with a value of true meaning the FileStream instance gets exclusive control. With further parameters, you can specify the size of the buffer (the default size is 8,192 bytes).

You can obtain a file handle from a FileStream object by using its Handle property:

```
//Create FileStream instance
FileStream inF = new FileStream("C:\\Networking\\MyStream.txt", FileMode.Open);
//Get the file handle
IntPtr fHandle = inF.Handle;
```

Reading and Writing with the FileStream Class

We've spent enough time covering the methods and properties of the Stream-derived classes that we can use, so let's actually start reading from and writing to a FileStream. We'll take a look at both synchronous and asynchronous modes of operation.

Synchronous I/O

Stream provides Read and Write methods for performing synchronous read/write operations on a stream.

The following example performs synchronous I/O operations on a file. It also uses the Seek method to set the position within the stream. We begin by adding the System.IO namespace for I/O operations and the System.Text namespace for the methods to convert strings to byte arrays (we detail these later in the chapter).

```
using System;
using System.IO;
using System.Text ;
class SyncIO
{
   public static void Main(string[] args)
   {
```

We then create a FileStream instance, specifying its FileMode as OpenOrCreate. This will open our file if it exists; otherwise, a new file is created. When you first run this example, a file called SyncDemo.txt is created in the same folder as the executable.

```
      // Create FileStream instance
      FileStream syncF = new FileStream("SyncDemo.txt",FileMode.OpenOrCreate);
```

Now we're ready to examine various synchronous methods. We'll start with WriteByte. In the example, a character is converted to a byte and then written in a file by using the WriteByte method. After the byte is written, the file position is automatically incremented by 1.

```
      syncF.WriteByte(Convert.ToByte('A'));
```

By using the Write method, we can write more than one character to the file. Here we convert a string to a byte array (with the GetBytes method of the Encoding class in the System.Text namespace), and this byte array is then written to the file with the Write method. Write takes three parameters: the byte array to write, the position or offset in the array from where to start writing, and the length of data to be written. In this case, we write the entire byte array from the start:

```
Console.WriteLine("--Write method demo--");
byte[] writeBytes = Encoding.ASCII.GetBytes(" is the first character.");
syncF.Write(writeBytes, 0, writeBytes.Length);
```

Thus, we've written a single byte with the WriteByte method and an entire string (converted to a byte array) with the Write method. Now we'll read this information back in the corresponding Read methods.

When you perform a read or write operation on a FileStream, the current position (or pointer) of the file automatically increases by the number of bytes read or written. We want to read the bytes just written, so we'll use the Seek method to set the current position in the stream, in this case back to the beginning of the stream:

```
// Set pointer at origin
syncF.Seek (0,SeekOrigin.Begin);
```

Now we can read. We'll read a single byte with the ReadByte method first. A byte is read from the stream (with the position automatically increased by 1) and converted back into a char:

```
Console.WriteLine ("--Readbyte method demo--");
// Read byte and display
Console.WriteLine("First character is ->" +
   Convert.ToChar(syncF.ReadByte()));
```

Now we read the remainder of the file with the Read method. This method takes three parameters: a byte array that will store the data read, the position or offset in the array from where to start reading, and the number of bytes to read. Here we'll read in all the remaining bytes in the file. We're at position 1 in the file, so we want to read in syncF.Length - 1 bytes:

```
// Use of Read method
Console.WriteLine("----Read method demo----");
// Allocate buffer
byte[] readBuf = new byte[syncF.Length-1];
// Read file
syncF.Read(readBuf,0,(Convert.ToInt32(syncF.Length))-1);
```

The byte array of data just read in is converted to a string with the GetString method of the Encoding class and displayed:

```
      // Display contents
      Console.WriteLine("The rest of the file is : " +
                        Encoding.ASCII.GetString(readBuf));
      syncF.Close();
   }
}
```

The output of this code is shown in Figure 2-2.

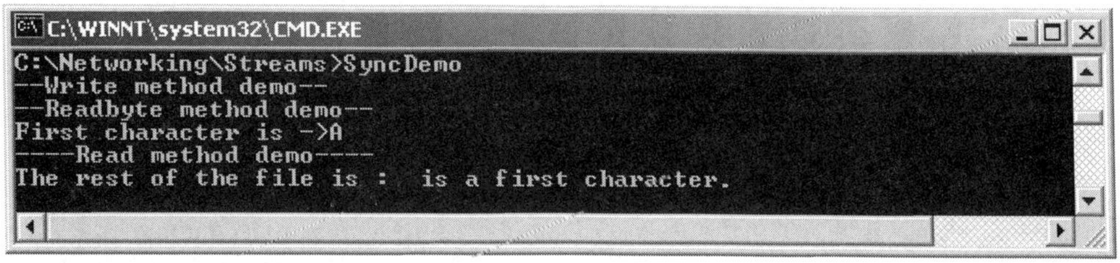

```
C:\WINNT\system32\CMD.EXE
C:\Networking\Streams>SyncDemo
--Write method demo--
--Readbyte method demo--
First character is ->A
----Read method demo----
The rest of the file is :  is a first character.
```

Figure 2-2. *Synchronous I/O output*

Asynchronous I/O

One of the overloads for the `FileStream` constructor provides the `useAsync` flag, which defines synchronous or asynchronous state. `FileStream` opens asynchronously when you pass `true` to this flag. Note that the operating system must support asynchronous I/O operations, otherwise it works as synchronous I/O. Windows NT, 2000, and XP support both synchronous and asynchronous I/O.

Asynchronous I/O is bit complex compared to synchronous I/O. We'll only sketch out the basics of how to implement asynchronous operations here, and we'll examine the topic in further depth in Chapter 4.

A special callback mechanism is needed to implement asynchronous I/O, and an `AsyncCallback` delegate provides a way for client applications to implement this callback mechanism. This callback delegate is supplied to the `BeginRead` or `BeginWrite` method.

Let's look at an example for asynchronous reading. We begin with the usual namespaces and some static fields to hold a `FileStream` object and a byte array:

```
using System;
using System.IO;
using System.Text;
using System.Threading;
public class AsyncDemo
{
   // Stream object for reading
   static FileStream fileStm;
   // Buffer to read
   static byte[] readBuf;
```

We declare an `AsyncCallback` delegate field for the callback function:

```
   // AsyncCallback delegate
   static AsyncCallback Callback;
```

In the `Main` method, we initialize our callback delegate to point to the `CallBackFunction` method—this is the method that will be called when the end of the asynchronous read operation is signaled. We'll delve into this process more in Chapter 4.

```
   public static void Main(String[] args)
   {
      Callback = new AsyncCallback(CallBackFunction);
```

Now we can initialize our `FileStream` object, specifying asynchronous operations with the final `true` value:

```
      fileStm = new FileStream("Test.txt",
                               FileMode.Open, FileAccess.Read,
                               FileShare.Read, 64, true);
      readBuf= new byte[fileStm.Length];
```

We can use the `BeginRead` method to initiate asynchronous read operations on the stream. The callback delegate is passed to the `BeginRead` method as its second-to-last parameter.

```
      // Call async read
      fileStm.BeginRead(readBuf, 0, readBuf.Length, Callback, null);
```

Data will be read from `FileStream` while we continue with other activities. Here we simply give the appearance of doing some other work by looping and every so often putting the main thread to sleep. Once the loop has finished, the `FileStream` object is closed.

```
      // Simulation of main execution
      for (long i = 0; i < 5000; i++)
      {
         if (i % 1000 == 0)
         {
            Console.WriteLine("Executing in Main - " + i.ToString());
            Thread.Sleep(10);
         }
      }
       fileStm.Close();
   }
```

Note that if the loop completes before reading has finished, then the `FileStream` object is closed anyway—the main thread of the program isn't waiting for `BeginRead` to finish. In Chapter 4, we'll look at an example that waits for an asynchronous operation to finish before continuing with the next activity. This can be very important if you need to perform asynchronous operations in a particular order or rely upon one operation completing before you can start the next one.

The callback function, suitably named `CallBackFunction` here, is called when the read operation has completed. `EndRead` is called to complete the asynchronous read. If the end of the file hasn't been reached, `BeginRead` is called again, to continue reading, and the contents of the current read are displayed:

```
   static void CallBackFunction(IAsyncResult asyncResult)
   {
      // Gets called when read operation has completed
      int readB = fileStm.EndRead(asyncResult);
      if (readB > 0)
      {
         Console.WriteLine(Encoding.ASCII.GetString(readBuf, 0, readB));
      }
   }
}
```

Figure 2-3 shows the typical output of this example. Note that your processor speed, file size, and buffer size may give you different results.

```
C:\WINNT\system32\CMD.EXE
C:\Networking\Streams>ASyncDemo
Executing in Main - 0
Executing in Main - 1000
This is a test file - it is intended for the Streams chapter to demonstrate
riety of ways of reading from streams. It sure is a good file.
Executing in Main - 2000
Executing in Main - 3000
Executing in Main - 4000
```

Figure 2-3. *Asynchronous I/O output*

BufferedStream Class

A *buffer* is a reserved area of memory used for storing temporary data. Its main purpose is to improve I/O performance, and it's often used to synchronize data transfer between devices of different speeds. Many online media applications use buffers as intermediate storage. Devices such as printers have their own buffers for storing the data.

In .NET, you can implement buffering through the `BufferedStream` class. A `BufferedStream` object wraps another `Stream` object. `BufferedStream` is generally used with .`NetworkStream` to store data in memory. `FileStream` already has its own internal buffer, and `MemoryStream` doesn't require buffering

A default buffer of 4,096 bytes is allocated when you create a buffer with the first `Buffered-Stream` constructor, but you can also specify a custom size for the buffer through the second constructor.

The following example shows the method for reading buffered stream. This method takes a `Stream` object parameter, wraps it in a `BufferedStream` object, and performs a read operation. In same way, you can perform other operations on `BufferedStream`.

```
// Reading BufferedStream
public static void readBufStream(Stream st)
{
   // Compose BufferedStream
   BufferedStream bf = new BufferedStream(st);
   byte[] inData = new Byte[st.Length];
   // Read and display buffered data
   bf.Read(inData, 0, Convert.ToInt32(st.Length));
   Console.WriteLine(Encoding.ASCII.GetString(inData));
}
```

MemoryStream Class

There are situations in which an application needs data frequently, such as in a lookup table for reference data. In such cases, storing the data in a file can cause delays and reduce the performance of an application. The `MemoryStream` class is the solution for such cases where data needs to be stored in memory.

MemoryStream is useful for fast, temporary storage. A good example is transferring serialized objects within a process—you can use MemoryStream for temporarily storing serialized objects. This gives better performance than using the FileStream or BufferedStream class.

Creating a MemoryStream object is quite different from creating a FileStream or BufferedStream. An instance can be created in several ways.

The following example shows how to create and use a MemoryStream instance. We use the WriteTo method to write the entire memory stream to a file.

```
using System;
using System.IO;
using System.Text ;
public class memStreamDemoClass
{
   public static void Main(String[] args)
   {
```

The MemoryStream instance is created without passing any parameter. Reading and writing data in the MemoryStream is the same as you saw in the FileStream example. Here we're using the Write method to write a simple string.

```
      // Create empty Memory stream
      MemoryStream mS = new MemoryStream();
      byte[] memData = Encoding.ASCII.GetBytes("This will go in Memory!!");
      // Write data
      mS.Write(memData,0,memData.Length);
```

After we write a string, we read it using the Read method. Note that before reading, we set the current position to 0.

```
      // Set pointer at origin
      mS.Position = 0;
      byte[] inData = new byte[100];
      // Read memory
      mS.Read(inData, 0, 100);
      Console.WriteLine(Encoding.ASCII.GetString(inData));
```

We use the WriteTo method to write the entire contents of this memory stream to the file stream.

```
      Stream strm = new FileStream("MemOutput.txt",
                              FileMode.OpenOrCreate, FileAccess.Write);
      mS.WriteTo(strm);
      strm.Close();
   }
}
```

NetworkStream Class

Across a network, the data transferred between locations is in the form of a continuous flow or stream. For handling such a stream, .NET has a special class, NetworkStream in the

System.Net.Sockets namespace, which is used for sending and receiving data through network sockets.

NetworkStream is an unbuffered stream, and it does not support random access to data. You cannot change the position within the stream, and therefore the use of Seek and Position throws an exception. The CanSeek property always returns false for a NetworkStream object.

As NetworkStream is unbuffered, BufferedStream is usually used along with this class as an intermediate storage medium.

Table 2-10 describes some of important members of NetworkStream.

Table 2-10. *Properties of NetworkStream*

Property	Description
DataAvailable	Returns a Boolean value indicating whether or not data is available on the stream for reading. A value of true indicates that data is available on the stream.
Readable	Used to get or set a Boolean value indicating whether or not read access is given to the stream. This property works the same as the CanRead property in other streams.
Socket	Returns the underlying Socket.
Writeable	Used for checking whether or not the stream can be written to. A value of true indicates that the stream is writeable. This property works the same as the CanWrite property in other streams.

Each NetworkStream constructor requires at least one Socket. In addition, you can specify a Boolean value indicating ownership of the stream and/or a value from the FileAccess enumeration you saw earlier to control read and write permissions. Setting the ownership flag to true gives control of the socket to the NetworkStream object, and by using the Close method, you can close the underlying socket.

A NetworkStream object can also be retrieved from a TcpClient. Chapter 5 is devoted to TCP, but we'll make use of it here to illustrate NetworkStream in a client/server scenario. The TcpClient.GetStream method creates a NetworkStream object, passing in its underlying Socket as the constructor parameter.

Let's look at the code for a simple TCP listener using a NetworkStream. The TCP classes are found in the System.Net.Sockets namespace.

```
using System;
using System.IO;
using System.Text;
using System.Net;
using System.Net.Sockets;
class TCPListenerDemo
{
   public static void Main()
   {
      try
      {
```

The first thing we do is create our TcpListener object to listen on port 5001 and start listening with the Start method. We get the local IP address by resolving the localhost name against the DNS, and we pass it to the TcpListener constructor. AcceptClient accepts a connection request, returning a TcpClient. We use its GetStream to create our NetworkStream object.

```
            // Create TCP listener
            IPAddress ipAddress=Dns.Resolve("localhost").AddressList[0];
            TcpListener listener = new TcpListener(ipAddress,5001);
            listener.Start();
            TcpClient tc = listener.AcceptClient();
            NetworkStream stm = tc.GetStream();
```

Now we can read data as we have with the other streams, using the Read method.

```
            byte[] readBuf = new byte[100];
            stm.Read(readBuf,0,100);
            //Display Data
            Console.WriteLine(Encoding.ASCII.GetString(readBuf));
            stm.Close();
         }
         catch (Exception e )
         {
            Console.WriteLine(e.ToString());
         }
      }
   }
```

To follow along with this example, you need a client application for sending some data. Remember to start the listener application before the client application!

Here's the code for the TCP client:

```
using System;
using System.IO;
using System.Text;
using System.Net;
using System.Net.Sockets;
class TcpClientExample
{
   static void Main(string[] args)
   {
      try
      {
```

We create our TcpClient and connect to the localhost on port 5001. Once again, we use the GetStream method to return the underlying NetworkStream:

```
         // Create TCP Client
         TcpClient client = new TcpClient();
         //Connect using hostname and port
```

```
        client.Connect ("localhost", 5001);
        //Get NetworkStream instance for sending data
        NetworkStream stm = client.GetStream();
```

Now that we have our NetworkStream, sending the data follows the same process as we've used with the other streams:

```
        byte[] sendBytes = Encoding.ASCII.GetBytes("This data has come from" +
                                                  " another place!!!");
        stm.Write (sendBytes, 0, sendBytes.Length);
```

Finally, our TcpClient is closed:

```
        client.Close();
      }
      catch (Exception e )
      {
        Console.WriteLine(e.ToString());
        Console.WriteLine("The listener has probably not started");
      }
    }
}
```

You'll see many more examples of creating client/server applications of varying complexity in upcoming chapters.

CryptoStream Class

The need to secure the content of certain types of data is a major consideration when transforming or storing it, and the need to secure data is increasing day by day. To make data secure, it is generally encrypted with some secret key into an unreadable form. To get back the original contents, the data is decrypted with a secret key. The secret key used for decryption may be the same as that used for encryption, or it could be different depending on the encryption algorithm used.

.NET provides the CryptoStream class to link streams to cryptographic transformations. CryptoStream is not actually in the System.IO namespace, but it does indeed derive from Stream. The CryptoStream class can be used to perform cryptographic operations on a Stream object.

The CryptoStream constructor takes three parameters: the stream to be used, the cryptographic transformation, and a specification of read or write access to the cryptographic stream.

We have a variety of cryptographic transformations at our disposal—any cryptographic service provider that implements the ICryptoTransform interface can be used. The following example demonstrates the use of various cryptographic providers that reside in the System.Security.Cryptography namespace.

```
using System;
using System.IO;
using System.Text ;
using System.Security.Cryptography;
```

```
public class crypt
{
   public static void Main()
   {
```

First, we ask the user to choose a service provider. All service providers derived from the SymmetricAlgorithm class have a single secret key that is used for both encryption and decryption.

```
      Console.WriteLine("Select Service Provider for CryptoStream");
      Console.WriteLine("1 = DESCryptoServiceProvider");
      Console.WriteLine("2 = RC2CryptoServiceProvider");
      Console.WriteLine("3 = RijndaelManaged");
      Console.WriteLine("4 = TripleDESCryptoServiceProvider");
      Console.WriteLine("5 = SymmetricAlgorithm");
      // Create des object
      SymmetricAlgorithm des = null;
      switch (Console.ReadLine())
      {
         case "1":
            des = new DESCryptoServiceProvider();
            break;
         case "2":
            des  = new RC2CryptoServiceProvider();
            break;
         case "3":
            des  = new RijndaelManaged();
            break;
         case "4":
            des  = new TripleDESCryptoServiceProvider();
            break;
         case "5":
            des= SymmetricAlgorithm.Create(); //uses default algorithm
            break;
         default:
            Console.WriteLine ("Wrong selection");
            return;
      }
```

A FileStream object is created to save the encrypted data, around which we wrap our CryptoStream object. The ICryptoTransform interface helps to define the basic operations of the cryptographic transformation that's created using the CreateEncryptor method of the SymmetricAlgorithm class.

```
      FileStream fs  = new FileStream("SecretFile.dat", FileMode.Create,
                                      FileAccess.Write);
      ICryptoTransform desencrypt = des.CreateEncryptor();
      CryptoStream cryptostream = new CryptoStream(fs, desencrypt,
                                                   CryptoStreamMode.Write);
```

Now we encrypt our message. We use a simple string, which we convert to a byte array with the GetBytes method of the Encoding class of the System.Text namespace (we cover this class in more detail later in this chapter). Once we have our byte array, it is written to the CryptoStream with its Write method.

```
string theMessage = "A top secret message";
byte[] bytearrayinput = Encoding.Unicode.GetBytes(theMessage);
Console.WriteLine("Original Message : {0}",theMessage);
cryptostream.Write(bytearrayinput, 0, bytearrayinput.Length);
cryptostream.Close();
fs.Close();
```

After closing our streams, we can proceed to decrypt our message. In the second part of our code, the encrypted message is read from the file and then converted back into the original.

```
/***********Time to Decrypt...************/
// Create file stream to read encrypted file back
FileStream fsread = new FileStream("SecretFile.dat", FileMode.Open,
                                   FileAccess.ReadWrite);

byte[] encByte = new byte[fsread.Length ];
fsread.Read(encByte,0,encByte.Length );
```

Here we have defined the size of our byte array by using the Length property of the FileStream to determine the length of the data written to our file. We read the data into this byte array with the Read method. Before we decrypt the data, we display the encrypted message to the console, and then set the Position within the FileStream back to 0 before continuing.

```
Console.WriteLine ("Encrypted Message :" +
                    Encoding.ASCII.GetString(encByte));
fsread.Position =0;
```

Decrypting the data involves a similar procedure to encrypting the data. The main difference is that the CreateDecryptor method is used to create the specified decryptor object. We create a new byte array into which we read from the CryptoStream, and then we use the GetString method of the Encoding class to turn the byte array into a string for display.

```
      // Create DES Decryptor from our des instance
      ICryptoTransform desdecrypt = des.CreateDecryptor();
      CryptoStream cryptostreamDecr = new CryptoStream(fsread, desdecrypt,
                                                  CryptoStreamMode.Read);
      byte[] decrByte = new byte[fsread.Length];
      cryptostreamDecr.Read(decrByte,0,(int)fsread.Length);
      string output = Encoding.Unicode.GetString(decrByte);
      Console.WriteLine("Decrypted Message : {0}" ,output);
      cryptostreamDecr.Close();
      fsread.Close();
   }
}
```

Figure 2-4 shows the output of the preceding code when it is run twice with the `SymmetricAlgorithm` encryption method.

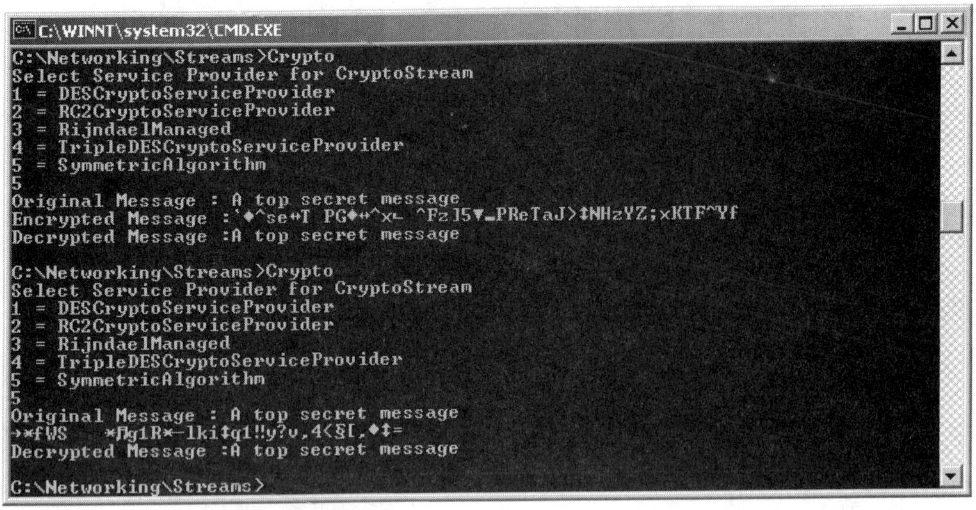

```
C:\WINNT\system32\CMD.EXE
C:\Networking\Streams>Crypto
Select Service Provider for CryptoStream
1 = DESCryptoServiceProvider
2 = RC2CryptoServiceProvider
3 = RijndaelManaged
4 = TripleDESCryptoServiceProvider
5 = SymmetricAlgorithm
5
Original Message : A top secret message
Encrypted Message :`♦^se↔T PG♦↔^x∟ ^Fz]5▼▬PReTaJ>‡NHzYZ;xKTF^Yf
Decrypted Message :A top secret message

C:\Networking\Streams>Crypto
Select Service Provider for CryptoStream
1 = DESCryptoServiceProvider
2 = RC2CryptoServiceProvider
3 = RijndaelManaged
4 = TripleDESCryptoServiceProvider
5 = SymmetricAlgorithm
5
Original Message : A top secret message
→×fWS    *ƒg1R×─lki‡q1‼y?v,4<§[,♦‡=
Decrypted Message :A top secret message

C:\Networking\Streams>
```

Figure 2-4. *Decryption output*

Stream Manipulation

We've looked at the different types of streams, how to create them, and how to read to and write from them. However, we've only been able to read and write byte arrays, and this is a somewhat cumbersome way of reading data. For example, if we wanted to write some decimal values to a file, we'd have to break these down into bytes ourselves. There must be an easier way! Sure enough, the `System.IO` namespace provides classes and methods for manipulating different data types in streams.

In this section, we look at the following classes for stream manipulation:

- `BinaryReader` and `BinaryWriter` for manipulating binary files
- `StreamReader` and `StreamWriter` for manipulating text files

Before we examine these classes, we need to consider encoding. This is something we alluded to earlier in the chapter when we were converting to and from byte arrays for transferring data from streams.

Encoding String Data

Although the data transported through streams is in byte form, without your knowing what these bytes mean, the information is meaningless. For example, if the bytes are to be converted back into characters, then you need to know how these bytes map to characters—a particular type of character may require more than 1 byte.

The Encoding class in the System.Text namespace is provided for performing such operations. The Encoding class handles sets of Unicode characters. *Unicode* is a worldwide character-encoding standard that allows universal data exchange and improves multilingual text processing. Many languages, such as Japanese, cannot be represented without Unicode. The wider range of characters supported by the Unicode format means that Unicode information typically requires 16-bit space instead of the standard 8-bit character strings.

The .NET Framework has several classes derived from the Encoding class for performing encoding between different formats. Table 2-11 presents these classes and their use.

Table 2-11. *Encoding Classes and Uses*

Class	Use
ASCIIEncoding	Encodes Unicode characters as single, 1-byte ASCII characters. This encoding has limitations because it supports 7-bit character values, and it is not a good choice for applications that support multilingual text processing.
UnicodeEncoding	Encodes each Unicode character in 2 bytes (16-bit).
UTF7Encoding	Encodes in 7-bit Unicode encoding. UTF-7 (UTF stands for *Universal Translation Format*) is a commonly used format to send Unicode-based data across networks. UTF-7 was originally invented to efficiently transmit Unicode characters through e-mail systems optimized for US-ASCII text messages.
UTF8Encoding	This class supports 8-bit encoding, or UTF-8. This encoding is widely used with applications that support multilingual text processing. XML uses UTF-8 encoding by default.

Some of the principal methods of the Encoding class appear in Table 2-12. The general aim of these methods is to convert between byte arrays and character arrays or strings.

Table 2-12. *Encoding Class Methods*

Method	Description
GetCharCount	Takes an array of bytes and returns the calculated number of characters produced by decoding.
GetChars	Decodes a byte array into a character array. This method can be used in different ways depending upon overload. Each overload takes a byte array and decodes it into an array of characters.
GetByteCount	Number of bytes required for encoding a character array. Overloads of this method can take either a character array or a string and return the number of bytes required to encode.
GetBytes	Encodes a string or character array into a byte array.
GetDecoder	Gets a Decoder. Decoder is an abstract class used for converting bytes into Unicode characters. This method returns a Decoder object that can be used for decoding a sequence of bytes into characters.
GetEncoder	Gets an Encoder. Encoder is an abstract class used for converting Unicode characters into a byte array. This method returns an Encoder object that can be used for encoding a sequence of characters into bytes.

Let's look at a quick example that converts a string into a byte array using the different formats, and then displays the values in the byte array.

```
using System;
using System.IO;
using System.Text;
class EncodingTest
{
   public static void Main(string[] args)
   {
      string test = "This is our test string.";

      byte[] ascb;
      byte[] unicb;
      byte[] utfb;
```

We've created three byte arrays. Now we'll convert our test string into these byte arrays using ASCII, Unicode, and UTF-7 encoding. After each conversion, our `DisplayArray` method will simply output all the bytes in the byte array.

```
      ascb = Encoding.ASCII.GetBytes(test);
      Console.WriteLine("ASCII Encoding : {0} bytes",ascb.Length);

      DisplayArray(ascb);

      unicb = Encoding.Unicode.GetBytes(test);
      Console.WriteLine("Unicode Encoding : {0} bytes",unicb.Length);
      DisplayArray(unicb);

      utfb = Encoding.UTF7.GetBytes(test);
      Console.WriteLine("UTF Encoding : {0} bytes",utfb.Length);
      DisplayArray(utfb);
```

Now that the bytes in the byte array have been displayed, let's see the effect of converting back from the byte array into a string. For these conversions, we specify an encoding different from that originally used.

```
      string unics = Encoding.Unicode.GetString(ascb);
      Console.WriteLine(unics);

      string ascs = Encoding.ASCII.GetString(unicb);
      Console.WriteLine(ascs);
   }

   static void DisplayArray(byte[] b)
   {
      for (int i=0;i<b.Length;i++)
```

```
            Console.Write(b[i]+" ");

         Console.WriteLine();
      }
   }
```

The output of this procedure is shown in Figure 2-5. Note the use of 2 bytes in the Unicode-encoded byte array for each character in the string. Note also that the reconverted strings illustrate the importance of using the correct encoding at each stage.

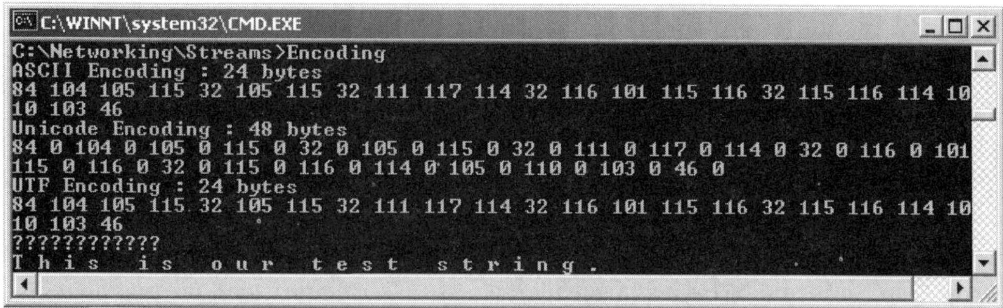

Figure 2-5. *Encoded stream*

Binary Files

The `BinaryReader` and `BinaryWriter` classes of the `System.IO` namespace are used for working with primitive data types from streams. Each class is created around an existing `Stream`.

BinaryReader

`BinaryReader` is used for reading primitive data types. By default, it uses UTF-8 encoding for reading the stream. You can specify custom encoding when you create an instance.

`BinaryReader` has various methods for reading primitive data types. The `Read` method reads bytes from the stream and advances the position in the stream, returning `-1` if the end of the stream is reached. Two other overloads allow you to read into a byte array or a character array, specifying the start position in the stream and then the number of bytes to read in. To read without advancing the position in the stream, the `PeekChar` method returns the next character from the stream, or `-1` if the end of the stream is reached or if the stream does not support seeking.

For each primitive data type, there is a method to read data of that type from the stream and advance the position of stream according to the length of the data type. Table 2-13 presents these methods.

Table 2-13. *Read Methods for Data Types*

Method	Bytes Read from Stream
bool ReadBoolean	1
byte ReadByte	1
byte[] ReadBytes(int count)	count
char ReadChar	Depends on the encoding used
decimal ReadDecimal	16
double ReadDouble	8
short ReadInt16	2
int ReadInt32	4
long ReadInt64	8
float ReadSingle	4
string ReadString	Depends on the length of the string

While performing a read operation on the stream, the end of the stream can be detected with the PeekChar method. This method reads the next character from the stream without advancing the position. A value of -1 is returned if no more characters are available.

The Close method closes the reader. The underlying stream can be returned from the BaseStream property of the BinaryReader.

You can create a BinaryReader instance by providing a stream with or without an encoding type.

```
//Create Stream instance
Stream strm = new FileStream("MyStream.txt",
                             FileMode.Open, FileAccess.Read);
//Use Stream instance for creating binary reader
BinaryReader br = new BinaryReader(strm);
```

You can also specify the encoding type when you create a BinaryReader object.

```
// Create Stream instance
Stream strm = new FileStream("Book.txt", FileMode.Open,
                             FileAccess.Read);
// Use stream instance for creating binary reader
BinaryReader br = new BinaryReader(strm,Encoding.ASCII);
```

BinaryWriter

The BinaryWriter class is used for writing primitive types in a binary format to a stream.

Writing to the stream is achieved with the Write method. There is an overload for writing each primitive data type to the stream, advancing the position in the stream according to the length of the data type. To move around the stream, the Seek method sets the position in the stream as with the Seek method of Stream. In fact, BinaryWriter.Seek simply calls the Seek method on the underlying Stream object (which can also be returned from the BaseStream property).

There are also Close and Flush methods for the standard management of the writer's resources.

Binary Reading and Writing Example

In following example, a FileStream is created for performing binary read and write operations. In the first part of the code, data is written to a file, and in the second part of the code, this data is read in and displayed.

```
using System;
using System.IO;
class BinaryGetting
{
   static void Main(string[] args)
   {
      double angle, sinAngle
      FileStream fStream = new FileStream("Sines.dat",
                                    FileMode.Create, FileAccess.Write);
      BinaryWriter bw = new BinaryWriter(fStream);
```

First, we create our FileStream object, a file called Sines.dat, and we specify write access, since we'll be writing some data to the stream. Then we create our BinaryWriter object around this FileStream. We calculate the sine of angles between 0 and 90 degrees at 5 degree intervals (we have to convert the angle in degrees to radians before we can calculate the sine), and then we use Write to output these values to the stream.

```
      for (int i=0;i<=90;i+=5)
      {
         double angleRads = Math.PI*i/180;
         sinAngle = Math.Sin(angleRads);
         bw.Write((double)i);
         bw.Write(sinAngle);
      }

      bw.Close();
      fStream.Close();
```

The BinaryWriter and FileStream objects are closed, and we can begin the process of retrieving the data with the BinaryReader. First, we create new FileStream and BinaryReader objects.

```
      FileStream frStream = new FileStream("Sines.dat",
                                    FileMode.Open, FileAccess.Read);
      BinaryReader br = new BinaryReader(frStream);
      int endOfFile;
```

We use the ReadDouble method to read the data back in. If this method tries to read beyond the end of the stream, an exception will be thrown, so we use the PeekChar method to detect the end of the file without advancing the position.

```
            do
            {
               endOfFile = br.PeekChar();
               if(endOfFile != -1)
               {
                  angle = br.ReadDouble();
                  sinAngle = br.ReadDouble();
                  Console.WriteLine("{0} : {1}",angle,sinAngle);
               }
            }
            while(endOfFile!= -1);
```

Finally, we close the BinaryReader and the underlying stream.

```
            br.Close();
            frStream.Close();
         }
      }
```

Figure 2-6 shows the output.

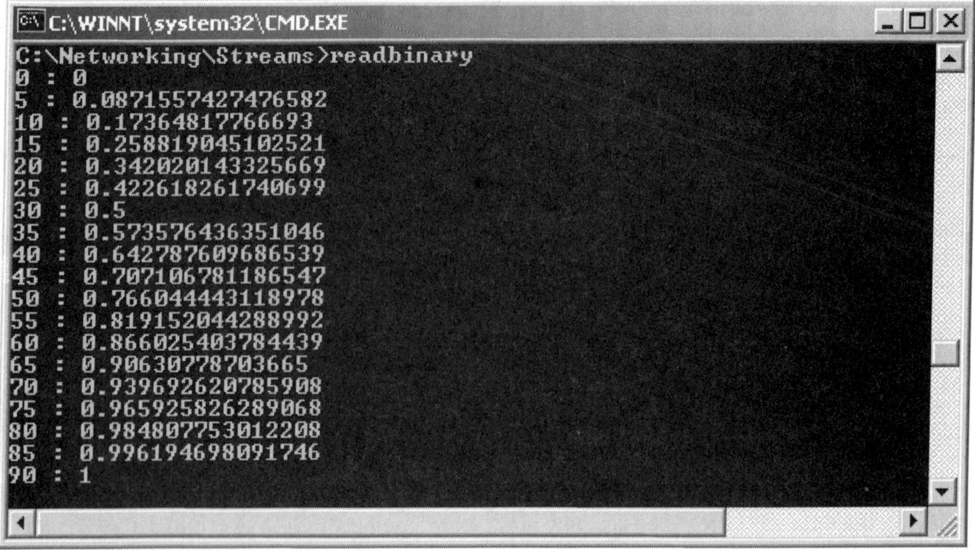

Figure 2-6. *Binary stream output*

TextReader

The TextReader class is used for reading text or characters in a stream. It's an abstract class from which StreamReader and StringReader derive. The text read in by a StringReader is stored as a StringBuilder, rather than a plain string.

Table 2-14 shows some of the important methods of TextReader.

Table 2-14. *TextReader Class Methods*

Method	Description
`Peek`	Returns the next character from the stream/string, without advancing the position
`Read`	Reads the characters/bytes from the stream/string
`ReadBlock`	Reads a specified number of characters from the current stream from a given starting point
`ReadLine`	Reads all characters up to the end of the line (signified by a carriage return or linefeed)
`ReadToEnd`	Reads all characters up to the end of the stream/string
`Synchronized`	Creates a thread-safe wrapper so that more than one thread can use the `TextReader`
`Close`	Closes the current reader

Working with StreamReader

It probably comes as no surprise to you that `StreamReader` is used to read characters from a byte stream. The `StreamReader` class uses encoding (specified in the constructor) or, if no encoding is specified, then it uses UTF-8 encoding. More than that, it essentially provides forward-only access to the stream, unlike the `BinaryReader` class, which allows random access with its `Seek` method. It is possible to change the position in the underlying stream by accessing it through the `BaseStream` property of the `StreamReader` class; however, the current position in the stream and the current position of the reader may not be the same for buffering reasons.

The following example demonstrates the use of `StreamReader`. It reads in text from a file called `TextOut.txt`. We actually create this file in the forthcoming `StreamWriter` example, but for now any text file will do.

```
using System;
using System.IO;
class TextReadingExample
{
   static void Main(string[] args)
   {
      Stream fS = new FileStream("TextOut.txt", FileMode.Open, FileAccess.Read);

      // Using Stream Object
      StreamReader sReader = new StreamReader(fS);
      string data;
      int line=0;
```

Now begins the central loop to read in each line. We use the `ReadLine` method to read a line from the stream. If no lines are available, `null` is returned. Thus, we test for this in our `while` loop:

```
      while ((data = sReader.ReadLine()) != null)
```

We display more information than just the line read in. We display a line count, which we increment ourselves, then the line read in, and then the position in the stream:

```
{
   Console.WriteLine("Line {0} : {1} : Position = {2}",
                     ++line, data,  sReader.BaseStream.Position);
}
```

Next, we reset the position to the start of the stream and read the entire contents in with the ReadToEnd method:

```
      // Set position using seek property of underlying stream
      sReader.BaseStream.Seek(0, SeekOrigin.Begin);
      Console.WriteLine("* Reading entire file using ReadToEnd \n" +
                                    sReader.ReadToEnd());

      sReader.Close();
      fS.Close();
   }
}
```

When you run the preceding code with the TextOut.txt file created next, you'll see output similar to that shown in Figure 2-7.

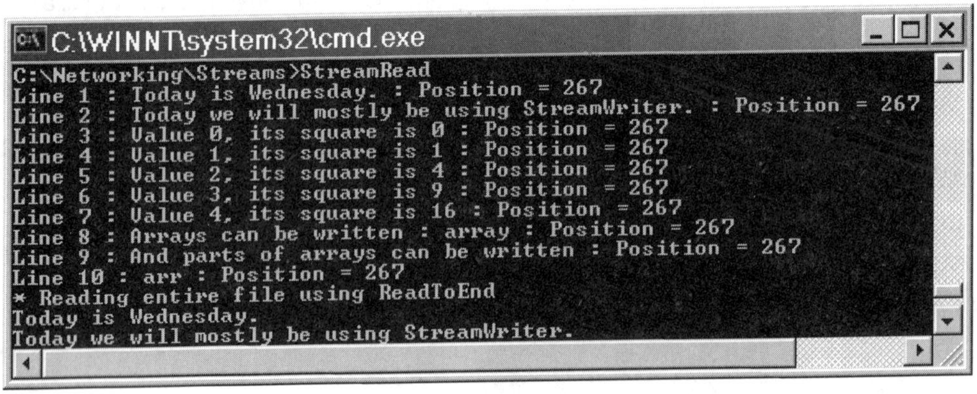

```
C:\WINNT\system32\cmd.exe
C:\Networking\Streams>StreamRead
Line 1 : Today is Wednesday. : Position = 267
Line 2 : Today we will mostly be using StreamWriter. : Position = 267
Line 3 : Value 0, its square is 0 : Position = 267
Line 4 : Value 1, its square is 1 : Position = 267
Line 5 : Value 2, its square is 4 : Position = 267
Line 6 : Value 3, its square is 9 : Position = 267
Line 7 : Value 4, its square is 16 : Position = 267
Line 8 : Arrays can be written : array : Position = 267
Line 9 : And parts of arrays can be written : Position = 267
Line 10 : arr : Position = 267
* Reading entire file using ReadToEnd
Today is Wednesday.
Today we will mostly be using StreamWriter.
```

Figure 2-7. *StreamReader output*

The interesting thing to note here is the Position, which doesn't change between any of the lines and is fixed at the value 267. This value is the length of the entire file, and it's a good illustration of how the stream position and the reader position often don't agree. The contents of the file have been buffered—you can see this by adding the following line in the while loop:

```
{
   Console.WriteLine("Line {0} : {1} : Position = {2}",
                     ++line, data,  sReader.BaseStream.Position);
   sReader.DiscardBufferedData();
}
```

The DiscardBufferedData method discards the reader's data. If you add this line, then running the preceding code with the same file as before will display only one line, since the remaining lines are all jettisoned following the DiscardBufferedData call.

TextWriter

TextWriter is an abstract class used for writing text, and it outputs a sequential series of characters. StreamWriter and StringWriter are derived from TextWriter. Like StringReader, StringWriter deals with StringBuilder objects rather than plain strings.

The TextWriter methods presented in Table 2-15 allow management of the writer and perform the actual writing.

Table 2-15. *TextWriter Class Methods*

Method	Description
Close	Closes the current writer.
Flush	Clears the buffers and writes to the underlying device.
Synchronized	Creates a thread-safe wrapper.
Write	Writes given data.
WriteLine	Similar to the Console.WriteLine method, this method writes data with a line terminator. The WriteLine method can be used in a number of ways depending on the parameters passed.

Working with StreamWriter

The StreamWriter class is used for writing characters in a stream. By default, it uses UTF-8 character encoding.

There are several ways to create an instance of the StreamWriter class depending on overloading parameters. One way allows you to pass a Stream object. If you are using a FileStream object, this means that you have more control over the file's accessibility than is possible through the other StreamWriter constructors.

The following example demonstrates the use of various StreamWriter properties and should make their use clearer.

```
using System;
using System.IO;
class TextWritingExample
{
   static void Main(string[] args)
   {
      Stream fS = new FileStream("TextOut.txt",
      FileMode.OpenOrCreate, FileAccess.Write);

      // Using Stream Object
      StreamWriter sWriter = new StreamWriter(fS);
```

We start by displaying some properties of the StreamWriter class, namely the Encoding type (we haven't specified any, so the default will be UTF-8) and the format provider:

```
// Display the encoding type
Console.WriteLine("Encoding type : " + sWriter.Encoding.ToString());
//Display Format Provider
Console.WriteLine("Format Provider : " +
sWriter.FormatProvider.ToString());
```

Now we write to the file, using the WriteLine method first. As you can see, its use is similar to that of the Console.WriteLine method in that it allows us to easily write out the values of variables or properties.

```
sWriter.WriteLine("Today is {0}." ,DateTime.Today.DayOfWeek);

sWriter.WriteLine("Today we will mostly be using StreamWriter.");

for (int i=0;i<5;i++)
  sWriter.WriteLine("Value {0}, its square is {1}",i,i*i);
```

Now we use the Write method to write out character arrays and parts of character arrays. Since Write doesn't attach a newline to the end of the output, we can use the escape sequence \r\n at the start of a line to ensure a newline before the text is written.

```
      sWriter.Write("Arrays can be written : ");
      char[] myarray = new char[]{'a','r','r','a','y'};
      sWriter.Write(myarray);
      sWriter.WriteLine("\r\nAnd parts of arrays can be written");
      sWriter.Write(myarray,0,3);

      sWriter.Close();
      fS.Close()
   }
}
```

When you view the result in Notepad, you can see that the content in Figure 2-8 is written to the output file.

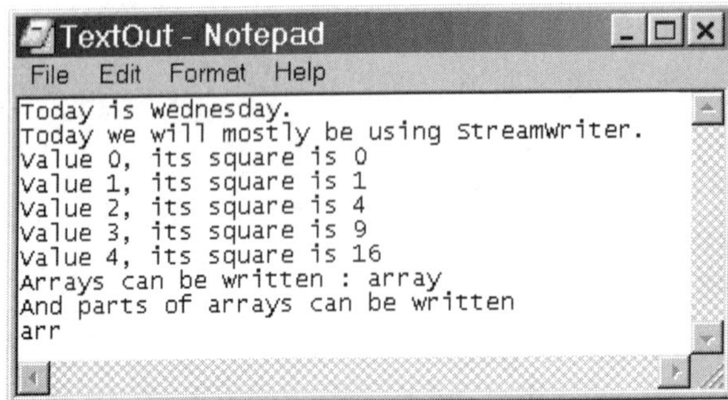

Figure 2-8. *StreamWriter output*

Serialization

Serialization is the process of taking objects and converting their state information into a form that can be stored or transported. The stored or transported object can be then deserialized to re-create the original state of object. Thus, you can serialize an object, transmit this information across a network, and then restore the object and its original state from another application or system.

Here are some key areas where serialization is beneficial:

- *Object availability*: A component can be saved in a file made available whenever required.
- *Object lifetime*: Saving the object with its state increases its life. In normal practice, when you close an application, all associated objects are destroyed automatically.
- *Object use within networked applications*: The complex form of the object has been transformed to a format that is suitable for transferring across a network and possibly through firewalls.
- *Object reliability*: The saved object can be re-created as is.

In this section, we examine two ways of serializing objects:

- Serializing into XML format
- Serializing with formatter objects into binary format

Serializing into XML Format

Serializing an object into XML format has certain advantages. One is that you have transformed system-specific state information into text, which can be easily sent across a network and through firewalls. However, the XML produced does not preserve the type of the various fields involved; instead, it serializes properties/fields or return values of an object in XML format. This feature is useful when you want to pass values instead of the details of the actual object itself.

The `XmlSerializer` class in the `System.Xml.Serialization` namespace provides the functionality for serializing and deserializing objects in XML format.

There are two simple rules for serializing a class:

- *The class must support a default public constructor with no parameters.* This is required because when the object is re-created through the deserialization process, the object is first instantiated with the default constructor, and then the public properties are set from the incoming data stream. If there is no default constructor, the .NET Framework will not know how to create the object.
- *Only public properties that support both* `get` *and* `set` *operations and public data members are persisted.* This is because the serialization process cannot access the private and read-only data members. There are ways to serialize this data, but they involve changes to the class itself.

To save all the public properties and data members of an object, nothing extra needs to be done to the class itself.

In the following example, a Customer class with fields for storing data about a customer is serialized using XML format. Note the presence of the private field.

```
using System;
using System.IO;
using System.Text ;
using System.Xml.Serialization;
public class XmlSerialExample
{
   public class Customer
   {
      public int CustomerID;
      public string CustomerName;
      public DateTime SignUpDate;
      private decimal currentCredit;
      public void SetCurrentCredit(decimal c)
      {
         currentCredit = c;
      }
      public decimal GetCurrentCredit()
      {
         return currentCredit;
      }
   }
```

Our Customer class is defined, so we create a new instance and set some of the fields.

```
   public static void Main()
   {
      // Prepare object for serialization
      Customer cm = new Customer();

      cm.CustomerID = 12;
      cm.CustomerName = "Ward Littell";
      cm.SignUpDate=DateTime.Now;
      cm.SetCurrentCredit(76.23M);
```

Now we begin the serialization process. We create a StreamWriter to output the produced XML to a file, Customer.xml. Then we create the XmlSerializer object, passing in the type of the object we want serialized. All that remains is to call the Serialize method of the XmlSerializer, passing in the StreamWriter and the object whose state we wish to persist.

```
      Console.WriteLine("Now Serializing....");
      // Create stream writer object
      StreamWriter writer = new StreamWriter("Customer.xml");
      // Create serializer
      XmlSerializer serializer = new XmlSerializer(typeof(Customer));
```

```
        // Serialize the object
        serializer.Serialize(writer, cm);
        writer.Close();
```

Our serialization process is now complete. To test it, we deserialize from the `Customer.xml` file and create a new object with the same state as our current `Customer` object.

```
        Console.WriteLine("Now Deserializing....");
        // Open and create stream
        Stream streamOut = new FileStream("Customer.xml", FileMode.Open,
                                          FileAccess.Read);
```

Our stream for reading the data from the `Customer.xml` file has been created. All we need to do now is call the `Deserialize` method of our `XmlSerializer` object. For purposes of illustration, we create a new `XmlSerializer` called `deserializer`. `Deserialize` returns an `object`. This needs a cast to `Customer`, and we have our re-created `Customer`.

```
        XmlSerializer deserializer = new XmlSerializer(typeof(Customer));
        // Deserialize the stored stream
        Customer recm = (Customer)deserializer.Deserialize(streamOut);
        streamOut.Close();
```

Finally, we display the state of our newly created object:

```
        // Display state of object
        Console.WriteLine ("Customer ID = {0}", recm.CustomerID);
        Console.WriteLine ("Customer Name = {0}", recm.CustomerName);
        Console.WriteLine ("Sign up date = {0}", recm.SignUpDate);
        Console.WriteLine ("Current Credit = {0}", recm.GetCurrentCredit());
        Console.Read();
    }
}
```

The output of this program is shown in Figure 2-9. Note that the value for `CurrentCredit` is 0 and not 76.23 as we set it originally. You'll see why this is so when cover the XML output next.

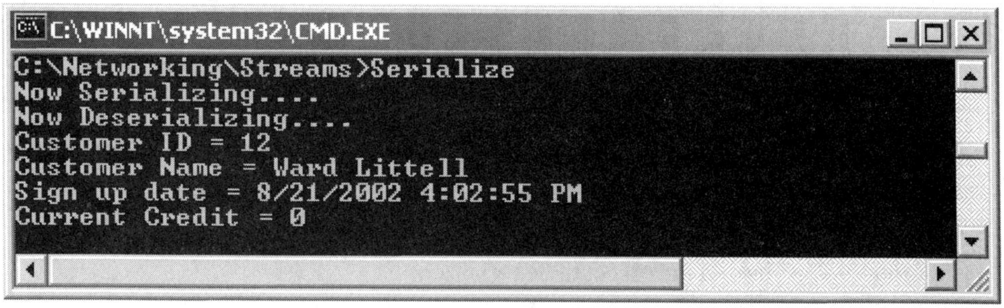

```
C:\WINNT\system32\CMD.EXE
C:\Networking\Streams>Serialize
Now Serializing....
Now Deserializing....
Customer ID = 12
Customer Name = Ward Littell
Sign up date = 8/21/2002 4:02:55 PM
Current Credit = 0
```

Figure 2-9. *Serialize output*

Figure 2-10 shows the serialized `Customer.xml` file. Note that this image shows that the exact type of each field is not preserved here—the XML contains only the values of the fields. Note also that the value of the private field `currentCredit` has not been serialized.

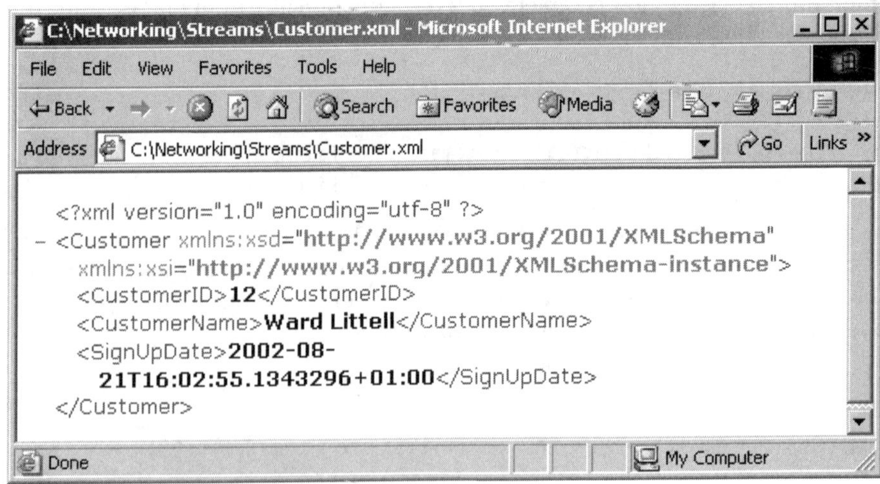

Figure 2-10. *Serialized XML file*

Serializing with Formatter Objects

Within the `System.Runtime.Serialization.Formatters` namespace lie the tools for serializing object state into formats such as binary or SOAP. The `BinaryFormatter` class provides functionality for serializing objects into binary format, and the `SoapFormatter` class serializes into SOAP format. We look at both of these classes in this section.

Binary format serializes object state and also assembly information, allowing exact reproduction of an object and its types. It also produces a compact format. The SOAP format is more verbose, but it allows your object state to be passed to a web service, for example.

The formatter objects allow the serialization of private fields, and the key to their use is the `[Serializable]` attribute, with which you mark a class to indicate that it can indeed be serialized.

Here are the steps for serializing an object:

1. Mark the class with the `[Serializable]` attribute to make it serializable.

2. Prepare the object's state for serialization.

3. Create a new formatter object: `BinaryFormatter` for binary format or `SoapFormatter` for SOAP.

4. Call the `Serialize` method of the formatter object, passing in the stream to which to output the results and the object to be serialized.

Deserializing is quite simple: you specify the format for deserializing the object with the relevant formatter object, call the `Deserialize` method of this formatter object, and cast the object returned to the type you wish to re-create.

Before we look at some serialization examples, here are a few points about serialization in general and the use of the [Serializable] attribute.

For a class to be successfully serialized, each field must be serializable. Thus, if our Customer class, marked as [Serializable], had a field of type Address

```
[Serializable]
public class Customer
{
   ...
   public Address HomeAddress;
}
public class Address
{
   public string StreetName;
   ...
}
```

then the Address class would itself have to be marked [Serializable], or serialization would fail.

Note also that the [Serializable] attribute is not inherited, thus derived types are not automatically serializable. To ensure that derived types can be serialized, they should also be marked as [Serializable].

In some situations, you may not want to serialize certain fields of a class—for example, if they are easily computed from other fields or if they contain confidential data. You can use the [NonSerialized] attribute to mark any such fields, and they will not be serialized.

```
[Serializable]
public class Customer
{
   public string CustomerName;
   ...
   [NonSerialized]
   public string FirstName;
}
```

Here's an example that uses a binary formatter object. (We'll look at the SOAP formatter shortly.)

```
using System;
using System.IO;
using System.Text;
using System.Runtime.Serialization;
using System.Runtime.Serialization.Formatters.Binary;
public class BinSerialExample
{
   [Serializable]
   public class Customer
   {
      public int CustomerID;
```

```
        public string CustomerName;
        public DateTime SignUpDate;
        private decimal currentCredit;
        public void SetCurrentCredit(decimal c)
        {
            currentCredit = c;
        }
        public decimal GetCurrentCredit()
        {
            return currentCredit;
        }
    }
    public static void Main()
    {
        // Prepare object for serialization
        Customer cm = new Customer();

        cm.CustomerID = 12;
        cm.CustomerName = "Ward Littell";
        cm.SignUpDate=DateTime.Now;
        cm.SetCurrentCredit(76.23M);

        Console.WriteLine("Now Serializing....");
        // Create stream object for storage
        Stream stm = new FileStream("BinCustomer.bin", FileMode.Create,
                                    FileAccess.Write);
```

Our stream is created, and now we create our BinaryFormatter object and serialize it.

```
        // Serialize object using Binary format
        BinaryFormatter inFormatter = new BinaryFormatter();
        inFormatter.Serialize(stm, cm);

        stm.Close();
        Console.WriteLine("Now Deserializing....");

        // Open and create stream
        Stream streamOut = new FileStream("BinCustomer.bin", FileMode.Open,
                                          FileAccess.Read);
```

To deserialize, we create our BinaryFormatter object, call the Deserialize method, and then cast the resulting object to our desired Customer type.

```
        // Perform deserialization on stored stream
        BinaryFormatter outFormatter = new BinaryFormatter();

        Customer recm = (Customer)outFormatter.Deserialize(streamOut);

        streamOut.Close();
```

```
        // Display state of object
        Console.WriteLine ("Customer ID = {0}", recm.CustomerID);
        Console.WriteLine ("Customer Name = {0}", recm.CustomerName);
        Console.WriteLine ("Sign up date = {0}", recm.SignUpDate);
        Console.WriteLine ("Current Credit = {0}", recm.GetCurrentCredit());
    }
}
```

When you run this code, you'll see that the `currentCredit` field has been serialized. The file produced is `BinCustomer.bin`. If you open this file in Visual Studio .NET, you should see something similar to Figure 2-11.

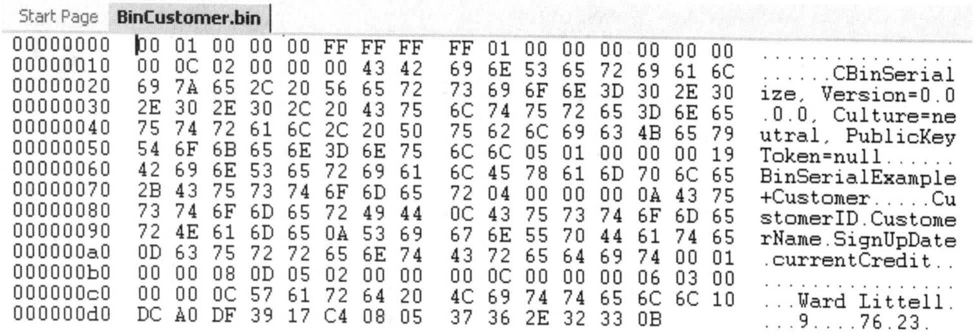

```
Start Page   BinCustomer.bin
00000000  00 01 00 00 00 FF FF FF  FF 01 00 00 00 00 00 00  ................
00000010  00 0C 02 00 00 00 43 42  69 6E 53 65 72 69 61 6C  ......CBinSerial
00000020  69 7A 65 2C 20 56 65 72  73 69 6F 6E 3D 30 2E 30  ize, Version=0.0
00000030  2E 30 2E 30 2C 20 43 75  6C 74 75 72 65 3D 6E 65  .0.0, Culture=ne
00000040  75 74 72 61 6C 2C 20 50  75 62 6C 69 63 4B 65 79  utral, PublicKey
00000050  54 6F 6B 65 6E 3D 6E 75  6C 6C 05 01 00 00 00 19  Token=null......
00000060  42 69 6E 53 65 72 69 61  6C 45 78 61 6D 70 6C 65  BinSerialExample
00000070  2B 43 75 73 74 6F 6D 65  72 04 00 00 00 0A 43 75  +Customer.....Cu
00000080  73 74 6F 6D 65 72 49 44  0C 43 75 73 74 6F 6D 65  stomerID.Custome
00000090  72 4E 61 6D 65 0A 53 69  67 6E 55 70 44 61 74 65  rName.SignUpDate
000000a0  0D 63 75 72 72 65 6E 74  43 72 65 64 69 74 00 01  .currentCredit..
000000b0  00 00 08 0D 05 02 00 00  00 0C 00 00 00 06 03 00  ................
000000c0  00 00 0C 57 61 72 64 20  4C 69 74 74 65 6C 6C 10  ...Ward Littell.
000000d0  DC A0 DF 39 17 C4 08 05  37 36 2E 32 33 0B        ...9....76.23.
```


Figure 2-11. *Serialized formatted binary*

All the contents of the file are stored in binary format. Note the assembly information, including the version information, for matching the correct version of the component to avoid any compatibility issues.

To use the SOAP formatter object, minor changes are required to the preceding code. First, we need to use the SOAP formatter namespace:

```
using System.Runtime.Serialization.Formatters.Soap;
```

We also need to change the formatter object (we use the `SoapFormatter` class for serializing into SOAP format) and the name of the file to which we serialize.

```
        // Create stream object for storage
        Stream stm = new FileStream("SoapCustomer.xml", FileMode.Create,
                                    FileAccess.Write);

        // Serialize object using SOAP format
        SoapFormatter inFormatter = new SoapFormatter();
        inFormatter.Serialize(stm, cm);

        stm.Close();
        Console.WriteLine("Now Deserializing....");

        // Open and create stream
```

```
Stream streamOut = new FileStream("SoapCustomer.xml", FileMode.Open,
                                  FileAccess.Read);

// Perform deserialization on stored stream
SoapFormatter outFormatter = new SoapFormatter();
Customer recm = (Customer)outFormatter.Deserialize(streamOut);

streamOut.Close();
```

Running this code produces the file shown in Figure 2-12, SoapCustomer.xml. This is a valid SOAP message that can be passed to a web service, for example.

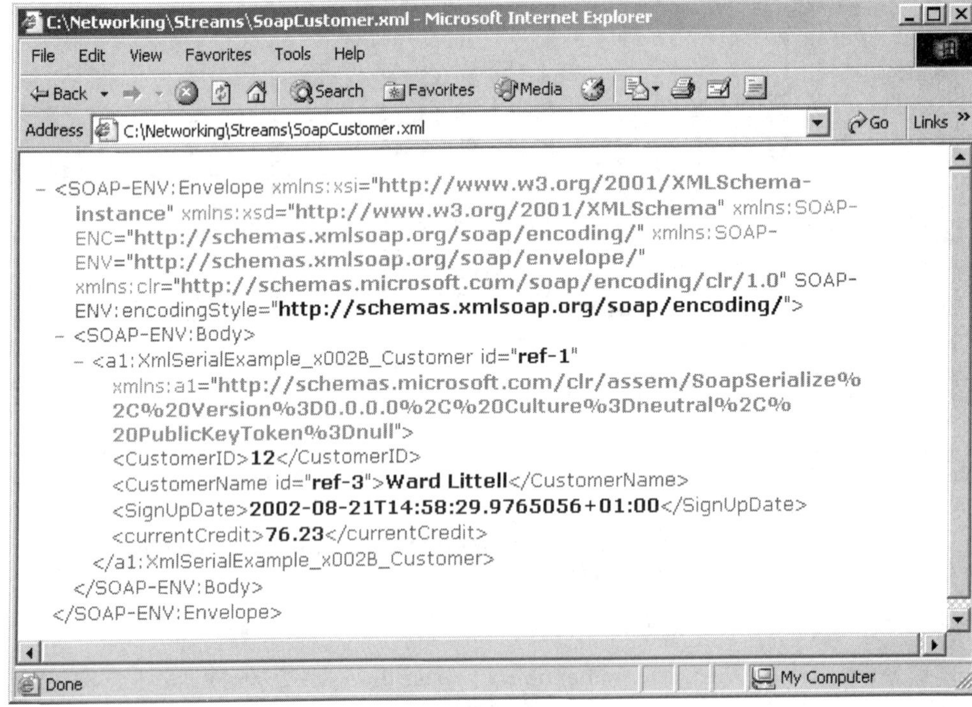

Figure 2-12. *Serialized formatted SOAP message*

Summary

In this chapter, we looked at the Stream class in the System.IO namespace and some of the classes derived from it that represent specific types of streams, characterized by their underlying device. We discussed the FileStream class, which allows access to a file on a disk; the MemoryStream class; and the NetworkStream class, among others. We showed that the methods they each inherit from Stream makes stream manipulation reasonably straightforward.

.NET provides various other classes in the System.IO namespace for stream manipulation and transferring data more complex than simple bytes. We looked at the BinaryReader and BinaryWriter classes for working with binary files, and the StreamReader and StreamWriter classes for working with text files.

Finally, we demonstrated how to serialize and deserialize objects into XML format, and how to use formatter objects to serialize into binary or SOAP format.

In the next chapter we'll present an overview of network programming with the .NET classes available within the System.Net namespace.

CHAPTER 3

■ ■ ■

Network Programming in .NET

In Chapter 1, we presented an overview of networking and looked at the structure and usage of different network protocols such as TCP, UDP, IP, and DNS. In this chapter, we start with network programming using classes from the `System.Net` namespace.

First, we briefly discuss all the classes from the `System.Net` namespace. Then we go into some of these classes in more detail. For the classes that are not covered here, we reference the corresponding chapter where they are covered in more detail. The networking classes discussed in this chapter play a fundamental role in all the remaining chapters of this book.

In particular, we discuss the following topics:

- The `System.Net` classes
- URIs
- IP addresses
- DNS lookups
- Requests and responses
- Authentication and authorization
- Permissions

System.Net Classes Overview

In the `System.Net` namespace, we have networking classes for IP address lookups, network authentication, and permissions, and classes for sending and receiving data.

Let's look at these classes by assigning them into some groups.

Name Lookup

To get an IP address from a DNS host name or to get a host name from an IP address, the `Dns` class can be used. The `DnsPermission` class represents the permission required for name lookups. `DnsPermissionAttribute` is an attribute class to mark assemblies, classes, or methods that need this privilege.

IP Addresses

IP addresses are handled within the class `IPAddress` (see Figure 3-1). A single host can have multiple IP addresses and alias names. All this information is contained within the class `IPHostEntry`. The `Dns` class returns an object of type `IPHostEntry` when you do a name lookup.

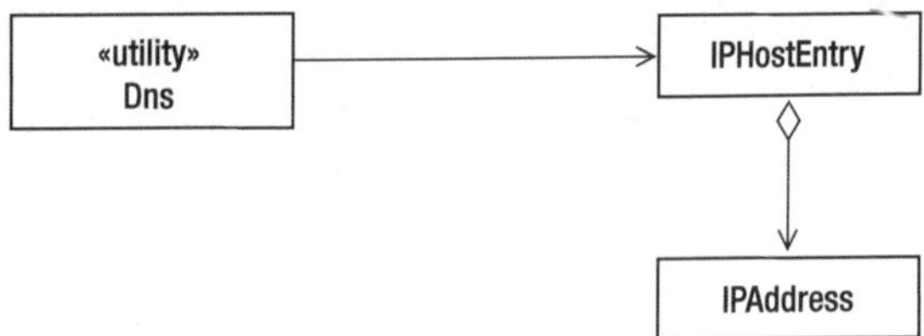

Figure 3-1. *IPAddress and name lookup classes*

Authentication and Authorization

The `AuthenticationManager` class has static methods to authenticate the client user. This utility class uses modules that implement the `IAuthenticationModule` interface. The `AuthenticationManager` asks these modules to authenticate the user. The authentication modules get request information and the user credentials with the `ICredentials` interface, and return an `Authorization` object for authorized users that are allowed to use the resource.

■ **NOTE** In this chapter, we present an overview of the authentication and authorization mechanism. We look into it in more detail in Chapter 13.

The client application can pass credentials to the server with an instance of the `NetworkCredential` class. User credentials can be cached in `CredentialCache`.

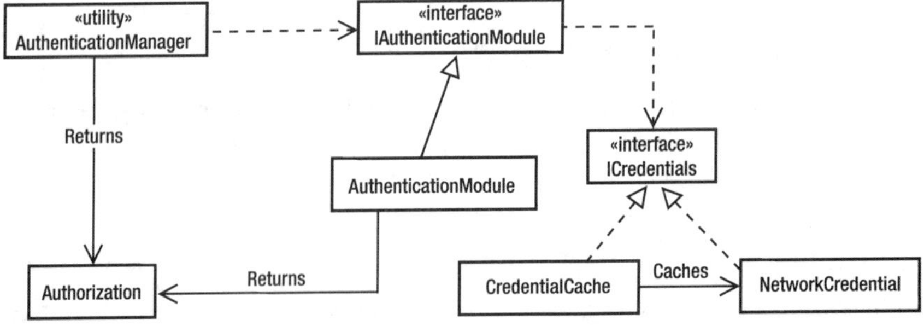

Figure 3-2. *Authentication and authorization classes*

Requests and Responses

The abstract base classes for sending requests to a server and receiving responses are WebRequest and WebResponse. In the System.Net namespace, we have some specific implementations of these classes for HTTP and file access (see Figure 3-3): HttpWebRequest, HttpWebResponse, FileWebRequest, and FileWebResponse.

■NOTE In this chapter we discuss the functionality of the WebRequest and WebResponse classes, and the specific implementations FileWebRequest and FileWebResponse. We discuss the HTTP protocol and related classes in Chapter 10.

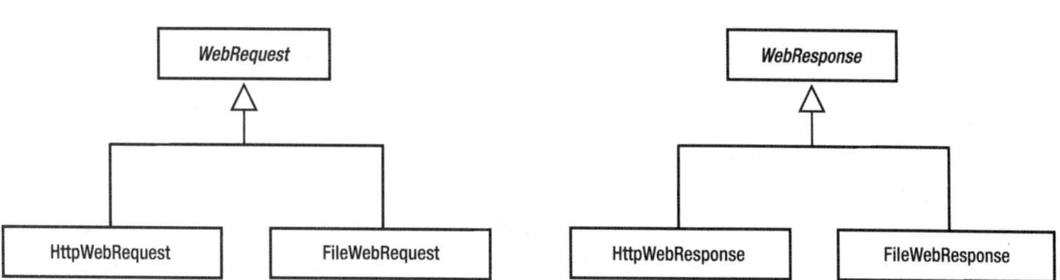

Figure 3-3. *Request and response classes*

The HttpXXX classes also make use of another class in the System.Net namespace: the HttpVersion class is used to specify the HTTP version. The HttpWebRequest and HttpWebResponse classes both have a ProtocolVersion property that defines the HTTP version: HttpVersion .Version10 or HttpVersion.Version11. HTTP 1.0 was used in the early days of the Internet and is still used by some web servers. HTTP 1.1, the current version, has more features than version 1.0, such as keeping a connection open for multiple requests.

The permissions needed with the request and response classes are defined with the WebPermission class and the attribute class WebPermissionAttribute.

A component class that makes it easy to use WebRequest and WebResponse from the Visual Studio .NET designer is the WebClient class. This class derives from the Component class, so it can be used with drag-and-drop functionality from the Toolbox. However, it is not configured to the Toolbox by default. With the WebClient class, it is easy to download files from and upload files to a server.

Connection Management

The ServicePoint and ServicePointManager classes (see Figure 3-4) play an important role for HTTP connections. An instance of the ServicePoint class is associated with a URI to a resource and can handle multiple connections. The utility class ServicePointManager manages ServicePoint objects by creating new objects or finding existing ones.

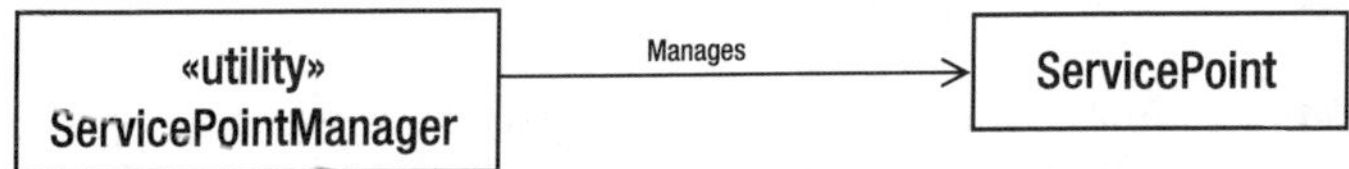

Figure 3-4. *Connection management classes*

You can increase the throughput of an application that requests a lot of data from a server simultaneously by increasing the number of connections on an application basc. By default, the maximum number of connections to the same server has a value of 2 to limit the network resources needed. Later in this chapter in the "Connection Pooling" section, we look at where the default value is specified and how it can be changed.

Creating connection pools is useful for middle-tier applications that connect to Internet resources on behalf of a specific user. You can reuse connections in connection groups where each group is associated with user credentials.

Cookies

Cookies are sets of data stored on the client side and used by the server to remember some information between requests. When you're using a web browser like Internet Explorer to request some data from a web server, Internet Explorer itself manages the acceptance and storage of cookies, and sends the cookies back to the web server. If you create a custom application that requests data from a web server that sends cookies, you can read these in an object of the class `CookieCollection` that is returned from the `Cookies` property of an `HttpWebResponse` (see Figure 3-5). You can pass cookies to the server with the help of the `CookieContainer` class. A cookie itself is represented in the `Cookie` class.

■ NOTE Cookies are sent within the header of the HTTP protocol, so we cover cookies again when we look at the HTTP protocol in Chapter 10.

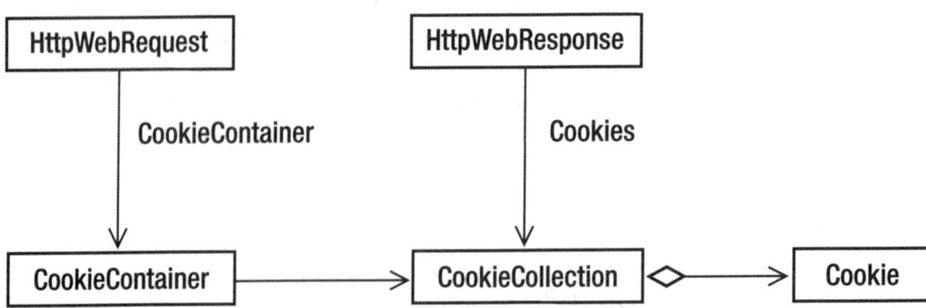

Figure 3-5. *Cookie management classes*

Proxy Server

A *proxy server* is used in a network environment to direct connection to the Internet through a single system (or multiple systems depending on the network size). The proxy server can cache pages that are requested by users, so if the same page is requested several times, a request to the web server is not needed anymore because the web proxy can answer the request itself.

The `WebProxy` class (see Figure 3-6) is used to define the proxy server that should be consulted for Internet requests. With the `GlobalProxySelection` class, you can define a default proxy server that should be used for all requests if not specified otherwise for a specific request.

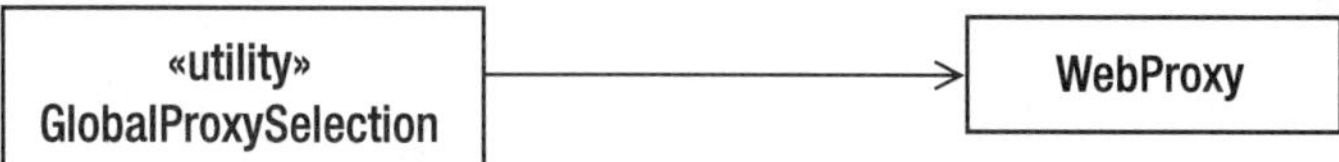

Figure 3-6. *WebProxy class*

Sockets

Instead of using the web classes, you can get more features and flexibility—but also more complexity—with socket classes. Most of the classes that are used with socket programming can be found in the namespace `System.Net.Sockets`.

With socket programming, you can do not only connection-oriented programming as is used with HTTP, but also connectionless programming as is used with UDP broadcasts and multicasts. Socket programming is extremely flexible and allows the use of different protocols such as GGP, ICMP, IGMP, IPX, and SPX.

In the following chapters, we discuss socket programming with both the TCP and UDP protocols, with connection-oriented data transfer and connectionless data transfer for broadcasts and multicasts.

Now that you have an understanding of the most important classes in the `System.Net` namespace, let's take a more detailed look at some of these classes, as they are the foundation for the rest of the book.

Working with URIs

We use *Uniform Resource Identifiers* (URIs) every day when browsing the Web. We need such URIs to identify and request different kind of resources. With a URI, we can access not only web pages, but also FTP servers, web services, and local files.

■ **NOTE** For URIs, the term URL (Uniform Resource Locator) is often used. URI is a generic term that is used to refer to resources. A URL is a URI that is associated with popular URI schemes such as `http`, `ftp`, and `mailto`. In technical documentation, the term "URL" is no longer used.

■ NOTE Another term that you may know already is URN (Uniform Resource Name). A URN is a standardized URI and is used to specify a resource independent of its network location.

URI is defined in RFC 2396 (`http://www.ietf.org/rfc/rfc2396.txt`). The RFC for URN is RFC 2142 (`http://www.ietf.org/rfc/rfc2141.txt`).

Some examples of URIs are shown here. This URI uses the `http` scheme to reference a website:

```
http://www.christiannagel.com
```

The `mailto` scheme is used for e-mail addresses:

```
mailto:christian@christiannagel.com
```

Usenet newsgroups can be accessed with the `news` scheme:

```
news:msnews.microsoft.com
```

Let's analyze the parts of a URI referencing a page at the ASP.NET website:

```
http://www.asp.net/Default.aspx?tabindex=0&tabid=1
```

The first part of the URI is the *scheme*. The scheme defines the namespace of the URI, and it may restrict the syntax that follows. Many schemes are named the same as the protocol they are using (such as `http`, `ftp`, etc.), but this is not a requirement. In our example, `http` is the scheme identifier. The scheme delimiter (`://` in the example) separates the scheme from the remaining URI.

After the scheme delimiter (`://` for the `http` scheme), the name of the server or the IP address in dotted quad notation follows: `www.asp.net`.

After the server name or IP address is the port number for connecting to a specific application on the server. If the port number is not specified, the default port number of a protocol is used (for example, port number 80 for HTTP).

The *path* defines a page (and directory) of the requested resource. This is not necessarily a physical file on the server, but it can be created dynamically. Here the path is `/Default.aspx`.

Separated from the path with a ? character is the last part of this URI, the *query*. In our example, the query is defined with `tabindex=0&tabid=1`. A query string can have multiple query components, each specifying a variable and a value connected with the `=` character. Multiple query components can be combined with the character `&`. Thus in our example, the first component is `tabindex=0`, with the variable `tabindex` and the value `0`, and the second component is `tabid=1`.

Sections inside a resource can be identified with *fragments*. Fragments are used to reference a section within an HTML page. With web page developments, fragments are also known as *bookmarks*. The # character separates a fragment identifier from the path. With the URL `http://www.microsoft.com/net/basics/glossary/glossary_a_z.asp#managed_code`, the fragment is `#managed_code`.

If a # character is added to a query string, then it is not a fragment; instead, it belongs to the query string. With a URL, you can have a query string or a fragment, but not both.

The use of some characters is reserved in a URI—these characters may not be contained within host names or a path because these are special separator characters. Reserved characters in a URI are as follows:

```
; / ? : @ & = + $ ,
```

Uri Class

The `Uri` class in the `System` namespace encapsulates a URI. It has properties and methods for parsing, comparing, and combining URIs.

Constructing Uri Objects

You can create a `Uri` object by passing a URI string to the constructor:

```
Uri uri = new Uri("http://msdn.microsoft.com/code/default.asp");
```

If you already have a base `Uri` object, you can create a new URI by combining the base URI with a relative URI:

```
Uri baseUri = new Uri("http://msdn.microsoft.com");
Uri newUri = new Uri(baseUri, "code/default.asp");
```

■ NOTE If the base URI already contains a path, this is ignored. Only the scheme, port, and server name are taken as a base for the new URI.

Commonly Used Schemes

The `Uri` class has read-only static fields to get some commonly used schemes:

- `Uri.UriSchemeFile`: The `file` scheme is used to access files locally or on network shares where Universal Naming Convention (UNC) names can be used.
- `Uri.UriSchemeFtp`: With the `ftp` scheme, the FTP protocol is used to get files from and put files on an FTP server.
- `Uri.UriSchemeGopher`: The Gopher protocol is a predecessor of the HTTP protocol. It offered some hierarchical browsing with text information about the content that was an advantage to the FTP protocol, but it was soon replaced by HTTP.
- `Uri.UriSchemeHttp` and `Uri.UriSchemeHttps`: These two schemes are well known: `http` and `https`. `https` is used for secure communication. We'll discuss the HTTP protocol in Chapter 8.
- `Uri.UriSchemeMailto`: The `mailto` scheme is used for sending e-mail.
- `Uri.UriSchemeNews` and `Uri.UriSchemeNntp`: Both the `news` and `nntp` schemes are used for newsgroup discussions using the NNTP protocol.

Checking for a Valid Host Name and Scheme

The `Uri` class has static methods to check for a valid scheme and host name. `Uri.CheckSchemeName` returns `true` if the scheme name is valid, and `Uri.CheckHostName` not only checks the host name, but also returns the type of the host with a value of the `UriHostNameType` enumeration.

Table 3-1 lists possible values of `UriHostNameType`.

Table 3-1. *UriHostNameType Enumeration*

Value	Description
`Basic`	The host name is set, but the type cannot be determined.
`Dns`	This will be the type returned most often. Passing a string either with or without domain extensions will return this type value.
`IPv4`	If a string passed contains dotted quad notation (for example, `204.148.170.161`), `IPv4` is returned.
`IPv6`	Passing an IPv6 string for the host name, `IPv6` is returned. IPv6 has 128 bits for the host identification, whereas IPv4 has only 32 bits. An IPv6 address string looks like this: `1080:0:0:0:8:800:200C:417A`.
`Unknown`	If the host name contains invalid characters, `Unknown` is returned.

You can use `Uri.CheckHostName` to check if the user entered a valid string for a host name, but this method doesn't check if the host name exists or can be reached. You can verify the existence of a host name by translating the host name to an IP address with the `Dns` class, as shown later in this chapter.

Properties of the Uri Class

The `Uri` class has a lot of read-only properties to access all parts of a URI.

Table 3-2 uses the following URI as an example to show the results of the properties:

```
http://www.globalknowledge.net:80/training/generic.asp?pageid=1078&country=DACH
```

Table 3-2. *Uri Class Properties*

Property	Description
`AbsoluteUri`	The absolute URI shows the complete URI. If the port number specified is the default port number for the protocol, the `Uri` constructor automatically removes it. With our example, the value of the `AbsoluteUri` property looks like this: `http://www.globalknowledge.net/training/generic.asp?pageid=1078&country=DACH`. If a file name is passed to the constructor of the `Uri` class, the `AbsoluteUri` property automatically prefixes the file name with the scheme `file://`.
`Scheme`	The scheme can be seen first in the URI. Here it is `http`.
`Host`	The `Host` property shows the host name of the URI: `www.globalknowledge.net`.
`Authority`	The `Authority` property shows the same as the `Host` property if the port number used is the default for the protocol. If a different port number is used, the `Authority` property shows the port number as well.

Property	Description
HostNameType	The type of the host name depends on the name that is used. Here, we get the same value of the enumeration UriHostNameType that we discussed previously. In this case it is UriHostNameType.Dns.
Port	With the property Port we can get the port number, 80.
AbsolutePath	The absolute path starts after the port number of the URI and excludes the query string. Here it is /training/generic.asp.
LocalPath	The local path is /training/generic.asp. As you can see, with an HTTP request there is no difference between AbsolutePath and LocalPath. A difference can be seen if the URI references a network share. With a URI such as file:\\server\share\directory\file.txt the LocalPath property just returns the directory and file name, whereas the AbsolutePath property includes the server and share names.
Query	The Query property shows the string that follows the path: ?pageid=1078&country=DACH.
PathAndQuery	PathAndQuery is a combination of both the path and the query string: /training/generic.asp?pageid=1078&country=DACH.
Fragment	If a fragment follows the path, it is returned with the Fragment property. Only a query string or a fragment can follow the path. The fragment is identified by the # character.
Segments	The Segments property returns a string array formed from the path. Here we have three segments: /, training/, and generic.asp.
UserInfo	If a user name is set in the URI, it can be read with the UserInfo property. Passing user names is common with the FTP protocol. If the anonymous user is not used, such as ftp://myuser@ftp.myserver.com, then the UserInfo property returns myuser.

In addition to the properties in Table 3-2, there are some properties that return a Boolean value if the URI represents a file, a UNC path, or a loopback address, or if the default port number for a specific protocol is used: IsFile, IsUnc, IsLoopback, and IsDefaultPort.

Modifying URIs with the UriBuilder Class

After you create an instance of the Uri class with the constructor, it cannot be modified anymore. The properties of the Uri class are read-only. To change values in a URI dynamically, you can use the UriBuilder class. It has similar properties to the Uri class, but here the properties are read/write. For read-only access, the Uri class is a lot faster than the UriBuilder class. You are probably familiar with such a concept from the String and StringBuilder classes.

In the following example, an instance of UriBuilder is constructed by passing the scheme, host name, port number, and path. Then, we change the path by setting the Path property. The Uri property of the UriBuilder returns a read-only Uri instance.

```
UriBuilder uri1 = new UriBuilder("http", "www.gotdotnet", 80,
                                 "team/codewise/default.aspx");
uri1.Path = "team/codewise/association.aspx";
Uri uri2 = uri1.Uri;
```

Absolute and Relative URIs

URIs can be *absolute* or *relative*. An absolute URI starts with the scheme, followed by the host name and the optional port number. The absolute URI can have a path, but the path is ignored if it is used together with a relative URI. A relative URI is defined only with a path, so it requires an absolute URI as its base to know the exact resource location. If you have one URI in use, a relative URI is sufficient to access another resource from the same host. Relative URIs are shorter, so you need fewer characters.

If you read a link from an HTML page that is represented in an anchor tag `<A>`, the link can include an absolute or a relative URI. If it includes a relative URI that you want to use with a query, you have to create an absolute URI from it because the `Uri` class stores only absolute URIs.

In the following code example, we create a base URI with the string `http://www.gotdotnet.com` and store it in the variable `baseUri`. The second object of type `Uri` that is created uses the variable `baseUri` as a base. The path `/team/libraries` is appended in the constructor. If the base URI were to include a path as well, that path would be ignored. The third URI in this example uses `resource1` as a base URI and appends `/userarea/default.aspx`. `resource1` already includes a path, but because it is used as a base URI, the path is ignored.

```
Uri baseUri = new Uri("http://www.gotdotnet.com");
Uri resource1 = new Uri(baseUri, "team/libraries");
Uri resource2 = new Uri(resource1, "/userarea/default.aspx");
Console.WriteLine(resource1.AbsoluteUri);
Console.WriteLine(resource2.AbsoluteUri);
```

Figure 3-7 shows the output of the demonstration application with the resultant absolute URIs that are stored in the `Uri` objects. As you can see, a missing / between the base URI and the path is added automatically, and the path in the base URI is ignored.

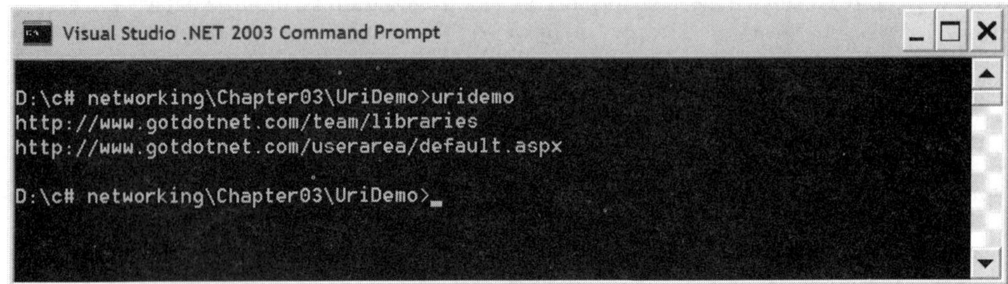

Figure 3-7. *UriDemo.exe output with absolute URIs*

Not only does the `Uri` class support creating absolute URIs by using a relative one, but it also has a method, `MakeRelative`, that creates a relative URI out of an absolute one.

The following code example shows the creation of a relative URI from two absolute ones. `resource1.MakeRelative(resource2)` returns a string that shows how we can go from the URI of `resource1` to the URI of `resource2`.

```
Uri resource1 =
      new Uri("http://www.gotdotnet.com/userarea/default.aspx");
Uri resource2 =
      new Uri("http://www.gotdotnet.com/team/libraries/");
Console.WriteLine(resource1.MakeRelative(resource2));
Console.WriteLine(resource2.MakeRelative(resource1));
Uri resource3 =
      new Uri("http://msdn.microsoft.com/vstudio/default.asp");
Console.WriteLine(resource2.MakeRelative(resource3));
```

Figure 3-8 shows the result. If we want to go from the absolute URI `http://www.gotdotnet.com/userarea/default.aspx` to the URI `http://www.gotdotnet.com/team/libraries`, the resultant relative URI is `../team/libraries`. For the way back, the relative URI `../../userarea/default.aspx` is needed. When working with the local file system, `..` references the parent directory. With the third string, you can see that if a completely different URI is passed to the method `MakeRelative`, the absolute URI is returned because the absolute URI is needed to access the resource.

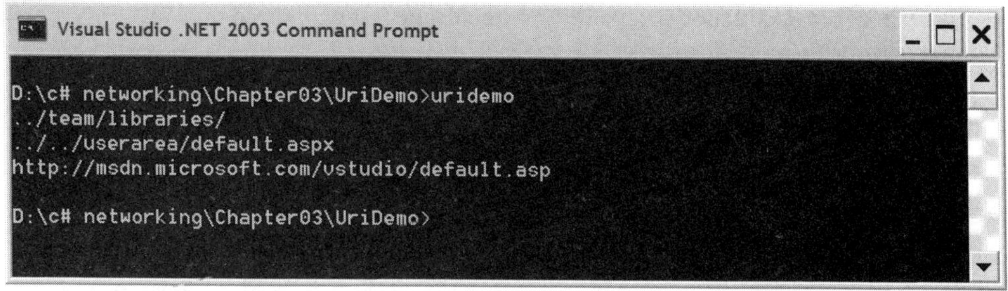

Figure 3-8. *UriDemo.exe output with relative URIs*

IP Addresses

In a TCP/IP network a computer can be uniquely identified with an IP address. IPv4 addresses are contained within 32 bits. For easier reading of an IP address, it is usually represented by dotted quad notation, such as 3204.148.170.161, making it easier to differentiate between networks and subnetworks, as you saw in Chapter 1.

The `IPAddress` class encapsulates an IP address to use it with many other classes from the `System.Net` namespace, and it supports conversion functionality from network to host byte order, and vice versa.

To create an IPAddress object with dotted quad notation, you could in .NET 1.0 use the static method Parse:

```
IPAddress address = IPAddress.Parse("204.148.170.161");
```

Here the IPAddress class itself stores the IP address within an integer that can be accessed with the Address property. In .NET 1.1, however, the Address property is obsolete. Use GetAddressBytes instead:

```
Byte[] bytes = address.GetAddressBytes();
for (int i = 0; i < bytes.Length; i++)
Console.Write(bytes[i]);
```

The ToString method returns dotted quad notation.

Predefined Addresses

The IPAddress class has some public read-only fields that return predefined IP addresses.

- IPAddress.None returns an address indicating that no network interface should be used. This is used by the Socket class to indicate that the server should not listen for client activity.
- IPAddress.IPv6None is equivalent to 0:0:0:0:0:0:0:0 in colon-hexadecimal notation or ::0 in compact notation for the IPv6 protocol, and it is supported only in .NET Framework 1.1.
- IPAddress.Loopback returns the predefined loopback address 127.0.0.1. This loopback address is used not to connect to the network, but to stay locally on a machine.
- IPAddress.IPv6Loopback is equivalent to 0:0:0:0:0:0:0:1 in colon-hexadecimal notation or ::1 in compact notation for the IPv6 protocol, and it is supported only in .NET Framework 1.1.
- IPAddress.Broadcast returns the IP broadcast address. With broadcast messages, you can send a message to every PC in the local network.
- A computer can have multiple network cards with multiple IP addresses. IPAddress.Any is used by a socket to listen to any network interface.
- IPAddress.IPv6Any is equivalent to 0:0:0:0:0:0:0:0 in colon-hexadecimal notation or :: in compact notation for the IPv6 protocol, and it is supported only in .NET Framework 1.1.

Host or Network Byte Order

Networking is about connecting computers—computers that can use different CPUs and operating systems. Depending on the CPU used, the ordering of bytes inside a short, an integer, or a long can be different between the systems. The terms *little endian* and *big endian* apply to this situation.

With little endian, the least significant byte is stored at a lower memory address. With big endian, it is the other way around: the most significant byte is stored at a lower memory address. Motorola CPUs use big endian, whereas Intel-compatible CPUs use little endian.

Defining the order of the bytes is an important issue when these different systems are connected. Fortunately, there is a standard for the byte representation on the network—the *network byte order*—and it's the same as big endian.

Using IP addresses that are stored within integers and port numbers that are stored within shorts, you have to convert the little endian version of the Intel system to the network byte order. The `IPAddress` class offers some static methods to convert `short`, `int`, and `long` data types from the host byte order (which is little endian in case of Intel CPUs) to the network byte order, and the other way around.

`IPAddress.NetworkToHostOrder` converts a multibyte integer value from network byte order to host byte order. `IPAddress.HostToNetworkOrder` converts a multibyte integer value from host byte order to network byte order.

■ **NOTE** For IP addresses and port numbers that are used with sockets, network byte order is needed. The .NET `Socket` class deals itself with the correct byte order. However, the byte order used for the data you send across the network is entirely your own concern. If you don't plan to communicate with systems of a different CPU architecture, there's no need to check for the byte order, but if you do communicate with different systems, you have to deal with it somehow.

■ **NOTE** You can look at Unicode text files for one example of how the network byte order can be resolved. Unicode has 2-byte characters, so the order is an issue. A Unicode text file has a beginning marker `FFFE`. With this marker, it can be easily detected if the file arrives in the wrong order, because the marker would show `FEFF`. Seeing the marker `FEFF`, all pairs of bytes must be reversed. A Unicode editor can reverse the order of the bytes, so there's no need to convert the data before sending it.

Dns Class

To connect to a server, the IP address of the server is needed. Because IP addresses are not easy to remember and can change, you use DNS names. In Chapter 1, you saw the functionality of DNS and how a DNS server resolves names to IP addresses.

For .NET applications, you can use the `Dns` class to resolve domain names to IP addresses. This class uses DNS servers to resolve names to IP addresses, and you will see that there are other mechanisms, too.

Resolving a Name to an IP Address

To get an IP address from a host name, you can use the static method `Dns.Resolve`. For a single host name, multiple IP addresses can be configured. So `Resolve` returns not only an `IPAddress`, but also an `IPHostEntry` object. `IPHostEntry` holds an array of addresses, alias names, and the host name itself.

In the following example, we resolve the IP addresses of the host name `www.microsoft.com` with `Dns.Resolve`. The IP addresses are written to the console by accessing the `AddressList` property that returns an array of `IPAddress` objects. Next, we loop through all registered names with the `Aliases` property, and finally we write the real host name to the console.

```
string hostname = "www.microsoft.com";
IPHostEntry entry = Dns.Resolve(hostname);
Console.WriteLine("IP Addresses for {0}: ", hostname);
foreach (IPAddress address in entry.AddressList)
   Console.WriteLine(address.ToString());
Console.WriteLine("\nAlias names:");
foreach (string aliasName in entry.Aliases)
   Console.WriteLine(aliasName);
Console.WriteLine("\nAnd the real hostname:");
Console.WriteLine(entry.HostName);
```

The output of this sample program (see Figure 3-9) shows that the host name `www.microsoft.com` is only an alias for `www2.microsoft.akadns.com`, and it has eight IP addresses.

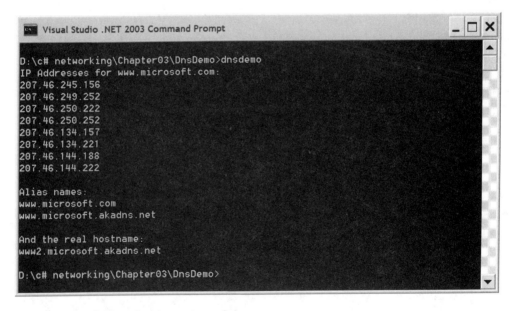

Figure 3-9. *DNS lookup for www.microsoft.com*

The `Dns` class has more static methods that return `IPHostEntry` objects. They differentiate mainly in the way the host name can be passed, as Table 3-3 shows.

Table 3-3. *Dns Class Static Methods*

Method	Description
Resolve	This method accepts a DNS host name or IP address in dotted quad notation to resolve IP addresses.
GetHostByName	This method accepts only the DNS host name, but not an IP address.
GetHostByAddress	This method returns an IPHostEntry object by passing an IP address either as a string in dotted quad notation or as an IPAddress object.

To get the host name of the local computer, you can use the method Dns.GetHostName.

How Is an IP Address Resolved?

There are many ways that an IP address can be resolved. You may have already wondered why a name was resolved although it was never configured with a DNS server. Let's look at the ways in which IP addresses can be resolved.

With early versions of the TCP/IP network, host names were resolved only by a HOSTS file. A HOSTS file has a mapping from an IP address to the name of the host with optional additional alias names. Such a host file named hosts can also be found on a Windows XP system in the directory <windir>\system32\drivers\etc.

Later, the Domain Name System was introduced with DNS servers that know about the mapping of host names to IP addresses and also the other way around. Getting the host name from an IP address is known as *reverse lookup*. Instead of changing every HOSTS file when a new IP address should be added, the new IP address need only be added to the DNS server. The client systems only need to be aware of the DNS server; therefore, the IP addresses can be resolved by asking the DNS server. The DNS server can be configured with the TCP/IP properties of the network configuration.

To free network administrators from the tiresome task of manually assigning IP addresses to every client on the network, a Dynamic Host Configuration Protocol (DHCP) server can be used. DHCP introduced dynamic IP addresses for PC clients. With DHCP, a client PC no longer has a fixed IP address. This brought about a new challenge for DNS servers and was the reason *dynamic DNS* was introduced with Windows 2000. Using dynamic DNS, the IP address and host name of a client PC can be set automatically in the DNS server as soon as the DHCP address is received.

To summarize, IP addresses are resolved with HOSTS files and DNS servers, but there are other ways. In a local network, in addition to a DNS name, a NetBIOS host name is used. If the DNS lookup fails, some NetBIOS naming mechanisms are used to get an IP address. Let's look at how this works in the following section.

NetBIOS Host Names

In a Microsoft network, PCs have not only DNS host names, but also NetBIOS host names. NetBIOS functionality can also be used with TCP/IP; here it is called NBT (NetBIOS over TCP/IP). Normally, the NetBIOS name is the same as the DNS name without the domain name extension.

For NetBIOS name resolution, an `LMHOSTS` file is used, similar to the `HOSTS` file. It's in the same directory as the `HOSTS` file, in fact. The file `LMHOSTS.SAM` you may find on your PC is just a sample file that shows what the `LMHOSTS` file can look like. If the host name cannot be resolved with the `LMHOSTS` file, the NetBIOS name resolution depends on the NetBIOS node type. We can differentiate between four different node types:

- *B-node (broadcast)*: With B-nodes, a broadcast is used to resolve the NetBIOS host name. If IP routers are used that don't forward name registration and name queries, the name can't be resolved. B-nodes are a bad option for large networks because they load the network with broadcasts.
- *P-node (point to point)*: Using P-nodes, a WINS server is used to register the host name. A WINS server is similar to a DNS server, except that it resolves NetBIOS names to IP addresses rather than DNS names to IP addresses. A client can ask the WINS server to get the IP address for a host name. This method reduces the network traffic, but it fails if the WINS server cannot be reached.
- *M-node (mixed)*: M-node configuration is a mixture of B-node and P-node. As a first try, a broadcast is used. If the broadcast doesn't work because the target host isn't in the same network, a WINS server is asked to resolve the host name. This configuration is useful with many small subnetworks that communicate across slow links.
- *H-node (hybrid)*: H-node is also a mixture of B-node and P-node, but here the P-node mechanism is used first, before the B-node mechanism. A broadcast is used as a last resort if other mechanisms fail.

You can look at the node type that is configured for your system with the command-line utility `ipconfig /all`. The default is the typically the best performing node type, H-node.

■ **NOTE** If the naming resolution is not complex enough, it is also possible to edit some entries in the Registry to change the order of DNS name lookup and NetBIOS name lookup. However, proceed cautiously, as it's not a good idea to mess up these Registry keys. You can find the configuration of these values in `HKLM\System\CurrentControlSet\Services\NetBT\Parameters`.

■ **NOTE** If the variable `DhcpNodeType` is set to `4`, this specifies H-node.

Resolving the IP Address Asynchronously

Querying a DNS server can take some time. The methods we have presented so far have all been synchronous. The `Dns` class has built-in support for asynchronous DNS lookups; the methods `Resolve` and `GetHostByName` have asynchronous versions. We discuss only the asynchronous versions of the `GetHostByName` method here, but the `Resolve` method is similar.

The asynchronous versions of the `GetHostByName` method are `BeginGetHostByName` and `EndGetHostByName`. The `BeginGetHostByName` method starts the name query but doesn't wait for a successful query or a timeout—it returns immediately. Besides passing the host name (similar to GetHostByName), this method accepts an AsyncCallback delegate that defines what method should be called as soon as the host name is resolved or the timeout happens. Here we're using the class method DnsLookupCompleted that has the return type and signature as it is defined by the AsyncCallback delegate:

```
using System;
using System.Net;
class AsyncDnsDemo
{
   private static string hostname = "www.apress.com";
   static void Main(string[] args)
   {
      if (args.Length != 0)
         hostname = args[0];
      Dns.BeginGetHostByName(hostname,
         new AsyncCallback(DnsLookupCompleted), null);
      Console.WriteLine("Waiting for the results...");
      Console.ReadLine();
   }
```

As soon as the DNS lookup is finished, the DnsLookupCompleted method is called, and we get the result of the name lookup by calling Dns.EndGetHostByName. Then we can access all IP addresses, alias names, and the real host name as in the synchronous example:

```
      private static void DnsLookupCompleted(IAsyncResult ar)
      {
         IPHostEntry entry = Dns.EndGetHostByName(ar);
         Console.WriteLine("IP Addresses for {0}: ", hostname);
         foreach (IPAddress address in entry.AddressList)
            Console.WriteLine(address.ToString());
         Console.WriteLine("\nAlias names:");
         foreach (string aliasName in entry.Aliases)
            Console.WriteLine(aliasName);
         Console.WriteLine("\nAnd the real hostname:");
         Console.WriteLine(entry.HostName);
      }
   }
```

As an alternative to passing a delegate to the BeginGetHostByName method, we can use a reference to the IAsyncResult interface that is returned to check for the completed DNS lookup using the IsCompleted property. As soon as the lookup is finished, we invoke the same method we previously used to read the IP addresses and host name, DnsLookupCompleted.

```
   static void Main(string[] args)
   {
      if (args.Length != 0)
         hostname = args[0];
      IAsyncResult ar = Dns.BeginGetHostByName(hostname, null, null);
```

```
      while (!ar.IsCompleted)
      {
         Console.WriteLine("Can do something else...");
         System.Threading.Thread.Sleep(100);
      }
      DnsLookupCompleted(ar);
   }
```

Requests and Responses

After the name of the host is resolved, the client and server can start communicating. The server creates a socket and listens for incoming clients, the client connects to a server, and then the client and the server can send and receive data. In Chapter 4 when we discuss sockets, you will see all the behind-the-scenes action. Here we use the WebRequest and WebResponse classes, where all socket issues are handled in the implementation of these classes—consequently, these classes are very simple to use.

In this small code example, we create a WebRequest object with the static method WebRequest.Create. The Create method accepts a Uri object or a URI string. The GetResponse method returns a WebResponse object and connects to the server to return some data. To read the data that is returned from the server, we use a StreamReader to read line by line.

```
Uri uri = new Uri("http://www.apress.com");
WebRequest request = WebRequest.Create(uri);
WebResponse response = request.GetResponse();
Stream stream = response.GetResponseStream();
StreamReader reader = new StreamReader(stream);
string line;
while ((line = reader.ReadLine()) != null)
{
   Console.WriteLine(line);
}
response.Close();
reader.Close();
```

Now that you've seen a simple application using WebRequest and WebResponse objects, let's look at these classes in detail.

WebRequest and WebResponse

The base classes for requests and responses to servers are WebRequest and WebResponse, respectively.

First let's look at the WebRequest class's methods and properties in Tables 3-4, 3-5, and 3-6.

Table 3-4. *WebRequest Class Static Methods*

Method	Description
Create CreateDefault	The WebRequest class has no public constructor. Instances can be created using the static methods Create and CreateDefault instead. These methods do not really create a new object of type WebRequest, but a new object of a class that derives from WebRequest, such as HttpWebRequest or FileWebRequest.
RegisterPrefix	With RegisterPrefix, you can register a class to handle a specific protocol. Objects of this class will be created with the WebRequest.Create method. This mechanism is called *pluggable protocols* and is described later in this chapter.

Table 3-5. *WebRequest Class Instance Methods*

Method	Description
GetRequestStream	GetRequestStream returns a stream object that can be used to send some data to the server.
BeginGetRequestStream	Getting access to the request stream in an asynchronous way is done with BeginGetRequestStream and EndGetRequestStream.
GetResponse	GetResponse returns a WebResponse object that can be used to read the data that is received from the server.
BeginGetResponse	Similar to the request stream, you have asynchronous methods to get the response stream.
EndGetResponse	EndGetResponse completes an asynchronous request started with the BeginGetResponse method.
Abort	If an asynchronous method is started with a BeginXXX method, it can be stopped prematurely with the Abort method.

Table 3-6. *WebRequest Class Properties*

Property	Description
RequestUri	RequestUri is a read-only property that returns the URI associated with the WebRequest. The URI can be set in the static Create method of this class.
Method	The Method property is used to get or set a method for a specific request. The HttpWebRequest supports the HTTP methods GET, POST, HEAD, and so on.
Headers	Depending on the protocol used, different header information can be passed to and received from the server. The protocol header information is contained within a WebHeaderCollection that can be accessed with the Header property.
ContentType	The type of data sent to the server is defined with the ContentType property. You can have any different type of data as long as it can be represented in a byte array. The content type usually defines the MIME type of the data, such as image/jpeg, image/gif, text/html, or text/xml.
ContentLength	This property contains the number of bytes of data sent to the Internet resource.

continues

Table 3-6. *Continued*

Property	Description
Credentials	If the server requires user authentication, the user credentials can be set with the Credentials property.
PreAuthenticate	For protocols that support preauthentication, the property PreAuthenticate can be set to true. By default, a web browser first tries to access the page of a website without authentication. If the website requires authentication, the server returns that access is denied for nonauthenticated users. The next request done by the client is with authentication information. This additional round-trip can be avoided by setting the property PreAuthenticate to true.
Proxy	With the Proxy property, you can set the web proxy that is used for this request.
ConnectionGroupName	With the ConnectionGroupName property, you can define the connection pool that should be used with this WebRequest object.
Timeout	The Timeout property defines the time in milliseconds you wait for a response from the server. The default value is 100,000 milliseconds. If the server doesn't respond within the timeout value, a WebException is thrown.

The WebResponse class is used to read data from the server. An object of this class is returned with the GetResponse method, as you have seen with the WebRequest class. Tables 3-7 and 3-8 show the members of the WebResponse class.

Table 3-7. *WebResponse Class Methods*

Method	Description
GetResponseStream	GetResponseStream returns a stream object that is used to read the response from the server. We discussed stream objects in Chapter 2.
Close	If the response object is no longer needed, it should be closed with the Close method.

Table 3-8. *WebResponse Class Properties*

Property	Description
ResponseUri	With the ResponseUri property, you can read the URI that is associated with the response object. This can be the same as the URI of the WebRequest object, or it can be different if the server redirected the request to another resource.
Headers	The Headers property returns a WebHeaderCollection that includes the protocol-specific header information returned from the server.
ContentType	Similar to the WebRequest class, you have ContentType and Content-Length properties. Here these properties define the nature of the data that is returned from the server.
ContentLength	This property contains the length, in bytes, of the response from the Internet resource.

Now that you know the properties and methods of the WebRequest and WebResponse classes, let's look at some of the features of these classes.

Pluggable Protocols

The WebRequest class is abstract, so the WebRequest.Create method cannot create an object of type WebRequest—an object of a class that is derived from WebRequest is created instead. Passing an HTTP request to the WebRequest.Create method creates an HttpWebRequest object. We'll discuss the HttpWebRequest class with detailed information about the HTTP protocol in Chapter 8. Passing a request with the file scheme creates a FileWebRequest object.

The http, https, and file schemes are predefined within the .NET configuration file machine.config as shown in the following code. You can find this configuration file in the directory <windows>\Microsoft.NET\Framework\<version>\CONFIG.

```
<configuration>
  <system.net>
    <webRequestModules>
      <add prefix="http" type="System.Net.HttpRequestCreator, System,
            Version=1.0.5000.0, Culture=neutral,
            PublicKeyToken=b77a5c561934e089" />
      <add prefix="https" type="System.Net.HttpRequestCreator, System,
            Version=1.0.5000.0, Culture=neutral,
            PublicKeyToken=b77a5c561934e089" />
      <add prefix="file" type="System.Net.FileWebRequestCreator, System
            Version=1.0.5000.0, Culture=neutral,
            PublicKeyToken=b77a5c561934e089" />
    </webRequestModules>
  </system.net>
</configuration>
```

Adding a configuration file entry allows you to extend the protocols used by the WebRequest class, or you can extend them programmatically.

To support a different protocol from the http, https, and file schemes, a new class that derives from WebRequest must be created, such as FtpWebRequest for the FTP protocol. This class must override methods and properties of the base class to implement protocol-specific behavior. In addition, a factory class that creates objects of the FtpWebRequest class must be defined. Such a factory class that is used by WebRequest must implement the IWebRequestCreate interface. We'll call this class FtpWebRequestCreator. An instance of this class must be registered for the ftp scheme with the WebRequest class:

```
WebRequest.RegisterPrefix("ftp", new FtpWebRequestCreator());
```

If the ftp scheme is now used with the WebRequest.Create method, a new instance of FtpWebRequest is created and returned:

```
FtpWebRequest request =
      (FtpWebRequest)WebRequest.Create("ftp://ftp.microsoft.com");
```

This request object can now be used to copy files from and to the FTP server similar to the request objects we use in the next section. In this chapter, we are not going to implement the FtpWebRequest class, but you can do it yourself after reading Chapters 4 and 5. Programming an FTP client requires using socket classes with a TCP connection.

FileWebRequest and FileWebResponse

Reading and writing files locally or by using file shares is not very different from reading and writing files from web servers. To read and write files, you can use the `FileWebRequest` and `FileWebResponse` classes. However, many methods and properties that are defined in the base classes `WebRequest` and `WebResponse` are not used with the derived classes, and the MSDN documentation just lists them as "reserved for future use."

To demonstrate how `FileWebRequest` and `FileWebResponse` can be used, we'll create a simple Windows Forms application (see Figure 3-10) in which the name of a file to be opened is entered in a text box, and then the file is opened and displayed in a multiline text box (the big white space in Figure 3-10). The opened file can then be saved with a different file name.

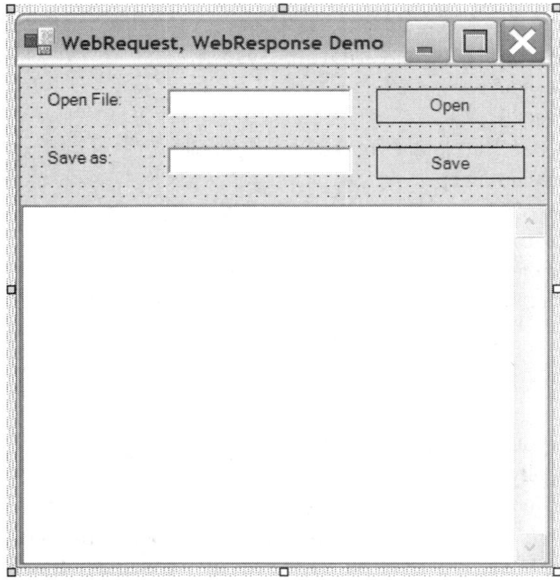

Figure 3-10. *Form design of the WebRequest sample application*

To make the code easier to read, the controls that are used with this application are shown in Table 3-9.

Table 3-9. *Controls of the WebRequest Demonstration Application*

Control Type	Name
`TextBox`	`textfileOpen`
`TextBox`	`textFileSave`
`Button`	`buttonOpenFile`
`Button`	`buttonSaveFile`
`TextBox`	`textData`

Reading from Files

The `Click` handler of the Open button opens the file and writes the content of the file to the multiline text box. We pass the file name to the `WebRequest.Create` method. It is not necessary to prefix the file name with the schema `file://`. The `WebRequest` class creates a `Uri` object and uses the `AbsolutePath` property of the `Uri` class. As you saw earlier, the `Uri` class automatically prefixes the file name with the correct scheme. So, passing a file name the `WebRequest` class creates a `FileWebRequest` object, and we can successfully cast it. The `GetResponse` method returns a `FileWebResponse` that we use immediately to get a `Stream` object with the method `GetResponseStream`. The `StreamReader` class is used to read the stream with simple methods. We read the complete file data into a string and pass the string to the `Text` property of the multiline text box, `textData`.

```
private void buttonOpenFile_Click(object sender, System.EventArgs e)
{
   string fileName = textFileOpen.Text;
   FileWebRequest request =
         (FileWebRequest)WebRequest.Create(fileName);
   Stream stream = request.GetResponse().GetResponseStream();
   StreamReader reader = new StreamReader(stream);
   textData.Text = reader.ReadToEnd();
   reader.Close();
}
```

Starting the application, we can enter a file name, and the file is opened and displayed in the multiline text box (see Figure 3-11).

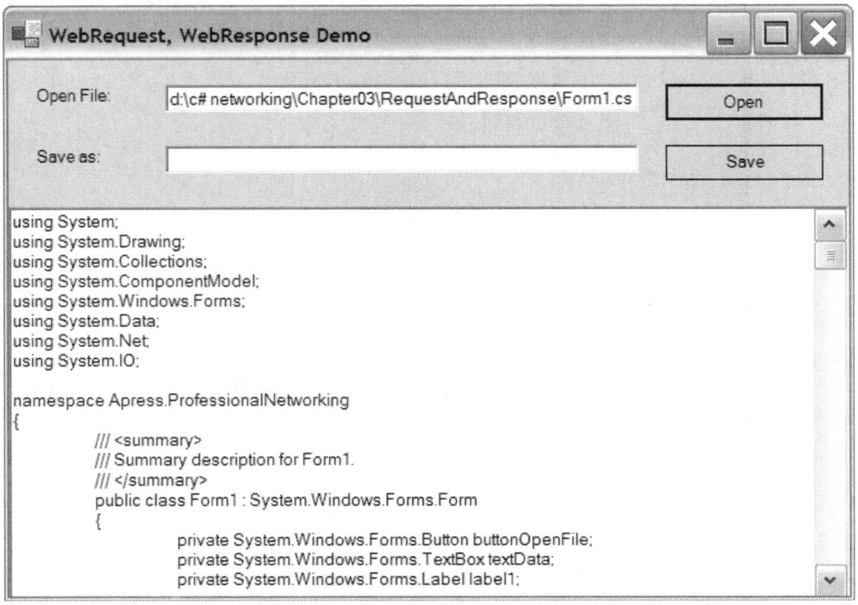

Figure 3-11. *WebRequest sample application*

There's just a simple change necessary and we can read files from both the file system and the Web. If we enter an HTTP request into the current program, it will result in an invalid cast exception because we cast the object that is returned from `WebRequest.Create` to the class `FileWebRequest`. Changing the program to not cast to a `FileWebRequest`, we can use any scheme:

```
string fileName = textFileOpen.Text;
WebRequest request = WebRequest.Create(fileName);
Stream stream = request.GetResponse().GetResponseStream();
```

■ **NOTE** If you don't use specific methods or properties of the derived class, it isn't necessary to cast the `WebRequest` object that is returned from the method `WebRequest.Create` to the specific class.

With .NET 1.1, the class `FileWebRequest` has no methods or properties that are specific to this class and are not defined in the base class `WebRequest`. However, the `HttpWebRequest` class has some specific methods and properties, which we'll deal with in Chapter 8.

Writing to Files

To write the data back to a file, we implement a `Click` handler for the Save button. As before, we create a `WebRequest` object, passing the file name. Now we use a `StreamWriter` instead of a `StreamReader`. There's one other important change: to make the stream writable, the `Method` property must be set to `"PUT"`. The default method is `"GET"`, which specifies that the stream is read-only.

```
private void OnFileSave(object sender, System.EventArgs e)
{
   string fileName = textFileSave.Text;
   WebRequest request = WebRequest.Create(fileName);
   request.Method = "PUT";
   Stream stream = request.GetRequestStream();
   StreamWriter writer = new StreamWriter(stream);
   writer.Write(textData.Text);
   writer.Close();
}
```

Now you've seen how the classes `WebRequest` and `WebResponse` can be used, but there are some other features of these classes that we'll look at next.

Connection Pooling

The default number of connections that can be opened to the server at one time is defined in the configuration file `machine.config`, as shown in the following code. With the default configuration, we have a maximum of two simultaneous connections to the same host.

```
<configuration>
  <system.net>
    <connectionManagement>
      <add address="*" maxconnection="2" />
    </connectionManagement>
  </system.net>
</configuration>
```

We can override the settings not only by adding entries to the configuration file, but also programmatically for specific requests using the `ServicePoint` and `ServicePointManager` classes. We can create multiple connection pools and use them by name with the `ConnectionGroupName` property. This is useful if we make multiple requests to the same server simultaneously. These classes are discussed in more detail in Chapter 8.

Using a Web Proxy

In a local network, a proxy server can be used to route Internet access to specific servers. A proxy server can reduce the transfer and network connections from the Internet, and increase the performance for local clients by caching resources.

The proxy server can perform active and passive caching.

- With *passive caching*, the web resources are stored in the cache of the proxy server as soon as a client requests a resource. If a second client requests the same resource again, it is not necessary to get the resource from the web server again, as the web proxy can answer directly from the cache created by the first request.
- Using *active caching*, the system administrator can configure specific web servers and directories that should be cached automatically following a specific schedule, such as during the night. This way, the network bandwidth needed for the Internet can be reduced during the day, and users will see a better performance for often-used pages.

The default proxy server is set through the Internet Options in the Control Panel. You can also access this configuration from Internet Explorer Tools ➤ Internet Options ➤ Connections ➤ LAN Settings, as shown in Figure 3-12.

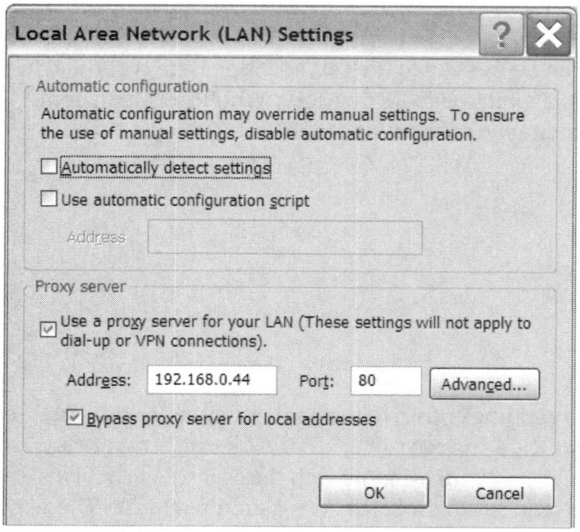

Figure 3-12. *Internet Explorer LAN settings*

Here the web proxy server has the IP address 192.168.0.44 and listens to port 80. For web servers in an intranet, the proxy server should not be used. This is marked with the "Bypass proxy server for local addresses" option. By clicking the Advanced button it is possible to configure different proxy servers for different protocols (such as HTTP, HTTPS, or FTP), and it is also possible to select specific websites that should not be accessed by the proxy server.

WebProxy Class

The `WebProxy` class is used to define a proxy server. This class has properties that are similar to the settings you've seen with the proxy server configuration. The properties are shown in Table 3-10.

Table 3-10. *WebProxy Class Properties*

Property	Description
`Address`	The Address is of type `Uri` and defines the URI to the proxy server, IP address, or name and port number.
`BypassList`	With the property `BypassList`, a string array can get and set URIs that should not use the proxy server.
`BypassArrayList`	`BypassArrayList` is a read-only property that returns an object of type `ArrayList` that represents the URIs you set with the property `BypassList`.
`BypassProxyOnLocal`	`BypassProxyOnLocal` is a Boolean property that specifies whether or not local addresses should be used with the proxy server.
`Credentials`	If the proxy server requires user authentication, you can pass the user credentials with the `Credentials` property.

Default Web Proxy

The default proxy server that is used for all connections is set with the `GlobalProxySelection` class. By default, the web proxy that is set with the Internet Options you have just seen is used. With the `Select` property, you can set a different proxy for all uses of `WebRequest.GetResponse`.

In the following program, we access the information from the default web proxy and write it to the console. The `Select` property of the `GlobalProxySelection` class returns an `IWebProxy` interface. To access the properties of the `WebProxy` class, we have to cast this interface to the `WebProxy` class. Then we access the URI of the proxy server that is defined with the `Address` property. The `BypassList` property returns a string array that we write out inside the `foreach` loop. Finally, we use the `BypassProxyOnLocal` property to write a message to the console that states whether or not the proxy is used for local addresses.

```
WebProxy proxy = (WebProxy)GlobalProxySelection.Select;
Console.WriteLine("Address of the proxy server: {0}", proxy.Address);
foreach (string bypassAddress in proxy.BypassList)
{
   Console.WriteLine("Not using the proxy server for this " +
                     "address: {0}", bypassAddress);
}
Console.WriteLine ("For local addresses the proxy server is {0}used",
                   proxy.BypassProxyOnLocal ? "not " : "");
```

The output to the console is shown in Figure 3-13.

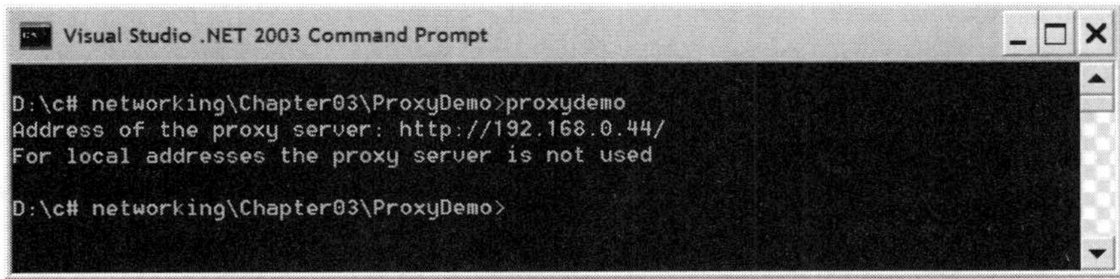

Figure 3-13. *ProxyDemo output*

Changing the Web Proxy for Specific Requests

Rather than using the default web proxy for all requests, you can use a different proxy for specific requests. In a network, multiple proxy servers can be used either to distribute the load or because of security requirements. To select a different proxy, you just have to set the `Proxy` property of the `WebRequest` class.

```
WebRequest request = WebRequest.Create("http://www.apress.com");
request.Proxy = new WebProxy("172.31.24.28", 8080);
```

The `Proxy` property of the `WebRequest` class accepts an object that implements the `IWebProxy` interface. Of course, the `WebProxy` class implements the `IWebProxy` interface. The constructor of the `WebProxy` class is overloaded and accepts a URI to the proxy server, and also all the parameters to configure a `WebProxy` object that you know already—for example, the user credentials and the list of URIs where the proxy server should be bypassed, among others.

Authentication

If the web server requires user authentication, you can create user credentials and pass them to the web request. The interfaces and classes that are of use here are `ICredentials`, `NetworkCredential`, and `CredentialCache`.

For user authentication, you can create an object of type `NetworkCredential`. This class provides credential information for basic, digest, NTLM, and Kerberos authentication.

In the constructor of the `NetworkCredential` class, you can pass a user name, password, and optionally a domain that authorizes the user.

```
NetworkCredential credentials =
      new NetworkCredential("UserName", "Password");
```

This credential information can be set with the `Credentials` property of the `WebRequest` class to authorize the user:

```
WebRequest request =
      WebRequest.Create("http://requireslogon.com/myfile.aspx");
request.Credentials = credentials;
```

If you want to use multiple credential information for different URIs, you can use the `CredentialCache` class as follows. With this cache you can also define the authentication type for a specific connection. Here, we're using basic authentication for the website `http://www.unsecure.com` and digest authentication for the website `http://www.moresecure.com`, where a hash is sent across the network instead of the password.

```
CredentialCache credentialCache = new CredentialCache();
credentialCache.Add(new Uri("http://www.unsecure.com"), "Basic",
                    new NetworkCredential("username", "password"));
credentialCache.Add(new Uri("http://www.moresecure.com"), "Digest",
                    new NetworkCredential("username", "password",
                                          "domain"));
```

To use the Windows logon credentials of the currently logged-on user, you can use the default credentials that can be accessed with ``CredentialCache.DefaultCredentials`. For security reasons, these credentials can be used only for the NTLM, Negotiate, and Kerberos authentication types, and it is not possible to read the user name and the domain from it.

Permissions

Whenever networking classes are used, permissions are required. For networking issues, you have three permissions to consider:

- `DnsPermission`
- `WebPermission`
- `SocketPermission`

The DnsPermission is required to do DNS name lookups with the Dns class. The WebPermission is used by classes from the System.Net namespace that use URIs to send and receive data from the Internet. The SocketPermission is used to accept data on a local socket or to connect to a host using a transport protocol.

Applications that are installed locally on a system have full trust, so all permissions are available by default. .NET applications can also be started from a network share, or assemblies can be downloaded from the Internet. In these situations, many permissions are not available by default; therefore, you have to configure the security settings for these applications.

In this section, we first discuss the programmatic aspects of the security, and then we examine how the permissions can be configured.

DnsPermission

Using the Dns class to make an IP address lookup, you need the DnsPermission. With this permission, you differentiate only between allow and deny. Making DNS queries can be either completely unrestricted or not allowed at all.

WebPermission

The WebPermission is required for classes such as WebRequest and WebResponse for sending data to and receiving data from the Internet.

Here you differentiate between Accept and Connect permissions. Accept is needed for URIs used inside classes and methods. Client applications that use URIs to connect to a server need the Connect privilege. The WebPermission class also has a list for URIs that you can connect to and a list for URIs that are accepted.

SocketPermission

The SocketPermission is needed for socket classes from the System.Net.Sockets namespace, which we deal with in Chapter 4. This is the most flexible permission of the three network permission classes.

For server applications that wait for clients to be connected, you can pass the NetworkAccess.Accept enumeration value in the constructor; client applications that connect to servers use the value NetworkAccess.Connect. You can restrict the connection to specific host and port numbers, and also define a transport protocol used.

Using Permission Attributes

If a required permission is not available, the program fails with an exception of type SecurityException as soon as the privileged method is called. The user may have been using the application for some time when the exception is thrown, and she may possibly lose some data if you don't handle the exception gracefully. A good way of avoiding this is to mark the assembly with the permissions that you need.

If you use the WebRequest class to get some data from the Internet, you need the WebPermission permission. You can mark classes and methods that require the permission with the WebPermission attribute (that's implemented in the class WebPermissionAttribute) as follows:

```
[WebPermission(SecurityAction.Demand,
               ConnectPattern="http://www.apress.com")]
class PermissionDemo
{
```

In this case, the SecurityException happens as soon as the PermissionDemo class is instantiated. If you want this check at program start-up, you can apply the WebPermission attribute to the assembly scope:

```
[assembly: WebPermission(SecurityAction.RequestMinimum,
           ConnectPattern="http://www.apress.com")]
```

If this WebPermission attribute is applied to the assembly, the runtime checks if the program has the required permission at program start-up. If it doesn't have the required permission, it stops immediately prior to the user entering (and losing) information.

Using the command-line utility permview that's part of the .NET Framework SDK, you can display the required assembly permissions, as shown in Figure 3-14.

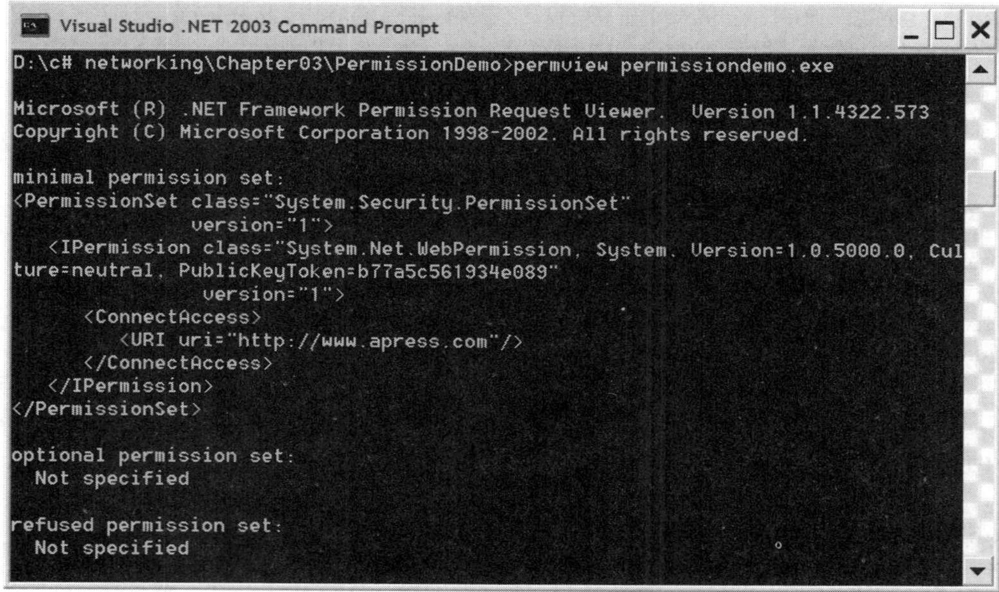

Figure 3-14. *Showing permissions*

Permission Attribute Parameters

With all permission attributes, you can pass a value of the enumeration SecurityAction in the constructor. Table 3-11 shows only the most important enumeration values.

Table 3-11. *SecurityAction Enumeration Values*

Values	Description
Demand Deny	The enumeration values SecurityAction.Demand and SecurityAction.Deny can be used with classes and methods. With Demand, you specify that the class or method needs the permission. Deny indicates that you don't want this permission.
RequestMinimum RequestOptional RequestRefused	The RequestXXX enumeration values can be used only for assembly scope; they can't be specified with classes and methods. RequestMinimum defines that this permission is mandatory to use the program. With RequestOptional, the program can do some useful work without this permission. Here you have to handle a SecurityException gracefully. RequestRefuse defines that you don't want to have this permission. This is used in cases where there can be some misuse of permissions, such as calling some assemblies when you don't have the sources and you don't trust them fully.

With the WebPermission attribute in addition to SecurityAction, you can set the properties shown in Table 3-12.

Table 3-12. *WebPermission Attribute Properties*

Properties	Description
Accept AcceptPattern	With the Accept property, you can define a URI to a resource that can be used within a class, method, or assembly where this attribute applies. With the AcceptPattern property, you can specify a regular expression to allow or deny access to URIs.
Connect ConnectPattern	The two ConnectXXX properties are similar to the AcceptXXX properties, with the difference being that these properties are used for a URI connection string.

The class SocketPermissionAttribute defines the additional properties shown in Table 3-13.

Table 3-13. *SocketPermission Attribute Properties*

Property	Description
Access	With this property, you can define the allowed network access method. Just two string values are allowed: Accept and Connect. Accept is used for a server application that listens to and accepts client connections, and Connect is for a client connecting to a server.
Host	With the Host property, you can set the host name with DNS syntax or an IP address where the permission applies.
Port	Port is a string property to specify the port number where you need permission. This can be used to restrict client applications to some specific servers. This property is of type string because different protocols don't necessary define the port number as an integer.
Transport	With the Transport property, you can restrict the network connection to a specific transport protocol. Possible values are All, ConnectionLess, ConnectionOriented, Tcp, and Udp. ConnectionLess allows the use of all connectionless protocols such as UDP; ConnectionOriented allows the use of connection-oriented protocols such as TCP.

Strong Name Assemblies

If you start network applications from an intranet or the Internet, you have to assign the permissions just discussed. However, it wouldn't be a pleasant task if you had to assign these permissions to all Internet or intranet applications—this would be a lot of work and add tremendous complexity. It would be much better to identify the specific assembly or a group of assemblies to configure permissions only for them.

With .NET, *strong names* may be used to uniquely identify assemblies. They also are a way to prevent tampering with assemblies.

To create a strong name, you can create a public/private key pair with the `sn` utility:

```
>sn - k mykey.snk
```

Using the assembly attribute `AssemblyKeyFile` (the class `AssemblyKeyFileAttribute` is in the namespace `System.Reflection`), add a public key and a signature to the assembly:

```
[assembly: AssemblyKeyFile("../../mykey.snk")]
```

This strongly named assembly can now be used for security configuration, as you will see next.

Configuring Permissions

Applications that are installed locally have full trust by default; configuring these applications is not necessary. If an application is downloaded from the Internet, it has no permissions by default, and you have to add the permissions explicitly. When starting applications from an intranet, you have `Dns` permissions by default, but you must configure the `WebPermission` and `SocketPermission` permissions explicitly.

For permission configurations, you have the command-line utility `caspol.exe` and the .NET Framework Configuration Tool Windows application in the Control Panel.

First, you have to create a new permission set that will be used by your networking application. If you are happy with an existing permission set that already has the required permissions included, it's not necessary to create a new one. With the .NET Framework Configuration Tool, we create a new permission set called Network Permissions, as shown in Figure 3-15.

Clicking Next brings up a dialog box for assigning the permissions to the permission set itself (see Figure 3-16). This permission set includes the required permissions: DNS for name lookups and Web Access for the `WebXXX` classes. We configure these permissions as unrestricted here, but you can also restrict the Web Access to a specific URI. The User Interface permission is needed for Windows applications.

For the assembly that needs these permissions, we create a new code group, Professional .NET Networking Zone, as shown in Figure 3-17.

With this code group, the condition type can be specified to define the assemblies that belong to this code group. The condition can be an application directory, a URI, or a site, for example. Here we select the Strong Name condition and import the strong name of the assembly created earlier. Selecting the check boxes for the name and version would restrict the code group to this specific assembly. Without selecting these options, the code group includes all assemblies that use the same public key, as shown in Figure 3-18.

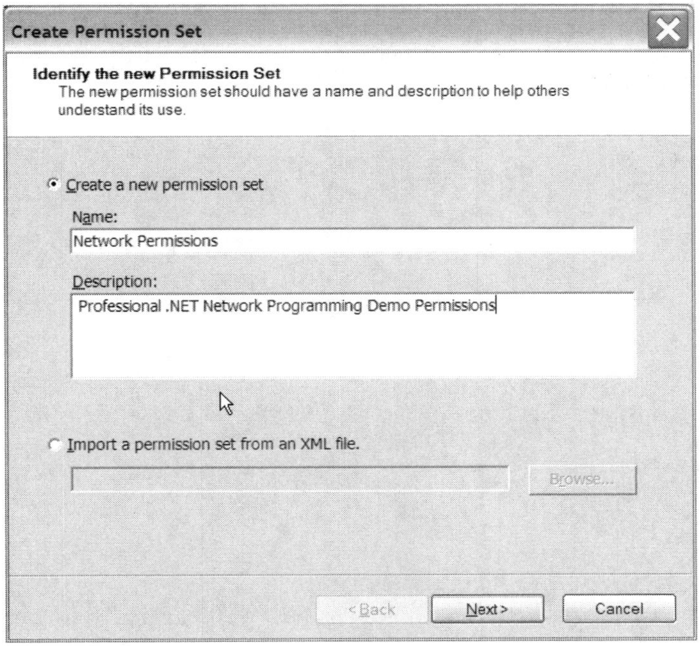

Create Permission Set

Identify the new Permission Set
The new permission set should have a name and description to help others understand its use.

Create a new permission set

Name:

Network Permissions

Description:

Professional .NET Network Programming Demo Permissions

Import a permission set from an XML file.

Browse...

< Back Next > Cancel

Figure 3-15. *Create a permission set*

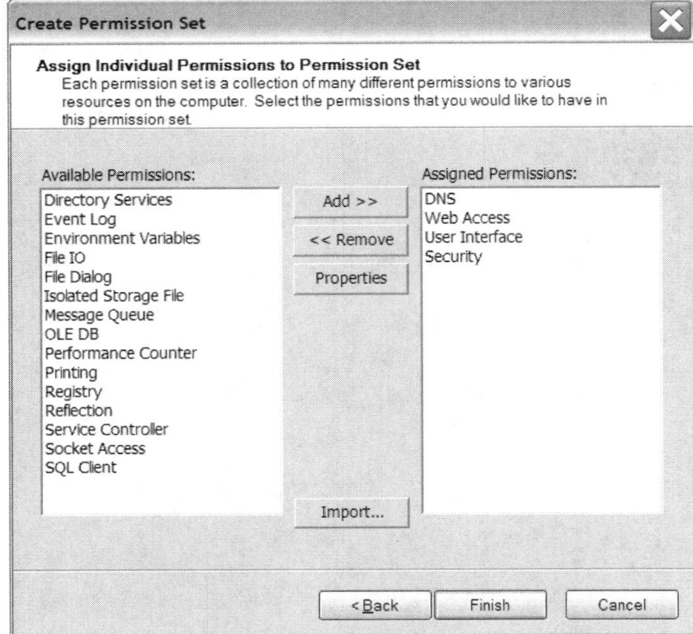

Figure 3-16. *Adding permissions to a permission set*

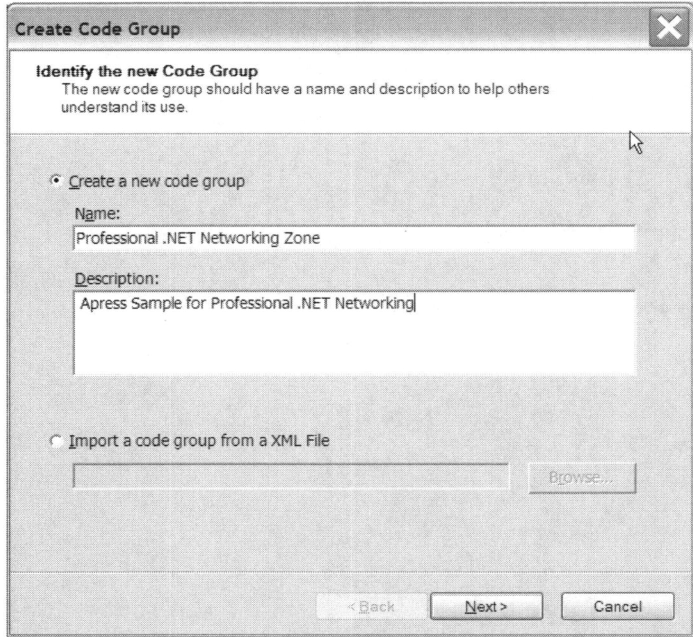

Figure 3-17. *Creating a code group*

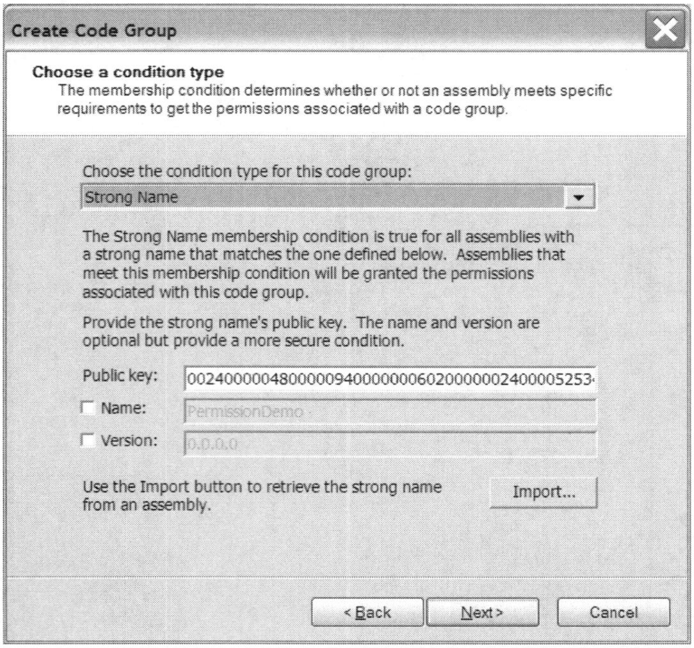

Create Code Group

Choose a condition type
The membership condition determines whether or not an assembly meets specific requirements to get the permissions associated with a code group.

Choose the condition type for this code group:
Strong Name

The Strong Name membership condition is true for all assemblies with a strong name that matches the one defined below. Assemblies that meet this membership condition will be granted the permissions associated with this code group.

Provide the strong name's public key. The name and version are optional but provide a more secure condition.

Public key: 00240000048000009400000006020000002400005253
Name: PermissionDemo
Version: 0.0.0.0

Use the Import button to retrieve the strong name from an assembly. Import...

< Back Next > Cancel

Figure 3-18. *Code group condition type*

Clicking Next selects the previously created permission set for this code group.

With this configuration, it is now possible to start the network application from a network share or download it with a link from a web server.

Summary

In this chapter, we presented an overview of network programming with the .NET classes available within the `System.Net` namespace. We then discussed the `Uri` class for working with absolute and relative URIs, and split up a URI into its constituent parts. After that, we looked at the features of the `IPAddress` class that not only wraps IP addresses, but also has support to convert the network byte order. Next, we used the `Dns` class to resolve host names to IP addresses. Because name lookups can take a while, we looked at doing that asynchronously.

We introduced the major topics of requests and responses, and we'll cover these more fully in later chapters, particularly in Chapter 8. We discussed the base classes `WebRequest` and `WebResponse`, and we used them to read and write simple files. Finally, we discussed two aspects of security: authentication to connect to websites that require user logon and the permissions needed by a networking application.

Thus we've laid the foundation to continue with socket programming in subsequent chapters, and then we'll move on to Internet programming.

CHAPTER 4

Socket Programming in .NET

The preceding chapters talked generally about .NET support for network programming. They showed you how to manipulate streams in .NET applications, and how to use the classes to work with IP addresses and DNS lookups. In this chapter, we'll start programming with sockets.

In particular, we'll discuss the following topics:

- An overview of sockets and socket types
- Socket support in .NET (the `System.Net.Sockets.Socket` class)
- A TCP socket server application
- Socket options
- An asynchronous TCP socket server application
- Socket permissions

An Overview of Sockets

A *socket* is one end of a two-way communication link between two programs running on a network. By connecting the two sockets together, you can pass data between different processes (either local or remote). The socket implementation provides the encapsulation of the network and transport level protocols.

Sockets were originally developed for UNIX at the University of California at Berkeley. In UNIX, the input/output method for communication follows an open/read/write/close algorithm. Before a resource can be used, it needs to be opened, by specifying the relevant permissions and other parameters. Once the resource is opened, it can be read from or written to. After using the resource, the user can finally call the `Close` method, signaling to the operating system that it has finished its tasks with the resource.

When Inter-Process Communication (IPC) and Networking facilities are added to the UNIX operating system, they adopt the familiar pattern as that of input/output (I/O). All the resources opened for communication are identified by a *descriptor* in UNIX and Windows. These descriptors (also called *handles*) can be a pointer to a file, memory, or any other channel, and actually point to an internal data structure primarily used by the operating system. A socket, being a resource, is also represented by a descriptor. Therefore, for sockets, a descriptor's life can be divided into three phases: open/create the socket, receive and send to the socket, and close the socket.

The IPC interface for communicating between different processes is built on top of the I/O methods. They facilitate sockets to send and receive data. Each target is specified by a socket address; therefore, this address can be specified in the client to connect with the target.

Socket Types

There are two basic types of sockets: stream sockets and datagram sockets. There is also a generalized form of sockets, called raw sockets.

Stream Sockets

A *stream socket* is a connection-oriented socket that consists of a stream of bytes that can be bidirectional, meaning that the application can both transmit and receive through the end-point. A stream socket guarantees error correction, handles delivery, and preserves data sequence. It can be relied on to deliver sequenced, unduplicated data. Stream sockets achieve this level of quality through the use of the Transmission Control Protocol (TCP), which makes sure that your data arrives on the other side in sequence and error-free.

A stream socket is suitable for transmitting large amounts of data. The overhead of establishing a separate connection for sending each message can be unacceptable for small amounts of data.

In stream sockets, a path is formed before communicating messages. This ensures that both sides taking part in the communication are alive and responding. If your application sends two messages to the recipient, the messages are guaranteed to be received in sequence. However, individual messages can be broken up into several packets, and there is no way to determine record boundaries. A stream socket depends on TCP to ensure the delivery of messages to their destinations. Under TCP, it's up to the protocol to disassemble the transmission of data into packets of appropriate sizes, send them over, and put them back together on the other side. An application knows only that it's sending a certain number of bytes to the TCP layer and that the other side gets those bytes. Effectively, TCP breaks up that data into appropriately sized packets, receives the packets on the other side, unwraps the data, and then puts it back together. We'll talk more about TCP in Chapter 7.

■ **NOTE** Streams are based on explicit connections: socket A requests a connection to socket B, and socket B accepts or rejects the connection request.

Stream sockets are preferable to datagram sockets (described in the next section) when the data must be guaranteed delivery on the other side and when the data size is large. Therefore, if the reliability of the connection between two applications is paramount, use stream sockets. An e-mail server is one example of an application that must deliver content in the correct order and without duplications or omissions.

Datagram Sockets

Datagram sockets are sometimes called *connectionless sockets*, because no explicit connection is established. With datagram sockets, a message is sent to the specified socket without checking if the socket is listening.

The use of datagram sockets requires the User Datagram Protocol (UDP) to pass the data from a client to the server. There are some limitations on the size of the message in this protocol, and unlike with stream sockets, where a message can be reliably sent to the destination server, datagram sockets offer no such guarantee. There are no errors returned from the server if the data is lost in between. We'll talk more about UDP in Chapter 8.

Using stream sockets is a more reliable method than using datagram sockets, but with some applications, the overhead incurred by establishing an explicit connection is unacceptable. A day/time server, which provides day/time synchronization to its clients, is an example of an application that might not require explicit connections. After all, it takes some time to establish a reliable connection with the server, which merely delays the service. To reduce the overhead, you would use datagram sockets.

Raw Sockets

A *raw socket*, by definition, is a socket that takes packets, bypassing the TCP and UDP layers in the TCP/IP stack and sending them directly to the application. The main purpose of using raw sockets is to bypass the mechanism by which the computer handles TCP/IP. It works by providing a custom implementation of the TCP/IP stack, replacing the mechanism provided by the TCP/IP stack on the kernel. The packet is passed directly to the application that needs it, and therefore it is much more efficient than going through the client's main network stack.

For such sockets, the packet is not passed through the TCP/IP filter, meaning that there is no processing on the packet, and it comes out in its raw form. This means that the receiving application is responsible for handling all the data appropriately and dealing with actions such as stripping off the headers and parsing; it's like making a small TCP/IP stack in the application.

Raw sockets are mainly used when writing custom low-level protocol applications. For example, various TCP/IP utilities such as `traceroute`, `ping`, and `arp` use raw sockets. You'll learn all about raw sockets in the next chapter.

Sockets and Ports

A *port* is defined to solve the problem of communicating with multiple applications simultaneously; it basically expands the notion of an IP address. A computer running simultaneous applications that receives a packet though the network can identify the target process using a unique port number that is determined when the connection is being made.

The socket is composed of the IP address of the machine and the port number used by the TCP application; this is also called an *endpoint*. Because the IP address is unique across the Internet and the port numbers are unique on the individual machine, endpoints are also unique across the entire Internet. This enables a process to talk to another process across the network, based entirely on the sockets.

Certain services have port numbers reserved for them; these are the *well-known port numbers*, such as FTP on port number 21. Your application can use any port number that hasn't been reserved or is already in use. The Internet Assigned Numbers Authority (IANA) prescribes the list of well-known port numbers.

Normally, a client/server application using sockets consists of two different applications: a client that initiates the connection with the target (the server) and the server, which waits for the connection from the client. For example, on the client side, the client must know the target's address and the port number. To make the connection request, the client tries to establish the connection with the server.

If everything goes well, provided that the server is already running before the client tries to connect to it, the server accepts the connection. Upon acceptance, the server application creates a new socket to deal specifically with the connected client.

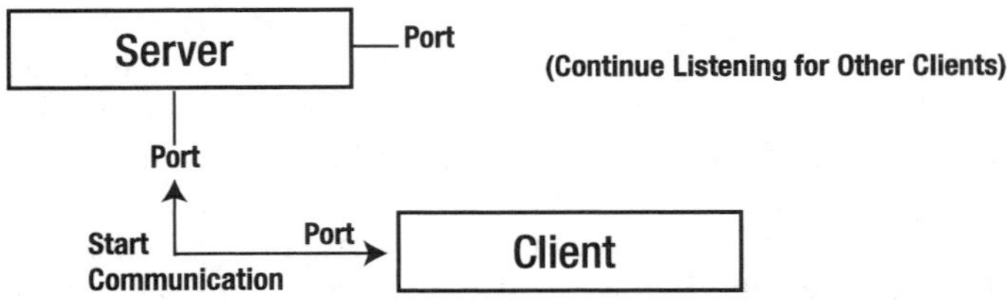

The client and server can now communicate with each other by reading from and writing to their respective sockets.

Working with Sockets in .NET

The classes in the `System.Net.Sockets` namespace provide sockets support in .NET. Table 4-1 provides a brief description of each of the classes in this namespace.

Table 4-1. *Classes in the System.Net.Sockets Namespace*

Class	Description
`MulticastOption`	Sets IP address values for joining or leaving an IP multicast group. This class is discussed in Chapter 9.
`NetworkStream`	Implements the underlying stream class from which data is sent or received. It is a high-level abstraction representing a connection to a TCP/IP communication channel. `NetworkStream` was discussed in Chapter 2.
`TcpClient`	Builds on the `Socket` class to provide TCP services at a higher level. `TcpClient` provides several methods for sending and receiving data over a network. Chapter 7 discusses `TcpClient` in more detail.

Class	Description
TcpListener	Builds on the low-level Socket class. Its main purpose is in server applications. This class listens for the incoming client connections and notifies the application of any connections. We'll look into this class when we talk about TCP in Chapter 7.
UdpClient	Implements UDP services. UDP is a connectionless protocol, therefore a different type of functionality is required to implement UDP services in .NET. We'll look more at this class in Chapter 8.
SocketException	The exception thrown when an error occurs in a socket. We'll look at this class later in this chapter.
Socket	Provides the basic functionality of a socket application.

■ NOTE With the 1.1 version of the .NET Framework, a few classes are added to the `System.Net.Sockets` namespace. These classes are related to IPv6 and the IrDA protocol. The classes related to IPv6 are covered in Chapter 6. The IrDA protocol is available only for the .NET Compact Framework for infrared connections; the `IrDAClient` and the `IrDAListener` classes are not covered in this book.

The `System.Net.Sockets.Socket` class plays an important role in network programming, performing both client and server operations. Typically, method calls to this class handle the necessary security checks, such as checking security permissions, and then are marshaled to counterparts in the Windows Sockets API. Table 4-2 lists the major `Socket` class properties, and Table 4-3 lists some important methods of this class.

Table 4-2. *System.Net.Sockets.Socket Properties*

Property	Description
AddressFamily	Gets the address family of the socket. The value is from the Socket.AddressFamily enumeration.
Available	Returns the amount of available data to read.
Blocking	Gets or sets the value that indicates whether the socket is in blocking mode.
Connected	Returns the value that informs whether the socket is still connected with the remote host.
LocalEndPoint	Gets the local endpoint.
ProtocolType	Get the protocol type of the socket.
RemoteEndPoint	Gets the remote endpoint of a socket.
SocketType	Gets the type of the socket.
SupportsIPv4	Returns a Boolean value indicating whether IPv4 is available on the current host. This property is supported in only version 1.1 of the Framework.
SupportsIPv6	Returns a Boolean value indicating whether IPv6 is supported and available on the current host. This property is supported in only version 1.1 of the Framework.

Table 4-2. *System.Net.Sockets.Socket Methods*

Method	Description
`Accept`	Creates a new socket to handle the incoming connection request.
`Bind`	Associates a socket with the local endpoint for listening for incoming connections.
`Close`	Forces the socket to close itself.
`Connect`	Establishes a connection with the remote host.
`GetSocketOption`	Returns the value of a `SocketOption`.
`IOControl`	Sets low-level operating modes for the socket. This method provides low-level access to the underlying socket instance of the `Socket` class.
`Listen`	Places the socket in listening mode. This method is exclusively used to server applications.
`Receive`	Receives data from a connected socket.
`Poll`	Determines the status of the socket.
`Select`	Checks the status of one or more sockets.
`Send`	Sends data to the connected socket.
`SetSocketOption`	Sets a `SocketOption`.
`Shutdown`	Disables send and receive functions on a socket.

Creating a TCP Stream Socket Application

In the following example, we use TCP to provide sequenced, reliable, two-way byte streams. We'll build a complete application involving both the client and the server. First, we demonstrate how to construct a TCP stream-based socket server, and then how to create a client application to test our server.

Building a TCP-based Server

The program shown in Listing 4-1 creates a server that receives connection requests from clients. The server is built synchronously; therefore, the execution of the thread is blocked until it accepts a connection from the client. The application demonstrates a simple server that replies to the client. The client ends its connection by sending `<TheEnd>` to the server. Figure 4-1 illustrates the server tasks.

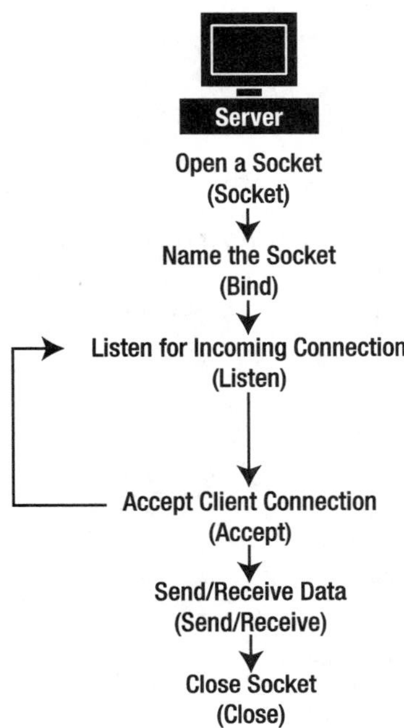

Figure 4-1. *The workflow of a TCP-based server*

Listing 4-1. *Server Application Using Sockets (SocketServer.cs)*

```
using System;
using System.Net.Sockets;
using System.Net;
using System.Text;
public class SocketServer
{
   public static void Main(string [] args)
   {
      // Establish the local endpoint for the socket
      IPHostEntry ipHost = Dns.Resolve("localhost");
      IPAddress ipAddr = ipHost.AddressList[0];
      IPEndPoint ipEndPoint = new IPEndPoint(ipAddr, 11000);

      // Create a TCP/IP socket
      Socket sListener = new Socket(AddressFamily.InterNetwork,
                                    SocketType.Stream, ProtocolType.Tcp);

      // Bind the socket to the local endpoint and
      // listen to the incoming sockets

      try
      {
```

```
         sListener.Bind(ipEndPoint);
         sListener.Listen(10);

         // Start listening for connections
         while (true)
         {
            Console.WriteLine("Waiting for a connection on port {0}",ipEndPoint);

            // Program is suspended while waiting for an incoming connection
            Socket handler = sListener.Accept();

            string data = null;
            // We got the client attempting to connect
            while(true)
            {
               byte[] bytes = new byte[1024];

               int bytesRec = handler.Receive(bytes);
               data += Encoding.ASCII.GetString(bytes,0,bytesRec);

               if (data.IndexOf("<TheEnd>") > -1)
               {
                  break;
               }
            }

            // Show the data on the console
            Console.WriteLine("Text Received: {0}",data);
            string theReply = "Thank you for those " + data.Length.ToString()
                              + " characters...";
            byte[] msg = Encoding.ASCII.GetBytes(theReply);

            handler.Send(msg);
            handler.Shutdown(SocketShutdown.Both);
            handler.Close();
         }
      }
      catch(Exception e)
      {
         Console.WriteLine(e.ToString());
      }
   } // End of Main
}
```

The first step is to establish the local endpoint for the socket. Before opening a socket for listening, a socket must establish a local endpoint address. The unique address of a TCP/IP service is defined by combining the IP address of the host with the port number of the service to create an endpoint for the service. The Dns class provides methods that return information about the network addresses supported by the local network device. When the local network device has more than one network address, or if the local system supports more than one network device, the Dns class returns information about all network addresses, and the application must choose the proper address for the service from the array.

We create an IPEndPoint for a server by combining the first IP address returned by Dns.Resolve for the host computer with a port number.

```
// Establish the local endpoint for the socket
IPHostEntry ipHost = Dns.Resolve("localhost");
IPAddress ipAddr = ipHost.AddressList[0];
IPEndPoint ipEndPoint = new IPEndPoint(ipAddr, 11000);
```

The IPEndPoint class here represents the localhost on port number 11000.

Next, we create a stream socket with a new instance of the Socket class. Having establishing a local endpoint for listening, we can create the socket:

```
// Create a TCP/IP socket
Socket sListener = new Socket(AddressFamily.InterNetwork,
                              SocketType.Stream, ProtocolType.Tcp);
```

The AddressFamily enumeration indicates the addressing schemes that a Socket instance can use to resolve an address. The following are some important AddressFamily parameters:

- InterNetwork is the address for IPv4.
- InterNetworkV6 is the address for IPv6.
- Ipx is the IPX or SPX address.
- NetBios is the NetBIOS address.

The SocketType parameter distinguishes between a TCP and a UDP socket. Other possible values are as follows:

- Dgram supports datagrams. Dgram requires the Udp ProtocolType and the InterNetwork AddressFamily.
- Raw supports access to the underlying transport protocol.
- Stream supports stream sockets. Stream requires the Tcp ProtocolType and the InterNetwork AddressFamily.

The third and last parameter defines the protocol type that is the requested protocol for the socket. The following are some important values for the ProtocolType parameter:

- Raw represents the raw packet protocol.
- Tcp represents TCP.
- Udp represents UDP.
- Ip represents IP.

Our next step is to name the socket with the Bind method. When you open the socket with the constructor, the socket has no name assigned to it. However, a descriptor is reserved for the socket created. To assign a name to the server socket, we call Bind. To be identified by a client socket, a TCP stream socket server must name its socket.

```
try
{
   sListener.Bind(ipEndPoint);
```

The Bind method associates a socket with a local endpoint. You must call Bind before any attempt to call Listen or Accept.

Now that our socket is created and a name has been bound to it, we can listen for incoming connections with Listen. In the listening state, the socket will poll for incoming connection attempts.

```
   sListener.Listen(10);
```

The parameter defines the backlog, which specifies the maximum number of *pending* connections in the queue. In the code shown here, the parameter allows a queue of ten connections.

Now that we're listening, our next step is to accept the client connection with Accept. Accept is used to receive the client connection that completes the name association between client and server. The Accept method blocks the caller thread until the connection is present.

The Accept method extracts the first connection request from the queue of pending requests and creates a new socket to handle it. Although a new socket is created, the original socket continues to listen and can be used with multithreading to accept multiple client connections. Any server application must close the listening socket, along with the incoming client sockets created by Accept.

```
   while (true)
   {
      Console.WriteLine("Waiting for a connection on port {0}",ipEndPoint);

      // Program is suspended while waiting for an incoming connection
      Socket handler = sListener.Accept();
```

Once the client and server are connected with each other, you can send and receive messages using the Send and Receive methods of the Socket class. The Send method writes outgoing data to the connected socket. The Receive method reads the incoming data on a stream-based socket. When using a TCP-based system, the sockets must be connected before using Send or Receive. The exact protocol definition between the two communicating entities needs to be made clear beforehand, so that there will be no deadlocks between the client and server applications caused by not knowing who will send the data first.

```
      string data = null;

      // We got the client attempting to connect
      while(true)
      {
         byte[] bytes = new byte[1024];
```

```
            // The data received from the client
            int bytesRec = handler.Receive(bytes);
            // Bytes are converted to string
            data += Encoding.ASCII.GetString(bytes,0,bytesRec);
            // Checking the end of message
            if (data.IndexOf("<TheEnd>") > -1)
            {
               break;
            }
         }

         // Show the data on the console
         Console.WriteLine("Text Received: {0}",data);
```

The Receive method receives the data from the socket and fills the byte array passed as an argument. The return value of the method actually determines the number of bytes read. In the preceding code, after receiving the data, we check for the end-of-message characters in the converted string. If the end-of-message characters are not found in the string, the code again starts to listen for incoming data; otherwise, we display the message to the console.

After exiting from the loop, we prepare a new byte array with our reply to pass back to the client. After conversion, the Send method is used to send to it the client.

```
         string theReply = "Thank you for those " + data.Length.ToString()
                         + " characters...";
         byte[] msg = Encoding.ASCII.GetBytes(theReply);

         handler.Send(msg);
```

When data exchange between the server and the client ends, close the socket with Close. To ensure that no data is left behind, always call Shutdown before calling Close. There should always be a corresponding Close call to each successful socket instance.

```
         handler.Shutdown(SocketShutdown.Both);
         handler.Close();
      }
   }
```

SocketShutdown is an enumeration, which can specify three different values for shutting down the socket:

- Both shuts down a socket for both sending and receiving.
- Receive shuts down a socket for receiving.
- Send shuts down a socket for sending.

The socket is closed when the Close method is called, which also sets the Connected property of the socket to false.

Building a TCP-based Client

The functions used to make a client application are more or less similar to the server application. We employ the same methods for establishing the endpoint, creating a socket instance, sending and receiving data, and closing the socket. Figure 4-2 illustrates the functions of the client application.

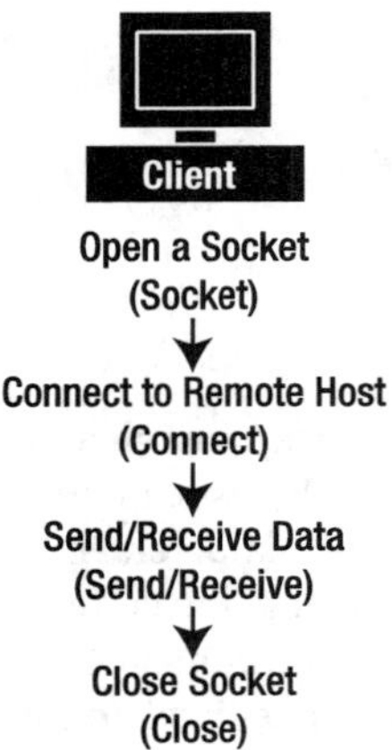

Figure 4-2. *The workflow of a TCP-based client*

Listing 4-2 shows the complete code for SocketClient.cs.

Listing 4-2. *Client Application Using Sockets (SocketClient.cs)*

```
using System;
using System.Net.Sockets;
using System.Net;
using System.Text;
public class SocketClient
{
   public static void Main(string [] args)
   {
      // Data buffer for incoming data
      byte[] bytes = new byte[1024];

      // Connect to a remote device
      try
      {
         // Establish the remote endpoint for the socket
         IPHostEntry ipHost = Dns.Resolve("127.0.0.1");
         IPAddress ipAddr = ipHost.AddressList[0];
         IPEndPoint ipEndPoint = new IPEndPoint(ipAddr, 11000);
```

```
        Socket sender = new Socket(AddressFamily.InterNetwork,
                                   SocketType.Stream, ProtocolType.Tcp);

        // Connect the socket to the remote endpoint
        sender.Connect(ipEndPoint);

        Console.WriteLine("Socket connected to {0}",
                          sender.RemoteEndPoint.ToString());
        string theMessage = "This is a test";
        byte[] msg = Encoding.ASCII.GetBytes(theMessage+"<TheEnd>");

        // Send the data through the socket
        int bytesSent = sender.Send(msg);

        // Receive the response from the remote device
        int bytesRec = sender.Receive(bytes);

        Console.WriteLine("The Server says : {0}",
                          Encoding.ASCII.GetString(bytes,0, bytesRec));

        // Release the socket
        sender.Shutdown(SocketShutdown.Both);
        sender.Close();
      }
      catch(Exception e)
      {
        Console.WriteLine("Exception: {0}", e.ToString());
      }
    }
}
```

The only new method used here is the Connect method, which is used to connect to the remote server. Let's look at how it's used in the client. First, we need to establish the remote endpoint:

```
try
{
   // Establish the remote endpoint for the socket
   IPHostEntry ipHost = Dns.Resolve("127.0.0.1");
   IPAddress ipAddr = ipHost.AddressList[0];
   IPEndPoint ipEndPoint = new IPEndPoint(ipAddr, 11000);

   Socket sender = new Socket(AddressFamily.InterNetwork,
                              SocketType.Stream, ProtocolType.Tcp);
```

Now we can connect our socket to the remote endpoint:

```
   sender.Connect(ipEndPoint);
```

Given the socket, the Connect method establishes the connection between the socket and the remote host specified by the endpoint parameter. Once we're connected, we can send our data and receive a response:

```
string theMessage = "This is a test";
byte[] msg = Encoding.ASCII.GetBytes(theMessage+"<TheEnd>");

// Send the data through the socket
int bytesSent = sender.Send(msg);

// Receive the response from the remote device
int bytesRec = sender.Receive(bytes);

Console.WriteLine("The Server says : {0}",
                  Encoding.ASCII.GetString(bytes,0, bytesRec));
```

Finally, we release the socket by calling Shutdown, shutting it down for both sending and receiving, and then call Close:

```
sender.Shutdown(SocketShutdown.Both);
sender.Close();
```

Figures 4-3 and 4-4 show our server and client in action.

Figure 4-3. *Running the TCP/IP-based server*

```
C:\WINNT\system32\CMD.EXE
C:\Networking\Sockets>socketclient
Socket connected to 127.0.0.1:11000
The Server says : Thank you for those 22 characters...

C:\Networking\Sockets>
```

Figure 4-4. *Running the TCP/IP-based client*

Managing Exceptions with System.Net.Sockets

The `Socket` class generally throws the `SocketException` when some error occurs in the network. `SocketException` may be thrown for a variety of reasons. We'll look at two cases here: problems in the `Socket` constructor and problems when connecting to ports.

The `Socket` constructor takes three parameters: `AddressFamily`, `SocketType`, and `ProtocolType`. It throws a `SocketException` if there is a mismatch or incompatibility between the three combinations. For example, attempting to create a `Socket` instance with the following parameters throws a `SocketException`:

```
Socket sSocket = new Socket(AddressFamily.InterNetworkV6,
                            SocketType.Stream,
                            ProtocolType.Tcp);
```

When the exception is thrown, its `Message` property (inherited from `Exception`) is the following:

```
An address incompatible with the requested protocol was used
```

IPv6 is not supported by TCP, so the `AddressFamily` parameter `InterNetworkV6` is incompatible with a `ProtocolType` of `Tcp`.

Another good candidate for this exception-handling mechanism is the `Connect` method. This method throws an exception if it fails to establish a connection between the local and remote endpoints specified in the `Connect` parameters. Let's put this to use.

Constructing a Port Scanner

We've looked at a simple client/server application in the previous section. Now let's make something more interesting with the help of the `SocketException`.

In the following example, we make our own port scanner, which tries to connect to the local host on each port specified in the loop. The scanner scans the first 1024 ports for our demonstration. We report successful connections, and if the connection fails, we catch the `SocketException` that is thrown. Listing 4-3 shows the complete code for `PortScanner.cs`.

■ TIP This port scanner can be used to check out open ports on *your* computer. These open ports could be a potential weakness in your system, exploitable by "rogue" applications.

Listing 4-3. *Port Scanner (PortScanner.cs)*

```
using System;
using System.Net.Sockets;
using System.Net;
public class SocketConn
{
   public static void Main(string [] args)
   {
      IPAddress address = IPAddress.Parse("127.0.0.1");
```

```
        // Loop through ports 1 to 1024
        for (int i=1; i <= 1024; i++)
        {
           Console.WriteLine("Checking port {0}",i);

           try
           {
              // Establish the remote endpoint for the socket
              IPEndPoint endPoint = new IPEndPoint(address,i);
              Socket sSocket = new Socket(AddressFamily.InterNetwork,
                                          SocketType.Stream,
                                          ProtocolType.Tcp);

              // Connect the socket to the remote endpoint
              sSocket.Connect(endPoint);

              Console.WriteLine("Port {0} is listening",i);
           }
           catch(SocketException ignored)
           {
              if (ignored.ErrorCode != 10061)
                Console.WriteLine(ignored.Message);
           }
        }
     }
}
```

The code works by making a connection with each port specified in the loop. If the port is opened, then the socket establishes a connection and prints the line giving information about the port. If the port is closed, a `SocketException` will be thrown. When such an exception is thrown, its `Message` property will return the following to indicate that a connection could not be made with the server:

```
No connection could be made because the target machine actively refused it
```

The `SocketException` has an `ErrorCode` property that holds an integer value that represents the last operating system error to occur. In the case of the exception thrown when an attempt is made to connect to a closed port, the `ErrorCode` value is `10061`. In our `catch` block to handle the `SocketException`, we check if the `ErrorCode` is different from this value and display the actual error message. This is to advise the reader in case something other than a failure to connect to the specified port happens:

```
catch(SocketException ignored)
{
   if (ignored.ErrorCode != 10061)
     Console.WriteLine(ignored.Message);
}
```

The `ErrorCode` property actually calls the native method `GetLastError` to get the error number. You can find the list of error codes in the `WinError.h` file in the `Microsoft Visual Studio .NET\Vc7\PlatformSDK\Include` folder.

Here's a summary of the output when I ran this piece of code on my machine running Windows 2000 Server.

```
Checking port 1
Checking port 2
...
Port 21 is listening
...
Port 25 is listening
...
Port 80 is listening
```

Cleaning Up Connections

Code in a `finally` block will be executed regardless of whether an exception is thrown or not, making it an ideal candidate for `Shutdown` and `Close` methods. This will ensure that the socket is always closed before the program ends.

```
try
{
   ...
}
catch( .. )
{
   ...
}
finally
{
   if (socketOpened.Connected)
   {
      socketOpened.Shutdown(SocketShutdown.Both);
      socketOpened.Close();
   }
}
```

Here, we use the `Connected` property to determine if the socket is still open. The `Connected` property returns the connection state of the socket, with a value of `true` indicating that the socket is open. If this is the case, the socket is closed.

Setting and Retrieving Socket Options

The .NET Framework provides `SetSocketOption` and `GetSocketOption` methods to set and retrieve socket options.

The `SetSocketOption` method calls through to the `setsockopt` function of the Windows Socket API. The `SetSocketOption` method requires a `SocketOptionLevel`, a `SocketOptionName`, and the value to set for the socket option—a byte array, `int`, or `object`.

Socket Option Levels

The SocketOptionLevel enumeration defines the option level for the socket. When you set or retrieve an option for a socket, this enumeration is used to specify at which level in the OSI model the option is applied (for example, whether the option is set at the TCP level, at the level of the individual socket, and so on). The following are the values possible for SocketOptionLevel:

- IP means that socket options apply to IP sockets.
- Socket means that socket options apply to the socket itself.
- Tcp means that socket options apply to TCP sockets.
- Udp means that socket options apply to UDP sockets.
- IPv6 means that sockets options apply to IPv6 sockets.

Socket Option Names

The second required parameter of SetSocketOptions is SocketOptionName. This parameter defines the name of the parameter whose value is being set. The values for the SocketOptionName enumeration can be found in the .NET Framework SDK Documentation. We'll look at a couple of SocketOptionName options here: ReuseAddress and Linger.

ReuseAddress

By default, only one socket may be bound to a local address that is already in use. However, you may want to bind more than one socket to a local address. Consider the following code that attempts to bind two sockets to the same local endpoint:

```
// Establish the local endpoint for the socket
IPEndPoint ipEndPoint =
      new IPEndPoint(Dns.GetHostByName(Dns.GetHostName()).AddressList[0], 11000);

// Create a TCP/IP socket
Socket sListener = new Socket(AddressFamily.InterNetwork,
SocketType.Stream, ProtocolType.Tcp);

// Bind the socket to the local endpoint and
// Listen to the incoming sockets

sListener.Bind(ipEndPoint);

sListener.Listen(10);

// Create a new socket
Socket sListener2 = new Socket(AddressFamily.InterNetwork,
      SocketType.Stream, ProtocolType.Tcp);
```

```
// Bind the socket to the local endpoint and
// Listen to the incoming sockets

sListener2.Bind(ipEndPoint);

sListener2.Listen(10);
```

Trying to bind two sockets to a single endpoint will throw a `SocketException` with the following `Message`:

```
Only one usage of each socket address (protocol/network address/port)
is normally permitted
```

The solution to this is the `ReuseAddress` option. Using this option and a nonzero integer value, you can set the socket to allow multiple bindings:

```
sListener2.SetSocketOption(SocketOptionLevel.Socket,
                           SocketOptionName.ReuseAddress, 1);
sListener2.Bind(ipEndPoint);
```

Note the use of the nonzero integer. This will actually be interpreted as a Boolean value of `true` by the Windows Sockets API `setsockopt` function, which is called by `SetSocketOption`.

Linger

Through the `Linger` value of `SocketOptionName`, you can determine how the socket should behave when there is some data queued to be sent and the socket is closed. The `LingerOption` class contains information about the socket's linger time. Two of its important members are as follows:

- `Enabled` determines whether to linger after the socket is closed.
- `LingerTime` is the time (in seconds) to linger if the `Enabled` property is `true`.

If `Enabled` is `false`, the socket will immediately close itself whenever a call to `Close` method is executed. If `Enabled` is `true`, the remaining data will continue to be sent to the destination until the time specified by the `LingerTime` property has passed. The connection will then be closed when either the time is over or all the data is sent. If there is no data is present in the queue, the socket is immediately closed, regardless of the `Enabled` property. The socket is also closed immediately if the `LingerTime` is specified as zero.

These two properties can also be set in the `LingerOption` class's constructor. The first parameter sets the `Enabled` property, and the second sets the `LingerTime` property. The value held by the `LingerOption` object is then passed to the `SetSocketOption` method:

```
// Create a new LingerOption class and set properties in the constructor
LingerOption lingerOpts = new LingerOption(true,5);
mySocket.SetSocketOption(SocketOptionLevel.Socket, SocketOptionName.Linger,
      lingerOpts);
```

Let's see how to use the `GetSocketOption` method to retrieve the value for the `LingerTime`. `GetSocketOption` has three overloads, each returning a different data type: void, byte array, or object. The overload that returns the object requires only the SocketOptionLevel and SocketOptionName as parameters. The overload that has no return value fills a byte array that you specify as an extra parameter. The overload that returns the byte array requires you to specify the length of the information you expect returned with an extra int parameter. We use the overload that returns an object—a cast to a LingerOption object allows us to retrieve the LingerTime property:

```
object o = mySocket.GetSocketOption(SocketOptionLevel.Socket,
                                    SocketOptionName.Linger);
Console.WriteLine(((LingerOption)o).LingerTime);
```

Asynchronous Programming

Most of the socket functions in the original library take an indefinite amount of time to complete execution. In such situations, the function is said to be *blocked*; this means that calling the function would block the current thread of execution. If there is only one thread in the application, the whole application will need to wait for the function to return before continuing execution. For example, the send and receive functions are said to be blocked because they do not return immediately.

The *asynchronous programming* model is designed for applications that cannot afford to hang around waiting for network operations to complete before moving ahead. With asynchronous programming, a connection does not block an application while waiting for network processes to complete. Instead of blocking the current thread, it uses the .NET asynchronous model to process the network connections on another thread, while the application continues to run in the original thread. When the second thread has completed its execution, it sends an event object to the original thread to indicate the status of the task. Events can be either *signaled*, in which case methods that are waiting on the event will return immediately, or *nonsignaled*. If the event is nonsignaled, the waiting method will be blocked until the event is signaled.

There are two types of events:

- Automatic events, which set themselves back to the nonsignaled state whenever they are signaled
- Manual reset events, which stay signaled until they are manually reset to the nonsignaled state

.NET has a ManualResetEvent class that you can use to indicate to your program that you want to continue. By setting a ManualResetEvent object to the signaled state, it will stop blocking any waiting methods, and the program can continue. We will use this object to facilitate our asynchronous programming in the next example.

In the world of .NET, there is a complete set of methods for asynchronous operations. For example, BeginSend is used instead of the normal Send method when doing asynchronous programming.

The asynchronous model uses the callback method to return the result of the operation. The .NET Framework has a set of methods responsible for initiating a task in an asynchronous manner but they require a callback function to end the operation. For example the Connect method uses BeginConnect to start a connection to the network device and the corresponding callback function is required to complete the connection.

The .NET Framework provides a delegate class for asynchronous operations. The class, which is called `AsyncCallback`, provides a way for applications to complete an asynchronous operation.

```
AsyncCallback aCallback = new AsyncCallback(AsyncCallback);
```

This delegate is supplied as an argument to the asynchronous function when the operation is initiated. The function pointer referenced by `AsyncCallback` contains program logic to finish processing the asynchronous task for the client.

This programming model uses multiple threads to process network connections. To facilitate synchronization between these different threads, you use the `ManualResetEvent` class to suspend execution of the main class and signal when execution can continue.

To demonstrate asynchronous operations, we'll build an asynchronous client application, which will be tested with the socket server we built earlier. Then we'll build an asynchronous server.

Creating an Asynchronous Client Application

Figure 4-5 illustrates the flow of an asynchronous client application.

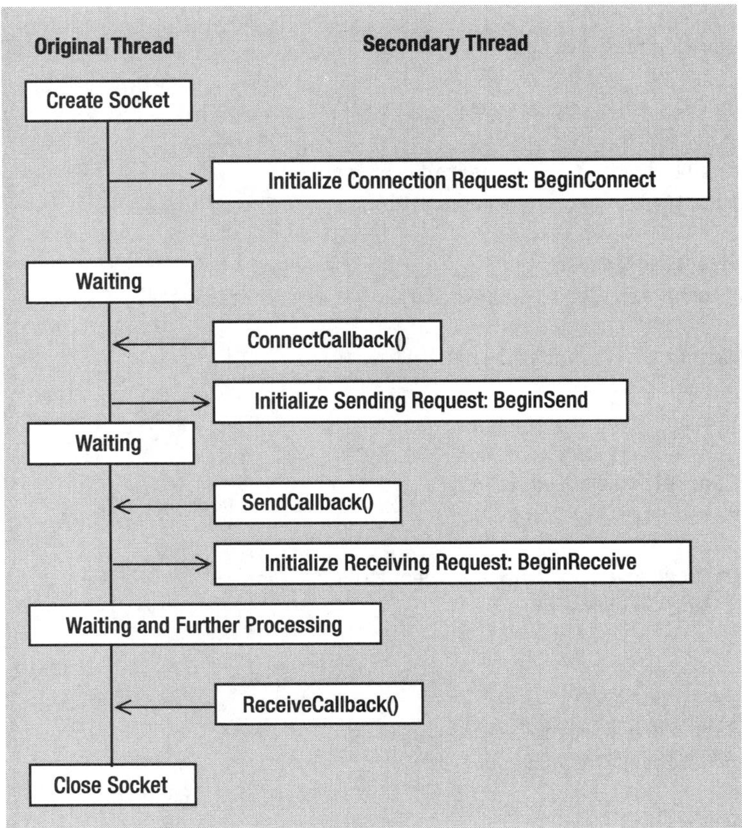

Figure 4-5. *The flow of an asynchronous client application*

As shown in the figure, we have three tasks to accomplish asynchronously here: connecting to the server, sending data to the server, and receiving data from the server.

Listing 4-4 shows the complete source code of the application.

Listing 4-4. *Asynchronous Client (AsyncClient.cs)*

```
using System;
using System.Net.Sockets;
using System.Net;
using System.Text;
using System.Threading;

public class AsyncClient
{
   public static ManualResetEvent ConnectDone = new ManualResetEvent(false);
   public static ManualResetEvent SendDone = new ManualResetEvent(false);
   public static ManualResetEvent ReceiveDone = new ManualResetEvent(false);

   public static String response = String.Empty;

   public static String sb = String.Empty;

   public static byte[] buffer = new byte[1024];

   // ConnectCallback is called when the connection is ready
   public static void ConnectCallback(IAsyncResult ar)
   {
      Thread thr = Thread.CurrentThread;
      Console.WriteLine("ConnectCallback Thread State:" + thr.ThreadState);

      Socket sClient = (Socket) ar.AsyncState;

      sClient.EndConnect(ar);

      Console.WriteLine("Socket connected to {0}",
            sClient.RemoteEndPoint.ToString());

      // Signal the ConnectDone event to inform the other thread
      // that the connection is ready for use
      ConnectDone.Set();
   }

   // SendCallback is called when sending is complete
   public static void SendCallback(IAsyncResult ar)
   {
      Thread thr = Thread.CurrentThread;
      Console.WriteLine("SendCallback Thread State:" + thr.ThreadState);
```

```
    Socket sClient = (Socket) ar.AsyncState;
    int bytesSent = sClient.EndSend(ar);

    Console.WriteLine("Sent {0} bytes to server.", bytesSent);
    // Signal the SendDone event
    SendDone.Set();
}

// ReceiveCallback is called when receiving is complete
public static void ReceiveCallback(IAsyncResult ar)
{
    Thread thr = Thread.CurrentThread;
    Console.WriteLine("ReceiveCallback Thread State:" + thr.ThreadState);

    Socket sClient = (Socket) ar.AsyncState;

    int bytesRead = sClient.EndReceive(ar);
    if (bytesRead > 0)
    {
        sb += Encoding.ASCII.GetString(buffer, 0 , bytesRead);

        // There might be more data to read
        sClient.BeginReceive(buffer, 0 , buffer.Length ,0 ,
                        new AsyncCallback(ReceiveCallback), sClient);
    }
    else
    {
        // Signal the ReceiveDone event
        ReceiveDone.Set();
    }
}

public static void Main(string [] arg)
{
    try
    {
        Thread thr = Thread.CurrentThread;
        Console.WriteLine("Main Thread State:" + thr.ThreadState);

        IPHostEntry ipHost = Dns.Resolve("127.0.0.1");
        IPAddress ipAddr = ipHost.AddressList[0];
        IPEndPoint endPoint = new IPEndPoint(ipAddr, 11000);

        Socket sClient = new Socket(AddressFamily.InterNetwork,
                              SocketType.Stream, ProtocolType.Tcp);

        // Create a new thread to initiate the connection to the server
```

```
            // ConnectCallback is called when the connection is done
            sClient.BeginConnect(endPoint, new AsyncCallback(ConnectCallback),
                                 sClient);

            // Wait until the connection is ready to use
            ConnectDone.WaitOne();

            string data = "This is a test.";

               for (int i=0;i<72;i++)
                  data += i.ToString()+":" + (new string('=',i));

            byte[] byteData = Encoding.ASCII.GetBytes(data+"<TheEnd>");

            // Send the data in a separate thread
            sClient.BeginSend(byteData, 0 , byteData.Length, SocketFlags.None,
                              new AsyncCallback(SendCallback), sClient);

            // Do something in the main thread
            for (int i=0;i<5;i++)
            {
                  Console.WriteLine(i);
                  Thread.Sleep(10);
            }
            // Wait until all sending is done
            SendDone.WaitOne();

            // Start receiving data in a separate thread
            sClient.BeginReceive(buffer, 0  , buffer.Length, SocketFlags.None,
                                 new AsyncCallback(ReceiveCallback), sClient);

            // Wait
            ReceiveDone.WaitOne();

            Console.WriteLine("Response received: {0} ", sb);
            sClient.Shutdown(SocketShutdown.Both);
            sClient.Close();
         }
         catch(Exception e)
         {
            Console.WriteLine(e.ToString());
         }
      }
   }
```

First, let's discuss how we're going to synchronize everything. The code will need to be synchronized because of its asynchronous nature. You cannot work with the socket if you haven't finished connecting to the server; otherwise, a deadlock could result if you were to attempt to receive data when you should instead be sending it. We will use the ManualEventReset class to synchronize the different threads that will be created.

```
public class AsyncClient
{
   public static string theResponse = "";
   public static byte[] buffer = new byte[1024];
   public static ManualResetEvent ConnectDone = new ManualResetEvent(false);
   public static ManualResetEvent SendDone = new ManualResetEvent(false);
   public static ManualResetEvent ReceiveDone = new ManualResetEvent(false);
```

A ManualResetEvent object can have its state set and reset (that is, be set to the signaled or nonsignaled state) with its Set and Reset methods. Each of three tasks—connecting, sending, and receiving—will have a ManualResetEvent object attached, and the main thread can wait for the relevant task to complete by calling the WaitOne method of the relevant ManualResetEvent object. This method blocks the current thread until the object is signaled.

When we create the ManualResetEvent objects in this example, the value of false indicates that the initial state is not set. Of course, the main thread can continue with other processing, but before the next task begins, we must be certain that the previous one has completed. This is precisely where WaitOne comes in.

Before we look at our first task, let's see how we create and initialize the socket we're going to use.

```
IPHostEntry ipHost = Dns.Resolve("127.0.0.1");
IPAddress ipAddr = ipHost.AddressList[0];
IPEndPoint endPoint = new IPEndPoint(ipAddr, 11000);

Socket sClient = new Socket(AddressFamily.InterNetwork,
                            SocketType.Stream, ProtocolType.Tcp);
```

Our first task is to connect to the server. This is achieved with the BeginConnect method. The BeginConnect method starts an asynchronous connection request with the remote host. It requires a callback method that implements the AsyncCallback delegate. This callback method should call EndConnect to end the pending connection request and return the connected socket.

```
sClient.BeginConnect(endPoint, new AsyncCallback(ConnectCallback), sClient);
```

There are three parameters to this method: the first represents the remote host using the IPEndPoint class, the second is the AsyncCallback delegate that is used for passing the function pointer, and the third is an object containing state information to be passed to the callback method specified. Here, the socket instance is being passed.

Let's look at the ConnectCallBack method:

```
public static void ConnectCallback(IAsyncResult ar)
{
   Thread thr = Thread.CurrentThread;
   Console.WriteLine("ConnectCallback Thread State:" + thr.ThreadState);
```

First, we inspect the thread in which our asynchronous method is running. Thread information can be obtained from the CurrentThread property of the Thread object. This will show that the code in our asynchronous method runs in the background thread.

Next, let's see how to retrieve the Socket that we're actually working on. The IAsyncResult parameter contains information about the state of the asynchronous operation. Using the AsyncState property of the IAsyncResult interface, we can retrieve the argument that we passed as the third parameter of the BeginConnect method. The value retrieved needs to be cast to a Socket.

```
Socket sClient = (Socket) ar.AsyncState;
```

Next, the EndConnect method is called to complete the asynchronous request. If some error occurred when accessing the socket, EndConnect will throw a SocketException.

```
sClient.EndConnect(ar);

Console.WriteLine("Socket connected to {0}",
                  sClient.RemoteEndPoint.ToString());
```

Finally, we call the Set method of the ConnectDone ManualResetEvent. This will indicate to the main thread that we've finished connecting.

```
   ConnectDone.Set();
}
```

Now that we've connected to the server, the next step is to communicate with the server by sending and receiving data.

The BeginSend method is used to send data asynchronously to the connected Socket.

```
sClient.BeginSend(byteData, 0 , byteData.Length, SocketFlags.None,
                  new AsyncCallback(SendCallback), sClient);
```

The first three parameters are about the data to send. The first parameter is a byte array buffer containing the data to send, the second argument represents the position in the buffer from which to begin sending data, and the third parameter is the buffer size. The fourth parameter specifies a value from the SocketFlags enumeration. Here, specifying SocketFlags.None is fine. The fifth parameter is the AsyncCallback delegate. The last parameter is used to store state information.

The BeginSend method calls the callback function passed through the AsyncCallback delegate:

```
public static void SendCallback(IAsyncResult ar)
{
```

```
   Thread thr = Thread.CurrentThread;
   Console.WriteLine("SendCallback Thread State:" + thr.ThreadState);

   Socket sClient = (Socket) ar.AsyncState;

   int bytesSent = sClient.EndSend(ar);

   Console.WriteLine("Sent {0} bytes to server.", bytesSent);

   SendDone.Set();
}
```

The code is similar to the ConnectCallback function, apart from the call to EndSend, which ends the asynchronous send request, and the setting of the SendDone ManualResetEvent.

The BeginReceive method starts asynchronously receiving data from a Socket:

```
sClient.BeginReceive(buffer, 0  , buffer.Length , SocketFlags.None,
                     new AsyncCallback(ReceiveCallback), sClient);
```

The arguments are similar to the BeginSend method. The callback method should use the EndReceive method to return the data read from the Socket.

```
public static void ReceiveCallback(IAsyncResult ar)
{
   Thread thr = Thread.CurrentThread;
   Console.WriteLine("ReceiveCallback Thread State:" + thr.ThreadState);

   Socket sClient = (Socket) ar.AsyncState;

   int bytesRead = sClient.EndReceive(ar);

   if (bytesRead > 0)
   {
      theResponse += Encoding.ASCII.GetString(buffer, 0 , bytesRead);

      sClient.BeginReceive(buffer, 0 , buffer.Length , SocketFlags.None,
                           new AsyncCallback(ReceiveCallback), sClient);
   }
   else
   {
      ReceiveDone.Set();
   }
}
```

To ensure that we've received all of the data, BeginReceive is called inside the callback. The EndReceive method returns the number of bytes, so we can check if there is some data back in the queue. The returned data is then stored in a string field, theResponse.

Let's look at the Main method that ties everything together. We've already seen some of this code. We start by displaying information about the current thread, to distinguish between the thread on which the socket is operating and the main thread. Then we create our socket, as you've seen earlier:

```
public static void Main(string [] arg)
{
   try
   {

      Thread thr = Thread.CurrentThread;
      Console.WriteLine("Main Thread State:" + thr.ThreadState);

      IPHostEntry ipHost = Dns.Resolve("127.0.0.1");
      IPAddress ipAddr = ipHost.AddressList[0];
      IPEndPoint endPoint = new IPEndPoint(ipAddr, 11000);

      Socket sClient = new Socket(AddressFamily.InterNetwork,
                              SocketType.Stream, ProtocolType.Tcp);
```

We can now begin establishing our connection. We call the BeginConnect method, specifying the ConnectCallBack method, and wait for the operation to be completed before sending a message to the connected socket. The main thread is blocked with ConnectDone.WaitOne. This means that we will not move onto sending data before the connection has completed successfully. This is signaled with the Set method of the ConnectDone object in ConnectCallBack.

```
sClient.BeginConnect(endPoint, new AsyncCallback(ConnectCallback),
                     sClient);

ConnectDone.WaitOne();
```

Now we'll define the message to send to the server. We bloat it with some string concatenation to create a bigger message. This will give us more of an opportunity to see the asynchronous operations in action.

```
string data = "This is a test.";
for (int i=0;i<72;i++)
   data += i.ToString()+":" + (new string('=',i));
byte[] byteData = Encoding.ASCII.GetBytes(data+"<TheEnd>");
```

Now we can start the asynchronous send operation. We have our message, and we know that a connection has been established:

```
sClient.BeginSend(byteData, 0 , byteData.Length, 0 ,
                  new AsyncCallback(SendCallback), sClient);
```

We "perform some other processing" to demonstrate that our client is genuinely running asynchronously. Here, we simply put the current thread to sleep for a hundredth of a second while looping. This provides a convenient simulation of some processor-hungry computations.

```
for (int i=0;i<5;i++)
{
   // Perform some other processing
   Console.WriteLine(i);
   Thread.Sleep(10);
}
```

Before we try to receive data from the server, all the data needs to have been sent. Thus, we use `SendDone.WaitOne` to block the thread until `SendCallBack` signals sending is finished with `SendDone.Set`.

```
// Before we can receive, we must have finished sending
SendDone.WaitOne();
sClient.BeginReceive(buffer, 0  , buffer.Length, 0,
                     new AsyncCallback(ReceiveCallback), sClient);
```

Finally, we wait for the data to be received before displaying it, and then shut down and close our socket.

```
      ReceiveDone.WaitOne();

      Console.WriteLine("Response received: {0} ", theResponse);

      sClient.Shutdown(SocketShutdown.Receive);
      sClient.Close();
   }
   catch(Exception e)
   {
      Console.WriteLine(e.ToString());
   }
}
```

Figure 4-6 shows the output of our asynchronous client when running with the (synchronous) socket server we developed earlier in the chapter.

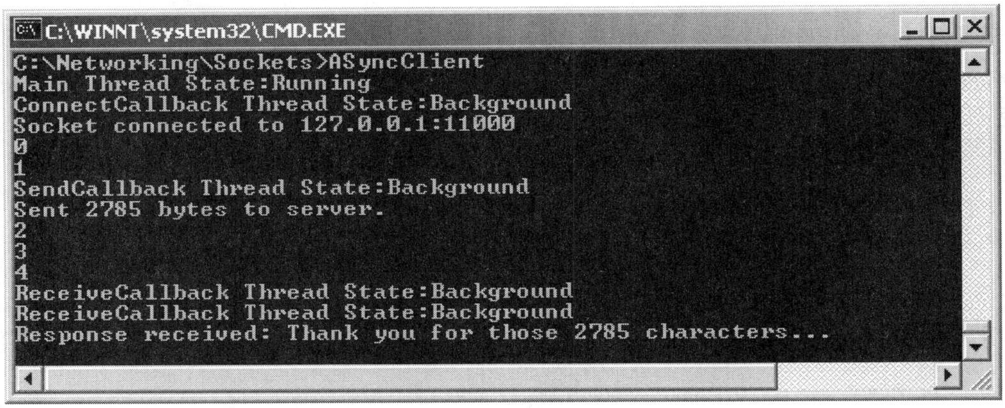

```
C:\WINNT\system32\CMD.EXE
C:\Networking\Sockets>ASyncClient
Main Thread State:Running
ConnectCallback Thread State:Background
Socket connected to 127.0.0.1:11000
0
1
SendCallback Thread State:Background
Sent 2785 bytes to server.
2
3
4
ReceiveCallback Thread State:Background
ReceiveCallback Thread State:Background
Response received: Thank you for those 2785 characters...
```

Figure 4-6. *Asynchronous client output*

Creating an Asynchronous Server Application

Figure 4-7 illustrates the flow for our asynchronous server application.

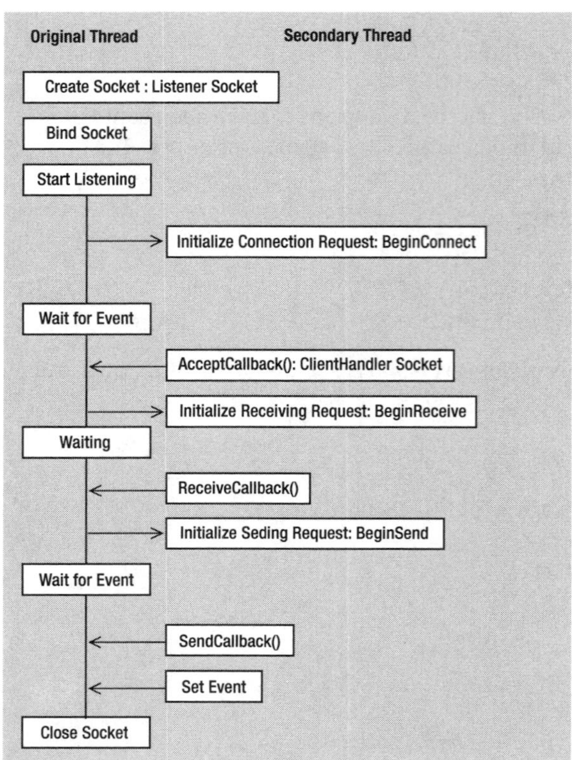

Figure 4-7. *The flow of an asynchronous server application*

Listing 4-5 shows the complete source for the `AsyncServer.cs`.

Listing 4-5. *Asynchronous Socket Server (AsyncServer.cs)*

```
using System;
using System.Net.Sockets;
using System.Net;
using System.Text;
using System.Threading;
public class AsyncServer
{
   // Buffer to receive and send data
   public static byte[] buffer = new byte[1024];

   // The event class to support synchronization
   public static ManualResetEvent socketEvent = new ManualResetEvent(false);
```

```
public static void Main(string [] args)
{
   Console.WriteLine("Main Thread ID:" + AppDomain.GetCurrentThreadId());

   byte[] bytes = new byte[1024];

   IPHostEntry ipHost = Dns.Resolve(Dns.GetHostName());
   IPAddress ipAddr = ipHost.AddressList[0];

   IPEndPoint localEnd = new IPEndPoint(ipAddr, 11000);

   Socket sListener = new Socket(AddressFamily.InterNetwork,
                              SocketType.Stream,
                              ProtocolType.Tcp);
   // Bind a socket
   sListener.Bind(localEnd);
   // Start listening
   sListener.Listen(10);
   Console.WriteLine("Waiting for a connection...");
   AsyncCallback aCallback = new AsyncCallback(AcceptCallback);
   // Asynchronous function for accepting connections
   sListener.BeginAccept(aCallback,sListener);
   // Waiting for the other threads to finish
   socketEvent.WaitOne();
}

public static void AcceptCallback(IAsyncResult ar)
{
   Console.WriteLine("AcceptCallback Thread ID:" +
                     AppDomain.GetCurrentThreadId());
   // Retrieved the socket
   Socket listener = (Socket)ar.AsyncState;
   // New socket
   Socket handler = listener.EndAccept(ar);

   handler.BeginReceive(buffer, 0 , buffer.Length, 0,
                        new AsyncCallback(ReceiveCallback), handler);
}

public static void ReceiveCallback(IAsyncResult ar)
{
   Console.WriteLine("ReceiveCallback Thread ID:" +
                     AppDomain.GetCurrentThreadId());

   string content = String.Empty;

   Socket handler = (Socket) ar.AsyncState;
```

```
        int bytesRead = handler.EndReceive(ar);

        // If there is some data ..
        if (bytesRead > 0)
        {
           // Append it to the main string
           content += Encoding.ASCII.GetString(buffer, 0, bytesRead);

           // If we encounter the end of message character ...
           if (content.IndexOf(".") > -1)
           {
              Console.WriteLine("Read {0} bytes from socket. \n Data: {1}",
                                content.Length, content);
              byte[] byteData = Encoding.ASCII.GetBytes(content);

              // Send the data back to the client
              handler.BeginSend(byteData, 0 , byteData.Length, 0 ,
                               new AsyncCallback(SendCallback), handler);
           }
           else
           {
              // Otherwise receive the remaining data
              handler.BeginReceive(buffer, 0 , buffer.Length, 0,
                                  new AsyncCallback(ReceiveCallback), handler);
           }
        }
     }

     public static void SendCallback(IAsyncResult ar)
     {
        Console.WriteLine("SendCallback Thread ID:" +
                          AppDomain.GetCurrentThreadId());

        Socket handler = (Socket) ar.AsyncState;

        // Send data back to the client
        int bytesSent = handler.EndSend(ar);

        Console.WriteLine("Sent {0} bytes to Client.", bytesSent);

        // Close down socket
        handler.Shutdown(SocketShutdown.Send);
        handler.Close();

        // Set the main thread's event
        socketEvent.Set();
     }
  }
```

The server starts by creating a socket, and then listening to the port that it is bound to. The asynchronous server application requires BeginAccept to accept connections asynchronously, and after the connection is established, it uses the BeginReceive and BeginSend methods to send data to and receive it from the client socket.

After BeginAccept is called, we set an event in the waiting state, so that a different thread in the application continues to execute when a client tries to connect to it. If we don't do this, the application finishes before the client because of the asynchronous nature of the server. The ManualResetEvent class is used here to set and wait for events:

```
AsyncCallback aCallback = new AsyncCallback(AcceptCallback);
// sListener is an instance of the Socket class
sListener.BeginAccept(aCallback, sListener);

// Assume that socketEvent is an instance of ManualResetEvent() class
socketEvent.WaitOne();
```

The BeginAccept method takes two parameters: an asynchronous delegate, which references the callback method, and a parameter that is used to pass data to the callback function (in this case, the listener socket itself). The BeginAccept method calls the AcceptCallback function when a new connection is received on the socket. This callback function calls the EndAccept method to return the new socket for the client.

Asynchronous sockets programming uses threads for different asynchronous operations. The main thread is responsible for initiating the listener socket, one thread is responsible for accepting incoming requests, and another thread is responsible for receiving and sending data. We can get the thread ID of the current thread using the GetCurrentThreadID function of the AppDomain class. We display this number in the console, so you can see that the different operations are running on different threads:

```
Console.WriteLine("Main Thread ID: " + AppDomain.GetCurrentThreadId());
```

Notice that we don't need to start the separate threads explicitly. This is done for us by the .NET Framework.

After accepting the connection by calling EndAccept, the new socket can communicate with the client by calling the asynchronous BeginReceive and the BeginSend methods:

```
Socket handler = listener.EndAccept(ar);

handler.BeginReceive(buffer, 0, buffer.Length, 0, new
                     AsyncCallback(ReceiveCallback), handler);
```

The ReceiveCallback function first calls the EndReceive function to complete the pending asynchronous task. Then we check whether the end-of-message character is found. If so, we use BeginSend to send the data back to the client; otherwise, we call BeginReceive to receive any data left:

```
int bytesRead = handler.EndReceive(ar);

if (bytesRead > 0)
{
   content += Encoding.ASCII.GetString(buffer, 0, bytesRead);
```

```
      if (content.IndexOf(".") > -1)
      {
         Console.WriteLine("Read {0} bytes from socket. \n Data: {1}",
                        content.Length, content);
         byte[] byteData = Encoding.ASCII.GetBytes(content);

         handler.BeginSend(byteData, 0 , byteData.Length, 0 ,
                        new AsyncCallback(SendCallback), handler);
      }
      else
      {
         handler.BeginReceive(buffer, 0 , buffer.Length, 0,
                          new AsyncCallback(ReceiveCallback), handler);
      }
   }
```

The SendCallback method completes the operation by calling EndSend, closing the handler socket, and setting the ManualResetEvent on the main thread so that the application can proceed:

```
int bytesSent = handler.EndSend(ar);

Console.WriteLine("Sent {0} bytes to Client.", bytesSent);

handler.Shutdown(SocketShutdown.Send);
handler.Close();

socketEvent.Set();
```

Socket Permissions

The .NET Framework provides many classes that help you to develop secure code within your applications. Many of these classes offer role-based security and cryptography. The .NET Framework also provides code-access permission objects, which are the building blocks for protecting against unauthorized code access. They are fundamental for enforcing security on managed code. Only code that has permission to run in the current context can be executed.

Each code-access permission demonstrates one of the following rights:

- The right to access protected resources such as files
- The right to perform a protected operation such as accessing managed code

For the Internet world, particularly for network applications, the System.Net classes provide built-in support for authentication and code-access permissions. The .NET Framework provides the SocketPermission class for enforcing code-access permissions.

The SocketPermission class is used to control rights to make or accept connections, controlling access to a network via sockets. A SocketPermission consists of a host specification and a set of "actions" specifying ways to connect to that host. It enforces secure code by monitoring the values of the host name, IP address, and transport protocol.

There are two ways to enforce security permission in C# sockets:

- *Imperatively*, using the `SocketPermission` class, Imperative security syntax implements permissions by creating a new instance of the `SocketPermission` class to demand a particular permission when the code is executed, such as the right to make a TCP connection. It is generally used when the security settings are changed at runtime.
- *Declaratively*, using the `SocketPermissionAttribute`. Declarative syntax uses attributes to place security information into the metadata of your code, so that the client that calls your code can use reflection to see what permissions are required by the code.

Using Imperative Security

The imperative type of security syntax creates a new instance of the `SocketPermission` class to enforce security. You can use imperative security syntax to perform demands and overrides, but not requests. Before calling the corresponding security measure, it is necessary to initialize the state of the `SocketPermission` class through the constructor so that it represents the particular form of permission that you want to use. This kind of security syntax is useful only when you have some information needed for security that is available only at runtime; for example, if you want to secure some host over a port but don't know the host name and port number until the program executes.

The application shown in Listing 4-6 demonstrates the basic use of the `SocketPermission` class. This code behaves as a client, so the `SocketServer.cs` application created earlier in the chapter must be running before executing this program. Otherwise, it will throw a `SocketException` when the `Connect` method is called. The program takes an optional command-line parameter that can either be `assert` (the default if no option is specified) or `deny`. We use this option to either grant or deny permission to the program to make a connection to the server.

Listing 4-6. *Client Application Using Imperative Security*

```
using System;
using System.Net.Sockets;
using System.Net;
using System.Text;
using System.Security;
using System.Security.Permissions;
public class ImpSecurity
{
   public static void Main(String [] arg)
   {
      // Option could be either Assert or Deny passed on the command line
      // If option is Assert, then the program executes successfully
      // Otherwise, it triggers a SecurityException
      String option = null;

      if (arg.Length > 0)
      {
         option = arg[0];
```

```
        }
        else
        {
            option = "assert";
        }

        Console.WriteLine("option:" + option);

        MethodA(option);
    }
    public static void MethodA(String option)
    {
        Console.WriteLine("MethodA");

        IPHostEntry ipHost = Dns.Resolve("127.0.0.1");
        IPAddress ipAddr = ipHost.AddressList[0];
        IPEndPoint ipEndPoint = new IPEndPoint(ipAddr, 11000);

        Socket sender = new Socket(AddressFamily.InterNetwork, SocketType.Stream,
                                   ProtocolType.Tcp);

        SocketPermission permitSocket = new SocketPermission(NetworkAccess.Connect,
                         TransportType.Tcp, "127.0.0.1",
                         SocketPermission.AllPorts);

        // Select Assert or Deny on the basis of parameter passed
        if (option.Equals("deny"))
        {
            permitSocket.Deny();
        }
        else
        {
            permitSocket.Assert();
        }

        try
        {
            // Connect the socket to the remote endpoint. Catch any errors
            sender.Connect(ipEndPoint);
            Console.WriteLine("Socket connected to {0}",
                              sender.RemoteEndPoint.ToString());

            byte[] bytes = new byte[1024];

            byte[] msg = Encoding.ASCII.GetBytes("This is a test<EOF>");
```

```
            // Send the data through the socket
            int bytesSent = sender.Send(msg);

            // Receive the response from the remote device
            int bytesRec = sender.Receive(bytes);

            Console.WriteLine("Echoed Test = {0}", Encoding.ASCII.GetString(bytes,
                              0, bytesRec));

         }
         catch(SocketException se)
         {
            Console.WriteLine("Socket Exception:"  + se.ToString());
         }
         catch(SecurityException sece)
         {
            Console.WriteLine("Socket Exception:"  + sece.ToString());
         }
         finally
         {
            if (sender.Connected)
            {
               // Release the socket
               sender.Shutdown(SocketShutdown.Both);
               sender.Close();
            }
         }
         Console.WriteLine("Closing MethodA");
      }
   }
```

The code in Listing 4-6 shows how to implement code-access security using the imperative syntax. The important part of the code is a single method call to either the Assert or Deny method of SocketPermission. The program basically follows two different paths of execution, depending on the command-line argument passed in. One path demonstrates a successful connection, and the other illustrates a failed connection request due to the security implications of the code.

In the program shown in Listing 4-6, we restrict the code from making a TCP connection to a server. This restriction is performed by calling the Deny method of the SocketPermission class. But before calling any methods of that class, we first need to initialize the SocketPermission object. This initialization is performed in the constructor:

```
SocketPermission permitSocket = new SocketPermission(NetworkAccess.Connect,
      TransportType.Tcp, "127.0.0.1", SocketPermission.AllPorts);
```

The constructor creates a new instance of the SocketPermission class and initializes it for the given transport address with the specified permission. The parameters denote the network access for which we want to grant/deny permissions (here, connecting to a server), the transport type (TCP), the host name, and the port number. The NetworkAccess value can be one of the following:

- Accept indicates that the application is allowed to accept connections from the Internet on a local resource.
- Connect indicates that the application is allowed to connect to specific Internet resources.

The TranportType parameter represents the transport protocol; it can be All, Tcp, Udp, and so on. The third parameter is the host name. The port number is the last parameter.

After the preceding code line is executed, a new SocketPermission object is created. This object controls access to the specified host name and port using the specified TransportType.

Once we have initialized the SocketPermission in this way, we can call Assert or Deny to allow or prevent the code from performing the specified NetworkAccess.

Passing "deny" as a parameter to this application (that is, running the application by entering ImpSecurity deny at the command line) produces the following output:

```
C:\Networking\Sockets>ImpPermissions deny
option:deny
MethodA
Socket Exception:System.Security.SecurityException: Request for the permission
of type System.Net.SocketPermission, System, Version=1.0.3300.0, Culture=neutral,
 PublicKeyToken=b77a5c561934e089 failed.
   at System.Security.SecurityRuntime.FrameDescHelper(FrameSecurityDescriptor
secDesc, IPermission demand, PermissionToken permToken)
   at System.Security.CodeAccessSecurityEngine.Check(PermissionToken permToken,
CodeAccessPermission demand, StackCrawlMark& stackMark, Int32 checkFrames, Int32
 unrestrictedOverride)
   at System.Security.CodeAccessSecurityEngine.Check(CodeAccessPermission cap,
StackCrawlMark& stackMark)
   at System.Security.CodeAccessPermission.Demand()
   at System.Net.Sockets.Socket.CheckCacheRemote(SocketAddress socketAddress,
EndPoint remoteEP, Boolean isOverwrite)
   at System.Net.Sockets.Socket.Connect(EndPoint remoteEP)
   at ImpSecurity.MethodA(String option)
The state of the failed permission was:
<IPermission class="System.Net.SocketPermission, System, Version=1.0.3300.0,
             Culture=neutral, PublicKeyToken=b77a5c561934e089"
             version="1">
   <ConnectAccess>
      <ENDPOINT host="127.0.0.1"
                transport="Tcp"
                port="11000"/>
   </ConnectAccess>
</IPermission>
Closing MethodA
```

Using Declarative Security

Declarative security uses .NET attributes to place security information inside the metadata of the code. Attributes can be placed at the assembly, class, or member level to indicate the type of request, demand, or override that is needed. In order to use this security syntax, the state data must be initialized first for the `SocketPermissionAttribute` object through the declarative syntax, so that it represents the form of permission that is being enforced on the code.

The example in Listing 4-7 demonstrates how to enforce permissions using `SocketPermissionAttribute`. We define two methods, called `LegalMethod` and `IllegalMethod`, which both attempt to connect to a server via TCP. On the first method, we place a `SocketPermissionAttribute` that grants the necessary permission to the method. On the second, we place an attribute to deny connect permission.

Listing 4-7. *Client Application Using Declarative Security*

```
using System;
using System.Net.Sockets;
using System.Net;
using System.Text;
using System.Security;
using System.Security.Permissions;
public class DecSecurity
{
   public static void Main(String [] arg)
   {
      LegalMethod();
      IllegalMethod();
   }
   [SocketPermission(SecurityAction.Assert, Access = "Connect",
                    Host = "127.0.0.1", Port = "All", Transport = "Tcp")]
   public static void LegalMethod()
   {
      Console.WriteLine("LegalMethod");

      IPHostEntry ipHost = Dns.Resolve("127.0.0.1");
      IPAddress ipAddr = ipHost.AddressList[0];
      IPEndPoint ipEndPoint = new IPEndPoint(ipAddr, 11000);

      Socket sender = new Socket(AddressFamily.InterNetwork, SocketType.Stream,
                                 ProtocolType.Tcp);

      try
      {
         // Connect the socket to the remote endpoint. Catch any errors
         sender.Connect(ipEndPoint);
         Console.WriteLine("Socket connected to {0}",
                           sender.RemoteEndPoint.ToString());
      }
```

```
      catch(SecurityException se)
      {
         Console.WriteLine("Security Exception:" + se);
      }
      catch(SocketException se)
      {
         Console.WriteLine("Socket Exception:"  + se);
      }
      finally
      {
         if (sender.Connected)
         {
            // Release the socket
            sender.Shutdown(SocketShutdown.Both);
            sender.Close();
         }
      }
   }

   [SocketPermission(SecurityAction.Deny, Access = "Connect",
                     Host = "127.0.0.1", Port = "All", Transport = "Tcp")]
   public static void IllegalMethod()
   {
      Console.WriteLine("IllegalMethod");

      IPHostEntry ipHost = Dns.Resolve("127.0.0.1");
      IPAddress ipAddr = ipHost.AddressList[0];
      IPEndPoint ipEndPoint = new IPEndPoint(ipAddr, 11000);

      Socket sender = new Socket(AddressFamily.InterNetwork,
                                 SocketType.Stream, ProtocolType.Tcp);

      try
      {
         // Connect the socket to the remote endpoint. Catch any errors
         sender.Connect(ipEndPoint);
         Console.WriteLine("Socket connected to {0}",
                           sender.RemoteEndPoint.ToString());
      }
      catch(SocketException se)
      {
         Console.WriteLine("Socket Exception:" + se );
      }
      catch(SecurityException se)
      {
         Console.WriteLine("Security Exception:" + se );
      }
```

```
            finally
         {
            if (sender.Connected)
            {
               // Release the socket
               sender.Shutdown(SocketShutdown.Both);
               sender.Close();
            }
         }
      }
   }
```

The program in Listing 4-7 is similar in functionality to the one in Listing 4-6. This program, however, uses the declarative security syntax instead of the imperative security demonstrated earlier. The code contains two different methods for connecting to the server, because the attributes couldn't be dynamically manipulated.

The SocketPermissionAttribute declaration is placed on each method that we need to secure:

```
[SocketPermission(SecurityAction.Deny, Access = "Connect",
                  Host = "127.0.0.1", Port = "All", Transport = "Tcp")]
```

This code declares and initializes the SocketPermissionAttribute, very much as we did in the SocketPermission's constructor. The properties of the SocketPermissionAttribute must have values that are not a null reference or invalid. Also, once set, these properties cannot be changed. The properties' values are the same as in the SocketPermission class. The declarative code, once compiled, is stored inside the metadata of the application code, so calling code can use reflection to see what permissions the code requires to run.

Summary

In this chapter, we looked at developing client and server applications with the Socket class. We began by explaining what a socket is and how sockets are introduced into the operating system. We described the two main types of sockets: stream sockets and datagram sockets. You learned that there is another type of socket, used for custom, lower-level programming, which is known as a raw socket. You also saw how sockets and ports are connected and socket numbers are built.

Next, we talked about the socket support in .NET, which is implemented in the System.Net.Sockets namespace. You learned that all the socket support is provided through the System.Net.Sockets.Socket class. We also discussed exception management for network applications, which is provided by the SocketException class. You learned that the Close and Shutdown methods should generally be placed inside the finally block. Then we covered the basic socket options and outlined how to set and get them using SetSocketOption and Get-SocketOption.

We also covered .NET's asynchronous programming model, and applied it to build an asynchronous socket-based client/server application. We used the AsyncCallback delegate for providing callback functions for asynchronous processing. You saw how the ManualResetEvent class is used for synchronizing different threads inside an asynchronous application.

Finally, we looked at the declarative and imperative security syntax for providing code-level security in networking applications. The imperative syntax should be used when the permissions needed are only known at runtime. Use declarative security if the permissions needed are known at compile-time.

CHAPTER 5

Raw Socket Programming

In this chapter, I discuss raw socket programming—I'll cover the basics of the Internet Control Message Protocol (ICMP) and Simple Network Management Protocol (SNMP). We'll look at each of these protocols in turn, and build some useful applications to demonstrate the fundamentals of raw socket programming.

ICMP is used by some network utility applications to communicate with the remote host on a network. The `ping` and `traceroute` utilities, for example, send data packets using the ICMP to the host, which in turn sends the data packets back as a reply. The time taken to send and receive a data packet is calculated in milliseconds, and this is used to determine the speed of the connection between the two hosts.

SNMP is another popular protocol used for network administration. SNMP is used to query and control network devices from a central management station. You'll see how the details of ICMP and SNMP compare throughout the chapter.

The first half of this chapter is about ICMP and raw socket programming: I'll show you the details of ICMP packets, packet formats and types, and I'll translate those details into practical ICMP classes and raw socket programming techniques. I'll show you practical code to send and receive packets, and the core techniques for formatting packets once you can send and receive them with no trouble. I'll build a `PingHost` ICMP class and a `TraceRoute` utility to show you these techniques at work in practice.

The second half of this chapter looks at the SNMP, and how its details compare with the ICMP. We'll take a look at SNMP structure, packet details, and SNMP commands. We'll then build a simple SNMP class to get the SNMP system name, so that you can see the techniques involved in some working code and how it differs from the ICMP techniques you learned.

The ICMP Protocol

The Network Working Group's RFC 792, written in 1981, first defined ICMP. The aim of RFC 792, which you can read for yourself at `http://www.faqs.org/rfcs/rfc792.html`, was to allow network devices to report errors in datagram processing. Since then, the original ICMP has undergone some changes that have made it a very robust means of communicating errors and network information between hosts.

ICMP uses the Internet Protocol (IP) to communicate across the network. ICMP is an indispensable part of IP and is implemented by every IP module. Although ICMP uses IP, it is an entirely separate protocol from TCP or UDP: an IP packet helps to identify the subsequent layer protocol that is enclosed in the data section by the protocol type field.

ICMP Packet Format

ICMP packets are recognized by the IP protocol type 1. The whole of the ICMP packet is then contained within the data section of the IP packet. Figure 5-1 shows how the ICMP packet fields are placed in an IP packet.

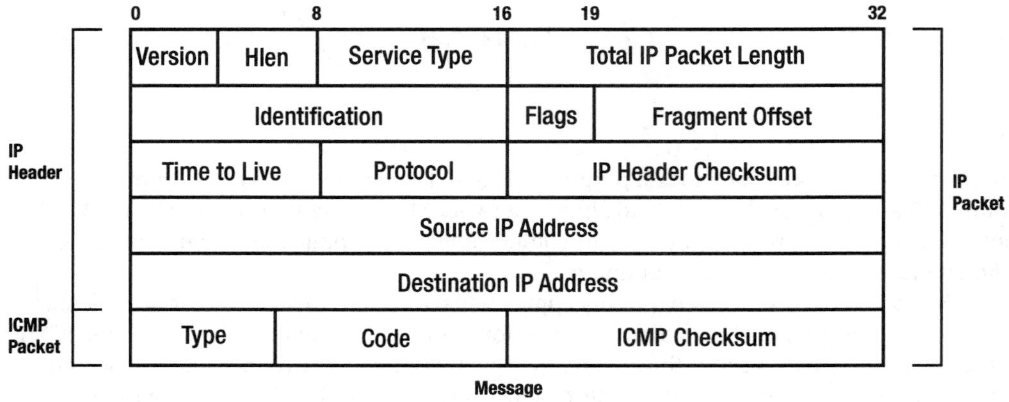

Figure 5-1. *ICMP packet in an IP packet*

Analogous to TCP and UDP, ICMP uses a specific packet format in order to identify the information in the packet. An ICMP packet contains the following fields:

- *Type*: The 1-byte Type element helps to define the kind of ICMP message that is present in the packet. Many types of ICMP packets are used to send the control request messages to the remote hosts. Each message type has its own format and data requirements.
- *Code*: An assorted ICMP message type requires specific control and data options. These options are defined in the single byte Code field.
- *Checksum*: A Checksum element is used to ensure that the ICMP packet reaches the destination without corruption or tampering. The checksum is computed on only the ICMP portion of the packet, using a specific algorithm defined in RFC 792. While computing the checksum value, the Checksum field is set to zero. The length of the checksum is 2 bytes.
- *Message*: The Message element holds diverse data elements that are unique to each ICMP message type. The Message data field is used to hold information that is sent to and from the remote host. The first two fields in the Message element are defined as an Identifier and Sequence number. These fields are used to uniquely identify the ICMP packet to the hosts.

ICMP Packet Types

There are various ICMP packet types, and the type is defined by the 1-byte value in the Type element. The most commonly used ICMP packet types include

- Echo request and Echo Reply packets
- Destination Unreachable packets

It's important to know some of the details and differences between these two core packet types, so let's take a look at each of these now.

Echo Request and Echo Reply Packets

So the most commonly used ICMP packets are Echo Request and Echo Reply. These packets enable a device to request an ICMP response from a remote device on the network.

The Echo Request packet exercises ICMP type 8 with a code value of 0. The Message data area holds the following three elements:

- An Identifier of 1 byte that uniquely identifies the Echo Request packet.
- A Sequence number of 1 byte that provides additional identification for the ICMP packet in a stream
- A multibyte data element containing the data that should be returned by the receiving host

When a device receives an Echo Request packet, it should respond with an Echo Reply packet, ICMP type 0. The Echo Reply packet must contain the same Identifier and Sequence number values as that of the Echo Request packet to which it is responding. The data element value must also be same as that received in the Echo Request packet. You'll see this and the other types in action later on, by the way, when I put some example code together.

Destination Unreachable Packet

The Destination Unreachable ICMP packet of type 3 is returned by a router device if it receives an IP packet indicating that it could not be forwarded to the appropriate destination. The data portion of the Destination Unreachable packet contains the IP header, along with the first 64 bits of the datagram.

The Code field identifies the reason why the packet could not be forwarded by the router.

Using Raw Sockets

ICMP packets don't use TCP or UDP, so the socket helper classes `TcpClient` and `UdpClient` aren't available to us. But raw sockets, which are a feature of the `Socket` class, can be used, and they very usefully allow you to define a network packet above the IP layer.

To create a raw socket, the `SocketType.Raw` socket type is used when the socket is created. There are several protocol type values that are used to match the raw socket type itself. Some of the most common are shown in Table 5-1.

Table 5-1. *Protocol Type Values and Their Protocol Description*

Protocol Value	Protocol Description
`Ggp`	Gateway-to-Gateway Protocol
`Icmp`	Internet Control Message Protocol
`Idp`	IDP Protocol
`Igmp`	Internet Group Management Protocol
`IP`	A raw IP packet
`ND`	Net Disk Protocol
`Raw`	A raw IP packet
`Unspecified`	An unspecified protocol
`Unknown`	An unknown protocol

Now if you use the `ProtocolType.Icmp` value, as detailed here, the IP packet created by the raw socket defines the consequent layer protocol as ICMP IP. This enables the remote host to instantly identify the packet as an ICMP packet, and process it accordingly.

I will now translate this table of values into some example code that creates a socket for ICMP packets.

```
using System;
using System.Net;
using System.Net.Sockets ;
namespace RawSocket
{
  // SimpleICMP.cs
  public class SimpleICMP
  {
    public static void Main(string[] args)
    {
      IPHostEntry host = null;
      host = Dns.Resolve("name");
      Socket tmpS = new
        Socket(host.AddressList[0].AddressFamily,
        SocketType.Raw, ProtocolType.Icmp);
    }
  }
}
```

This code creates a socket for ICMP packets—the key part being, of course, the declaration using the ICMP protocol type value from Table 5-1, where you create the new socket, `tmpS`, passing the host details, socket type, and protocol type value as detailed:

```
Socket tmpS = new
  Socket(host.AddressList[0].AddressFamily,
  SocketType.Raw, ProtocolType.Icmp);
```

Sending Raw Packets

ICMP is a connectionless protocol, which means that you have to bind the socket to a specific local port to send a packet, or you have to use the Connect method to connect the socket to a specific remote host. You also need to use the SendTo method to specify the IPEndPoint object of the destination address. But note that, since ICMP doesn't use ports, the value of the port property of the IPEndPoint object is not important.

With this in mind, the following code extract creates an IPEndPoint destination object with no port, and sends a packet to that IPEndPoint destination:

```
IPEndPoint iep = new IPEndPoint(IPAddress.Parse("192.168.0.1"), 0);
sock.SendTo(packet, iep);
```

Because the raw socket doesn't format the data, the value entered in the packet byte array is forwarded "as is" to the remote host. This means that you must manually create the ICMP packet in the byte array and then send it to the remote host. Be aware that a mistake in creating the packet would thus result in an error on the receiving host, and there would be no return ICMP packet!

Receiving Raw Packets

Receiving data from a raw socket is more difficult than sending data. To receive data from the raw socket, you use the ReceiveFrom method. Now since the raw socket does not identify a higher-layer protocol, the data returned from a ReceiveFrom method call holds the whole of the IP packet contents. The data must then duly be extracted from the raw IP packet information to create the ICMP packet elements.

The IP packet data starts at byte 20; therefore, to extract the ICMP packet data and header, you need to start reading the byte array at the 20th position in the received data packet. Here is a code extract that literally does just this process:

```
static void Main(string[] args)
{
  // Sets up our socket as previously demonstrated
  IPHostEntry lipa = Dns.Resolve("127.0.0.1");
  IPEndPoint lep = new IPEndPoint(lipa.AddressList[0], 80);
  Socket s = new Socket(lep.Address.AddressFamily,
        SocketType.Raw, ProtocolType.Icmp);
  byte[] msg = Encoding.ASCII.GetBytes("This is a test");
  try
  {
    s.SendTo(msg, 0, msg.Length, SocketFlags.None, lep);

    // Creates an IpEndPoint to capture the identity
    // of the sending host.
    IPEndPoint sender = new IPEndPoint(IPAddress.Any, 0);
    EndPoint tempRemoteEP = (EndPoint)sender;

    // Creates a byte buffer to receive the message.
    byte[] buffer = new byte[1024];
```

```
      // Receives datagram from a remote host.  This call blocks.
      s.ReceiveFrom(buffer, SocketFlags.None, ref tempRemoteEP);

      // Displays the information received to the screen.
      Console.WriteLine(" I received the following message : "
                + Encoding.ASCII.GetString(buffer));
      Console.ReadLine();
    }
    catch(Exception e)
    {
      Console.WriteLine("Exception : " + e.ToString());
    }
  }
```

The key parts of this code I want to draw your attention to are how you create an IPEndPoint to capture the identity of the sending host, create a buffer to receive the message, and then once you've received it, process it as detailed previously.

It's important to remember, from the preceding discussion, that the ReceiveFrom method returns the entire IP packet, so you must declare the receiving buffer size to be at least 20 bytes larger than the expected data.

Creating an ICMP Class—Formatting ICMP Packets

So far you've seen how to send and receive packets—but what about formatting them? The raw socket does not automatically format the ICMP packet—you have to do this format work yourself. The good news, however, is that because C# is an object-oriented language, it conveniently allows you to create a C# ICMP class to format an ICMP packet, and manipulate the packet contents as necessary.

With this technique, you can use the ICMP class in any network applications that use the ICMP packets. I will now take you through this technique part by part, and create some example code as we go along, to keep this discussion grounded in coding practice rather than just the details of the protocols.

The ICMP Class Constructors

The ICMP class should define a data variable for each element in the ICMP packet. The data variables that need to be defined, to represent generic ICMP packets, are as listed in Table 5-2.

Table 5-2. *ICMP Packet Constructor*

Data Variable	Size	Type
Type	1 byte	Byte
SubCode	1 byte	Byte
Checksum	2 bytes	Unsigned 16-bit integer
Identifier	2 bytes	Unsigned 16-bit integer
SequenceNumber	2 bytes	Unsigned 16-bit integer
Data	Multibyte	Byte array

The default ICMP constructor creates an instance of the ICMP class, but doesn't assign any values to the data variables. These are assigned within the ICMP application program whenever an ICMP packet is created.

The following code extract shows you the format of the ICMP class default constructor:

```
public class IcmpPacket
{
// Type of message
  public Byte Type;

// Type of subcode
  public Byte SubCode;

// One's complement checksum of struct
  public UInt16 CheckSum;

// Identifier
  public UInt16 Identifier;

// Sequence number
  public UInt16 SequenceNumber;
public Byte [] Data;

}
```

This ICMP class default constructor obviously correlates directly to Table 5-2—so far so good.

ICMP Serialize Method

Next, you build a method named Serialize. This method helps to calculate the total size of the packet from the packet information passed to it as the parameter. The total size is calculated by converting the packet into a byte array.

```
///  This method gets the packet and calculates the total size
///  of the packet by converting it to byte array

public static Int32 Serialize( IcmpPacket packet,
          Byte [] Buffer, Int32 PacketSize, Int32 PingData )
{
  Int32 cbReturn = 0;

  // Serialize the struct into the array
  int Index=0;

  Byte [] b_type = new Byte[1];
  b_type[0] = (packet.Type);

  Byte [] b_code = new Byte[1];
  b_code[0] = (packet.SubCode);
```

```
    Byte [] b_cksum = BitConverter.GetBytes(packet.CheckSum);
    Byte [] b_id = BitConverter.GetBytes(packet.Identifier);
    Byte [] b_seq = BitConverter.GetBytes(packet.SequenceNumber);

    // Serialize type
    Array.Copy( b_type, 0, Buffer, Index, b_type.Length );
    Index += b_type.Length;

    // Serialize subcode
    Array.Copy( b_code, 0, Buffer, Index, b_code.Length );
    Index += b_code.Length;

    // Serialize cksum
    Array.Copy( b_cksum, 0, Buffer, Index, b_cksum.Length );
    Index += b_cksum.Length;

    // Serialize id
    Array.Copy( b_id, 0, Buffer, Index, b_id.Length );
    Index += b_id.Length;

    Array.Copy( b_seq, 0, Buffer, Index, b_seq.Length );
    Index += b_seq.Length;

    // Copy the data
    Array.Copy( packet.Data, 0, Buffer, Index, PingData );
    Index += PingData;
    if( Index != PacketSize/* sizeof(IcmpPacket)  */) {
      cbReturn = -1;
      return cbReturn;
      }
    cbReturn = Index;
    return cbReturn;
  }
```

I have commented the code directly, so you can see the key points where you need to serialize the data variables in this method, and then actually copy the data.

ICMP Checksum Method

The next part of creating an ICMP packet is to calculate the checksum value of the packet. The easiest way to do this task is to create a self-contained method for calculating the checksum, and place that method within the ICMP class that is to be used by the ICMP application program.

The ICMP RFC I referred to earlier defines the Checksum element as "the 16-bit one's complement of the one's complement sum of the ICMP message, starting with the ICMP type."

For computing the checksum, the Checksum element should be set to zero. The following code extract will give you a solid example of calculating the checksum:

```
/// This method has the algorithm to make a checksum

public static UInt16 checksum( UInt16[] buffer, int size )
{
  Int32 cksum = 0;
  int counter;

  counter = 0;

  while ( size > 0 ) {
    UInt16 val = buffer[counter];
    cksum += Convert.ToInt32( buffer[counter] );
    counter += 1;
    size -= 1;
    }

  cksum = (cksum >> 16) + (cksum & 0xffff);
  cksum += (cksum >> 16);
  return (UInt16)(~cksum);
}
```

ICMP Packet Creation

Now let's draw all these parts together—you've created your default class constructor, and you've built your `Serialize` and `Checksum` methods.

I will in a moment therefore present a fleshed-out method that I have called `PingHost`. This method takes the hostname of the server and then pings it and shows the response time, using the technique we have been building.

In the first part of this `PingHost` method, I create an ICMP packet, by defining the ICMP Type element as 8 and the SubCode element as 0. This creates an Echo Request packet that uses the Identifier and Sequence elements to track the individual ping packet, and allows entering any text into the data element.

The returned ICMP packet (if there is one) creates a new ICMP object, which can then be used to determine if the received packet is the match for the sent ICMP packet. The Identifier, Sequence, and data elements of the received packet should match the same values of the ICMP packet sent. You'll see further down the `PingHost` method that if these do not match, you can safely conclude that you've intercepted an ICMP packet from another application running on the same device, and so you simply keep listening for the correct ICMP packet to be returned.

You'll also see that you need to check for the response timeout, and if no ICMP packet is received from the remote host within 10 seconds, throw an error message. Here then is the `PingHost` method—I have placed more detailed commentary within the code itself to make it easier to follow:

```
/// This method takes the hostname of the server
/// and then it pings it and shows the response time

public static void PingHost(string host)
{
  // Declare the IPHostEntry
  IPHostEntry serverHE, fromHE;
  int nBytes = 0;
  int dwStart = 0, dwStop = 0;

  // Initialize a socket of the type ICMP
  Socket socket = new Socket(AddressFamily.InterNetwork,
           SocketType.Raw, ProtocolType.Icmp);

  // Get the server endpoint
  try
  {
    serverHE = Dns.GetHostByName(host);
  }
  catch(Exception)
  {
    Console.WriteLine("Host not found"); // fail
    return ;
  }

  // Convert the server IP_EndPoint to an EndPoint
  IPEndPoint ipepServer = new
        IPEndPoint(serverHE.AddressList[0], 0);
  EndPoint epServer = (ipepServer);

  // Set the receiving endpoint to the client machine
  fromHE = Dns.GetHostByName(Dns.GetHostName());
  IPEndPoint ipEndPointFrom = new
        IPEndPoint(fromHE.AddressList[0], 0);
  EndPoint EndPointFrom = (ipEndPointFrom);

  int PacketSize = 0;
  IcmpPacket packet = new IcmpPacket();

  // Construct the packet to send
  packet.Type = 8;
  packet.SubCode = 0;
  packet.CheckSum = UInt16.Parse("0");
```

```
packet.Identifier    = UInt16.Parse("45");
packet.SequenceNumber  = UInt16.Parse("0");
int PingData = 32; // sizeof(IcmpPacket) - 8;
packet.Data = new Byte[PingData];

// Initialize the Packet.Data
for (int i = 0; i < PingData; i++)
{
  packet.Data[i] = (byte)'#';
}

// Variable to hold the total packet size
PacketSize = PingData + 8;
Byte [] icmp_pkt_buffer = new Byte[ PacketSize ];
Int32 Index = 0;

// Call the Serialize method you built earlier which
// counts the total number of bytes in the packet
Index = Serialize(packet,
                  icmp_pkt_buffer,
                  PacketSize,
                  PingData );
if( Index == -1 )
{
  // Error in packet size
  Console.WriteLine("Error in Making Packet");
  return ;
}

// Now get this critter into a UInt16 array

// Get the half size of the packet
Double double_length = Convert.ToDouble(Index);
Double dtemp = System.Math.Ceiling( double_length / 2);
int cksum_buffer_length = Convert.ToInt32(dtemp);

// Create a byte array
UInt16 [] cksum_buffer = new UInt16[cksum_buffer_length];

// Code to initialize the Uint16 array
int icmp_header_buffer_index = 0;
for( int i = 0; i < cksum_buffer_length; i++ ) {
  cksum_buffer[i] =  BitConverter.ToUInt16
         (icmp_pkt_buffer,icmp_header_buffer_index);
  icmp_header_buffer_index += 2;
  }
```

```
// Call the checksum method you built, which will
// return a checksum

UInt16 u_cksum = checksum(cksum_buffer, cksum_buffer_length);

// Save the checksum to the Packet
packet.CheckSum  = u_cksum;

// Now that you have the checksum, serialize the packet again
Byte [] sendbuf = new Byte[ PacketSize ];

// Again check the packet size
Index = Serialize(packet,
                  sendbuf,
                  PacketSize,
                  PingData );

// If there is a error report it
if( Index == -1 )
{
  Console.WriteLine("Error in Making Packet");
  return ;
}

// Start timing
dwStart = System.Environment.TickCount;

// Send the packet over the socket
try
{
  if ((nBytes = socket.SendTo(sendbuf,
     PacketSize, 0, epServer)) == -1)
  {
    Console.WriteLine("Socket Error cannot Send Packet");
  }
}

// Gracefully handle host unreachable situations
catch(SocketException ex)
{
if(ex.ErrorCode==10065)
    Console.WriteLine("Destination host unreachable.");
}

// Initialize the buffers.
// The receive buffer is the size of the
// ICMP header plus the IP header (20 bytes)
```

```
  Byte [] ReceiveBuffer = new Byte[256];
  nBytes = 0;
  // Receive the bytes
  bool recd =false;
  int timeout=0;

  // Loop for checking the time of the server responding
  while(!recd)
  {
    nBytes = socket.ReceiveFrom
        (ReceiveBuffer, 256, 0, ref EndPointFrom);
    if (nBytes == -1)
    {
      Console.WriteLine("Host not responding") ;
      recd=true ;
      break;
     }
    else if(nBytes>0)
    {
      // Stop timing
      dwStop = System.Environment.TickCount - dwStart;
      Console.WriteLine("Reply from "
         + epServer.ToString()+" in "
         + dwStop+"ms :Bytes Received: "+nBytes);
      recd=true;
      break;
    }

    // Time out check
    timeout=System.Environment.TickCount - dwStart;
    if(timeout>1000)
    {
      Console.WriteLine("Time Out") ;
      recd=true;
    }
   }

// Close the socket
socket.Close();
}
```

To recap, in the first part of this `PingHost` method I create an ICMP packet, which creates an Echo Request packet that uses the Identifier and Sequence elements to track the individual ping packet, and allows entering data into the data element. The returned ICMP packet (if there is one) creates a new ICMP object, which can then be used to determine if the received packet is the match for the sent ICMP packet. The Identifier, Sequence, and data elements of the received packet should match the same values of the ICMP packet sent. If these do not match, you simply keep listening for the correct ICMP packet to be returned. You also check for the response timeout, and if no ICMP packet is received from the remote host within 10 seconds, you give an error message.

This method is the culmination of the technique I set out to demonstrate in the previous few sections to cover the concept of packet formatting and manipulation. You'll see in this PingHost method the drawing together of the ICMP class constructor, the Serialize method, and the Checksum method.

Finally, this PingHost method can be tested with a simple console application, such as this:

```
public static void Main(string[] args)
{
  // Here you are passing localhost IP
  // But you can check the ping progam by passing either
  // Internet IP or Network IP
  PingHost("127.0.0.1") ;
}
```

Now you've created a PingHost method, let's now move on to create another ICMP-based application—a tracing utility.

Using ICMP to Create a Tracing Application

Tracing is closely related to pinging. To trace a request, you look into the ICMP header. Each ICMP header consists of a field called time to live (TTL). The TTL field is decremented at each machine in which the datagram is processed. Thus if a packet routes through Machine 1, Machine 2, and Machine C, and if I set initial TTL to 3, then TTL at Machine 2 would be 2, and TTL at Machine 3 would be 1. If the gateway processing a datagram finds the TTL field is zero, it discards the datagram. The gateway also notifies the source host through the time-exceeded message.

To get the tracing utility working, I'm going to send a packet containing an Echo Request to the destination machine, with an increasing number for TTL starting from 1. Each time TTL goes to zero, the machine that was currently processing the datagram will return the packet with a time-exceeded message. I'll remember the IP of this machine, and I'll send the packet back with incremented TTL. I'll then repeat this until I successfully receive an echo reply.

So the following TraceHost program sends an ICMP Echo Request to a remote host. In order to determine what routers the ICMP packet uses to travel to reach its destination, this code exploits another ICMP message packet. I will be using the previous ICMP class and its methods Serialize and Checksum for this trace program. Here's the code, with comments inline:

```
public static void TraceHost(string host)
{
  // Declare the IPHostEntry
  IPHostEntry serverHE, fromHE;
  int nBytes = 0;
  int dwStart = 0, dwStop = 0;

  //Initialize a Socket of the Type ICMP
  Socket socket = new
       Socket(AddressFamily.InterNetwork ,
```

```
    SocketType.Raw, ProtocolType.Icmp);

// Get the server endpoint
try
{
  serverHE = Dns.GetHostByName(host);
}
catch(Exception)
{
  Console.WriteLine("Host not found");
  return ;
}

// Convert the server IP_EndPoint to an EndPoint
IPEndPoint ipepServer = new
        IPEndPoint(serverHE.AddressList[0], 0);
EndPoint epServer = (ipepServer);

// Set the receiving endpoint to the client machine
fromHE = Dns.GetHostByName(Dns.GetHostName());
IPEndPoint ipEndPointFrom = new
        IPEndPoint(fromHE.AddressList[0], 0);
EndPoint EndPointFrom = (ipEndPointFrom);
int PacketSize = 0;
IcmpPacket packet = new IcmpPacket();

// Construct the packet to send
packet.Type = 8;    //8
packet.SubCode = 0;
packet.CheckSum = UInt16.Parse("0");
packet.Identifier   = UInt16.Parse("45");
packet.SequenceNumber  = UInt16.Parse("0");
int PingData = 32;  // sizeof(IcmpPacket) - 8;
packet.Data = new Byte[PingData];

// Initialize the Packet.Data
for (int i = 0; i < PingData; i++)
{
  packet.Data[i] = (byte)'#';
}

// Variable to hold the total packet size
PacketSize = PingData + 8;
Byte [] icmp_pkt_buffer = new Byte[ PacketSize ];
Int32 Index = 0;
```

```
// Call the method Serialize which counts
// the total number of bytes in the packet
Index = Serialize(packet,
                  icmp_pkt_buffer,
                  PacketSize,
                  PingData );

// Error in packet size
if( Index == -1 )
{
  Console.WriteLine("Error in Making Packet");
  return ;
}
for(int ittl=1; ittl<= 256; ittl++)
{
  Byte[] ByteRecv = new Byte[256];

  // Socket options to set TTL and Timeouts
  socket.SetSocketOption(SocketOptionLevel.IP,
         SocketOptionName.IpTimeToLive, ittl);
  socket.SetSocketOption(SocketOptionLevel.Socket,
         SocketOptionName.SendTimeout,10000);
  socket.SetSocketOption(SocketOptionLevel.Socket,
         SocketOptionName.ReceiveTimeout,10000);

  // Get current time
  DateTime dt= DateTime.Now;

  // Send request
  int iRet= socket.SendTo(icmp_pkt_buffer,
         icmp_pkt_buffer.Length, SocketFlags.None,
         epServer);

  // Check for Win32 SOCKET_ERROR
  if(iRet== -1)
    Console.WriteLine("error sending data");

  // Receive
  iRet= socket.ReceiveFrom(ByteRecv, ByteRecv.Length,
         SocketFlags.None, ref EndPointFrom );

  // Calculate time required
  TimeSpan ts= DateTime.Now- dt;

  // Check if response is OK
  if(iRet== -1)
    Console.WriteLine("error getting data");
  Console.WriteLine("TTL= {0,-5} IP= {1,-20}
```

```
            Time={2,3}ms",ittl,((IPEndPoint)epServer)
            .Address,ts.Milliseconds);

    if((iRet == 32+ 8 +20)&&
            (BitConverter.ToInt16(ByteRecv,24) ==
            BitConverter.ToInt16(icmp_pkt_buffer,4))
            && (ByteRecv[20] == 0))
      break;

    // Time out
    if(ByteRecv[20] != 11)
    {
      Console.WriteLine("Unexpected Error");
      break;
    }
  }

// Close the socket
socket.Close();
}
```

The methods and techniques for working with ICMP in this way should be clear to you now if you compare the similarities in both the `PingHost` method and now the `TraceRoute` program here. It's now time to move on and take a look at SNMP.

SNMP

Simple Network Management Protocol is a protocol used for network management. SNMP helps you in querying and controlling the network devices from a central management area.

SNMP is different from other network protocols. It doesn't follow the byte-by-byte protocol layout, but changes according to the type of the query and the type of data queried.

Impending SNMP

During the initial stage of the Internet, its designers realized the imperative for an easy way to monitor network devices. Many monitoring protocols were developed over years, which challenged those who wanted to standardize network monitoring. Ultimately SNMP became the most robust and widely accepted way for monitoring network devices.

The principle of SNMP is that every network device maintains a database of network statistics that can be queried from a remote device. The main database is called the Management Information Base (MIB) and was defined in RFC 1155. Each of the network devices that implements SNMP contains the same basic MIB structure. The MIB contains records for simple network statistics; for instance:

- The network name of the device
- The number of network interfaces on the device
- Error rates of each network interface

SNMP encloses procedures for querying and setting values in the database. Because of this feature, you'll often find a lot of network paraphernalia using the SNMP database to store network device configuration settings for all the devices on the network in a single place. This makes SNMP supple in the network environment, but also makes the SNMP database more convoluted.

SNMP Commands

SNMP uses the MIB database to do the work, rather than using a large set of commands to control network devices. Every controllable aspect of the network device is given a record in the database. SNMP takes care of the retrieval and setting up of the database values, rather than having to interpret lots of individual commands to perform actions on the network device.

Use of the MIB database reduces the complexity of the SNMP packets. Each part of an SNMP command is called a *Protocol Data Unit* (PDU). In Version 1 of the SNMP, there are five types of PDUs that are used for retrieval and setting database values on network devices; these are as follows:

- `GetRequest`: This PDU queries the remote SNMP device for a single data value in the MIB database.
- `GetNextRequest`: The `GetNextRequest` PDU is used to query the remote SNMP device for a series of data values starting at a specified point in the MIB. As each data value is returned, the next MIB object in the series is returned to point the querying device to the next related object in the query. This helps SNMP clients to navigate through the entire table of MIB database entries on the remote SNMP device.
- `GetResponse`: This PDU returns the information that was requested in a `GetRequest` or `GetNextRequest` query.
- `SetRequest`: The `SetRequest` PDU sets a value in the MIB database on the remote SNMP device. The sending device should have the proper access authority to write to the remote device MIB database.
- `Trap`: This PDU sends an impetuous data value to a remote SNMP management post. It is used for allowing devices to report error conditions automatically to a central management station on the network, without having to be constantly queried.

Community Names

SNMP provides a method of authentication through the *community name* system, in order to prevent the modification of a network device's MIB database by an unauthorized user.

An SNMP application running on a network device contains an individual MIB database. The community name is the password that grants a specific access level to particular area in the MIB database. Community names can grant access levels to various MIB databases. SNMP allows two access modes to the MIB database elements; these are read-only, and read-write.

The pairing of an SNMP with an SNMP MIB view is called a *community profile*. The pairing of a community name with a community profile is called an *SNMP access policy*.

The community name is described as a byte string. Two of the famous community names are public (for read-only access) and private (for read-write access).

Common Management Information Base (MIB)

The Common MIB is the standard database used for SNMP implementations on network devices. It was first defined in RFC 1155 and provides for a set database format for network devices.

MIB Structure

The MIB uses a treelike hierarchical database structure that describes data records as *objects*. Each object is referenced by an object identifier, and each object has an object value.

The object identifier follows the Abstract Syntax Notation, version 1 (ASN.1) naming convention. This syntax assigns a numerical value to each object and references objects in the tree based on a hierarchical naming convention. The naming convention is similar to the way DNS names are referenced, with dots separating name levels, except that for SNMP the root node is specified first.

In SNMP, the root object is named as `iso`, which is an acronym for the International Organization for Standardization. The `iso` is termed as an object identifier of `1`.

All MIB entries are located under the `iso` object. The `iso` object has a child node called `org`, which is referenced by name (`iso.org`) or by its object identifier (`1.3`).

The third-level object, `dod`, has an object identifier of `1.3.6`.

■ **NOTE** The Internet Activities Board (IAB) assigns all MIB object identifiers under the `Internet` object.

Every child node under an object is dispensed with a unique object identifier in this way. To refer to an individual object, it's necessary to list every object identifier for each object level, starting at the top level.

MIB Object Values

Once the object identifier of the information is recognized, it is then necessary to use the data retrieved. In order to do this, you need to know the way the information is stored in the database—which means it's time for us to start looking at packets again.

SNMP Packets

Each of the SNMP packets is described as a *sequence*. This sequence has three basic parts:

- The SNMP version number
- The community name used for the query
- The SNMP Protocol Data Unit (SNMP PDU)

Version and community name are at the beginning of SNMP packets. The beginning of an SNMP packet is standard for all PDU types. The version number is always set to zero for an SNMP version 1 packet. The community name is also standard for all PDU types. Every character in the community name is placed in a byte. However, if the community name passed in the SNMP packet is invalid, there will be no response from the network device.

The SNMP PDU is the final part of the packet sequence. This holds the information specific to the PDU type of the packet. There is only one PDU section contained by an SNMP packet, since only one PDU type can be present.

There are five PDU types of SNMP version 1, which have their own formats. Three of these PDU types use the same PDU format however, and these are `GetRequest`, `GetNextRequest`, and `GetResponse`.

SMTP Class

You already know enough about SNMP packets to get up and working, so let's build an SNMP class. This class will simply get the SNMP system name, but it will require many of the same techniques, with differences for SNMP, that you saw in the discussion of ICMP.

So the SNMP class that I've built to show you here is a little different from the ICMP class developed earlier. Most importantly, you'll notice that in an SNMP class, you don't know the set byte format for the SNMP packet. This makes it difficult to build a class constructor, and you need to build the packet on the fly. You'll also see that you need to send and receive the SNMP packets within a method.

Three pieces of information need to be packed inside the SNMP packet. These are the PDU Type, the MIB Object Identifier to Query, and the Valid Community name to gain access to the MIB database. Once the packet is built, it is sent of course—and then the return information is unpacked and the return data examined.

■ **NOTE** The SNMP class I'm going to build here has a single method named `GetSNMP`. This method can be split into four parts and I will explain each part in detail as I go along so that you can follow the technique I am using with SNMP here.

In the first part of this SNMP class, I convert the MIB object identifier into a byte array. The MIB object, which is in string format, will be converted to integer format, and then individually converted into a 16-bit signed integer. If this value fits into a single byte, it is placed in the byte array without any change; otherwise, if it requires two bytes, then the high byte is placed first in the packet, followed by the low byte. Here then is the first part of this class; I have included further comments so you can follow the code.

```
int iSnmpLength;
int iCommunityLength = Community.Length;
int ibyteMIBLength = byteMIBvals.Length;
int iCount = 0;
int iTemp;
int i;
int iInitialbyteMIBLength = ibyteMIBLength;
```

```
int iPosition = 0;
string[] byteMIBvals = MIBData.Split('.');
byte[] bytePacket = new byte[1024];
byte[] byteMIB = new byte[1024];

// Convert the string byteMIB into a byte array of integer values
for (i = 0; i < iInitialbyteMIBLength; i++)
{
  iTemp = Convert.ToInt16(byteMIBvals[i]);
  if (iTemp > 127)
  {
    byteMIB[iCount] = Convert.ToByte(128 + (iTemp / 128));
    byteMIB[iCount + 1] = Convert.ToByte
            (iTemp - ((iTemp / 128) * 128);
    iCount += 2;
    ibyteMIBLength++;
  }
  else
  {
    byteMIB[iCount] = Convert.ToByte(iTemp);
    iCount++;
  }
}
```

Once the byte array of the MIB object identifier is built for the PDU, you then need to create the entire package. You add each SNMP packet individually to the packet byte array. You'll be placing the community name into this byte array, but first convert the string and add it to the byte array through a loop (as you did in the MIB byte array conversion).

In order to make the `SNMPGet` method work with both the `GetRequest` and `GetNextRequest` type, you collect a request parameter for the method, and set the packet value according to that parameter:

```
// Length of entire SNMP bytePacket
iSnmpLength = 29 + iCommunityLength + ibyteMIBLength - 1;

// The SNMP sequence start
bytePacket[iPosition++] = 0x30; //Sequence start
bytePacket[iPosition++] = Convert.ToByte(iSnmpLength - 2);

// Sequence size
// SNMP version
bytePacket[iPosition++] = 0x02; // Integer type
bytePacket[iPosition++] = 0x01; // Length
bytePacket[iPosition++] = 0x00; // SNMP version 1

// Community name
bytePacket[iPosition++] = 0x04; // String type
bytePacket[iPosition++] = Convert.ToByte(iCommunityLength);
```

```
// Length
// Convert community name to byte array
byte[] data = Encoding.ASCII.GetBytes(Community);
for (i = 0; i < data.Length; i++)
{
      bytePacket[iPosition++] = data[i];
}

// Add GetRequest or GetNextRequest value
if (Request == "GetRequest")
      bytePacket[iPosition++] = 0xA0;
else
      bytePacket[iPosition++] = 0xA1;
bytePacket[iPosition++] = Convert.ToByte(20 + ibyteMIBLength - 1);

// Size of total byteMIB
//Request ID
bytePacket[iPosition++] = 0x02; // Integer type
bytePacket[iPosition++] = 0x04;
bytePacket[iPosition++] = 0x00; // SNMP Request ID
bytePacket[iPosition++] = 0x00;
bytePacket[iPosition++] = 0x00;
bytePacket[iPosition++] = 0x01;

// Error status
bytePacket[iPosition++] = 0x02; //Integer type
bytePacket[iPosition++] = 0x01; bytePacket[iPosition++] = 0x00;

// SNMP error status
// Error index
bytePacket[iPosition++] = 0x02; // Integer type
bytePacket[iPosition++] = 0x01; // Length
bytePacket[iPosition++] = 0x00; // SNMP error index

// Start of variable bindings
bytePacket[iPosition++] = 0x30;
bytePacket[iPosition++] = Convert.ToByte(6 + ibyteMIBLength - 1);

// Size of variable binding
bytePacket[iPosition++] = 0x30; bytePacket[iPosition++] = Convert.ToByte(6 +
ibyteMIBLength - 1 - 2); // Size
bytePacket[iPosition++] = 0x06; // Object type
bytePacket[iPosition++] = Convert.ToByte(ibyteMIBLength - 1);

// Start of byteMIB
bytePacket[iPosition++] = 0x2b;
```

```
// Place byteMIB array in bytePacket
for(i = 2; i < ibyteMIBLength; i++)
      bytePacket[iPosition++] = Convert.ToByte(byteMIB[i]);
bytePacket[iPosition++] = 0x05;    //Null object value
bytePacket[iPosition++] = 0x00;    //Null
```

After creating the package, send the packet using the Socket class available in the namespace System.Net.Socket. Here you use the UDP protocol type with port 161. You use the Socket class's ReceiveFrom method to get the response from the server. Here is the code:

```
// Send bytePacket to destination
Socket sock = new Socket(AddressFamily.InterNetwork, SocketType.Dgram,
ProtocolType.Udp);
sock.SetSocketOption(SocketOptionLevel.Socket,
      SocketOptionName.ReceiveTimeout, 5000);
IPHostEntry ihe = Dns.Resolve(Host);
IPEndPoint iep = new IPEndPoint(ihe.AddressList[0], 161);
EndPoint ep = (EndPoint)iep;
sock.SendTo(bytePacket, iSnmpLength, SocketFlags.None, iep);

// Receive response from bytePacket
try
{
  int recv = sock.ReceiveFrom(bytePacket, ref ep);
}
catch (SocketException)
{
  bytePacket[0] = 0xff;
}
return bytePacket;
```

Next you'll build a simple test program that helps to get the system name using the SNMP class. Comments are inline, and I'll describe what's going on in more detail at the end; here's the code:

```
public static void Main(string[] argv)
{
  if(argv.Length<2) return;
  string strInfo = string.Empty ;
  int iCommLength;
  int iMIBLength;
  int iDataType;
  int iDataLength;
  int iStartData;
  byte[] byteResponse = new byte[1024];
  SNMP objSNMP = new SNMP();
```

```
  Console.WriteLine("SNMP information:");

  // Setting the parameter for GetRequest method
  // and getting the byteResponse
  byteResponse = objSNMP.SNMPGet
            ("GetRequest", argv[0], argv[1],
           "1.3.6.1.2.1.1.5.0");
  if (byteResponse[0] == 0xff)
  {
    Console.WriteLine("No Response Received from {0}", argv[0]);
    return;
  }

// Get the community name and MIB lengths
// from the packet
  iCommLength = Convert.ToInt16(byteResponse[6]);
  iMIBLength = Convert.ToInt16
           (byteResponse[23 + iCommLength]);

// Decode the MIB data from the SNMP byteResponse
  iDataType = Convert.ToInt16(byteResponse
           [24 + iCommLength + iMIBLength]);
  iDataLength = Convert.ToInt16(byteResponse
           [25 + iCommLength + iMIBLength]);
  iStartData = 26 + iCommLength + iMIBLength;
  strinfo = Encoding.ASCII.GetString
           (byteResponse, iStartData, iDataLength);
  Console.WriteLine(" sysName - iDataType:
           {0}, Value: {1}",
  iDataType, strInfo);
}
```

Here you pass the SysName object identifier, community name, and the network IP along with the Request Type parameter. Once the parameters are passed, you receive the response packet that needs to be decoded. First you need for this to get the community name length and MIB length. Community name length is easy to get since it is in the same spot in the packet. The MIB length depends upon the community name length. Next you need to get the data type length. It is simple enough to get the string's data type length in the case of SysName, since it returns a string data type.

You can test this program against any network device or hub that supports SNMP. You can also test it with Windows NT and Windows 2000/2003 OS. But in Windows OS, SNMP is not preinstalled, so you will need to install it as a Windows component through the usual Management and Monitoring Tools options.

Summary

The Internet Control Message Protocol is used by a network utility for communicating with the remote host on the network. The Internet Protocol is used for a host-to-host datagram service in a system of interconnected networks. Occasionally a destination host communicates with a source host and reports an error in datagram processing. ICMP is used for this purpose. Some networking utilities such as `ping` and `traceroute` are based on the ICMP. You saw in this chapter how to use raw socket programming techniques to build your own `PingHost` class and `TraceRoute` utility, once you understood how ICMP packets are organized and the building block techniques of how to send, receive, and format ICMP packets.

The Simple Network Management Protocol (SNMP) is used for network administration. SNMP is used to query and control network devices from a central management station. In this chapter, you looked at SNMP and how it requires different techniques from ICMP to code against. I've shown you how to build a simple SNMP class through to the end of this chapter, which allowed you to compare and contrast the coding techniques for SNMP against ICMP.

CHAPTER 6

■ ■ ■

IPv6

The Internet Protocol (IP) is the foundation of every networked-based application in the world. The current version, Internet Protocol version 4 (IPv4), has several unanticipated design issues. Internet Protocol version 6 (IPv6) is the next-generation protocol and resolves the design issues of IPv4.

In 1990, the Internet Engineering Task Force (IETF) started working on a new version of IPv6, also known as Next Generation Internet Protocol (IPng). Now several application vendors have started their application development in IPv6, including Microsoft.

Microsoft has introduced IPv6 in several products, including Windows Server 2003, Internet Explorer 6.0, IIS, RPC, .NET Framework, and Visual Studio .NET. Microsoft has also launched beta service packs that include IPv6 for Windows Server 2000 and Windows XP Professional. Currently, Microsoft and other companies are working to integrate IPv6 in other applications for more efficient and effective wireless communications. Microsoft promises to give strong IPv6 features and support in Longhorn and the next generation of application development tools, technologies, and languages. In this chapter, we will use Windows Server 2003 for demonstrating how to work with IPv6.

In this chapter, we'll discuss the following topics:

- Key features and differences between IPv4 and IPv6
- An introduction to IPv6
- How to install, configure, and verify IPv6 on Microsoft Windows 2003
- .NET support for IPv6, with some coding examples

The Need for a New Protocol

The current protocol, IPv4, has existed for the past 20 years. It now has problems related to address depletion, security, auto-configuration, extensibility, and more.

Network addresses are used to uniquely identify a node, usually a host or a router, on a network. Currently, every machine connected to the Internet using IPv4 has a unique IP address. This IP address has maximum limit of 32 bits and is displayed in human-readable decimal form as *xxx.xxx.xxx.xxx* (for example, 255.255.255.255) and gives 4,294,967,296 (2^{32}) unique values.

Although Network Address Translation (NAT) allows a certain number of machines on a private network to share one public IP address, according to the IETF, IPv4 addresses will be exhausted sometime around the year 2008.

Therefore, in 1992, the IETF began efforts to find a next-generation protocol for the Internet. Two years later, Simple Internet Protocol Plus (SIPP) was adopted and, in 1995, it was named Internet Protocol version 6 (IPv6). IPv6 is designed to overcome the core limitations of IPv4. An IPv6 address is displayed in human-readable hexadecimal form as follows:

```
xxxx:xxxx:xxxx:xxxx:xxxx:xxxx:xxxx:xxxx
```

where each divided bit can have a maximum decimal store of 65,535 or hex FFFF (16 bits). This means an IPv6 address is 128 bits long, allowing 3.4x1038 (2^{128}) unique values!

Moreover, the IPv6 offers scalability, increased security features, a Cluster Address field (which identifies topological regions), real-time traffic support, and auto-configuration (so that even a novice user can connect a machine to the Internet).

So, with that historical introduction established, let's now take a look at the various features that IPv6 offers for the future.

Features of IPv6

The IPv6 feature set is designed to overcome the weaknesses of IPv4. Here are the key features of IPv6:

- New header format, large address space, thereby supporting billions of hosts, even with inefficient address space allocation
- Efficient and hierarchical addressing and routing infrastructure, thereby reducing the size of the routing table
- Built-in security, thus providing better security, authentication, and confidentiality of data at the IP level
- Support for multicasting
- Support for auto-configuration
- Better support for quality of service (QoS) needed by multimedia applications
- Backward compatibility, so that the old and new versions of IP can coexist

Table 6-1 summarizes the differences between IPv4 and IPv6.

Table 6-1. *Differences Between IPv4 and IPv6*

Feature	IPv4	IPv6
IP address length	32 bits (4 bytes)	128 bits (16 bytes)
IPSec support	Optional.	Must
Packet flow identification	No identification of packet flow for QoS.	Packet flow identification for QoS
Fragmentation	Done by both routers and the sending host.	Done by only the sending host.
Header checksum	Present	Not present in header
Optional data	Present in header	Present in IPv6 extension headers
Link-layer address resolution	Address Resolution Protocol (ARP)	Multicast Neighbor Discovery (MND) messages
Group Management	Internet Group Management Protocol (IGMP) used to manage local subnet group membership	Multicast Listener Discovery (MLD) messages used to manage local subnet group membership
Broadcast addresses	Used to send traffic to all nodes on a subnet	Not used; a link-local scope all-nodes multicast address used instead
IP configuration	Must be configured either manually or through DHCP	Does not require manual configuration or DHCP
DNS name queries	Use A records	Use AAAA or A6 records
DNS reverse queries	Use IN-ADDR.ARPA	Use IP6.INT or IP6.ARPA
Packet size support (MTU)	576-byte (possibly fragmented).	1280-byte (without fragmentation)

■ NOTE For more details on the differences between IPv4 and IPv6, see `http://www.microsoft.com/technet/prodtechnol/winxppro/maintain/xpmanaged/15_xpip6.mspx`.

The following sections discuss the IPv6 header and addressing.

The IPv6 Header

In Chapter 1, we examined the IPv4 header, which is illustrated in Figure 6-1. If you compare the IPv4 header to the IPv6 header, shown in Figure 6-2, you'll see that the IPv6 header is simplified by eliminating unnecessary fields. This allows for more efficient processing. The IPv4 header has a variable length of 20 bytes, whereas IPv6 has a fixed length of 40 bytes.

4 bit Version	4 bit Header Length	8 bit (TOS) Type of Service	16 bit Total Length	
16 bit Identification			3 bit Flag	13 bit Fragment Offset
8 bit TTl		8 bit Protocol	16 bit Header Checksum	
32 bit Source Address				
32 bit Destination Address				

Figure 6-1. *The IPv4 header*

6 bit Version	8 bit Traffic class	20 bit Flow Label	
16 bit Payload Length		8 bit Next Header	8 bit Hop Limit
128 bit Source Address			
128 bit Destination Address			

Figure 6-2. *The IPv6 header*

IPv6 Addressing

IPv6 uses the 128-bit addressing model, using more space than 32-bit IPv4 addresses. In this section, we'll look at IPv6 address representation and various address types.

IPv6 Address Representation

The three forms of address representation are colon-hexadecimal form, compressed form, and mixed form. Let's first look at the colon-hexadecimal form.

Colon-Hexadecimal Form

IPv6 addresses are represented in hexadecimal format, making them easier to read than IPv4 addresses. For example, an IPv4 decimal address might look like this:

```
26312.423.256.61020.65535.55234.6123.56432
```

The IPv6 representation in colon-hexadecimal format would look like this:

```
66CB:01A7:0100:EE5C:FFFF:D7C2:17EB:DC70
```

Typical IPv6 addresses consist of eight groups of 16-bit hexadecimal values, separated by colons, in the following format:

```
xxxx:xxxx:xxxx:xxxx:xxxx:xxxx:xxxx:xxxx
```

where *xxxx* is a 16-bit hexadecimal value, and each *x* is a 4-bit hexadecimal value.

The maximum IP address for IPv6 is as follows:

```
FFFF:FFFF:FFFF:FFFF:FFFF:FFFF:FFFF:FFFF
```

Here is an example of an actual IPv6 address in this form:

```
80FF:10FE:0E00:00FF:0000:0000:0000:0001
```

Compressed Form

As well as colon-hexadecimal form, an IPv6 address can be in a compressed form. To minimize the address length, you can omit the leading zeros. Therefore, the previous address example:

```
80FF:10FE:0E00:00FF:0000:0000:0000:0001
```

can be compressed to become:

```
80FF:10FE:E00:FF:0:0:0:1
```

To reduce the size of the address even further, you can compress 16-bit groups of zeros to `::`. Our address example can thus be further compressed to become:

```
80FF:10FE:E00:FF::1
```

Note that the symbol `::` appears only once in an address.

Mixed Form

The mixed form consists of a combination of an IPv6 and IPv4 address, in this format:

```
x:x:x:x:x:x:d:d:d:d
```

where each *x* represents the hexadecimal values of the six IPv6 high-order 16-bit address elements, and each *d* represents the decimal value of an IPv4 address.

IPv6 Address Types

IPv6 has several address types, which can be identified by the leading bits in an address, called the format prefix (FP). The various IPv6 addresses and their subtypes include unicast, multicast, and anycast. Table 6-2 shows examples of the address types in colon-hexadecimal and compressed formats. These types are described in more detail in the following sections.

Table 6-2. *IPv6 Address Type Examples*

Address Type	Colon-Hexadecimal Form	Compressed Form
Multicast	FFED:0:0:0:0:BA98:3210:4562	FFED::BA98:3210:4562
Unicast	3FFE:FFFF:0:0:8:800:20C4:0	3FFE:FFFF::8:800:20C4:0
Loopback	0:0:0:0:0:0:0:1	::1
Anycast (unspecified)	0:0:0:0:0:0:0:0	::

Unicast Addresses

A *unicast address* is a typical IP address that denotes a single host interface. There are several forms of unicast addresses, depending on scope. These include the neutral-interconnect unicast address, NSAP address, IPX hierarchical address, link-local address, site-local address, and global address. The following are some of the most common IPv6 addresses

- :*Link-local address*: These addresses never pass through router and are valid only on a single link of an interface. Link-local addresses are prefixed with FE8*x*, FE9*x*, FEA*x*, or FEB*x*. FE80 is the only one in use at the time of writing. Link-local addresses are equivalent to Automatic Private IP Addressing (APIPA) addresses. They are automatically configured for each interface. These addresses are used when you start your system and it has not yet acquired its addresses. Link-local addresses are also used to check who is present on this link.

- *Site-local address*: These addresses are used for addressing internally within the single site of an organization. They are prefixed with FEC*x*, FED*x*, FEE*x*, or FEF*x*. FEC0 is most commonly used at the time of writing. Site-local addresses are equivalent to private IPv4 addresses.

- *Global address*: These addresses are public addresses and used for IPv6 Internet. Global addresses are equivalent to public IPv4 addresses.

Multicast Addresses

A *multicast address* is an identifier for a group of addresses, and it's used for broadcasting. The multicast address can be defined based on geographical location, network location, and other information—which is not possible with IPv4. A multicast address sends packets to all associated interfaces. The multicast addresses are also used to transmit streams of video, audio, and other group data.

Anycast Address

An *anycast address* is assigned to more than one interface. The packet sent to an anycast address is routed to the nearest interfaces, such as the nearest DNS server, DHCP server, or other arbitrary groups having that address. The anycast address provides a flexible, cost-effective model for enabling application robustness and load balancing. Anycasting is a feature of IPv6 and architecturally not available in IPv4.

Installing IPv6 on Windows Server 2003

The first prerequisite for installing IPv6 is, of course, to make sure you have the appropriate privileges to change your network configuration.

As noted at the beginning of this chapter, the Windows Server 2003 family has support for IPv6. You can install the IPv6 protocol for Windows Server 2003 in two ways: by using the `netsh` command or through the Local Connection Properties dialog box. Let's look at each of these methods.

Installing IPv6 with the netsh Command

To install IPv6 using the `netsh` command, at the command prompt, type the following command:

```
netsh interface ipv6 install
```

When the system successfully installs IPv6, it prints `Ok` at the command prompt. You can verify the installation using the `ping` or `ipconfig` command.

Here is an example of the output of the `netsh interface ipv6 install` command and then the `ipconfig` command:

```
C:\>netsh interface ipv6 install
Ok.

C:\>ipconfig

Windows IP Configuration

Ethernet adapter Local Area Connection:

   Connection-specific DNS Suffix  . : localdomain
   IP Address. . . . . . . . . . . . : 192.168.19.131
   Subnet Mask . . . . . . . . . . . : 255.255.255.0
   IP Address. . . . . . . . . . . . : fe80::20c:29ff:fe5e:bb71%4
   Default Gateway . . . . . . . . . :

Tunnel adapter Automatic Tunneling Pseudo-Interface:

   Connection-specific DNS Suffix  . : localdomain
   IP Address. . . . . . . . . . . . : fe80::5efe:192.168.19.131%2
   Default Gateway . . . . . . . . . :
```

To uninstall IPv6, you can use the following command:

```
netsh interface ipv6 uninstall
```

Note that you must restart the server for your changes to take effect.

Installing IPv6 through Local Area Connection Properties

To install IPv6 through the Local Area Connection Properties dialog box, follow these steps:

1. Right-click the My Network Places icon on your desktop and click Properties.
2. You will see a new window, showing all the connections for your server. Right-click Local Area Connection and select Properties.
3. Click the Install button. In the Select Network Component Type dialog box, click Protocol, and then click Add.
4. In the Select Network Protocol dialog box, select Microsoft TCP/IP version 6, and then click OK. Microsoft TCP/IP version 6 should now be listed in the Local Area Connection Properties dialog box, as shown in Figure 6-3.
5. Close the window to save your changes, and then restart the system.

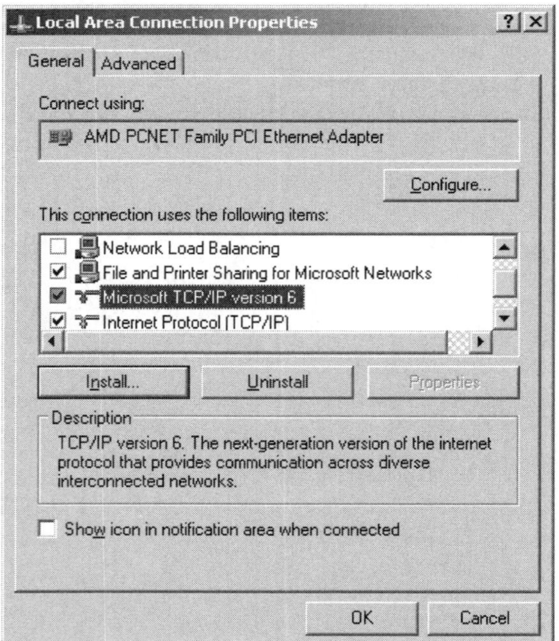

Figure 6-3. *Installing IPv6*

To uninstall IPv6, select the Microsoft TCP/IP version 6 entry in the Local Area Connection Properties dialog box, and then click the Uninstall button.

Verifying IPv6 Configuration

In Windows Server 2003, the Local Area Connection Properties dialog box shows the protocols installed on your machine. Verify that the Microsoft TCP/IP version 6 is present and checked in this dialog box, as shown in Figure 6-3.

Alternatively, you can check that the IPv6 protocol is installed by using the `ping` or `ipconfig` command. To ping the loopback IPv6 address, use `ping ::1`. The `::1` indicates that you are pinging to a loopback address; that is, the local host address. The `ping ::1` command doesn't work if you have not installed IPv6 properly on your machine.

Here is the output of the `ping` command:

```
C:\>ping ::1

Pinging ::1 from ::1 with 32 bytes of data:

Reply from ::1: time<1ms
Reply from ::1: time<1ms
Reply from ::1: time<1ms
Reply from ::1: time<1ms

Ping statistics for ::1:
    Packets: Sent = 4, Received = 4, Lost = 0 (0% loss),
Approximate round trip times in milli-seconds:
    Minimum = 0ms, Maximum = 0ms, Average = 0ms
```

.NET Support for IPv6

Microsoft .NET version 1.1 supports IPv6 and offers various interfaces that will communicate with IPv6. .NET 1.1 supports IPv6 for the following functions:

- Sockets
- DNS
- HTTP
- XML web services
- ASP.NET and managed applications

To use IPv6 in .NET, you must first make sure that you have installed IPv6 on your machine, as discussed in the previous section. Next, you will need to change settings in the machine configuration file for your system to enable IPv6.

Enabling IPv6 in Machine.config

For .NET applications, you need to enable IPv6 through your machine.config file. Go to the .NET machine configuration directory, typically located in the Windows root directory at %Windir%\Framework\version\CONFIG, such as:

```
C:\WINDOWS\Microsoft.NET\Framework\v1.1.4322\CONFIG
```

Next, open the machine.config file and change <ipv6 enabled=false/> to <ipv6 enabled=true/>, as shown in Figure 6-4.

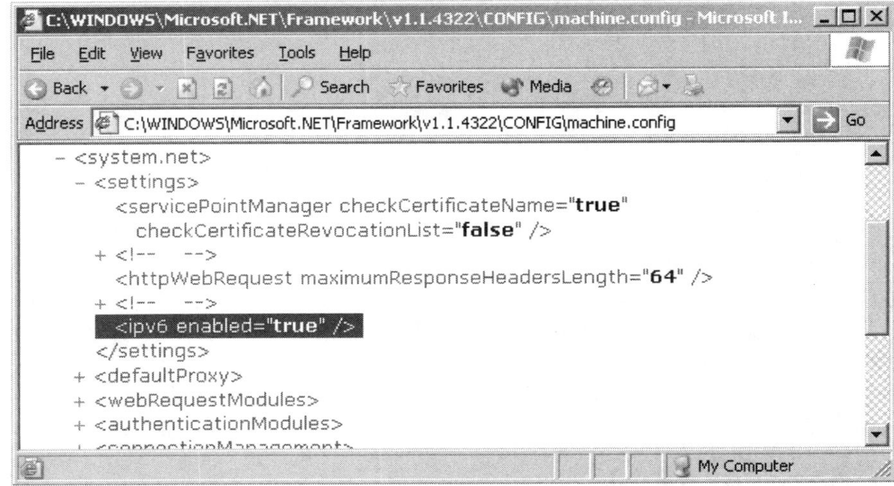

Figure 6-4. *Enabling IPv6 in the machine.config file*

Note that when you make changes to the machine configuration file, your .NET application can use the IPv4 programming interfaces. Also, if you want your application to support only IPv4, you can make changes in the app.config file, as follows

```
<settings>
                    <ipv6 enabled=false/>
</settings>
```

In the next section, you'll see various classes and methods specific to the IPv6, as well as some examples of how to use them in your applications.

Reviewing IPAddress Class Support for IPv6

In previous chapters, you have seen the IPAddress class in use. Now we'll take a look at various IPAddress interfaces that support IPv6:

- AddressFamily property
- IPv6Any field

- `IPv6Loopback` field
- `IPv6None` field
- `IsLoopback` method
- `Parse` method
- `ScopeId` property

The code in Listing 6-1 demonstrates the use of the various interfaces available for IPv6.

Listing 6-1. *IPv6 Interfaces*

```
using System;
using System.Net ;
using System.Net.Sockets;

namespace ipv6
{
  public class ipv6details
  {
    public static void getIPV6details()
    {
      try
      {
        if (!Socket.SupportsIPv6)
        {
          Console.WriteLine ("Your System Doesn't Support IPV6 \r\nCheck
          you have IPv6 enabled and have changed machine.config");
        }
        else
        {
          Console.WriteLine ("Your System Supports IPV6");

          // Display the server Any address.
          Console.WriteLine("\r\nServer Any address - IPv6Any = " +
      IPAddress.IPv6Any.ToString());

          // Display the server default loopback address.
          Console.WriteLine("Server loopback address - IPv6Loopback = " +
      IPAddress.IPv6Loopback.ToString());

          // Used during auto-configuration first phase.
          Console.WriteLine("None address in standard compressed format -
      IPv6None = " + IPAddress.IPv6None.ToString());

          // Check whether the current address is loopback address.
          Console.WriteLine("Is current address is loopback address -
```

```
    IsLoopback = " + IPAddress.IsLoopback(IPAddress.IPv6Loopback));

        Console.WriteLine("\n--------------------------------\n");

        // Get other server related information.
        IPHostEntry hostServ = Dns.Resolve (Dns.GetHostName());

        // Loop on the AddressList.
        foreach (IPAddress currentAdr in hostServ.AddressList)
        {
          // Display the type of address family supported by the server.
          Console.WriteLine("AddressFamily of Server = " +
        currentAdr.AddressFamily.ToString());

          // Display the ScopeId property for IPV6 addresses.
          if(currentAdr.AddressFamily.ToString() ==
        ProtocolFamily.InterNetworkV6.ToString())
            Console.WriteLine("Scope Id = " +
        currentAdr.ScopeId.ToString());


          // Display the server IP address in the standard format.
          Console.WriteLine("Server IP address in the standard format ="
         + currentAdr.ToString());

          // Display the server IP address in byte format.
          Console.Write("Server IP address in the byte format = ");

          Byte[] bytes = currentAdr.GetAddressBytes();
          for (int i = 0; i < bytes.Length; i++)
          {
            Console.Write(bytes[i]);
          }

          Console.WriteLine("\r\n");

        }
      }
    }
    catch(Exception Er)
    {
      Console.WriteLine(Er.ToString());
    }
  }
  public static void Main(string[] args)
  {
    getIPV6details();
```

```
        }
    }
}
```

Figure 6-5 shows the output of this code.

```
C:\IPv6.exe
Your System Supports IPV6

Server Any address - IPv6Any = ::
Server loopback address - IPv6Loopback = ::1
None address in standard compressed format - IPv6None = ::
Is current address is loopback address - IsLoopback = True

-------------------------------

AddressFamily of Server = InterNetworkV6
Scope Id = 0
Server IP address in the standard format = fe80::20c:29ff:fe5e:bb71
Server IP address in the byte format = 2541280000002124125525494187113

AddressFamily of Server = InterNetworkV6
Scope Id = 0
Server IP address in the standard format = fe80::1
Server IP address in the byte format = 25412800000000000001

AddressFamily of Server = InterNetworkV6
Scope Id = 0
Server IP address in the standard format = fe80::5efe:192.168.19.131
Server IP address in the byte format = 254128000000009425419216819131

AddressFamily of Server = InterNetwork
Server IP address in the standard format = 192.168.19.131
Server IP address in the byte format = 19216819131
```

Figure 6-5. *Using IPv6 interfaces*

NOTE Other than the `IPAddress` class, some other networking classes like `Socket` and `IPv6Multicast-Option` support IPv6. These are discussed later in this chapter. Using the `Sockets` class is demonstrated in the "Creating an IPv6-Based Client/Server Application" section, and using `IPv6MulticastOption` is demonstrated in the "The IPv6MulticastOption Class" section.

AddressFamily

The `AddressFamily` property of the `IPAddress` class returns the family of the IP address. This property returns `InterNetwork` for IPv4 or `InterNetworkV6` for IPv6. While creating an instance of the `Socket` class, this property is used to resolve an address. The following code displays the `AddressFamily` property of the system:

```
// Display the type of address family supported by the server.
Console.WriteLine("AddressFamily of Server = " +
currentAdr.AddressFamily.ToString());
```

IPv6Any

The Socket class uses the IPv6Any field to listen for a client on all network interfaces. The IPv6Any field is equivalent to 0:0:0:0:0:0:0:0 in colon-hexadecimal notation, or to :: in compact notation. The following code prints the IPv6Any address at the command prompt:

```
// Display the server Any address.
Console.WriteLine("\r\nServer Any address - IPv6Any = " +
IPAddress.IPv6Any.ToString());
```

IPv6Loopback

IPv6Loopback is a read-only field that returns the IP loopback address. It is equivalent to 0:0:0:0:0:0:0:1 in colon-hexadecimal notation and to ::1 in compact notation. The following code displays the system's default loopback address:

```
// Display the server default loopback address.
Console.WriteLine("Server loopback address - IPv6Loopback = " +
IPAddress.IPv6Loopback.ToString());
```

IPv6None

The IPv6None read-only field is used with the Socket class to indicate that it should not listen for client activity; that is, the IP address provided by this field indicates that no network interface should be used. The IPv6None field is equivalent to 0:0:0:0:0:0:0:0 in colon-hexadecimal notation and to ::0 in compact notation. The following code shows the IPv6None output at the command prompt.

```
// Used during auto-configuration first phase.
Console.WriteLine("None address in standard compressed format - IPv6None = " +
IPAddress.IPv6None.ToString());
```

IsLoopback

The IsLoopback method checks whether the specified IP address is the loopback address and returns a Boolean value. It returns true if the address is loopback address; otherwise, it returns false. The following command checks whether the specified IP address is the loopback address and returns true or false.

```
// Check whether the current address is loopback address.
Console.WriteLine("Is current address is loopback address - IsLoopback = " +
IPAddress.IsLoopback(IPAddress.IPv6Loopback));
```

Parse

The Parse method is used to convert an IP address in string format to an IPAddress instance. IPv6 addresses are hexadecimal, and therefore a string containing an IP address should be in colon-hexadecimal notation.

```
//An example of a valid address is fe80:0000:0000:0011:0260:0300:93ff:62cc
Console.Writeline ("Enter IP to Parse");
string sendIPv6Addr = Console.Readline();
IPAddress ip = IPAddress.Parse(sendIPv6Addr);
```

ScopeId

The `ScopeId` property is used to set or to get IPv6 address scope identifier. This property has a different meaning depending on the address scope. For example, for site-local addresses, the `ScopeId` property indicates the site identifier; for link-local addresses, it indicates the interface identifier.

Creating an IPv6-Based Client/Server Application

In Chapter 4, you learned how to use socket for IPv4 based client-server model. In this section, you'll see how to use the `Socket` class and IPv6 interfaces to create a client/server application.

The code we'll look at here demonstrates how to pass text from the client to the server. The entire code is divided in two parts. The first part is an IPv6-based server, which uses the `Socket` class for receiving text from the second part of code, which is the client. So let's start with the server.

Creating an IPv6 Server

Listing 6-2 shows the code for the IPv6-based server.

Listing 6-2. *IPv6 Server*

```
using System;
using System.Text ;
using System.Net.Sockets;
using System.Net;

namespace IPV6Server
{
  class server
  {

    [STAThread]
    static void Main(string[] args)
    {

      const int receivingPort = 5001;
      if(!Socket.SupportsIPv6)
      {
        Console.Error.WriteLine("Your system does not support IPv6");
        return;
      }
```

```
        Socket receiver = new Socket(
          AddressFamily.InterNetworkV6,
          SocketType.Stream,
          ProtocolType.Tcp);

        receiver.Bind(new IPEndPoint(IPAddress.IPv6Any, receivingPort));
        receiver.Listen(0);
        Socket socket = receiver.Accept();

        Console.WriteLine ("<< Received Data >>");

        string recvData;
        do
        {
          byte[] recvBytes =  new byte[1024];
          int byteLen = socket.Receive (recvBytes);
          recvData=(Encoding.ASCII.GetString(recvBytes,0,byteLen));
          Console.WriteLine (recvData);
        }while(recvData.Length != 0);

        receiver.Close();
        socket.Close();
      }
    }
  }
```

In the code in Listing 6-2, we first check whether the host system supports IPv6 by using the `SupportsIPv6` property, as you can see here:

```
if(!Socket.SupportsIPv6)
{
  Console.Error.WriteLine("Your system does not support IPv6");
  return;
}
```

Next, we create an instance of the `Socket` class. Note that the parameters we use for creating the `Socket` instance are specific to IPv6. The first parameter, `AddressFamily.InterNetworkV6`, indicates that we are creating a connection for IPv6 protocol. The second and third parameters indicate the type of socket and protocol, which are `Stream` and `Tcp`, respectively:

```
Socket receiver = new Socket(
  AddressFamily.InterNetworkV6,
  SocketType.Stream,
  ProtocolType.Tcp);
```

In the next step, we bind the socket for listening and accepting from the specified IP address and port. `IPAddress.IPv6Any` indicates that the socket will listen on all addresses of the system:

```
receiver.Bind(new IPEndPoint(IPAddress.IPv6Any, receivingPort));
receiver.Listen(0);
Socket socket = receiver.Accept();
```

Finally, we process the data that we accepted on the specified port. The data is processed until the client doesn't send a blank character:

```
string recvData;
      do
      {
        byte[] recvBytes =  new byte[1024];
        int byteLen = socket.Receive (recvBytes);
        recvData=(Encoding.ASCII.GetString(recvBytes,0,byteLen));
        Console.WriteLine (recvData);
      }while(recvData.Length != 0);
```

Creating an IPv6 Client

Listing 6-3 shows the complete code for the IPv6-based client.

Listing 6-3. *IPv6 Client*

```
using System;
using System.Net;
using System.Net.Sockets;
using System.Text;

namespace IPV6Client
{
  class client
  {
    [STAThread]
    static void Main(string[] args)
    {
      const int sendPort=5001;
      const string sendIPv6Addr =":;1"; //loopback address

      if(!Socket.SupportsIPv6)
      {
        Console.Error.WriteLine("Your system does not support IPv6");
        return;
      }

      IPAddress ip = IPAddress.Parse(sendIPv6Addr);
      IPEndPoint ipEndPoint = new IPEndPoint(ip, sendPort);

      Socket socketCnn = new Socket(
        AddressFamily.InterNetworkV6,
```

```
          SocketType.Stream,
          ProtocolType.Tcp);

        socketCnn.Connect(ipEndPoint);

        Console.WriteLine ("Enter Data to Send\r\n----------------------");
        bool exitFlag =false;
        do
        {
          byte[] sendByte = Encoding.ASCII.GetBytes(Console.ReadLine() );
          socketCnn.Send(sendByte);
          if (sendByte.Length == 0)
            exitFlag = true;
         }while(!exitFlag);
        socketCnn.Close();
      }
    }
  }
```

In the client code, the first step is the same as in Listing 6-2 for the server: we check for IPv6 support. The second step is to create the IPEndPoint instance using IPAddress. IPEndPoint takes two parameters: the first defines the sending address and the second defines the port:

```
IPAddress ip = IPAddress.Parse(sendIPv6Addr);
IPEndPoint ipEndPoint = new IPEndPoint(ip, sendPort);
```

Next, we create an instance of Socket class, just as we did in the server:

```
Socket socketCnn = new Socket(
  AddressFamily.InterNetworkV6,
  SocketType.Stream,
  ProtocolType.Tcp);
```

The created Socket instance is now used for connecting to the specified address using the Connect method:

```
socketCnn.Connect(ipEndPoint);
```

Finally, the code takes data from the user, processes it, and sends a response using our created Socket instance. To stop the client, the user must press the Enter key without typing any characters:

```
bool exitFlag =false;
do
{
  byte[] sendByte = Encoding.ASCII.GetBytes(Console.ReadLine() );
  socketCnn.Send(sendByte);
  if (sendByte.Length == 0)
    exitFlag = true;
 }while(!exitFlag);
```

Figures 6-6 and 6-7 show the IPv6 server and client in action.

C:\Server\IPV6Server.exe

<< Received Data >>
This is from client!!
I'm using IPv6 !!!!!!

Figure 6-6. *Using the IPv6-based server*

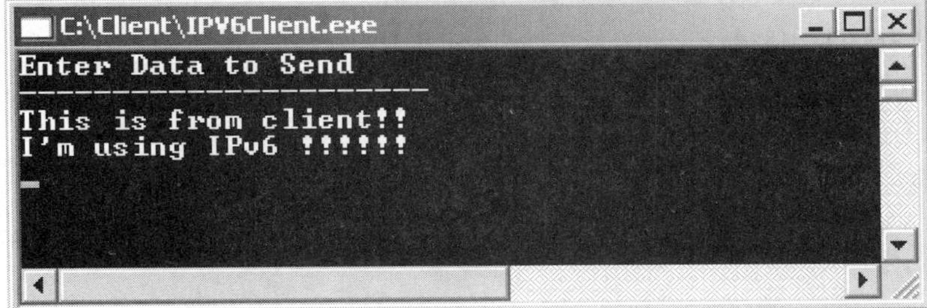

Figure 6-7. *Using the IPv6-based client*

Using the IPv6MulticastOption Class

The `IPv6MulticastOption` class provides options for joining the multicast group. In a normal broadcasting scenario, only one sender sends data to many hosts. In a multicasting scenario, everyone can send data and is visible to everyone else. But by using the `IPv6MulticastOption` class, you can control groups and interfaces of hosts. This is useful for "controlled" multicasting.

The `IPv6MulticastOption` has two properties:

- `Group`: Used to get or set the IP address of multicast group. You can group the various multicast IP addresses for communication.
- `InterfaceIndex`: Used to get or set an index associated with multicast group. The limit for indexes is from 0 to 4294967295.

To understand the `IPv6MulticastOption` class, let's build an example that has a multicast sender and multicast receiver. The sender sends data on a multicast IP address, and the receiver receives data from it. Multicasting is the topic of Chapter 9, so we won't go into the details of the technology here.

Creating a Multicast Sender

Let's start with a walk-through of the sender code. The entire code for the sender is shown in Listing 6-4.

Listing 6-4. *IPv6-based Multicast Sender*

```
using System;
using System.Net;
using System.Net.Sockets;
using System.Text;

namespace multiCastSender
{
  public class multiSender
  {
    static void Main(string[] args)
    {
      try
      {
        // Create UdpClient for sending data with port address and IPv6 address
family.
        UdpClient udpSender = new UdpClient(2000, AddressFamily.InterNetworkV6);

        // Create IPAddress using multicast address.
        IPAddress multiIP = IPAddress.Parse("FF01::1");

        // Instantiate IPv6MulticastOption.
        IPv6MulticastOption mcoIPv6 = new IPv6MulticastOption(multiIP);

         // Join the specified multicast group using interface index and group.
        udpSender.JoinMulticastGroup((int)mcoIPv6.InterfaceIndex, mcoIPv6.Group);

        // Define endpoint for sending data.
         IPEndPoint endpoint = new IPEndPoint(multiIP,1000);

        Console.WriteLine ("Enter data to send\r\n---------------");
        string strData;
        do
        {
          // Get data, process and send to specified port.
          strData=Console.ReadLine();
          byte [] b=Encoding.ASCII.GetBytes(strData);
          udpSender.Send (b,b.Length,endpoint); //send data
        }while(strData!="");

        // Drop multicast group.
        udpSender.DropMulticastGroup(multiIP);
```

```
            }
            catch (Exception e)
            {
              Console.WriteLine (e.ToString());
            }
          }
        }
      }
```

In the code in Listing 6-4, we first create an instance of `UdpClient` by specifying the port address and address family for IPv6. The `InterNetworkV6` enumeration of `AddressFamily` shows that we are using the IPv6 protocol for communication:

```
UdpClient udpSender = new UdpClient(2000, AddressFamily.InterNetworkV6);
```

Next, an instance of `IPAddress` class is created by parsing a multicast address as shown. You can use any valid multicast address for multicast communication:

```
// Create IPAddress using multicast address.
IPAddress multiIP = IPAddress.Parse("FF01::1");
```

An instance of the `IPv6MulticastOption` class is created using the `IPAddress` created in the previous step:

```
// Instantiate IPv6MulticastOption.
IPv6MulticastOption mcoIPv6 = new IPv6MulticastOption(multiIP);
```

In the next step, an instance of `UdpClient` joins the multicast group by using the `InterfaceIndex` and `Group` properties:

```
// Join the specified multicast group using interface index and group.
udpSender.JoinMulticastGroup((int)mcoIPv6.InterfaceIndex, mcoIPv6.Group);
```

Lastly, our code receives data from user, processes it, and sends on the specified port, as shown here:

```
Console.WriteLine ("Enter data to send\r\n---------------");
string strData;
do
{
  // Get data, process and send to specified port.
  strData=Console.ReadLine();
  byte [] b=Encoding.ASCII.GetBytes(strData);
  udpSender.Send (b,b.Length,endpoint); //send data
}while(strData!="");
```

Creating a Multicast Receiver

Listing 6-5 shows the code for the multicast receiver.

Listing 6-5. *IPv6-based Multicast Receiver*

```
class multiReceiver
  {

    [STAThread]
    static void Main(string[] args)
    {
      try
      {
        // Create UdpClient for listening with port and IPv6 as address family type.
        UdpClient udpListener = new UdpClient(1000, AddressFamily.InterNetworkV6);

        // Create a multicast IPAddress.
        IPAddress multiIP = IPAddress.Parse("FF01::1");

        // Join the group.
        udpListener.JoinMulticastGroup(multiIP);

        // Define endpoint to receive data.
        IPEndPoint endpoint = new IPEndPoint(IPAddress.IPv6Any,1000);
        string recData;
        do
        {
          // Receive the data and process.
          Byte[] byteData = udpListener.Receive(ref endpoint);
          recData = Encoding.ASCII.GetString(byteData);
          Console.WriteLine (recData);
        }while (!recData.Equals("")) ;
        // Drop multicast group
       udpListener.DropMulticastGroup(multiIP);

      }
      catch (Exception e)
      {
        Console.WriteLine(e.ToString ());
      }
    }

  }
}
```

In the receiver, we first create an instance of `UdpClient` and a multicast IP address, just as we did in the sender. Next, we join the multicast group using the multicast IP address:

```
// Join the group
udpListener.JoinMulticastGroup(multiIP);
```

In the next step, we create an instance of IPEndPoint to receive the data. The received data is processed in do-while loop, until the sender sends a blank message:

```
// Define endpoint to receive data
        IPEndPoint endpoint = new IPEndPoint(IPAddress.IPv6Any,1000);
        string recData;
        do
        {
          // Receive the data and process
          Byte[] byteData = udpListener.Receive(ref endpoint);
          recData = Encoding.ASCII.GetString(byteData);
          Console.WriteLine (recData);
        }while (!recData.Equals("")) ;
```

Summary

In this chapter, you learned about some of the history and basic concepts of IPv6, the differences between IPv4 and IPv6. We then looked at how to configure and verify IPv6 on Windows Server 2003.

Next, we covered the .NET version 1.1 support for IPv6 through various interfaces. To demonstrate how to use the IPv6 protocol in .NET applications, we walked through several examples, including IPv6 client/server code and an IPv6 multicast communication example.

CHAPTER 7

TCP

In Chapter 5, we looked at low-level sockets programming for performing network-related tasks. In this chapter, we will look in detail at the higher-level network classes provided in the .NET Framework.

In this chapter, we'll discuss the following topics:

- A general introduction to TCP, including its architecture and data structures
- The `TcpClient` and `TcpListener` classes provided in the .NET Framework for working with TCP
- The TCP channel with .NET Remoting

An Overview of TCP

Transmission Control Protocol (TCP) is used as a reliable protocol for communications in an interconnected network of computers. TCP verifies that the data is properly delivered to the destination in the correct sequence. We'll look briefly at how TCP achieves this in a moment.

TCP is a connection-oriented protocol designed to provide reliable transmission of data from one process to another process running on the same or different computers. The term *connection-oriented* means that the two processes or applications must establish a TCP connection prior to exchanging any data. This is in contrast to the User Datagram Protocol (UDP, which we'll look at in the next chapter), which is a *connectionless* protocol, allowing data to be broadcast to an unknown number of clients.

Before looking at how TCP works, you should know the definitions of the following terms:

- A *segment* is the unit of data that TCP sends to IP.
- A *datagram* is the unit of data that IP sends to the network interface layer.
- Every TCP segment sent over a connection has a *sequence number* assigned to it. This is used to ensure that the data arrives in the correct order.

Encapsulation

When an application sends data using TCP, it travels down the protocol stack. The data is passed through each of the layers and finally transferred across the network as a stream of bits.

Each layer in the TCP/IP protocol suite adds some information in the form of headers and/or trailers, as illustrated in Figure 7-1.

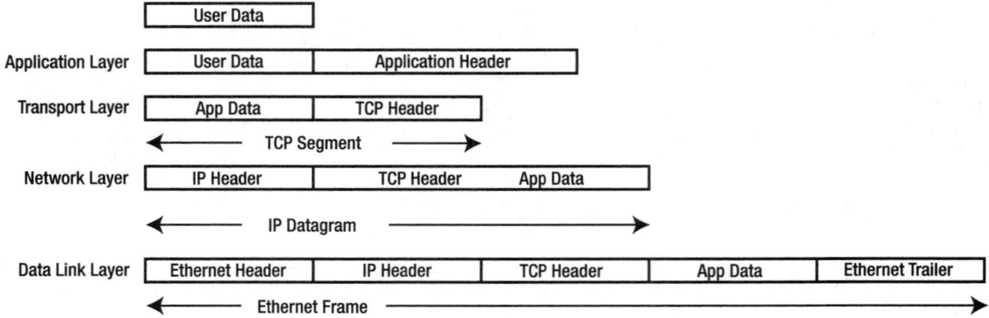

Figure 7-1. *Information added by TCP/IP*

When the packet arrives on the other side of the network, it is again passed through each layer, from bottom to top. Each layer strips out its header/trailer information to verify the data, and finally, it reaches the server application in the same form as it left the client application.

TCP Headers

To understand how TCP works, we also need to look quickly at the structure of a TCP header, which is illustrated in Figure 7-2.

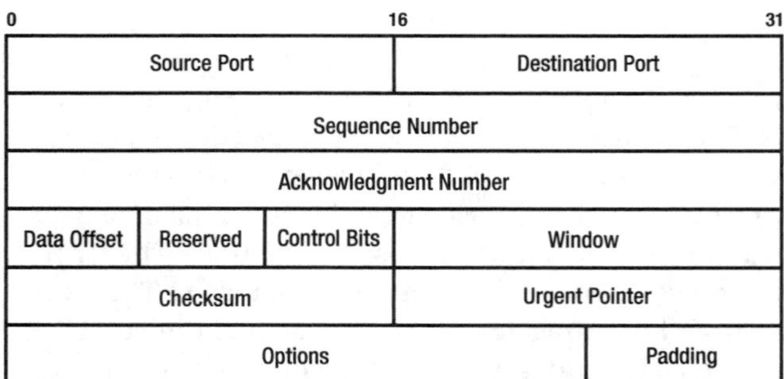

Figure 7-2. *The TCP/IP header structure*

TCP uses the sequence and acknowledgment numbers to ensure that all the data arrives in the correct order and the control bits contain various flags to indicate the status of the data. There are six of these control bits (usually represented by three-letter abbreviations):

- `URG` indicates that the segment contains urgent data.
- `ACK` indicates that the segment contains an acknowledgment number.

- `PSH` indicates the data is to be pushed through to the receiving user.
- `RST` resets the connection.
- `SYN` is used to synchronize sequence numbers.
- `FIN` indicates the end of data.

TCP Connections

TCP uses a process called a *three-phase handshake* to establish a connection. As the name suggests, and illustrated in Figure 7-3, this process consists of three steps:

1. The client initiates communication with the server by sending a segment to the server with the `SYN` control bit set. This segment contains the client's initial sequence number.
2. The server responds by sending a segment with both the `SYN` and `ACK` bits set. This segment contains the server's initial sequence number (unrelated to that of the client) and the acknowledgment number, which will be equal to the client's sequence number plus one (that is, it is the next sequence number expected from the client).
3. The client must acknowledge this segment by sending back a segment with the `ACK` bit set. The acknowledgment number will be the server's sequence number plus one, and the sequence number will be the same as the server's acknowledgment number (that is, the client's original sequence number plus one).

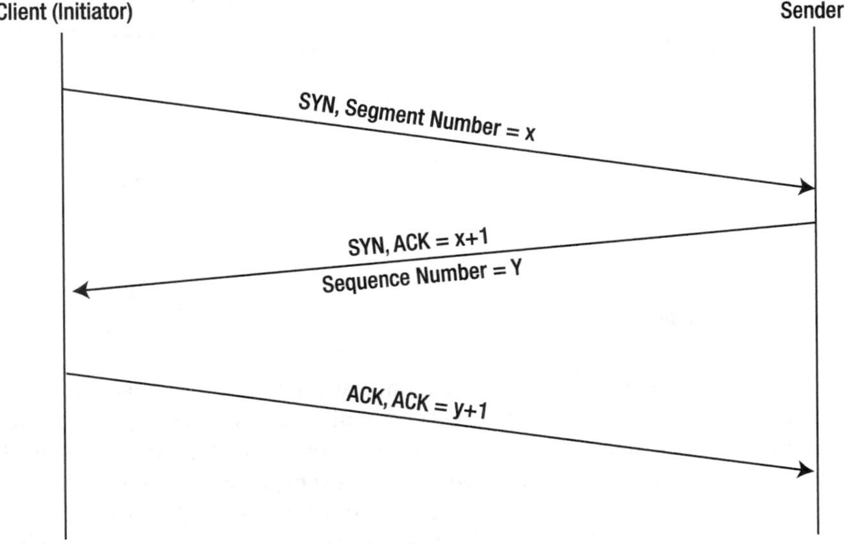

Figure 7-3. *A three-way handshake*

TCP Operations

Now that we've covered the basics of how TCP establishes connections, let's look at a few TCP operations to see how TCP transfers data.

Basic Stream Data Transfer

TCP transfers data in byte chunks known as *segments*. In order to ensure that segments are received correctly and in the correct order, a sequence number is assigned to each segment. The receiver sends an acknowledgment that the segment has been received. If the acknowledgment is not received before the timeout interval expires, the data is resent. Figure 7-4 illustrates the process.

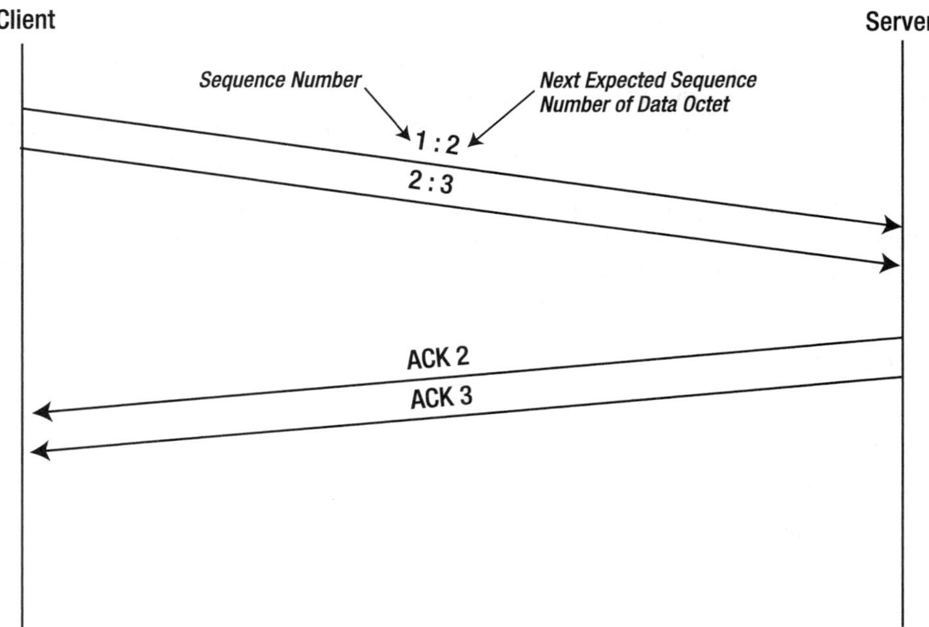

Figure 7-4. *Segment transfer*

Each octet (8 bits) of data is assigned a sequence number. The sequence number of the segment is the sequence number of the first octet of data within the segment, and this number is sent in the TCP header for the segment. Segments can also have an acknowledgment number, which is the sequence number for the next expected data segment.

TCP uses the sequence numbers to ensure that duplicate data isn't passed on to the receiving application and that the data is delivered in the correct order. The TCP header contains a checksum, which is used to ensure that the data hasn't been corrupted in transit. If a segment with an invalid checksum is received, it is simply discarded, and no acknowledgment is sent. This means that the sender will resend the segment when the timeout value expires.

Flow Control

TCP governs the amount of data sent to it by returning a window size with every acknowledgment. A *window* is the amount of data that the receiver can accept. A data buffer is placed between the application program and the network data flow. The window size is actually the difference between the size of the buffer and the amount of data stored in it. This number is sent to inform the remote host about the current window size. This is called a *sliding window*. The sliding window algorithms control the flow for network data transfers, as shown in Figure 7-5.

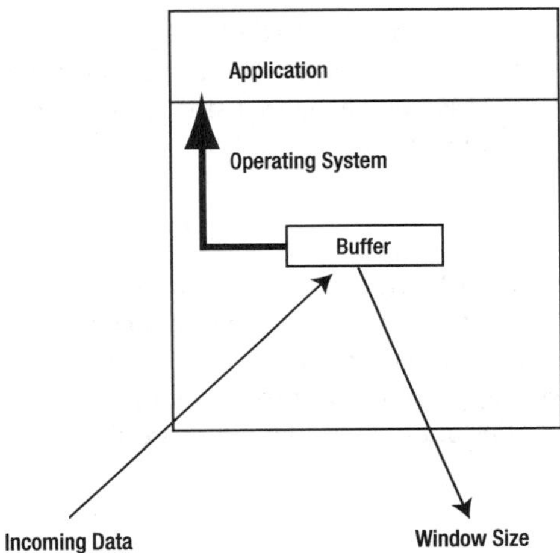

Figure 7-5. *The TCP/IP header structure*

The data received is stored in this buffer, and the application can access and read the data from the buffer at its own speed. As the application reads data, the buffer empties itself to accept more input from the network.

If the application is too slow reading the data from the buffer, the window size will drop to zero and the remote host will be told to stop sending the data. As soon as the local application processes the data in the buffer, the window size increases and can start receiving data from the network again.

If the size of the window is greater than the packet size, the sender knows that the receiver can hold multiple packets at once, improving the performance.

Multiplexing

TCP allows many processes on a single machine to use a TCP socket simultaneously. A TCP socket consists of a host address and a unique port number, and a TCP connection comprises two sockets on different ends of a network. A port may be used for simultaneous multiple connections; a single socket on one end may be used for several connections with different sockets on the other end. An example of this is a web server listening on port 80 answering requests from more than one computer.

.NET Support for TCP

.NET support for TCP sockets is a great improvement over the previous programming model. Previously, most developers using Visual C++ have either employed the CSocket and CAsyncSocket classes for manipulating all types of socket communication or used third-party programming libraries. There was almost no built-in support for higher-level TCP programming. In .NET, there is a separate namespace provided for working with sockets: the System.Net.Sockets namespace (as discussed in the previous chapters). This namespace contains low-level classes, such as Socket, as well as higher-level classes, such as TcpClient and TcpListener, to offer simple interfaces to TCP communication.

The TcpClient and TcpListener classes follow the stream model for sending and receiving data, as opposed to the Socket class, which employs the byte-level approach. In these classes, all communication between the client and the socket is based on a stream, using the NetworkStream class. However, you can also work with bytes where necessary.

The TcpClient Class

The TcpClient class provides client-side connections for TCP services. It is built on the Socket class to provide TCP services at a higher level. TcpClient has a private data member called m_ClientSocket, which is used to communicate with the TCP server. The TcpClient class provides simple methods for connecting to another socket application over the network, and for sending and receiving data to it. The important properties of the TcpClient class are shown in Table 7-1.

Table 7-1. *TcpClient Properties*

Name	Type	Description
LingerState	LingerOption	A public property that sets or returns a LingerOption object that holds information about whether the connection will remain open after the socket is closed, and if so, for how long.
NoDelay	bool	A public property that specifies whether the socket will delay sending or receiving data if the send or receive buffer isn't full. If set to false, TCP will delay sending the packet until there is sufficient data, to avoid the inefficiency of sending very small packets over the network.
ReceiveBufferSize	int	A public property that specifies the size of the buffer for incoming data (in bytes). This property is used when reading data from a socket.
ReceiveTimeout	int	A public property that specifies the length of time in milliseconds that the TcpClient will wait to receive data once initiated. A SocketException will be thrown after this time has elapsed if no data is received.
SendBufferSize	int	A public property that specifies the size of the buffer for outgoing data.
SendTimeout	int	A public property that specifies the length of time in milliseconds that the TcpClient will wait to receive confirmation of the number of bytes sent to the remote host from the underlying Socket after a send is initiated. A SocketException will be thrown if the SendTimeOut expires.

Name	Type	Description
Active	bool	A protected property that specifies whether there is an active connection to a remote host.
Client	Socket	A protected property that specifies the underlying Socket used by the TcpClient. Because this property is protected, the underlying socket can be accessed only if you derive your own class from TcpClient.

The TcpClient class has the following methods:

- The Close method closes the TCP connection.
- The Connect method connects to a remote TCP host.
- The GetStream method returns the NetworkStream used for transferring data between the client and the remote host.

Instantiating a TcpClient

The constructor for the TcpClient class has three overloads:

```
public TcpClient();
public TcpClient(IPEndPoint ipEnd);
public TcpClient(string hostname, int port);
public TcpClient(AddressFamily family);
```

The default constructor initializes a TcpClient instance:

```
TcpClient newClient = new TcpClient();
```

If a TcpClient is instantiated in this way, you must call the Connect method with an IPEndPoint to establish a connection to a remote host.

The second overload takes a single parameter of type IPEndPoint. This initializes a new instance of the TcpClient class bound to the specified endpoint. Notice that this IPEndPoint is the local endpoint, not the remote endpoint. If you try to pass a remote endpoint to the constructor, an exception will be thrown, stating that the IP address isn't valid in this context.

If you use this constructor, you still must call the Connect method with the remote endpoint after creating the TcpClient object:

```
// Create a local endpoint
IPAddress ipAddr = IPAddress.Parse("192.168.1.51");
IPEndPoint endPoint = new IPEndPoint(ipAddr, 11100);
TcpClient newClient = new TcpClient(endPoint);
IPAddress hostIp = IPAddress.Parse("192.168.1.52");
// You must call connect() to make a connection with the server
newClient.Connect(hostIp, 11000);
```

The parameter passed to the TcpClient constructor is the local endpoint, whereas the Connect method actually connects the client with the server, so it takes the remote endpoint as a parameter.

The last overload creates a new instance of the TcpClient class and establishes a remote connection using DNS name and port number parameters passed in as arguments:

```
TcpClient newClient = new TcpClient("localhost", 80);
```

This is the most convenient method, as it allows you to initialize the TcpClient, resolve the DNS name, and connect with the host in one easy step. However, notice that you can't specify the local port to which you want to bind using this overload. This method is also not recommended if you know the IP address of the host to which you are trying to connect, because it will waste some time trying to resolve the DNS in every case.

In .NET 1.1, there is a fourth constructor, which takes the IP AddressFamily. The local endpoint is specified as in the earlier example. Currently, only IPv4 and IPv6 are supported by the .NET Framework.

Establishing a Connection with the Host

Once you've instantiated a TcpClient, the next step is to establish a connection with the remote host. The Connect method is provided to connect the client with the TCP host. You need to call this method only if you used the default constructor or a local endpoint to instantiate the TcpClient; otherwise, if you passed a host name and port number into the constructor, attempting to call Connect will cause an exception.

There are three overloads for the Connect method:

```
public void connect(IPEndPoint endPoint);
public void Connect(IPAddress ipAddr, int port);
public void Connect(string hostname, int port);
```

These are fairly self-explanatory, but we'll quickly demonstrate examples of using each overload. First, here's how to pass in an IPEndPoint object representing the remote endpoint you want to connect to:

```
// Create a new instance of the TcpClient class
TcpClient newClient = new TcpClient();
// Establish a connection with the IPEndPoint
IPAddress ipAddr = IPAddress.Parse("127.0.0.1");
IPEndPoint endPoint = new IPEndPoint(ipAddr, 80);
// Connect with the host using IPEndPoint
newClient.Connect(endPoint);
```

Passing in an IPAddress object and a port number looks like this:

```
// Create a new instance of the TcpClient class
TcpClient newClient = new TcpClient();
// Establish a connection with the IPEndPoint
IPAddress ipAddr = IPAddress.Parse("127.0.0.1");
// Connect with the host using IPAddress and port number
newClient.Connect(ipAddr, 80);
```

Finally, the following example shows passing in a host name and port number:

```
// Create a new instance of the TcpClient class
TcpClient newClient = new TcpClient();
// Connect with the host using host name as string and port
newClient.Connect("127.0.0.1", 80);
```

If there is a connection failure or other problem, a SocketException will be thrown:

```
try
{
   TcpClient newClient = new TcpClient();
   // Connect to the server
   newClient.Connect("192.168.0.1", 80);
                                 // Socket raises exception here
                             // if there is some problem with the
                             // connection
}
catch(SocketException se)
{
   Console.WriteLine("Exception: " + se);
}
```

Sending and Receiving Messages

The NetworkStream class is used for stream-level processing as a communication channel between two connected applications. This class has already been discussed in Chapter 2, so here we'll just look at using it with a TcpClient object.

Before sending and receiving any data, you need to get the underlying stream. TcpClient provides a GetStream method exclusively for this purpose. GetStream creates an instance of the NetworkStream class using the underlying socket and returns it to the caller. In the following example, we assume that newClient is an instance of the TcpClient and that a connection with the host has already been established. Otherwise, an InvalidOperation exception would be thrown.

```
NetworkStream tcpStream = newClient.GetStream();
```

After getting the stream, we can use the NetworkStream's Read and Write methods to actually read from the host application and write to it. The Write method takes three parameters: a byte array containing the data to send to the host, the position in the stream to start writing, and the length of the data:

```
byte[] sendBytes = Encoding.ASCII.GetBytes("This is a Test<EOF>");
tcpStream.Write(sendBytes, 0, sendBytes.Length);
```

The Read method has the same set of parameters: a byte array to store the data to read from the stream, the position to start reading, and the number of bytes to read:

```
byte[] bytes = new byte[newClient.ReceiveBufferSize];
int bytesRead = tcpStream.Read(bytes, 0, newClient.ReceiveBufferSize);

// Convert from bytes to string
// returnData will contain the incoming data from socket
string returnData = Encoding.ASCII.GetString(bytes);
```

The TcpClient's ReceiveBufferSize property allows you to get or set the size of the receive buffer (in bytes), so you can use it as the size of the byte array. Note that setting this property doesn't restrict the number of bytes you can read in each operation, as the buffer will be dynamically resized if necessary, but it does reduce overhead if you specify a buffer size.

Closing a TCP Socket

After communicating with the client, the Close method should be called to free all resources:

```
// Close client socket
newClient.Close();
```

That is all that is required to use the TcpClient class to communicate with the server.

Using the Protected Properties

Apart from this basic functionality, if you need to access the socket instance underlying the TcpClient object, for example to set options by calling SetSocketOption, you can call the Client property to access the members of the underlying Socket. You can also use the Client property to set the TcpClient's underlying socket to an existing Socket object. But since this is a protected member of the TcpClient class, you must inherit from TcpClient before using it.

The Client property allows protected access to the private m_ClientSocket member we mentioned earlier. The TcpClient class passes calls made on it to the Socket class's parallel method after checking the validity of parameters and initializing the socket instance. The m_ClientSocket object is instantiated in the constructor. The constructor calls the private initialize method that constructs the new Socket object and then calls the set_Client method to assign it to the Client property. The method sets the m_Active Boolean value, which is used to track the state of the Socket instance. It also checks for redundant Socket connections and for any operations that require the connection. A separate protected property, Active, is provided for setting and getting the value of the private m_Active member.

There are a lot of socket options that the TcpClient class does not cover. If you want to set or get any of these properties that are not exposed by the TcpClient (such as Broadcast or KeepAlive), you need to derive a class from TcpClient and use its Client member.

The following code demonstrates how to use these protected properties:

```
using System;
using System.Net;
using System.Net.Sockets;
```

```
using System.IO;
using System.Text;
public class PSocket : TcpClient
{
   public PSocket() : base()
   {
   }
   public PSocket(string ipaddress, int port) : base(ipaddress, port)
   {
   }
   public static void Main()
   {
      // Creating a TcpClient object but not connecting
      PSocket ps2 = new PSocket();
      // Showing the state of the socket
      Console.WriteLine("trackActive: " + ps2.Active);
      // Connecting with the client
      ps2.Connect("127.0.0.1", 11000);
      // Checking the state of the socket
      Console.WriteLine("trackActive: " + ps2.Active);
      // Creating another TcpClient class, this time connecting
      // within the constructor
      PSocket newClient = new PSocket("127.0.0.1", 11000);
      // Checking the state of the other socket
      Console.WriteLine("trackActive: " + newClient.Active);
      // Getting the internal protected socket member
      Socket s = newClient.Client;
      // Use the socket to set an option
      s.SetSocketOption(SocketOptionLevel.Socket, SocketOptionName.KeepAlive, 1);
   }
}
```

Building a Simple E-mail Client Application

To demonstrate the use of the `TcpClient` class, we'll build a simple e-mail client implementing two of the most common protocols in the Internet world: Simple Mail Transfer Protocol (SMTP) and Post Office Protocol (POP3). Both of these protocols are discussed in detail in Chapter 11. Here, we'll just provide an introduction to SMTP before describing how the application works.

■ **NOTE** As you'll learn in Chapter 11, .NET does provide classes for sending e-mail over SMTP. However, it's important to see how to implement application-level protocols such as this, and SMTP provides a useful example because of its simplicity.

An Introduction to SMTP

Figure 7-6 shows the basic model involved in completing a mail transaction with SMTP. The process starts when the user sends the mail. The sending system contacts the receiving system on TCP port 25 to establish a communication link. The receiving system, which may be the final destination or an intermediate system, replies back with status messages to inform the sender that it's ready to receive the message. These responses consist of a three-digit status code and a human-readable message. The receiving system continues by sending commands followed by the original e-mail. The receiving system responds appropriately with status messages and commands. The link is terminated when the sender has finished sending the message and disconnects itself from the receiving system.

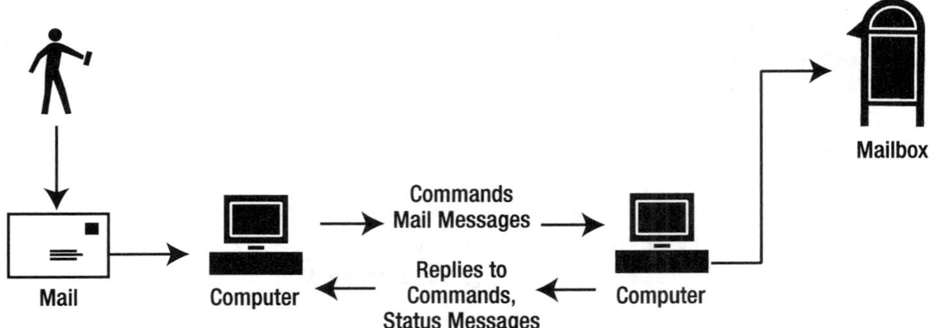

Figure 7-6. *A mail transaction with SMTP*

The command syntax for SMTP isn't very difficult, and it contains only a few commands: `HELO`, `MAIL`, `RCPT`, `DATA`, and `QUIT`.

The `HELO` command is used to initiate communications between the sending and receiving hosts. This command is accompanied by a parameter identifying the sending host. The receiving host then identifies itself back to the sending host; this places both machines into the ready state to begin communications. If successful, this command should be met with the reply code 250, which indicates that the command completed without error:

```
Sending System:     HELO apress.com
Receiving System:   250 gg.mail.com
```

The `MAIL` command lets the receiving system know who is sending the mail message so that any error in delivering the mail message can be directed back to the original e-mail sender. Since mail can be intercepted en route by more than one host, it is used to identify the final destination of the e-mail. Most e-mail servers put some restriction on this parameter, such as ensuring that the user's domain name is the same as the e-mail server's domain, to prevent anonymous e-mail and spamming.

```
Sending System:     MAIL FROM:<noman@csquareonline.com>
Receiving System:   250 OK
```

The RCPT command is used to send the mailbox names of the users to whom the mail is being sent. It's possible to have more than one recipient for a particular mail message.

```
Sending System:     RCPT TO:<noman@csquareonline.com>
Receiving System:   250 OK
```

The DATA command indicates that the information that follows contains the body of the message file. The message end is indicated by the sending system's transmission of a line containing only a period (.). The following example shows the transaction between the sending and the receiving system. Note that the subject of the mail is specified within this data by adding a SUBJECT: line just after sending the DATA command. The text between SUBJECT: and the carriage return and linefeed character (CRLF sequence) constructs the subject of the message.

```
Sending System:     DATA
Receiving System:   354 Ready to receive data...
Sending System:     SUBJECT:Subject of the message<CR><LF>This
is a test message. <CR><LF>.<CR><LF>
Receiving System:   250 OK
```

After the receiving system gets the end of message line, it replies to the sender about the status of the message.

Finally, the QUIT command indicates that the sending system is ready to close down the communication link between the sender and the receiver.

```
Sending System:     QUIT
Receiving System:   221 web.akros.net closing connection.
```

The following is an example of a successful SMTP session between a sending and receiving system. For each command and response, CLIENT represents the system that will be initiating and sending the mail, and SERVER represents the system to which the mail is sent.

```
[Establish Connection with SMTP Server]
Connection Established with xyz.com
SERVER: 220 web1.xyz.com ESMTP SendMail
CLIENT: HELO xyz.com
SERVER: 250 OK
CLIENT: MAIL FROM: <noman@csquareonline.com><CR><LF>
SERVER: 250 <noman@csquareonline.com>... Sender OK
CLIENT: RCPT TO: <noman@csquareonline.com><CR><LF>
SERVER: 250 <noman@csquareonline.com>... Recepient OK
CLIENT: DATA<CR><LF>
SERVER: 354 Enter mail, end with "." on a line by itself
CLIENT: SUBJECT: test<CR><LF>
test<CR><LF>
.<CR><LF>
SERVER: 250 asdkauy83 Message accepted for delivery
CLIENT: QUIT<CR><LF>
SERVER: 221 web.xyz.com Closing Connection
```

To test this, you can use a telnet application and connect to your local SMTP server on port 25. (See Chapter 1 for a discussion of the Microsoft Telnet client.) Then you can manually type the client portion of the example into the telnet application to get a feel for the process. We look at a sample SMTP telnet session in Chapter 11.

The E-mail Client

Our e-mail client application is a Windows application, with a very simple user interface, as shown in Figure 7-7. It includes single-line text boxes to specify the SMTP server we want to connect to, the From and To fields for the e-mail, and the subject of the e-mail. We'll also have a multiline text box for the body of the e-mail and a list box where we'll display status messages.

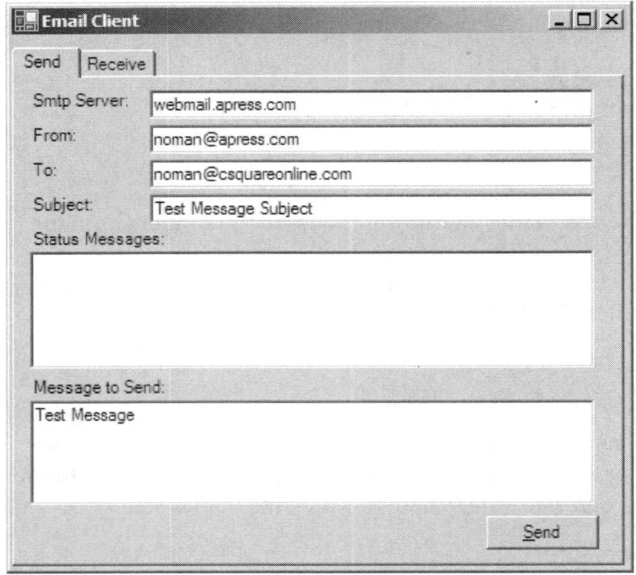

Figure 7-7. *The Send tab of the e-mail client interface*

The form has two tabs: one for sending e-mail via SMTP and the other for retrieving them from an inbox via POP. The SMTP tab contains the controls listed in Table 7-2.

Table 7-2. *E-mail Client Form Controls*

Name	Type	Associated Label Text
`txtSmtpServer`	Text box	Smtp Server:
`txtFrom`	Text box	From:
`txtTo`	Text box	To:
`txtSubject`	Text box	Subject:
`lstLog`	List box	Status Messages:
`txtMessage`	Text box	Message to Send:
`btnSend`	Button	Send

■NOTE The complete code for this application, as well as the other examples presented in this chapter, is available from the Downloads section of the Apress website: `http://www.apress.com`.

All the code for connecting to the server and sending the message is implemented in the `Click` event handler for the Send button. We start by making a connection to the SMTP server:

```
private void btnSend_Click(object sender, System.EventArgs e)
{
   // Create an instance of the TcpClient class
   TcpClient smtpServer = new TcpClient(txtSmtpServer.Text, 25);
   lstLog.Items.Add("Connection Established with " + txtSmtpServer.Text);
```

The next step is to build the `Stream` classes to communicate with the SMTP server. We have used a `NetworkStream` for writing a stream to the server, but a `StreamReader` for reading from the server. This provides a `ReadLine` method that is much easier to use than calling the `NetworkStream`'s `Read` method, which reads the stream into bytes that we then need to convert into a string using the `Encoding` class. The `StreamReader`'s `ReadLine` method returns a string.

```
   // Create the stream classes for communication
   NetworkStream writeStream = smtpServer.GetStream();
   StreamReader readStream = new StreamReader(smtpServer.GetStream());
```

Once we've connected to the server, it will send us a message to tell us that the connection has been made. We read this message using the `StreamReader.ReadLine` method and display it in the list box:

```
   // Retrieve connection success message
   receiveData = readStream.ReadLine();
   // Add it to the list box
   lstLog.Items.Add(receiveData);
```

After that, we send the `HELO` command followed by the sending host name to start the session. This command is not required by all SMTP servers, but it's best practice to follow the proper command sequence:

```
     sendString = "HELO "+Dns.GetHostName()+"\r\n";
     dataToSend = Encoding.ASCII.GetBytes(sendString);
     writeStream.Write(dataToSend,0,dataToSend.Length);
   // Display response message
     receiveData = readStream.ReadLine();
     lstLog.Items.Add(receiveData);
```

Next, we send the user's e-mail address to the server by writing an SMTP `MAIL FROM` command to our `NetworkStream` object. Again, the server will send a response message, which we retrieve from the `StreamReader` and add to the list box:

```
   // Send 'From' E-mail Address
   sendString = "MAIL FROM: " + "<" + txtFrom.Text + ">\r\n";
```

```
dataToSend = Encoding.ASCII.GetBytes(sendString);
writeStream.Write(dataToSend, 0, dataToSend.Length);
// Display response message
receiveData = readStream.ReadLine();
lstLog.Items.Add(receiveData);
```

Then we send the destination e-mail address in a `RCPT TO` command and again display the server's response:

```
// Sending 'To' E-mail Address
sendString = "RCPT TO: " + "<" + txtTo.Text + ">\r\n";
dataToSend = Encoding.ASCII.GetBytes(sendString);
writeStream.Write(dataToSend, 0, dataToSend.Length);
// Display response message
receiveData = readStream.ReadLine();
lstLog.Items.Add(receiveData);
```

Now, after both the e-mail addresses have been authenticated, the actual data (including the e-mail's subject) is sent following the `DATA` SMTP command:

```
// Send data
sendString = "DATA " + "\r\n";
dataToSend = Encoding.ASCII.GetBytes(sendString);
writeStream.Write(dataToSend, 0, dataToSend.Length);
// Display response message
receiveData = readStream.ReadLine();
lstLog.Items.Add(receiveData);
// Sending Message Subject and Text
sendString = "SUBJECT: " + txtSubject.Text + "\r\n" +
             txtMessage.Text + "\r\n" + "." + "\r\n";
dataToSend = Encoding.ASCII.GetBytes(sendString);
writeStream.Write(dataToSend, 0, dataToSend.Length);
receiveData = readStream.ReadLine();
lstLog.Items.Add(receiveData);
```

The last step is to send the `QUIT` command to the server and free any resources used by the application:

```
   // Send disconnect message to server
   sendString = "QUIT " + "\r\n";
   dataToSend = Encoding.ASCII.GetBytes(sendString);
   writeStream.Write(dataToSend,0,dataToSend.Length);
   receiveData = readStream.ReadLine();
   lstLog.Items.Add(receiveData);
   // Close all open resources
   writeStream.Close();
   readStream.Close();
   smtpServer.Close();
}
```

The second tab of our e-mail client application, shown in Figure 7-8, allows us to read e-mail from an inbox using the POP3 protocol. Since we present a similar example in Chapter 11, we won't show the code here.

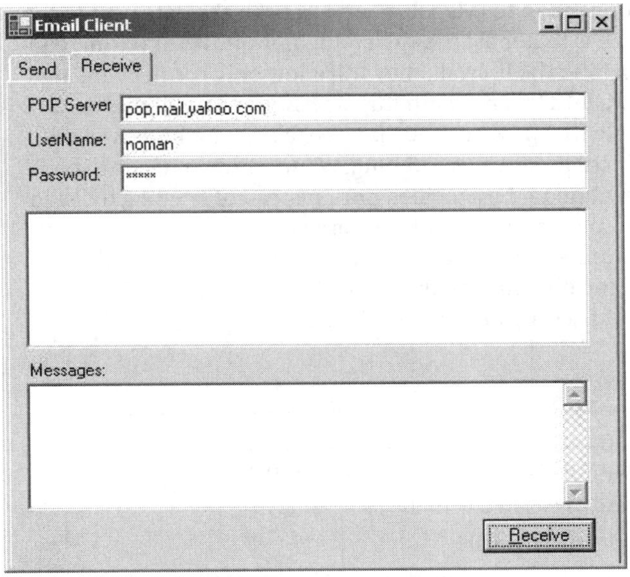

Figure 7-8. *The Receive tab of the e-mail client interface*

Creating an FTP Client

The second example we'll look at in this chapter is a bit more complicated than the previous one. We'll implement `FtpWebRequest` and `FtpWebResponse` classes, which will allow us to download files from or upload them to an FTP server in much the same way that we can access files using the `FileWebRequest` and `FileWebResponse` classes discussed in Chapter 3.

An Introduction to FTP

File Transfer Protocol (FTP) is an application-level protocol built on top of a transport-level protocol, usually TCP. It is used for uploading and downloading files on a remote server. In many ways, implementing an FTP client is very similar to implementing an SMTP client, as in the previous example. You open a TCP connection to the server and send text commands to perform actions such as retrieving a file from the server, and the server returns a three-digit code (along with a human-readable message) to indicate the status of the requested action.

Where FTP differs from SMTP is that two different connections are used:

- The control connection, on which you send the commands and receive the server's responses
- The data connection, which is used for the actual transfer of the files to be downloaded or uploaded

By default, the server listens on port 21 for commands from the client. When it needs to send data, the server will open a second connection to port 20 of the client. The data connection is opened only when a command has been sent to upload or download a file.

In *active* mode (the default), the client must listen for connections. When data needs to be sent, the FTP server will open a connection to this socket and transfer the data over to the client. The problem with this approach is that most firewall configurations won't permit connections from outside to machines behind the firewall; they will allow only connections that were initialized from behind the firewall. FTP's answer to this is *passive* mode. In this case, the client sends a command to indicate that passive mode is to be used, and the server will respond with the port number on which the server is listening. When the data needs to be sent, the client can now open a connection to the specified port, instead of needing to listen for the server's request. Our sample implementation will use passive mode.

The FTP specification defines a number of commands for authentication, uploading and downloading files, and changing the directory on the server. We won't use all of these commands in our code. The ones we do use are described in Table 7-3.

Table 7-3. *Some Common FTP Commands*

Command	Description
`USER` *<username>*	The user name to be authenticated on the server
`PASS` *<password>*	The password associated with the user name
`RETR` *<filename>*	Download the specified file
`STOR` *<filename>*	Upload a file and store it in the specified location
`TYPE` *<type indicator>*	The format for the data: `A` for ASCII, `E` for EBCDIC, `I` for Image (binary data), or `L` *<byte size>* for local byte size
`PASV`	Use passive mode
`STAT`	Causes the server to send a status message to the client; can be used while data is being transferred to indicate the status of the operation
`QUIT`	Close the connection to the server

As with SMTP reply codes, the three-digit FTP codes are ordered according to the granularity of detail provided by the digit. The first digit gives a general indication of the status of the command; the second digit indicates the general type of error that occurred; and the third digit gives more specific information. The following are the possible first digits:

- 1 indicates a positive preliminary response. The requested action is being initiated, and another response will be sent before the client should send a new command.
- 2 indicates a positive completion response. The requested action has been completed.
- 3 indicates a positive intermediate response. The command has been accepted, but the server requires more information before proceeding.
- 4 indicates a temporary negative response. The command was rejected, but the error is temporary, and the command can be resent.
- 5 indicates a permanent negative response. The command was rejected.

Some of the specific responses that we will handle in our example are listed in Table 7-4.

Table 7-4. *Common FTP Response Codes*

Code	Description
125	Data connection open; starting transfer
150	About to open data connection
200	Command accepted
220	Service ready for new user
227	Entering passive mode
230	User logged in
331	User name accepted; send password

The FTP Client

As we mentioned earlier, to make the FTP client as intuitive as possible for developers using it, we'll implement an `FtpWebRequest` class that inherits from `WebRequest` and can be used in the same way. This is implemented as a Class Library project, and consists of five classes:

- `FtpRequestCreator` is used when we register the `ftp` prefix with `WebRequest`.
- `FtpWebRequest` represents a request to download or upload a file on an FTP server.
- `FtpWebResponse` represents the response from the server.
- `FtpWebStream` represents the stream between the client and server.
- `FtpClient` is the utility class we use for connecting to the server and executing the FTP commands.

The following sections describe the implementation of each of these classes.

The FtpRequestCreator Class

The first thing we need to do is create an implementation of the `IWebRequestCreate` interface. This interface has one method, `Create`, which is called by the `WebRequest.Create` static method. In this method, we simply return a new instance of our `FtpWebRequest` class:

```
using System;
using System.Net;
namespace Apress.Networking.TCP.FtpUtil
{
   public class FtpRequestCreator : IWebRequestCreate
   {
      public FtpRequestCreator()
      {
      }
      public System.Net.WebRequest Create(System.Uri uri)
      {
```

```
            return new FtpWebRequest(uri);
        }
    }
}
```

When we want to create an FtpWebRequest object, we need to register the ftp prefix and pass in an FtpRequestCreator object, so that the WebRequest class knows that it must use this class to handle any web requests beginning with ftp.

The FtpWebRequest Class

Next, we can define the FtpWebRequest class itself. This will have five data members, to store the user name and password of the user we will connect as, the URI we want to connect to, a Boolean value indicating whether the data is to be in binary rather than ASCII format, and a string representing the method for the request. This last field represents the command we want to execute against the server; to make this more accessible to users who aren't familiar with the FTP protocol, we will allow this to be set to GET instead of RETR, and PUT instead of STOR. These values are also exposed as public properties of the class. The constructor of the class simply sets the uri field to the Uri passed in. The only other method in the class is the GetResponse method, which simply instantiates and returns a new FtpWebResponse object, passing the current FtpWebRequest as a parameter:

```
using System;
using System.Net;
namespace Apress.Networking.TCP.FtpUtil
{
   public class FtpWebRequest : WebRequest
   {
      private string username = "anonymous";
      internal string password = "someuser@somemail.com";
      private Uri uri;
      private bool binaryMode = true;
      private string method = "GET";
      internal FtpWebRequest(Uri uri)
      {
         this.uri = uri;
      }
      public string Username
      {
         get { return username; }
         set { username = value; }
      }
      public string Password
      {
         set { password = value; }
      }
      public bool BinaryMode
      {
```

```
         get { return binaryMode; }
         set { binaryMode = value; }
      }
      public override System.Uri RequestUri
      {
         get { return uri; }
      }
      public override string Method
      {
         get { return method; }
         set { method = value; }
      }
      public override System.Net.WebResponse GetResponse()
      {
         FtpWebResponse response = new FtpWebResponse(this);
         return response;
      }
   }
}
```

The FtpWebResponse Class

Next, we define the `FtpWebResponse` class. This has two private data members: the `FtpWebRequest` object with which it is associated and an instance of a class called `FtpClient`, where we will implement most of the actual code for communicating with the FTP server. The class's constructor simply sets the `request` field to the `FtpWebRequest` object that is passed in:

```
using System;
using System.IO;
using System.Net;
using System.Net.Sockets;
namespace Apress.Networking.TCP.FtpUtil
{
   public class FtpWebResponse : WebResponse
   {
      private FtpWebRequest request;
      private FtpClient client;
      internal FtpWebResponse(FtpWebRequest request)
      {
         this.request = request;
      }
```

The `GetResponseStream` method is where we actually connect to the server and download or upload the data. This method first separates the URI we want to connect to into its component parts: the name of the server and the path/name of the file we want to download or save to the server. Next, we create an instance of the `FtpClient` class, passing in the user name and password from the `FtpWebRequest` object, and we use this object to connect to the server. Next, we execute the command represented by the `FtpWebRequest` object. This could be either

GET/RETR to download a file or PUT/STOR to upload a file. In either case, we retrieve a NetworkStream object that is used to represent the stream between the client and the server. If the method isn't one of these, we throw an exception to state that the method isn't supported. Finally, we create a new FtpWebStream object from this NetworkStream and return it to the caller:

```
public override System.IO.Stream GetResponseStream()
{
   // Split up URI to get host name and file name
   string hostname;
   string filename;
   GetUriComponents(request.RequestUri.ToString(), out hostname,
                    out filename);
   // Connect to the FTP server and get a stream
   client = new FtpClient(request.Username, request.password);
   client.Connect(hostname);
   NetworkStream dataStream = null;
   switch (request.Method)
   {
      case "GET":
      case "RETR":
         dataStream = client.GetReadStream(filename,
                                           request.BinaryMode);
         break;
      case "PUT":
      case "STOR":
         dataStream = client.GetWriteStream(filename,
                                            request.BinaryMode);
         break;
      default:
         throw new WebException("Method " + request.Method +
                                " not supported");
   }
   // Create and return an FtpWebStream
   // (to close the underlying objects)
   FtpWebStream ftpStream = new FtpWebStream(dataStream, this);
   return ftpStream;
}
```

The GetUriComponents method parses a URI in string format and populates two output parameters with the host name and the file name components from this:

```
private void GetUriComponents(string uri, out string hostname,
                              out string fileName)
{
   // Check that URI has at least 7 characters, or we'll get an error
   uri = uri.ToLower();
   if (uri.Length < 7)
```

```
            throw new UriFormatException("Invalid URI");
         // Check that URI starts "ftp://", and remove that from the start
         if (uri.Substring(0, 6) != "ftp://")
            throw new NotSupportedException(
                                        "Only FTP requests are supported");
         else
            uri = uri.Substring(6, uri.Length - 6);
         // Divide the rest of the URI into the host name and the file name
         string[] uriParts = uri.Split(new char[] { '/' }, 2);
         if (uriParts.Length != 2)
            throw new UriFormatException("Invalid URI");
         hostname = uriParts[0];
         fileName = uriParts[1];
      }
```

Finally, the Close method simply calls Close on the FtpClient object:

```
      public override void Close()
      {
         client.Close();
      }
   }
}
```

The FtpWebStream Class

The FtpWebStream class inherits from Stream. It has two private fields: the FtpWebResponse object that returns it to the client application and the underlying NetworkStream between the client and the FTP server. Again, the constructor just populates these fields:

```
using System;
using System.IO;
using System.Net.Sockets;
namespace Apress.Networking.TCP.FtpUtil
{
   internal class FtpWebStream : Stream
   {
      private FtpWebResponse response;
      private NetworkStream dataStream;
      public FtpWebStream(NetworkStream dataStream,
                  FtpWebResponse response)
      {
         this.dataStream = dataStream;
         this.response = response;
      }
```

The remaining methods and properties simply pass on the call to the underlying NetworkStream, or if the functionality isn't supported, throw a NotSupportedException:

```
      public override void Close()
```

```
        {
            response.Close();
            base.Close();
        }
        public override void Flush()
        {
            dataStream.Flush();
        }
        public override int Read(byte[] buffer, int offset, int count)
        {
            return dataStream.Read(buffer, offset, count);
        }
        public override long Seek(long offset, System.IO.SeekOrigin origin)
        {
            throw new NotSupportedException("Seek not supported");
        }
        public override void SetLength(long value)
        {
            throw new NotSupportedException("SetLength not supported");
        }
        public override void Write(byte[] buffer, int offset, int count)
        {
            dataStream.Write(buffer, offset, count);
        }
        public override bool CanRead
        {
            get { return dataStream.CanRead; }
        }
        public override bool CanSeek
        {
            get { return false; }
        }
        public override bool CanWrite
        {
            get { return dataStream.CanWrite; }
        }
        public override long Length
        {
            get { throw new NotSupportedException("Length not supported"); }
        }
        public override long Position
        {
            get { throw new NotSupportedException("Position not supported"); }
            set { throw new NotSupportedException("Position not supported"); }
        }
    }
}
```

The FtpClient Class

The final class in our project, `FtpClient`, is where most of the actual work is done. This class is intended to be called only from within our application, so we've set its accessibility to `internal` and also made the class `sealed`. The class has seven private fields:

- `bufferSize` is a constant representing the size of the buffer we'll use for reading from and writing to the `NetworkStream`.
- `controlStream` is the `NetworkStream` that is used to send commands and receive responses from the FTP server.
- `dataStream` is the `NetworkStream` used to send data to and receive it from the FTP server.
- `username` is a string representing the name of the user, for authenticating against the FTP server.
- `password` is the password associated with the user name.
- `client` is a `TcpClient` object used to make the control connection to the FTP server.
- `dataClient` is a `TcpClient` object used to make the data connection to the FTP server.

```
using System;
using System.Net;
using System.Net.Sockets;
using System.IO;
using System.Text;
namespace Apress.Networking.TCP.FtpUtil
{
   internal sealed class FtpClient
   {
      private const int bufferSize = 65536;
      private NetworkStream controlStream;
      private NetworkStream dataStream;
      private TcpClient client;
      private string username;
      private string password;
      private TcpClient dataClient = null;
```

The constructor takes the user name and password as parameters, and stores these in the data members:

```
public FtpClient(string username, string password)
{
   this.username = username;
   this.password = password;
}
```

The `Connect` method makes the initial connection with the FTP server. It opens a connection to port 21 (the default port for the control connection to an FTP server) using the `TcpClient` class and retrieves the `NetworkStream` for this connection. We then call the `GetResponse` method, which retrieves the status code and message from the stream. If all is well, this should be a 220 "service ready for new user" response, so we log on using the user name and password. If any other status code is returned, something has gone wrong, so we throw an exception:

```
public void Connect(string hostname)
{
   // Set the private fields representing the TCP control connection to
   // the server and the NetworkStream used to communicate with the
   // server
   client = new TcpClient(hostname, 21);
   controlStream = client.GetStream();
   string responseMessage;
   if (GetResponse(out responseMessage) != 220)
   {
      throw new WebException(responseMessage);
   }
   Logon(username, password);
}
```

We use the GetResponse method to read a response from the FTP server on the control connection. It returns the three-digit status code as an integer and populates an output parameter with the response message:

```
public int GetResponse(out string responseMessage)
{
   // Read the respose from the server, trim any nulls, and return it.
   byte[] response = new byte[client.ReceiveBufferSize];
   controlStream.Read(response, 0, response.Length);
   responseMessage = Encoding.ASCII.GetString(response).Replace(
                                                         "\0", "");
   return int.Parse(responseMessage.Substring(0, 3));
}
```

The Logon method sends a USER command to the server. If the server requires a password, it will respond with a 331 response, in which case we send a PASS command with the user's password. Otherwise, it should return a 230 response to say that the user has logged in successfully. If any other response is returned, we throw an UnauthorizedAccessException.

■ **CAUTION** FTP has no built-in security features for protecting passwords, so passwords must be sent in plain text format. For this reason, sensitive passwords should not be sent.

```
private void Logon(string username, string password)
      {
         // Send a USER FTP command. The server should respond with a 331
         // message to ask for the user's password.
         string respMessage;
```

```
        int resp = SendCommand("USER " + username, out respMessage);
        if (resp != 331 && resp != 230)
           throw new UnauthorizedAccessException(
                                      "Unable to login to the FTP server");
        if (resp != 230)
        {
           // Send a PASS FTP command. The server should respond with a 230
           // message to say that the user is now logged in.
           resp = SendCommand("PASS " + password, out respMessage);
           if (resp != 230)
              throw new UnauthorizedAccessException(
                                 "FTP server can't authenticate username");
        }
     }
```

The next two methods simply return a NetworkStream for downloading or uploading a file via the data connection, by calling the DownloadFile or UploadFile method (we'll look at these next):

```
     public NetworkStream GetReadStream(string filename, bool binaryMode)
     {
        return DownloadFile(filename, binaryMode);
     }
     public NetworkStream GetWriteStream(string filename, bool binaryMode)
     {
        return UploadFile(filename, binaryMode);
     }
```

The DownloadFile method opens the data connection to the FTP server, and then sets the binaryMode to specify whether we're expecting binary or ASCII data. Next, we send a RETR command to tell the server we want to download a file. This should be met with a 125 or 150 response to signal that the data connection is either already open or is about to be opened. If it isn't, we throw a WebException; otherwise, we return the NetworkStream from our dataClient TcpClient:

```
     private NetworkStream DownloadFile(string filename, bool binaryMode)
     {
        if (dataClient == null)
           dataClient = CreateDataSocket();
        SetBinaryMode(binaryMode);
        string respMessage;
        int resp = SendCommand("RETR " + filename, out respMessage);
        if(resp != 150 && resp != 125)
           throw new WebException(respMessage);
        dataStream = dataClient.GetStream();
        return dataStream;
     }
```

The UploadFile method is almost identical, except that a STOR command is sent instead of a RETR command:

```
private NetworkStream UploadFile(string filename, bool binaryMode)
{
   if (dataClient == null)
      dataClient = this.CreateDataSocket();
   // Set binary or ASCII mode
   SetBinaryMode(binaryMode);
   // Send a STOR command to say we want to upload a file
   string respMessage;
   int resp = SendCommand("STOR " + filename, out respMessage);

   // We should get a 150 response to say that the server is
   // opening the data connection
   if (resp != 150 && resp != 125)
      throw new WebException("Cannot upload files to the server");
   dataStream = dataClient.GetStream();
   return dataStream;
}
```

The SetBinaryMode method allows us to specify whether we want to retrieve binary or text (ASCII) data. We do this by sending a TYPE command to the FTP server with the parameter A for ASCII data or I for image (binary) data. We should receive a 200 response code if all went well:

```
private void SetBinaryMode(bool binaryMode)
{
   int resp;
   string respMessage;
   if(binaryMode)
      resp = SendCommand("TYPE I", out respMessage);
   else
      resp = SendCommand("TYPE A", out respMessage);
   if (resp != 200)
      throw new WebException(respMessage);
}
```

The CreateDataSocket method is the most complicated of our methods. First, we send a PASV command to the server to say that we want to use passive mode; the server responds with a message similar to the following:

```
227 Entering Passive Mode (192,168,0,1,177,147).
```

The first four values in the parentheses represent the IP address, and the last two represent the port number the server is listening on. We use these values to retrieve the IP address and port number used by the server for data connections. These are returned as 8-bit values, so we calculate the IP address by concatenating the values (separated by periods) into a string in the normal quad format (for example, "192.168.0.1"), and the port number by shifting the fifth value left by 8 bits, and adding the sixth value. Once we've done this, we can create and return a TcpClient object to open the data connection to the specified IP address and port number:

```
private TcpClient CreateDataSocket()
{
   // request server to listen on a data port (not the default data
   // port) and wait for a connection
   string respMessage;
   int resp = SendCommand("PASV", out respMessage);
   if (resp != 227)
      throw new WebException(respMessage);
   // The response includes the host address and port number
   // IP address and port number separated with ','
   // Create the IP address and port number
   int[] parts = new int[6];
   try
   {
      int index1 = respMessage.IndexOf('(');
      int index2 = respMessage.IndexOf(')');
      string endPointData = respMessage.Substring(index1 + 1,
                                            index2 - index1 - 1);
      string[] endPointParts = endPointData.Split(',');
      for (int i = 0; i < 6; i++)
      {
         parts[i] = int.Parse(endPointParts[i]);
      }
   }
   catch
   {
      throw new WebException("Malformed PASV reply: " + respMessage);
   }
   string ipAddress = parts[0] + "." + parts[1] + "." + parts[2] +
                      "." + parts[3];
   int port = (parts[4] << 8) + parts[5];
   // Create a client socket
   TcpClient dataClient = new TcpClient();
   // Connect to the data port of the server
   try
   {
      IPEndPoint remoteEP = new IPEndPoint(IPAddress.Parse(ipAddress),
                                           port);
      dataClient.Connect(remoteEP);
   }
   catch(Exception)
   {
      throw new WebException("Can't connect to remote server");
   }
   return dataClient;
}
```

The `Close` method simply reads any outstanding responses from the server, logs off, and cleans up the resources we've opened:

```
public void Close()
{
   if (dataStream != null)
   {
      dataStream.Close();
      dataStream = null;
   }
   string respMessage;
   GetResponse(out respMessage);
   Logoff();
   // Close the control TcpClient and NetworkStream
   controlStream.Close();
   client.Close();
}
```

The `Logoff` method simply sends a `STAT` command to the server for debugging purposes, and then sends a `QUIT` command. There will be two responses to the `STAT` command, so we need to call `GetResponse` to read the second:

```
public void Logoff()
{
   // Send the QUIT command to log off from the server
   string respMessage;
   SendCommand("STAT", out respMessage);  // Test only
   GetResponse(out respMessage);  // STAT has 2 response lines!
   SendCommand("QUIT", out respMessage);
}
```

The last method, `SendCommand`, is where we actually write the command to the control stream. We add the final CRLF combination to the command before sending it, so that we don't need to do this every time we call the method. Once we've sent the command, we call `GetResponse` to read the server's response:

```
      internal int SendCommand(string command, out string respMessage)
      {
         // Convert the command string (terminated with a CRLF) into a
         // byte array, and write it to the control stream
         byte[] request = Encoding.ASCII.GetBytes(command + "\r\n");
         controlStream.Write(request, 0, request.Length);
         return GetResponse(out respMessage);
      }
   }
}
```

That completes the code for the class library, so now let's write a simple console application to test it.

A Client Console Application

The first thing we need to do in our Main method is register the ftp prefix with WebRequest. We do this by calling the WebRequest.RegisterPrefix static method, and passing in the prefix associated with our new WebRequest extension, and an IWebRequestCreate implementation that will create an instance of our FtpWebRequest. After this, we call two methods to demonstrate uploading and downloading files, respectively:

```
using System;
using System.IO;
using System.Net;
using Apress.Networking.TCP.FtpUtil;
namespace TestClient
{
   class Class1
   {
      const int bufferSize = 65536;
      static void Main(string[] args)
      {
         // Register the ftp schema
         // Alternatively, a config file could be used
         WebRequest.RegisterPrefix("ftp", new FtpRequestCreator());
         UploadDemo();
         DownloadDemo();
      }
```

The UploadDemo method creates a new instance of our FtpWebRequest class and sets its properties to specify the user name and password used to make the connection, to specify the data format for the file (here, we want to use binary format, so we set the BinaryMode property to true), and the method to execute against the server. As we want to upload a file, this could be either PUT or STOR. Next, we call the GetResponseStream method of the associated FtpWebResponse object to retrieve an FtpWebStream that we can use to write the file content to the FTP server. In order to do this, we open a FileStream object pointing to the file we want to upload and copy it in 65,536-byte chunks into the FtpWebStream. Finally, we close the FtpWebStream (which will close the associated response and log off from the server) and the FileStream:

```
      // Upload a file using FtpWebRequest
      public static void UploadDemo()
      {
         FtpWebRequest req = (FtpWebRequest)WebRequest.Create(
                                         "ftp://192.168.0.1/demofile.bmp");
         req.Username = "Administrator";
         req.Password = "secret";
         req.Method = "PUT";  // STOR or PUT
         req.BinaryMode = true;
         Stream writeStream = req.GetResponse().GetResponseStream();
         FileStream fs = new FileStream(@"c:\temp\cool.bmp", FileMode.Open);
         byte[] buffer = new byte[bufferSize];
```

```
        int read;
        while ((read = fs.Read(buffer, 0, bufferSize)) > 0)
        {
            writeStream.Write(buffer, 0, bufferSize);
        }
        writeStream.Close();
        fs.Close();
    }
```

CAUTION You will need the appropriate permissions on the FTP server to upload files. By default, uploading files to the server is not permitted.

The `DownloadDemo` method is similar, but the way we use it depends on whether we're downloading binary or text data. If it's binary data, we copy the file data into a `FileStream` object in 65,536-byte chunks as in `UploadDemo`. If it's a text file, we can use the far simpler `StreamReader`:

```
    // Download a file using FtpWebRequest
    public static void DownloadDemo()
    {
        FtpWebRequest req = (FtpWebRequest)WebRequest.Create(
                                        "ftp://192.168.0.1/sample.bmp");
        // defaults:
        /* req.Username = "anonymous";
            req.Password = "someuser@somemail.com";
            req.BinaryMode = true;
            req.Method = "GET";    */
        FtpWebResponse resp = (FtpWebResponse)req.GetResponse();
        Stream stream = resp.GetResponseStream();
        // Read a binary file
        FileStream fs = new FileStream(@"c:\temp\sample.bmp",
                                   FileMode.Create);
        byte[] buffer = new byte[bufferSize];
        int count;
        do
        {
            Array.Clear(buffer, 0, bufferSize);
            count = stream.Read(buffer, 0, bufferSize);
            fs.Write(buffer, 0, count);
        } while (count > 0);
        stream.Close();
        fs.Close();
        /* read a text file
            StreamReader reader = new StreamReader(stream);
            string line;
```

```
            while ((line = reader.ReadLine()) != null)
            {
               Console.WriteLine(line);
            }
            reader.Close(); */
        }
    }
}
```

And that completes the project! This isn't the most robust possible implementation, and we haven't implemented every possible command, but it should give you a clear idea of what's involved in implementing an FTP client. It also shows how you can integrate your classes with the existing `WebRequest` framework, so that it's very intuitive to call.

Now that you've seen how the `TcpClient` class works, let's look at the other .NET class used with TCP, which is the `TcpListener class`.

The TcpListener Class

Typically, a server-side application starts by binding to the local endpoint and listening to incoming requests from clients. As soon as a client is found knocking on the port, the application activates by accepting the request and then creating a channel that is then responsible for communicating with the client. The application continues to listen for more incoming client requests on the main thread. The `TcpListener` class does exactly that: it listens to the client's request, accepts it, and then creates a new instance of the `Socket` class or the `TcpClient` class that you can use to communicate with the client. Just like `TcpClient`, `TcpListener` also encapsulates a private `Socket` object, `m_ServerSocket`, available only to derived classes.

Table 7-5 lists the important `TcpListener` properties.

Table 7-5. *TcpListener Properties*

Name	Type	Description
`LocalEndpoint`	`IPEndpoint`	A public property that returns an `IPEndpoint` object that contains information about the local network interface and the port number which is being used to listen for incoming client requests
`Active`	`bool`	A protected property that indicates whether the `TcpListener` is currently listening for connection requests
`Server`	`Socket`	A protected property that returns the underlying `Socket` object used by the listener to listen for connection requests

The `TcpListener` class has the following methods:

- The `AcceptSocket` method accepts a pending connection request and returns a `Socket` object to use to communicate with the client.
- The `AcceptTcpClient` method accepts a pending connection request and returns a `TcpClient` object to use to communicate with the client.

- The Pending method indicates whether there are any connection requests pending.
- The Start method causes the TcpListener to start listening for connection requests.
- The Stop method closes the listener.

Instantiating a TcpListener

The TcpListener constructor has three overloads:

```
public TcpListener(int port);
public TcpListener(IPEndPoint endPoint);
public TcpListener(IPAddress ipAddr, int port);
```

The first simply specifies on which port you want to listen. The IP address is this case is IPAddress.Any, which provides an address that the server should listen for client activity on all network interfaces. This field is equivalent to 0.0.0.0:

```
int port = 11000;
TcpListener newListener = new TcpListener(port);
```

This constructor is obsolete in .NET Framework 1.1.

The second overload takes an IPEndPoint object that specifies the IP address and port you want to listen on:

```
IPAddress ipAddr = IPAddress.Parse("127.0.0.1");
IPEndPoint endPoint = new IPEndPoint(ipAddr, 11000);
TcpListener newListener = new TcpListener(endPoint);
```

The third overload takes an IPAddress object and a port number:

```
IPAddress ipAddr = IPAddress.Parse("127.0.0.1");
int port = 11000;
TcpListener newListener = new TcpListener(ipAddr, port);
```

Listening for Clients

The next step after creating a socket is to start listening for client requests. The TcpListener class has a Start method that binds a socket using the IP address and port provided as arguments in the TcpListener constructor, and then begins listening for client connections by calling the Listen method on the underlying Socket.

```
TcpListener newListener = new TcpListener(ipAddr, port);
newListener.Start();
```

Once you've started listening to the socket, you can check whether there are already connections in the queue by calling the Pending method. This allows you to check for any waiting clients before the accept method is called, which will then block the running thread:

```
...
if (newListener.Pending())
{
   Console.WriteLine("There are connections pending in queue");
}
```

Accepting Connections from a Client

A typical server program uses two sockets: one used by the TcpListener class and another, which is returned when the listener accepts a client's connection, that is used to communicate individually with that client. The AcceptSocket or the simpler AcceptTcpClient method can be used to accept any request that is currently pending in the queue. These methods return a Socket or TcpClient, respectively, to accept client requests.

```
Socket sAccepted = newListener.AcceptSocket();
TcpClient sAccepted = newListener.AcceptTcpClient();
```

Sending and Receiving Messages

The actual communication between the client and the server socket can be performed using the Socket's Send and Receive methods or by writing to/reading from the NetworkStream, depending on the type of socket created when accepting the connection. This topic was covered in detail earlier in the section on the TcpClient class, so we will skip the code here.

Stopping the Server

After communicating with the client, the last step is to stop the listening socket. Calling the Stop method of the TcpListener class performs this step:

```
newListener.Stop();
```

Building a Multithreaded Client/Server Application

As an example of using the TcpListener class, we'll build a simple multithreaded echo server that can serve multiple echo clients using threads. Before showing the code, we will provide a short introduction to multithreading. As the topic is not directly connected with network programming, we won't attempt to cover multithreaded programming in detail, and we will assume familiarity with the basic concepts of threading.

An Introduction to Multithreading

The multithreading support in .NET is provided through the System.Threading namespace. The Thread class in this namespace represents an individual thread. The thread needs an entry point for running an alternative flow of code. This entry point is the method where the thread will begin execution. Naturally enough, this method is represented by a delegate—specifically, the ThreadStart delegate. Therefore, before creating an instance of the Thread class, you need to create an instance of the ThreadStart delegate, specifying the method name in the constructor.

After specifying the method using the delegate in the Thread constructor, the next step is to inform the operating system about the change in the thread state. The Start method of the Thread class notifies the operating system that the thread is changing its state to running:

```
// Threading.cs
using System;
using System.Threading;
public class MultiThread
{
   public static void runThread()
   {
      Console.WriteLine("Thread is running");
   }
   public static void Main(string [] arg)
   {
      // The ThreadStart specifying the delegate function
      ThreadStart threadMethod = new ThreadStart(runThread);
      // Create a thread instance with the ThreadStart delegate
      Thread newThread = new Thread(threadMethod);
      Console.WriteLine("Starting Thread");
      // Start the thread, which calls the runThread method in a separate thread
      newThread.Start();
   }
}
```

This is all that you need to know about using threads in a basic multithreaded server, although you will need a more intensive usage of the Thread class to build a more robust server application, with support for synchronization techniques such as locking and advanced thread manipulation such as thread pooling.

The Echo Client

The client for our example is a simple application, similar to the one shown in the previous section on the TcpClient class, so we don't need to look at it in too much detail here. Listing 7-1 shows the client for our application.

Listing 7-1. *Echo Client for the Multithreaded Server*

```
using System;
using System.Net;
using System.IO;
```

```
using System.Net.Sockets;
using System.Text;
public class EchoClient
{
   const int ECHO_PORT = 8080;
   public static void Main(string [] arg)
   {
      Console.Write("Your UserName:");
      string userName = Console.ReadLine();
      Console.WriteLine("-----Logged In----->");
      try
      {
         // Create a connection with the ChatServer
         TcpClient eClient = new TcpClient("127.0.0.1", ECHO_PORT);
         // Create the stream classes
         StreamReader readerStream = new StreamReader(eClient.GetStream());
         NetworkStream writerStream = eClient.GetStream();
         string dataToSend;
         dataToSend = userName;
         dataToSend += "\r\n";
         // Send user name to the server
         byte[] data = Encoding.ASCII.GetBytes(dataToSend);
         writerStream.Write(data,0,data.Length);
         while(true)
         {
            Console.Write(userName + ":");
            // Read line from server
            dataToSend = Console.ReadLine();
            dataToSend += "\r\n";
            data = Encoding.ASCII.GetBytes(dataToSend);
            writerStream.Write(data, 0, data.Length);
            // If QUIT is sent, then quit application
            if (dataToSend.IndexOf("QUIT") > -1)
               break;
            string returnData;
            // Receive response from server
            returnData = readerStream.ReadLine();
            Console.WriteLine("Server: " + returnData);
         }
         // Close TcpClient
         eClient.Close();
      }
      catch(Exception exp)
      {
         Console.WriteLine("Exception: " + exp);
      }
   }
}
```

The Multithreaded Server

The server application uses multiple threads for serving more than one client simultaneously. Figure 7-9 shows the flow of the server application.

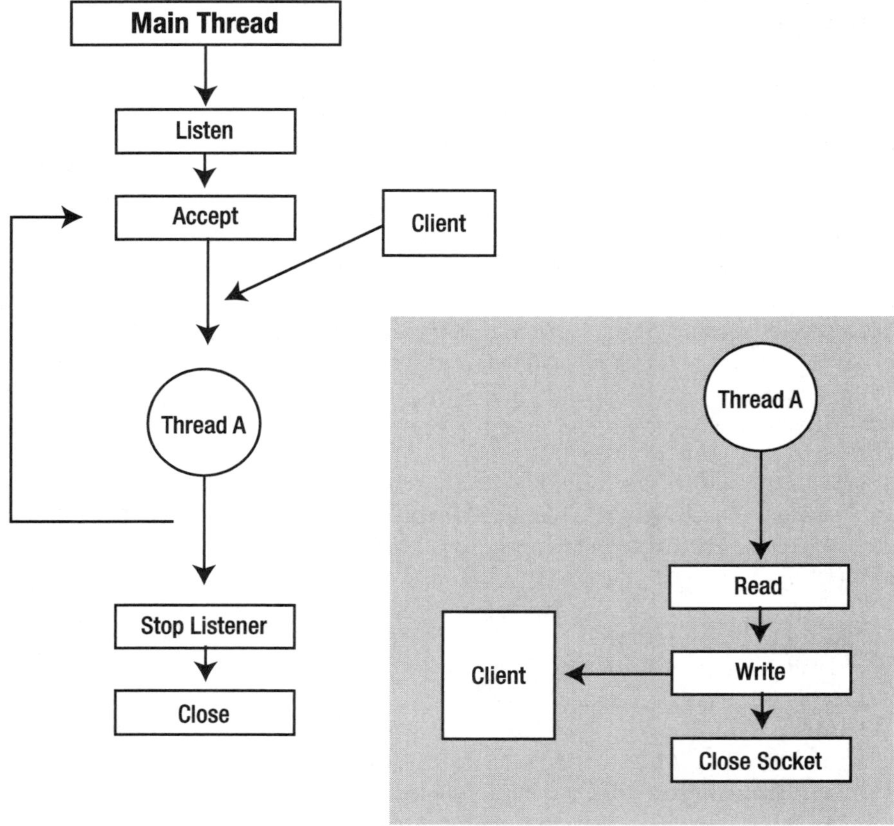

Figure 7-9. *The flow of the multithreaded server application*

Listing 7-2 shows the complete code for the server application.

Listing 7-2. *Multithreaded Echo Server*

```
// MEchoServer.cs
using System;
using System.Net;
using System.Net.Sockets;
using System.IO;
using System.Threading;
using System.Collections;
using System.Text;
public class ClientHandler
{
```

```
    public TcpClient clientSocket;
    public void RunClient()
    {
        // Create the stream classes
        StreamReader readerStream = new StreamReader(clientSocket.GetStream());
        NetworkStream writerStream = clientSocket.GetStream();
        string returnData = readerStream.ReadLine();
        string userName = returnData;
        Console.WriteLine("Welcome " + userName + " to the Server");
        while (true)
        {
            returnData = readerStream.ReadLine();
            if (returnData.IndexOf("QUIT") > -1)
            {
                Console.WriteLine("Bye Bye " + userName);
                break;
            }
            Console.WriteLine(userName + ": " + returnData);
            returnData += "\r\n";
            byte[] dataWrite = Encoding.ASCII.GetBytes(returnData);
            writerStream.Write(dataWrite,0,dataWrite.Length);
        }
        clientSocket.Close();
    }
}
public class EchoServer
{
    const int ECHO_PORT = 8080;
    public static int nClients = 0;
    public static void Main(string [] arg)
    {
        try
        {
            IPAddress ip=IPAddress.Parse("127.0.0.1");

            // Bind the server to the local port
            TcpListener clientListener = new TcpListener(ip,ECHO_PORT);
            // Start to listen
            clientListener.Start();
            Console.WriteLine("Waiting for connections...");
            while (true)
            {
                // Accept the connection
                TcpClient client = clientListener.AcceptTcpClient();
                ClientHandler cHandler = new ClientHandler();
                // Pass value to the ClientHandler object
                cHandler.clientSocket = client;
                // Create a new thread for the client
```

```
                Thread clientThread = new Thread(new ThreadStart(cHandler.RunClient));
                clientThread.Start();
            }
            clientListener.Stop();
        }
        catch(Exception exp)
        {
            Console.WriteLine("Exception: " + exp);
        }
    }
}
```

We start by creating an instance of the TcpListener class and specifying the port number to bind the socket to. The listener socket then starts listening and accepting client requests. The change in the code from that for a single-threaded server appears when the listener accepts a client's request. In a single-user server model, which only serves a single client at a time, a Stream object is built to communicate directly with the client. After wrapping up the existing client, the server would be able to start listening for a new client. All the tasks performed in this type of application are executed on a single thread. In a multithreaded application, as soon as the listener accepts a client's socket, it starts a new thread, which is responsible for negotiating with the client. The main server thread continues to listen for further requests.

The method that executes on the secondary thread is implemented in a different class, called ClientHandler. We use a member variable to pass data between the main thread and this secondary thread. When the listener accepts a TcpClient object, we instantiate a new object of the ClientHandler class and assign the TcpClient object to its public field. We then execute the RunClient method on a new thread. Since this is a member of the ClientHandler class, it can access the TcpClient object that we set from the main thread.

The RunClient method in the ClientHandler class is completely responsible for negotiating with a single client. It performs the procedure of creating streams and then reading and writing messages to the socket.

You can test the application by running the server first and then running multiple instances of the client and logging on with different names. Although this is the simplest of servers, built just for demonstration purposes, it can be used as a framework for developing a more robust server application.

.NET Remoting

Operating systems typically protect applications from the effects of other applications. Microsoft Windows provides this protection by implementing processes for each application. Each application is loaded in a separate process space. The code and memory running in a process cannot access another code running in a different process, although there are well-defined methods regulated by the operating system to achieve this.

In the .NET Framework, *application domains* (*AppDomains*) are the units used to provide isolation between two different applications. It is possible to run multiple AppDomains in a single process. The existence of different AppDomains within a single process means that if any piece of code in an AppDomain malfunctions for any reason, it won't harm the other AppDomains in the same process. You can also stop a piece of code included in an AppDomain. However, the most important advantage is that the code running in an AppDomain cannot access other code in a different AppDomain.

The process that is used to provide communication between different objects in different AppDomains is called *.NET Remoting*. The applications that are communicating can be on the same computer, on a single LAN, on the Internet, or in any other geographically located area connected with some protocol.

One of the advantages of . NET Remoting comes from the fact that, unlike the proprietary protocols employed by Microsoft DCOM and Java RMI, Remoting is built on accepted industry standards, such as Simple Object Access Protocol (SOAP), Hypertext Transfer Protocol (HTTP), and TCP. This makes it possible for different applications on the Internet to communicate as if they were making the connection over a private network.

However, while Remoting *can* use the SOAP and HTTP protocols, it doesn't have to. In fact, it's probably worth thinking twice if you're using SOAP with Remoting, as you lose some of the performance benefits of Remoting over ASP.NET web services. If you're using Remoting rather than web services, efficiency is probably a significant factor, and for best performance, you should use binary encoding with the TCP channel.

How Remoting Works

In order to use the Remoting framework, the hosting application must first be loaded, and you must register a channel and port to listen connections. The client also needs to register the same channel.

A *channel* is a transport medium between the server and the client. Channels use network protocols like TCP or HTTP to send data from one object to other. When a client calls a method on the server object, the parameters and other details for the method are packed inside a message object and transported through the channel to the remote object. A client can select any channel type that is registered on the server to be used as the transport medium. This allows developers to choose the best channel for their needs. There are two types of channels provided by the .NET Framework: the TCP transport channel and the HTTP transport channel. The TCP channel is discussed here, and the HTTP channel is discussed in Chapter 10. You can extend these built-in transport channel types, or even to create an altogether new channel type to be used in specialized environments or scenarios. The results are returned from the server in a similar way.

After the client has registered the channel, it creates a new instance of the remote class. If the client succeeds in instantiating a remote object, it then receives a reference to the server object, through which it can call methods on the remote object, as if it were part of the client process. The Remoting system uses a proxy to implement this. When the client creates an instance of the remote object, the Remoting framework intercepts the call and creates a proxy object with the same public interface as the real object, and then returns this proxy object to the client. The client then makes methods calls on this proxy. These calls are intercepted by the Remoting framework and routed to the server process. The server process then instantiates the object, calls the method, and sends the return value to the client application via the client proxy. Figure 7-10 illustrates the Remoting process.

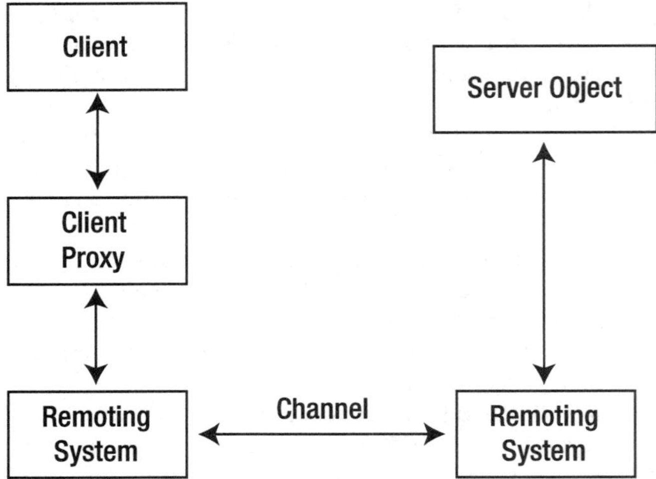

Figure 7-10. *The .NET Remoting process*

Channel Sinks

Channels route each message through a series of *channel sinks*. Each sink changes or filters the message, and then passes it on to the next sink in the chain, to the receiving application, or to the channel itself. There can be any number of sinks that process the messages sent over the channel, such as a security sink (for encrypting the message) or a logging sink (for tracking the Remoting process).

On the client side, the first sink is the *formatter sink*; this passes the message onto any custom sinks implemented in the sink chain. Finally, the message reaches the *transport sink*, which writes it to the transport channel.

On the server side, the whole process is reversed. The transport sink retrieves the message from the channel and forwards it to the channel sink chain. The last sink in the chain is the formatter sink, which routes the message to the Remoting infrastructure, so that it can be passed to the receiving application.

Formatter sinks are used for encoding and decoding of messages before the channel transports them. Two formatters are provided with the .NET Remoting framework:

Binary formatter: When binary formatting is used for messages, both the client and server require the .NET Framework to process messages. The type system maintains its state when transmission is performed using the binary formatter. Because the binary formatter depends on the .NET Framework, it can preserve the type system information by serializing or deserializing the object.

SOAP XML-based formatter: The SOAP formatter follows the SOAP specifications outlined by the W3C (`http://www.w3.org/TR/2002/WD-soap12-part1-20020626/`). This allows interoperability with other clients or servers. Because the SOAP formatter can include different implementations from different languages, it is not possible for it to preserve the type system information.

The binary formatter has better performance than the SOAP formatter because less data is sent over the network, and because it requires less time for serialization and deserialization. The SOAP formatter is designed for interoperability rather than performance.

Figure 7-11 shows how the channel sinks work.

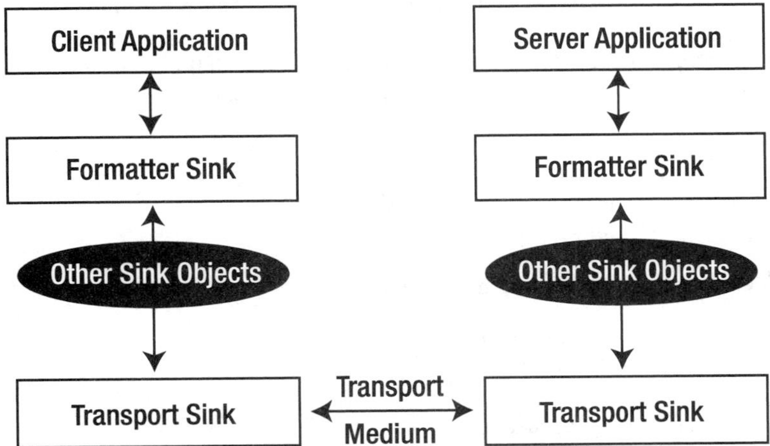

Figure 7-11. *Channel sinks*

The TCP Transport Channel

By default, the TCP transport channel uses the binary formatter to serialize all messages to the binary stream and transport them to the target using the TCP protocol. The .NET Framework provides the `System.Runtime.Remoting.Channels.Tcp` namespace to be used in applications that use the TCP transport channel. There are three classes in the namespace:

- .`TcpChannel` provides an implementation for a sender/receiver channel that uses TCP to transmit messages
- .`TcpClientChannel` provides an implementation for a client channel that uses TCP to transmit messages
- .`TcpServerChannel` provides an implementation for a server channel that uses TCP to transmit messages

Building a Simple Remoting Application

In this section, we'll demonstrate how to write a simple Remoting application. The client passes a string to the remote object, which echoes back the same string to the client.

There are three steps required to build a Remoting application: create the remote object, create the hosting application for the remote object, and then create the client application.

Creating the Remote Object

The remote object is a simple class instance. The only extension that it needs is that the class must inherit from the MarshalByRefObject class. We can convert all our existing classes to remote classes just by deriving them from MarshalByRefObject. There can be any number of methods and properties in the class. Here, we define a simple class that can be used to instantiate a remote object.

The first step before starting any Remoting application is to include all the namespaces required. The following namespaces are used for a TCP transport-based Remoting application:

```
// ServerObj.cs
using System.Runtime.Remoting;
using System.Runtime.Remoting.Channels;
using System.Runtime.Remoting.Channels.Tcp;
```

The next step is to define the class for the remote object:

```
// Notice that the class is derived from MarshalByRefObject
public class ServerObj : MarshalByRefObject
{
   public string ServerMethod(string argument)
   {
      Console.WriteLine(argument);
      return argument;
   }
}
```

We must build this class as a dynamic link library (DLL), so we use the following command to compile the remote object:

```
csc /target:library /out:ServerObj.dll ServerObj.cs
```

Creating the Hosting Application

After creating the remote object, the next step is to create an application that hosts our remote object on the server. The application that we build here is a simple console-based application (although for production, you might need to consider using Windows Services as a better alternative).

The first step is to include all the necessary using directives in the preceding code. The next step is to create and register the TcpChannel. (You should close the server created in the previous section before doing this, because we use Remoting on the same port.)

```
TcpChannel tcpChannel = new TcpChannel(8080);
```

The TcpChannel constructor is used to specify the port number for listening for client connections.

Next, we register the TCP channel:

```
ChannelServices.RegisterChannel(tcpChannel);
```

The ChannelServices class provides static methods for registering channels, getting registered channels, unregistering channels, creating the channel sink chain, dispatching messages to the sink chain, and URL discovery. All the channels that are registered can be accessed through the RegisteredChannels property, which returns an array of IChannel objects. The most important member of this class is the RegisterChannel method. It performs the registration of a channel with the channel services. It takes a single argument, which is the channel object we created earlier:

```
public static void RegisterChannel(IChannel channelObject);
```

It is important to note here that you cannot register two channels with the same name in the application domain. By default, the names of the HttpChannel and TcpChannel are http and tcp, respectively. If you need to register two channels, you must change the name of the respective channel by altering the ChannelName property of the channel object.

After creating and registering the channel, the RegisterWellKnownServiceType method of the RemotingConfiguration class is called to register the class with the Remoting framework:

```
RemotingConfiguration.RegisterWellKnownServiceType(
     typeof(RemoteSample.ServerObj),
     "EchoMessage",
     WellKnownObjectMode.SingleCall);
```

The RemotingConfiguration class provides static methods for configuring the Remoting options.

The RegisterWellKnownServiceType method takes three parameters that indicate the type of the Remoting class, the string to identify the Remoting object (that is, its URI), and the object activation mode. There are two types of activation for remote objects:

- *Server-activated objects* are created by the server only when they are needed, for instance when the client invokes the first method on that server. There are two activation modes for server-activated objects: Singleton and SingleCall. Singleton objects have only one instance, regardless of how many clients there are for that object. When an object is specified as SingleCall, a new instance is created every time for each client method invocation.

- *Client-activated objects* are created on the server when the client calls new or Activator.CreateInstance.

In the code sample, we created a server-activated object with SingleCall mode.

Finally, we wait for the client to connect with the server by blocking the input stream through Console.ReadLine:

```
Console.ReadLine();
```

Listing 7-3 shows the complete source code for the Remoting service application.

Listing 7-3. *Remoting Server Application with Server-Activated Objects*

```
// ServerApp.cs
using System;
using System.Runtime.Remoting;
using System.Runtime.Remoting.Channels;
using System.Runtime.Remoting.Channels.Tcp;
namespace RemoteSample
{
   public class ServerApp
   {
      public static void Main(string [] arg)
      {
         TcpChannel tcpChannel = new TcpChannel(8080);
         ChannelServices.RegisterChannel(tcpChannel);
         RemotingConfiguration.RegisterWellKnownServiceType(
              typeof(RemoteSample.ServerObj),
              "EchoMessage",
              WellKnownObjectMode.SingleCall);

         Console.WriteLine("Hit <enter> to continue...");
         Console.ReadLine();
      }
   }
}
```

Creating the Client Application

The last step in implementing the sample Remoting application is to create the client application. As with the server application, the client must also register the TCP channel with the channel services:

```
TcpChannel tcpChannel = new TcpChannel();
ChannelServices.RegisterChannel(tcpChannel);
```

Being a sharp reader, you may have noticed that the server IP address and port number have been omitted. Normally, a client requires two pieces of information to connect with the server: the server IP address and the port number. Here, we don't specify either of those. You will see in the next step how the Remoting framework handles this.

The next step is the most important for the client. Here, the object is created on the server and a reference to that object is returned to the client:

```
ServerObj obj = (ServerObj)Activator.GetObject(typeof(RemoteSample.ServerObj),
"tcp://localhost:8080/EchoMessage");
```

The `Activator` class provides methods to create types of objects remotely or locally, or to obtain references to existing remote objects. The `GetObject` method creates a proxy for a currently running remote server-activated well-known object. The object type and the URL are passed as parameters. Notice the URL, which is used to define the protocol, the port number, and the IP address for the remote object—all the information required to connect with a remote server that was missing from the TcpChannel constructor.

Here, we are trying out the example on a single PC, so we specified localhost, but it can be replaced with any server IP address on which you want to host your remote object.

After creating the proxy and getting the reference to the remote object by means of the proxy, we can call any of the methods declared in our remote object:

```
obj.ServerMethod("Apress Remoting Sample");
```

The complete client code is shown in Listing 7-4.

Listing 7-4. *Remoting Client Application with Server-Activated Objects*

```
// ClientApp.cs
using System;
using System.Runtime.Remoting;
using System.Runtime.Remoting.Channels;
using System.Runtime.Remoting.Channels.Tcp;
namespace RemoteSample
{
   public class ClientApp
   {
      public static void Main(string[] arg)
      {
         TcpChannel tcpChannel = new TcpChannel();

         ChannelServices.RegisterChannel(tcpChannel);

         ServerObj obj = (ServerObj)Activator.GetObject(
                              typeof(RemoteSample.ServerObj),
                              "tcp://localhost:8080/EchoMessage");

         Console.WriteLine(obj.ServerMethod("Apress Remoting Sample"));
      }
   }
}
```

When compiling both the client and server applications, we need to include a reference to the server object DLL, or we will receive an error stating, "The type or namespace name ServerObj does not exist in the class." The server is compiled using the following:

```
csc /r:ServerObj.dll ServerApp.cs
```

And the client application is compiled using the following:

```
csc /r:ServerObj.dll ClientApp.cs
```

After compiling all the files, you must execute the server application first to start listening for the client request.

Creating a Client-Activated Remote Object

The Remoting example demonstrates the remote instantiation of server-activated objects. For a client-activated object, although the remote object remains the same, there are some changes required in the server and client applications.

In the server application, shown in Listing 7-5, we call the `RegisterActivatedServiceType` method instead of `RegisterWellknownServiceType`. The `RegisterActivatedServiceType` takes a single argument that represents the type of the remote object. The URI in this case is assigned using the `ApplicationName` property of the `RemotingConfiguration` class.

Listing 7-5. *Remoting Server Application with Client-Activated Objects*

```
using System;
using System.Runtime.Remoting;
using System.Runtime.Remoting.Channels;
using System.Runtime.Remoting.Channels.Tcp;
namespace RemoteSample
{
   public class ServerApp
   {
      public static void Main(string [] arg)
      {
         TcpChannel tcpChannel = new TcpChannel(8080);
         ChannelServices.RegisterChannel(tcpChannel);
         RemotingConfiguration.ApplicationName = "EchoMessage";
         RemotingConfiguration.RegisterActivatedServiceType(
                                             typeof(RemoteSample.ServerObj));
         Console.WriteLine("Hit <enter> to continue...");
         Console.ReadLine();
      }
   }
}
```

On the client side, shown in Listing 7-6, we have two different methods to access the remote objects: `Activator.CreateInstance` and `RemotingConfiguration.RegisterActivatedClientType`. To create an instance of the remote object using the `new` keyword, you must first register the object type on the client by calling the `RegisterActivatedClientType` method. Calling `CreateInstance` gives us a new instance of the server object and requires the URL of the remote application as a parameter. The `UrlAttribute` class is used to pass attributes to `CreateInstance`. The `CreateInstance` method returns an `ObjectHandle` object that acts as a wrapper for the remote object; we can call this object's `UnWrap` method to get the remote object itself.

Listing 7-6. *Remoting Client Application with Client-Activated Objects*

```
using System;
using System.Runtime.Remoting;
using System.Runtime.Remoting.Channels;
using System.Runtime.Remoting.Channels.Tcp;
```

```
using System.Runtime.Remoting.Activation;
namespace RemoteSample
{
   public class ClientApp
   {
      public static void Main(string [] arg)
      {
         TcpChannel tcpChannel = new TcpChannel();
         ChannelServices.RegisterChannel(tcpChannel);

         // Method 1
         object[] attrs = {new UrlAttribute("tcp://localhost:8080/EchoMessage")};
         ObjectHandle handle = Activator.CreateInstance(
             "ServerObj", "RemoteSample.ServerObj", attrs);
         ServerObj obj = (ServerObj)handle.Unwrap();
         Console.WriteLine("Client:" + obj.ServerMethod("Apress Remoting Sample"));
         // Method 2
         RemotingConfiguration.RegisterActivatedClientType(
             typeof(RemoteSample.ServerObj), "tcp://localhost:8080/EchoMessage");
         ServerObj obj2 = new ServerObj();
         Console.WriteLine("Client2:" + obj2.ServerMethod(
                                               "Apress Remoting Sample"));
      }
   }
}
```

Although this sample application does perform all the basic steps involved in .NET Remoting, it could be greatly improved. You can see that there is no error checking performed in the code. There is an exception class called RemotingException provided especially for the Remoting framework, which can be used to help out with most of the hiccups involved in these types of applications. As the TCP channel employs the Socket class to connect to the server, a SocketException will be thrown if the server is not listening to the port. If you forget to inherit the remote class from MarshalByRefObject, the client code will throw a RemotingException when calling GetObject to create a proxy for the running remote object. A RemotingException is also thrown when you try to register a channel that is already registered. In this case, you can call the ChannelServices.GetChannel method, which will return the channel interface if it is already registered; otherwise, null is returned.

Summary

In this chapter, we looked into the TCP core architecture. We then covered client/server applications built using the higher level TcpClient and TcpListener classes. To demonstrate the power of TcpClient, we created a fully functional e-mail client. We also built a multithreaded echo server with the support of the .NET multithreading classes. Next, we covered the .NET Remoting framework, focusing on the TcpChannel transport channel provided with the .NET Framework. Finally, we demonstrated a simple Remoting application that instantiates an object on the server from a remote client.

CHAPTER 8

UDP

In Chapter 4, we looked at socket programming in .NET, and you learned how to use the `Socket` class to connect to remote hosts using different protocols. In Chapter 7, we looked at the `TcpClient` and `TcpListener` classes, which provide a higher-level implementation for connecting over TCP. The Microsoft .NET Framework also provides a special class called `UdpClient` specifically for implementing the User Datagram Protocol (UDP). In this chapter, we'll look at the basics of UDP, and then see how to use the `UdpClient` class.

In the previous chapter, you saw the *three-phase handshake* that TCP uses to ensure that data is transmitted correctly. While this does make TCP far more reliable, it also adds a lot of overhead. UDP has none of this overhead, so it's much faster. This makes it well suited for multimedia transmissions such as video streams, where the precise order in which packets arrive may not be critical.

In fact, UDP is an exceptionally simple protocol; the specification (RFC 768) is only three pages long! (This compares to 85 pages for the TCP specification, RFC 793.)

In this chapter we'll look at the following topics:

- A basic introduction to UDP, including its advantages and disadvantages
- Implementation of UDP in .NET using the `UdpClient` class
- Higher-level UDP-based protocols

An Overview of UDP

UDP is a simple, connectionless, datagram-oriented protocol and provides a fast but not necessarily reliable transport service. It supports and is often used for one-to-many communications, using broadcast or multicast IP datagrams. UDP is situated in the transport layer on top of IP (a network-layer protocol), as shown in Figure 8-1. See Chapter 1 for a discussion of how the OSI model maps to the TCP/IP architecture and the TCP/IP protocol suite.

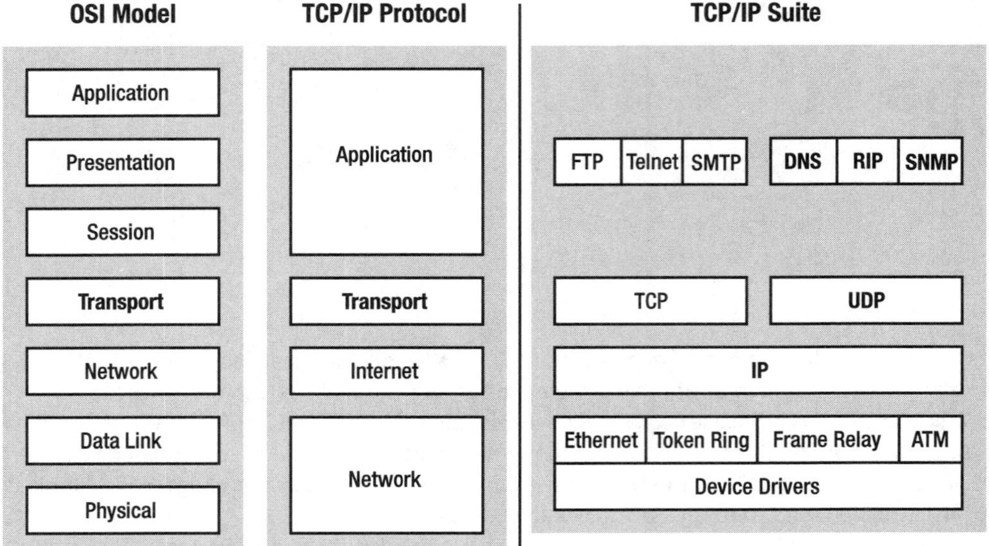

Figure 8-1. *The OSI model, TCP/IP protocol, and TCP/IP suite*

UDP Datagrams

A *datagram* is a self-contained, independent packet of data. It carries sufficient data to be routed from the source to the destination without further information, so no exchanges between the source and destination computers and the transporting network are required. The IP datagram consists of 32-bit source and destination IP addresses. The destination IP address specifies the endpoint for the UDP datagram, whereas the source IP address is used to check who sent the message. At the destination, packets are filtered, and those from restricted source IP addresses are discarded, without notifying the sender.

The *maximum transmission unit* (MTU) is a characteristic of the data link layer that describes the maximum number of bytes of data that can be transferred in a single packet. In other words, the MTU is the largest packet that a given network medium can carry. Ethernet, for example, has a fixed MTU of 1,500 bytes. In UDP, if the size of a datagram is larger than the MTU, IP performs fragmentation, breaking up the datagram into smaller pieces (*fragments*), so that each fragment is smaller than the MTU.

The *time-to-live* (TTL) value allows you to set an upper limit of routers through which a datagram can pass. The TTL value prevents packets from getting caught in routing loops forever. The TTL is initialized by the sender, and the value is decremented by every router that handles the datagram. When the TTL reaches zero, the datagram is discarded.

UDP Ports

UDP uses ports to map incoming data to a particular process running on a computer. UDP routes the packet at the appropriate location using the port number specified in the UDP header of the datagram.

UDP ports can receive more than one message at a time. In some cases, TCP and UDP services may use the same port numbers, such as port 7 (Echo) or port 23 (Telnet). UDP has the well-known ports listed in Table 8-1.

Table 8-1. *Well-Known UDP Ports*

UDP Port Number	Description
15	NETSTAT—Network Status
53	DNS—Domain Name Server
69	TFTP—Trivial File Transfer Protocol
137	NetBIOS Name Service
138	NetBIOS datagram service
161	SNMP—Simple Network Management Protocol

■ **NOTE** The list of UDP and TCP ports is maintained by Internet Assigned Numbers Authority (IANA). For more information about the associated ports, see `http://www.iana.org/assignments/port-numbers`.

How UDP Works

When a UDP-based application sends data to another networked host, UDP adds an 8-byte header containing the destination and source port number, along with the total length of the data and a checksum. IP adds its own header on top of the UDP datagram to form an IP datagram, as illustrated in Figure 8-2.

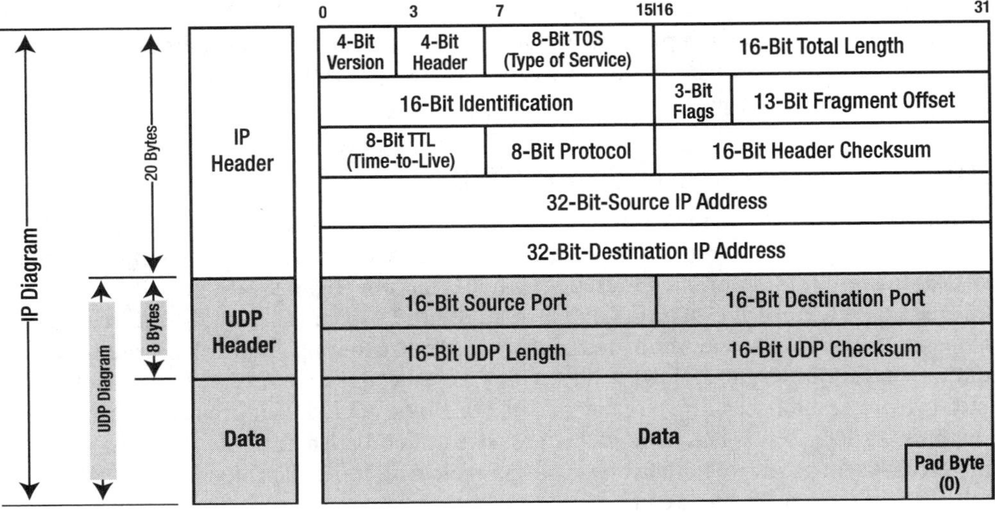

Figure 8-2. *The UDP and IP datagrams*

In Figure 8-2, the total length of the UDP header is specified as 8 bytes. Theoretically, the maximum size of an IP datagram is 65,535 bytes. Allowing for an IP header of 20 bytes and a UDP header of 8 bytes, the maximum size for user data is 65,508 bytes. However, most programs use a smaller size than this maximum value. For example, the default size for most applications is around 8,192 bytes because that is the amount of user data that the Network File System (NFS) reads and writes by default. You can set the size of receive and send buffers.

The checksum is used to check whether the data has properly arrived at the destination without being corrupted. The checksum covers both the UDP header and data. A pad byte is used if the checksum of the datagram is odd. If the checksum transmitted is zero, the receiver detects a checksum error and the datagram is discarded. The checksum is optional, but it is recommended that you always keep it enabled.

■ **NOTE** The checksum can't be enabled or disabled using the `UdpClient` class. To do this, you need to use the low-level `Socket` class (covered in Chapter 4) and set the `NoChecksum` option by calling its `SetSocketOption` method.

In the next step, the IP layer adds 20 bytes of header that includes the TTL, the source and destination IP addresses, and other information. This is known as *IP encapsulation*.

As we mentioned, the maximum size of a packet is 65,508 bytes. If the size of the packet exceeds the default size or the maximum size of the MTU, the IP layer breaks it into segments. These segments are called *fragments*, and the process of breaking the data into segments is known as *fragmentation*. The IP header contains all the information about the fragments.

When the sender application puts a datagram on the network, the datagram is routed to the destination IP address specified in the IP header. While passing through the router, the TTL value in the IP header is decreased by one.

When the datagram arrives at the correct destination and port, the IP layer checks whether the datagram is fragmented from the IP header. If it is fragmented, the datagram is reassembled using the information available in the header. Finally, the application layer retrieves the filtered data by removing the header.

Differences Between TCP and UDP

The main difference between TCP and UDP is that TCP is a connection-oriented protocol that verifies the success of communications, and UDP is connectionless protocol that provides fast, lower-overhead communications, but without guaranteeing delivery.

One major feature of UDP that is not available with TCP is multicasting. *Multicasting* is an open, standards-based method for simultaneously distributing identical information to multiple users. Multicasting allows you to achieve one-to-many communications, such as sending news or mail to multiple recipients, relaying Internet radio, or providing online demo programs. Multicasting is less bandwidth-intensive than broadcasting, because data for multiple users is sent at once. Multicasting is not possible with the TCP protocol. We'll look at multicasting in detail in the next chapter.

Table 8-2 summarizes the differences between TCP and UDP, and the following sections describe the advantages and disadvantages of UDP compared with TCP, as well as when to use UDP.

Table 8-2. *Features of UDP and TCP*

Characteristics	UDP	TCP
Connection-oriented	No	Yes
Use of session	No	Yes
Reliability	No	Yes
Acknowledgment	No	Yes
Sequencing	No	Yes
Flow control	No	Yes
Secure	Less	More
Data checksum	Optionally	Yes
Overhead	Less	More
Speed	Fast	Slower
Topology	One-to-one *and* one-to-many	One-to-one
Header size	8 bytes	20 bytes

Disadvantages of UDP

Compared to TCP, UDP has the following disadvantages:

Lack of handshaking signals: Before sending a segment, UDP does not use handshaking signals between sending and receiving the transport layer. The sender therefore has no way of knowing whether the datagram reaches the end system. As a result, UDP cannot guarantee that the data will actually be delivered at the destination (for example, in cases where the end system is off or the network is down). In contrast, TCP is a connection-oriented service and provides communication between a networked host using packets. TCP uses handshaking signals to check whether the transportation of data was successful.

No support for sessions: UDP doesn't have any support for sessions due to its connection-less nature. To make TCP connection-oriented, sessions are maintained between hosts. TCP uses session IDs to keep track of connections between two hosts.

No guarantee of sequenced data delivery: UDP does not guarantee that only one copy of the data will be delivered to the destination. To send large amounts of data to the end system, UDP breaks it into small segments. UDP does not guarantee that these segments will be delivered to the destination in the same order as they were created at the source. In contrast, TCP uses sequence numbers, along with port numbers and frequent acknowledgment packets, to guarantee sequenced delivery of data.

Reduced security: TCP is more secure than UDP. In many organizations, firewalls and routers do not allow UDP packets. This is because hackers can use UDP ports, as explicit connections aren't required.

Lack of flow control: UDP doesn't have flow control; as a result, a poorly designed UDP application can tie up a big chunk of network bandwidth.

Advantages of UDP

Compared to TCP, UDP has the following advantages:

Lower overhead requirements: TCP has higher overhead requirements; UDP has comparatively low overhead requirements. UDP is a connectionless protocol, so the overhead of making connections can be avoided. TCP uses substantially more operating resources than UDP does, and as a result, UDP is widely used in environments where servers handle many simultaneous clients. For example, this is why DNS prefers UDP over TCP; DNS would be much slower if it ran over TCP.

Speed: UDP is fast compared to TCP. As UDP does not use any handshaking signals, the delay in making connections can be avoided. Because of this, many applications prefer UDP over TCP. The features that make TCP more robust than UDP (such as handshaking signals) also make it slower.

Topology support: UDP supports both one-to-one and one-to-many (multicast) connections, whereas TCP supports only one-to-one communication.

Smaller header size: UDP has only 8-byte headers for every segment, whereas TCP has 20-byte headers, so UDP consumes less network bandwidth.

When to Use UDP

Many applications on the Internet use UDP. UDP is known as a "best-effort service" protocol. Looking at the advantages and disadvantages of UDP, we can conclude that UDP is beneficial for the following applications:

- For broadcasting or multicasting purposes, where the application wants to communicate with multiple hosts
- Where the datagram size is small and the sequence of fragments is not important
- Where connection setup is not required
- When the application doesn't want to send important bulk data (as UDP has no flow control)
- If retransmission of packets is not required
- Where low overhead on the operating system is required
- Where network bandwidth is crucial

.NET Support for UDP

In .NET, you can implement UDP by using the `Socket` class or the `UdpClient` class. We looked at using the `Socket` class in Chapter 4. This class gives you access to more options than the higher-level `UdpClient` class (such as the ability to disable the checksum, as we mentioned earlier), but it does make the code slightly more complex. However, the `UdpClient` class is built on top of the `Socket` class, and by inheriting from `UdpClient`, you can access the underlying `Socket`.

■ **NOTE** The WinSock control and WinSock unmanaged API can also be used to implement UDP. These rely on COM interoperability and P/Invoke, respectively, and are not covered in this book. The `System.Net.Sockets` namespace is essentially a wrapper for the WinSock API, so it is preferable to use the .NET classes. The WinSock control may be a good option for former Visual Basic programmers who want to keep their programming as visual as possible, but it adds the overhead of COM interoperability, so it's not a good solution.

The .NET classes for working with UDP reside in the `System.Net.Sockets` namespace. This namespace provides managed classes for TCP, UDP, and generic sockets programming, as you learned in Chapter 4.

The UdpClient Class

The Microsoft .NET Framework provides the `UdpClient` class for implementing UDP on a network. As with the `TcpClient` and `TcpListener` classes, this class is built on the `Socket` class, but it hides unnecessary members that aren't required for implementing a UDP-based application.

■ **NOTE** Before implementing `UdpClient`, you must be familiar with some of the other primary classes in .NET and understand the basics of working with sockets in .NET. These topics are covered in Chapters 3 and 4.

Using `UdpClient` is quite simple, requiring only four basic steps, as illustrated in Figure 8-3. First, create an instance of `UdpClient`. Next, connect to the remote host by calling its `Connect` method. These two steps can be achieved in one line of code by specifying the remote IP address and remote port number in the `UdpClient`'s constructor. We said earlier that UDP is a connectionless protocol. So, you might be wondering, why do we need to connect? In fact, the `Connect` method does not actually establish a connection to the remote host prior to sending and receiving data. When you send a datagram, the destination needs to be known; the specified IP address and port number serve this purpose. The third step is to send or receive the data using the `Send` or `Receive` method. Finally, the `Close` method closes the UDP connection.

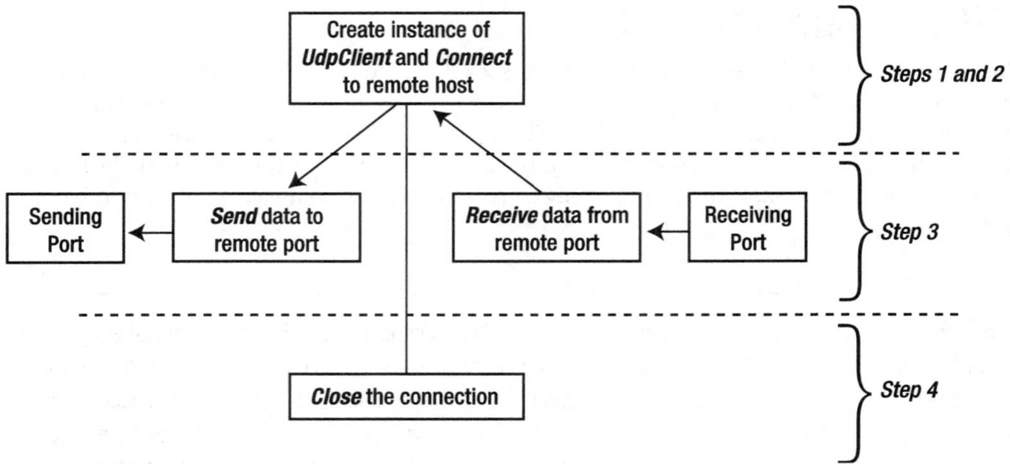

Figure 8-3. *Using the UdpClient class*

Table 8-3 lists the methods of the `UdpClient` class. We'll look at the important methods and properties in detail as we discuss using the `UdpClient` class.

Table 8-3. *UdpClient Methods*

Name	Description
`Connect`	A public method that provides connection information used to send data to a remote host.
`Send`	A public method that sends data via UDP
`Receive`	A public method that receives data from a remote host via UDP
`Close`	A public method that closes an open UDP connection
`JoinMulticastGroup`	A public method used to join a multicast group
`DropMulticastGroup`	A public method used to disconnect a `UdpClient` from a multicast group
`GetHashCode`	A public method inherited from `System.Object`
`Equals`	A public method inherited from `System.Object`
`ToString`	A public method inherited from `System.Object`
`GetType`	A public method inherited from `System.Object`
`Finalize`	A protected method inherited from `System.Object`
`MemberwiseClone`	A protected method inherited from `System.Object`

The `UdpClient` class has the following protected properties:

- The `Active` property is used to check the connection with the remote host.
- This `Client` property is used for retrieving the underlying `Socket` object that is used by the `UdpClient`.

Instantiating a UdpClient Class

A UdpClient instance can be created in a number of different ways, depending on the parameters passed in. How you use the UdpClient object depends on how it was created. You can create a UdpClient instance in the following ways:

- Use the default constructor
- Specify a port number as a parameter
- Use an IPEndPoint instance to represent the local IP address and port number to use for the connection
- Pass both a host name and a port number into the constructor

Using the Default Constructor

The simplest way to create a UdpClient instance is to use the default constructor (passing in no parameters). When you use an instance created in this way, you need to either call the Connect method to establish a connection or specify the connection information when you send data.

```
// Instantiate UdpClient using the default constructor
UdpClient udpClient = new UdpClient();
```

If you use this constructor, an arbitrary free port number will be chosen, and the IP address 0.0.0.0 will be used.

Specifying a Port Number

You can also specify a port number as a parameter when you create a UdpClient instance.

```
// Instantiate UdpClient using port number
try
{
   UdpClient udpClient = new UdpClient(5001);
}
catch (ArgumentOutOfRangeException e)
{
   Console.WriteLine("Invalid port number");
}
catch (SocketException e)
{
   Console.WriteLine("Port is already in use");
}
```

In this case, the UdpClient will listen on all local interfaces (that is, it will use the IP address 0.0.0.0). If the port number is not within the range specified by the MinPort and MaxPort fields of the IPEndPoint class, an ArgumentOutOfRangeException (derived from ArgumentException) is thrown. If the port is already in use, a SocketException will be thrown.

Using an IPEndPoint Instance

You can also use an IPEndPoint instance representing the local IP address and port number that you want to use for the connection. The first step here is to instantiate the IPEndPoint; the IPEndPoint instance can be created using a long IP address or an IPAddress object.

```
// Creates an instance of IPEndPoint.
IPAddress ipAddress = IPAddress.Parse("127.0.0.1");
IPEndPoint ipLocalEndPoint = new IPEndPoint(ipAddress, 5001);
try
{
   // Use IPEndPoint instance to create the UdpClient instance
   UdpClient udpClient = new UdpClient(ipLocalEndPoint);
}
catch (Exception e)
{
   Console.WriteLine(e.ToString());
}
```

The IP address must be one of the interfaces of the local machine, or a SocketException will be thrown with the error "The requested address is not valid in its context." If a null instance of IPEndPoint is passed into the constructor, an ArgumentNullException is thrown.

Specifying a Host Name and Port Number

If you pass both a host name and a port number into the constructor, the constructor is initialized using the host name and port number of the remote host. This allows you to eliminate the step of calling the Connect method, as this method is called from within this constructor.

```
// Instantiate UdpClient using remote host name and a port number.
try
{
   UdpClient udpClient = new UdpClient("remoteHostName", 5001);
}
catch (Exception e)
{
   Console.WriteLine(e.ToString());
}
```

Specifying the Connection Information

The second step in using UdpClient, once you've created a UdpClient object, is to provide the connection information that is used if you want to send any data to a remote host. Remember that UDP is a connectionless protocol, so this information isn't needed if you only want to receive data; it's used only to indicate where you want to send data.

This information can be specified in any of three places: in the UdpClient constructor, as you've just seen, in an explicit call to UdpClient's Connect method, or in your call to the Send method when you actually send the data.

The Connect method has three overloads:

- Using an IPEndPoint instance
- Establishing a connection using the IP address and the port number of the remote host
- Using a DNS or machine name and the port number of the remote host

Using an IPEndPoint Object

The first overload for Connect uses an instance of the IPEndPoint class to connect to the remote host, so you should create an IPEndPoint instance before calling the Connect method.

```
// Create instance of UdpClient
UdpClient udpClient = new UdpClient();
// Get the IP address of the remote host
IPAddress ipAddress = IPAddress.Parse("224.56.0.1");
// Create instance of IPEndPoint using IPAddress and port number
IPEndPoint ipEndPoint = new IPEndPoint(ipAddress, 1234);
try
{
   // Connect using this IPEndPoint instance
   udpClient.Connect(ipEndPoint);
}
catch (Exception e)
{
   Console.WriteLine("Error while connecting: " + e.ToString());
}
```

If any error occurs while connecting, a SocketException will be thrown.

Using an IP Address and Port Number

The second overload takes an IPAddress object and the port number of the remote host. If you know the remote IP address and the remote UDP port, you can make the connection to the remote UDP host, as shown in this example:

```
// Create instance of UdpClient
UdpClient udpClient = new UdpClient();
// Get the IP address of remote host
IPAddress ipAddress = IPAddress.Parse("224.56.0.1");
try
{
   // Connect using created IPAddress instance and remote port
   udpClient.Connect(ipAddress, 1234);
}
catch (Exception e )
{
   Console.WriteLine("Error while connecting: " + e.ToString());
}
```

Using the Host Name and Port Number

The other Connect overload uses the DNS or machine name and the port number of the remote host. This method is quite easy, as you do not need to create an IPAddress or IPEndPoint instance.

```
// Create instance of UdpClient
UdpClient udpClient = new UdpClient();
try
{
   udpClient.Connect("remoteMachineName", 1234);
}
catch (Exception e)
{
   Console.WriteLine("Error while connecting: " + e.ToString());
}
```

Sending Data Using UdpClient

Once you've created a UdpClient instance and (optionally) supplied the connection details, you can start to send data. Unsurprisingly, you do this by calling the Send method, which is used to send a datagram from the client to the remote host. One important point about UDP is that it does not receive any type of acknowledgment after sending data to a remote host. Like the Connect method, Send has several overloads. Send returns the length of the data, which can be used to check whether the data was sent properly.

The basic procedure for sending data with the UdpClient class, illustrated in Figure 8-4, involves four steps: create a UdpClient instance, connect to the remote host (optional), send the data, and then close the connection.

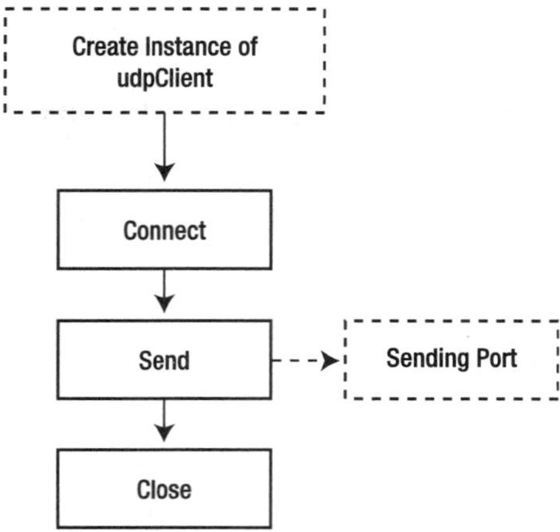

Figure 8-4. *Sending data using UdpClient*

Here is an example that shows this general process:

```
// Example of sending data
private static void Send(string datagram)
{
    // Remote IP address
    IPAddress remoteAddress = IPAddress.Parse("127.0.0.1");
    // Port we want to connect to
    int remotePort = 5001;
    // ** STEP 1 ** Create the UdpClient instance
    UdpClient sender = new UdpClient();
    try
    {
        // ** STEP 2 ** Connect to remote host
        sender.Connect(remoteAddress, remotePort);
        Console.WriteLine("Sending datagram: {0}", datagram);
        byte[] bytes = Encoding.ASCII.GetBytes(datagram);
        // ** STEP 3 ** Send data to connected host
        sender.Send(bytes, bytes.Length);
        // ** STEP 4 ** Close the connection
        sender.Close();
    }
    catch (Exception e)
    {
        Console.WriteLine(e.ToString());
    }
}
```

Although this example shows the general approach, the `Send` method can be used in various ways, depending on how the `UdpClient` was connected to the remote port and how the `UdpClient` instance was created. If no connection information has been specified before you call `Send`, you need to include this information within the call.

The `Send` method has three overloads:

- Using an `IPEndPoint` instance
- Specifying the host name and port number of the remote host
- Sending just the data (assumes a connection has already been made)

Using an IPEndPoint Object

The first overload takes three parameters: the data as an array of bytes, the length of the data as an `int`, and an `IPEndPoint` object. Note that you cannot call this overload if you called the `Connect` method manually or if you supplied connection information in the `UdpClient`'s constructor. To use this overload of `Send`, first create an `IPEndPoint` instance by specifying the endpoint you want to connect to—the remote IP address and port number. Then pass this IPEndPoint object into the Send method.

```
// Create udpClient instance. Note how instance is created.
UdpClient udpClient = new UdpClient();
// Get the remote IPAddress
IPAddress ipAddress = IPAddress.Parse("148.182.27.1");
// Create instance of IPEndPoint by passing IP address and remote port
IPEndPoint ipEndPoint = new IPEndPoint(ipAddress, 5005);
// Create data in byte[] format
byte[] sendBytes = Encoding.ASCII.GetBytes("Apress UDP Send Example");
try
{
   // Send data using the IPEndPoint instance.
   udpClient.Send(sendBytes, sendBytes.Length, ipEndPoint);
}
catch (Exception e)
{
   Console.WriteLine("Error: " + e.ToString());
}
```

Using the Host Name and Port Number

The second overload allows you to specify the host name and port number of the remote endpoint, as well as the actual data and its length in bytes. Again, Send assumes that the connection has not been established between the client and the remote host, so this overload cannot be called if you have already called the Connect method or specified connection information in the UdpClient constructor.

```
// Create udpClient instance. Note how instance is created.
UdpClient udpClient = new UdpClient();
// Create data in byte[] format
byte[] sendBytes = Encoding.ASCII.GetBytes("Apress UDP Send Example");
try
{
   // Send data by specifying remote machine name and remote port
   udpClient.Send(sendBytes, sendBytes.Length, "remoteHostName", 5001);
}
catch (Exception e)
{
   Console.WriteLine("Error: " + e.ToString());
}
```

Sending Just the Data

The final overload assumes that the UDP client is already connected to the remote host, so it only remains for you to send the data and an int representing the data length using the Send method. This is the only overload that can be used in conjunction with the Connect method.

```
// Create udpClient instance. Note how instance is created.
UdpClient udpClient = new UdpClient("remoteHostName", 5001);
// Create data in byte[] format
byte[] sendBytes = Encoding.ASCII.GetBytes("Apress UDP Send Example");
try
{
   // Send data
   udpClient.Send(sendBytes, sendBytes.Length);
}
catch (Exception e)
{
   Console.WriteLine("Error: " + e.ToString());
}
```

Receiving Data Using UdpClient

To receive data from a remote host via UDP, you (naturally) call the `Receive` method. This method takes one reference parameter, an instance of `IPEndPoint`, and returns the received data as a `byte` array. It is generally advised to execute this method on a separate thread, since this method polls the underlying socket for incoming datagrams and blocks until data is received. If this is run on the main thread, your program execution will halt until it receives the datagram packet.

If you've already specified connection information for the `UdpClient` instance, either in the constructor or by calling `Connect`, only data from the specified remote endpoint will be accepted and returned to your application; connections from other sources will be rejected. If no connection information has been specified, all incoming connections to the local endpoint will be accepted.

After receiving a datagram, the method returns the sent data as a `byte` array (with the header information stripped off) and populates the `IPEndPoint` reference parameter with information about the remote host that sent the data.

The process for receiving data from a remote host is very similar to that for sending data. As illustrated in Figure 8-5, it involves three general steps: create a `UdpClient` instance, receive data, and close the `UdpClient` instance.

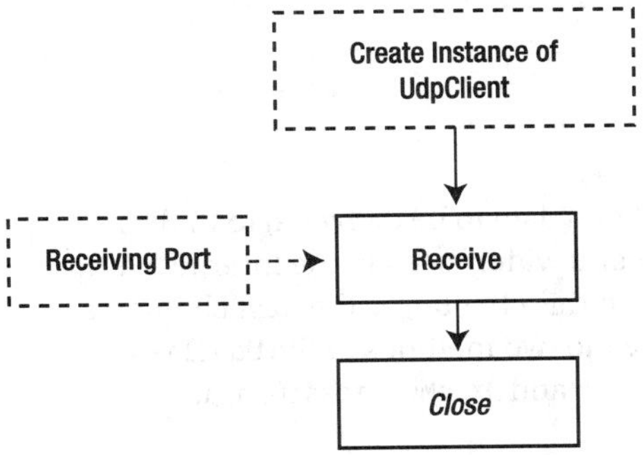

Figure 8-5. *Receiving messages with UdpClient*

The following example shows the general process:

```
// Example of receiving data
private static void Receive()
{
   // ** STEP 1 ** Create a UdpClient for reading incoming data.
   UdpClient receivingUdpClient = new UdpClient(5001);  // Listening on port 5001
   // Create IPEndPoint variable to pass into Receive() as ref parameter
   IPEndPoint RemoteIpEndPoint = null;
   try
   {
      Console.WriteLine("Listening on port 5001...");
      // ** STEP 2 ** Without thread, blocks until the socket finishes
      // receiving the data
      byte[] receiveBytes = receivingUdpClient.Receive(ref RemoteIpEndPoint);

      // Convert the data
      string returnData = Encoding.ASCII.GetString(receiveBytes);
      Console.WriteLine("{0} bytes received from {1}",
                  receiveBytes.Length, RemoteIpEndPoint.ToString());
      Console.WriteLine(returnData);
      // ** STEP 3 ** Close the UdpClient
      receivingUdpClient.Close();
   }
   catch (Exception e)
   {
      Console.WriteLine(e.ToString());
   }
}
```

Closing the Connection

The last step in working with `UdpClient` is to close the connection. The `Close` method is used to close an open UDP connection. If any error occurs while closing the connection, a `SocketException` is thrown. Closing a connection is very simple:

```
udpClient.Close();
```

Joining and Leaving Multicast Groups

As mentioned earlier in this chapter, multicasting allows data to be delivered to multiple destinations. Multicasting is a characteristic of UDP and widely used in the Internet world.

We're not going to look at multicasting in depth in this chapter, as the next chapter is dedicated solely to that topic. Here we will introduce the two methods of the `UdpClient` class that are used for multicasting: `JoinMulticastGroup` and `DropMulticastGroup`.

The JoinMulticastGroup Method

The `JoinMulticastGroup` method is used to join a multicast group. With this method, the `UdpClient` can receive multicast datagrams broadcast to the specified IP address. This method has two overloads.

The first overload just takes an `IPAddress` object representing the IP address of the multicast group to join. The `UdpClient` will receive any datagrams broadcast to this IP address.

```
// Create instance of UdpClient
UdpClient udpClient = new UdpClient();
// IPAddress with multicast ip
IPAddress multicastIP = IPAddress.Parse ("224.123.32.64");
try
{
   // Join multicast group
   udpClient.JoinMulticastGroup(multicastIP);
}
catch (Exception e)
{
   Console.WriteLine(e.ToString());
}
```

The second overload takes the multicast IP address with the TTL value as an `int`:

```
UdpClient udpClient = new UdpClient();
// Create an IPAddress to use to join
IPAddress multicastIP = Dns.Resolve("mutliCastHost").AddressList[0];
try
{
    // The life of packet is 30 router hops
    UdpClient.JoinMulticastGroup(multicastIP, 30);
}
catch (Exception e)
{
   Console.WriteLine(e.ToString());
}
```

■NOTE To send a multicast datagram, specify an IP multicast address within the range 224.0.0.0 to 239.255.255.255.

The DropMulticastGroup Method

The DropMulticastGroup method can be used to disconnect a UdpClient instance from a multicast group. This method takes one parameter: the IP address of the multicast group from which the client is to be dropped.

```
try
{
   // Drop multicast group by sending instance of IPAddress
   udpClient.DropMulticastGroup(multicastIP);
}
catch (Exception e)
{
   Console.WriteLine("Error while using DropMulticastGroup :" +
                     e.ToString());
}
```

Using the Active and Client Protected Properties

The UdpClient class has two protected properties—Active and Client—which are accessible from within the class in which the property is declared and from within a derived class. This means that you cannot directly use the UdpClient instance to access the protected properties.

The Active property is used to check the connection with the remote host. This property returns true if the connection is active.

The Client property is used to retrieve the underlying Socket object that is used by the UdpClient instance. As we mentioned earlier, the UdpClient class is built on top of the Socket class. The Client property allows you to access the underlying socket, and therefore, to access all the members of the Socket class that are not available through the UdpClient class. This is the biggest advantage of this property. For example, you can use the Blocking property of the Socket class to specify whether or not the Socket is in blocking mode. You cannot do this with the available members of the UdpClient class.

The following example uses both the Active and the Client properties.

```
// Using the Active and Client properties
using System;
using System.Net;
using System.Net.Sockets;
class UdpDerived : UdpClient
{
   public void insideSocket()
   {
      // Uses the protected Active property belonging to the UdpClient base
      // class to determine if a connection is established.
      if (this.Active)
      {
         Console.WriteLine("Connection is Active!");
         // Retrieve underlying Socket instance to get rich set of all
         // methods and properties of Socket class
         Socket richSock = this.Client;
```

```
            // e.g. following Socket property returns socket type you used
            Console.WriteLine("Socket Type is: " + richSock.SocketType.ToString());
         }
      }
      [STAThread]
      static void Main(string[] args)
      {
         UdpDerived derivedInstance = new UdpDerived();
         // Connect to test Active property
         IPEndPoint endPoint = new IPEndPoint(IPAddress.Parse("127.0.0.1"), 5001);
         // Connect using instance of derived class
         derivedInstance.Connect(endPoint);
         // Call protected method
         derivedInstance.insideSocket();
      }
   }
```

Creating a Chat Application Using UDP

To demonstrate using the UdpClient class, we'll develop a simple chat application in C#. The chat application uses a separate thread for listening for messages from the remote hosts. The Thread class is in the System.Threading namespace, so we will add the following using directive to the project:

```
using System.Threading;
```

■ **NOTE** The complete code for this application, as well as the other examples presented in this chapter, is available from the Downloads section of the Apress website: http://www.apress.com.

The full code for the chat application is shown in Listing 8-1.

Listing 8-1. *UDP Chat Application*

```
using System;
using System.Net;
using System.Net.Sockets;
using System.Text;
using System.Threading;
namespace Apress.Networking.UDP.ChatApp
{
   class Chat
   {
      private static IPAddress remoteIPAddress;
      private static int remotePort;
      private static int localPort;
```

```
[STAThread]
static void Main(string[] args)
{
   try
   {
      // Get necessary data for connection
      Console.WriteLine("Enter Local Port");
      localPort = Convert.ToInt16(Console.ReadLine());
      Console.WriteLine("Enter Remote Port");
      remotePort = Convert.ToInt16(Console.ReadLine());
      Console.WriteLine("Enter Remote IP address");
      remoteIPAddress = IPAddress.Parse(Console.ReadLine());

      // Create thread for listening
      Thread tRec = new Thread(new ThreadStart(Receiver));
      tRec.Start();

      while(true)
      {
         Send(Console.ReadLine());
      }
   }
   catch (Exception e)
   {
      Console.WriteLine(e.ToString());
   }
}
private static void Send(string datagram)
{
   // Create UdpClient
   UdpClient sender = new UdpClient();
   // Create IPEndPoint with details of remote host
   IPEndPoint endPoint = new IPEndPoint(remoteIPAddress, remotePort);
   try
   {
      // Convert data to byte array
      byte[] bytes = Encoding.ASCII.GetBytes(datagram);
      // Send data
      sender.Send(bytes, bytes.Length, endPoint);
   }
   catch (Exception e)
   {
      Console.WriteLine(e.ToString());
   }
   finally
   {
      // Close connection
      sender.Close();
```

```
            }
        }
        public static void Receiver()
        {
            // Create a UdpClient for reading incoming data.
            UdpClient receivingUdpClient = new UdpClient(localPort);
            // IPEndPoint with remote host information
            IPEndPoint RemoteIpEndPoint = null;
            try
            {
                Console.WriteLine(
                       "-----------*******Ready for chat!!!*******-----------");
                while(true)
                {
                    // Wait for datagram
                    byte[] receiveBytes = receivingUdpClient.Receive(
                                                     ref RemoteIpEndPoint);
                    // Convert and display data
                    string returnData = Encoding.ASCII.GetString(receiveBytes);
                    Console.WriteLine("-" + returnData.ToString());
                }
            }
            catch (Exception e)
            {
                Console.WriteLine(e.ToString ());
            }
        }
    }
}
```

The application is divided into three logical parts: specifying connection information, receiving data, and sending data. In the first part, the user is asked to enter information about the local and remote ports and the remote IP address to use. Figure 8-6 shows a possible setup for the ports that allows the application to be tested on a single machine. Port 5001 is used as the sending port for host A and the receiving port for client B, and vice versa for port 5002.

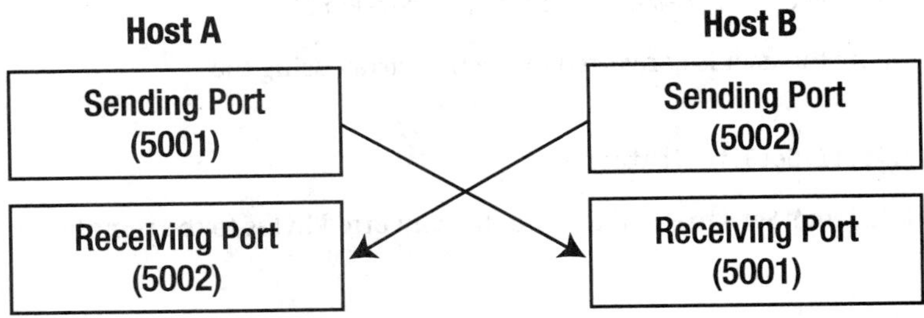

Figure 8-6. *A setup for testing the chat application on a single machine*

In the second part, the application listens for incoming data from the remote host. As we discussed earlier, the Receive method polls for the incoming datagrams and blocks the execution of the thread until a message returns from a remote host. To separate this process from the main flow, a new thread is created. The ThreadStart delegate references the Receiver method, which is invoked when the thread starts:

```
Thread tRec = new Thread(new ThreadStart(Receiver));
tRec.Start();
```

In the Receiver method, the UdpClient instance is created using the specified localPort:

```
UdpClient receivingUdpClient = new UdpClient(localPort);
```

Next, we create a new instance of the IPEndPoint class and assign it the value null, so that we can pass it into the Receive method as a reference parameter:

```
IPEndPoint RemoteIpEndPoint = null;
```

We then start an infinite while loop in order to receive data using the Receive method. The data is returned as a byte array, which we convert back into the original string using the Encoding.ASCII class:

```
while(true)
{
   // Wait for datagram
   byte[] receiveBytes = receivingUdpClient.Receive(ref RemoteIpEndPoint);
   // Convert and display data
   string returnData = Encoding.ASCII.GetString(receiveBytes);
   Console.WriteLine("-" + returnData);
}
```

The third logical block in the application accepts the data entered by the user and sends it to the specified remote port. This executes on the main thread while the worker thread continues to listen for incoming data. To send data to the remote port, the first step is to create the UdpClient instance:

```
UdpClient sender = new UdpClient();
```

Next, the IPEndPoint instance is created using the specified remote IP address and port:

```
IPEndPoint endPoint = new IPEndPoint(remoteIPAddress, remotePort);
```

The string data entered by the user is converted into a byte array using the Encoding.ASCII class:

```
byte[] bytes = Encoding.ASCII.GetBytes(datagram);
```

Finally, we call the UdpClient's Send method to send the converted bytes to the remote endpoint:

```
sender.Send(bytes, bytes.Length, endPoint);
```

Figure 8-7 shows an example of using the chat application.

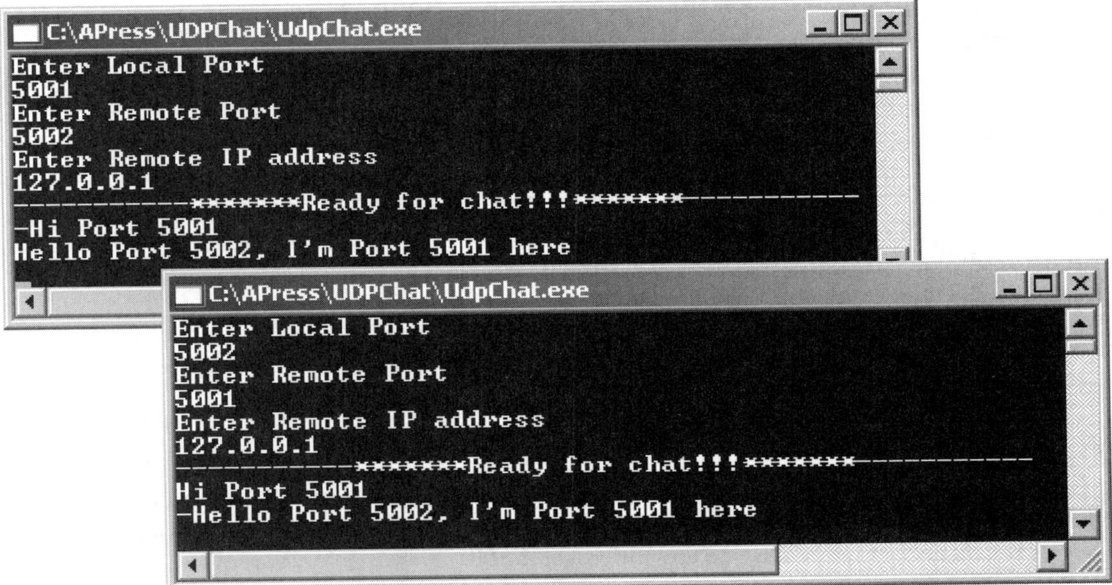

Figure 8-7. *Using the UDP chat application*

Building a UDP File Transfer Application

You have seen how to use the `UdpClient` class to send and receive datagrams, and we created a chat application using the same principal. Next, you'll see how to transfer a file and serialized object using `UdpClient`.

The sender and receiver programs in this example are divided into two logical parts. In the first part, the sender sends file details (namely the file extension and file size) to the receiver as a serialized object, and in the second part, the actual file is sent to the destination. In the receiver, the first part accepts the serialized object with the associated information, and in the second part, it creates the file on the destination machine. To make the application more interesting, we'll open the saved file using the associated program (for example, a `.doc` file might be opened with Microsoft Word or an `.htm` file with Internet Explorer).

Coding the File Server

The file server is a simple console application implemented in a class named `FileSender`. This has a nested class called `FileDetails` that contains the information about the file (the file size and the file type). We start by importing the necessary namespaces and declaring the fields for the class. The class has five private fields: an instance of our `FileDetails` class, a `UdpClient` object, plus information about the connection to the remote client, and a `FileStream` object for reading in the file we'll send to the client.

```
using System;
using System.IO;
using System.Net;
using System.Net.Sockets;
```

```
using System.Text;
using System.Xml.Serialization;
using System.Diagnostics;
using System.Threading;
public class FileSender
{
   private static FileDetails fileDet = new FileDetails();
   // UdpClient-related fields
   private static IPAddress remoteIPAddress;
   private const int remotePort = 5002;
   private static UdpClient sender = new UdpClient();
   private static IPEndPoint endPoint;

   // Filestream object
   private static FileStream fs;
```

Next, we define the FileDetails class. Our FileDetails object will need to be serialized for sending over the network, so we add the [Serializable] attribute. The class just has two public fields, to store the type and the size of the file:

```
   // File details (required for receiver)
   [Serializable]
   public class FileDetails
   {
      public string FILETYPE = "";
      public long FILESIZE = 0;
   }
```

Now we come to the Main method for the server. In this method, we invite the user to input a remote IP address to send the file to, and then to enter the path and filename of the file to send. We open up this file with the FileStream object and check its length. If this is greater than the maximum permitted size of 8,192 bytes, we close the UdpClient and the FileStream, and exit the application. Otherwise, we send the file information, wait two seconds by calling the Thread.Sleep method, and then send the file itself.

```
   [STAThread]
   static void Main(string[] args)
   {
      try
      {
         // Get remote IP address and create IPEndPoint
         Console.WriteLine("Enter Remote IP address");
         remoteIPAddress = IPAddress.Parse(Console.ReadLine().ToString());
         endPoint = new IPEndPoint(remoteIPAddress, remotePort);

         // Get file path. (Important: file size should be less than 8K)
         Console.WriteLine("Enter File path and name to send.");
         fs = new FileStream(@Console.ReadLine().ToString(), FileMode.Open,
                                                             FileAccess.Read);
```

```
        if (fs.Length > 8192)
        {
            Console.Write("This version transfers files with size < 8192 bytes");
            sender.Close();
            fs.Close();
            return;
        }
        SendFileInfo();        // Send file info to receiver
        Thread.Sleep(2000);    // Wait for 2 seconds
        SendFile();            // Send actual file
    }
    catch (Exception e)
    {
        Console.WriteLine(e.ToString());
    }
}
```

The SendFileInfo method populates the fields of the FileDetails object, and then serializes this object into a MemoryStream, using an XmlSerializer object. This is then read into a byte array, which is passed into the UdpClient's Send method, to send the file information to the client.

```
public static void SendFileInfo()
{
    // Get file type or extension
    fileDet.FILETYPE = fs.Name.Substring((int)fs.Name.Length - 3, 3);
    // Get file length (future purpose)
    fileDet.FILESIZE = fs.Length;

    XmlSerializer fileSerializer = new XmlSerializer(typeof(FileDetails));
    MemoryStream stream = new MemoryStream();

    // Serialize object
    fileSerializer.Serialize(stream, fileDet);
    // Stream to byte
    stream.Position = 0;
    byte[] bytes = new byte[stream.Length];
    stream.Read(bytes, 0, Convert.ToInt32(stream.Length));
    Console.WriteLine("Sending file details...");
    // Send file details
    sender.Send(bytes, bytes.Length, endPoint);
    stream.Close();
}
```

The SendFile method just reads the file content from the FileStream into a byte array, and then sends this to the client.

```
private static void SendFile()
{
```

```
        // Creating a file stream
        byte[] bytes = new byte[fs.Length];
        // Stream to bytes
        fs.Read(bytes, 0, bytes.Length);

        Console.WriteLine("Sending file...size = " + fs.Length + " bytes");
        try
        {
           sender.Send(bytes, bytes.Length, endPoint); // Send file
        }
        catch (Exception e)
        {
           Console.WriteLine(e.ToString());
        }
        finally
        {
           // Clean up
           fs.Close();
           sender.Close();
        }
        Console.Read();
        Console.WriteLine("File sent suceessfully.");
     }
  }
```

Coding the File Receiver

The file receiver is also a console application, and it is implemented in a class named `FileRecv`. Again, we start by importing the necessary namespaces and declaring the fields for the class.

```
using System;
using System.IO;
using System.Net;
using System.Diagnostics;
using System.Net.Sockets;
using System.Text;
using System.Xml.Serialization;
public class FileRecv
{
   private static FileDetails fileDet;
   // UdpClient vars
   private static int localPort = 5002 ;
   private static UdpClient receivingUdpClient = new UdpClient(localPort);
   private static IPEndPoint RemoteIpEndPoint = null ;
   private static FileStream fs;
   private static byte[] receiveBytes = new byte[0];
```

We will need to deserialize the file information sent from the server into a FileDetails object, so we need to define that class within the client application, too.

```
[Serializable]
public class FileDetails
{
   public string FILETYPE = "";
   public long FILESIZE = 0;
}
```

The Main method for the application just calls two methods, to get the file details and the file itself.

```
[STAThread]
static void Main(string[] args)
{
   // Get the file details
   GetFileDetails();
   // Receive file
   ReceiveFile();
}
```

The GetFileDetails method calls the Receive method of the UdpClient object. This receives the serialized FileDetails object from the server, which we save to a MemoryStream. We use an XmlSerializer object to deserialize this stream back into a FileDetails object, and then display the retrieved information in the console.

```
private static void GetFileDetails()
{
   try
   {
      Console.WriteLine(
         "-----------*******Waiting to get File Details!!*******-----------");
      // Receive file info
      receiveBytes = receivingUdpClient.Receive(ref RemoteIpEndPoint);
      Console.WriteLine("----Received File Details!!");

      XmlSerializer fileSerializer = new XmlSerializer(typeof(FileDetails));
      MemoryStream stream1 = new MemoryStream();
      // Received byte to stream
      stream1.Write(receiveBytes, 0, receiveBytes.Length);
      stream1.Position = 0; // IMP
      // Call the Deserialize method and cast to the object type.
      fileDet = (FileDetails)fileSerializer.Deserialize(stream1);
      Console.WriteLine ("Received file of type ." + fileDet.FILETYPE +
               " whose size is " + fileDet.FILESIZE.ToString () + " bytes");
   }
```

```
        catch (Exception e)
        {
            Console.WriteLine (e.ToString ());
        }
    }
```

The ReceiveFile method retrieves the file from the server and saves it to disk with the filename temp, plus the extension retrieved from the FileDetails object. We then call the Process.Start static method to open the document with the associated program.

```
    public static void ReceiveFile()
    {
        try
        {
            Console.WriteLine(
                        "-----------*******Waiting to get File!!*******-----------");
            // Receive file
            receiveBytes = receivingUdpClient.Receive(ref RemoteIpEndPoint);
            // Convert and display data
            Console.WriteLine("----File received...Saving...");
            // Create temp file from received file extension
            fs = new FileStream("temp." + fileDet.FILETYPE, FileMode.Create,
                                    FileAccess.ReadWrite, FileShare.ReadWrite);
            fs.Write(receiveBytes, 0, receiveBytes.Length);
            Console.WriteLine("----File Saved...");
            Console.WriteLine("-------Opening file with associated program------");
            Process.Start(fs.Name);    // Opens file with associated program
        }
        catch (Exception e)
        {
            Console.WriteLine(e.ToString ());
        }
        finally
        {
            fs.Close();
            receivingUdpClient.Close();
        }
    }
}
```

Figure 8-8 shows the file transfer application in action.

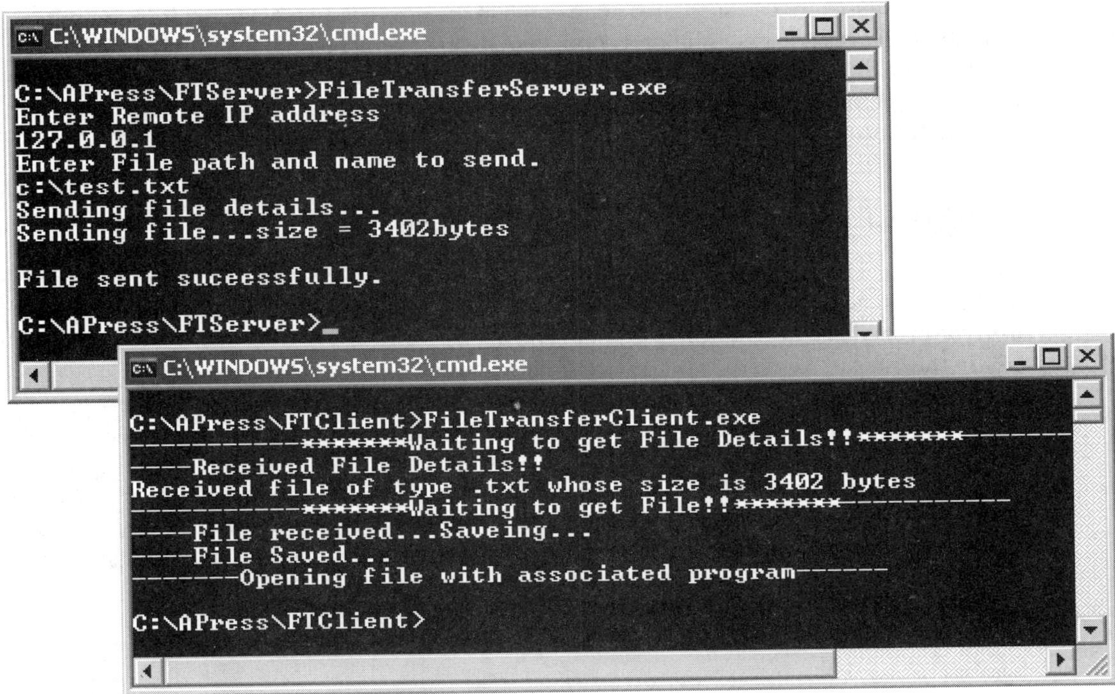

Figure 8-8. *Running the file transfer application*

This application has some limitations. One is that the size of the file depends on the size of the internal message buffer or network limit. The default buffer size is 8,192 bytes, so you cannot send files larger than that. This could be overcome by dividing the file into multiple segments, each with a buffer size of 8,192 bytes. By calling the `Read` method with the required buffer size, you can divide the file into multiple segments.

As UDP does not use acknowledgment signals, you would need to implement a separate mechanism to check whether each segment was received correctly before sending the next segment. You could do this by creating another instance of `UdpClient` in both the sender and receiver, which will check for acknowledgment messages.

Broadcasting

When you run the sample file transfer application, you can specify an individual IP address to send the file to, but you can also specify a broadcast address, to send the file to all machines on the subnet or on the entire network.

A *broadcast address* consists of the subnet ID, with all remaining bits set to 1. For example, if you want to broadcast a message to all hosts with IP addresses in the range 192.168.0, you would use the broadcast address 192.168.0.255. To send a message to all machines on the network, regardless of the subnet mask, you can use the address 255.255.255.255. With broadcasts, the message is sent to every machine in the network; it is for the client to decide whether or not it wants to process the data.

We'll discuss broadcasts in a bit more detail in the next chapter, where we look at multicasting. Unlike broadcasts, multicast connections can cross over a firewall. Multicasts also are less bandwidth-intensive than broadcasts, and using multicasting rather than broadcasting is generally recommended. We will therefore concentrate on multicasting rather than broadcasts in the next chapter.

Higher-Level UDP-Based Protocols

UDP is useful where the order of delivery is not important and does not need to be guaranteed. As the sender does not know which destination is active, it uses a port number to specify the type of service required from the remote host.

In the Internet world of today, many applications use UDP services, including Internet phone, Internet videoconferencing, and real-time audio/video broadcasting. Most people don't know that the preferred transport protocol of the Distributed Component Object Model (DCOM) is UDP. The connectionless nature of UDP allows DCOM to perform several optimizations by merging many low-level acknowledgment packages with actual data and pinging messages. This minimizes network round-trips as much as possible, and therefore improves speed and performance. Microsoft networking uses UDP for logon, browsing, and name resolution.

Table 8-4 lists some of higher-level protocols based on UDP.

Table 8-4. *Some Higher-Level Protocols Based on UDP*

Protocol	Use
RTP (Real-Time Protocol)	Real-time media
NFS (Network File System)	Remote file server
SNMP (Simple Network Management Protocol)	Network management
RIP (Routing Information Protocol)	Routing protocol
DNS (Domain Name Service)	Host name resolution
TFTP (Trivial File Transfer Protocol)	File transfer
RPC (Remote Procedure Call)	Typical client/server model
LDAP (Lightweight Directory Access Protocol)	Directory services

Let's take a closer look at some of the more common protocols listed in Table 8-4:

Real-Time Protocol (RTP): This is an application-layer protocol designed for delivering real-time media such as audio/video over unicast or multicast private and public IP networks. One example is Microsoft NetMeeting, which uses RTP for sending real-time information across the Internet. The RTP-based application implements RTP by using UDP and by adding some functionality. The added functionality provides sequence numbering, payload identification, source identification, and time-stamping.

Network File System (NFS): Another popular application that uses UDP, NFS provides transparent file access to files and file systems across the network. The advantage of NFS over FTP is that it provides transparent access to files; that is, NFS can access the portion of the file that is referenced by an application or process. NFS is built using Sun Remote Procedure Call (RPC), and it uses the reserved UDP port number 2049 for performing file operations.

Simple Network Management Protocol (SNMP): As its name indicates, SNMP is a network-management protocol widely used in networks. SNMP allows administrators to monitor and control remote hosts and gateways on a network. The SNMP service can handle one or more requests from the host. It communicates between a management program run by an administrator and the network management agent running on a host. SNMP uses ports 161 and 162 for the manager and agent, respectively.

Domain Name System (DNS): This is a distributed database used by TCP/IP applications to map host names to IP addresses. UDP is the preferred protocol for DNS applications, and it uses port 53 for sending DNS queries to a name server.

Trivial File Transfer Protocol (TFTP): This is an application-layer protocol that is useful for transferring files between remote hosts. This protocol is intended to be used when bootstrapping diskless systems. It uses UDP port number 69 for its file-transfer activity.

Summary

In this chapter, we discussed the basics of UDP and saw how it compares with TCP. We covered how to implement the UDP protocol in .NET using the `UdpClient` class. We looked at the members of the `UdpClient` class, and saw how to use them within programs. We then looked at two longer applications: a chat application, which demonstrated the use of the `UdpClient` class for two-way communication, and a file server/receiver application that could be used to send files to a specific address or to broadcast a file to all addresses in the network/subnet. Lastly, we discussed some higher-level UDP-based protocols, which demonstrate the sort of tasks that UDP is ideally suited to perform.

CHAPTER 9

Multicast Sockets

In 1994, the Rolling Stones transmitted a live concert over the Internet for free. This was made possible due to *multicasting*, the same technology that enables us to watch astronauts in space, to hold meetings over the Internet, and much more.

Multicasting can be used for group communications over the Internet, where every node participating in the multicast must join the group set up for the purpose. Routers can forward messages to all interested nodes.

Unicasting would be inappropriate for these types of applications; if it were used for events attended by thousands of clients, the load on the server and on the network would be excessive. Multicasting means that the server needs to send messages just once, and they will be distributed to a whole group of clients. Only systems that are members of the group participate in the network transfers.

In the past few chapters, we discussed socket programming using connection-oriented and connectionless protocols. Chapter 8 showed how you can send broadcasts with the User Datagram Protocol (UDP). In this chapter, UDP again rears its head, but now we are using multicasts.

In this chapter, we will create two Windows applications using multicasting features. With one application, it will be possible to chat with multiple systems, where everyone is both a sender and a receiver. The second application, in the form of a picture show, demonstrates how large data packets can be sent to multiple clients without using a high percentage of the network bandwidth.

In particular, we will cover the following topics:

- Compare unicasts, broadcasts, and multicasts
- Examine the architecture of multicasting
- Implement multicast sockets with .NET
- Create a multicast chat application
- Create a multicast picture show application

Unicasts, Broadcasts, and Multicasts

The Internet Protocol (IP) supports three kinds of IP addresses: unicast, broadcast, and multicast. Let's see how these methods compare.

Unicast Addresses

With *unicast* addresses, network packets are sent to a single destination. If multiple clients connect to a single server, all clients maintain a separate connection on the server. The server needs resources for each of these simultaneous connections and must communicate individually with every client.

The Transmission Control Protocol (TCP) provides a connection-oriented communication where two systems communicate with each other; with TCP, you can send only unicast messages (as discussed in Chapter 7). UDP can also be used to send unicast messages (as discussed in Chapter 8). Unlike with TCP, UDP uses connectionless communication, making it faster than TCP, but without TCP's reliability.

Broadcast Addresses

With *broadcast* addresses, broadcast datagrams are sent to all nodes in a subnetwork. Broadcast addresses are identified by IP addresses where all bits of the host are set to 1. For instance, to send messages to all hosts in a subnet with a mask of 255.255.255.0 in a network with the address 192.168.0, the broadcast address would be 192.168.0.255. Any host with an IP address beginning 192.168.0 will then receive the broadcast messages.

Broadcasts are *always* performed with connectionless communication using UDP. The server sends the data regardless of whether any client is listening. Due to performance issues, it wouldn't be possible to set up a separate connection to every client. Connectionless communication means that the server does not need to allocate resources for every single client; no matter how many clients are listening, the same server resources will be consumed. Of course, there are disadvantages to the connectionless mechanism. For one, there is no guarantee that the data is received by anyone. If you want reliability, you need to add a handshaking mechanism of your own at a higher level than UDP.

Broadcasts introduce a performance issue for every system on the destination subnet, because each system on that subnet must check whether the receiving packet is of interest. A broadcast may be of interest to any system in the network, and it passes all the way up to the transport layer in the protocol stack of each system before its relevancy can be determined.

There is another issue with broadcasts: they don't cross subnets. Routers don't let broadcasts cross them. You would soon reach network saturation if routers forwarded broadcasts, so this is desired behavior. Thus, broadcasts can be used only inside a particular subnet.

■ **NOTE** Broadcast communication is useful if multiple nodes in the same subnet should get information simultaneously. The Network Time Protocol (NTP) is an example of where broadcasts are useful.

Multicast Addresses

With *multicast* addresses, multicast datagrams are sent to all nodes, possibly on different subnets, that belong to a group. Multicasts packets can pass across different networks through routers, so it is possible to use multicasts in an Internet scenario, as long as your network provider supports multicasting.

Hosts that want to receive particular multicast messages must register their interest using the Internet Group Management Protocol (IGMP). Multicast messages are *not* sent to networks where no host has joined the multicast group.

Class D IP addresses (in the range 224.0.0.0 to 239.255.255.255) are used for multicast groups, to differentiate them from normal host addresses, allowing nodes to easily detect if a message is of interest.

Application Models with Multicasting

Multicasting is a good choice for many types of applications. Two basic models with multicasting are many-to-many applications and one-to-many applications.

Many-to-Many Applications

A *many-to-many application* allows every system in a group to send data to every other system in the group. Using multicasting means that each system doesn't need to create a connection to every other system; instead, a multicast address can be used.

For example, a peer-to-peer chat application would benefit from using multicasting. The chat sender could send a message to every node of the group by sending a single message to the network, as shown in Figure 9-1.

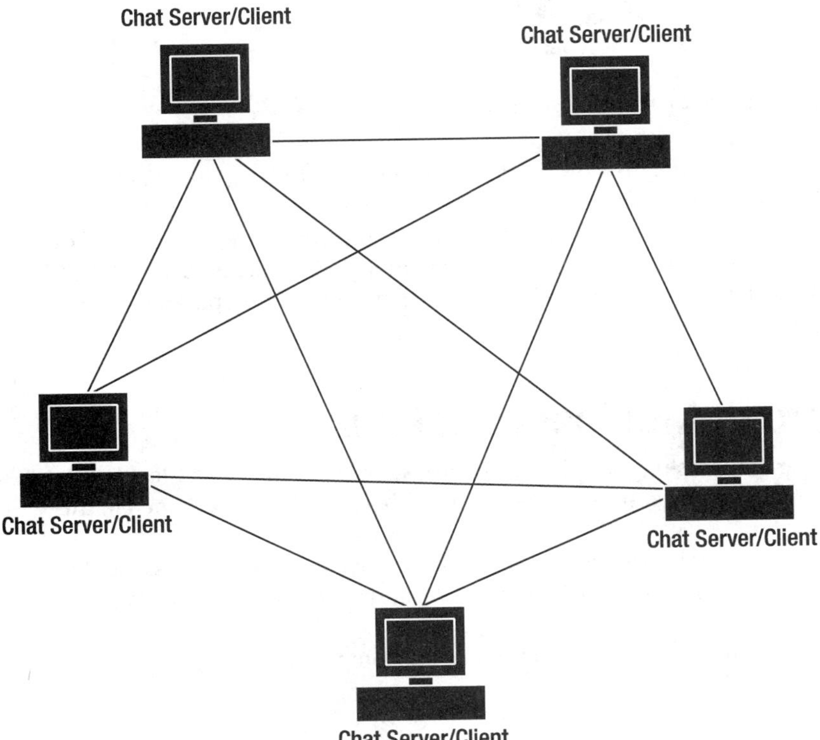

Figure 9-1. *A multicasting many-to-many application*

One-to-Many Applications

Another scenario where multicasts play an important role is if one system wants to send data to a group of systems. This is known as a *one-to-many application* and is illustrated in Figure 9-2. This approach can be useful for sending audio, video, or other large data types. The server sends the data only once, to the multicast address, and a large number of systems can listen.

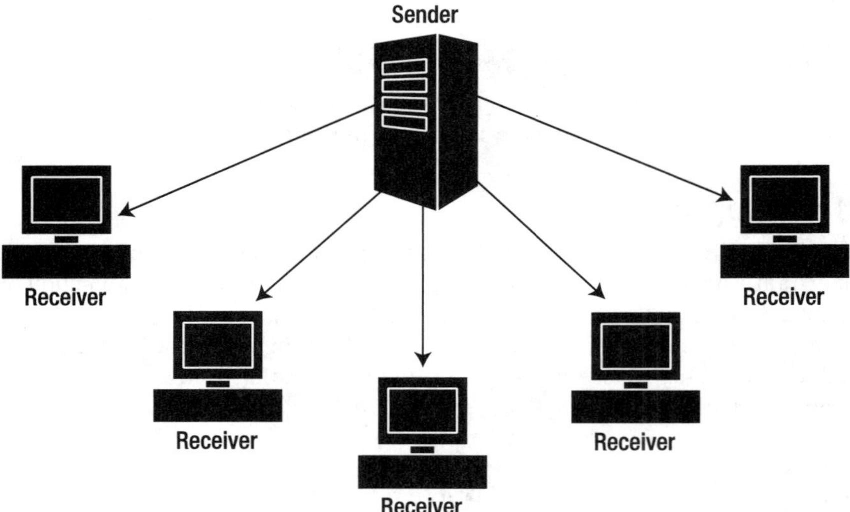

Figure 9-2. *A multicasting one-to-many application*

The Rolling Stones concert in November 1994, mentioned at the beginning of this chapter, was the first time audio and video of a live rock concert was transmitted over the Internet using multicast. This was a big success, and it demonstrated the usefulness of multicasting. The same technology is used in a local network to install applications on hundreds of PCs simultaneously, without the server needing to send a big installation package to every client system separately.

Architecture of Multicast Sockets

Multicast messages are sent, using UDP, to a group of systems identified by a Class D subnet address. Certain Class D address ranges are reserved for specific uses, as explained in this section.

In addition to UDP, IGMP is used to register clients that want to receive messages for a specific group. This protocol is built into the IP module, and it allows clients to leave a group as well as join a group.

In this section, we'll cover the following multicasting components and issues:

- IGMP
- Multicast address allocation
- Routing

- Scoping
- Routing protocols
- Scalability
- Reliability
- Security

IGMP

IGMP is used by IP hosts to report group memberships to any immediately neighboring routers that are multicast-enabled. Similar to the ICMP protocols, IGMP is implemented in the IP module. IGMP messages are encapsulated in IP datagrams with the IP protocol number 2. As explained in Chapter 1, the protocol number is listed in the IP header, and the value 2 denotes IGMP. Figure 9-3 shows the protocol stack with IGMP.

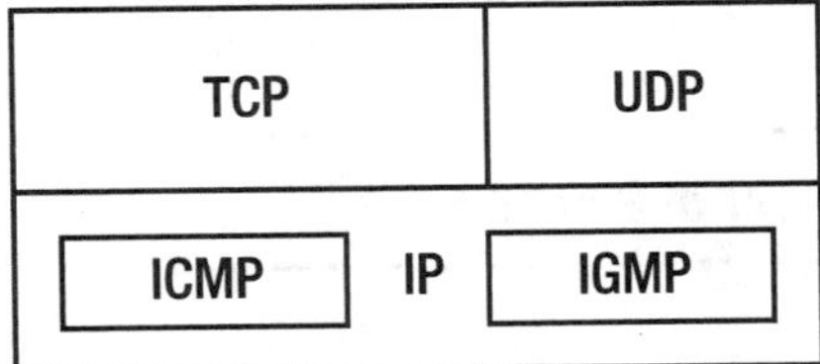

Figure 9-3. *Protocol stack with IGMP*

Currently, two versions of IGMP are commonly used:

IGMP version 2 (IGMPv2): This version added the leave group message so that a client can explicitly leave the group. IGMPv1 had to wait for a timeout that could take up to five minutes. During this time, unwanted multicast transmissions were sent to the network, and for large data such as audio or video streams, this could consume a substantial part of the available bandwidth. With IGMPv2, latency is reduced to just a few seconds when leaving the group.

IGMP version 3 (IGMPv3): This version (defined in RFC 3376, `http://www.ietf.org/rfc/rfc3376.txt`) is available with Windows XP and adds specific joins and leaves with the source address(es). This capability makes the Source-Specific Multicast (SSM) protocol possible. With an IGMPv2 multicast, every member of the group can send multicast messages to every other member. SSM makes it possible to restrict the sender (source) of the group to a specific host or multiple hosts, which is a great advantage in the one-to-many application scenario. The layout of IGMPv3 messages is different from that of IGMPv2 messages, and the size of an IGMPv3 message depends on how many source addresses are used.

An IGMPv2 message consists of 64 bits and contains the type of the message, a maximum response time (used only for membership queries), a checksum, and the group address. You can see the IGMPv2 message in the first 64 bits in Figure 9-4.

The IGMPv3 message, illustrated in Figure 9-4, adds a varying number of 32-bit values to the message. The 32 bits that follow the group address are separated as follows:

- A 4-bit reserved field
- A 1-bit S flag that defines that the router should suppress updating the time field
- A 3-bit QRV (querier's robustness variable) that defines the robustness value of the sender of the query
- An 8-bit QQIC (querier's query interval code) value that specifies the number of seconds of the query interval
- A 16-bit number that defines the number of source addresses that continue with the following bytes of the message

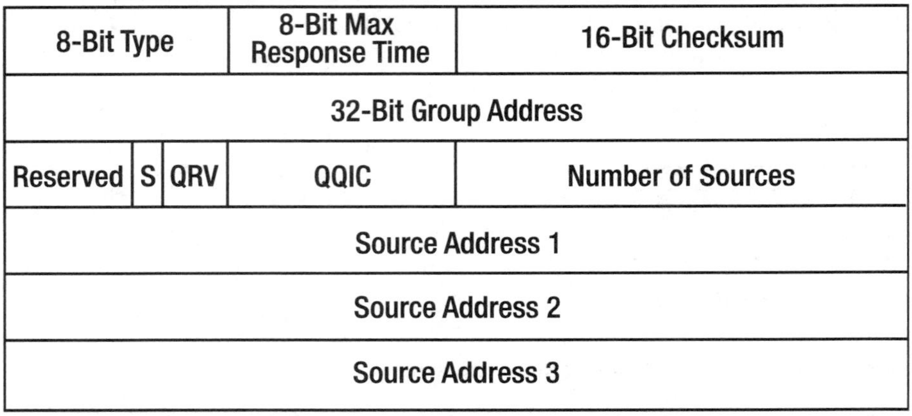

<table>
<tr><td colspan="3">8-Bit Type</td><td>8-Bit Max Response Time</td><td>16-Bit Checksum</td></tr>
<tr><td colspan="5">32-Bit Group Address</td></tr>
<tr><td>Reserved</td><td>S</td><td>QRV</td><td>QQIC</td><td>Number of Sources</td></tr>
<tr><td colspan="5">Source Address 1</td></tr>
<tr><td colspan="5">Source Address 2</td></tr>
<tr><td colspan="5">Source Address 3</td></tr>
</table>

Figure 9-4. *The IGMPv3 message format*

The message types used for communication between a host and a router are defined by the first 8 bits of IGMP message headers, as described in Table 9-1.

Table 9-1. *IGMP Message Header*

Hex Value	Message	Description
0x11	Membership Query	These are used by the router to see whether any group members exist. Two types of membership queries can be differentiated by the group address in the 32-bit group address field. A *general query* has a group address in the IGMP header of all zeros, and asks which groups have members on an attached network. A *group-specific query* returns information about whether a particular group has members.

Hex Value	Message	Description
0x22	Version 3 Membership Report	When a host joins a multicast group, a membership report is sent to the router to inform the router that a system on the network is listening to multicast messages. The values for IGMPv1 and v2 membership reports are 0x12 and 0x16. IGMPv3 implementations must also understand membership reports for IGMPv1 and IGMPv2.
0x17	Leave Group	The last host of a multicast group inside a subnet must send a leave group message to all routers (224.0.0.2) when it leaves a group. A host may remember the hosts of the multicast group (received in membership reports in response to membership queries) so that it knows when it is the last one in the group, but this is not a requirement. If the group members are not remembered, every host leaving a group sends a leave group message. In any case, the router checks if it was the last host in the group, and stops forwarding multicast messages if so.

Multicast Address Allocation

A Class D multicast address starts with the binary values 1110 in the first four bits, making the address range from 224.0.0.0 to 239.255.255.255.

However, not every address of this range is available for multicasting; for example, the multicast addresses 224.0.0.0 through 224.0.0.255 are special purpose, and routers do not pass them across networks. Unlike normal IP addresses, where every country has a local representation to assign IP addresses, only the Internet Assigned Names and Numbers Authority (IANA, `http://www.iana.org`) is responsible for assigning multicast addresses. RFC 3171 defines the use of specific ranges of IP multicast addresses and their purposes.

■ NOTE RFC 3171 uses Classless InterDomain Routing (CIDR) addresses for a shorthand notation of a range of IP addresses. The CIDR notation 224.0.0/24 is similar to the address range with the dotted quad-notation 224.0.0.0 through 224.0.0.255. In the CIDR notation, the first part shows the fixed range of the dotted quad-notation followed by the number of fixed bits, so 232/8 is the shorthand CIDR notation for 232.0.0.0 through 232.255.255.255.

As a quick overview of multicast addresses, let's look at the three main ways in which they can be allocated: static, dynamic, and scope-relative.

Static Multicast Addresses

A *static multicast address* is one of global interest, used for protocols that need well-known addresses. Static multicast addresses that are needed globally are assigned by the IANA. These addresses may be hard-coded into applications and devices.

■TIP The IANA website offers a form that allows you to request multicast addresses for applications that need a globally unique IP address, at `http://www.iana.org/cgi-bin/multicast.pl`.

Two blocks of static multicast addresses are used:

Local Network Control Block: This includes all systems on the subnet. Addresses starting with 224.0.0 belong to this block, and they are never forwarded by a router. Examples of these are 224.0.0.1 to send a message to all systems on the subnet and 224.0.0.2 to send a message to all routers on the subnet. The Dynamic Host Configuration Protocol (DHCP) server answers messages on the IP address 224.0.0.12, but only on a subnet.

Internetwork Control Block: The addresses in the CIDR range 224.0.1/24 belong to this block. Messages sent to these addresses can be forwarded by a router. Examples are Network Time Protocol (NTP) and Windows Internet Name Service (WINS) requests.

■NOTE A complete list of actually reserved multicast addresses and their owners in the ranges defined by RFC 3171 can be found at the IANA website: `http://www.iana.org/assignments/multicast-addresses`.

Dynamic Multicast Addresses

Often, a *dynamic multicast address* would better suit your purpose than a fixed, static address. These requested-on-demand addresses have a specific lifetime. The concept of requesting dynamic multicast addresses is similar to DHCP requests, and indeed, these requests in the first versions of the Multicast Address Dynamic Client Allocation Protocol (MADCAP) were based on DHCP. Later MADCAP versions (defined by RFC 2730) are completely independent of DHCP, as they have quite different requirements.

With MADCAP, the client sends a unicast or a multicast message to a MADCAP server to request a multicast address. The server answers with a lease-based address.

■NOTE A MADCAP server comes with Windows Server 2003, and Windows 2000 Server and can be configured as part of the DHCP server services.

Scope-Relative Multicast Addresses

Scope-relative multicast addresses are multicast addresses that are used only within a local group or organization. The address range 239.0.0.0 to 239.255.255.255 is reserved for administrative scope-relative addresses. These addresses (defined in RFC 2365) can be reused with other local groups. Routers are typically configured with filters to prevent multicast traffic in this address range from flowing outside the local network.

Another way to define the scope of multicast addresses is by using a time to live (TTL) value. We will look at TTL values in the next section.

Routing

Adding multicast capabilities to the Internet was not a straightforward task. When the multicast protocol was defined, router manufacturers didn't implement multicasting functionality because they didn't know if multicasting had a real use. Instead, they preferred to wait until they knew whether their customers actually wanted multicasting technology. This meant that it wasn't possible to use multicasting over the Internet. To resolve this dilemma, the Multicast Backbone (MBone) was created in 1992. The MBone started with 40 subnetworks in 4 different countries, and it now spans 3,400 subnets in 25 countries.

The MBone connects together islands of subnetworks capable of multicasting through *tunnels*, as illustrated in Figure 9-5. Multicast messages are forwarded using a unicast connection between both tunnel ends to connect multiple islands across the Internet where multicasting is not supported.

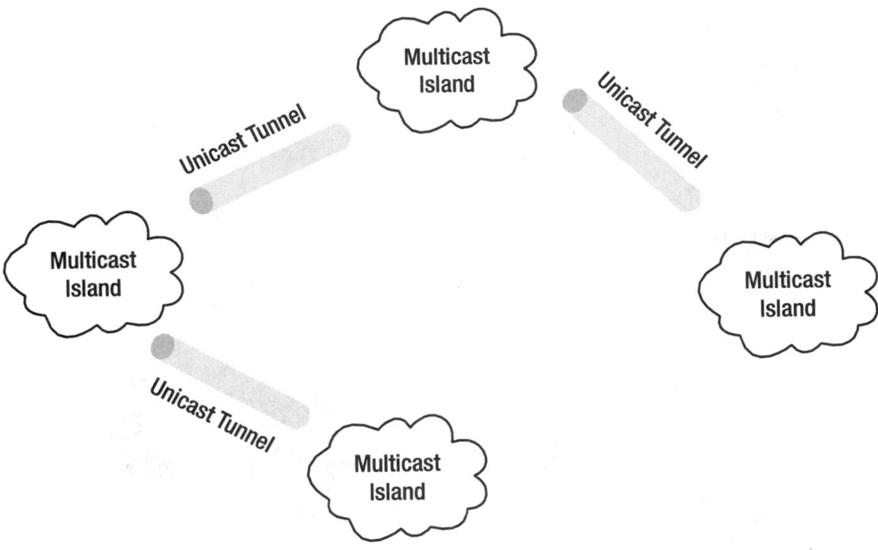

Figure 9-5. *The MBone connects multicast islands.*

Today, routers are capable of routing multicast messages, but many Internet providers still don't support multicasts, and so the MBone remains a useful facility. The MBone is used for audio and video multicasts, technical talks, seminars, NASA space shuttle missions, and so on. MBone tools (such as `sdr` and `multikit`) provide information about planned multicast events.

■ NOTE For the actual status of multicast-enabled networks in the Internet, see `http://www.multicasttech.com/status`.

How is a multicast packet sent to a client? Figure 9-6 shows a server that sends multicast messages to a specific multicast group address. A client that wants to receive multicast packets for the defined multicast address must join the multicast group. Suppose client E joins the multicast group by sending an IGMP request to the routers on its local network. All routers of a subnet can be reached using the IP address 224.0.0.2. In Figure 9-6, only router Z is in client E's subnet. The router registers the client as a member of the multicast group and informs other routers using a different protocol in order to pass information about multicast members across routers. Multicast-enabled routers pass the information about the member in this group on to other routers. The server just needs to send a UDP message to the group address. Because router X now knows that a client wants to receive those messages, it forwards the multicast message to router Z, which, in turn, forwards the message to the subnetwork of client E. Client E can read the multicast message. The message is never transmitted to the network of router Y, because no client of that network joined the multicast group.

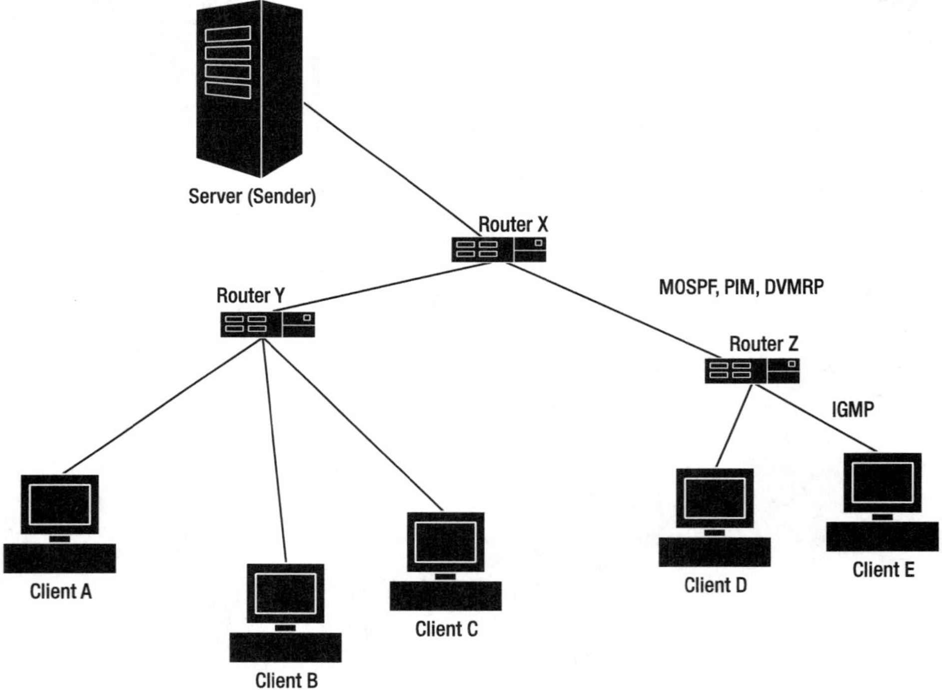

Figure 9-6. *A network with multicasts*

The scope of the multicast determines how many times multicast messages are forwarded by routers. Let's look at how the scope can be influenced.

Scoping

We discussed scoping when we looked at administrative scope-relative multicast addresses, which belong to a specific Class D address range assigned by IANA. However, there's another way to scope multicast messages.

When the client sends a multicast group report to join a multicast group, it defines a TTL value that is sent in the IP packet. The TTL value defines how many hops the membership report should be forwarded. A TTL value of 1 means that the group report never leaves the local network. Every router receiving the group report decrements the TTL value by 1 and discards the packet when the TTL reaches zero.

There's a problem defining the exact number of hops to a sender, as different routes may need a different number of hops, and so the hop count may be different from one package to the next. This problem doesn't exist with administrative scope-relative multicast addresses.

Routing Protocols

Different protocols can be used by routers to forward multicast membership reports and to find the best way from the sender to the client. When the MBone was created, the Distance Vector Multicast Routing Protocol (DVMRP) was the only protocol used. Now Multicast Open Shortest Path First (MOSPF) and Protocol-Independent Multicast (PIM) are also widely used protocols for multicasting. These routing protocols work as follows:

DVMRP: This protocol uses a reverse path-flooding algorithm, where the router sends a copy of the network packet out to all paths, except the one from where the packet originated. If no node in a router's network is a member of the multicast group, the router sends a prune message back to the sending router so that it knows it does not need to receive packets for that multicast group. DVMRP periodically refloods attached networks to reach new nodes that may be added to the multicast group. Now you can see why DVMRP doesn't scale too well!

MOSPF: This protocol is an extension of the Open Shortest Path First (OSPF) protocol. With MOSPF, all routers must be aware of all available links to networks hosting members of multicast groups. MOSPF calculates routes when multicast traffic is received. This protocol can be used only in networks where OSPF is used as a unicast routing protocol, because MOSPF routes are exchanged between routers using OSPF. Also, MOSPF won't scale well if many multicast groups are used or if the groups change often, because this can consume a lot of the router's processing power.

PIM: This protocol uses two different algorithms for sending messages to group members. When the members are widely distributed across different networks, PIM-SM (Sparse Mode) is employed; when a group uses only a few networks, PIM-DM (Dense Mode) is used. PIM-DM uses a reverse path-flooding algorithm similar to DVMRP, except that any unicast routing protocol can be used. PIM-SM defines a registration point for proper routing of packets.

Scalability

A great advantage of multicasting is scalability. Multicasting is the most efficient and scalable way to send messages to multiple clients.

For example, suppose that you want to send 123 bytes to 1,000 clients. Using unicast, the network is loaded with 123,000 bytes, because the message must be sent once for every client. With multicasting, sending the same 123 bytes to 1,000 clients requires only 123 bytes to be sent to the network, because all of the clients will receive the same message. On the other hand, if you send the 123 bytes using a broadcast, the network load would be low—123 bytes, similar to multicast. But broadcasting not only has the disadvantage that messages can't cross different networks, but also that clients who are not interested in the broadcast message need to handle the broadcast packet up to the transport layer before they can determine that no socket is listening to the message and discard the packet.

Reliability

IP multicasting doesn't offer any compatible transport-level protocol that is both reliable and implements a flow mechanism. UDP, on the other hand, neither guarantees that messages arrive nor that they arrive in the correct order.

In many scenarios, it's not a problem if some messages are lost. For example, when listening to a live concert on the Internet, users expect to miss a few packets, and it is preferable to a faithful reproduction that pauses while data is resent.

However, a high-quality listening application that caches a lot of data in advance would probably prefer a reliable mechanism. If you want to use multicasting to install an application on multiple workstations simultaneously, a reliable mechanism is essential. If some messages were lost, the installed application may not run or could even produce harmful effects.

If guaranteed delivery is needed for a multicast, you must add custom handshaking using a reliable protocol. One way to do this is by adding packet numbers and a checksum to the data that is sent as part of the multicast. If the receiver detects a corrupted packet because of an incorrect checksum, or a packet is missing, it sends an NACK message to the sender, and the sender can resend the corrupted or missing packet. Note that the use of an NACK message in the event of an error is far more scalable than the alternative of sending acknowledgment messages for every packet correctly received.

Windows XP uses NACK messages in this way, as part of its reliable multicasting, provided through Message Queuing. If you use Windows XP (or Windows 2003 Server) on both the client and the server, you won't need to implement an NACK mechanism yourself.

Security

What about multicasting and security? We can differentiate multicasting security issues according to whether the Internet or an intranet is used, and whether you're securing multicast communication within a group.

A firewall acts as a security gateway between the Internet and an intranet. We'll assume that your Internet provider supports the MBone on the Internet side, and that multicasting is enabled in the intranet. Your firewall would stop multicast messages passing from the Internet to the intranet, and vice versa, and you must explicitly enable the multicast address and the port to pass through the firewall.

Regarding secure communication within a multicast group, the Internet Engineering Task Force (IETF) working group on Multicast Security (MSEC) has made a proposal for multicasting group key management that promises to establish a standard way for secure communication among authorized group members. This proposal would prevent anyone outside the group from reading the group's messages. At the time of writing, the IETF has a draft document originating from June 2004 describing secure group key management: `http://www.ietf.org/internet-drafts/draft-ietf-msec-gkmarch-08.txt`.

Using Multicast Sockets with .NET

Now that we've covered the basic principles and issues of multicasting, let's look at the .NET classes that support it. This section describes the code needed for a multicast sender and a multicast receiver.

Multicast Sender Applications

The sending application has no special tasks that we haven't already talked about in previous chapters, and you can simply use the `UdpClient` class to send multicast messages. The only difference from what we've done in Chapter 8 is that we must now use a multicast address. The `IPEndPoint` object `remoteEP` will point to the group address and the port number that will be used by the group:

```
IPAddress groupAddress = IPAddress.Parse("234.5.6.11");
int remotePort = 7777;
int localPort = 7777;
IPEndPoint remoteEP = new IPEndPoint(groupAddress, remotePort);
UdpClient server = new UdpClient(localPort);
server.Send(data, data.Length, remoteEP);
```

The multicast group address must also be made known to clients joining the group. You can do this by using a fixed address defined in a configuration file that clients can access, but you can also use a MADCAP server to get a multicast address dynamically. In that case, you need to implement a way to tell the client about the dynamically assigned addresses. You could do this by using a stream socket that the client connects to and sending the multicast address to the client. We will implement a stream socket to tell the client about the multicast address later in this chapter, when we create a picture show application.

Multicast Receiver Applications

The receiving application joins and leaves the group. You can use the `UdpClient` class or the `Socket` class for these tasks.

Using the UdpClient Class

Clients must join the multicast group. The method `JoinMulticastGroup` of the `UdpClient` class already implements this. This method sets the socket options `AddMembership` and `MulticastTimeToLive`, and sends an IGMP group report message to the router. The first parameter of `JoinMulticastGroup` denotes the IP address of the multicast group, and the second parameter represents the TTL value (the number of routers that should forward the report message).

```
UdpClient udpClient = new UdpClient();
udpClient.JoinMulticastGroup(groupAddress, 50);
```

To drop a group membership, call `UdpClient.DropMulticastGroup`, which takes an IP address parameter specifying the same multicast group address as used with `JoinMulticastGroup`:

```
udpClient.DropMulticastGroup(groupAddress);
```

Using the Socket Class

Instead of using the `UdpClient` class, you can also use the `Socket` class directly. The following code does practically the same task as the `UdpClient` class.

```
public void SetupMulticastClient(IPAddress groupAddress, int timeToLive)
{
   Socket socket = new Socket(AddressFamily.InterNetwork,
         SocketType.Dgram, ProtocolType.Udp);
   MulticastOption multicastOption =
         new MulticastOption(groupAddress);
   socket.SetSocketOption(SocketOptionLevel.IP,
          SocketOptionName.AddMembership,
          multicastOption);
   socket.SetSocketOption(SocketOptionLevel.IP,
          SocketOptionName.MulticastTimeToLive,
          timeToLive);
}
```

A UDP socket is created with the constructor of the `Socket` class, and then the socket options `AddMembership` and `MulticastTimeToLive` are set with the method `SetSocketOption`. We have already used this method in Chapter 4; now we'll use it with multicast options. The first argument you pass is `SocketOptionLevel.IP`, because the IGMP protocol is implemented in the IP module. The second argument specifies a value of the `SocketOptionName` enumeration. The `AddMembership` value is used to send an IGMP group membership report, and `MulticastTimeToLive` sets the number of hops that the multicast report should be forwarded. For the group membership report, you also must specify the IP address of the multicast group. The IP address can be specified with the helper class MulticastOption.

Leaving the multicast group is done by calling SetSocketOption with the enumeration value SocketOptionName.DropMembership:

```
public void StopMulticastClient(IPAddress groupAddress, int timeToLive)
{
   Socket socket = new Socket(AddressFamily.InterNetwork,
         SocketType.Dgram, ProtocolType.Udp);
   MulticastOption multicastOption =
         new MulticastOption(groupAddress);
   socket.SetSocketOption(SocketOptionLevel.IP,
          SocketOptionName.DropMembership,
          multicastOption);
}
```

The advantage of the Socket class over UdpClient is that you have more options available for multicasting. In addition to the options you have seen for joining and dropping a group, Windows XP has the enumeration value SocketOptionName.AddSourceGroup to join a multicast source group using SSM.

Creating a Chat Application

Now we can start writing a full multicast application. The first of our sample applications is a simple chat application that multiple users can use to send messages to all other chat clients. In this application, every system acts as both client and server. Every user can enter a message that is sent to all multicast participants.

The chat application is created as a Windows Forms project called MulticastChat, creating an executable with the name MulticastChat.exe. The main form class in this application is ChatForm.cs.

■ **NOTE** The complete multicast chat application is available for download from the Downloads section of the Apress website (http://www.apress.com).

Setting Up the User Interface

The user interface of the chat application, shown in Figure 9-7, allows the user to enter a chat name, and then to join the network communication by clicking the Start button. When this button is clicked, the multicast group is joined, and the application starts listening to the group address. Messages are entered in the text box below the Message label, and they are sent to the group when the user clicks the Send button.

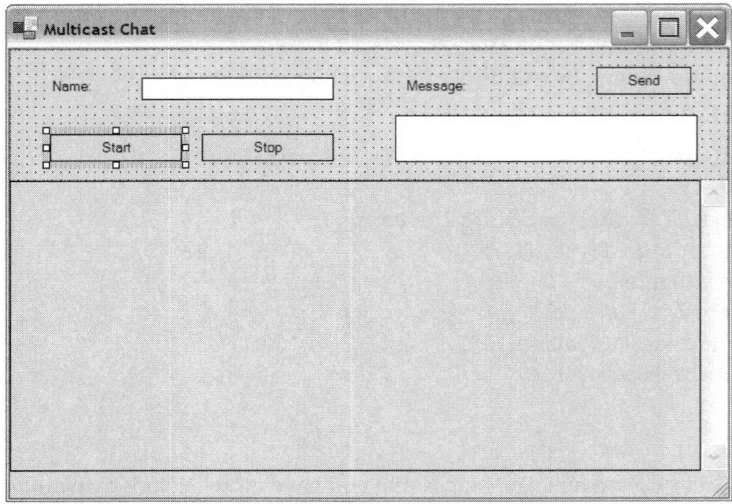

Figure 9-7. *User interface of the multicast chat application*

Table 9-2 shows the major controls of the form with their name and any nondefault property values.

Table 9-2. *Controls for the Multicast Chat Application*

Control Type	Name	Properties
TextBox	`textName`	Text = ""
Button	`buttonStart`	Text = "Start"
Button	`buttonStop`	Enabled = false Text = "Stop"
Button	`buttonSend`	Enabled = false Text = "Send"
TextBox	`textMessage`	Multiline = true Text = ""
TextBox	`textMessages`	Multiline = true ReadOnly = true Scrollbars = Vertical Text = ""
StatusBar	`statusBar`	

`ChatForm` is the main class of the application, as you can see in the following code. The code shows the .NET namespaces and private fields that will be used by all the methods that we'll add to the class as we progress:

```
using System;
using System.Configuration;
using System.Collections.Specialized;
```

```
using System.Net;
using System.Net.Sockets;
using System.Text;
using System.Threading;
using System.Windows.Forms;
namespace Apress.Networking.Multicast
{
   public class ChatForm : System.Windows.Forms.Form
   {
      private bool done = true;        // Flag to stop
                                       // listener thread
      private UdpClient client;        // Client socket
      private IPAddress groupAddress;  // Multicast group
                                       // address
      private int localPort;           // Local port to
                                       // receive messages
      private int remotePort;          // Remote port to send
                                       // messages
      private int ttl;
      private IPEndPoint remoteEP;
      private UnicodeEncoding encoding =
            new UnicodeEncoding();
      private string name;             // User name in chat
      private string message;          // Message to send
      //...
```

Creating the Configuration File

The multicast address and port numbers should be easily configurable, so we'll create an XML application configuration file. With Visual Studio .NET, you just need to create an `app.config` file, which will automatically be renamed to `MulticastChat.exe.config` in the `Debug\bin` directory. With the chat application, the following content is needed:

```
<?xml version="1.0" encoding="utf-8" ?>
<configuration>
   <appSettings>
      <add key="GroupAddress" value="234.5.6.11" />
      <add key="LocalPort" value="7777" />
      <add key="RemotePort" value="7777" />
      <add key="TTL" value="32" />
   </appSettings>
</configuration>
```

The value of the `GroupAddress` key must be a Class D IP address, as discussed earlier in the chapter. `LocalPort` and `RemotePort` use the same values to make the chat application both a receiver and a sender with the same port number.

■ **NOTE** To start this application twice on the same system for testing purposes, you will need to copy the application and the configuration file into two different directories. Because two running applications on one system cannot listen to the same port number, you will also need to change the port numbers for `LocalPort` and `RemotePort` in the configuration file to two different ports. Each application will need `RemotePort` to be set to the value of `LocalPort` in the second application.

We've set the TTL value in this file to 32. If you don't want to forward group membership reports across routers in your multicast environment, change this value to 1.

This configuration file is read by the `ChatForm` class constructor using the class `System.Configuration.ConfigurationSettings`. If the configuration file doesn't exist, or if it is incorrectly formatted, an exception is thrown, which we catch to display an error message:

```
      public ChatForm()
      {
         //
         // Required for Windows Form Designer support
         //
         InitializeComponent();
         try
         {
            // Read the application configuration file
            NameValueCollection configuration =
                  ConfigurationSettings.AppSettings;
            groupAddress =
                  IPAddress.Parse(
                  configuration["GroupAddress"]);
            localPort =
                  int.Parse(configuration["LocalPort"]);
            remotePort =
                  int.Parse(configuration["RemotePort"]);
            ttl = int.Parse(configuration["TTL"]);
         }
         catch
         {
            MessageBox.Show(this,
                  "Error in application configuration" +
                  "file!",
                  "Error Multicast Chat",
                  MessageBoxButtons.OK,
                  MessageBoxIcon.Error);
            buttonStart.Enabled = false;
         }
      }
   }
}
```

Joining the Multicast Group

In the `Click` handler of the Start button, we read the name that was entered in the text box `textName` and write it to the `name` field. Next, we create a `UdpClient` object and join the multicast group by calling the method `JoinMulticastGroup`. Then we create a new `IPEndPoint` object referencing the multicast address and the remote port for use with the `Send` method to send data to the group:

```
private void OnStart(object sender, System.EventArgs e)
{
   name = textName.Text;
   textName.ReadOnly = true;
   try
    {
      // Join the multicast group
      client = new UdpClient(localPort);
      client.JoinMulticastGroup(groupAddress, ttl);
      remoteEP = new IPEndPoint(groupAddress,
            remotePort);
```

In the next section of code, we create a new thread that will receive messages sent to the multicast address because the `UdpClient` class doesn't support asynchronous operations. An alternative way of achieving asynchronous operations would be to use the raw `Socket` class. The `IsBackground` property of the thread is set to `true` so that the thread will be stopped automatically when the main thread quits.

After starting the thread, we send an introduction message to the multicast group. To convert a string to the byte array that the `Send` method requires, we call `UnicodeEncoding.GetBytes`:

```
// Start the receiving thread
Thread receiver = new Thread(
      new ThreadStart(Listener));
receiver.IsBackground = true;
receiver.Start();
// Send the first message to the group
byte[] data = encoding.GetBytes(name +
      " has joined the chat");
client.Send(data, data.Length, remoteEP);
```

The last action performed by the `OnStart` method is to enable the Stop and Send buttons, and disable the Start button. We also write a handler for the `SocketException` that could occur if the application is started twice and listening on the same port:

```
      buttonStart.Enabled = false;
      buttonStop.Enabled = true;
      buttonSend.Enabled = true;
   }
   catch (SocketException ex)
   {
      MessageBox.Show(this, ex.Message,
```

```
            "Error MulticastChat",
            MessageBoxButtons.OK, MessageBoxIcon.Error);
   }
}
```

Receiving Multicast Messages

In the method of the listener thread that we created earlier, we wait in the `client.Receive` method until a message arrives. With the help of the class `UnicodeEncoding`, the received byte array is converted to a string.

The returned message should now be displayed in the user interface. There is an important issue to pay attention to when using threads and Windows controls. In native Windows programming, it is possible to create Windows controls from different threads, but only the thread that created the control may invoke methods on it, so all function calls on the Window control must occur in the creation thread. In Windows Forms, the same model is mapped to the .NET Windows Forms classes. All methods of Windows Forms controls must be called on the creation thread, with the exception of the method `Invoke` and its asynchronous variants, `BeginInvoke` and `EndInvoke`. These can be called from any thread, as it forwards the method that should be called to the creation thread of the Window control. That creation thread then calls the method.

So, instead of displaying the message in the text box directly, we call the `Invoke` method of the `Form` class to forward the call to the creation thread of the `Form` class. Because this is the same thread that created the text box, this fulfills our requirements.

The `Invoke` method requires an argument of type `Delegate`, and because any delegate derives from this class, every delegate can be passed to this method. We want to invoke a method that doesn't take parameters: `DisplayReceivedMessage`, and there's already a predefined delegate in the .NET Framework to invoke a method without parameters: `System.Windows.Forms.MethodInvoker`. This delegate accepts methods without parameters, such as our `DisplayReceivedMessage` method.

With the exception handler block, exceptions with the error code 10004 will be ignored. This exception will be thrown when the receiving thread is stopped, which occurs when a user clicks the Stop button.

```
// Main method of the listener thread that receives the data
private void Listener()
{
   done = false;
   try
   {
      while (!done)
      {
         IPEndPoint ep = null;
         byte[] buffer = client.Receive(ref ep);
         message = encoding.GetString(buffer);
         this.Invoke(
               new MethodInvoker (DisplayReceivedMessage));
      }
   }
   catch (SocketException ex)
```

```
   {
      if (ex.ErrorCode == 10004)
      {
         // Ignore cancel blocking call error messages
      }
      else
      {
         MessageBox.Show(this, ex.Message,
               "Error MulticastChat",
               MessageBoxButtons.OK, MessageBoxIcon.Error);
      }
   }
}
```

In the DisplayReceivedMessage implementation, we write the received message to the textMessages text box, and write some informational text to the status bar:

```
private void DisplayReceivedMessage()
{
   string time = DateTime.Now.ToString("t");
   textMessages.Text = time + "  " + message + "\r\n" +
         textMessages.Text;
   statusBar.Text = "Received last message at " + time;
}
```

Sending Multicast Messages

Our next task is to implement the message-sending functionality in the Click event handler of the Send button. As you have already seen, a string is converted to a byte array using the UnicodeEncoding class:

```
private void OnSend(object sender, System.EventArgs e)
{
   try
   {
      // Send a message to the group
      byte[] data = encoding.GetBytes(name + ": " +
            textMessage.Text);
      client.Send(data, data.Length, remoteEP);
      textMessage.Clear();
      textMessage.Focus();
   }
   catch (Exception ex)
   {
      MessageBox.Show(this, ex.Message,
            "Error MulticastChat",
            MessageBoxButtons.OK, MessageBoxIcon.Error);
   }
}
```

Dropping the Multicast Membership

The Click event handler for the Stop button, the method OnStop, stops the client listening to the multicast group by calling the DropMulticastGroup method. Before the client stops receiving the multicast data, a final message is sent to the group, indicating that the user has left the conversation:

```
private void OnStop(object sender, System.EventArgs e)
{
   StopListener();
}
private void StopListener()
{
   // Send a leaving message to the group
   byte[] data = encoding.GetBytes(name + " has left the chat");
   client.Send(data, data.Length, remoteEP);
   // Leave the group
   client.DropMulticastGroup(groupAddress);
   client.Close();
   // Tell the receiving thread to stop
   done = true;
   buttonStart.Enabled = true;
   buttonStop.Enabled = false;
   buttonSend.Enabled = false;
}
```

Because the multicast group should be left not only when the user clicks the Stop button, but also when the user exits the application, we will handle the Closing event of the form in the OnClosing method. If the server has not already been stopped, we again call the StopListener method to stop listening to the group after sending a final message to the group:

```
private void OnClosing(object sender,
                       System.ComponentModel.CancelEventArgs e)
{
      if (!done)
   StopListener();
}
```

Starting the Chat Application

Now we can run the chat application on multiple systems and start the conversation. Figure 9-8 shows an example of the application in action. Note that newer messages appear toward the top of the chat window.

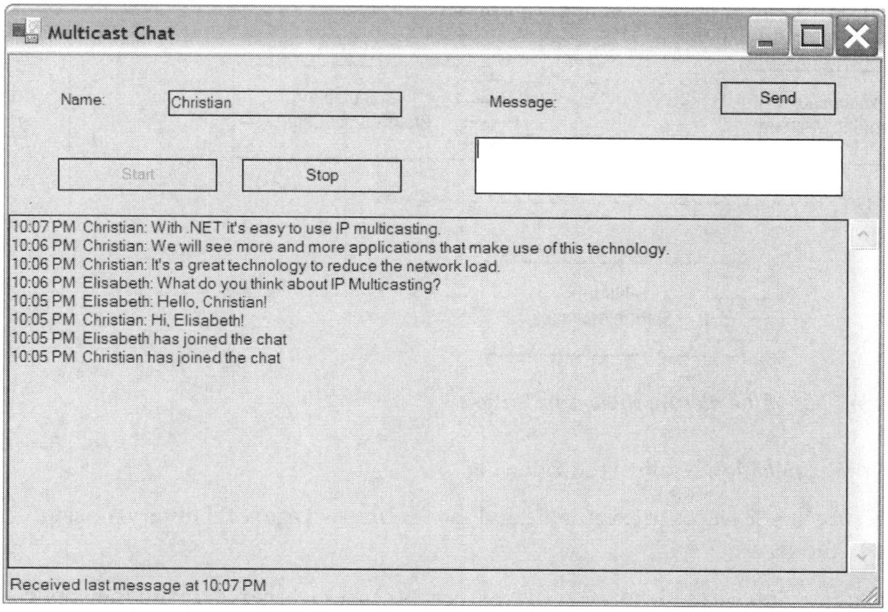

Figure 9-8. *Using the multicast chat application*

Creating a Picture Show Application

The second application we will look at in this chapter is a picture show application. This application illustrates a multicast scenario where a single application sends messages to multiple clients. This application is a little more challenging than the chat application, because the messages that can be sent are larger and won't necessarily fit into datagram packets.

The picture show server allows pictures on its file system to be selected for multicasting to all clients that have joined the multicast group.

■NOTE The picture show is a large application, and so rather than try to cover it in its entirely, we'll focus on the most important aspects related to network communications. The complete working application is available for download from the Downloads section of the Apress website (`http://www.apress.com`).

The complete picture show application consists of three Visual Studio .NET projects:

- `PictureShowServer`, a Windows server application
- `PictureShowClient`, a Windows client application
- `PicturePackager`, a class library used by both client and server

Figure 9-9 shows the dependency of these projects.

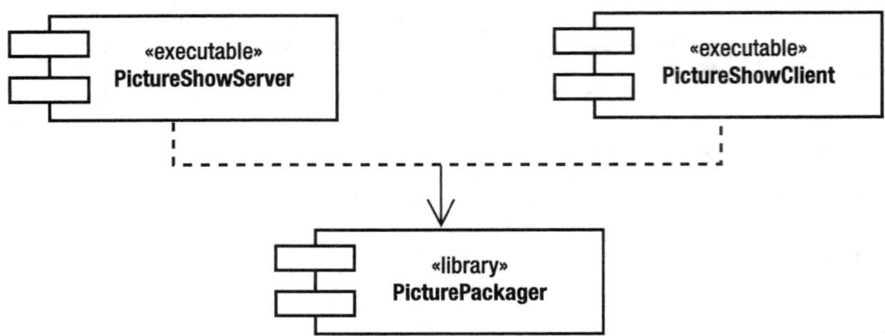

Figure 9-9. *Assemblies of the picture show application*

Running the application requires the following:

- The `PictureShowServer.exe` executable and the `PicturePackager.dll` library must be copied to the server.
- The client systems need `PictureShowClient.exe`, `PicturePackager.dll`, and the application configuration file `PictureShowClient.exe.config`.
- The server application must be started and initialized before the client applications can run.
- You must set the server name in the client application to that of your server.

The first consideration is how we're going to send pictures to our application's users.

Creating a Picture Protocol

Some of the pictures sent to the multicast group will be too large to fit in a datagram packet. We need to split the picture into multiple packages. Also, we want to send some more data in addition to the picture stream. So, we need some layout of the data that is sent across the wire.

To make it easy to parse the data with classes from the `System.Xml` namespace, and also to make the format extensible for future versions of the application, we'll use an XML format for the packages that contain the picture data.

■ **NOTE** To save space, we could define a custom binary format for the data packet, but when sending a picture, the XML overhead is not large compared to the size of the picture. Using XML gives us the advantage of an existing parser, and this format makes it easy to add more elements in future versions.

One of our XML packages will fit into a single IP datagram. The root element is `<PicturePackage>` with an attribute called `Number`, which identifies the fragments that belong together. `<Name>` and `<Data>` are child elements of the `<PicturePackage>` element. The `<Name>` element is informational and can be used for a name of the picture; the <Data> element is the base-64 encoded binary data segment of the picture. The attribute SegmentNumber allows us to work out how to put the segments together in order to create a complete picture; LastSegmentNumber informs us how many segments are needed:

```
<PicturePackage Number="4">
   <Name>hello.jpg</Name>
   <Data SegmentNumber="2" LastSegmentNumber="12"
         Size="2400">
      <!-- base-64 encoded picture data -->
   </Data>
</PicturePackage>
```

The PicturePackager assembly contains two classes:

PicturePackage: This is an entity class. A single PicturePackage object corresponds to an XML <PicturePackage> file, as in the preceding example. We can produce the XML representation for a single picture segment using the GetXml method on the class. The PicturePackage class offers two constructors. The first is for use on the server, creating a picture fragment from native data types (int, string, and byte[]).The second constructor is designed for use on the client, and it creates a fragment from an XML source.

PicturePackager: This is a utility class that has static methods only. It splits up a complete picture into multiple segments with the GetPicturePackages method, and it re-creates a complete picture by merging the constituent segments with the GetPicture method.

Setting Up Picture Packages

So, the PicturePackage class represents one segment of a complete picture, and here it is reproduced in full. It starts by defining read-only properties that map to XML elements of the format described in the previous section:

```
using System;
using System.Xml;
using System.Text;
namespace Apress.Networking.Multicast
{
   public class PicturePackage
   {
      private string name;
      private int id;
      private int segmentNumber;
      private int numberOfSegments;
      private byte[] segmentBuffer;
      public string Name
      {
         get
         {
            return name;
```

```
      }
   }
   public int Id
   {
      get
      {
         return id;
      }
   }
   public int SegmentNumber
   {
      get
      {
         return segmentNumber;
      }
   }
   public int NumberOfSegments
   {
      get
      {
         return numberOfSegments;
      }
   }
   public byte[] SegmentBuffer
   {
      get
      {
         return segmentBuffer;
      }
   }
```

Next, we deal with the two constructors. One takes multiple arguments to create a `PicturePackage` object by the sender, and the other takes XML data received from the network to re-create the object on the receiver:

```
// Creates a picture segment from data types
// Used by the server application
public PicturePackage(string name, int id, int segmentNumber,
                      int numberOfSegments, byte[] segmentBuffer)
{
   this.name = name;
   this.id = id;
   this.segmentNumber = segmentNumber;
   this.numberOfSegments = numberOfSegments;
   this.segmentBuffer = segmentBuffer;
}
// Creates a picture segment from XML code
// Used by the client application
```

```
public PicturePackage(XmlDocument xml)
{
   XmlNode rootNode = xml.SelectSingleNode("PicturePackage");
   id = int.Parse(rootNode.Attributes["Number"].Value);
   XmlNode nodeName = rootNode.SelectSingleNode("Name");
   this.name = nodeName.InnerXml;
   XmlNode nodeData = rootNode.SelectSingleNode("Data");
   numberOfSegments = int.Parse(nodeData.Attributes[
                           "LastSegmentNumber"].Value);
   segmentNumber = int.Parse(nodeData.Attributes[
                           "SegmentNumber"].Value);
   int size = int.Parse(nodeData.Attributes["Size"].Value);
   segmentBuffer = Convert.FromBase64String(nodeData.InnerText);
}
```

The only other item in this class is the `GetXml` method, which converts the picture segment into an `XmlDocument` object with the help of classes from the `System.Xml` namespace. The XML representation is returned as a string:

```
      // Return XML code representing a picture segment
      public string GetXml()
      {
         XmlDocument doc = new XmlDocument();
         // Root element <PicturePackage>
         XmlElement picturePackage =
               doc.CreateElement("PicturePackage");
         // <PicturePackage Number="number">
         // </PicturePackage>
         XmlAttribute pictureNumber =
               doc.CreateAttribute("Number");
         pictureNumber.Value = id.ToString();
         picturePackage.Attributes.Append(pictureNumber);
         // <Name>pictureName</Name>
         XmlElement pictureName = doc.CreateElement("Name");
         pictureName.InnerText = name;
         picturePackage.AppendChild(pictureName);
         // <Data SegmentNumber="" Size=""> (base-64 encoded
         //                                     fragment)
         XmlElement data = doc.CreateElement("Data");
         XmlAttribute numberAttr =
               doc.CreateAttribute("SegmentNumber");
         numberAttr.Value = segmentNumber.ToString();
         data.Attributes.Append(numberAttr);
         XmlAttribute lastNumberAttr =
               doc.CreateAttribute("LastSegmentNumber");
         lastNumberAttr.Value = numberOfSegments.ToString();
         data.Attributes.Append(lastNumberAttr);
         data.InnerText =
```

```
                Convert.ToBase64String(segmentBuffer);
            XmlAttribute sizeAttr =
                doc.CreateAttribute("Size");
            sizeAttr.Value = segmentBuffer.Length.ToString();
            data.Attributes.Append(sizeAttr);
            picturePackage.AppendChild(data);
            doc.AppendChild(picturePackage);
            return doc.InnerXml;
        }
    }
}
```

Creating the Picture Packager

As noted earlier, the PicturePackager class is a utility class that consists of static methods only. It is used by both the sender and receiver. The GetPicturePackages method splits up an image into multiple packages in the form of an array of PicturePackage objects, where every segment of the picture is represented by a single PicturePackage object:

```
using System;
using System.Drawing;
using System.Drawing.Imaging;
using System.IO;
namespace Apress.Networking.Multicast
{
    public class PicturePackager
    {
        protected PicturePackager()
        {
        }
        // Return picture segments for a complete picture
        public static PicturePackage[]
            GetPicturePackages(string name,
                               int id,
                               Image picture)
        {
            return GetPicturePackages(name, id, picture, 4000);
        }
        // Return picture segments for a complete picture
        public static PicturePackage[]
            GetPicturePackages(string name, int id,
                               Image picture,
                               int segmentSize)
        {
            // Save the picture in a byte array
            MemoryStream stream = new MemoryStream();
            picture.Save(stream, ImageFormat.Jpeg);
            // Calculate the number of segments to split the
            // picture
```

```
   int numberSegments = (int)stream.Position /
         segmentSize + 1;
   PicturePackage[] packages = new
         PicturePackage[numberSegments];
   // Create the picture segments
   int sourceIndex = 0;
   for (int i=0; i < numberSegments; i++)
   {
      // Calculate the size of the segment buffer
      int bytesToCopy = (int)stream.Position -
            sourceIndex;
      if (bytesToCopy > segmentSize)
         bytesToCopy = segmentSize;
      byte[] segmentBuffer = new byte[bytesToCopy];
      Array.Copy(stream.GetBuffer(), sourceIndex,
            segmentBuffer,
            0, bytesToCopy);
      packages[i] = new PicturePackage(name, id,
            i + 1, numberSegments, segmentBuffer);
      sourceIndex += bytesToCopy;
   }
   return packages;
}
```

The receiver uses the inverse `GetPicture` method, which takes all `PicturePackage` objects for a single picture and returns the complete image object:

```
// Returns a complete picture from the segments passed
// in
public static Image GetPicture(
      PicturePackage[] packages)
{
   int fullSizeNeeded = 0;
   int numberPackages = packages[0].NumberOfSegments;
   int pictureId = packages[0].Id;
   // Calculate the size of the picture data and check
   // for consistent picture IDs
   for (int i=0; i < numberPackages; i++)
   {
      fullSizeNeeded +=
            packages[i].SegmentBuffer.Length;
      if (packages[i].Id != pictureId)
         throw new ArgumentException(
            "Inconsistent picture ids passed",
            "packages");
   }
   // Merge the segments to a binary array
   byte[] buffer = new byte[fullSizeNeeded];
   int destinationIndex = 0;
```

```
            for (int i = 0; i < numberPackages; i++)
            {
               int length = packages[i].SegmentBuffer.Length;
               Array.Copy(packages[i].SegmentBuffer, 0, buffer,
                     destinationIndex, length);
               destinationIndex += length;
            }
            // Create the image from the binary data
            MemoryStream stream = new MemoryStream(buffer);
            Image image = Image.FromStream(stream);
            return image;
         }
      }
   }
```

> **NOTE** The `System.Drawing` and `System.Xml` assemblies must be referenced by the `PicturePackager` assembly.

Building the Picture Show Server

Now that we have the assembly to split and merge pictures, we can start with the implementation of the server application. The server project is `PictureShowServer`, and its main form class is `PictureServerForm`, contained in the `PictureShowServer.cs` file. Figure 9-10 shows the main form for the server.

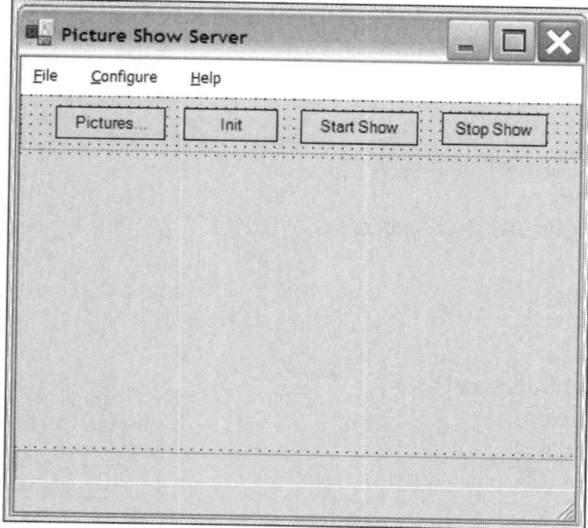

Figure 9-10. *The picture show server user interface*

The controls on this form are listed in Table 9-3.

Table 9-3. *Picture Show Server Controls*

Control Type	Name	Comments
MainMenu	`mainMenu`	The menu has the main entries File, Configure, and Help. The File menu has the submenus Init, Start, Stop, and Exit. The Configure menu allows configuration of the Multicast Session, the Show Timings, and Pictures. The Help menu just offers an About option.
Button	`buttonPictures`	The Pictures… button will allow the user to configure the pictures that should be presented.
Button	`buttonInit`	The Init button will publish the multicast address and port number to clients using a TCP socket.
Button	`buttonStart`	The Start button starts sending the pictures to the multicast group address.
Button	`buttonStop`	The Stop button stops the picture show prematurely.
PictureBox	`pictureBox`	The picture box will show the picture that is currently being transferred to clients.
ProgressBar	`progressBar`	The progress bar indicates how many pictures of the show have been transferred.
StatusBar	`statusBar`	The status bar shows information about what's currently going on.
ImageList	`imageList`	The image list holds all images that make up the show.

The `PictureServerForm` class contains the `Main` method, and there are three other dialog classes and the `InfoServer` class:

- `ConfigurePicturesDialog` allows the user to select image files from the server's file system to make up the picture show.
- `MulticastConfigurationDialog` sets up the multicast address and port number, and the interface where the pictures should be sent in case the server system has multiple network cards.
- `ConfigureShowDialog` allows the time between pictures to be specified.
- `InfoServer.cs` is a class that starts its own thread, which acts as an answering server for a client application. This thread returns information about the group address and port number to clients.

Let's look at the code for the startup class for the application, which is called `PictureServerForm` and resides in the `PictureShowServer.cs` source file. You'll see the namespaces and fields that the class will require for the methods covered in subsequent sections.

```
using System;
using System.Drawing;
using System.Windows.Forms;
using System.Net;
```

```
using System.Net.Sockets;
using System.Text;
using System.IO;
using System.Xml;
using System.Threading;
namespace Apress.Networking.Multicast
{
   public class PictureServerForm :
         System.Windows.Forms.Form
   {
      private string[] fileNames;      // Array of picture
                                       // file names
      private object filesLock = new object();  // Lock to
                                       // synchronize access
                                       // to fileNames
      private UnicodeEncoding encoding =
            new UnicodeEncoding();
      // Multicast group address, port, and endpoint
      private IPAddress groupAddress =
            IPAddress.Parse("231.4.5.11");
      private int groupPort = 8765;
      private IPEndPoint groupEP;
      private UdpClient udpClient;
      private Thread senderThread;     // Thread to send
                                       // pictures
      private Image currentImage;      // Current image sent
      private int pictureIntervalSeconds = 3; // Time
                                       // between sending
                                       // pictures
      //...
```

Opening Files

One of the first actions the picture show server application must do is to configure the pictures that are to be presented. `OnConfigurePictures` is the handler for the Configure ➤ Pictures menu item and the `Click` event of the Pictures... button:

```
private void OnConfigurePictures(object sender, System.EventArgs e)
{
   ConfigurePicturesDialog dialog = new ConfigurePicturesDialog();
   if (dialog.ShowDialog() == DialogResult.OK)
   {
      lock (filesLock)
      {
         fileNames = dialog.FileNames;
         progressBar.Maximum = filenames.Length;
      }
   }
}
```

This opens a Configure Pictures dialog box, shown in Figure 9-11, which offers a preview of the pictures in a ListView with a LargeIcon view.

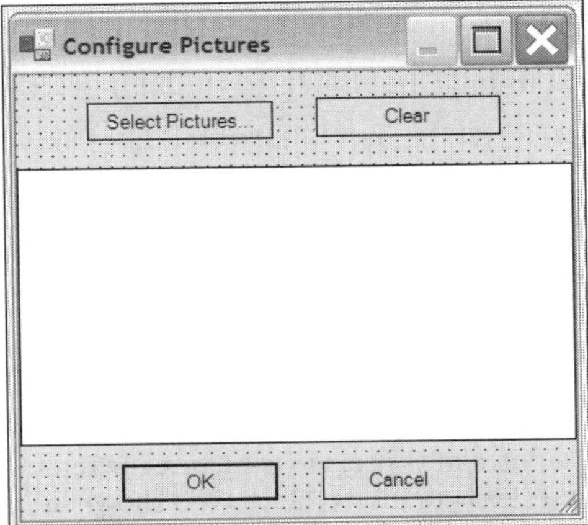

Figure 9-11. *Configure Pictures dialog box*

The controls used for the Configure Pictures dialog box are detailed in Table 9-4.

Table 9-4. *Controls in the Configure Pictures Dialog Box*

Control Type	Name	Comments
Button	`buttonSelect`	The Select Pictures… button displays `openFileDialog` so the user can select the pictures for the show.
OpenFileDialog	`openFileDialog`	
Button	`buttonClear`	The Clear button removes all selected images.
Button	`buttonOK`	The OK button sends the selected files the main form and closes the dialog box.
Button	`buttonCancel`	The Cancel button closes the dialog box. All file selections are ignored.
ImageList	`imageList`	The `imageList` Windows Forms component collects all selected images for display in the `listViewPictures` list view, showing a preview for the user.
ListView	`listViewPictures`	

`OnFileOpen` is the handler for the `Click` event of the Select Pictures… button. It is where we create `Image` objects from the files selected by `OpenFileDialog` for adding them to the `imageList` associated with the ListView:

```
private void OnFileOpen(object sender, System.EventArgs e)
      {
   if (openFileDialog.ShowDialog() == DialogResult.OK)
   {
      fileNames = openFileDialog.FileNames;
```

```
            int imageIndex = 0;
            foreach (string fileName in fileNames)
            {
               using (Image image = Image.FromFile(fileName))
               {
                  imageList.Images.Add(image);
                  listViewPictures.Items.Add(fileName,
                        imageIndex++);
               }
            }
        }
    }
```

Configuring Multicasting

Another configuration dialog box of the server application allows users to configure the multicast address and multicast port number. The Multicast Configuration dialog box is shown in Figure 9-12.

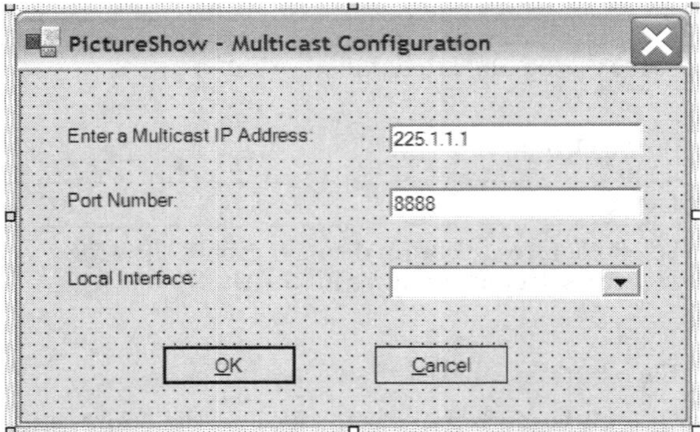

Figure 9-12. *Multicast Configuration dialog box*

The controls used for the Multicast Configuration dialog box are detailed in Table 9-5.

Table 9-5. *Controls in the Multicast Configuration Dialog Box*

Control Type	Name	Comments
TextBox	`textBoxIPAddress`	This text box allows the user to enter a multicast IP address.
TextBox	`textBoxPortNumber`	This text box allows the user to enter the port number for multicasting.
ComboBox	`comboBoxLocalInterface`	The user can select a local interface here. The combo box list is filled at form startup.

This dialog box allows users to select the local interface that should be used for sending multicast messages. This can be useful if the system has multiple network cards or if it is connected to both a dial-up network and a local network.

The combo box listing the local interfaces is filled at form startup. First, we call `Dns.GetHostName` to retrieve the host name of the local host, and then we call `Dns.GetHostByName` to get an `IPHostEntry` object containing all the IP addresses of the local host. If the host has multiple IP addresses, the string `"Any"` is added to the combo box to allow the user to send multicast messages across all network interfaces. If there is only one network interface, the combo box is disabled, as it will not be possible to select a different interface.

Here is the constructor in `MulticastConfigurationDialog.cs`:

```
public MulticastConfigurationDialog()
{
   //
   // Required for Windows Form Designer support
   //
   InitializeComponent();
   string hostname = Dns.GetHostName();
   IPHostEntry entry = Dns.GetHostByName(hostname);
   IPAddress[] addresses = entry.AddressList;
   foreach (IPAddress address in addresses)
   {
      comboBoxLocalInterface.Items.Add(address.ToString());
   }
   comboBoxLocalInterface.SelectedIndex = 0;
   if (addresses.Length > 1)
   {
      comboBoxLocalInterface.Items.Add("Any");
   }
   else
   {
      comboBoxLocalInterface.Enabled = false;
   }
}
```

Another interesting aspect of this class is the validation of the multicast address. The text box `textBoxIPAddress` has the `OnValidateMulticastAddress` handler assigned to the `Validating` event. The handler checks that the IP address entered is in the valid range of multicast addresses:

```
private void OnValidateMulticastAddress(object sender,
                        System.ComponentModel.CancelEventArgs e)
{
   try
   {
      IPAddress address = IPAddress.Parse(textBoxIPAddress.Text);
      string[] segments = textBoxIPAddress.Text.Split('.');
      int network = int.Parse(segments[0]);
      // Check address falls in correct range
```

```
        if ((network < 224) || (network > 239))
           throw new FormatException("Multicast addresses " +
                 "must have the range 224.x.x.x to " +
                 "239.x.x.x");
        // Check address is not a reserved Class D
        if ((network == 224) && (int.Parse(segments[1]) == 0)
            && (int.Parse(segments[2]) == 0))
           throw new FormatException("The Local Network " +
                 "Control Block cannot be used for " +
                 "multicasting groups");
     }
     catch (FormatException ex)
     {
        MessageBox.Show(ex.Message);
        e.Cancel = true;
     }
  }
```

We now return to the events in the main `PictureServerForm` class in the file `PictureShow-Server.cs`. When the Init button is clicked in the main dialog box (see Figure 9-10), we want the listening server to start up so that it can send the group address and port number to requesting clients. We do this by creating an `InfoServer` object with the IP address and the port number, and then invoke `Start`. This method starts a new thread to handle client requests, as you will see next. `OnInit` finishes by calling some helper methods that enable the Start button and disable the Init button:

```
// PictureShowServer.cs
      private void OnInit(object sender, System.EventArgs e)
      {
         InfoServer info = new InfoServer(groupAddress,
               groupPort);
         info.Start();
         UIEnableStart(true);
         UIEnableInit(false);
      }
```

The `InfoServer` class does all the work of responding to client requests by sending the multicast group address and port number to the clients in a separate thread. The class constructor initializes the `InfoServer` object with the group address and the group port. The `Start` method (invoked by the `OnInit` in the `PictureShowServer` class) creates the new thread. The main method of the newly created thread, `InfoMain`, sets up a TCP stream socket, where we simply place the multicast address and the port number separated by a colon (`:`) for sending them to the client as soon as one connects to the server (see Chapter 4 for details on stream sockets):

```
// InfoServer.cs
using System;
using System.Net;
using System.Net.Sockets;
```

```
using System.Text;
using System.Threading;
namespace Apress.Networking.Multicast
{
   public class InfoServer
   {
      private IPAddress groupAddress;
      private int groupPort;
      private UnicodeEncoding encoding =
            new UnicodeEncoding();
      public InfoServer(IPAddress groupAddress,
            int groupPort)
      {
         this.groupAddress = groupAddress;
         this.groupPort = groupPort;
      }
      public void Start()
      {
         // Create a new listener thread
         Thread infoThread = new Thread(
               new ThreadStart(InfoMain));
         infoThread.IsBackground = true;
         infoThread.Start();
      }
      protected void InfoMain()
      {
         string configuration = groupAddress.ToString() +
               ":" + groupPort.ToString();
         // Create a TCP streaming socket that listens to
         // client requests
         Socket infoSocket = new Socket(
               AddressFamily.InterNetwork,
               SocketType.Stream,
               ProtocolType.Tcp);
         try
         {
            infoSocket.Bind(new IPEndPoint(IPAddress.Any,
                  8777));
            infoSocket.Listen(5);
            while (true)
            {
               // Send multicast configuration information
               // to clients
               Socket clientConnection =
                     infoSocket.Accept();
               clientConnection.Send(
                     encoding.GetBytes(configuration));
```

```
                  clientConnection.Shutdown(
                        SocketShutdown.Both);
                  clientConnection.Close();
               }
            }
            finally
            {
               infoSocket.Shutdown(SocketShutdown.Both);
               infoSocket.Close();
            }
         }
      }
   }
```

The UIEnableStart helper method enables or disables the Start button to prevent the user from clicking the wrong button. This method is called in the method OnInit, and, as you would expect, is very similar to UIEnableInit:

```
// PictureShowServer.cs
      private void UIEnableStart(bool flag)
      {
         if (flag)
         {
            buttonStart.Enabled = true;
            buttonStart.BackColor = Color.SpringGreen;
            miFileStart.Enabled = true;
         }
         else
         {
            buttonStart.Enabled = false;
            buttonStart.BackColor = Color.LightGray;
            miFileStart.Enabled = false;
         }
      }
```

Sending Pictures

OnStart is the method that handles the Click event of the Start button, and this is where the sending thread is initialized and started. The start method of this thread is SendPictures, which we look at next.

```
// PictureShowServer.cs
      private void OnStart(object sender,
            System.EventArgs e)
      {
         if (fileNames == null)
         {
            MessageBox.Show("Select pictures before " +
```

```
                "starting the show!");
            return;
        }
        // Initialize picture sending thread
        senderThread = new Thread(
              new ThreadStart(SendPictures));
        senderThread.Name = "Sender";
        senderThread.Priority = ThreadPriority.BelowNormal;
        senderThread.Start();
        UIEnableStart(false);
        UIEnableStop(true);
    }
```

The list of file names that we receive from the Configure Pictures dialog box is used by the SendPictures method of the sending thread. Here, we load a file from the array fileNames to create a new Image object that is passed to the SendPicture method. Then the progress bar is updated with the help of a delegate to reflect the ongoing progress. When building the multicast chat application earlier in the chapter, we discussed issues relating to the use of Windows controls in multiple threads, and now we use the Invoke method again:

```
// PictureShowServer.cs
    private void SendPictures()
    {
        InitializeNetwork();
        lock (filesLock)
        {
            int pictureNumber = 1;
            foreach (string fileName in fileNames)
            {
                currentImage = Image.FromFile(filename);
                Invoke(new MethodInvoker(SetPictureBoxImage);
                SendPicture(image, fileName, pictureNumber);
                Invoke(new MethodInvokerInt(
                      IncrementProgressBar),
                      new object[] {1});
                Thread.Sleep(pictureIntervalSeconds);
                pictureNumber++;
            }
        }
        Invoke(new MethodInvoker(ResetProgress));
        Invoke(new MethodInvokerBoolean(UIEnableStart),
               new object[] {true});
        Invoke(new MethodInvokerBoolean(UIEnableStop),
               new object[] {false});
    }
```

We've already discussed the MethodInvoker delegate in the System.Windows.Forms namespace when we used it in the multicast chat application. The MethodInvoker delegate allows you to call methods that take no arguments. Now we also need methods that take an int, a string, or a bool argument to set specific values and to enable or disable certain user interface elements. The delegates for these purposes are placed at the top of the PictureShowServer.cs file:

```
namespace Apress.Networking.Multicast
{
  public delegate void MethodInvokerInt(int x);
  public delegate void MethodInvokerString(string s);
  public delegate void MethodInvokerBoolean(bool flag);
  //...
```

The SendPicture method splits up a single picture image using the PicturePackager utility class. Every individual picture package is converted to a byte array with an encoding object of type UnicodeEncoding. This byte array is then sent to the multicast group address by the Send method of UdpClient:

```
// PictureShowServer.cs
      private void SendPicture(Image image, string name,
            int index)
      {
         string message = "Sending picture " + name;
         Invoke(new MethodInvokerString(SetStatusBar),
               new Object[] {message});
         PicturePackage[] packages =
               PicturePackager.GetPicturePackages(name,
               index, image, 1024);
         // Send all segments of a single picture to the
         // group
         foreach (PicturePackage package in packages)
         {
            byte[] data =
                  encoding.GetBytes(package.GetXml());
            int sendBytes = udpClient.Send(data,
                  data.Length);
            if (sendBytes < 0)
               MessageBox.Show("Error sending");
            Thread.Sleep(300);
         }
         message = "Picture " + name + " sent";
         Invoke(new MethodInvokerString(SetStatusBar),
                new object[] { message });
      }
```

Creating the Picture Show Client

The multicast picture show client has a simple user interface consisting of a menu, a picture box, and a status bar on a form, as shown in Figure 9-13. The status bar has three panels showing not only status messages but also the multicast address and port numbers. The File menu entry has Start, Stop, and Exit submenus.

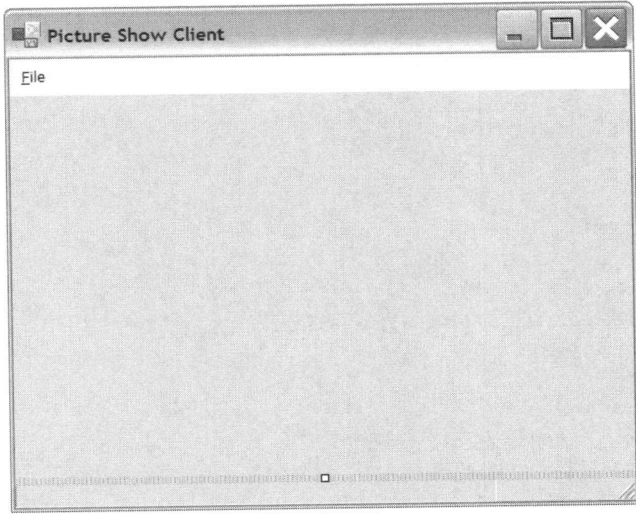

Figure 9-13. *The picture show client user interface*

The components on this form are described in Table 9-6.

Table 9-6. *Controls in the Picture Show Client Application*

Control Type	Name	Comments
MainMenu	`mainMenu`	The main menu has a single File menu entry with Start, Stop, and Exit submenus.
PictureBox	`pictureBox`	The picture box displays a picture as soon as all fragments that make it up have been received.
StatusBar	`statusBar`	The status bar is split into three panels with the `Panels` property. The first panel (`statusBarPanelMain`) shows normal status text; the second and third (`statusBarPanelAddress` and `statusBarPanelPort`) display the group address and port number.

The form class is `PictureClientForm` in the file `PictureShowClient.cs`. It houses the methods `GetMulticastConfiguration` (to request the multicast group information from the server), `OnStart` (to join the multicast group), and `Listener` (to start a new thread). It also contains the method `DisplayPicture`, which is called for each picture in the show, and `OnStop`, which terminates the listening thread.

Let's start with the namespaces and private fields that the client `PictureClientForm` class requires:

```
// PictureShowClient.cs
using System;
using System.Drawing;
using System.Collections;
using System.Windows.Forms;
using System.Collections.Specialized;
using System.Net;
using System.Net.Sockets;
using System.Threading;
using System.Text;
using System.Configuration;
namespace Apress.Networking.Multicast
{
   public delegate void MethodInvokerInt(int i);
   public delegate void MethodInvokerString(string s);
   public class PictureClientForm :
         System.Windows.Forms.Form
   {
      private IPAddress groupAddress; // Multicast group
                                      // address
      private int groupPort;          // Multicast group
                                      // port
      private int ttl;
      private UdpClient udpClient;    // Client socket for
                                      // receiving
      private string serverName;      // host name of
                                      // the server
      private int serverInfoPort;     // Port for group
                                      // information
      private bool done = false;      // Flag to end
                                      // receiving thread
      private UnicodeEncoding encoding =
           new UnicodeEncoding();
      // Array of all pictures received
      private SortedList pictureArray = new SortedList();
```

Receiving the Multicast Group Address

As in the multicast chat application, we use a configuration file for setting up the client picture show application. In this case, it is used to configure the name and address of the server so clients can connect to the TCP socket that returns the multicast address and port number:

```
<?xml version="1.0" encoding="utf-8" ?>
<configuration>
   <appSettings>
```

```
    <add key="ServerName" value="localhost" />
    <add key="ServerPort" value="7777" />
    <add key="TTL" value="32" />
  </appSettings>
</configuration>
```

The values in this configuration file are read by the `PictureClientForm` form class constructor, which also invokes the `GetMulticastConfiguration` method:

```
// PictureShowClient.cs
      public PictureClientForm()
      {
         //
         // Required for Windows Form Designer support
         //
         InitializeComponent();
         try
         {
            // Read the application configuration file
            NameValueCollection configuration =
                  ConfigurationSettings.AppSettings;
            serverName = configuration["ServerName"];
            serverInfoPort =
                  int.Parse(configuration["ServerPort"]);
            ttl = int.Parse(configuration["TTL"]);
         }
         catch
         {
            MessageBox.Show("Check the configuration file");
         }
         GetMulticastConfiguration();
      }
```

We connect to the server in the `GetMulticastConfiguration` method. After connecting, we can call `Receive`, as the server immediately starts to send once a connection is received. The byte array received is converted to a string using an object of the `UnicodeEncoding` class. The string contains the multicast address and the port number separated by a colon (`:`), so we split the string and set the member variables `groupAddress` and `groupPort`.

As mentioned earlier, the status bar has two additional panels, `statusBarPanelAddress` and `statusBarPanelPort`, where the multicast address and multicast port number are displayed:

```
// PictureShowClient.cs
      private void GetMulticastConfiguration()
      {
         Socket socket = new Socket(
               AddressFamily.InterNetwork,
                SocketType.Stream, ProtocolType.Tcp);
         try
         {
```

```
            // Get the multicast configuration info from the
            // server
            IPHostEntry server =
                Dns.GetHostByName(serverName);
            IPAddress ipAddress=null;
            foreach(IPAddress ipa in server.AddressList)
            {
                if(ipa.AddressFamily==
                    AddressFamily.InterNetwork)
                {
                    ipAddress=ipa;
                    break;
                }
            }
            socket.Connect(new IPEndPoint(ipAddress,
                serverInfoPort));
            byte[] buffer = new byte[512];
            int receivedBytes = socket.Receive(buffer);
            if (receivedBytes < 0)
            {
                MessageBox.Show("Error receiving");
                return;
            }
            socket.Shutdown(SocketShutdown.Both);
            string config = encoding.GetString(buffer);
            string[] multicastAddress = config.Split(':');
            groupAddress = IPAddress.Parse(
                multicastAddress[0]);
            groupPort = int.Parse(multicastAddress[1]);
            statusBarPanelAddress.Text =
                groupAddress.ToString();
            statusBarPanelPort.Text = groupPort.ToString();
        }
        catch (SocketException ex)
        {
            if (ex.ErrorCode == 10061)
            {
                MessageBox.Show(this, "No server can be " +
                    "found on " +  serverName +
                    ", at port " + serverInfoPort,
                    "Error Picture Show",
                    MessageBoxButtons.OK,
                    MessageBoxIcon.Error);
            }
            else
            {
```

```
                MessageBox.Show(this, ex.Message,
                    "Error Picture Show",
                    MessageBoxButtons.OK,
                    MessageBoxIcon.Error);
            }
        }
        finally
        {
            socket.Close();
        }
    }
```

Joining the Multicast Group

Once we have the multicast address and the port number, we can join the multicast group. The constructor of the `UdpClient` class creates a socket listening to the port of the group multicast, and then we join the multicast group by calling `JoinMulticastGroup`.

The task of receiving the messages and packaging the pictures together belongs to the newly created listener thread that invokes the `Listener` method:

```
// PictureShowClient.cs
    private void OnStart(object sender,
        System.EventArgs e)
    {
        udpClient = new UdpClient(groupPort);
        try
        {
            udpClient.JoinMulticastGroup(groupAddress, ttl);
        }
        catch (Exception ex)
        {
            MessageBox.Show(ex.Message);
        }
        Thread t1 = new Thread(new ThreadStart(Listener));
        t1.Name = "Listener";
        t1.IsBackground = true;
        t1.Start();
    }
```

Receiving the Multicast Picture Data

The listener thread waits in the `Receive` method of the `udpClient` object until data is received. The byte array received is converted to a string with the encoding object, and, in turn, a `PicturePackage` object is initialized, passing in the XML string that is returned from the encoding object.

We need to merge all the picture fragments of a single picture received together to create full images for the client. This is done by using the `pictureArray` member variable of type `SortedList`. The key of the sorted list is the picture ID; the value is an array of `PicturePackage` objects that make up a complete picture.

We then check whether the pictureArray already contains an array of PicturePackages for the received picture. If it does, the fragment is added to the array; if not, we allocate a new array of PicturePackage objects.

After updating the status bar with information about the picture fragment, we invoke the DisplayPicture method if we have already received all the fragments of a picture:

```
// PictureShowClient.cs
      private void Listener()
      {
         while (!done)
         {
            // Receive a picture segment from the
            // multicast group
            IPEndPoint ep = null;
            byte[] data = udpClient.Receive(ref ep);
            PicturePackage package = new PicturePackage(
                  encoding.GetString(data));
            PicturePackage[] packages;
            if (pictureArray.ContainsKey(package.Id))
            {
               packages = (PicturePackage[])
                     pictureArray[package.Id];
               packages[package.SegmentNumber - 1] =
                     package;
            }
            else
            {
               packages =
                     new PicturePackage[
                     package.NumberOfSegments];
               packages[package.SegmentNumber - 1] =
                     package;
               pictureArray.Add(package.Id, packages);
            }
            string message = "Received picture " +
                  package.Id + " Segment " +
                  package.SegmentNumber;
            Invoke(new MethodInvokerString(SetStatusBar),
                  new object[] {message});
            // Check if all segments of a picture are
            // received
            int segmentCount = 0;
            for (int i = 0; i < package.NumberOfSegments;
                  i++)
            {
                if (packages[i] != null)
                segmentCount++;
            }
```

```
            // All segments are received, so draw the
            // picture
            if (segmentCount == package.NumberOfSegments)
            {
               this.Invoke(new MethodInvokerInt(
                     DisplayPicture),
                     new object[] {package.Id});
            }
         }
      }
```

All we need to do in DisplayPicture is re-create the picture with the help of the Picture-Packager utility class. The picture is displayed in the picture box on the form. Because the picture fragments are no longer needed, we can now free some memory by removing the item representing the PicturePackage array of the sorted list collection:

```
private void DisplayPicture(int id)
{
   PicturePackage[] packages = (PicturePackage[])pictureArray[id];
   Image picture = PicturePackager.GetPicture(packages);
   pictureArray.Remove(id);
   pictureBox.Image = picture;
}
```

Starting the Picture Show

Now we can start the server and client picture show applications. First, select the pictures using the Pictures… button on the server interface. Figure 9-14 shows the Configure Pictures dialog box after some pictures have been selected.

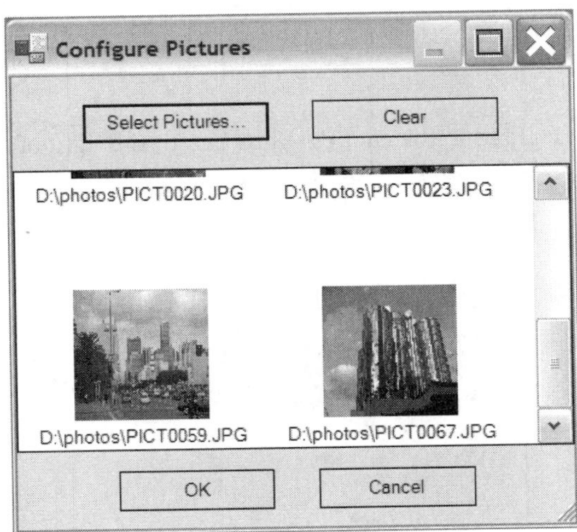

Figure 9-14. *The Configure Pictures dialog box with some photos selected*

Clicking the Init button in the main dialog box starts the InfoServer thread, listening for client requests. Before starting this thread, the multicast addresses can be changed, but the defaults should be enough to get started.

Once the InfoServer thread is started, clients can join the session by selecting File ➤ Start from their menus. Figure 9-15 shows the server application in action.

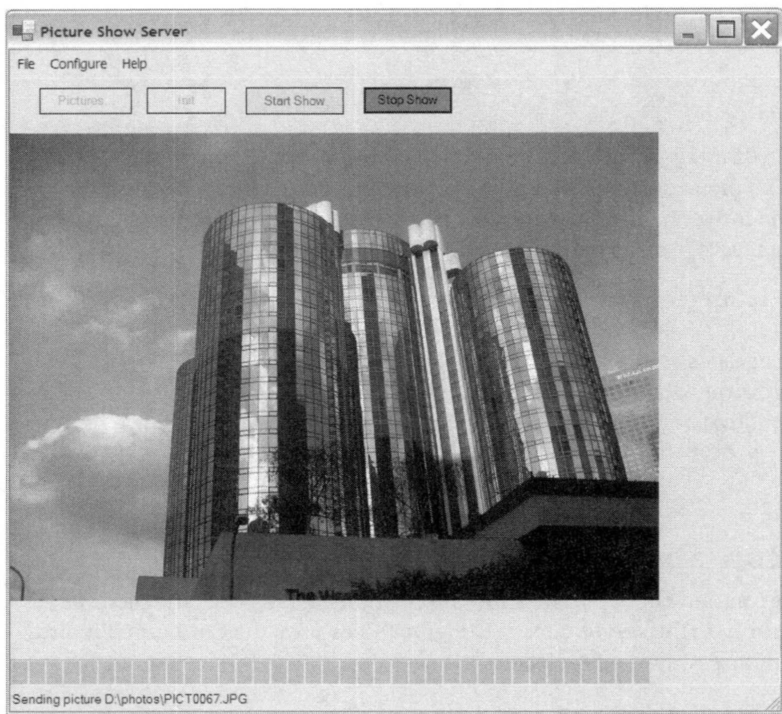

Figure 9-15. *Running the picture show server application*

As picture segments are received, they are detailed in the client's status bar, to the right of the multicast group address and port number, as shown in Figure 9-16.

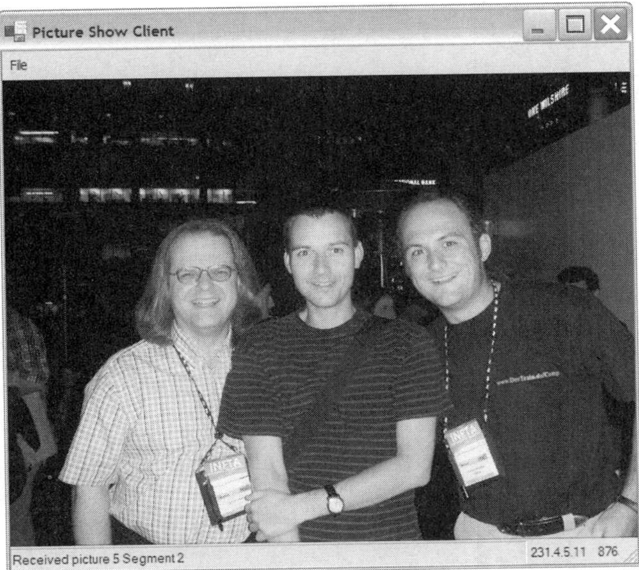

Figure 9-16. *Running the picture show client application*

Summary

In this chapter, we've looked at the architecture and issues of multicasting, and saw how multicasting can be implemented with .NET classes.

To demonstrate multicasting, we built two multicast applications. The first was a chat application in a many-to-many scenario. The second was a picture server in a one-to-many scenario, sending large data to the multicast group. You saw how easy it is to use the built-in multicast methods of the `UdpClient` class for multicasting in .NET.

Multicasting is a fairly young technology, and it has a bright future. We expect many issues, such as security and reliability, will be resolved by the standards fairly soon. For multicasting to be truly viable across the Internet, a few more improvements are required. However, multicasting already has many useful applications. Using multicasting to send data in a one-to-many or many-to-many group application considerably reduces the network load when compared to unicasting.

CHAPTER 10

HTTP

The advent of the World Wide Web, in 1990, brought about a massive increase in the use of the Internet. This was made possible by the introduction of the HyperText Transport Protocol (HTTP). Tim Berners-Lee first implemented HTTP in 1990–91 at CERN, the European Center for High-Energy Physics in Geneva, Switzerland.

HTTP's importance as an application protocol is significant, since a large share of web traffic today uses this protocol. The .NET classes support most of the features of the latest HTTP version, HTTP 1.1. The advanced features include pipelining, chunking, authentication, pre-authentication, encryption, proxy support, server-certificate validation, connection management, and HTTP extensions. NET also provides support for creating applications that use Internet protocols to send and receive data.

In this chapter, you will see how .NET exposes a robust implementation of HTTP. In particular, we'll discuss the following topics:

- An overview of HTTP, including HTTP headers, HTTP requests, and HTTP responses
- HTTP in .NET, including using the `HttpWebResponse`, `HttpWebRequest`, `WebClient`, `ServicePoint`, and `ServicePointManager` classes
- Reading and writing cookies in .NET
- Creating an HTTP server with ASP.NET support
- Using the HTTP transport channel with .NET Remoting

An Overview of HTTP

The Web depends on two essential components: the TCP/IP network protocol and HTTP. HTTP is a lightweight, application-level protocol that sits on top of TCP. Although HTTP is known chiefly as the transport channel of the Web and local intranets, it is a generic protocol that is used for many other tasks, such as for name servers and distributed object management systems through its request methods, error codes, and headers.

HTTP messages are in a MIME-like format. They contain metadata about the message (such as the type of content it contains and its length) and information about the request and response, such as the method used to send the request.

HTTP is a client/server protocol through which two systems communicate, usually over a TCP/IP connection. An HTTP server is a program that listens on a port on the machine for incoming HTTP requests. An HTTP client opens a connection to the server through a socket, sends a request message for a particular document, and waits for a reply from the server. The server sends a response message containing a success or error code, headers containing information about the response, and (if the request was successful) the requested document. The general format of an HTTP message is the same for both requests and responses:

```
start-line
message-header(s)
[message-body]
```

There may be any number of headers, each on separate line; that is, each one is preceded by a carriage return and linefeed character (CRLF sequence). The message body is optional, but if present, is separated from the headers by two CRLF sequences.

HTTP uses both persistent and nonpersistent connections. Nonpersistent connections are the default mode for HTTP 1.0, whereas persistent connections are the default mode for HTTP 1.1. A connection is said to be *nonpersistent* if each of the TCP connections is closed immediately after the server sends the requested object to the client. This means that the connection is used for exactly one request and one response, and it does not persist for other requests. With *persistent* connections, the server leaves the TCP connection open after sending the response, and hence subsequent requests and responses between the same client and server can be sent over the same connection. The server closes the connection only when it isn't used for a certain time.

Let's look briefly at a sample request from an HTTP client (such as a web browser) and the response from the web server (we'll look at the individual parts of these in more detail shortly). The following message is a request for the page `http://www.dotnetforce.com/default.aspx`, sent from the Internet Explorer 6.0 (IE 6) browser:

```
GET /default.aspx HTTP/1.1
Connection: Keep-Alive
User-Agent: Mozilla/4.0 (compatible; MSIE 6.0; Windows NT 5.1; .NET CLR 1.0.3705)
Host: www.dotnetforce.com
Accept: image/gif, image/x-xbitmap, image/jpeg, image/pjpeg, */*
<CRLF><CRLF>
```

The first line specifies the HTTP method to use, the relative address of the document to retrieve, and the HTTP protocol version to use. This is followed by a set of headers containing information about the request. In this case, the request doesn't include a message body, so the request ends with two CRLF sequences.

The response from an Internet Information Server (IIS) version 5 web server to this request might look like this:

```
HTTP/1.1 200 OK
Server: Microsoft-IIS/5.0
Date: Thu, 08 Aug 2002 19:07:29 GMT
Content-Type: text/html
Accept-Ranges: bytes
Last-Modified: Tue, 22 May 2001 11:19:22 GMT
ETag: "7e9623db1e2c01:a3d"
Content-Length: 2499
<html>
   <!-- HTML content here -->
</html>
```

Here, the first line contains the HTTP version, a status code, and a message, followed by the message headers, a blank line, and the message body. The message body typically consists of the content of the requested document (or content generated by an ASP.NET page or a server-side script).

In the following sections, we'll examine the construction of HTTP headers, HTTP requests, and HTTP responses.

HTTP Headers

As you've seen, an HTTP message consists of a start line, followed by a set of headers, an empty line, and some data. The start line specifies the action required of the server, the type of data being returned, or a status code.

HTTP headers can be divided into three broad categories: headers that are sent in the request, those that are sent in the response, and those that may be sent with either.

Request headers specify the capabilities of the client, such as the type of documents that the client can handle. Table 10-1 describes the most important request headers.

Table 10-1. *Common HTTP Request Headers*

Header	Description	Example
`Accept`	A list of MIME types that the client accepts, in the format *type/subtype*. Each item in this list should be separated by commas.	`Accept: text/html, image/gif, */*`[1]
`From`	Indicates the Internet e-mail address of the user account under which the requesting client is running.	`From: response@dotnetforce.com`
`Referer`	Allows the client to specify the address (URI) of the resource from which the requested URI is obtained. This allows a server to generate lists of back links to resources of interest, such as logging, optimized caching, and so on. It also allows obsolete or mistyped links to be traced for maintenance.	`Referer: http://www.dotnetforce.com/Default.aspx`
`User-Agent`	A string that identifies the client application (typically a browser), as well as the platform on which it's running. The general format is *software/version library/version*, but this can vary. This information can be used for statistical purposes, to trace protocol violations, and for automated recognition of the client. This allows a response to be tailored to avoid particular client limitations, such as the inability to support HTML tables.	IE 6 string: `User-Agent: Mozilla/4.0 (compatible; MSIE 6.0; Windows NT 5.1; .NET CLR 1.0.3705)`

1 **/* indicates that files of all types will be accepted and handled by the client. If the file type requested can't be handled by the client, an HTTP 406 Not Acceptable error will be returned.*

Response headers provide information about the document returned. Table 10-2 shows the response header types.

Table 10-2. *HTTP Response Headers*

Header	Description	Example
`Content-Type`	Used to indicate the media type of the data that is sent to the recipient or, in the case of the `HEAD` method, the media type that would have been sent had the request been a `GET`.	`Content-Type: text/html`
`Expires`	The date after which the information in the document ceases to be valid. Caching clients, including proxies, must not cache this copy of the resource beyond the date given, unless its status has been updated by a later check of the origin server.	`Expires: Fri, 06 Aug 2004 16:00:00 GMT`
`Location`	Defines the exact location of another resource to which the client is to be redirected. If the value is a full URL, the server returns a "redirect" to the client to retrieve the specified object directly. If a reference to another file must be made on the server, a partial URL must be specified.	`Location: http://www.dotnetforce.com/WS/Default.aspx` `Location: /Tutorial/HTTP/index.html`
`Server`	Contains information about the software used by the origin server to handle the request.	`Server: Microsoft-IIS/5.0`

A few headers can be included in either the response or request. For example, `Date` is used to set the date and time at which the message was originated:

```
Date: Tue, 03 Aug 2004 18:12:31 GMT
```

In HTTP 1.0, you could use the `Connection` header in the request to indicate that you wanted to keep the connection alive after the response had been sent. This is now the default behavior in HTTP 1.1, so you can use the `Connection` header to indicate that you *do not* want a persistent connection:

```
Connection: close
```

HTTP Requests

Each client makes a request, and the server responds to that request. Every request and response has three parts: the request or response line, a header section, and the entity-body (the *entity-body* is any content sent with the message, such as an HTML page to display in the browser or form data to send to the server).

The client contacts the server at a designated port number (the default is 80) and requests a document from the server by specifying an HTTP command called a method, followed by the document address and an HTTP version number. The client also sends the optional header information to the server in order to inform the server of its configuration and the document formats that it accepts. The header information is given in a line, along with header name and value. The client sends a blank line to end the header. After this, the client sends additional data. This could be form data sent to the server using the POST method or a file to upload with the PUT method.

Client request lines are divided into three sections. The first line of a message should always contain an HTTP method, followed by a URI, which identifies the file or resource that the client queries, and the HTTP version number:

```
GET /default.aspx HTTP/1.1
```

Let's examine each of these sections now.

HTTP Methods

A *method* is an HTTP command that begins the first line of a client request. The method informs the server of the purpose of the client request. Seven methods are defined for HTTP:

GET: This method is used to request information that is located at a specified URI on the server. It is the method commonly used by browsers to retrieve documents for viewing. The result of a GET request is generated in different ways. It could be a file accessible by the server, the output of a program, the output from a hardware device, and so on. When a client uses the GET method in its request, the server sends a response containing a status line, headers, and the requested data. If the server cannot process the request due to an error or lack of authorization, the server sends a textual explanation in the data portion of the response. The entity-body portion of a GET request is always empty. The file or program that the client requests is identified by its full path name on the server. Any additional information, such as form values, that the client needs to send to the server is appended to the URL as a query string:

```
GET /default.aspx?name=Vinod HTTP/1.1
```

CAUTION Method names are case-sensitive. For example, get won't be recognized as a valid method.

HEAD: This method is functionally similar to the GET method, except that the server does not send anything in the data portion of the reply. The HEAD method requests only the header information on a file or resource. The HTTP server should send the same header information for a HEAD request as it would for a GET request. This method is used when the client needs information about the document but doesn't need to retrieve it.

POST: This method allows data to be sent to the server in a client request. The data is sent to a data-handling program to which the server has access. The POST method can be used for many applications, such as providing input to network services, command-line interface programs, and so on. The data is sent to the server in the entity-body section of the client's request. After the server has processed the POST request and headers, it passes the entity-body to the program specified by the URI.

DELETE: This method requests the named file to be deleted from the server.

PUT: This method requests that the document included as the request body be uploaded to the server and made available with the specified URI.

TRACE: This method is used for debugging the request/response chain; the server should return the entire request message in the response body.

OPTIONS: This method requests information about the HTTP support on the web server. OPTIONS can be used with a URL to retrieve information about a specific document or with the wildcard * to retrieve information about the server's capabilities in general. This information is returned in the response headers. The following response contains the information returned from a request for options for the postinfo.html page on an IIS version 5 server (OPTIONS /postinfo.html HTTP/1.1):

```
HTTP/1.1 200 OK
Server: Microsoft-IIS/5.0
Date: Fri, 09 Aug 2002 18:52:18 GMT
MS-Author-Via: DAV
Content-Length: 0
Accept-Ranges: bytes
DASL: <DAV:sql>
DAV: 1, 2
Public: OPTIONS, TRACE, GET, HEAD, DELETE, PUT, POST, COPY, MOVE,
MKCOL, PROPFIND, PROPPATCH, LOCK, UNLOCK, SEARCH
Allow: OPTIONS, TRACE, GET, HEAD, COPY, PROPFIND, SEARCH, LOCK, UNLOCK
Cache-Control: private
<CRLF><CRLF>
```

The Allow header indicates which HTTP methods are permitted for this particular document. The Public header specifies all of the methods supported by the server. For example, the response in this example shows that DELETE is supported by the server but not permitted for postinfo.html. The response also indicates the server's support for DAV (Distributed Authoring and Versioning) and DASL (DAV Searching and Locating).

■ **NOTE** DAV is a standard that extends HTTP 1.1 by providing a new set of methods to allow you to manage resources on a web server, such as setting and retrieving properties of the resources, and moving and copying files. DASL defines extensions to allow you to search DAV servers. DAV is defined in RFC 2518 (http://www.ietf.org/rfc/rfc2518.txt).

HTTP servers can also implement extension methods that aren't defined by HTTP.

URI

After the request method comes the URI specifying the file you want to retrieve, post data to, and so on. This may be an absolute URI, such as http://www.apress.com/default.aspx, or a path relative to the document root directory of the server, such as /default.aspx (the relative path *must* be prefixed by a forward slash). It is the responsibility of the server to map these URIs to file system paths such as C:\inetpub\wwwroot\default.aspx.

HTTP Version Number

The last component of a request line is the HTTP version number, which is used to specify the version of the HTTP specification used. Usually, this will be either `HTTP/1.1` or `HTTP/1.0` (although there is an older version, `HTTP/0.9`).

HTTP Responses

The server's response to a client request is divided into three parts. The first line is the server response line, which contains the HTTP version number, a number indicating the status of the request, and a short phrase describing the status. Then comes the header information, followed by an empty line and the entity-body (which may be empty, such as when responding to a `HEAD` or an `OPTIONS` request).

The HTTP version indicates the version of HTTP that the server uses to respond. The status code is a three-digit number that indicates the server's result of the client's request. The description following the status code is just a human-readable description of the status code. There are a number of predefined status codes, but the server can define additional codes. Some of the most common predefined status codes are listed in Table 10-3.

Table 10-3. *Common HTTP Status Codes*

Code	Description
200	OK—the request was received and processed.
301	The resource has been moved permanently.
302	The resource has temporarily been moved.
400	Bad request—the request message was not correctly formatted.
401	Unauthorized—the user doesn't have rights to access the requested document.
402	Payment required to access the resource.
408	The request timed out.
500	Internal server error—an error prevented the HTTP server from processing the request.

After the status line, the server sends header information to the client about itself and the requested document. A blank line (that is, two consecutive CRLF sequences) ends the header.

If the client requested data, and the request is successful, the requested data will be sent as the entity-body after the response headers. This data could be a copy of the requested file, or it could be content generated dynamically, such as by an ASP.NET page or a server-side script. If the client's request is not fulfilled, additional data may be provided to explain why the server could not fulfill the request.

In HTTP 1.0, after the server has finished sending the requested data, it disconnects from the client, and the transaction is over unless a `Connection: Keep-Alive` header is sent. However, in HTTP 1.1, the default is that the server should maintain the connection and allow the client to make additional requests, even if the `Connection` header isn't sent. If you don't want this behavior, you need to send a `Connection: close` header to specify that the connection should be closed after the response has been sent.

Using HTTP with .NET

Although you can implement HTTP manually using the standard Sockets or TCP classes, .NET provides a number of classes (mostly in the System.Net namespace) that are designed to facilitate communication with an HTTP server. These implement the generic request/response model, along with some additional properties that provide a greater level of control over the HTTP-specific features, such as access to HTTP in an object model for property-level control over headers, authentication, pre-authentication, encryption, proxy support, pipelining, and connection management. Table 10-4 shows these .NET classes.

Table 10-4. *.NET Support for HTTP*

Class	Namespace	Inherits From	Description
HttpWebRequest	System.Net	WebRequest	Represents an HTTP request
HttpWebResponse	System.Net	WebResponse	Represents an HTTP response
WebClient	System.Net	Component	Provides easy-to-use methods for sending files or data to a URI and receiving data from a URI
Uri	System	MarshalByRefObject	Represents a URI, allowing easy access to the component parts of the URI, such as the host name and absolute path
UriBuilder	System	Object	Utility class for creating and modifying Uri objects
ServicePoint	System.Net	Object	Handles connections to a given URI
Manager	System.Net	Object	Manager class for managing ServicePoint objects

The HttpWebRequest and HttpWebResponse Classes

The .NET Framework provides two basic classes for simplifying HTTP access: HttpWebRequest and HttpWebResponse. These classes handle most of the functionality provided through the HTTP protocol in a straightforward manner. They derive from the abstract WebRequest and WebResponse classes that we looked at in Chapter 3.

To demonstrate how these classes work, Listing 10-1 shows an example of using them to retrieve a web page from the Internet.

Listing 10-1. *A Simple Web Request*

```
using System;
using System.Net;
using System.IO;
using System.Text;
class SimpleWebRequest
{
   public static void Main()
   {
      string query = "http://www.apress.com";
```

```
        HttpWebRequest req = (HttpWebRequest)WebRequest.Create(query);
        HttpWebResponse resp = (HttpWebResponse)req.GetResponse();
        StreamReader sr = new StreamReader(resp.GetResponseStream(),Encoding.ASCII);
        Console.WriteLine(sr.ReadToEnd());
        resp.Close();
        sr.Close();
    }
}
```

In order to create an `HttpWebRequest` object, we need to call the static `WebRequest.Create` method (also inherited by the `HttpWebRequest` class). This method examines the format of the URI passed in and returns a `WebRequest` object representing an HTTP request or a file system request, as appropriate. Since the same method is used to create both HTTP and file system requests, the object returned is of type `WebRequest`, and it must be cast to `HttpWebRequest` or `FileWebRequest`. The `Create` method parses the URL and passes the resolved URL into the request object. The request portion structures the outbound HTTP request and also handles the configuration of the HTTP headers.

Once we have the request object, we can call its `GetResponse` method. This sends the request to the server and returns a `WebResponse` object (again, we need to cast this to `HttpWebResponse`). This object represents an HTTP response message, and it contains the HTTP header information such as `ContentType`, `ContentLength`, `StatusCode`, and `Cookies`, and the first part of the data, which is buffered internally until read from the stream itself. The `HttpWebResponse` object's properties are set with this data.

Next, a stream is returned using the `GetResponseStream` method. The stream points at the actual binary HTTP response from the web server (the entity-body of the response message). A stream provides a lot of flexibility in handling how data is retrieved from the web server. To retrieve the actual data and read the rest of the result document from the web server, the stream must be read. Here, we use a `StreamReader` object to return a string from the data. The encoding type is set to `ASCII` (although a more robust solution would check the `Content-Encoding` header and use the encoding specified there). The encoding is important because, if the data is transferred as a byte stream without the encoding, it results in invalid character translations for any extended characters.

The example in Listing 10-1 uses the `StreamReader` object's `ReadToEnd` method to retrieve the entire data from the web server as a string. However, the data could also be read in parts using the `StreamReader` object's `Read` method. See Chapter 2 for more information about reading data from streams.

Setting and Reading the HTTP Headers

Both the `HttpWebRequest` and `HttpWebResponse` classes have a `Headers` property that returns a `WebHeaderCollection` object containing information about the headers for the HTTP message. You can add headers to an HTTP request by calling either the `Add` method or the `Set` method of this object:

```
HttpWebRequest req = (HttpWebRequest)WebRequest.Create("http://localhost:81");
req.Headers.Add("Accept-Language: en-us");
// This is exactly equivalent
// req.Headers.Set("Accept-Language", "en-us");
```

As this example shows, the `Add` method takes a single string parameter representing the entire header field. The `Set` method takes two string values: the name of the header and the value you want it to have. Both of these methods can be used equally for standard and custom HTTP headers. However, the `HttpWebRequest` class also has a number of public properties that allow you to set a request header without accessing the `Headers` property, as listed in Table 10-5.

Table 10-5. *HttpWebRequest Public Properties*

Property	Data Type	HTTP Header
Accept	string	Accept
Connection	string	Connection
ContentLength	long	Content-Length
ContentType	string	Content-Type
Expect	string	Expect
IfModifiedSince	DateTime	If-Modified-Since
Referer	string	Referer
TransferEncoding	string	Transfer-Encoding
UserAgent	string	User-Agent

For example, to set the `User-Agent` header to `"User-Agent: SimpleHttpClient"`, use the following:

```
req.UserAgent = "SimpleHttpClient";
```

Note that where a property exists to set a header, this *must* be used. For example, if you attempt to set the `User-Agent` header using the following, a runtime exception will be thrown:

```
req.Headers.Add("User-Agent: SimpleHttpClient");
```

The `HttpWebResponse` object also contains a number of public properties (all read-only), which allow you to access the value of selected HTTP headers, as listed in Table 10-6.

Table 10-6. *HttpWebResponse Public Properties*

Property	Type	HTTP Header
ContentEncoding	string	Content-Encoding
ContentLength	long	Content-Length
ContentType	string	Content-Type
LastModified	DateTime	Last-Modified
Server	string	Server

Each individual header field can also be accessed as a name/value pair within the `WebHeaderCollection`. The names of the headers are the keys to the collection, and the header values are the associated values. You can access the value of a header using the indexer of the collection with the name of the header. The following code writes all the headers in the response to the console window:

```
foreach (string header in resp.Headers)
   Console.WriteLine("{0}: {1}", header, resp.Headers[header]);
```

Creating a Currency Converter Application

You have seen how to get the contents from the Web using the `HttpWebRequest` and `HttpWebResponse` objects, so now let's look at a sample application. Listing 10-2 shows an application that uses these objects to convert one currency to another, using live currency rates from the `http://finance.yahoo.com` website.

Listing 10-2. *A Currency Converter*

```
using System;
using System.IO;
using System.Net;
using System.Text;
class CurrencyConverter
{
   static void Main()
   {
      HttpWebRequest req;
      HttpWebResponse resp;
      StreamReader sr;
      char[] separator = { ',' };
      string result;
      string fullPath;
      string currencyFrom = "USD";   // US Dollar
      string currencyTo = "INR";     // Indian Rupee
      double amount = 100d;
      Console.WriteLine("Currency Converter");
      Console.WriteLine("Currency From : {0}", currencyFrom);
      Console.WriteLine("Currency To : {0}", currencyTo);
      Console.WriteLine("Amount : {0}", amount);
      // Build the URL that returns the quote
      fullPath = "http://finance.yahoo.com/d/quotes.csv?s=" + currencyFrom +
                 currencyTo + "=X&f=sl1d1t1c1ohgv&e=.csv";
      try
      {
         req = (HttpWebRequest)WebRequest.Create(fullPath);
         resp = (HttpWebResponse)req.GetResponse();
         sr = new StreamReader(resp.GetResponseStream(), Encoding.ASCII);
         result = sr.ReadLine();
         resp.Close();
         sr.Close();
         string[] temp = result.Split(separator);
         if(temp.Length > 1)
         {
            // Only show the relevant portions
```

```
                double rate = Convert.ToDouble(temp[1]);
                double convert = amount * rate;
                Console.WriteLine("{0} {1}(s) = {2} {3}(s)", amount,
                                  currencyFrom, convert, currencyTo);
             }
             else
             {
                Console.WriteLine("Error in getting currency rates " +
                                  "from website.");
             }
          }
          catch(Exception e)
          {
             Console.WriteLine("Exception occurred: "+e.Message);
          }
       }
    }
```

We retrieve the live currency rates by building a URL pointing to the `finance.yahoo.com` website, including a query string that specifies the currencies we want to convert to and from as three-character strings (in this example, USD for US dollars and INR for Indian rupees), together with some more cryptic information required by Yahoo's server. We use the `HttpWebRequest` object to send this request to the server, and we use the `HttpWebResponse` object to access the returned document. This is a comma-separated values (CSV) file, the second value of which is the current exchange rate. This is the only value we're interested in, so we convert it to a `double` and store it in the `rate` variable. We then use this variable to calculate the value of the converted currency. Figure 10-1 shows the application in action.

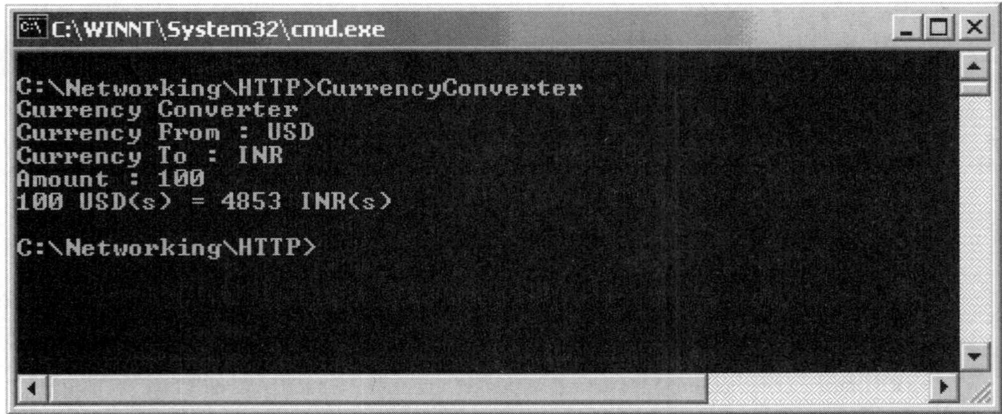

Figure 10-1. *Using the currency converter application*

Note that the currency converter example might not work correctly in some countries, where the period (.) is used as a thousands separator rather than a decimal point. A workaround would be to replace the decimal point with a comma before calling Convert.ToDouble on the value read from the CSV file:

```
double rate = Convert.ToDouble(temp[1].Replace(".", ","));
```

A more robust solution would be to check the CurrencyDecimalSeparator property of the NumberFormatInfo object for the current culture.

Posting Data

This currency converter application retrieves data using an HTTP GET request. If you want to post data to the server, use the HTTP POST method. POST data refers to the process of taking data and sending it to the web server as a part of the request payload. A POST operation not only sends data to the server, but also retrieves a response from the server indicating success or failure, and possibly other content such as a web page. Listing 10-3 demonstrates how to post data.

Listing 10-3. *Posting Data to a Server*

```
using System;
using System.IO;
using System.Net;
using System.Text;
using System.Web;
class PostData
{
   static void Main()
   {
      string SiteURL="http://www.dotnetforce.com/postsample.asp";
      StreamWriter sw = null;
      // Preparing the data to post
      string postData = "Posted=" + HttpUtility.UrlEncode("True") +
                        "&X=" + HttpUtility.UrlEncode("Value");
      HttpWebRequest req = (HttpWebRequest)WebRequest.Create(SiteURL);
      req.Method = "POST";
      req.ContentLength = postData.Length;
      req.ContentType = "application/x-www-form-urlencoded";
      sw = new StreamWriter(req.GetRequestStream());
      // Encoding the data
      byte[] sendBuffer = Encoding.ASCII.GetBytes(postData);
      // Posting the data
      sw.Write(postData);
      sw.Close();
      HttpWebResponse resp = (HttpWebResponse)req.GetResponse();
      StreamReader srData = new StreamReader(resp.GetResponseStream(),
                                             Encoding.ASCII);
```

```
        // Reading the output stream
        string outHtml = srData.ReadToEnd();
        Console.WriteLine(outHtml);
        // Close and clean up the StreamReader
        resp.Close();
        srData.Close();
    }
}
```

Posted data needs to be encoded properly before it's sent to the server. Data posted to a web page can have one of two different MIME types: `application/x-www-form-urlencoded` (as in this example) or `multipart/form-data`. In the former case, the data is encoded in the same way as for a query string: the data must be encoded in the buffer into key/value pairs, and you need to use URL encoding for the values. The static `UrlEncode` method of the `System.Web.HttpUtility` class can be used for encoding the data. The `multipart/form-data` type allows you to upload files from the client via an HTML form. As the name suggests, the data is divided into sections, which can contain binary or character data, or standard URL-encoded form data.

■ NOTE URL encoding should be used only when you post data to a web page. It's not needed for any other content—you can post the data directly.

The posted data must be encoded and saved to a byte array using the static `Encoding.ASCII` object with the `GetBytes` method, which returns a byte array. After setting the `ContentLength` property, which helps the remote server to handle the size of the data stream, the posted data is written to the server using a `StreamWriter` object. This object writes to the output stream returned from the `GetRequestStream` method of your `HttpWebRequest` object. Once you've sent the data, you use a `StreamReader` object to read the response returned from the server.

Up to now, we have just been looking at the basic use of `HttpWebRequest` and `HttpWebResponse` objects. However, to build a typical application that uses HTTP, you need to use some more advanced features, such as HTTP chunking, keep-alive connections, and connection management. In the next sections, we will look at these and other advanced features of HTTP.

HTTP Chunking

One of the features added to HTTP 1.1 is *chunking*. Chunking refers to the process of sending a message body in multiple fragments, rather than all at once. Each fragment must be prefixed by its size if the connection is persistent, and the header does not include a `Content-Length` field. Otherwise, there would be no way for the recipient to know when the message body has been completely sent and the connection is free for the next transaction.

Chunked transfer coding may be used by both requests and responses, although it is more commonly seen in the latter. It is used mainly when an application needs to send or receive data whose exact size is not known at the time when the download or upload begins.

This is most commonly the case when the data in question is created dynamically based on other application or server logic.

To send chunked data, the `SendChunked` property of the `HttpWebRequest` should be set to `true`, as shown in Listing 10-4.

Listing 10-4. *Sending Chunked Data*

```
using System;
using System.IO;
using System.Net;
using System.Text;
class ChunkingExample
{
  static void Main()
  {
    string query = "http://localhost/postsample.aspx";
    StreamWriter sw = null;
    string postData = "Posted=true&X=Value";
    HttpWebRequest req = (HttpWebRequest)HttpWebRequest.Create(query);
    // Setting the request method
    req.Method = "POST";
    // Setting the Content-Type header
    req.ContentType = "application/x-www-form-urlencoded";
    // Setting the Content-Length header
    req.ContentLength = postData.Length;
    // Setting the SendChunked property
    req.SendChunked = true;
    // Posting the data
    sw = new StreamWriter(req.GetRequestStream());
    sw.Write(postData);
    sw.Close();
    HttpWebResponse resp = (HttpWebResponse)req.GetResponse();
    StreamReader sr = new StreamReader(resp.GetResponseStream());
    // Reading the output stream
    string outHtml = sr.ReadToEnd();
    Console.WriteLine(outHtml);
    resp.Close();
    sr.Close();
  }
}
```

HTTP Pipelining

One of the most important features of HTTP 1.1 is *pipelining*. This feature allows the .NET classes to send simultaneous multiple HTTP requests to a back-end server over a persistent connection without waiting for a response from the server before the next request is sent. Figure 10-2 illustrates the use of pipelining in comparison to the traditional request/response behavior of HTTP.

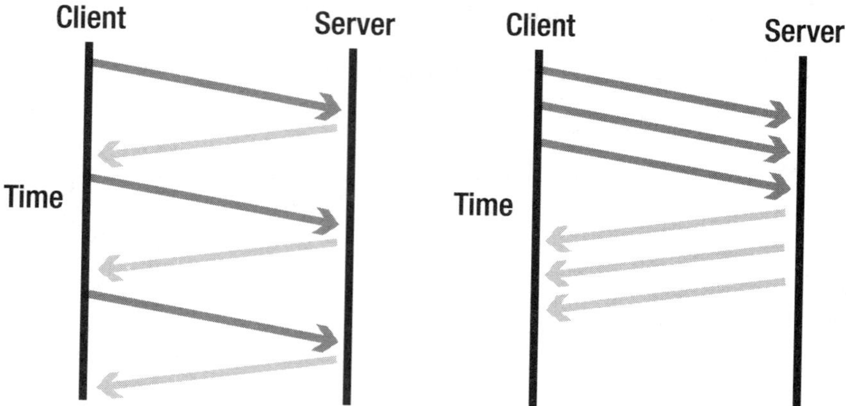

Figure 10-2. *HTTP pipelining (left) versus traditional request/response behavior (right)*

By enabling pipelining, an application requesting multiple resources from a server doesn't get blocked waiting for one particular resource, which may take longer to send than the others. This can therefore increase the performance of the application.

Pipelining is enabled by default in .NET, but it can be disabled by setting the `Pipelined` property of the `HttpWebRequest` to `false`. You might do this if it's important that you get the response to each request before sending the next request.

HTTP Keep-Alive Connections

Persistent connections (or *keep-alive* connections) were introduced in HTTP 1.0. They allow a client using HTTP to conserve network resources and behave in a more efficient manner by keeping an existing TCP connection to the server alive and reusing that connection, rather than closing it and creating a new one for each request.

As explained earlier in the chapter, the `Connection` header controls connection persistence. By default, all HTTP 1.1 connections are considered persistent, unless a request or response includes a `Connection: close` header. When a server or client receives a message with this header, it closes the connection as soon as the transaction is complete.

By default, the `KeepAlive` property of an `HttpWebRequest` object is set to `true`, causing a persistent connection to be created with the server, provided that the server supports this behavior. If you are accessing a back-end server from a middle-tier ASP.NET application, you should be aware that the connection to the back-end server stays open until the server times out the connection.

If `KeepAlive` is set to `true`, the connection won't be closed until the timeout duration elapses with no new request made or the server explicitly terminates the connection. In most cases, both the client and the server are permitted to close the connection by sending a `Connection: close` header in the request/response.

HTTP Connection Management

Connection management is an important feature for achieving maximum scalability and performance in a networked application. This is achieved by limiting the number of outbound sockets established and making use of advanced HTTP features such as persistent connections to optimize client/server interaction. .NET manages connections through the `ServicePoint` and `ServicePointManager` classes.

The `ServicePoint` class in the `System.Net` namespace manages connections to an Internet resource on the basis of the host information that is passed in the resource's URI. The initial connection to the resource determines the information that must be maintained by the `ServicePoint`, which, in turn, is shared by all the subsequent requests to that resource.

A `ServicePoint` object represents a connection to a URI with a particular protocol identifier (such as `http://`) and host name (such as `www.dotnetforce.com`). If two or more requests are made to access resources with the same protocol and host details, the same connection will be used for both requests. For example, if you make a request for `http://www.dotnetforce.com/default.aspx`, and then make a second request for `http://www.dotnetforce.com/SiteContent.aspx?Type=1`, the same connection will be used both times, because they share the same host details and protocol identifier.

You instantiate a `ServicePoint` using the `FindServicePoint` static method of the `ServicePointManager` class. This takes as a parameter a `Uri` object representing the Internet resource this service point will be used to connect to, or a `Uri` object or a URL in string format, together with an `IWebProxy` object. Here is an example:

```
// Get a Uri object to point to http://www.dotnetforce.com
Uri siteURL = new Uri("http://www.dotnetforce.com");
// Call FindServicePoint() to get a ServicePoint object for this URI
ServicePoint spSite = ServicePointManager.FindServicePoint(siteURL);
```

We'll look at proxy settings in the "Proxy Support" section later in this chapter.

Connection Timeout

When an instance of a `ServicePoint` is created, it maintains the connection to an Internet resource specified until the connection times out. You can change this timeout value for an individual `ServicePoint` object by setting the `MaxIdleTime` property. The default value of `MaxIdleTime` is set by the `ServicePointManager.MaxServicePointIdleTime` property. You can also find out how long has elapsed since the last connection was made to the service point through the `IdleSince` property:

```
// Get the date and time of the connection since it was last connected
DateTime idleTime = spSite.IdleSince;
// Setting the MaxIdleTime in Milliseconds
spSite.MaxIdleTime = 5000;
```

The default `MaxIdleTime` value is 900,000 milliseconds (15 minutes).

You can also set the MaxIdleTime property to Timeout.Infinite (in the System.Threading namespace) to indicate that the ServicePoint should never time out (although the connection can be terminated by the server, of course):

```
spSite.MaxIdleTime = Timeout.Infinite;
```

Connection Limit

The default maximum number of connections permitted from an application using the HttpWebRequest class to a given server is two. This number can be increased or decreased, depending on the actual conditions under which the application is running. The following code sets the client's maximum number of connections to four:

```
Uri SiteURL = new Uri("http://www.dotnetforce.com");
ServicePoint spSite = ServicePointManager.FindServicePoint(SiteURL);
spSite.ConnectionLimit = 4;
```

The maximum number of connections you should set depends on the criteria on which the application runs. It's better to get a baseline measurement of the application's throughput with the default setting, and then change the default and check how the performance is affected.

■ CAUTION It is recommended in the HTTP 1.1 specification that a client application should have no more than two simultaneous open connections to a server.

Generally, the number of concurrent connections shouldn't be too high, as there is a fine balance between the benefits of the application having multiple connections and the overhead of creating a new connection. At some point, an application that creates a lot of connections will actually perform slower than an application wisely using a fewer connections.

The WebClient Class

In most web applications, uploading and downloading data is a day-to-day task. Before .NET, you had to either buy a third-party component or use the WinSock API to do this, which was a tedious job. Now you can use a component in the .NET Framework class library for this task: the WebClient class, which can be instantiated directly.

```
WebClient client = new WebClient();
```

WebClient relies on the WebRequest class to provide access to Internet resources, so the WebClient class can use any registered pluggable protocol. In general, this class is a great way for accomplishing HTTP, HTTPS, and file protocol communications.

Residing in the System.Net namespace, the WebClient class exposes three methods for downloading data from a remote resource, and four methods for uploading raw data or files to a remote resource. In this section, you will see how to upload and download data using these methods.

The DownloadData Method

The `DownloadData` method takes a string value representing a URL address as an argument and returns a byte array of data from the specified address:

```
using System;
using System.Net;
using System.Text;
class WebTest
{
   static void Main()
   {
      WebClient client = new WebClient();
      byte[] urlData = client.DownloadData("http://www.dotnetforce.com");
      string data = Encoding.ASCII.GetString(urlData);
      Console.WriteLine(data);
   }
}
```

The DownloadFile Method

The `DownloadFile` method takes a URL address and a file name as parameters. The file will be downloaded to a local drive. The following code downloads an image file from a remote location to the local hard disk:

```
using System;
using System.Net;
using System.IO;
class DownloadFile
{
   static void Main(string[] args)
   {
      string siteURL = "http://www.dotnetforce.com/images/logo11.gif";
      string fileName = "C:\\ASP.gif";
      // Create a new WebClient instance.
      WebClient client = new WebClient();
      // Concatenate the domain with the web resource file name.
      Console.WriteLine("Downloading File \"{0}\" from \"{1}\" .......\n\n",
                        fileName, siteURL);
      // Download the Web resource and save it into the
      // current file system folder.
      client.DownloadFile(siteURL,fileName);
      Console.WriteLine("Successfully Downloaded File \"{0}\" from \"{1}\"",
                        fileName, siteURL);
      Console.WriteLine("\nDownloaded file saved in the following " +
                        "file system folder:\n\t" + fileName);
   }
}
```

Figure 10-3 shows the results of running this code.

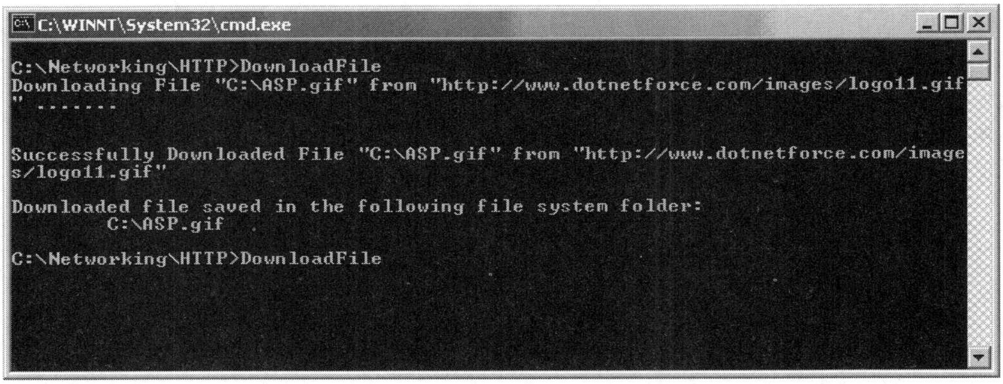

```
C:\WINNT\System32\cmd.exe
C:\Networking\HTTP>DownloadFile
Downloading File "C:\ASP.gif" from "http://www.dotnetforce.com/images/logo11.gif
" .......

Successfully Downloaded File "C:\ASP.gif" from "http://www.dotnetforce.com/image
s/logo11.gif"

Downloaded file saved in the following file system folder:
        C:\ASP.gif

C:\Networking\HTTP>DownloadFile
```

Figure 10-3. *Downloading a file*

The OpenRead Method

The OpenRead method is similar to the DownloadData method; the only difference is that it returns a Stream object that enables you to read the data from the target URL. Using this method, the data can be retrieved in parts with the help of the Stream object's Read and ReadBlock methods. This allows you to inform the user of the status of the download.

The following example uses the OpenRead method to read the data from the remote location.

```
using System;
using System.IO;
using System.Net;
class OpenRead
{
   static void Main(string[] args)
   {
      string siteURL = "http://www.rediff.com";
      // Create a new WebClient instance.
      WebClient client = new WebClient();
      // Concatenate the domain with the web resource file name.
      Console.WriteLine("Start Downloading Data From \"{0}\" .......\n\n",
                        siteURL);
      // Download the web resource from the RemoteURL.
      Stream stmData = client.OpenRead(siteURL);
      StreamReader srData = new StreamReader(stmData);
      // Create file
      FileInfo fiData = new FileInfo("C:\\Default.htm");
      StreamWriter st = fiData.CreateText();
      Console.WriteLine("Writing to the file...");
      // Write to file
      st.WriteLine(srData.ReadToEnd());
```

```
        st.Close();
        stmData.Close();
    }
}
```

The OpenWrite Method

The `OpenWrite` method is used to send data to the specified URL. This can be done using the `POST` method or through another supported method (such as a DAV method). `OpenWrite` takes a string address parameter and the name of the HTTP method to use, and it returns a stream that you can write to in order to place data into the specified URL.

The following example uploads a file from the hard disk to the remote location (assuming that you have the necessary permissions on the server).

```
using System;
using System.IO;
using System.Net;
using System.Text;
class OpenWrite
{
    static void Main(string[] args)
    {
        string siteURL = "http://localhost/postsample.aspx";
        // Create a new WebClient instance.
        string uploadData = "Posted=True&X=Value";
        // Apply ASCII encoding to obtain an array of bytes.
        byte[] uploadArray = Encoding.ASCII.GetBytes(uploadData);
        // Create a new WebClient instance.
        WebClient client = new WebClient();
        Console.WriteLine("Uploading data to {0}...", siteURL);
        Stream stmUpload = client.OpenWrite(siteURL, "POST");
        stmUpload.Write(uploadArray, 0, uploadArray.Length);
        // Close the stream and release resources.
        stmUpload.Close();
        Console.WriteLine("Successfully posted the data.");
    }
}
```

First, we create a `WebClient` object that points to the Internet resource (such as an ASP.NET page) where we want to post the data. Next, we convert the string data we want to post into a byte array and write this to the stream returned from our call to the `WebClient`'s `OpenWrite` method. Since we specified `"POST"` as the second parameter of `OpenWrite`, this has the effect of posting the data to the specified page.

The UploadData Method

The `UploadData` method sends data in the form of a byte array to the server without encoding it. This method takes the URL and optionally the upload method (`"POST"`, `"GET"`, and so on) as parameters.

The following example uploads a string using the POST method with UploadData.

```
using System;
using System.Net;
using System.IO;
using System.Text;
class UploadData
{
   static void Main(string[] args)
   {
      string siteURL;
      siteURL = "http://localhost/postsample.aspx";
      WebClient client = new WebClient();
      client.Credentials = System.Net.CredentialCache.DefaultCredentials ;
      string uploadString = "Hello Force..";
      // Adding the HTTP Content-Type Header
      client.Headers.Add("Content-Type",
                         "application/x-www-form-urlencoded");
      // Apply ASCII encoding to obtain the string as a byte array.
      byte[] sendData = Encoding.ASCII.GetBytes(uploadString);
      Console.WriteLine("Uploading to {0} ...", siteURL);
      // Upload the string using the POST method.
      byte[] recData = client.UploadData(siteURL, "POST", sendData);
      // Display the response.
      Console.WriteLine("\nResponse received was {0}",
                        Encoding.ASCII.GetString(recData));
   }
}
```

The UploadFile Method

The UploadFile method is similar to the UploadData method. This method uploads a file (for example, from the local hard drive). The UploadFile method accepts a URL, file name, and optionally the HTTP method to use as parameters. This method uploads the specified file to the specified location and optionally returns the response of the target URL as a byte array.

The following example uploads a file from the local disk to the remote location using the UploadFile method.

```
using System;
using System.Net;
using System.IO;
using System.Text;
class UploadFile
{
   static void Main(string[] args)
   {
```

```
        string siteURL="http://localhost/images/http.txt";
        string remoteResponse;
        // Create a new WebClient instance.
        WebClient client = new WebClient();
        NetworkCredential cred = new NetworkCredential("username",
                                                   "password", "domain");
        string fileName = "C:\\http.txt";
        Console.WriteLine("Uploading {0} to {1} ...", fileName, siteURL);
        // File uploaded using PUT method
        byte[] responseArray = client.UploadFile(siteURL, "PUT", fileName);
        // Response from the target URL
        remoteResponse = Encoding.ASCII.GetString(responseArray);
        Console.WriteLine(remoteResponse);
    }
}
```

Notice that we specify the account details using a NetworkCredential object, as the server may not allow anonymous uploads. We use the PUT HTTP method, which is specifically intended for uploading files to an HTTP server. The remote server response is sent in a byte array, which has to be transformed into a string. We use the static ASCII property of the Encoding class in the System.Text namespace for this task. This returns an ASCIIEncoding object, which has a GetString method that accepts the byte array as a parameter. The byte array is translated to a string, which is written to the console:

Also notice that the uploaded file will be sent as multipart/form-data and will contain metadata as well as the actual file data, so it will need to be trimmed on the server side. For example, suppose our original file contains the text:

```
Imagine some text about the HTTP protocol here...
```

This will be sent to the server in the following format:

```
-----------------------8c410e41d7c7730
Content-Disposition: form-data; name="file"; filename="HTTP.txt"
Content-Type: application/octet-stream
Imagine some text about the HTTP protocol here...
-----------------------8c410e41d7c7730
```

The first and last lines (the boundaries for the content) can be discovered from the boundary token in the Content-Type header of the request.

The UploadValues Method

The UploadValues method enables you to upload a name/value pair collection to an Internet resource. This method is useful when you need to emulate a POST request from an HTML form and retrieve the response. With this method, values are passed to the remote target using the NameValueCollection of the System.Collections.Specialized namespace. Optionally, you can also specify the method for sending the value. The method can be POST, GET, or any other supported method.

The following example gets the search result information from the web page SiteContent.aspx. The values Type and Keyword are passed to this page using the UploadValues method.

```
using System.Net;
using System.IO;
using System.Text;
using System.Collections.Specialized;
class UploadValues
{
   static void Main(string[] args)
   {
      string siteURL = "http://localhost/Force/SiteContent.aspx";
      string remoteResponse;
      // Create a new WebClient instance.
      WebClient client = new WebClient();
      NameValueCollection appendURL = new NameValueCollection();
      // Add the NameValueCollection
      appendURL.Add("Type", "14");
      appendURL.Add("Keyword", "WebService");
      Console.WriteLine("Uploading the Value pair");
      // Upload the NameValueCollection using POST method
      byte[] responseArray = client.UploadValues(siteURL, "POST",
                                                 appendURL);
      remoteResponse = Encoding.ASCII.GetString(responseArray);
      Console.WriteLine(remoteResponse);
   }
}
```

Authentication

HTTP provides for some simple security measures, such as credential-based access control. The .NET classes support a variety of client authentication mechanisms, including digest, basic, Kerberos, NTLM, and custom. To obtain this functionality, you can use the Credential-Cache class or the NetworkCredential class (both in the System.Net namespace). Both of these classes implement the ICredentials interface, so it's often possible to use either class.

A NetworkCredential object stores a single set of credentials for logging on to a network or an Internet resource. This object contains information about the user name and password for the user account it represents, and (for Windows-based authentication systems) the domain to which the user account belongs. The CredentialCache class can store multiple sets of authentication credentials. You can set or retrieve the default set of credentials for the application by calling the DefaultCredentials static property of the CredentialCache class.

Authentication is achieved by setting the Credentials object of the HttpWebRequest or WebClient class before making a request. In the case of digest and basic authentication, a user name and password are specified. For NTLM or Kerberos authentication, Windows security is used, and the Credential object can be set to a user name, password, and domain combination, or the system defaults can be requested. The best way to understand this is by looking at the code you would use to authenticate to an Internet resource that requires a login. We'll look at a few authentication examples here. However, we'll cover authentication and authorization in detail in Chapter 13, so we'll keep this discussion simple.

Basic Authentication

To make a request to an Internet site using basic authentication, you should specify the user name and password for accessing it. You do this by creating a new `NetworkCredential` object, passing in the user name and password as strings, and setting the `Credentials` property of the `HttpWebRequest` or of the `WebClient` object to point to this. Here is an example of using the `HttpWebRequest` class to make the request:

```
string query = "http://www.rediff.com/";
WebRequest request = (HttpWebRequest)WebRequest.Create(query);
request.Credentials = new NetworkCredential("Username", "Password");
HttpWebResponse response = (HttpWebResponse)request.GetResponse();
StreamReader reader = new StreamReader(response.GetResponseStream(),
                                       Encoding.ASCII);
Console.WriteLine(reader.ReadToEnd());
response.Close();
reader.Close();
```

Similarly, for a `WebClient` object, you would specify this:

```
WebClient client = new WebClient();
client.Credentials  = new NetworkCredential("Username", "Password");
```

NTLM Authentication

The following code makes a request to a secured internal site using NTLM authentication. In this case, we're using the application's default credentials, so we set the `HttpWebRequest` object's `Credentials` property to `CredentialCache.DefaultCredentials`.

```
using System;
using System.Net;
using System.IO;
using System.Text;
class Credential
{
   static void Main(string[] args)
   {
      string query= "http://www.rediff.com/";
      WebRequest request = (HttpWebRequest)WebRequest.Create(query);
      request.Credentials = CredentialCache.DefaultCredentials;
      HttpWebResponse response = (HttpWebResponse)request.GetResponse();
      StreamReader reader = new StreamReader(response.GetResponseStream(),
                                             Encoding.ASCII);
      Console.WriteLine(reader.ReadToEnd());
      response.Close();
      reader.Close();
   }
}
```

Similarly, for the WebClient class, we should specify the following:

```
WebClient objWeb = new WebClient();
objWeb.Credentials = CredentialCache.DefaultCredentials;
```

If we wanted to use a different Windows user account to log on, we could create a new NetworkCredential object, specifying the account's domain as well as the user name and password:

```
request.Credentials = new NetworkCredential("Username", "Password", "Domain");
```

You can add credentials to a CredentialCache by calling its Add method. This allows you to associate a particular set of credentials with a specific URI. The Add method takes three parameters: a Uri object representing the URI prefix for which this set of credentials is to be used, a string specifying the type of authentication, and a NetworkCredential object representing the user account to be used for this URI. Here is an example:

```
CredentialCache myCreds = new CredentialCache();
NetworkCredential localCred = new NetworkCredential("Username", "Password",
                                                     "Domain");
Uri localUri = new Uri("http://localhost");
myCreds.Add(localUri, "NTLM", localCred);
HttpWebRequest req = (HttpWebRequest)WebRequest.Create(
                                          "http://localhost/postinfo.html");
req.Credentials = myCreds;
```

When you set the HttpWebRequest's Credentials property to point to your new CredentialCache object, the objects in the cache are checked to find the set of credentials that is associated with the URI you want to access. The first set of credentials that matches both the URI and the authentication type required by the resource will be used to log on to the resource.

Proxy Support

HTTP proxy support in the .NET classes can be controlled on a per-request basis, or it can be set once globally for the lifetime of the application.

To set the default proxy for all web requests, use the GlobalProxySelection class:

```
GlobalProxySelection.Select = new WebProxy("proxyserver", 80);
```

The GlobalProxySelection object stores the default proxy settings that will be used to access remote resources beyond the local network. The default proxy settings are taken from the application's configuration file. However, these settings can be overridden for individual requests. You can also disable proxy support by setting the Proxy property of the HttpWebRequest object to the return value of the GlobalProxySelection object's static GetEmptyWebProxy method.

Alternatively, to set the proxy server for a specific web request, you can create a WebProxy object using the URI of the proxy server and the port on which it is running. Other overloads take the URI of the proxy, a Boolean value indicating whether the proxy is to be bypassed for local addresses, a string array of other URIs for which the proxy shouldn't be used, and an ICredentials object that is used to authenticate against the proxy server. Here is an example:

```
using System;
using System.Net;
using System.IO;
using System.Text;
class Proxy
{
   static void Main(string[] args)
   {
      WebProxy myProxy = new WebProxy("proxyserver", 80);
      myProxy.BypassProxyOnLocal = true;
      string query= "http://www.dotnetforce.com/";
      HttpWebRequest request = (HttpWebRequest)HttpWebRequest.Create(query);
      request.Proxy = myProxy;
   }
}
```

Reading and Writing Cookies

HTTP is stateless, so in principle, HTTP servers respond to each client's request without relating that request to previous or subsequent requests. To maintain state between the client and the server, you need to track the user's session programmatically, recording information about which resources the user accessed and keeping track of any information entered by the user.

Session tracking allows you to maintain a relationship between two successive requests made to a server on the Internet. There are many ways to maintain state over a session, such as `<hidden>` HTML form fields and URL query strings. However, *cookies* are perhaps the most widely used means of maintaining the state of an application.

Cookies work by storing tokens on the client. This means that the client is responsible for managing the cookies created. Normally, the browser manages all of this (although a few browsers don't support cookies, and users can disable cookie support), but when the application front-end isn't a browser, you need to perform tracking manually and manage the session state yourself.

Whenever the server assigns a cookie for one request, the client must retain it and send it back to the server on its next request. The `HttpWebRequest` and `HttpWebResponse` objects provide the container to hold cookies, both for sending and receiving, but they don't automatically persist them, so it becomes your responsibility to store the cookies and send them back to the server on its next request.

To manage the cookies, use the `CookieCollection` class in the `System.Net` namespace, which provides a mechanism for handling multiple cookies.

Writing Cookies on the Client

To demonstrate the use of cookies in .NET, we will build a sample application that will create a cookie, and then we will build an ASP.NET test page to check that the cookie has been created. For this, we need to create an IIS virtual directory named `CookieSample`.

The code in Listing 10-5 (WriteCookie.cs) sets a cookie called MyName with the value "Vinod" using the Cookie object, and sends it to the server as part of an HTTP request.

Listing 10-5. *Writing Cookies*

```
using System;
using System.Net;
using System.IO;
using System.Text;
class WriteCookie
{
   static void Main(string[] args)
   {
      CookieCollection cookies = new CookieCollection();
      // Creating the cookie
      Cookie cookie = new Cookie("MyName", "Vinod", "/", "localhost");
      string query = "http://localhost/CookieSample/CookiesText.aspx";
      HttpWebRequest request = (HttpWebRequest)WebRequest.Create(query);
      request.CookieContainer = new CookieContainer();
      request.CookieContainer.Add(cookie);
      HttpWebResponse response = (HttpWebResponse)request.GetResponse();
      StreamReader reader = new StreamReader(response.GetResponseStream(),
                                             Encoding.ASCII);
      Console.WriteLine(reader.ReadToEnd());
      reader.Close();
      response.Close();
   }
}
```

Notice that the Cookie object is only an in-memory representation of the cookie; it doesn't save any data to disk on the client. When we create the cookie, we also set the path (the URIs on the server to which the cookie will be sent) and domain name for which the cookie is valid.

Once we have a Cookie object, we can also set its Expires property to specify when the cookie will expire (and no longer be sent to the server). After setting these properties, the cookie is added into the request's CookieContainer. The CookieContainer is a collection of cookie collections that enables you to store cookies for multiple sites. Each cookie added to the CookieContainer is added to an internal cookie collection associated with a particular URI.

To test this code, we'll create a very simple ASP.NET page named CookiesTest.aspx. This page should be saved in the root of the CookieSample virtual directory, and it just gets the value of the cookie that we added in WriteCookie.cs. This is written to the response stream:

```
<%@ Page language="C#" %>
<%
HttpCookie cookie = Request.Cookies["MyName"];
if (cookie != null)
   Response.Write("Value for cookie MyName: " + cookie.Value);
else
   Response.Write("Cookie not set");
%>
```

Now compile and execute the WriteCookie.cs code. The program makes a request to CookiesTest.aspx, and the response is displayed in the console. Figure 10-4 shows the output of the content of this page when we execute the program. As you can see, the value of the cookie MyName has been retrieved by the ASP.NET page.

Figure 10-4. *Running the WriteCookie application*

Reading Cookies on the Client

Reading the cookie is as simple as writing the cookie using the .NET Framework's System.Net namespace. To test this, we'll again use a very simple ASP.NET page, WriteCookie.aspx. This file is again placed in the root of the CookieSample virtual directory, and it simply creates a new cookie and sends that cookie to the client.

```
<%@ Page language="C#" %>
<%
string username = "Vinod";
HttpCookie cookie = new HttpCookie("MyName", username);
Response.Cookies.Add(cookie);
Response.Write("Hello, " + username);
%>
```

If we request this page from the client, we can access the username cookie through the Cookies property of the HttpWebResponse class:

```
string query = "http://localhost/CookieSample/WriteCookie.aspx";
HttpWebRequest req = (HttpWebRequest)WebRequest.Create(query);
HttpWebResponse resp = (HttpWebResponse)req.GetResponse();
Console.WriteLine("Value of Cookie MyName :" +
                  resp.Cookies["MyName"].Value);
```

The cookie value can be retrieved once the request headers have been received after the call to GetResponse.

Note that the Cookies collection of the HttpWebResponse object will be populated only if the CookieContainer of the corresponding HttpWebRequest was set. Otherwise, you need to read the cookie from the Headers collection. Cookies are sent in the Set-Cookie header in a format similar to the following:

```
Set-Cookie: FirstName=Vinod; path=/,LastName=Kumar; path=/
```

You can find the value of a cookie by finding the name of the cookie in the header, calculating the positions of the next equal sign and the next semicolon, and retrieving the substring between these two characters:

```
string cookie = response.Headers["Set-Cookie"];
if (cookie != null)
{
   int start = cookie.IndexOf("FirstName");
   int equals = cookie.IndexOf('=', start);
   int end = cookie.IndexOf(';', equals);
   if (equals != -1 && end != -1)
   {
      string value = cookie.Substring(equals + 1, end - equals - 1);
   }
}
```

Maintaining State with Cookies

The easiest way to maintain state on the client is to store cookies sent from the server in a `CookieCollection`. Let's see how this works by making two consecutive requests. Listing 10-6 shows the example.

Listing 10-6. *Persisting Cookies*

```
using System;
using System.Net;
using System.IO;
using System.Text;
class CookiePersist
{
   static void Main()
   {
      // Make the first request (to WriteCookie.aspx)
      string query = "http://localhost/CookieSample/WriteCookie.aspx";
      HttpWebRequest request = (HttpWebRequest)WebRequest.Create(query);
      // Set the request's CookieContainer, or we won't be able to
      // read the cookies in the response header.
      request.CookieContainer = new CookieContainer();
      // Send the request and get the response
      HttpWebResponse response = (HttpWebResponse)request.GetResponse();
      // Save the response cookies in a CookieCollection object
      CookieCollection cookies = response.Cookies;
      // Display the response body in the console window
      StreamReader reader = new StreamReader(response.GetResponseStream());
      Console.WriteLine(reader.ReadToEnd());
      reader.Close();
      response.Close();
      // Make the second request (to CookiesTest.aspx)
```

```
        HttpWebRequest nextRequest = (HttpWebRequest)WebRequest.Create(
                        "http://localhost/CookieSample/CookiesTest.aspx");
        // Add our saved CookieCollection to the request's CookieContainer
        nextRequest.CookieContainer = new CookieContainer();
        nextRequest.CookieContainer.Add(cookies);
        // Send the request, and print out the response
        HttpWebResponse nextResponse = (HttpWebResponse)
                                       nextRequest.GetResponse();
        reader = new StreamReader(nextResponse.GetResponseStream());
        Console.WriteLine(reader.ReadToEnd());
        reader.Close();
        nextResponse.Close();
    }
}
```

First, we call `WriteCookie.aspx`, where the `MyName` cookie is set with the value `"Vinod"`. Once we receive the response for this request, we save the cookies in the response into a `CookieCollection`. Next, we create a new `HttpWebRequest` object and add our `CookieCollection` object to its `CookieContainer`. Then we send the request to our `CookiesTest.aspx` page, which reads the value of the `MyName` cookie and writes it to the response stream.

When you run this program, you should see that the value set for the `MyName` cookie in `WriteCookie.aspx` has been passed to the `CookiesText.aspx` page, as shown in Figure 10-5.

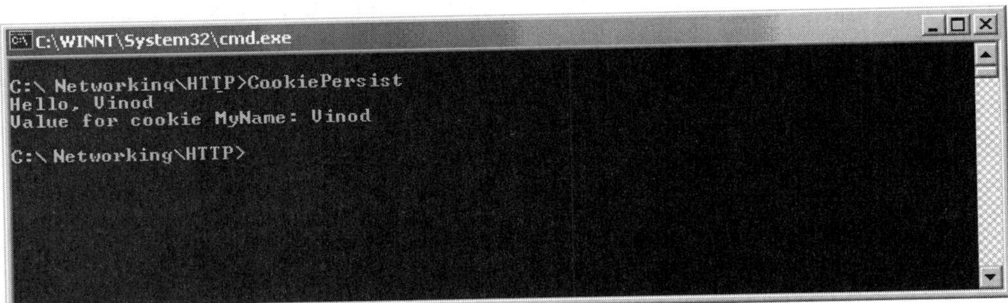

Figure 10-5. *Running the CookiePersist program*

Creating an HTTP Server with ASP.NET Support

One of the coolest features of ASP.NET is its ability to run outside IIS. Specifically, it supports a hosting framework (within the `System.Web.Hosting` namespace) that enables you to create your own web server with ASP.NET support. In this section, we will build an HTTP server that can process ASP.NET pages. We will call this server `APressServer`.

■ NOTE The code for the HTTP server application, as well as the other examples presented in this chapter, is available with this book's downloadable code, from the Download section of the Apress website (`http://www.apress.com`).

Storing the Server Configuration Information

Before we start to write any code, let's look at three XML files that will store the configuration information for our server: HostInfo.xml, Default.xml, and Mime.xml.

The HostInfo.xml file will store hosting information for the server: the virtual path and the port number. We use 8001 as the port, but we could choose any free port:

```
<HostLocation>
   <VDir>C:\\APressServer</VDir>
   <Port>8001</Port>
</HostLocation>
```

The default.xml file stores the default document names. These are the documents that the server will look for in a virtual directory if the browser request specifies only a directory, rather than an actual document. A default document could be the home page for a directory or an index page listing the documents in that directory.

```
<Document>
   <File>default.htm</File>
   <File>default.aspx</File>
   <File>Index.htm</File>
   <File>Home.aspx</File>
</Document>
```

The mime.xml file contains information about the different MIME types supported by the server and the file extensions associated with each type. This information will allow the server to set the Content-Type header correctly for each file type:

```
<Mime>
   <Values>
      <Ext>.htm</Ext>
      <Type>text/html</Type>
   </Values>
   <Values>
      <Ext>.html</Ext>
      <Type>text/html</Type>
   </Values>
   <Values>
      <Ext>.aspx</Ext>
      <Type>text/html</Type>
   </Values>
   <Values>
      <Ext>.gif</Ext>
      <Type>image/gif</Type>
   </Values>
   <Values>
      <Ext>.jpg</Ext>
      <Type>image/jpg</Type>
   </Values>
</Mime>
```

We're storing all the information in XML format for easy retrieval, but we could also use text files, the Registry, and so on to store the information.

Coding the Basic Server

Now let's see how our HTTP server works. The client initiates an HTTP request by opening a TCP/IP socket to the web server port (8001 for our server) and sending an ASCII request such as the following:

```
GET /Server.html HTTP/1.1
Accept: image/gif, image/x-xbitmap, image/jpeg, image/pjpeg, application/vnd.ms
powerpoint, application/vnd.ms-excel, application/msword, */*
Accept-Language: en-us
Accept-Encoding: gzip, deflate
User-Agent: Mozilla/4.0 (compatible; MSIE 6.0; Windows NT 5.0; .NET CLR 1.0.2914)
Host: localhost:8001
Connection: Keep-Alive
```

After receiving this request, the server writes a copy of the requested resource to the socket, where it is read by the client; it then closes the connection. Once the connection is closed, the server doesn't remember anything about this request.

The server is created as a new Visual C# Console Application project called `HttpServer` in Visual Studio .NET. This project contains three classes: `APressServer`, where we implement the HTTP server, and `Host` and `ASPXHosting`, which we will use to process any ASP.NET pages requested. Add a reference to `System.Web.dll` to the project.

We start by importing the namespaces required for the application and defining the `HttpServer` namespace. The first class in this namespace is the `APressServer` class. This class has two fields: a public enumeration, which we will use to specify which piece of configuration we want to retrieve from the `HostInfo.xml` file, and the `TcpListener` class, which will listen for requests from clients.

In the constructor for the `APressServer` class, we simply start the `TcpListener` on the port read from the `HostInfo.xml` configuration file. We then create a new thread and call the `StartListen` method on this thread. This method will accept any requests from clients.

```
using System;
using System.IO;
using System.Net;
using System.Net.Sockets;
using System.Text;
using System.Threading ;
using System.Web;
using System.Web.Hosting ;
using System.Xml;
namespace HttpServer
{
   class APressServer : MarshalByRefObject
   {
      // enum for HostInfo
      public enum HostInfo { VirtualDirectory, Port }
```

```
    private TcpListener myListener;
    // The constructor, which makes the TcpListener start listening on the
    // given port. It also calls a Thread on the method StartListen().
    public APressServer()
    {
       try
       {
          // Start listening on the given port
          IPHostEntry e=Dns.Resolve(Dns.GetHostName());
          IPAddress a=e.AddressList[0];
          myListener = new TcpListener(a,Int32.Parse(GetHostingInfo(
          HttpServer.APressServer.HostInfo.Port)));
          myListener.Start();
          Console.WriteLine("Web Server Running... Press ^C to Stop...");
          // Start the thread, which calls the method 'StartListen'
          Thread thread = new Thread(new ThreadStart(StartListen));
          thread.Start();
       }
       catch (NullReferenceException)
       {
          // Don't even ask me why they throw this exception
          // when this happens
          Console.WriteLine("Accept failed. Another process might be " +
                                                         "bound to port " +
                               HttpServer.APressServer.HostInfo.Port.ToString());
       }
    }
```

Reading from the Configuration Files

We get the port information from the `HostInfo.xml` in the `GetHostingInfo` method. This method takes a `HostInfo` value as an argument, and it returns either the virtual directory or the port number, depending on the argument:

```
public string GetHostingInfo(HostInfo InfoType)
{
   string retVal = "";
   string xPath = "";
   try
   {
      // Set the XPath expression to find the VDir or Port node,
      // depending on the argument passed into the method
      if (InfoType.Equals(HostInfo.VirtualDirectory))
         xPath = "HostLocation/VDir";
      else if (InfoType.Equals(HostInfo.Port))
         xPath = "HostLocation/Port";
      else
         return "";
```

```
        // Load the XML file
        XmlDataDocument xDHost = new XmlDataDocument();
        xDHost.Load("data\\HostInfo.xml");
        // Select the appropriate node
        XmlNode node = xDHost.SelectSingleNode(xPath);
        // Get the text value of the element
        retVal = node.InnerText.Trim();
    }
    catch(XmlException  eXML)
    {
        Console.WriteLine("An ConfigFile Exception Occurred : " +
                                                  eXML.ToString());
    }
    return retVal;
}
```

The GetTheDefaultFileName method retrieves the default file name from the default.xml file, if the user hasn't provided a file name. This method takes the directory path as input and looks for the file in the directory provided. If one of the default files is found, it returns the file name; otherwise, it returns an empty string:

```
public string GetTheDefaultFileName(string sLocalDirectory)
{
    string sLine = "";
    try
    {
        // Load the XML document
        XmlDataDocument xDFile = new XmlDataDocument();
        xDFile.Load("data\\Default.xml");
        // Select all the <File> elements
        XmlNodeList fileNodes = xDFile.SelectNodes("Document/File");
        // Iterate through the selected nodes, until we find one of the
        // default files
        foreach(XmlNode node in fileNodes)
              {
            if (File.Exists(sLocalDirectory + node.InnerText.Trim()))
            {
                sLine = node.InnerText.Trim();
                break;
            }
        }
    }
    catch(XmlException  eXML)
    {
        Console.WriteLine("A ConfigFile Exception Occurred : " +
                                                  eXML.ToString());
    }
    // Return the file name if a default file exists,
```

```
    // or an empty string otherwise
    if (File.Exists(sLocalDirectory + sLine))
        return sLine;
    else
        return "";
}
```

The next method, GetMimeType, is used to identify the MIME type, using the extension of the file requested by the user. This method takes the file name as an input argument, and it checks the file extension with the MIME information in the Mime.xml file. It returns the corresponding MIME type:

```
public string GetMimeType(string sRequestedFile)
{
    string sMimeType = "";
    string sFileExt = "";
    string sMimeExt = "";
    // Convert to lowercase
    sRequestedFile = sRequestedFile.ToLower();
    int iStartPos = sRequestedFile.IndexOf(".");
    sFileExt = sRequestedFile.Substring(iStartPos);
    try
    {
        // Load the Mime.xml file to find out the Mime type
        XmlDataDocument xDMime = new XmlDataDocument();
        xDMime.Load("data\\Mime.xml");

        // Select the <Type> element that has an <Ext> sibling
        // with the same value as the extension for our file
        string xPath = "Mime/Values/Type[../Ext='" + sFileExt +"']";
        XmlNode mimeNode = xDMime.SelectSingleNode(xPath);
        if (mimeNode != null)
        {
            sMimeType = mimeNode.InnerText.Trim();
            // Get the value of the previous <Ext> element
            sMimeExt = mimeNode.PreviousSibling.InnerText.Trim();
        }
    }
    catch (Exception e)
    {
        Console.WriteLine("An Exception Occurred : " + e.ToString());
    }
    if (sMimeExt == sFileExt)
        return sMimeType;
    else
        return "";
}
```

That finishes our set of methods for reading our configuration files. The next method we'll look at, WriteHeader, is used to build and send the HTTP header information to the browser.

Sending Data to the Client

WriteHeader takes as parameters the information used to build the headers, such as the HTTP version, the content type, and the content length. It also takes a Socket as a reference parameter. When we've built the header, we send it to the client using this socket:

```
public void WriteHeader(string sHttpVersion, string sMIMEHeader,
                        int iTotalBytes, string sStatusCode,
                        ref Socket mySocket)
{
   string sBuffer = "";
   // If Mime type is not provided, set default to text/html
   if (sMIMEHeader.Length == 0)
      sMIMEHeader = "text/html";
   sBuffer = sBuffer + sHttpVersion + sStatusCode + "\r\n";
   sBuffer = sBuffer + "Server: APressServer\r\n";
   sBuffer = sBuffer + "Content-Type: " + sMIMEHeader + "\r\n";
   sBuffer = sBuffer + "Accept-Ranges: bytes\r\n";
   sBuffer = sBuffer + "Content-Length: " + iTotalBytes + "\r\n\r\n";
   byte[] bSendData = Encoding.ASCII.GetBytes(sBuffer);
   SendToBrowser(bSendData, ref mySocket);
   Console.WriteLine("Total Bytes : " + iTotalBytes.ToString());
}
```

The SendToBrowser method is an overloaded method that sends the information to the client. This method takes as arguments either a string or a byte array and the socket reference. The HTML code generated after the ASP.NET file is processed using the ASPXHosting class is passed as a string argument and converted to a byte array using the System.Text.Encoding class; this in then passed to the other overload of SendToBrowser:

```
public void SendToBrowser(string data, ref Socket socket)
{
   SendToBrowser(Encoding.ASCII.GetBytes(data), ref socket);
}
```

The other overload of SendToBrowser simply sends the byte data to the client calling the Send method of the Socket that is passed in. If this returns –1, we know that an error has occurred:

```
public void SendToBrowser(Byte[] bSendData, ref Socket socket)
{
   int iNumByte = 0;
   try
   {
      if (socket.Connected)
      {
         if ((iNumByte = socket.Send(
```

```
                              bSendData, bSendData.Length,0)) == -1)
            Console.WriteLine("Socket error: cannot send packet");
         else
            Console.WriteLine("No. of bytes sent {0}", iNumByte);
      }
      else
         Console.WriteLine("Connection Dropped....");
   }
   catch (Exception  e)
   {
      Console.WriteLine("Error Occurred : {0} ", e );
   }
}
```

Accepting Connections

The methods that we have discussed so far are the building blocks of the application. Now let's look at the `StartListen` method. This is the key method that accepts the connection established between the client and server, processes the request from the client, and sends a response to it depending on the request:

```
public void StartListen()
{
   int iStartPos = 0;
   string sRequest;
   string sDirName;
   string sRequestedFile;
   string sErrorMessage;
   string sLocalDir;
   // Get the virtualDir info
   string sWebServerRoot = GetHostingInfo(
                 HttpServer.APressServer.HostInfo.VirtualDirectory);
   string sPhysicalFilePath = "";
   string sFormattedMessage = "";
   string sResponse = "";
   while(true)
   {
      // Accept a new connection
      Socket socket = myListener.AcceptSocket();
      Console.WriteLine("Socket Type " + socket.SocketType);
      if(socket.Connected)
      {
         Console.WriteLine("\nClient Connected!!\n" +
                           "=================\nCLient IP {0}\n",
                           socket.RemoteEndPoint);
         // Make a byte array and receive data from the client
         byte[] bReceive = new byte[1024];
         int i = socket.Receive(bReceive, bReceive.Length, 0);
```

```
// Convert Byte to string
string sBuffer = Encoding.ASCII.GetString(bReceive);
// Let's just make sure we are using HTTP;
// that's about all we care about
iStartPos = sBuffer.IndexOf("HTTP", 1);
// Get the HTTP text and version, e.g. "HTTP/1.1"
string sHttpVersion = sBuffer.Substring(iStartPos, 8);
sRequest = sBuffer.Substring(0, iStartPos - 1);
// Replace backslash with forward slash, if any
sRequest.Replace("\\","/");
// If a file name is not supplied, add a forward slash to
// indicate that it is a directory, and then we will look
// for the default file name...
if ((sRequest.IndexOf(".") < 1) && (!sRequest.EndsWith("/")))
   sRequest = sRequest + "/";
// Extract the requested file name
iStartPos = sRequest.LastIndexOf("/") + 1;
sRequestedFile = sRequest.Substring(iStartPos);
// Extract the directory name
sDirName = sRequest.Substring(sRequest.IndexOf("/"),
                              sRequest.LastIndexOf("/") - 3);
// Identify the physical directory
if (sDirName == "/")
   sLocalDir = sWebServerRoot;
else
{
   // Get the virtual directory
   sDirName =sDirName.Replace(@"/",@"\");
   sLocalDir = sWebServerRoot + sDirName;
}

Console.WriteLine("Directory Requested : " + sLocalDir);
```

This code is fairly self-explanatory. It accepts the connection and receives the request, and converts it into a string from a byte array. It then looks for the request type; extracts the HTTP version, file, and directory information; and also gets the virtual directory information from the `HostInfo.xml` file using the `GetHostingInfo` method.

If no file is specified, and a default file can't be found, we send an HTTP 404 Not Found error to the browser:

```
// Identify the file name. If the filename is not supplied,
// look in the default file list
if (sRequestedFile.Length == 0)
{
   // Get the default file name
   sRequestedFile = GetTheDefaultFileName(sLocalDir);
   if (sRequestedFile == "")
   {
```

```
            sErrorMessage = "<H2>Error!! No Default File Name " +
                            "Specified</H2>";
            WriteHeader(sHttpVersion, "", sErrorMessage.Length,
                        " 404 Not Found", ref socket);
            SendToBrowser(sErrorMessage, ref socket);
            socket.Close();
            return;
         }
      }
```

Similarly, the following code gets the MIME type from the Mime.xml file using the GetMimeType method, and then checks for the file extension. If the file extension is .aspx, then an instance of the ASPXHosting class will be created, and the HTML output will be passed as an argument to the SendToBrowser method (along with the Socket reference). This is generated by the CreateHost method, which takes the ASP.NET file name as an argument.

If the requested file is not an .aspx file, the file is read using the BinaryReader and sent to the browser using the SendToBrowser method. In both cases, the SendHeader method is called before the SendToBrowser method. After sending the data to the client, the connection is closed:

```
         else
         {
            int iTotBytes=0;
            sResponse = "";
            FileStream fs = new FileStream(sPhysicalFilePath,
                 FileMode.Open, FileAccess.Read, FileShare.Read);

            // Create a reader that can read bytes
            // from the FileStream
            BinaryReader reader = new BinaryReader(fs);
            byte[] bytes = new byte[fs.Length];
            int read;
            while ((read = reader.Read(
                                  bytes, 0, bytes.Length)) != 0)
            {
               // Read from the file and write the data
               // to the network
               sResponse = sResponse + Encoding.ASCII.GetString(
                                              bytes, 0, read);
               iTotBytes = iTotBytes + read;
            }
            reader.Close();
            fs.Close();
            WriteHeader(sHttpVersion,  sMimeType, iTotBytes,
                        " 200 OK", ref socket);
            SendToBrowser(bytes, ref socket);
         }
      }
      socket.Close();
```

```
        }
    }
}
```

Finally, we need the Main method to start the server running:

```
        static void Main()
        {
            APressServer server = new APressServer();
        }
    }
}
```

Now let's see the Host and ASPXHosting classes that will process any ASP.NET files requested.

Hosting ASP.NET Applications Outside IIS

As mentioned earlier, one of the more interesting features of ASP.NET is its ability to run outside IIS. Specifically, ASP.NET supports a hosting framework (within the System.Web.Hosting namespace) that allows you to run it on top of other web servers.

For our HTTP server, we use the SimpleWorkerRequest and ApplicationHost classes. The latter has a static method called CreateApplicationHost, which we use to create an instance of our Host class in the application domain used to host ASP.NET. This class allows us to marshal method calls between our web server's application domain (AppDomain) and the ASP.NET AppDomain. The SimpleWorkerRequest class is a simple predefined implementation of the HttpWorkerRequest abstract class, which provides methods and enumerations used by ASP.NET to process requests.

We need to pass an HttpWorkerRequest object into the ProcessRequest method of the HttpRuntime class (in the System.Web namespace) to process the ASP.NET page, so using SimpleWorkerRequest avoids the necessity of creating our own implementation.

```
using System;
using System.IO;
using System.Web;
using System.Web.Hosting;
using System.Xml;
public class Host : MarshalByRefObject
{
    public string HandleRequest(string fileName)
    {
        StringWriter wr = new StringWriter();
        Console.WriteLine("The output from the {0} file", fileName);
        // Create a Worker to execute the aspx file
        HttpWorkerRequest worker = new SimpleWorkerRequest(fileName, "" , wr);

        // Execute the page
        HttpRuntime.ProcessRequest(worker);
        return wr.ToString();
```

```
    }
}
public class ASPXHosting
{
    public enum HostInfo{VirtualDirectory, Port}
    public  string CreateHost(string fileName)
    {
        Host myHost = (Host)ApplicationHost.CreateApplicationHost(
                                    typeof(Host), "/", GetHostingInfo(
                                    ASPXHosting.HostInfo.VirtualDirectory));
        return myHost.HandleRequest(fileName);
    }
    public string GetHostingInfo(HostInfo InfoType)
    {
        // As in the APressServer class -
        // we won't repeat the code here
    }
}
```

Testing the Server

To test the application, let's execute an ASP.NET page named APressServerSample.aspx. This page is placed in the root directory of the web server. Since we use 8001 as our port, we call the file by specifying the URL http://localhost:8001/APressServerSample.aspx. This file simply has a Label web control that contains some information:

```
<%@ Page language="c#" %>
<!DOCTYPE HTML PUBLIC "-//W3C//DTD HTML 4.0 Transitional//EN" >
<html>
    <head>
        <title>APressServerSample</title>
    </head>
    <body MS_POSITIONING="GridLayout">
        <form id="APressServerSample" method="post" runat="server">
            <asp:Label id="Label1" runat="server" ForeColor="#C00000"
                    Font-Bold="True" Font-Names="verdana">
APressServerSample.aspx page Processed using APress Server</asp:Label>
        </form>
    </body>
</html>
```

Figure 10-6 shows the output of the APressServerSample.aspx file in a web browser.

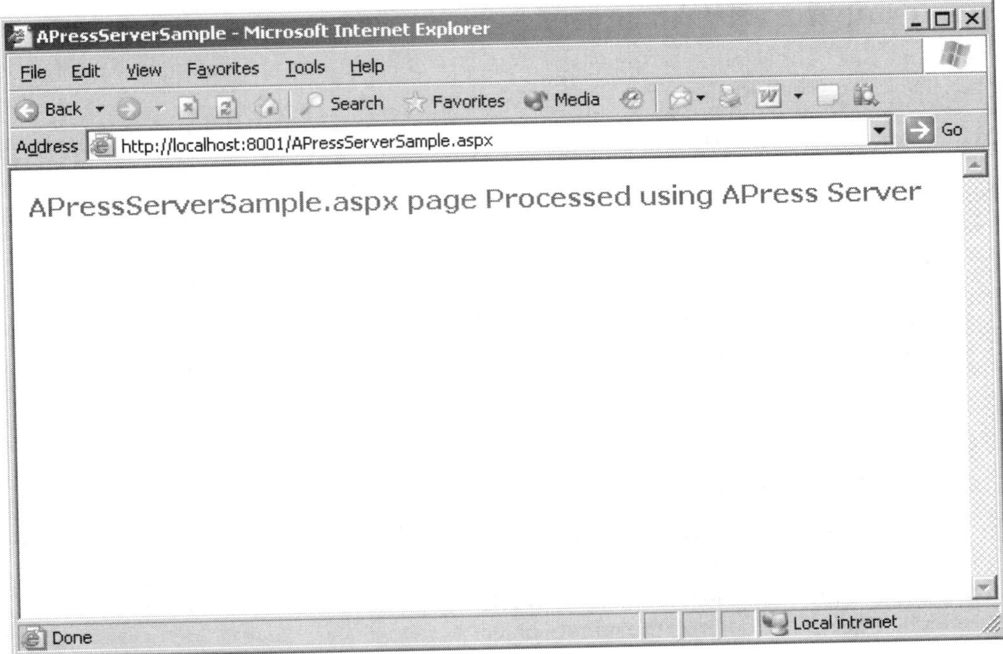

Figure 10-6. *Running the HTTP server*

This example demonstrates the power of the .NET classes and .NET's simple and straightforward support for most HTTP 1.1 features.

Building an HTTP Remoting Application

In Chapter 7, we introduced the basic concepts of .NET Remoting. The .NET Remoting Framework uses channels to connect applications together. The two channels that are currently available in the .NET Framework are `TcpChannel` and `HttpChannel`. As you learned in Chapter 7, the TCP channel should generally be used if the message is to be sent over the local network, because it has better performance. However, if the message is to be sent over the Internet, the HTTP channel is generally the better choice, because TCP connections won't usually be permitted over a firewall.

By default, messages sent over the HTTP channel are formatted using SOAP. This is good for interoperability, but has poorer performance than the binary channel used by default with TCP.

Since using Remoting with the HTTP channel is conceptually very similar to using the TCP channel, which we covered in Chapter 7, we won't rehash the theory. Rather, we'll just look at a short example of a simple application.

Registering the HTTP Channel

As with the TCP channel, we need to register the HTTP channel with channel services before we can use it in our applications:

```
public class LoadHttpChannel
{
   HttpChannel httpChannel;
   public void LoadChannel()
   {
      httpChannel =  new HttpChannel();
      // Register the HTTP Channel
      ChannelServices.RegisterChannel(httpChannel);
   }
}
```

Defining the Remote Class

First, we need to define the class that we will instantiate remotely. We'll keep this as simple as possible, and just define one method that writes a string passed in as a parameter to the console. This class will need to exist both on the client and on the remote server, as Remoting uses reflection to call methods on the remote object.

```
// APressLog.cs
using System;
namespace APressLog
{
   public class RemotingSample : MarshalByRefObject
   {
      public void RemoteLog(string value)
      {
         Console.WriteLine(value);
      }
   }
}
```

Compile this into a DLL using the command `csc /t:library APressLog.cs`.

To make a class accessible remotely, we should derive it from `MarshalByRefObject`. If an object is marshaled by reference, a reference to the object is passed from one AppDomain to another. In contrast, if an object is marshaled by value, a copy of the complete state of the object is passed to the target AppDomain. The remote application uses the object's metadata to create a "proxy" for the original object. We can make method calls against this proxy, which will then be marshaled to the real object.

Creating the Remote Server Application

Now let's create a simple server application that listens to the requests:

```
// RemoteServer.cs
using System;
using APressLog;
using System.Runtime.Remoting;
using System.Runtime.Remoting.Channels;
using System.Runtime.Remoting.Channels.Http ;
namespace RemoteServer
{
   class RemotingServer
   {
      public static void Main()
         {
         ChannelServices.RegisterChannel(new HttpChannel(8000));

         RemotingConfiguration.RegisterWellKnownServiceType(
                                    typeof(RemotingSample), "APressLog",
                                    WellKnownObjectMode.Singleton);
         Console.WriteLine("Log Server Listening on endpoints:\r\n" +
                           "\thttp://localhost:8000/APressLog\r\n");
         Console.WriteLine("Press enter to stop the server...");
         Console.ReadLine();
      }
   }
}
```

This should be compiled into a console application, referencing our `APressLog.dll` assembly:

```
csc RemoteServer.cs /r:APressLog.dll
```

In the server code, we register the HTTP channel to use as the transport mechanism and to listen on port 8000. After registering the channel, we register the object that will actually be instantiated on the remote server, using the `RegisterWellKnownServiceType` method. This method tells the Remoting infrastructure where to find the remote object. It takes as parameters the object type, URI, and `WellKnownObjectMode` as arguments for locating the object. Here, we use `Singleton` as the `WellKnownObjectMode`, which means that the same object instance will be used for each of the incoming messages.

When the call arrives at the server, the .NET Framework extracts the URI from the message, examines the Remoting tables to locate the reference for the object that matches the URI, and then instantiates the object if necessary, forwarding the method call to the object.

If the object is registered as `SingleCall`, it won't be reused after the method call is completed, left for the garbage collector to destroy, so a new instance of the object is created for each method call. The remote object itself is not instantiated by the registration process. This happens only when a client attempts to call a method on the object or activates the object from the client side.

Creating the Remote Client Application

Here is the client code to access our server application:

```
// RemoteClient.cs
using System;
using System.Runtime.Remoting;
using APressLog;
namespace RemotingClient
{
   class Client
   {
      static void Main()
      {
         RemotingSample httpAPressLog = (RemotingSample)Activator.GetObject(
                  typeof(RemotingSample), "http://localhost:8000/APressLog");
         httpAPressLog.RemoteLog("Client : Hello..Server");
      }
   }
}
```

Again, this should be compiled into a console application referencing our `APressLog.dll` assembly:

```
csc RemoteClient.cs /r:APressLog.dll
```

In the code, the `RemotingSample` object is created using the server-activation model, by calling the `Activator.GetObject` method. *Server-activated objects* are objects whose lifetimes are directly controlled by the server.

The server application domain creates these objects only when the client makes a method call on the object, not when the client first instantiates the object using the `new` keyword or `Activator.GetObject` (similar to late binding); this saves a network round-trip solely for the purpose of instantiating the object. A proxy is created in the client application domain only when a client requests an instance of a server-activated type.

Figure 10-7 shows the output on the server side when we start the server and then run the client application.

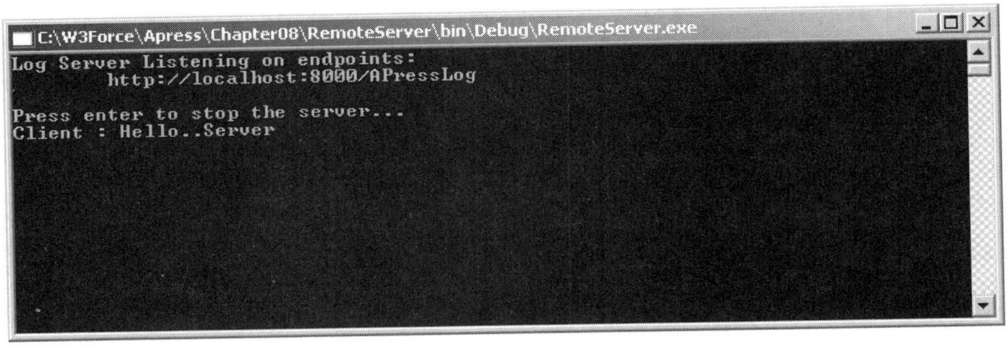

```
C:\W3Force\Apress\Chapter08\RemoteServer\bin\Debug\RemoteServer.exe
Log Server Listening on endpoints:
        http://localhost:8000/APressLog

Press enter to stop the server...
Client : Hello..Server
```

Figure 10-7. *Running the Remoting application*

Summary

This chapter covered HTTP programming in detail. The first step in Internet programming is to have a thorough knowledge of how HTTP works, so we started this chapter with an overview of HTTP, before looking at the support for HTTP programming in .NET.

Following the overview, we discussed using the .NET methods and classes to work with the HTTP protocol. We covered a wide range of topics, such as HTTP chunking, web client classes, and authentication. We then discussed reading and writing cookies in .NET.

To demonstrate working with HTTP, we created an HTTP server that can host ASP.NET applications outside IIS and a simple HTTP Remoting application.

CHAPTER 11

E-mail Protocols

Ever since the rise of Internet messaging, e-mail has been a cornerstone of electronic communication. If you're reading this book, you probably have some prior experience sending e-mail within a programming language, so we aren't really covering some new and exciting technology that .NET brings to the table. What is exciting is how easy and seamless .NET makes network programming, especially with regard to using the various e-mail protocols to send and retrieve e-mail, and to perform various tasks that may have been convoluted or difficult in the past.

In this chapter, we provide a high-level overview of the various e-mail protocols and how they are accessed and used in a .NET environment. We'll also develop some sample applications that implement the SMTP and NNTP protocols.

In particular, we'll discuss the following topics:

- An overview of how e-mail works
- How to send e-mail with SMTP
- The e-mail message structure
- How to retrieve e-mail with POP3 and IMAP
- .NET support for e-mail
- Examples of SMTP, POP3, and NNTP applications

How E-mail Works

It's quite easy to think of e-mail as similar to ordinary postal mail. The big difference is that no stamps are needed! Well, that and the fact that e-mail sending is almost instantaneous, and the postal service is usually very slow. Also, e-mail can be sent to many recipients at once, as well as forwarded to others very easily. However, in both cases, we know that there is a starting point and an endpoint to a communication session. There is also a delivery mechanism that transfers the mail from one point to another along its mail route until it reaches its final destination.

In the most generic sense, two components interact in e-mail delivery: the Message Transfer Agent (MTA) and the User Agent (the e-mail client). For snail mail, the transfer agent may be a postal or carrier company such as the United States Postal Service or Federal

Express. In the electronic world, the MTA is the Simple Mail Transport Protocol (SMTP), which is responsible for directing e-mail from the starting point (sender) to the endpoint (receiver), bouncing the e-mail across various machines on the Internet.

■NOTE The method described here stems from roots in TCP/IP. However, this is not the only system and standard used for messaging, but the most commonly used and accepted method. Other messaging standards, such as X.400, exist as alternatives to TCP/IP-related messaging. For more information about the X.400 protocol, see `http://www.itu.int/` and `http://www.alvestrand.no/x400/`.

When you think about how e-mail is actually sent across the Internet, you must first realize that the Internet is nothing more than hundreds of thousands of computers that are networked together, using the same standard protocols for communication. Endpoints are simply mailboxes or message stores on e-mail servers (although you could also view the sender and receivers as the starting point and endpoint, and the message stores as holding places for the messages until they are received by a client program). A mail server is simply the machine (or virtual machine) that handles sending and receiving messages, and communicates with other machines in the process of handling e-mail.

For example, a company may have employees using a Microsoft Outlook mail client that connects to the company's mail server (which may be running Exchange). All e-mail messages that come in and go out of that company are handled by the mail server, which acts as both the endpoint and starting point for any e-mail transmitted over the Internet. Figure 11-1 illustrates this simple situation, using one mail server (in practice, many companies have multiple servers to handle e-mail communications).

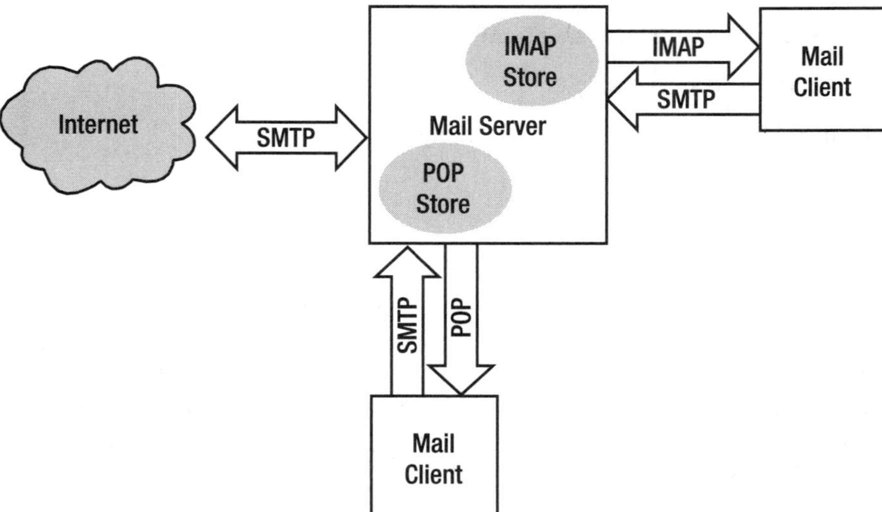

Figure 11-1. *Simple e-mail handing*

As shown in Figure 11-1, the mail clients (such as Outlook) communicate with the mail server using SMTP, and the mail server also communicates with other machines over the Internet using SMTP. The Post Office Protocol (POP3) and Internet Message Access Protocol (IMAP) are also depicted in the figure. These protocols allow mail clients to access and retrieve e-mail. To send mail, e-mail clients use SMTP. So, SMTP, POP3, and IMAP are the standard protocols for sending and retrieving e-mail.

Internet mail is largely defined by a number of standards and recommendations made by companies and individuals close to Internet technology research and design. These standards are endorsed by the Internet Mail Consortium (IMC, `http://www.imc.org/`) and the Internet Engineering Task Force (IETF, `http://www.ietf.org`). The current set of Internet mail standards is composed of many related RFCs, recommendations, and statements on common practices. Not all standards are fully endorsed or full IETF standards documents, but they are considered stable and are used throughout the industry for developing e-mail software.

Many RFCs are available on the IMC website (`http://www.imc.org/rfcs.html`). These documents provide details about every aspect of e-mail handling. In this chapter, we will touch on a few of these RFCs. In particular, we will look at RFC 2821, which defines the SMTP protocol, and RFC 2822, which defines what an e-mail message should look like. For more information about these RFCs, visit the IMC website.

Sending E-mail

SMTP (outlined in RFC 2821) defines the interaction between mail servers that are transporting e-mail. For the most part, SMTP uses TCP as a transport protocol (see RFC 1090 for SMTP over X.25).

SMTP Sessions

In essence, an SMTP session consists of a conversation between two machines that are trying to hand off or pass along an e-mail message. A simplified view of this is shown in Figure 11-2.

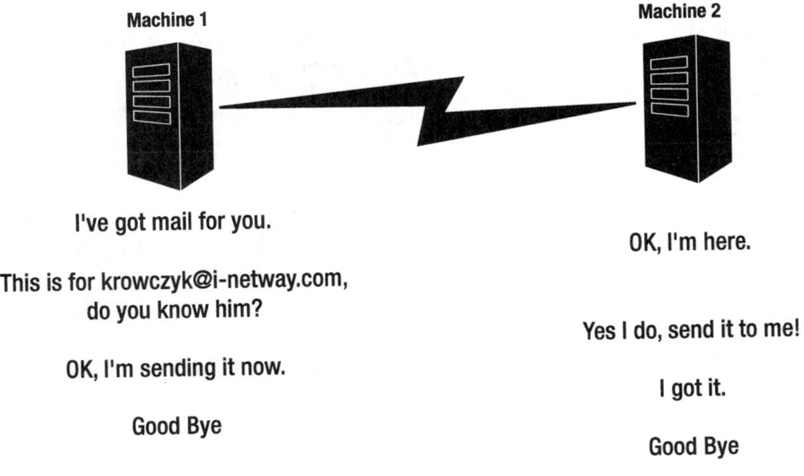

Figure 11-2. *Sending an e-mail message with SMTP*

As you can see, an SMTP session can be summed up in a simple communication between two computers. At this point, the e-mail will have bounced around the Internet to finally reach machine 2, which is the mail handler for `i-netway.com` in the example shown in Figure 11-2. If, for instance, there is no user at this e-mail address (the address was invalid) or the mail handler doesn't have any way to deliver the message, the machine will reply that the e-mail was undeliverable.

Another way to look at an SMTP e-mail session is as a telnet connection to an actual e-mail server. (See Chapter 1 for a brief discussion of using the Microsoft Telnet client.) If someone at Apress were trying to send me an e-mail via telnet, the conversation would look something like this:

```
open i-netway.com 25
Trying. . . Connected to i-netway.com
220 I-NETWAY.COM - Server ESMTP (PMDF v4.3-10 #2381)
helo apress.com
250 I-NETWAY.COM OK, APRESS.COM.
mail from:<editor@apress.com>
250 Address Ok.
rcpt to:<krowczyk@i-netway.com>
250 krowczyk@i-netway.com OK.
data
354 Enter mail, end with a single ".".
SUBJECT:E-mail Chapter
Andy, thanks for the chapter!
.
250 OK.
//by quitting, the message is sent
quit
221 Bye received. Goodbye.
```

■CAUTION Most ISPs disable telnet access, because it allows hackers and the like to easily spoof e-mail messages, which is not a good thing! This example is only meant to show the conversation between an SMTP e-mail server and a client.

The session begins with the `Telnet` command to open a connection to the `i-netway.com` e-mail server. This is followed by a few SMTP commands that are needed to send the e-mail message and the responses from the SMTP server.

We discussed the most common SMTP commands in Chapter 6, where we built a simple SMTP client, but now let's look at the complete list. Table 11-1 presents a quick summary of the various SMTP commands that are available (for more detailed explanations, refer to RFC 2821).

Table 11-1. *SMTP Commands*

Command	Description
HELO	Identifies the SMTP client to the SMTP server.
MAIL	Initiates a mail transaction to deliver an e-mail to one or more mailboxes.
RCPT	Identifies the recipient to whom the mail data is to be sent. If the data is to be sent to more than one recipient, multiple RCPT commands can be used.
DATA	Marks the start of the mail data. The data following the DATA command is appended to the mail buffer. The mail data may contain any of the 128 ASCII character codes. The end of the data is marked by a carriage return and linefeed, period, and then another carriage return and linefeed sequence (<CRLF>.<CRLF>).
SEND	Initiates a mail transaction to deliver an e-mail to one or more terminals.*
SOML	For SEND or MAIL, initiates a mail transaction to deliver an e-mail to one or more terminals or mailboxes. The e-mail is delivered to the terminal of each recipient if that recipient is active on the host and accepting terminal messages, or else it is delivered to the recipient's mailbox.*
SAML	For SEND and MAIL, initiates a mail transaction to deliver an e-mail to one or more terminals or mailboxes. The e-mail is delivered to the terminal of each recipient if that recipient is active on the host and accepting terminal messages, and to every recipient's mailbox.*
RSET	Aborts the current mail transaction. All data will be discarded and all buffers cleared. The receiver must send an OK reply.
VRFY	Asks the receiver to confirm that the following argument is a valid username. If it is, the full name of the user (if known) and the fully specified mailbox are returned.
EXPN	Asks the receiver to confirm that the following argument is a mailing list, and if so, to return the names of the members of that list. The full names of the users (if known) and the fully specified mailboxes are returned in a multiline reply. This command is similar to the VRFY command, but is used for multiple recipients.
HELP	Asks the receiver to send helpful information to the sender. The command can take an argument (such as a command name) and return more specific information as a response.
NOOP	This command has no effect, except that the receiver should send an OK reply. No operation takes place, and no other commands or data should be affected.
QUIT	On receiving a QUIT command, the receiver must send an OK reply, and then close the connection to the sender.
TURN	On receiving a TURN command, the receiver must either (1) send an OK reply and take on the role of the SMTP client; or (2) send a refusal reply and retain the role of the SMTP server. This command is deprecated because of security concerns. Poor authentication implementations would allow a client machine to take on the role of the SMTP server and divert e-mail messages.

* Terminal *refers to a user's terminal screen. Because most clients are not terminal clients nowadays, the* SEND, SOML, *and* SAML *commands are, for the most part, obsolete. They are included here for the sake of completeness, because they are part of the RFC.*

SMTP Reply Codes

If you look back at the previous example of sending an e-mail using SMTP through telnet, you will see that the server sends back a reply code for each SMTP command. Actually, the reply codes sent back by the server provide much information about the status of the current e-mail transaction. Figure 11-3 illustrates a typical reply code and the information it contains.

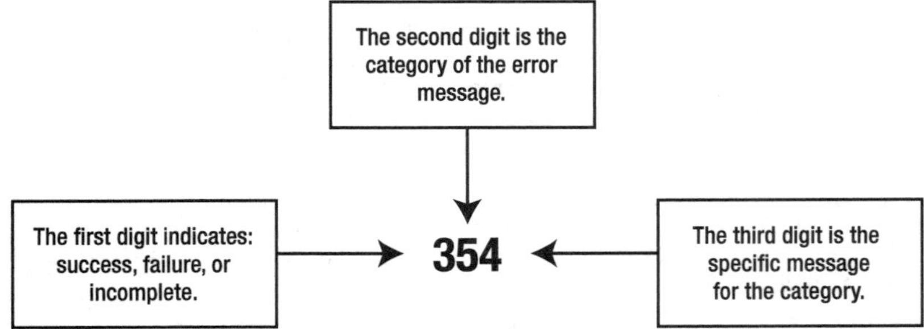

Figure 11-3. *An SMTP reply code*

The first two digits of the SMTP reply code are the most important. The first digit gives the status of the command, as follows:

- A 1 indicates preliminary acceptance of the command, pending confirmation.
- A 2 indicates successful completion of the command.
- A 3 indicates intermediate acceptance of the command, pending further information.
- A 4 indicates temporary negative status.
- A 5 indicates failure.

The second digit is the category of the error or status message:

- A 0 indicates a syntax error.
- A 1 indicates a connection error.
- A 5 indicates a mail error.

Table 11-2 shows some common reply codes that you might receive from an SMTP transaction call. The error or status messages may differ among SMTP servers, but the reply code means the same thing in each case. The status message is really just a human-readable description of the status or error.

■ **NOTE** RFC 2821 defines all of the reply codes available, and the numeric codes are definitive. This means that you can't define new codes as you see fit! However, since we are talking about an agreed-upon standard protocol, the response codes should be predefined and set in stone.

Table 11-2. *Examples of SMTP Reply Codes*

Reply Code	Message
500	Syntax error, command unrecognized
501	Syntax error in parameters or arguments
502	Command not implemented
503	Bad sequence of commands
220	<domain> Service ready
221	<domain> Service closing transmission channel
421	<domain> Service not available, closing transmission channel
250	Requested mail action OK, completed
354	Start mail input, end with <CRLF>.<CRLF>
550	Requested action not taken, mailbox unavailable
553	Requested action not taken, mailbox name not allowed
554	Transaction failed

E-mail Message Structure

Before we start talking about accessing e-mail with POP3 and IMAP, let's first look at the content and structure of a mail message (described in RFC 2822). Think of it as sort of a "schema" or outline of a typical mail message. The following is a typical mail message:

```
Received: from MAILCLUSTER [111.111.111.111] by mail.brinkster.com with ESMTP
(SMTPD32-6.05) id AF1F18B600FA; Thu, 08 Jan 2004 05:40:47 -0400
Received: by MAILCLUSTER with Internet Mail Service (5.5.2653.19)
id <NZPCN64X>; Thu, 08 Jan 2004 10:39:30 +0100
Message-ID: <E12F1784B51ED5119EA900D0B74D69240EFEAF87@MAILCLUSTER>
From: APress <editor@apress.com>
To: "'Andrew Krowczyk'" <krowczyk@i-netway.com>
Subject: C# Networking Chapter
Date: Thu, 08 Jan 2004 10:39:28 +0100
Importance: high
X-Priority: 1
MIME-Version: 1.0
X-Mailer: Internet Mail Service (5.5.2653.19)
Content-Type: text/plain
X-RCPT-TO: <krowczyk@i-netway.com>
X-UIDL: 323073316
Status: U
Andy, thanks for the work you've done!
- APress
```

This typical e-mail structure consists of both message headers and message text. Some information is required for the message to conform to the e-mail standards; other information is optional and can be included or excluded depending on many factors.

The following are headers that are generally required in all e-mail:

- *From*: The agent (person, system, or process) that created the message. This should be a single authenticated machine address generated by the sending agent. As you would imagine, this indicates who/what is sending the e-mail message.
- *Date*: The date the message was sent. The only optional parts of the date specification are the day of the week and the seconds. The time zone may be given in usual denotations such as CST, EDT, or GMT. The time zone is preferred as a numeric offset from the GMT. In the preceding message, +0100 denotes the GMT offset.
- *One recipient address*: At least one recipient address must be used, which can be To, Cc, or Bcc.

There are also other headers and information that may be optional and not required in every message, such as the following:

- *Reply-To*: The reply-to header is often used to designate the preferred e-mail address to which to send responses. This is often used by list mail and other processes to correctly identify the return e-mail address location.
- *Sender*: Why would the sender be optional? This is really the same thing as the required From field. The Sender field is intended for use when the sender of the e-mail is not the author of the e-mail or is one of a group of authors. This shouldn't be used if it's identical to the From field. The Sender field must be present if it's different from the From field. Here is an example:

  ```
  FROM: "Joe Someone" <joe@someone.com>
  SENDER: INFO-SAMPLE Discussion <INFO-SAMPLE@SOMEDOMAIN.COM>
  TO: Multiple recipients of list
  INFO-SAMPLE Discussion <INFOSAMPLE@SOMEDOMAIN.COM>
  ```

Received Headers

One of the most important parts of an e-mail message is the data that is transmitted in the received headers of the mail message. This provides debugging information, as well as a good look at where the e-mail came from and how it got from point A to point B.

Our example contains the following received lines:

```
Received: from MAILCLUSTER [111.111.111.111] by mail.brinkster.com with ESMTP
(SMTPD32-6.05) id AF1F18B600FA; Thu, 08 Jan 2004 05:40:47 -0400
Received: by MAILCLUSTER with Internet Mail Service (5.5.2653.19)
id <NZPCN64X>; Thu, 08 Jan 2004 10:39:30 +0100
```

The received lines provide the following information:

- They are the postmaster's primary debugging tool. By reading the header, you can find out much information about where the mail came from and how it got to the final destination.
- They tell which systems have touched or tampered with the mail.
- Each MTA that relays a message attaches its own received header line. RFC 2882 requires that MTAs add their own received line when they handle the mail, and they are prohibited by the RFC from touching the received lines put in by other mailers.
- The received headers show the path, hop by hop, that the mail took from the sender to the receiver.

An example of how the messages can be traced via the received lines in the headers is shown in Figure 11-4.

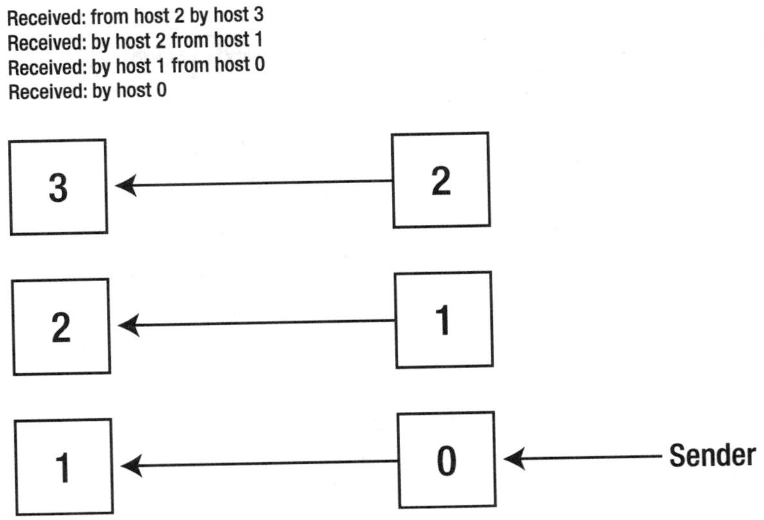

Figure 11-4. *Received lines in a header*

Since the headers contain so much information, it's worth knowing how to view header information using Microsoft Outlook. Simply right-click the message of interest and select Options. The Internet headers for the message are displayed at the bottom of the Message Options dialog box, as shown in Figure 11-5.

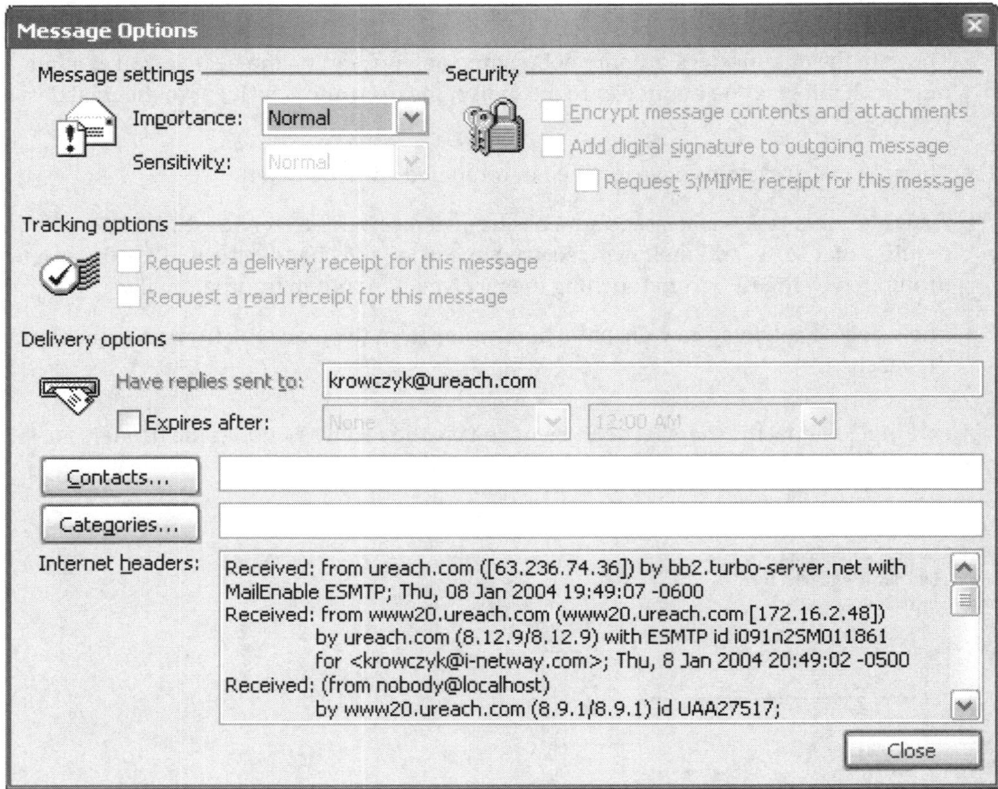

Figure 11-5. *Viewing headers in Outlook*

NOTE Internet headers might not be displayed for e-mail messages that are sent internally on the same network.

E-mail Attachments (MIME)

E-mail was originally a text-only messaging system using just ASCII characters. But people wanted to be able to "attach" binary files of different types to the e-mail messages and have the attachments transferred along with the ASCII text messages. So, to address this need, Multipurpose Internet Mail Extensions (MIME) was developed. MIME defines extensions to SMTP to support binary attachments of arbitrary format.

MIME actually encompasses two main functions:

- MIME encodes binary data so that it can be passed over the Internet. Remember that the Internet is a 7-bit ASCII world, so 8-bit extensions don't work, because there are issues with line length and file formatting.
- MIME attaches a label or tag to the encoded data so that the content can be determined and interpreted at the endpoint of the message; for example, this is a movie file or a Microsoft Excel document.

MIME uses a new encoding scheme that is called base-64. It also adds new SMTP headers that describe the attached document. The idea is actually quite simple: you are encoding the binary data into a different bit data representation, and then piggybacking that data with the e-mail itself as an attached bit of data. Once the endpoint e-mail client receives the message, the new headers tell it that there is an attached document (or documents) embedded within the e-mail message, and the client can properly decode and display the document. (RFC 2045 through RFC 2049 define MIME and its composition.)

Let's take a look at the headers that must be used when MIME is used to attach a bit of information. There is one required field, MIME-Version, and several optional fields:

- *MIME-Version*: This required field indicates which version of MIME is being used (currently 1.0).
- *Content-type*: This field describes what format this part of the message is in, such as text, message, application, multipart, image, audio, and so on. The default type is ASCII text. A few common content types are text/plain, text/html, application/binary, application/postscript, image/gif, and image/jpeg.
- *Content-transfer encoding*: This header tells how to decode the message. There are a few different encoding schemes that may be used. Base-64 encoding is used to encode binary data in 7-bit ASCII data. 7-bit is no encoding, case insensitive. 8-bit is no encoding. Binary also is no encoding. X-token is a proprietary encoding designation. The *x* designates that this is a nonstandard status encoding scheme. This simply means that the content is not encoded with a standardized coding scheme, which in most cases is bad, as it doesn't fall into interoperability guidelines.
- *Content-ID*: This field allows one body to refer to another. It's similar to the Message-ID field (unique identifier in the e-mail message structure). Generally, this field is optional.
- *Content-description*: A textual description about the encoded data. For example, an image content type might contain the description "a picture of the moon."
- *Content-disposition*: This field is used to tell the e-mail client if the content should be displayed inline with the message or as an attachment to the message. There is a parameter called Filename that is a suggestion for a name if the encoded data is detached from the mail message.

The following is a typical mail message that includes a MIME attachment:

```
From: krowczyk@i-netway.com (Andrew Krowczyk)
Subject: Sample message with Word Document Attachment
To: mailto:editor@apress.com
MIME-version: 1.0
Content-type: MULTIPART/MIXED;
BOUNDARY=
"Boundary_[ID_nf991kyavAuSo/HeKKQ]"—Boundary_[ID_nf991kyavAuSo/HeKKQ]
Content-type: text/plain; charset=us-ascii
Hi, please see the attached Word Document.
-Andy—Boundary_[ID_nf991kyavAuSo/HeKKQ]
Date: Thu, 08 Jan 2004 16:43:34 -0700
Content-type: application/mac-binhex40; name=sample_worddoc.doc
Content-disposition: attachment; filename=sample_worddoc.doc
PGh0bWw+DQo8aGVhZD4NCjx0aXRsZT6q967mpcC/y7hgrKGwyjwvdGl0bGU+DQo8bWV0YSBodHRw
LWVxdWl2PSJDb250ZW50LVR5cGUiIGNvbnRlbnQ9InRleHQvaHRtbDsgY2hhcnNldD1iaWc1Ij4N
CjxsaW5rIHJlbD0ic3R5bGVzaGVldCIgaHJlZj0iaHR0cDovL3d3dy5raW5nLmNvbS50dy9wbS5j
c3MiIHR5cGU9InRleHQvY3NzIj4NCjwvaGVhZD4NCjxzY3JpcHQgbGFuZ3VhZ2U9IkphdmFTY3Jp
cHQiPg0KZnVuY3Rpb24gZ290b3VybChkaXl0eXBlKSB7DQogdmFyIHB3PXdpbmRvdy5vcGVuKCdo
```

As you can see, the MIME sections and headers define the message boundaries and the binary content. For brevity, we've left out the actual binary encoding of the document. It would look like a bunch of garbled data in ASCII characters.

Later in the chapter, we'll look at an example of sending e-mail messages that include attachments from a .NET application.

Now that you've seen what happens when you send e-mail, we'll look at the protocols and methods for retrieving e-mail messages.

Retrieving Client/Server E-mail

In general, you can think about how e-mail messages are retrieved from mail server message stores as a client/server relationship. You use an e-mail client, such as Microsoft Outlook, Lotus Notes, or another mail package to retrieve messages from a central mail server mailbox. There are also Web-based e-mail services such as Hotmail that follow along the same lines.

There are generally three models of e-mail handling:

- *Offline (POP3 model)*: The client connects to the mail server and pulls or retrieves e-mail down to the client. In this instance, all the mail is stored on the client machine, not the server. Usually, e-mail is deleted from the server once it's retrieved, although some mail clients offer the ability to leave messages on the server.
- *Online (original IMAP model)*: The client application connects to the server for every transaction. Everything is stored on the server.
- *Disconnected (later IMAP model)*: The client and server share the storage of messages. The server is always correct, and the client application must synchronize the list of messages with the server.

One of the most important points to note is that POP and IMAP only *get* the mail messages from the server's mailbox. As with all e-mail transactions, sending mail requires the use of SMTP. In the next few sections, we'll look at using the POP and IMAP protocols for retrieving e-mail.

POP3

POP3 (outlined in RFC 1939) allows you to write nice-looking graphical user interface (GUI) applications that will present e-mail in a way that's easy to read and manage.

■ **NOTE** Actually, a few versions of POP have been around. The POP2 and POP3 standards are not even compatible from a protocol standpoint. Since the huge majority of POP clients are POP3, we'll restrict our discussion to that protocol.

In the POP3 world, the mail exists on the mail server when it's received by the system. It just sits there, waiting to be picked up by a mail client. Once you connect to the mail server with a client mail program, the POP3 client copies the mail from the server to the local machine's hard drive, as illustrated in Figure 11-6. This method locks you into reading the mail on the client machine, which might not be ideal.

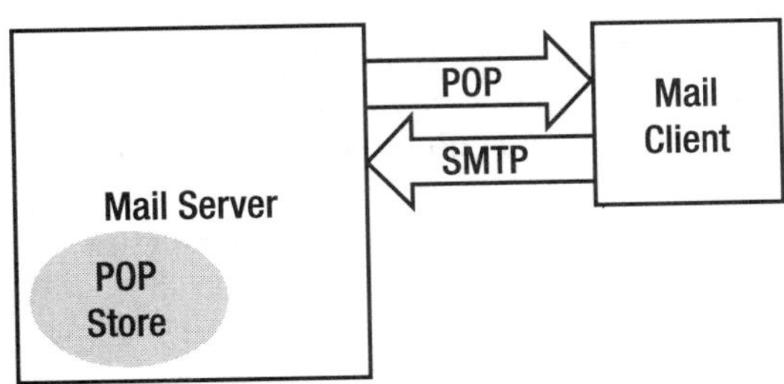

Figure 11-6. *POP3 e-mail retrieval*

For instance, suppose you have a mail account that you read both at work and at home. Let's suppose that you have Microsoft Outlook installed on both your office and home machines. If you connect at the office and Outlook downloads four new mail messages, those messages will generally be removed from the server and transported to the local hard drive on the office machine. This means that you've lost access to those messages from your home machine. Because POP3 moves the messages from the server to your client machine, sharing a POP3 e-mail system between multiple machines can be troublesome.

The following example demonstrates using POP3 over telnet, which shows the procedures that allow you to access a typical POP3 mailbox on a mail server. The internal methods used in the .NET C# `System.Web.Mail` namespace (discussed later in this chapter) would do something very similar to this while retrieving messages using the POP3 protocol. Although most of this is abstracted away by the .NET runtime components, it's interesting to see what happens behind the scenes.

```
open mail.i-netway.com 110
Trying. . . Connected to MAIL.I-NETWAY.COM
+OK test.someserver.COM MultiNet POP3 Server Process v4.0(1) at Mon 08-Jan-2004
3:21PM-CST
user krowczyk                                  // designate user
+OK User Name (krowczyk) ok. Password, please.
pass thisismypassword                          // enter password
+OK 3 messages in folder INBOX (V4.0)
list 2                                         // list gives message size
+OK 2 7124                                     // in bytes
stat                                           // stat gives total message
+OK 3 14749                                    // size in bytes
quit
+OK POP# MultiNet test.i-netway.COM Server exiting (3 INBOX messages left)
Connection closed by Foreign Host
```

A typical POP session consists of a client connecting to the POP3 server on TCP port 110 (the default). Once the client is connected, the POP3 server sends back a connection greeting message that acknowledges the connection and starts the POP3 session. Commands are then issued and responded to by the client and server, until the connection has been closed and the session ends.

POP3 commands consist of a keyword optionally followed by arguments. Some of the specifics for commands are as follows:

- Commands are terminated by a CRLF sequence.
- Keywords are separated by a space character.
- Keywords are three or four characters long.
- Each argument may be up to 40 characters in length.
- Responses may be up to 512 characters in length.
- `+OK` designates a positive response.
- `-ERR` designates a negative response or an error condition.

Table 11-3 summarizes the POP3 commands.

Table 11-3. *POP3 Commands*

Command	Description
`USER [name]`	User name sent to the server. This command is required.
`PASS [password]`	The password. This command is required.
`QUIT`	Terminates or ends the current session. This command is required.
`DELE [msg]`	Deletes mail from the server. This command is required.
`RSET`	Undoes any changes made during the current session. This command is required.
`STAT`	Returns the number of messages on the server. This command is required.
`RETR [msg]`	Retrieves the content of a message. This command is required.
`LIST [msg]`	Returns information about the message in parameter, such as size in bytes. If no parameter is given, a list with all messages and their sizes is returned. This command is required.
`NOOP`	Does nothing but cause the server to respond with a positive response. This command is required.
`TOP [msg] [n]`	The server sends the headers of the message, the blank line separating the headers from the body, and then the number of lines of the indicated message's body. *[msg]* is the message number desired. *[n]* specifies the top *n* lines to be retrieved. This command is optional.
`UIDL [msg]`	Called a "unique ID listing" for the message selected. If an argument is given, the server issues a positive response with a line containing information about the specified message. The unique ID of a message is an arbitrary server-determined string, consisting of 1 to 70 characters in the range 0x21 to 0x7E, which uniquely identifies a message within a mail drop. This command is optional.
`APOP [mailbox] [digest]`	A string identifying a mailbox and a MD5 digest string. The MD5 algo rithm takes a message of arbitrary length as an input and produces a 128-bit fingerprint message digest of the input. It is typically used within RSA cryptography and such. This command is optional.

POP3 provides basic functionality for retrieving messages from a mail server. It serves its purpose very well, and it is pretty much the standard that the majority of mail servers and clients use.

IMAP

IMAP (outlined and documented in RFC 2060) gives you everything that POP3 doesn't provide. You can use it for online, offline, or disconnected modes of operation. It allows you to control folders on both the client machine and the server. It also provides enhanced authentication (POP3 authentication is relatively weak). And it allows the use of multiple mail servers that can work together with the same mail client. Figure 11-7 shows an example of how an IMAP client and servers might interact.

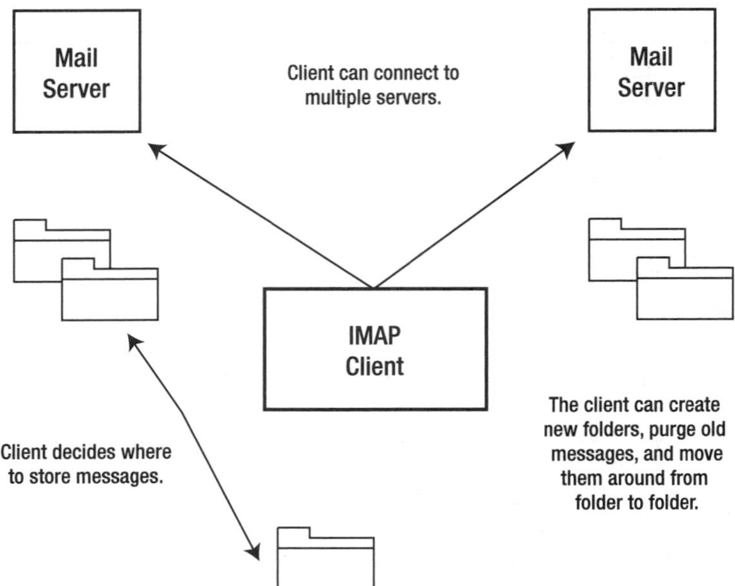

Figure 11-7. *IMAP e-mail retrieval*

The following are some of IMAP's features:

- *Server-side mailbox manipulation*: IMAP offers the ability to add messages to a remote mailbox. It also provides support for and notification of simultaneous updates in shared mailboxes, as well as new mail notification.
- *Multiple mailbox support*: IMAP allows remote folder management, including list, create, delete, and rename capabilities. It provides support for folder hierarchies. It also allows access to message types other than e-mail, such as NetNews.
- *Online performance optimization*: IMAP lets you determine the message structure without downloading the entire message. It also allows selected retrieval of MIME body parts, and offers server-based search and retrieval to minimize data transfer.
- *Roaming power user support*: Shared folders overcome the limitations of POP3 access on more than one machine. Also, performance optimization helps with slow mail server connections.

Although IMAP offers much more advanced functionality than POP3, you'll find that many of the e-mail users and clients in the world use POP3 servers for mail retrieval. IMAP is often much more complex to implement than POP3. For offline processing mode, POP3 and IMAP have almost equivalent possibilities, but for online or disconnected processing mode, IMAP is clearly superior. However, because of POP3's inherent simplicity, our examples in this chapter will use that protocol.

Now that you've had an overview of the e-mail protocols, we can get to the interesting part: exchanging e-mail with .NET applications.

.NET Support for E-Mail Exchange

In your past life (when you programmed without .NET), you may have used CDONTS to send e-mail within your applications. This was commonly done from within both ASP and Visual Basic. There were often third-party ActiveX components that took the place of CDONTS and made sending e-mail a bit easier than dealing with Microsoft's confusing objects.

In .NET, Microsoft has wrapped up all the SMTP e-mail functionality and rolled it directly into the .NET Framework under the `System.Web.Mail` namespace. Using the classes within this namespace, you can easily construct and send mail, with attachments if desired, using the SMTP service built into Internet Information Server (IIS).

The System.Web.Mail Namespace

Using the `System.Web.Mail` namespace actually allows you to send messages using the Collaboration Data Objects for Windows 2000 (CDOSYS) message component. In fact, .NET simply wraps the functionality of the underlying messaging components. This allows the e-mail messages to be delivered either through the SMTP mail service built into Windows 2000 or through an arbitrary SMTP server.

■ **TIP** If you need a component that contains more functionality than the `System.Web.Mail` namespace, you can take a look at the following components: EasyMail.NET (`http://www.quiksoft.com/emdotnet`), aspNetEmail (`http://www.aspnetemail.com`), and Smtp.NET (`http://www.exclamationsoft.com/exclamationsoft/smtp.net/default.asp`). EasyMail.net also provides a very nice parsing library and IMAP capabilities.

The `System.Web.Mail` namespace contains three classes and three enumerations, as shown in Table 11-4.

Table 11-4. *System.Web.Mail Classes and Enumerations*

Class/Enumeration	Description
`MailAttachment`	A class that represents the attachments of an e-mail
`MailMessage`	A class that represents the e-mail message itself
`SmtpMail`	A class that is responsible for sending a `MailMessage` via SMTP
`MailEncoding`	An enumeration that specifies the encoding of the message: `Base64` or `UUEncode`
`MailFormat`	An enumeration that specifies the format of the message: `HTML` or `Text`
`MailPriority`	An enumeration that specifies the priority of the message: `High`, `Normal`, or `Low`

Constructing a MailMessage Object

Sending a message using the `System.Web.Mail` namespace requires you to first construct a `MailMessage` object to represent the e-mail. Once you've set the properties of this object and populated it with the details of the e-mail message, you send it using the `SmtpMail` class. You are most likely to use the properties listed in Table 11-5 when initializing a `MailMessage` object.

Table 11-5. *Common MailMessage Properties*

Property	Description
`Attachments`	The list of attachments (`MailAttachment` objects) that are transmitted with the e-mail
`Bcc`	A semicolon-delimited list of e-mail addresses that receive a blind carbon copy (bcc) copy of the e-mail
`Body`	The body of the e-mail
`BodyEncoding`	Sets the encoding type of the body of the e-mail message
`BodyFormat`	Specifies the `MailFormat` of the e-mail: `MailFormat.Text` or `MailFormat.Html`
`Cc`	A semicolon-delimited list of e-mail addresses that receive a carbon copy (cc) of the e-mail
`From`	The e-mail address of the sender
`Priority`	Specifies the `MailPriority` of the e-mail
`Subject`	The subject of the e-mail
`To`	The e-mail address of the recipient
`UrlContentBase`	Gets or sets the `Content-Base` HTTP header, the URL base of all relative URLs used in an HTML body
`UrlContentLocation`	Gets or sets the `Content-Location` HTTP header for the e-mail message
`Headers`	Read-only property that consists of the list of custom headers to be trans mitted with the message

The first step in constructing a `MailMessage` object is to set a reference to the `System.Web.dll` assembly, since the `System.Web` and `System.Web.Mail` namespaces aren't available until the reference is set. Figure 11-8 shows this procedure.

After you have added the reference to `System.Web.dll`, you can include it in a `using` statement and instantiate your `MailMessage` object:

```
using System.Web.Mail;
// Create a mail message object
MailMessage email = new MailMessage();
```

Next, you can set up a few properties of the e-mail:

```
// Set message parameters
email.From = "someone@someone.com";
email.To = "krowczyk@i-netway.com";
```

```
email.Subject = "Test message using SmtpMail";
email.BodyFormat = MailFormat.Text;
email.Body = "This is just a test message";
```

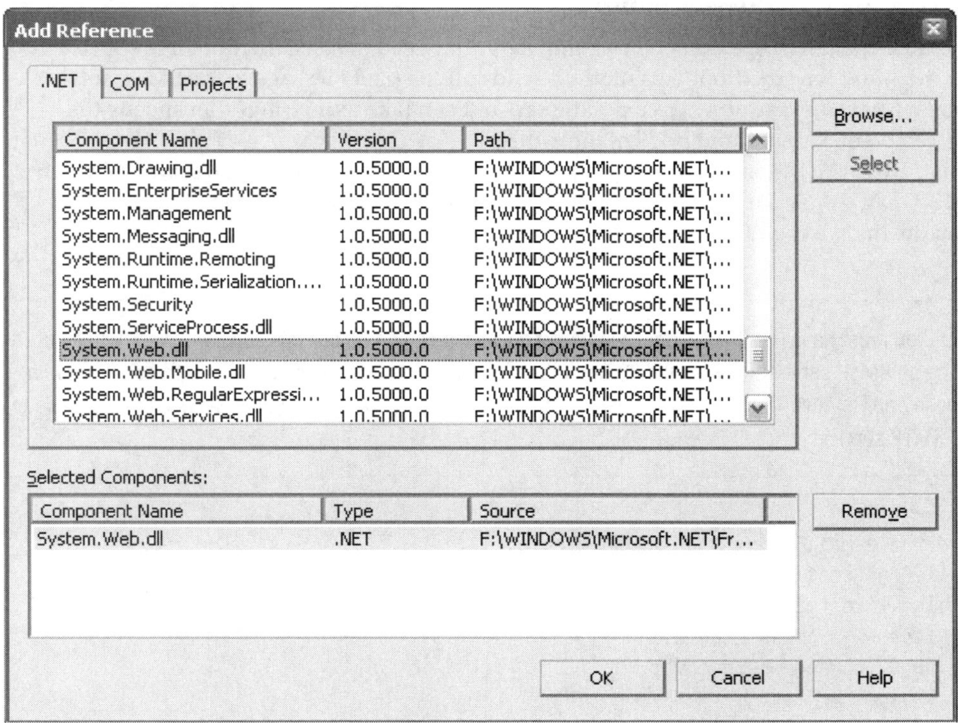

Figure 11-8. *Adding a reference to System.Web.dll*

Adding an Attachment

Adding an attachment is as easy as creating one or more `MailAttachment` objects and adding them to the `Attachments` list of the `MailMessage` object. The `MailAttachment` class has two properties:

- `Encoding` is the type of encoding for the e-mail attachment. This can be either `MailEncoding.Base64` or `MailEncoding.UUEncode`.
- `Filename` is the name of the attachment file.

You can add an attachment calling the `Add` method of the `Attachments` collection, passing in the path of the file that you want to attach to the mail and the `MailEncoding` to use:

```
email.Attachments.Add(new MailAttachment(@"c:\testfile.txt", MailEncoding.Base64));
```

You can add any number of attachments to the e-mail message in this way by continuing to add MailAttachment objects to the Attachments list of the MailMessage.

Sending an E-mail Message

To send an e-mail message that you've composed, you need to call a method of the SmtpMail object: the static Send method. This method sends off the mail message to the SMTP server. It can take a MailMessage object as a parameter, or it can take four strings that specify the sender, recipient, subject, and body of the e-mail.

The SmtpMail class also has one public property: SmtpServer. This is the server to which the SMTP mail should be sent. If this property is not set, the SmtpMail object defaults to sending the mail to the Windows SMTP service for delivery.

■ NOTE You must have the SMTP service installed on your machine before this code will work when not specifying an SMTP server. To install the IIS SMTP service, open the Control Panel's Add Remove Programs and choose Add Remove Windows Components. Then select the Internet Information Services and choose to add the SMTP service.

```
// Send the e-mail using the SmtpMail object
SmtpMail.Send(email);
// Or also like this - without a mail message object
string from = "from@somewhere.com";
string to = "to@somewhere.com";
string subject = "test";
string body = "test message";
SmtpMail.Send (from, to, subject, body);
```

As noted, if you don't set the SmtpServer property, the e-mail will be sent via the Windows SMTP service. To set the SmtpServer property, you can just use the following code:

```
// For example, here we want to set the SMTP server field before sending the mail
// message
SmtpMail.SmtpServer = "mail.testserver.com";
// Now send message as we did before
SmtpMail.Send(email);
```

These code snippets have shown the various parts of sending e-mail using the SMTP capabilities of .NET. Now we'll look at a sample application that ties it all together.

Creating an SMTP Mail Application

In this section, we'll create a sample SMTP mail application. It's a simple .NET Windows Form application that allows us to set various properties of an e-mail and send it using a designated SMTP server.

Figure 11-9 depicts the end result of the code we're going to cover. The form has five single-line text boxes, where the user can enter the name of the SMTP server to use, the e-mail addresses of the sender and recipient, the subject of the mail, and the path to any attachment to send with the mail. There is also a multiline text box, where the body of the mail can be typed.

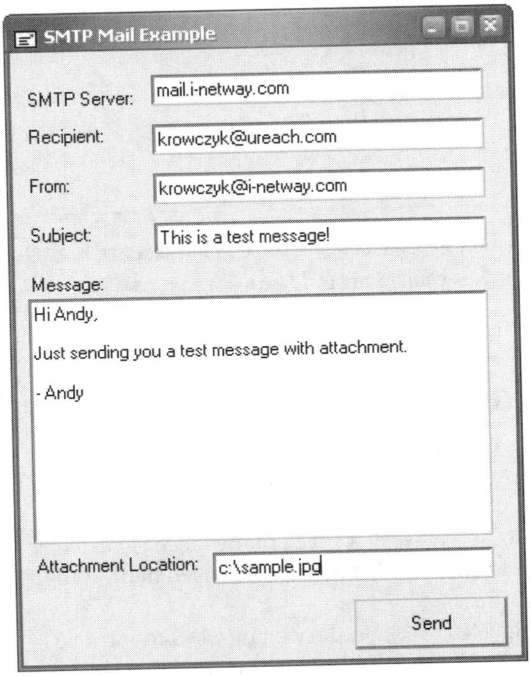

Figure 11-9. *The sample SMTP application*

There is really no magic to writing this sort of simple application. We basically just create a form with appropriate text boxes and enter some code in the `Click` event handler for the Send button that uses the SMTP mail capabilities we've been looking at to send the mail on its way.

First, add a reference to the `System.Web.dll` assembly, and add a `using` directive to point to the `System.Web.Mail` namespace. Apart from the standard Windows code (generated by Visual Studio .NET), we need to add only the code behind the Send button. This is very similar to the code you've already seen:

```
private void button1_Click(object sender, System.EventArgs e)
{
   // Create mail message
   MailMessage email = new MailMessage();
   // Set message parameters
   email.From = txtFrom.Text;
   email.To = txtRecipient.Text;
   email.Subject = txtSubject.Text;
   email.BodyFormat = System.Web.Mail.MailFormat.Text;
   email.Body = txtMessage.Text;
```

```
    // Add attachment
    if(txtMessage.Text != "")
        email.Attachments.Add(new MailAttachment(txtAttachment.Text,
                                        MailEncoding.Base64));
    // Set SMTP server
    SmtpMail.SmtpServer = txtSmtpServer.Text;
    // Now send message
    SmtpMail.Send(email);
}
```

■ **NOTE** The code for this application, and the other sample applications presented in this chapter, is available with this book's downloadable code, in the Downloads section of `http://www.apress.com`.

Creating a POP3 Application

If you've had any experience with .NET mail programming or development, you probably know that .NET doesn't provide inherent support for retrieving mail from POP3 and IMAP mailboxes. We've already covered the SMTP component of the .NET Framework that allows you to send e-mail. We have also mentioned that the `System.Web.Mail` namespace is basically just a wrapper for the CDOSYS component. This unmanaged component is used behind the scenes to send e-mail.

So how do we retrieve e-mail messages using .NET? We could try using CDO to retrieve mail, but that will work only for Microsoft Exchange Servers, and not all the mail servers out there are based on Exchange! What we really want to do, considering that this is a book about networking, is to code our own POP3 e-mail class that uses the POP3 protocol to retrieve e-mail. We'll use some of the networking namespaces that exist in .NET to accomplish this goal.

Creating a POP3 C# Class

Our first task in creating a class that handles POP3 messages is to determine what exactly makes up a message.

First, create a new Visual C# Windows Application project called `POPMail`. For this project, we'll create a class that represents the core of a POP3 e-mail message, so add a new class to the project called `POP3EmailMessage`:

```
public class POP3EmailMessage
{
   // Define public members
   public long msgNumber;
   public long msgSize;
   public bool msgReceived;
   public string msgContent;
}
```

This class contains a message number, the size of the message (in bytes), a flag indicating whether the message has been received from the server, and a string containing the actual content of the e-mail message. As explained earlier in the chapter, these fields are common within a typical e-mail message and are used when retrieving a message. For example, we need an index (`msgNumber`) to the message that we want to deal with when listing or retrieving from the POP3 server.

As you've seen in the past few chapters, the .NET Framework provides a rich base of classes to deal with low-level networking needs. In our case, we want to harness the `TcpClient` class, because we will make remote connections to the mail server using TCP. We will therefore create a class that is derived from the `System.Net.Sockets.TcpClient` namespace:

```
// Define the POP3 class
public class POP3 : System.Net.Sockets.TcpClient
{
```

Connecting to a Server

There are a few things that this class must be able to do, the first of which is connect to the POP3 server, passing in a user name and password. (What we're doing here is similar to the process you saw earlier in the telnet session shown in our discussion of the POP3 protocol.)

So, let's start by writing a `ConnectPOP` method. This takes three parameters: the name of the server to connect to, and the user name and password of the mailbox we want to access.

```
public void ConnectPOP(string sServerName, string sUserName, string sPassword)
{
   // Message and the server resulting response
   string sMessage;
   string sResult;
   // Call the connect method of the TcpClient class
   // Remember default port for server is 110
   Connect(sServerName, 110);
   // Get result back
   sResult = Response();
   // Check response to make sure it's +OK
   if (sResult.Substring(0,3) != "+OK")
      throw new POPException(sResult);
   // Got past connect, send username
   sMessage = "USER " + sUserName + "\r\n";
   // Write() sends data to the Tcp Connection
   Write(sMessage);
   sResult = Response();
   // Check response
   if (sResult.Substring(0,3) != "+OK")
   {
      throw new POPException(sResult);
   }
   // Now follow up with sending password in same manner
   sMessage = "PASS " + sPassword + "\r\n";
```

```
    Write(sMessage);
    sResult = Response();
    if (sResult.Substring(0,3) != "+OK")
       throw new POPException(sResult);
}
```

We connect to the POP3 server and send the user name and password using the Connect method of the TcpClient class and our methods Write and Response. As you saw in the POP3 telnet session shown earlier in the chapter, the POP3 server should send back an +OK response if we are successful, or an -ERR message if a failure occurs. If this happens, we throw an exception using the message sent back from the server.

Disconnecting from a Server

Since we're talking about connecting, we may as well also show the disconnect method now. To disconnect from the server, we simply need to issue the QUIT command. That makes our DisconnectPOP method really quite simple:

```
public void DisconnectPOP()
{
   string sMessage;
   string sResult;
   sMessage = "QUIT\r\n";
   Write(sMessage);
   sResult = Response();
   if (sResult.Substring(0,3) != "+OK")
      throw new POPException(sResult);
}
```

So far, we have a way to connect to the POP3 server, as well as a way to disconnect from it. The typical POP3 session will consist of a call to ConnectPOP, commands to get e-mail messages and so on, and then a call to DisconnectPOP.

Getting a List of Messages

We can get a list of messages in the POP3 inbox simply by issuing a LIST command to the server. The ListMessages method shows how we can do this.

■ NOTE In order to use the ArrayList, you must import the System.Collections namespace.

```
public ArrayList ListMessages()
{
   // Same sort of thing as in ConnectPOP and DisconnectPOP
   string sMessage;
   string sResult;
   ArrayList returnValue = new ArrayList();
```

```
    sMessage = "LIST\r\n";
    Write(sMessage);
    sResult = Response();
    if (sResult.Substring(0, 3) != "+OK")
       throw new POPException (sResult);
    while (true)
    {
       sResult = Response();
       if (sResult == ".\r\n")
       {
          return returnValue;
       }
       else
       {
          POP3EmailMessage oMailMessage = new POP3EmailMessage();
          // Define a separator
          char[] sep = { ' ' };
          // Use the split method to break out array of data
          string[] values = sResult.Split(sep);

          // Put data into oMailMessage object
          oMailMessage.msgNumber = Int32.Parse(values[0]);
          oMailMessage.msgSize = Int32.Parse(values[1]);
          oMailMessage.msgReceived = false;
          returnValue.Add(oMailMessage);
          continue;
       }
    }
}
```

As you saw in the telnet example, sending a `LIST` command to the POP3 server will cause the server to send back multiple lines of text. Each line represents an e-mail message that contains a message number and a number of bytes that the e-mail message contains. It's key to note that this method returns only an array of message objects that have very minimal data in them. The way that we receive more information and the message content is by creating a mirror of the `RETR` command that retrieves the actual message.

Retrieving a Specific Message

To retrieve a full message from the POP3 server, we need to issue the `RETR` command with the `msgNumber` of the message that we want to retrieve. This follows the same procedure as we described earlier:

```
public POP3EmailMessage RetrieveMessage(POP3EmailMessage msgRETR)
{
   string sMessage;
   string sResult;
   // Create new instance of object and set new values
```

```
    POP3EmailMessage oMailMessage = new POP3EmailMessage ();
    oMailMessage.msgSize = msgRETR.msgSize;
    oMailMessage.msgNumber = msgRETR.msgNumber;
    // Call the RETR command to get the appropriate message
    sMessage = "RETR " + msgRETR.msgNumber + "\r\n";
    Write(sMessage);
    sResult = Response();
    if (sResult.Substring(0, 3) != "+OK")
       throw new POPException (sResult);

    // Set the received flag equal to true since we got the message
    oMailMessage.msgReceived = true;
    // Now loop to get the message text until we hit the "." endpoint
    while (true)
    {
       sResult = Response();
       if (sResult == ".\r\n")
          break;
       else
          oMailMessage.msgContent = sResult;
    }
    return oMailMessage;
}
```

Deleting a Message

Since the POP3 protocol states that a message isn't deleted from the server when the message is retrieved, we need to call the DELE command explicitly to remove the message from the server. Writing that method is also quite simple:

```
public void DeleteMessage(POP3EmailMessage msgDELE)
{
   string sMessage;
   string sResult;
   sMessage = "DELE " + msgDELE.msgNumber + "\r\n";
   Write(sMessage);
   sResult = Response();
   if (sResult.Substring(0, 3) != "+OK")
      throw new POPException(sResult);
}
```

Writing the Message

The Write method takes a message as input and writes it out to the TCP network stream. This will, in effect, send our command to the POP3 server we are connected to. Since C# string data types cannot be directly buffered to the network stream, we must use the ASCIIEncoding class of the System.Text namespace to get the byte representation of the string data. Once this is done, we just write that out to the network stream:

```
private void Write(string sMessage)
{
   // Used for data encoding
   System.Text.ASCIIEncoding oEncodedData = new System.Text.ASCIIEncoding();
   // Now grab the message into a buffer for sending to the TCP network stream
   byte[] WriteBuffer = new byte[1024];
   WriteBuffer = oEncodedData.GetBytes(sMessage);
   // Take the buffer and output it to the TCP stream
   NetworkStream NetStream = GetStream();
   NetStream.Write(WriteBuffer, 0, WriteBuffer.Length);
}
```

Reading the Data

The flip side of the `Write` method is the `Response` method. This method allows us to read data back from the POP3 server connection. This is used throughout the class to grab the result codes sent back from the server in response to commands that we've sent with each `Write`. Again, we need to use the `ASCIIEncoding` class to get the string representation of the bytes being received across the network stream.

```
private string Response()
{
   System.Text.ASCIIEncoding oEncodedData = new System.Text.ASCIIEncoding();
   byte []ServerBuffer = new Byte[1024];
   NetworkStream NetStream = GetStream();
   int count = 0;
   // Here we read from the server network stream and place data into
   // the buffer (to later decode and return)
   while (true)
   {
     byte []buff = new Byte[2];
     int bytes = NetStream.Read( buff, 0, 1 );
     if (bytes == 1)
     {
        ServerBuffer[count] = buff[0];
        count++;
        if (buff[0] == '\n')
        {
            break;
         }
      }
      else
      {
         break;
      }
   }
   // Return the decoded ASCII string value
   string ReturnValue = oEncodedData.GetString(ServerBuffer, 0, count );
   return ReturnValue;
}
```

Creating a POP Exception

This class simply encapsulates an application exception that we may throw in our code:

```
namespace POPMailException
{
   public class POPException : System.ApplicationException
   {
      public POPException(string str) : base(str)
      {
      }
   }
}
```

Using the POP3 Class in an Application

The sample application adds a GUI front end to the POP3 class that we just wrote, but the basic use of this class can be seen by taking a look at the `Main` method of the console application, as shown here. This method steps through the items needed to instantiate the class and retrieve the message numbers and message text.

```
static void Main(string[] args)
{
   try
   {
      POP3 oPOP = new POP3();
      oPOP.ConnectPOP("mail.someserver.com", "username", "password");
      ArrayList MessageList = oPOP.ListMessages();
      foreach (POP3EmailMessage POPMsg in MessageList)
      {
         POP3EmailMessage POPMsgContent = oPOP.RetrieveMessage(POPMsg);
         System.Console.WriteLine("Message {0}: {1}",
         POPMsgContent.msgNumber, POPMsgContent.msgContent);
      }
      oPOP.DisconnectPOP();
   }
   catch ( POPException e )
   {
      System.Console.WriteLine(e.ToString());
   }
   catch ( System.Exception e)
   {
      System.Console.WriteLine(e.ToString());
   }
}
}
```

Figure 11-10 shows the sample PopMail application. It uses the POP3 class described in the previous sections to list the e-mail messages in the user's mailbox. The user can then retrieve the message text by inserting the number of the message to display. The entire message is then retrieved from the mailbox.

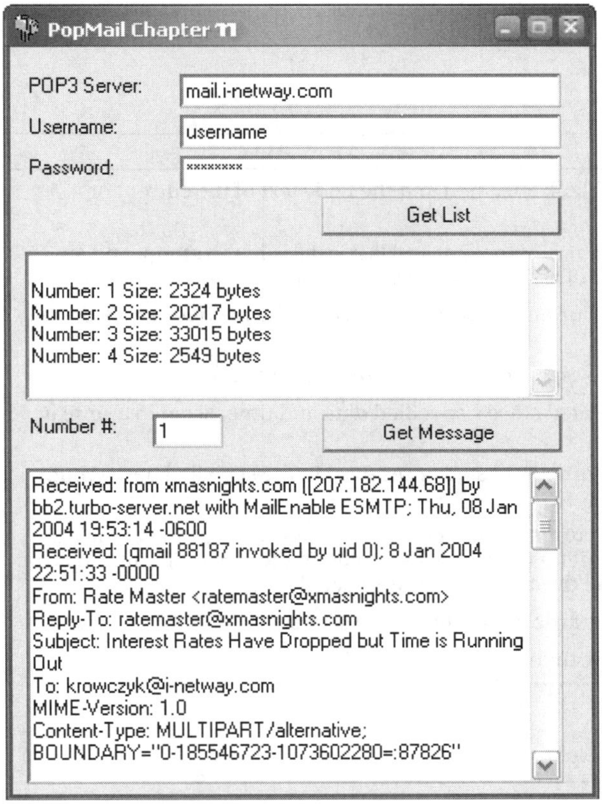

Figure 11-10. *The sample POP3 application*

■ **TIP** You could expand the `POP3EmailMessage` class to include much more functionality, using individual properties that describe the headers, subject, message, and so on. We made the class simple and tried to follow the same sort of design as you would see via logging in to a telnet session with the POP3 server, as this follows the design of the POP3 protocol and is easy to understand. There are also many popular third-party components that encapsulate this functionality very nicely. But what fun would buying one of those be?

Building an NNTP Application

The Network News Transport Protocol (NNTP, defined in RFC 977) is commonly used to access the content of newsgroups on the Internet. This protocol has been around for a while. It's a basic TCP network stream-based protocol, much like SMTP and other e-mail related protocols. Tables 11-6, 11-7, and 11-8 summarize NNTP commands, responses, and response codes.

Table 11-6. *Common NNTP Commands*

Command	Description
`ARTICLE`	Displays the header, a blank line, then and the body text of the current or specified article
`GROUP`	Returns the article numbers of the first and last articles in the group, and an estimate of the number of articles on file in the group
`LAST`	Internally maintained "current article pointer," set to the previous article in the current newsgroup
`LIST`	Returns a list of valid newsgroups and associated information
`NEWSGROUPS`	A list of newsgroups created since a specified data and time, listed in a similar format to `LIST`
`NEWNEWS`	A list of message IDs of articles posted or received in the specified newsgroup since the date specified
`NEXT`	Internally maintained "current article pointer," advanced to the next article in the current newsgroup (if no more articles remain in the current group, an error message is returned and the article remains selected)
`POST`	If posting is allowed, the article is posted to the server
`QUIT`	Closes the connection with the server

Table 11-7. *Digits That Compose NNTP Responses*

Response	Description
1*xx*	Informative message
2*xx*	Command OK
3*xx*	Command OK so far, send the rest of it
4*xx*	Command was correct, but couldn't be performed for some reason
5*xx*	Command unimplemented, or incorrect, or a serious program error occurred
*x*0*x*	Connection, setup, and miscellaneous messages
*x*1*x*	Newsgroup selection
*x*2*x*	Article selection
*x*3*x*	Distribution functions
*x*4*x*	Posting
*x*8*x*	Nonstandard (private implementation) extensions
*x*9*x*	Debugging output

Table 11-8. *Common NNTP Messages*

Message	Description
100	Help text
190 through 199	Debug output
200	Server ready—posting allowed
201	Server ready—no posting allowed
400	Service discontinued
500	Command not recognized
501	Command syntax error
502	Access restriction or permission denied
503	Program fault—command not performed

We'll briefly cover a class that encapsulates access to NNTP newsgroups and servers, which is based on and quite similar to the POP3 class that we described earlier. You'll see more specific responses and commands as we discuss the NNTP class in the following sections.

■ **NOTE** We won't go into more details about NNTP, since this chapter is primarily about .NET and e-mail access. If you would like more information about NNTP, refer to RFC 977, located at `http://www.ietf.org/rfc/rfc0977.txt?number=977`.

Creating an NNTP Class in C#

We derive the NNTP class from the same `System.Net.Sockets.TcpClient` class. First, we import the necessary namespaces:

```
using System;
using System.Net.Sockets;
using NNTPServerException;  // Our own exception class implementation
using System.Collections;
```

Connecting to the Server

As in the POP3 client, inheriting from the `TcpClient` gives us a wealth of functionality that we don't need to implement ourselves, such as the network transfer layers responsible for connecting to the server and allowing us to send data across the network stream.

```
public class NNTP : System.Net.Sockets.TcpClient
```

Our `ConnectNNTP` method simply calls the `TcpClient`'s `Connect` method, passing in the server name as well as the standard port number (119) for the NNTP server connection:

```
public void ConnectNNTP(string sServer)
{
   string sResult;
```

```
    // Connect to the server on the default port #119
    Connect(sServer, 119);
    sResult = Response();
    // In this case, a response code of 200 is an OK response
    if (sResult.Substring(0, 3) != "200")
        throw new NNTPException(sResult);
}
```

Disconnecting from the Server

Again, if we write a connect function, we must write a disconnect function. This simply sends the `QUIT` command to the NNTP server:

```
public void DisconnectNNTP()
{
    string sMessage;
    string sResult;
    // Send the QUIT command
    sMessage = "QUIT\r\n";
    Write(sMessage);
    sResult = Response();
    // We expect a code of 205 acknowledging the quit
    if (sResult.Substring( 0, 3) != "205")
        throw new NNTPException(sResult);
}
```

Getting the Newsgroups

As you might imagine, calling `GetNewsGroupListing` in our class will use the `LIST` command to return all of the groups that are available on the NNTP server. This may be a lot, depending on the server.

```
public ArrayList GetNewsGroupListing()
{
    string sMessage;
    string sResult;
    // Create an array for the return values
    ArrayList ReturnValue = new ArrayList();

    sMessage = "LIST\r\n";
    Write(sMessage);

    // Check the response, if OK continue
    sResult = Response();
    if (sResult.Substring(0, 3) != "215")
        throw new NNTPException(sResult);
    // While there are more results, loop and append to output array list
    while (true)
    {
```

```
      sResult = Response();
      if (sResult == ".\r\n" || sResult == ".\n")
      {
         return ReturnValue;
      }
      else
      {
         char[] separator = { ' ' };
         string[] values = sResult.Split(separator);
         ReturnValue.Add(values[0]);
         continue;
      }
   }
}
```

Getting News from a Group

To get the news from a specific newsgroup that is listed on the NNTP server, we simply need to create a method that calls the GROUP command, passing in the name of the newsgroup for which we want to retrieve the messages:

```
public ArrayList GetNews(string sNewsGroup)
{
   string sMessage;
   string sResult;
   ArrayList ReturnValue = new ArrayList();
   sMessage = "GROUP " + sNewsGroup + "\r\n";

   // Write the message to the server
   Write(sMessage);
   sResult = Response();

   // Check for successful operation
   if (sResult.Substring(0, 3) != "211")
      throw new NNTPException(sResult);
   char[] separator = { ' ' };
   string[] values = sResult.Split(separator);
   // For beginning and end
   long begin = Int32.Parse(values[2]);
   long end = Int32.Parse(values[3]);
   if (begin + 100 < end && end > 100)
      begin = end - 100;
   for (long i = begin; i<end; i++)
   {
      sMessage = "ARTICLE " + i + "\r\n";
      Write(sMessage);
      sResult = Response();
      if (sResult.Substring( 0, 3) == "423")
```

```
            continue;
        if (sResult.Substring( 0, 3) != "220")
            throw new NNTPException(sResult);
        string sArticle = "";
        while (true)
        {
            sResult = Response();
            if (sResult == ".\r\n")
                break;
            if (sResult == ".\n")
                break;
            if (sArticle.Length < 1024)
                sArticle += sResult;
        }
        ReturnValue.Add(sArticle);
    }
    return ReturnValue;
}
```

Posting to a Group

Posting to a newsgroup is also an easy task. It consists of simply calling the POST command with the name of the newsgroup, followed by the headers and the body of the message we want to post:

```
public void PostMessage(string sNewsGroup, string sSubject, string sFrom,
                        string sContent)
{
    string sMessage;
    string sResult;
    sMessage = "POST " + sNewsGroup + "\r\n";

    Write(sMessage);
    sResult = Response();
    if (sResult.Substring( 0, 3) != "340")
        throw new NNTPException(sResult);
    // Build message
    sMessage = "From: " + sFrom + "\r\n"
            + "Newsgroups: " + sNewsGroup + "\r\n"
            + "Subject: " + sSubject + "\r\n\r\n"
            + sContent + "\r\n.\r\n";
    Write(sMessage);
    sResult = Response();
    if (sResult.Substring( 0, 3) != "240")
        throw new NNTPException(sResult);
}
```

Writing and Reading the Data

Again, due to the encoding/decoding that must take place to allow the C# `string` type to be transported in bytes over the network stream, we need to come up with our own method that writes the data in a memory buffer to the server:

```
private void Write(string sMessage)
{
   System.Text.ASCIIEncoding oEncode = new System.Text.ASCIIEncoding();
   byte[] WriteBuffer = new byte[1024];
   WriteBuffer = oEncode.GetBytes(sMessage);
   NetworkStream oNetworkStream = GetStream();
   oNetworkStream.Write(WriteBuffer, 0, WriteBuffer.Length);
}
```

We also need to transform the data coming back from the server to an appropriate string format for our class representation:

```
private string Response()
{
   System.Text.ASCIIEncoding oEncode = new System.Text.ASCIIEncoding();
   byte []ServerBuffer = new Byte[1024];
   NetworkStream oNetworkStream = GetStream();
   int count = 0;
   while (true)
   {
      byte []LocalBuffer = new Byte[2];
      int bytes = oNetworkStream.Read(LocalBuffer, 0, 1);
      if (bytes == 1)
      {
         ServerBuffer[count] = LocalBuffer[0];
         count++;
         if (LocalBuffer[0] == '\n')
            break;
      }
      else
         break;
      string ReturnValue = oEncode.GetString(ServerBuffer, 0, count);
      return ReturnValue;
   }
}
```

Defining an NNTP Exception

Again, we define our own exception class for NNTP errors:

```
namespace NNTPServerException
{
   public class NNTPException : System.ApplicationException
   {
```

```
    public NNTPException(string str) : base(str)
    {
    }
}
```

Using the NNTP Class in an Application

Using the NNTP class is quite straightforward, as you can see from the following code (as with the POP3 example, the code shows the Main method for a simple console application). This takes you through the use of the different methods in the class.

```
static void Main(string[] args)
{
   try
   {
      // Create NNTP object
      NNTP oNNTP = new NNTP();
      // Connect to a server
      oNNTP.ConnectNNTP("news.testserver.com");
      // Get a list of newsgroups for the server
      ArrayList NewsGroupList = oNNTP.GetNewsGroupListing();
      foreach (string NewsGroupEntry in NewsGroupList)
         System.Console.WriteLine("Newsgroup :{0}", NewsGroupEntry);
      // Now let's get the news for an article called "this article"
      NewsGroupList = oNNTP.GetNews("msnews.microsoft.com");
      foreach (string sArticle in NewsGroupList)
         System.Console.WriteLine("{0}", sArticle);
      oNNTP.PostMessage("test", "test", "test@test.com (Test User)",
                        "test");
      oNNTP.DisconnectNNTP();
   }
   catch (NNTPException e)
   {
      System.Console.WriteLine(e.ToString());
   }
   catch (System.Exception)
   {
      System.Console.WriteLine("Unhandled Exception");
   }
}
```

The sample NNTP application you'll find with this book's downloadable code works much like the POPMail sample that you saw earlier. It follows the basic structure of the POPMail sample, but instead uses our NNTP class to retrieve posting from newsgroups. Figure 11-11 shows the NNTP sample application.

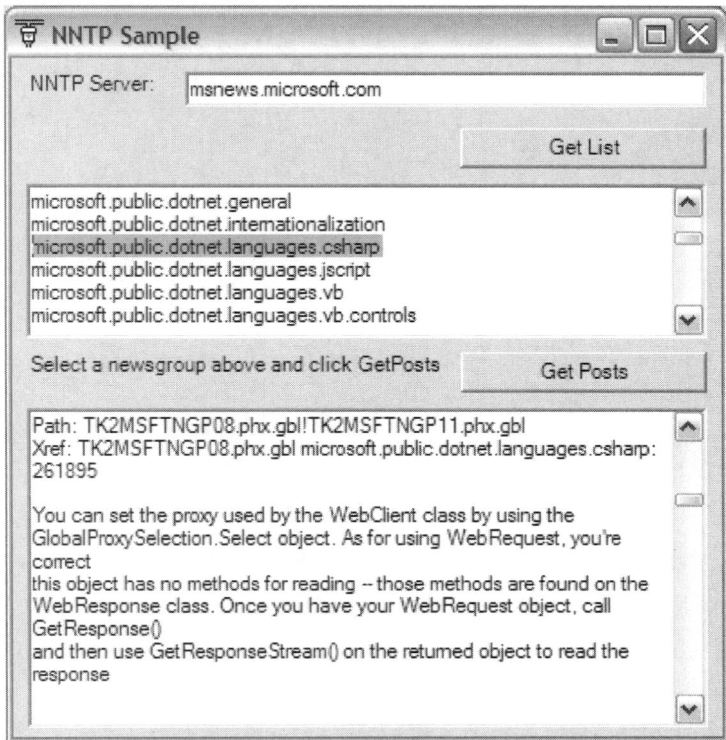

Figure 11-11. *The NNTP sample application*

■ **TIP** As with any bit of code, there is always room for improvement. The same improvements could be made for the NNTP class as for the POP3 class. Creating a better object representation of the NNTP message would be a place to start, as well as adding behind-the-scenes implementations of message retrieval and navigation. That would avoid any client applications needing to explicitly function at the protocol level to work with the newsgroups.

Summary

In this chapter, we covered the basics of the SMTP, POP3, IMAP, and NNTP protocols and saw how those protocols worked together in sending and receiving e-mail messages over the Internet. We also took a deeper look and presented sample code to send e-mail via the .NET Framework's built-in classes for transporting e-mail messages via SMTP, as well as developing some grassroots protocol implementation classes for POP3 and NNTP.

The IMAP and MIME protocols are deep and complex protocols. Implementing their functionality in .NET is not as easy as with POP3 and NNTP. Fortunately, third-party tools are available that allow you to use these protocols in .NET. For production use, using one of the third-party controls is an economical option.

CHAPTER 12

Cryptography in .NET

Every year computer crime increases dramatically, and it is always a challenge to keep up with the hackers. The `System.Security.Cryptography` namespace of the .NET Framework provides programmatic access to the variety of cryptographic services that we can incorporate into our applications to encrypt and decrypt data, ensure data integrity, and handle digital signatures and certificates. In this chapter, we'll explore the `System.Security.Cryptography` namespace so that we can utilize the cryptographic services in our applications.

In addition to our coverage of the `System.Security.Cryptography` namespace, we'll take a look at the following:

- A brief history of cryptography, just what it is, and why you might want to use it
- The three types of cryptographic algorithms and how they work
- Hashing with .NET
- Symmetric and asymmetric transformation with .NET
- How an X509 certificate is read
- How cryptography ties into network programming

Let's not waste another minute—let's dive right into the exciting world of cryptography!

History of Cryptography

Cryptography is the art and science of secret writing (encrypting and decrypting information). The term "cryptography" is originally derived from the two Greek words, "kryptos" and "graph," meaning hidden and writing. Much of cryptography is math oriented and uses patterns and algorithms to encrypt messages and other forms of communication. Cryptography is a branch of mathematics, and is a combination of *cryptology* and *cryptanalysis* studies.

NOTE *Cryptology* is the science of coding and decoding secret messages, which is concerned with "breaking" cryptosystems, or deciphering messages without prior detailed knowledge of the cryptosystem. *Cryptanalysis* is the flip-side of cryptography: it is the science of cracking codes, decoding secrets, violating authentication schemes, and in general breaking cryptographic protocols.

Historically, the use of cryptography dates back to 1900 BC when a scribe in Egypt first used a derivation of the standard hieroglyphics of the day to communicate ("Cryptography Timeline" by Carl Ellison). Fast-forward thousands of years, and in the late 1970s, Dr. Horst Feistel of IBM Research Laboratory creates the precursor of the famous Data Encryption Standard (DES) algorithm. Until 1998, the US government had tough restrictions preventing US companies exporting cryptographic software; that restriction was eased in 1998.

What Is Cryptography?

Cryptography is all about converting plaintext or clear text into cipher text through a process known as *encryption*. The cipher text is converted back to plaintext or clear text by the opposite process called decryption. Figure 12-1 illustrates the general process of cryptography.

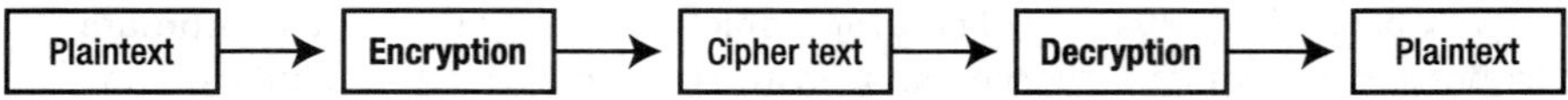

Figure 12-1. *The process of cryptography*

■ **NOTE** The mathematical cryptography algorithm that performs the encryption and decryption transformations is also called a *cipher* and the encrypted text is called the *cipher text*.

Let's look at a simple example by building a simple ASP.NET page:

```
<html>
<script language="C#" runat="server">
   public void Page_Load(Object sender, EventArgs E)
   {
      lblHello.Text = "Some information!";
   }
</script>

<body style="font: 10pt verdana" bgcolor="ffffcc">
   <form runat="server">
      <h3>Hacking!</h3>
      <asp:Label id="lblHello" Text="Default text" runat="server" />
   </form>
</body>
</html>
```

All this ASPX page does is to display "Some Information!" in a label server control in the `Page_Load()` event. Pretty simple, isn't it? Figure 12-2 shows how the page looks in IE6.

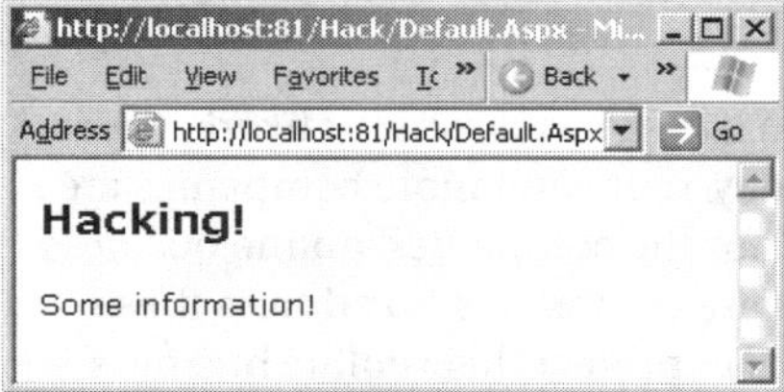

Figure 12-2. *Simple ASPX page*

Let's use a tool called `TCPTrace.exe`, which is a network-sniffing tool. Microsoft also ships a similar tool called Network Monitor with the Windows Server products. The `TCPTrace.exe` tool, shown in Figure 12-3, can be downloaded from `http://www.PocketSOAP.com`.

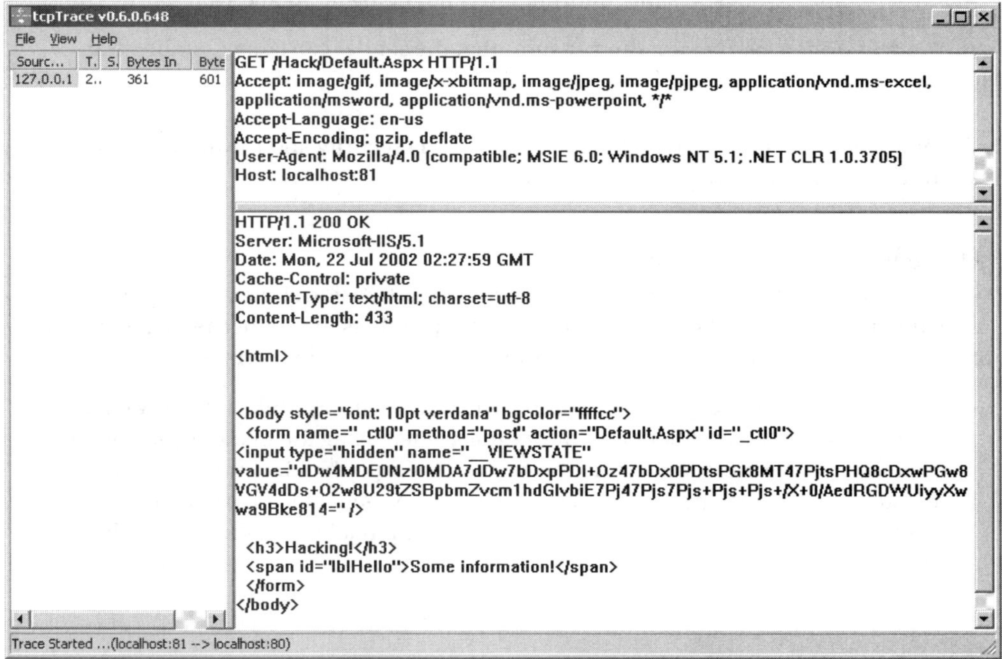

Figure 12-3. *TCPTrace.exe tool*

My web server (IIS 5.0) is running on port 80, and in order to sniff the packets sent to my web server, we have to change the port on the `TCPTrace` utility to 81, and the `TCPTrace` utility will forward all the requests received at port 81 to port 80 (to the web server). When accessing the site from IE, use port 81. For example, if you're accessing your local host, then you've to access it like this: `http://localhost:81/`.

As you can see, anyone who has access to a simple network-sniffing tool can read the information that you've transmitted over the public network. So how do you prevent this information leak? Cryptography plays a major role in network safety.

Why Use Cryptography?

If your computer is connected to or transmits information over an electronic network, your data is visible to everyone and is available for hackers. Today, more and more companies are doing business online, and this increases the security risk for the companies' online business as well as the customers and partners that interact with these companies. To address these problems, each and every company must take strong steps to protect their online business as well as their customers and partners.

When used properly, cryptography addresses the following problems:

- *Confidentiality*: Confidentiality ensures that your information is protected.
- *Authentication*: Authentication ensures that you know who is accessing your private network.
- *Integrity*: Integrity ensures that information is not being tampered with during transit.
- *Nonrepudiation*: Nonrepudiation ensures that the sender can't deny sending the message.

Cryptography provides all the services to address the security and privacy concerns of transmitting sensitive data over a public network.

Concepts of Cryptography

A cryptography algorithm is a mathematical function that transforms a readable plaintext message into unreadable text garbage, and reverses the process to produce readable text from an encrypted message. All cryptographic algorithms are based on two simple principles:

- *Substitution*: The concept of substitution is based on simply replacing every character in the message with another one. For example, when using the *Caesar cipher*, for a given letter in the message, shift to the right (in the alphabet) by three. That is, an "a" becomes "d," "b" becomes "e," and so on. This can be generalized to work for any number n not greater than 25 (assuming a 26-letter alphabet). In this cipher, the number n is the "key."

■ **NOTE** There are many varieties of substitution ciphers available, including mono-alphabetic substitution ciphers, polyalphabetic substitution ciphers, and perfect substitution ciphers.

- *Transposition*: The concept of transposition is based on scrambling the characters that are in the message. Some common forms of transposition algorithm involve writing the message into a table row by row and reading them column by column. Some of the transposition algorithms such as *Triple-DES* perform this process three times to create the cipher text.

The math formula of cryptography is simple. When you pass the plaintext message into the encryption function, the function should provide the `CipherMessage`, and when you pass the `CipherMessage` into the decryption function, it should return the original message:

```
Encryption(Message) = CipherMessage
```

And

```
Decryption(CipherMessage) = Message
```

In the same way, the following formula should also be true:

```
Decryption(Encryption(Message)) = Message
```

In the simple encryption/decryption algorithms, the algorithm is well known, and anyone who knows the algorithm should be able to decrypt the `CipherMessage`. Therefore, to provide more security for the algorithms, a key is added.

■ **NOTE** We need a key to lock and unlock a lock. In the same way, a cipher is a math algorithm and a key is sequence of bytes that is used to encrypt and decrypt the information. If we don't have the key, we can't unlock the lock. In the same way, if we lose the key, we can't decrypt the encrypted data. The keys come in different sizes based on the cryptography algorithms. For example, the DES algorithm is based on 56 bits and the RC2 algorithm is based on 128 bits.

In order to encrypt or decrypt the message, we have to pass the appropriate key into the function:

```
Encryption(Message, Key) = CipherMessage
```

And

```
Decryption(CipherMessage, Key) = Message
```

In the same way, the following formula should also be true:

```
Decryption(Encryption(Message, Key), Key) = Message
```

Cryptographic Algorithms

Cryptographic algorithms can be divided into three types:

- *Symmetric algorithms*: In symmetric cryptographic algorithms, the same key is used for encrypting and decrypting the message.
- *Asymmetric algorithms*: In asymmetric cryptography algorithms, different keys are used for encrypting and decrypting the messages. The asymmetric cryptography algorithms are also known as public key infrastructure (or PKI).

- *Hashing or message digest algorithms*: In hash cryptographic algorithms, the original text is transformed into a fixed-length cipher text. The hash algorithms also perform one-way encryption, meaning the hashed cipher text can't be decrypted to its original clear text version. The fixed length of the cipher text changes based on the algorithm from 128 to 256 bits.

Symmetric Algorithms

When encrypting and decrypting the information, the same key is used for the encrypting and decrypting process in symmetric algorithms, as shown in Figure 12-4.

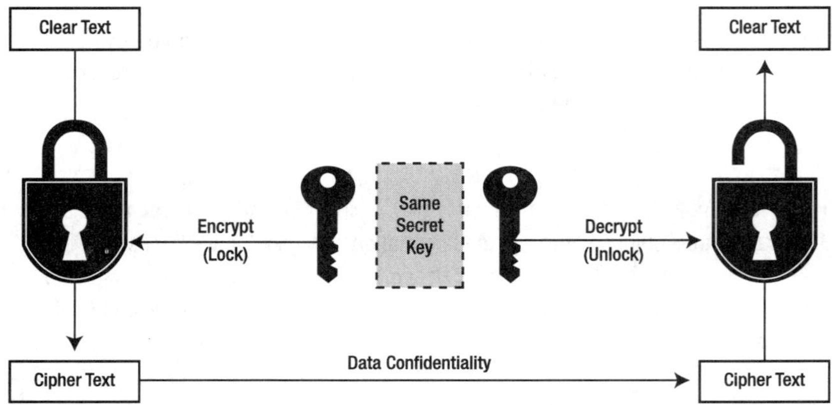

Figure 12-4. *Symmetric encryption*

With this method, the data can be transmitted in an insecure network and the receiver can decrypt the information using the same cryptography algorithm used by the sender. Of course, the key that is used to encrypt and decrypt should be kept secret if you want this method to work for you. Another problem with this approach is distributing the key to the other end where it needs to be encrypted or decrypted.

■ **NOTE** For more information about the key sizes, read the paper "Selecting Cryptographic Key Sizes" at `http://security.ece.orst.edu/koc/ece575/papers/cryptosizes.pdf`.

Some of the common symmetric encryption algorithms are as follows:

- *DES*: The Data Encryption Standard was adopted by the US government in 1977 and by ANSI in 1981. DES follows 56-bit key for encryption and decryption. DES is a very famous algorithm, but due to its small key length support, its use is very limited in today's world.

- *Triple-DES*: Triple-DES (or 3DES) is a very secure algorithm when compared with DES, since Triple-DES encrypts the message three times using the DES algorithm with different keys. The total key length of Triple-DES is 168 bits.
- *Blowfish*: Blowfish is a fast, compact, and simple encryption algorithm invented by the famous author Bruce Schneier, who wrote the celebrated book *Applied Cryptography* (John Wiley & Sons, 1995). This algorithm allows a variable key length up to 448 bits.
- *IDEA*: The International Data Encryption Algorithm (IDEA) was developed by James L. Massey and Xuejia Lai in Switzerland. Widespread use of this algorithm was hindered by several patent problems.
- *RC2, RC4, RC5*: The RC2 and RC4 algorithms were originally developed by Ronald Rivest for RSA Security. Both RC2 and RC4 allow key lengths between 1 and 2048 bits. On the other hand, RC5 allows a user-defined key length, data block size, and number of encryption rounds.
- *Rijndael (AES)*: This algorithm was originally developed by Joan Daemen and Vincent Rijmen. Rijndael is a fast and compact algorithm that supports keys of 128, 192, and 256 bits in length.

■ NOTE The .NET Framework supports DES, Triple-DES, RC2, and Rijndael symmetric encryption algorithms.

Symmetric key algorithms are much faster than PKI algorithms, so they are the preferred choice for encrypting and decrypting large blocks of data. On the other hand, they're also very easy to implement. The main disadvantage of symmetric encryption is that we need to protect the keys, and it is a challenge to exchange the keys between the encryption source and the decryption destination. The security of the algorithms is also related to the length of the key: the longer the key, the slimmer the probability of the information being decrypted. The possibility of information being decrypted is also based on the complexity of the key that you've chosen. The more complex the key, the slimmer the probability of the information being decrypted.

Asymmetric Algorithms

With asymmetric algorithms, one key encrypts the message and the other key decrypts the information as shown in Figure 12-5.

Both the keys are different, but they're related to each other. Therefore, we can publish the public key without worrying about the possibility of our encryption being compromised. This encryption is also called *public key encryption*, or *public key infrastructure*, since the public key is available publicly without compromising the integrity and security of the key or message. The decryption key is normally called the *private key* or *secret key*.

Public key cryptography and related standards and techniques underlie security features of many products, including signed and encrypted e-mail, form signing, object signing, single sign-on, and the most popular protocol, Secure Sockets Layer (SSL)/TLS.

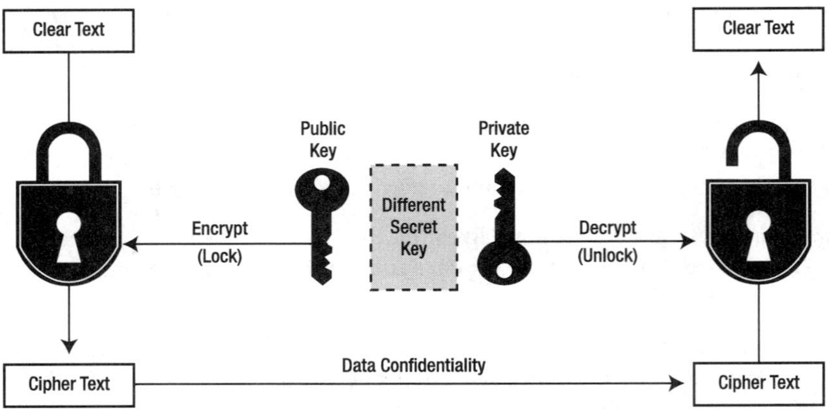

Figure 12-5. *Asymmetric encryption*

As shown in Figure 12-5, the public key can be freely distributed, but only you will be able to read a message encrypted using this key. When someone sends an encrypted message to you, that person encrypts the message with your public key, and upon receiving the encrypted data, you can decrypt it with the corresponding private key. The message encrypted with the public key can be decrypted only with the corresponding private key.

■ **NOTE** The PKI systems also use key exchange methods such as the *Diffie-Hellman key exchange*. The Diffie-Hellman key exchange is not an algorithm—it is a method that allows us to develop secure key exchange between two parties. The other methods are Digital Signature Standard (or DSS) and Elliptic Curve Cryptosystems.

The other way is to download the public key from an online repository. For example, if you get a client certificate from Thawte, you've an option to add your public key to the online repository. When someone wants to send something very secure, all he or she has to do is to get the your public key from you or from the online repository and sign the information with your public key and send it to you. When you receive the message, you decrypt it with your private key. This is one of the most common ways of exchanging keys.

Compared with symmetric key encryption, public key encryption requires more computation and is therefore not always appropriate for large amounts of data.

The .NET Framework supports two asymmetric algorithms:

- *DSA/DSS*: Digital Signature Standard (DSS) was developed by the National Security Agency. DSS is based on the Digital Signature Algorithm (DSA), and it supports any key length.
- *RSA*: RSA is a well-known public key algorithm developed by Ronald Rivest, Adi Shamir, and Leonard Adleman, and supports variable key length based on the implementation.

Message Digest Algorithms

Message digest algorithms (also known as MAC or hash algorithms) transform a variable-size input and return a fixed-size string as shown in Figure 12-6.

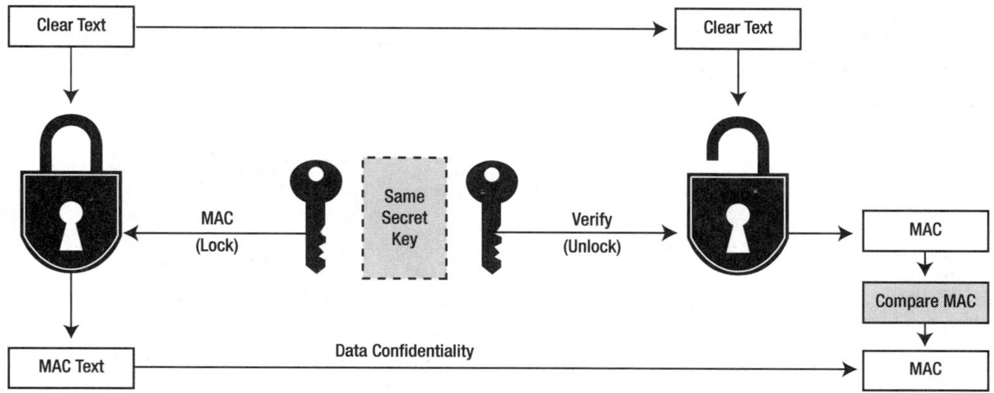

Figure 12-6. *Message digest or hash*

The hash algorithms are also called one-way hash, since the hashed string can't be converted back to the original state—once the original clear text value has been hashed, it is not possible to get the original hashed value from the MAC.

When we hash a clear text message with a hash algorithm, it uses a key to produce the hash value. Once the hash value is generated, we can send the clear text and the hash to the other end, where the clear text value can be hashed with the same key and algorithm—the generated hash value can then be compared with the one supplied by the other end. If the values match, we can be sure that the message has not been altered in transit.ASP.NET's Forms authentication module supports the one-way hash algorithms MD5 and SHA3 to authenticate the user names/passwords stored in the `web.config` file. The same functionality can also be extended by storing the hashed passwords in the database using the `HashPasswordForStoringInConfigFile` method of the `FormsAuthentication` class available in the `System.Web.Security` namespace.

Some of the common MAC functions are MD2, MD4, MD5, SHA, SHA-1, SHA-256, SHA-384, and SHA-512. The .NET Framework supports the following hash functions:

- HMACSHA-1
- MACTripleDES
- MD-5
- SHA-1
- SHA-256
- SHA-384
- SHA-512

■ **NOTE** A Hash Message Authentication Code (or HMAC) function is a technique for verifying the integrity of a message transmitted between two parties that agree on a shared key.

Digital Signatures

Although encryption and decryption address a few problems, there are two important problems they don't address:

- Tampering
- Impersonation

Digital signatures use the one-way hashing functions for tamper detection and related authentication problems. Since the value of the hash is unique for the hashed data, any change in the data, even deleting or altering a single character, results in a different value. Moreover, the content of the hashed data cannot, for all practical purposes, be deduced from the hash. This therefore becomes the best way to detect tampering.

In public key encryption, it's possible to use the private key for encryption and the public key for decryption. Since this could create problems when encrypting sensitive information, we can digitally sign any data, instead of encrypting the data itself. Signing the data creates a one-way hash of the data, which can then be encrypted using the private key. The encrypted hash, along with other information, such as the hashing algorithm, is known as a *digital signature*. Figure 12-7 shows a simplified view of the way a digital signature can be used to validate the integrity of signed data.

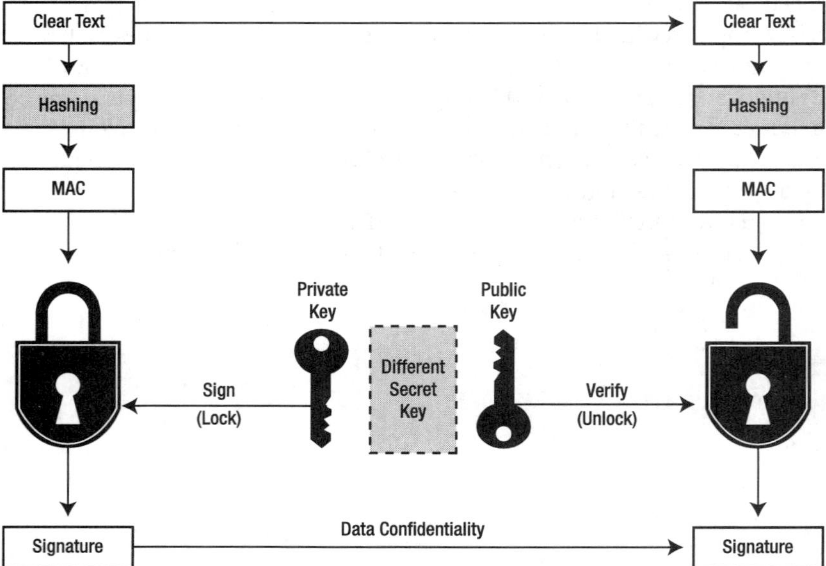

Figure 12-7. *Digital signature*

If you look at this figure, the sender sends the clear text message (or encrypted message) with the digital signature. The digital signature is computed based on the clear text message, the clear text message is hashed using a hashing algorithm such as MD5, and the hashed value will be signed by the private key. At the other end, we'll receive the clear text message (or encrypted message) with the digital signature. Then we'll compute a hash value for the clear text and compare it with the digital signature. If the digital signature verification process was successful then, we're assured that the data has not been tampered with in transit.

Cryptography Terminology

Before diving into the world of crypto coding, you need to understand some cryptographic terminology.

Block Ciphers and Stream Ciphers

Cryptographic ciphers handle data in two formats:

- Block ciphers
- Stream ciphers

Block ciphers are traditionally the most popular ones. A block cipher transforms a fixed-length block of plaintext data into a block of cipher text data of the same length and then repeats the process until the entire message has been processed. This transformation takes place under the action of a user-provided secret key. Decryption is performed by applying the reverse transformation to the cipher text block using the same secret key. The fixed length is called the *block size*, and for many block ciphers, the block size is 64 bits. Typically, symmetric algorithms are based on the block cipher format. For example, the DES and RC2 algorithm use 8 bytes, 3DES uses 16 bytes, and Rijndael uses 32 bytes as input. Using this scale, each algorithm splits the input into the blocks and performs the transformation.

More recent symmetric encryption algorithms are based on *stream ciphers*. Every stream cipher generates a *keystream*, and encryption is provided by combining the keystream with the plaintext (usually with the bitwise `XOR` operator). Stream ciphers can be designed to be exceptionally fast, much faster in fact than any block cipher. While block ciphers operate on large blocks of data, stream ciphers typically operate on smaller units of plaintext, usually bits. The encryption of any particular plaintext with a block cipher will result in the same cipher text when the same key is used. With a stream cipher, the transformation of these smaller plaintext units will vary, depending on when they are encountered during the encryption process.

Padding

Block ciphers deal with blocks of bits (usually 64 bits), and the last remaining bits may not fit in a block. For example, suppose we have 136 bits of information that we are trying to encrypt using a block cipher that takes 64 bits (or 8 bytes) at a time to encrypt. Figure 12-8 shows how the 136 bits input is split into 64-bit blocks for the padding process.

136 Bits		
64 Bits	64 Bits	8 Bits

Figure 12-8. *136 bits split into smaller blocks for the padding process*

In the process of encryption, the first two blocks will contain 128 bits, and the remaining 8 bits will not fit in the block cipher's buffer. To address the incomplete block, padding is needed. A padding scheme will define how the last incomplete block of data will be handled in the process of encryption. The padding will be addressed in the process of decryption by removing all the padded characters and restoring the original text.

■ **NOTE** PKCS#7 (or Public Key Cryptography Standard) is one of the most famous padding schemas, and it was published by RSA security, Inc. For more information, please visit the RSA website at `http://www.rsasecurity.com/products/bsafe/overview/IntroToPKCSstandards.pdf`.

The .NET Framework handles padding using the `PaddingMode` enumeration. The `PaddingMode` enumeration supports three values:

- `None`
- `PKCS7`
- `Zeros`

As the name suggests, when we use `None`, no padding is done. When `PKCS7` is used, the value of the remaining bytes in the block will be filled with the remaining number of bytes. For example, if 6 bytes are free in a given block, the last 6 bytes will be padded with the value 6. If 4 bytes are free, the last 4 bytes will be padded with the value 4, as shown in Figure 12-9.

Figure 12-9. *PKCS7 padding*

When PaddingMode.Zeros is used, the remaining bytes will be filled with the value zero, as shown in Figure 12-10.

Figure 12-10. *Zeros padding*

Modes

The mode of a cipher determines how blocks of plaintext will be encrypted into blocks of cipher text, and decrypted back. The CipherMode enumeration defines the block cipher mode to be used when performing the encryption or decryption process. You can specify the mode using the Mode property of many of the cipher algorithms. The .NET Framework supports CBC, CFB, CTS, ECB, and OFB modes.

When using ECB (or Electronic Code Book) mode, each block of plaintext is encrypted to a block of cipher text. The main drawback to ECB mode is that the same plaintext will always encrypt to the same cipher text when the same key is used.

The CBC (or Cipher Block Chaining) mode overcomes the drawbacks of ECB mode. When using CBC mode, each block of plaintext is combined with the previous block's cipher text (using an XOR operation), which produces encrypted blocks of cipher text, as shown in Figure 12-11.

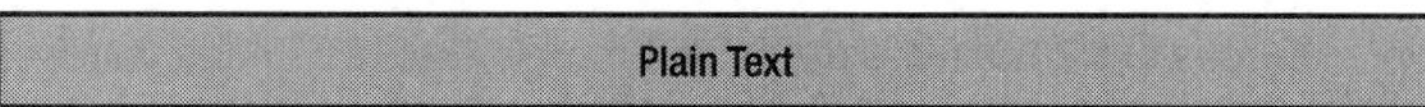

Figure 12-11. *CBC mode*

NOTE Since there is no previous cipher text block when starting the process, an initialization vector (or IV) is used for the first block of plaintext.

The CFB (or Cipher Feedback) mode allows a block cipher to act like a stream cipher by processing the small increment of plaintext into cipher text instead of processing it block by block. CFB mode also uses an IV to process the initial plaintext.

The CTS (or Cipher Text Stealing) mode is a very versatile mode that behaves pretty much like CBC mode. The CTS mode handles any length of plaintext and produces cipher text that matches the length of the plaintext.

The OFB (or Output Feedback) mode works pretty much like CFB mode; the only difference is the way that the internal buffer (shift register) is handled.

The System.Security.Cryptography Namespace

The `System.Security.Cryptography` namespace provides a simple way to implement security in your .NET application using the cryptography classes. Some of the cryptography classes are pure .NET managed code, and some of them are wrappers for the unmanaged Microsoft Crypto API. You can find out if the cryptography class is managed or unmanaged code by looking at the class name. All the unmanaged providers end with the suffix `CryptoServiceProvider`, and all managed providers end with the `Managed` suffix. For example, if you look at the hashing classes such as `MD5CryptoServiceProvider`, `SHA1Managed`, and `SHA256Managed`, you can figure out that `SHA1Managed` and `SHA256Managed` are pure .NET managed implementations of the SHA algorithm.

■ **NOTE** The Crypto API is Microsoft's API for accessing cryptographic functions built into the Windows platform. Microsoft recently released CAPICOM, an ActiveX wrapper around the Crypto API to simplify Crypto API programming in Visual Basic 6, but it implements only a subset of the API.

Note that the .NET Framework supports the use of strong key lengths in all encryption algorithms. However, for encryption algorithms that are implemented on top of Crypto API, you need to install a High Encryption Pack to upgrade your version of Windows.

- For Windows 2000 users, Service Pack 2 includes the High Encryption Pack. It can also be obtained from the following URL: `http://www.microsoft.com/windows2000/downloads/recommended/encryption/`.
- For Windows NT 4.0 users, Service Pack 6a includes the High Encryption Pack; this can be downloaded from `http://www.microsoft.com/ntserver/nts/downloads/recommended/SP6/allSP6.asp`.
- For Windows ME, Windows 98, and Windows 95 users, Internet Explorer 5.5 includes the High Encryption Pack, or you can download it from `http://www.microsoft.com/windows/ie/download/128bit/default.asp`.

Cryptography Class Hierarchy

The `System.Security.Cryptography` namespace provides three top-level classes, `SymmetricAlgorithm`, `AsymmetricAlgorithm`, and `HashAlgorithm`, representing the three main areas of cryptography as shown in Figure 12-12.

This model also brings the flexibility of extending the namespace. For example, the `System.Security.Cryptography` namespace doesn't currently support the *Blowfish* symmetric algorithm. If we wanted to add this algorithm to this namespace, all we would have to do is to derive our Blowfish algorithm class from the `SymmetricAlgorithm` class, and we'd get most of the standard functionality for free. The next advantage is that all the algorithm provider classes are inherited from their algorithm implementation classes. For example, the SHA1 hashing algorithm provider (the `SHA1Managed` class) is derived from the `SHA1` hash algorithms implementation (the `SHA1` class).

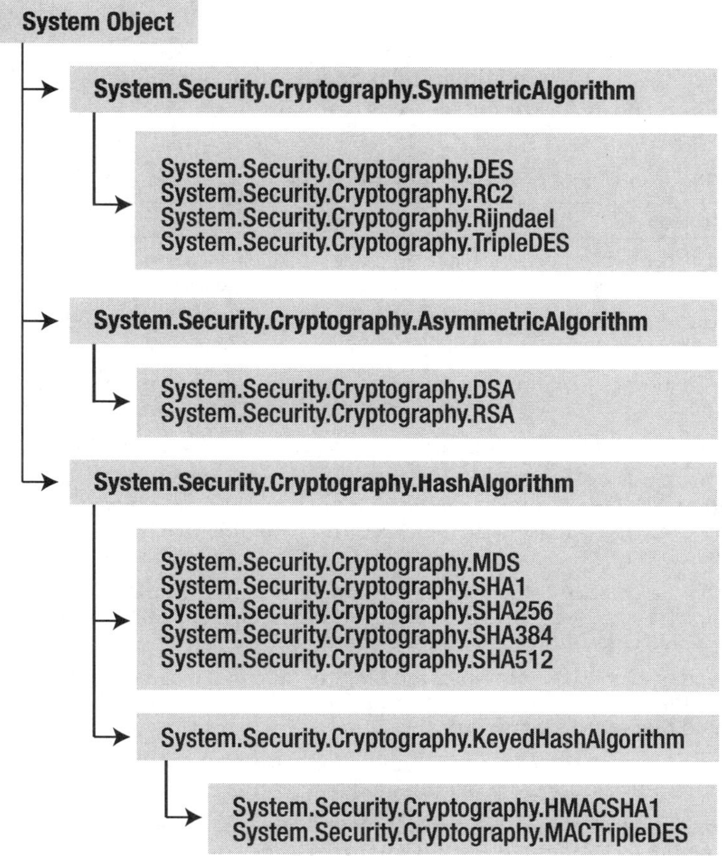

Figure 12-12. *The System.Security.Cryptography namespace and its classes*

Hashing with .NET

The `System.Security.Cryptography` namespace in the .NET Framework provides several interfaces, known as *Cryptographic Service Providers* (CSPs), which implement a variety of hashing algorithms and make hashing simple and straightforward.

As we saw earlier, the .NET Framework implements several well-known, secure hash algorithms, including Message Digest 5 (or MD5) and Secure Hash Algorithm (or SHA). The MD5 provider generates 128-bit hash values, and the SHA provider can generate 160-bit, 256-bit, 384-bit, and 512-bit hash values. The `ComputeHash` method of both the MD5 and SHA CSPs accepts a byte array or a `Stream` object, and returns a hash value.

■NOTE The .NET Framework also implements a key-based hash, which is often used to generate digital signatures.

The HashAlgorithm Class

All the hash algorithm classes are inherited from the `HashAlgorithm` abstract class. The `HashAlgorithm` class exposes some common methods and properties that can be used across all the hashing algorithms. Table 12-1 discusses a few of them.

Table 12-1. *Various Methods and Properties of the HashAlgorithm Class*

Class Member	Description
`Hash` `HashValue`	Returns the computed hash value in a byte array. `Hash` is a public property and `HashValue` is a protected field—both return a byte array.
`HashSize` `HashSizeValue`	Returns the size of the hash in bits. `HashSize` is a public property and `HashSizeValue` is a protected field: both return an integer value.
`InputBlockSize`	A public property that returns an integer representing the input block size in bits.
`OutputBlockSize`	A public property that returns an integer representing the output block size in bits.
`ComputeHash`	Computes the hash value for the given input byte array or `Stream`. `ComputeHash` is a public method that returns the output in a byte array or `Stream` object.
`Create`	Creates an instance of the hash algorithm that is currently in use. For example, if you are using MD5 hash algorithm, then it'll create an object type of that algorithm. `Create` is a static method.
`TransformBlock`	Generates the hash value for a given range of the input byte array and copies the result into another byte array. `TransformBlock` is a public method that returns a byte array.
`TransformFinalBlock`	Generates a hash value for a given range and returns a byte array. `TransformFinalBlock` is a public method that returns a byte array.
`State`	Returns the state of the hash computation. This property will contain a zero before the computations and a nonzero value after a successful hash computation. `State` is a protected field that returns an integer value representing the current state of the hash value computation.

Let's see a simple example of computing an MD5 hash. This method takes a byte array (clear text) and returns a byte array (hash value):

```
byte[] ComputeMD5(byte [] input)
{
   MD5CryptoServiceProvider md5Provider = new MD5CryptoServiceProvider();
   return md5Provider.ComputeHash(input);
}
```

As you can see, the MD5 provider is very easy to use. All we have to do is create a new object of the type `MD5CryptoServiceProvider` and pass the byte array to the `ComputeHash` method, which returns a byte array. The same technique can be used for all the hash algorithms available in the .NET Framework. Let's write a simple Windows application to hash a string using multiple hash algorithms. Figure 12-13 shows the application in action.

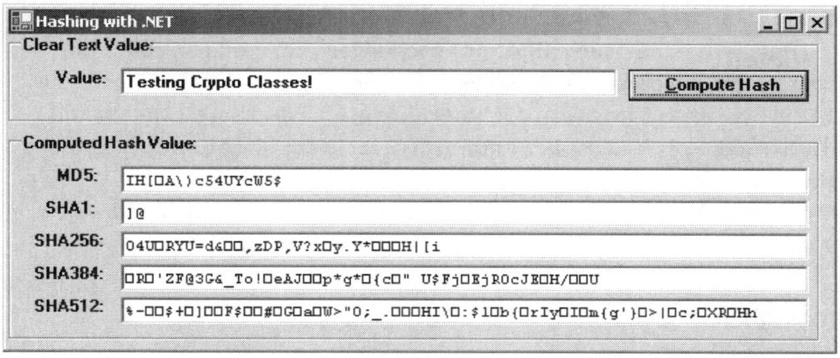

Figure 12-13. *Application that hashes a string through multiple hash algorithms*

The implementation of the application is quite simple. We accept a string from the user and hash it using different hash algorithms. Here is the code for the Compute Hash button's `Click` event handler:

```
private void btnCompute_Click(object sender, System.EventArgs e)
{
   if (txtHash.Text.Trim() != "")
   {
      // Generate bytes for the input string
      byte[] inputData = ASCIIEncoding.ASCII.GetBytes(txtHash.Text);

      // Display the hash value in text box
      txtMD5.Text = ASCIIEncoding.ASCII.GetString(new
                              MD5CryptoServiceProvider().ComputeHash(inputData));

      txtSHA1.Text = ASCIIEncoding.ASCII.GetString(new
                                          SHA1Managed().ComputeHash(inputData));

      txtSHA256.Text = ASCIIEncoding.ASCII.GetString(new
                                        SHA256Managed().ComputeHash(inputData));

      txtSHA384.Text = ASCIIEncoding.ASCII.GetString(new
                                        SHA384Managed().ComputeHash(inputData));

      txtSHA512.Text = ASCIIEncoding.ASCII.GetString(new
                                        SHA512Managed().ComputeHash(inputData));
   }
}
```

First, we call the `GetBytes` method of the `ASCIIEncoding` class to convert the string variable into a byte array. Then, we create a new object for each algorithm, and pass the input byte array to the `ComputeHash` method. Then, we call the `GetString` method of the `ASCIIEncoding` class again to convert the byte array into a string. Quite simple, isn't it—don't forget to add `using` directives for the `System.Text` namespace and `System.Security.Cryptography` namespaces to run this code.

If you're dealing with non-ASCII strings, you can use the `UnicodeEncoding` class in the `System.Text` namespace.

Using Hash Values for Authentication

Hashing techniques are very useful when it comes to authenticating users. We're going to see a simple authentication method for a Windows application using the MD5 algorithm. For the purposes of illustration, the user name and the password supplied by the user will be authenticated against an Access database.

Let's create an Access database called `DBAuth.mdb` with a single table called `Tbl_MA_Users`. The table is going to store the user ID, e-mail address, password, first name, and last name, as shown in Figure 12-14.

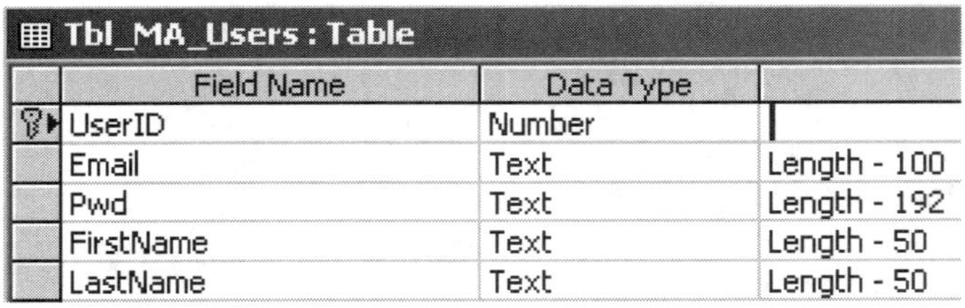

Tbl_MA_Users : Table

Field Name	Data Type	
UserID	Number	
Email	Text	Length - 100
Pwd	Text	Length - 192
FirstName	Text	Length - 50
LastName	Text	Length - 50

Figure 12-14. *Tbl_MA_Users table*

The e-mail address will be the login name for the users, and the password is stored in the database in the MD5 hash format, as shown in Figure 12-15.

UserID	Email	Pwd	FirstName	LastName
1	ssivakumar@chennai.net	{?□H!8□XJ~□N"H□S	Srinivasa	Sivakumar

Figure 12-15. *Login name and password in our example database*

This ensures the users that their password can't be hacked. For example, the user's password `MyPass` is stored in the database as `{?_H!8_XJ~_N"H_S` in MD5 hash format. Let's build a simple authentication screen to authenticate users against the Access database (see Figure 12-16).

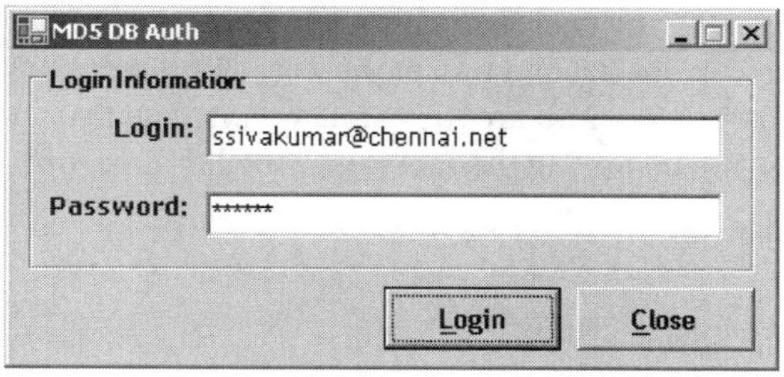

Figure 12-16. *Simple authentication screen*

Here is the code for the Login button:

```
private void btnLogin_Click(object sender, System.EventArgs e)
{
   if (txtEmail.Text.Trim() != "" && txtPwd.Text.Trim() != "")
      AuthenticateUser();
}
```

First, we check that something was entered in the user name and the password text boxes. If something was entered, we call the AuthenticateUser method. In the AuthenticateUser method, we're connecting to the Access database and querying the table that matches the login name entered by the users.

```
private bool AuthenticateUser()
{
   bool bRtnValue = false;
   string strConn = "PROVIDER=Microsoft.Jet.OLEDB.4.0;" +
                    "DATA SOURCE=DBAuth.mdb;";
   OleDbConnection Conn = new OleDbConnection(strConn) ;
   Conn.Open();

   String strSQL = "SELECT Pwd FROM Tbl_MA_Users WHERE Email = '" +
                                                        txtEmail.Text + "'";
   OleDbCommand Cmd = new OleDbCommand(strSQL,Conn);

   // Create a datareader, connection object
   OleDbDataReader Dr = Cmd.ExecuteReader(
                                 System.Data.CommandBehavior.CloseConnection);

   // Get the first row and check the password
   if (Dr.Read())
   {
```

Next, we pass the clear text password entered by the user into the GenerateMD5Hash method, which returns the hashed string. If the current hashed password stored in the database and the hash generated by the GenerateMD5Hash method are the same, we display the message "Password was successful!"; otherwise we displaying the message "Invalid password":

```
      if (Dr["Pwd"].ToString() == GenerateMD5Hash(txtPwd.Text))
      {
         MessageBox.Show(this,"Password was successful!");
         bRtnValue = true;
      }
      else
      {
         MessageBox.Show(this,"Invalid password.");
      }
   }
   else
   {
      MessageBox.Show(this,"Login name not found.");
   }

   Dr.Close();

   return bRtnValue;
}
```

The GenerateMD5Hash method is very simple. First, we convert the input string into a byte array using the ASCIIEncoding class. Next, we create a new object of type MD5CryptoServiceProvider and call its ComputeHash method to generate the hash value. Then, we convert the hash value into a string and send it back to the caller:

```
string GenerateMD5Hash(string input)
{
   // Generate bytes from our input string
   byte[] inputData = ASCIIEncoding.ASCII.GetBytes(input);

   // Compute the MD5 hash
   MD5 md5Provider = new MD5CryptoServiceProvider();
   byte[] hashResult = md5Provider.ComputeHash(inputData);

   return ASCIIEncoding.ASCII.GetString(hashResult);
}
```

This is a simple procedure to implement, and it gives us an excellent security model for applications. In this example, we've used the MD5 algorithm. In the same way, we could use any of the other hash algorithms such as SHA1 to implement the application.

NOTE The only problem with this approach is that if the user wants his or her password e-mailed back to him or her, we won't be able to do it, since we can't convert the hash value back to clear text. However, we can always reset the password and send the new password back to the user.

Keyed Hash Values

The keyed hash algorithms, or HMAC, are very similar to the hash algorithms, except that they generate the hash values based on a key. The HMAC algorithms are useful in the same way as the hash algorithms. For example, a HMAC value can be used to verify the integrity of a message transmitted between two parties that agree on a shared secret key. This is similar to the symmetric algorithm.

HMAC combines the original message with the key to compute a hash value. The sender computes the HMAC of the clear text and sends the HMAC with the clear text. The recipient recalculates the HMAC using the clear text and the sender's copy of the key. If the computed HMAC matches with the one sent from the other end, then the recipient knows that the original message has not been modified, since the message digest hasn't changed. In this way, the receiver can test the authenticity of the transmission. HMACs are commonly used as digital signatures (see Figure 12-17).

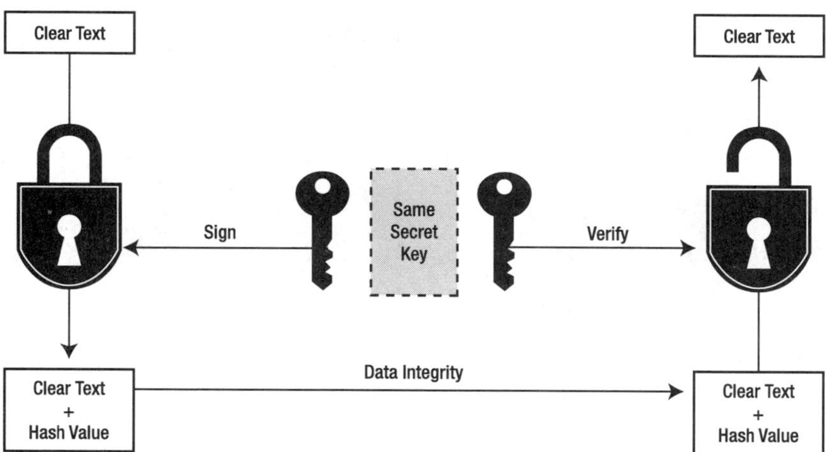

Figure 12-17. *Keyed hash*

The .NET Framework supports the `HMACSHA1` and `MACTripleDES` algorithms. The `HMACSHA1` algorithm computes keyed hash values using the SHA1 algorithm, and the `MACTripleDES` algorithm computes it based on the Triple-DES algorithm. We're going to see a simple example on how to use the HMAC classes. We'll build a Windows application that shows the HMAC value for the given clear text value and key.

First, we convert the input string and the key into byte arrays. Then we create an object of type HMACSHA1 and pass this object into a CryptoStream object. Then, we use the standard stream operations to read the input array and close the stream. The Hash property of the HMACSHA1 object returns the HMAC value. The same process is repeated for the MACTripleDES algorithm.

```
void ProcessKeyedHash(string input, string key)
{
   try
   {
      // Generate bytes for our input string
      byte[] inputData = ASCIIEncoding.ASCII.GetBytes(input);
      byte[] keyBytes = new byte[16];
      keyBytes = ASCIIEncoding.ASCII.GetBytes(key);

      // Compute HMACSHA1
      HMACSHA1 hmac = new HMACSHA1(keyBytes);
      CryptoStream cs = new CryptoStream(Stream.Null, hmac,
                                   CryptoStreamMode.Write);
      cs.Write(inputData, 0, inputData.Length);
      cs.Close();

      txtHMACSHA1.Text = ASCIIEncoding.ASCII.GetString(hmac.Hash);

      // Compute the MACTripleDES
      MACTripleDES macTripleDES = new MACTripleDES(keyBytes);
      txtMACTripleDES.Text = ASCIIEncoding.ASCII.GetString(
                                   macTripleDES.ComputeHash(inputData));
   }
   catch (Exception e)
   {
      MessageBox.Show(this, e.ToString());
   }
}
```

Figure 12-18 shows the application in action.

The only difference between these two algorithms is that the HMACSHA1 algorithm accepts keys of any size, and produces a hash value that is 20 bytes long. On the other hand, the MACTripleDES algorithm uses key lengths of 8, 16, or 24 bytes, and produces a hash value 8 bytes long. If the key length is different from the requirement, then an exception is thrown.

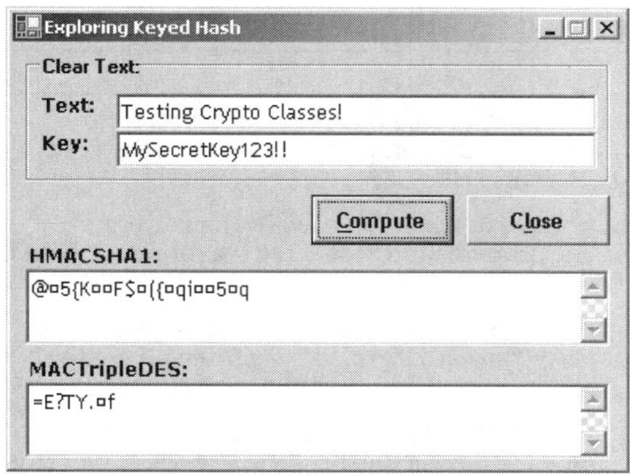

Figure 12-18. *Getting an HMAC value for the given clear text value and key*

Symmetric Transformation with .NET

The `System.Security.Cryptography` namespace supports the DES, Triple-DES, RC2, and Rijndael symmetric algorithms. In this list, only the Rijndael algorithm is a managed implementation; the other algorithms use their counterparts in the Microsoft Crypto API.

The SymmetricAlgorithm Class

All the symmetric algorithm classes are inherited from the `SymmetricAlgorithm` class. The `SymmetricAlgorithm` class exposes some common methods and properties that can be used across all the hashing algorithms. Table 12-2 discusses a few of them.

Table 12-2. *Various Methods and Properties of the SymmetricAlgorithm Class*

Class Member	Description
`Key` `KeyValue`	Specifies the secret key for the symmetric algorithm. `Key` is a public property and `KeyValue` is a protected field—both return a byte array.
`KeySize` `KeySizeValue`	Specifies the size of the secret key in bits. `KeySize` is a public property and the `KeySizeValue` is a protected field—both return an integer value representing the length of the key in bits.
`LegalKeySizes` `LegalKeySizesValue`	Specifies the valid key sizes in bytes for the current symmetric algorithm. `LegalKeySizes` is a public property and `LegalKeySizesValue` is a protected field—both return a `KeySizes` array.

`IV`
`IVValue`
array.
	Specifies the initialization vector for the symmetric algorithm. `IV` is a public property and `IVValue` is a protected field—both return a byte

`BlockSize` `BlockSizeValue`	Specifies the block size in bits for the current symmetric algorithm. `BlockSize` is a public property and `BlockSizeValue` is a protected field—both return an integer.

continues

Table 12-2. *Continued*

Class Member	Description
LegalBlockSizes LegalBlockSizesValue	Specifies the valid block size supported by the current symmetric algorithm. LegalBlockSizes is a public property and LegalBlockSizesValue is a protected field—both return a KeySizes array.
Mode ModeValue	Specifies the mode of symmetric operation used by the current algorithm. Mode is a public property and ModeValue is a protected field—both return a CipherMode.
Padding PaddingValue	Specifies the padding mode used by the current symmetric algorithm. Padding is a public property and PaddingValue is a protected field—both return a PaddingMode.
CreateEncryptor	The CreateEncryptor method creates a symmetric encryption object using the key and the initialization vector specified. CreateEncryptor is a public method and returns an ICryptoTransform interface.
CreateDecryptor	The CreateDecryptor method creates a symmetric decryption object using the key and the initialization vector specified. CreateDecryptor is a public method and returns an ICryptoTransform interface.
GenerateKey	The GenerateKey method generates a random key for the symmetric algorithm and overrides the value stored in the Key property. GenerateKey is a public method and returns a random key in a byte array.
GenerateIV	The GenerateIV method generates a random initialization vector for the symmetric algorithm and overrides the value stored in the IV property. GenerateIV is a public method and returns a random vector in a byte array.
ValidKeySize	Indicates whether the specified key size is valid for the current sym metric algorithm. ValidKeySize is a public method and returns an integer.

Let's start out by exploring the symmetric algorithms using the DES algorithm. Since symmetric algorithms tend to be faster than asymmetric ones, symmetric algorithms are good candidates for bulk encryption/decryption operations such as encrypting and decrypting entire files. We'll write a Windows application that will encrypt and decrypt files using the DES algorithm.

The user interface will provide options for locating a file using the Windows Common Dialog controls. There will be options provided to encrypt and decrypt a file with a secret key (see Figure 12-19).

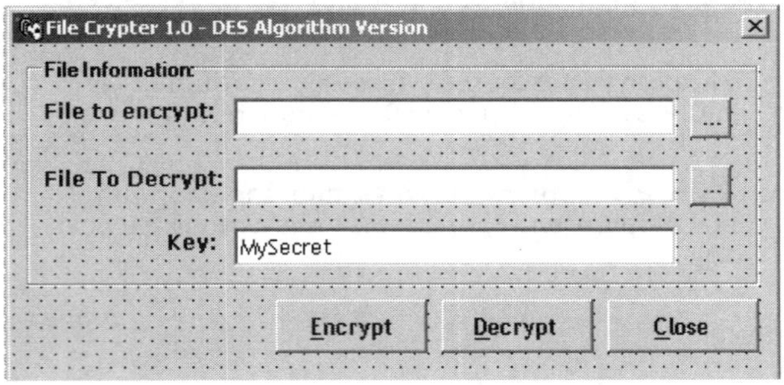

Figure 12-19. *Application that encrypts/decrypts files using DES*

The Encrypt button will add an .enc extension to the source file when generating the encrypted destination file. Here is how the code looks for the Encrypt button:

```
private void button1_Click(object sender, System.EventArgs e)
{
   if (EncryptData(encFile.Text, encFile.Text + ".enc" , txtKey.Text) == true)
      MessageBox.Show(this, "Done!", "Encryption Status", MessageBoxButtons.OK,
                      MessageBoxIcon.Information);
   else
      MessageBox.Show(this, "The encryption process failed!", "Fatal Error",
                      MessageBoxButtons.OK, MessageBoxIcon.Stop);
}
```

The Encrypt button event calls the EncryptData method, passing in the source file name, destination file name, and the secret key for the encryption operation. Let's take a look at the EncryptData method.

First, we create an object type of DESCryptoServiceProvider and assign the secret key supplied by the user to the Key property. Then we call the GenerateIV method to generate an initialization vector for the encryption operation. Next, we create the DES encryption object by calling the CreateEncryptor method of the DESCryptoServiceProvider class. After that, we instantiate two FileStream objects, one in read mode (the source file), and the other in write mode (the destination file) to encrypt the file.

```
// The EncryptData method will encrypt the given file using the DES algorithm
public bool EncryptData(string sourceFile, string destinationFile,
                        string cryptoKey)
{
   try
   {
      // Create the DES Service Provider object and assign the key and vector
      DESCryptoServiceProvider DESProvider = new DESCryptoServiceProvider();
      DESProvider.Key = ASCIIEncoding.ASCII.GetBytes(cryptoKey);
      // Initialize the initialization vector
      DESProvider.IV=this.iv;
      ICryptoTransform DESEncrypt = DESProvider.CreateEncryptor();

      // Open the source and destination file using the file stream object
      FileStream inFileStream = new FileStream(sourceFile,
                                          FileMode.Open, FileAccess.Read);
      FileStream outFileStream = new FileStream(destinationFile, FileMode.Create,
                                           FileAccess.Write);
```

■ **NOTE** The initialization vector (or IV) is always used to initialize the first block of plaintext for encryption. We've already talked about this in the "Modes" section.

Once we've created these objects, we need a CryptoStream object to which we write the encrypted file. We pass the DES encryption object and the output file stream into the CryptoStream's constructor. Then we read the content of the input file and write it back into the CryptoStream. Then, we close all the stream objects and return true.

```
      // Create a CrytoStream class and write the encrypted out
      CryptoStream cryptoStream = new CryptoStream(outFileStream, DESEncrypt,
                                                   CryptoStreamMode.Write);

      // Declare the byte array of the length of the input file
      byte[] bytearrayinput = new byte[inFileStream.Length];

      // Read the input file stream into the byte array and write
      // it back in the CryptoStream
      inFileStream.Read(bytearrayinput, 0, bytearrayinput.Length);
      cryptoStream.Write(bytearrayinput, 0, bytearrayinput.Length);

      // Close the stream handlers
      cryptoStream.Close();
      inFileStream.Close();
      outFileStream.Close();
      return true;
   }
   catch (Exception e)
   {
      MessageBox.Show(this, e.ToString(), "Encryption Error",
                      MessageBoxButtons.OK, MessageBoxIcon.Stop);
      return false;
   }
}
```

The decryption process does the opposite of the encryption process. Let's look at the Decrypt button code. First, we retrieve the original file name from the selected one by removing the .enc extension from the file name. Then we call the DecryptData method with the source, destination, and secret key.

```
private void button2_Click(object sender, System.EventArgs e)
{
   string decFileName = decFile.Text.Replace(".enc", "");
   if (DecryptData(decFile.Text, decFileName, txtKey.Text) == true)
      MessageBox.Show(this, "Done!", "Decryption Status", MessageBoxButtons.OK,
                      MessageBoxIcon.Information);
   else
      MessageBox.Show(this, "The decryption process failed!", "Fatal Error",
                      MessageBoxButtons.OK, MessageBoxIcon.Stop);
}
```

The DecryptData method works in a very similar way to EncryptData. We create an object of type DESCryptoServiceProvider and assign the key to it. Then, we generate a new IV and create a new DES decryption object by calling the CreateDecryptor method. Next, we read the source file into the CrytoStream and transform the content into a new file. Finally, we close the stream objects and return true.

```
// The DecryptData method will decrypt the given file using the DES algorithm
public bool DecryptData(string sourceFile, string destinationFile,
                        string cryptoKey)
{
   try
   {
      // Create the DES Service Provider object and assign the key and vector
      DESCryptoServiceProvider DESProvider = new DESCryptoServiceProvider();
      DESProvider.Key = ASCIIEncoding.ASCII.GetBytes(cryptoKey);
      // Initialize the initialization vector
      DESProvider.IV=this.iv;

      FileStream DecryptedFile = new FileStream(sourceFile, FileMode.Open,
                                          FileAccess.Read);
      ICryptoTransform desDecrypt = DESProvider.CreateDecryptor();

      CryptoStream cryptostreamDecr = new CryptoStream(DecryptedFile, desDecrypt,
                                                 CryptoStreamMode.Read);
      StreamWriter DecryptedOutput = new StreamWriter(destinationFile);
      DecryptedOutput.Write(new StreamReader(cryptostreamDecr).ReadToEnd());
      DecryptedOutput.Flush();
      DecryptedOutput.Close();
      DecryptedFile.Close();
      return true;
   }
   catch (Exception e)
   {
      MessageBox.Show(this, e.ToString(), "Decryption Error",
                      MessageBoxButtons.OK, MessageBoxIcon.Stop);
      return false;
   }
}
```

Using Other Symmetric Algorithms

Since all the symmetric algorithms are derived from the `SymmetricAlgorithm` class, it is very easy to implement the encryption/decryption process with the previous code base. For example, if you want to use the RC2, Triple-DES, or Rijndael algorithm, all you have to do is replace the following declaration in the `EncryptData` and `DecryptData` methods with the appropriate declarations shown here:

- *DES*:

```
DESCryptoServiceProvider DESProvider = new DESCryptoServiceProvider();
```

- *RC2*:

```
RC2CryptoServiceProvider RC2Provider = new RC2CryptoServiceProvider();
```

- *Triple-DES*:

```
TripleDESCryptoServiceProvider tDESProvider = new
                                    TripleDESCryptoServiceProvider();
```

- *Rijndael*:

```
RijndaelManaged RijndaelProvider = new RijndaelManaged();
```

If you make this change, the file encrypter/decrypter application will work fine.

The success of the symmetric encryption and decryption process is based on the key value. If you don't supply a proper key length to the algorithm, then a `CryptographicException` will be raised. The key sizes supported by the algorithm can be fetched by accessing the `LegalKeySizes` property. This property returns an array of the `KeySizes` class. The `KeySizes` class has three integer public properties—`MaxSize`, `MinSize`, and `SkipSize`. The `MaxSize` and `MinSize` properties specify the maximum key size (in bits) and the minimum key size (in bits) respectively. The `SkipSize` returns the interval between the valid key sizes in bits.

Table 12-3 lists the key sizes supported by the major algorithms.

Table 12-3. *Supported Key Sizes*

Algorithm	Key Size
DES	64 bits or 8 bytes
RC2	128 bits or 16 bytes
Triple-DES	192 bits or 24 bytes
Rijndael	256 bits or 32 bytes

The strength of the encryption is also based on the key. The larger the key, the better the encryption. Thus, the likelihood of a hacker being able to decrypt the data with a brute-force attack is decreased. However, there is one more constraint that we should remember—the bigger the key, the more time required for the encryption and decryption process.

Asymmetric Transformation with .NET

As we discussed earlier in the chapter, asymmetric algorithms are based on the concept of public and private keys, or PKI. The `System.Security.Cryptography` namespace supports two asymmetric algorithms: RSA and DSA.

The AsymmetricAlgorithm Class

Both the RSA and DSA algorithms inherit from the base class `AsymmetricAlgorithm`. The `AsymmetricAlgorithm` class exposes some common methods and properties that can be used across all the hashing algorithms, some of which are listed in Table 12-4.

Table 12-4. *Various Methods and Properties of the AsymmetricAlgorithm Class*

Class Member	Description
`KeySize` `KeySizeValue`	Specifies the size of the key modules in bits. `KeySize` is a public property and `KeySizeValue` is a protected field—both return an integer value representing the length of the key in bits.
`LegalKeySizes` `LegalKeySizesValue`	Specifies a valid key size in bits for the current asymmetric algorithm. `LegalKeySizes` is a public property and `LegalKeySizesValue` is a protected field—both return a `KeySizes` array.
`KeyExchangeAlgorithm`	Specifies the key exchange algorithm used when communicating between two ends and the way the public key and private key will be exchanged. This is a public property that returns a string representing the name of the key exchange algorithm used.
`SignatureAlgorithm`	Specifies the name of the algorithm used to sign the current object. This is a public property that returns a string representing the name of the signature algorithm used.
`FromXmlString`	Reconstructs an `Asymmetric` object from an XML file. This is a public method that takes a string as input.
`ToXmlString`	Returns an XML representation of the current algorithm object. This is a public method that returns a string.

As we've already discussed, many of the cryptography algorithms are implemented on top of the Crypto API library. The .NET Framework wraps the Crypto API library with sets of managed classes, called Cryptographic Service Providers (or CSPs). The `CspParameters` class is used to send values to and receive values from the unmanaged Crypto API.

■ **NOTE** The Cryptographic Service Providers are plug-ins for the Crypto API. These plug-ins are encryption engines that perform the encryption/decryption process.

The CSP operation is based on an enumeration value called `CspProviderFlags`. The `CspProviderFlags` enumeration supports two values: `UseDefaultKeyContainer` and `UseMachine-KeyStore`. If the `UseDefaultKeyContainer` option is specified, the key information is read from the default key container. If the `UseMachineKeyStore` option is specified, the key information is read from the computer's key container.

■ **NOTE** CSPs maintain a database to store public/private key pairs. Some CSPs maintain their key container in the Registry, whereas others maintain it in other locations, such as in Smart Cards or encrypted, hidden files.

Using the RSA Algorithm

The RSA algorithm is implemented in the `RSACryptoServiceProvider` class, which inherits from the `RSA` class. The `RSA` class inherits from the `AsymmetricAlgorithm` class. The RSA algorithm allows us to encrypt, decrypt, sign data with a digital signature, and verify the signature. We'll look at these one by one in this section.

Let's start with a simple encryption/decryption approach. Since the RSA algorithm is an asymmetric algorithm, it is slower than its symmetric counterpart. Therefore, the RSA algorithm is best for small amounts of message encryption. Accordingly, we'll build a Windows application that will encrypt and decrypt the message entered by the user using PKI technology.

Whenever you create a new default constructor instance of the `RSACryptoServiceProvider` class, it automatically creates a new set of public/private key information, ready to use. We can also store the PKI values into XML files. This demonstration will be our first example. Let's build a UI as shown in Figure 12-20.

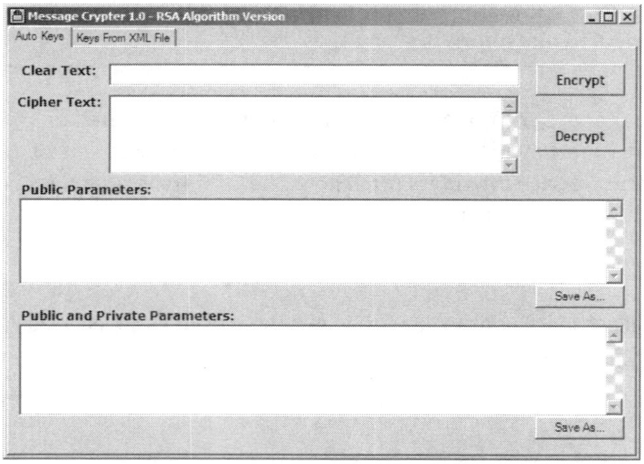

Figure 12-20. *Our example UI*

This UI allows us to see the clear text as well as the encrypted cipher text. Our code will also show the public and the private parameters used in this process, and we'll have an option to store the public and private parameters in different XML files.

Since we're going to use the RSA auto-generated public/private keys, we declare a class-level static object.

```
static RSACryptoServiceProvider rsaProvider;
```

Here is the code for the Encrypt button:

```
if (txtClearText.Text.Trim() != "")
{
   // Initialize the RSA Cryptography Service Provider (CSP)
   rsaProvider = new RSACryptoServiceProvider();

   UTF8Encoding utf8 = new UTF8Encoding();
   byte[] clearText = utf8.GetBytes(txtClearText.Text.Trim());

   // Encrypting the data received
   txtCipherText.Text = Convert.ToBase64String(rsaProvider.Encrypt(clearText,
                                                   false));

   // Show the public and private parameters
   txtPrvParams.Text = rsaProvider.ToXmlString(true);

   // Show the public parameters
   txtPubParams.Text = rsaProvider.ToXmlString(false);
}
```

We create a new object type of `RSACryptoServiceProvider`. Then we transform the user-entered message into a byte array using the `UTF8Encoding` class. Then we call the `Encrypt` method of the `RSACryptoServiceProvider` class, and pass the input byte array and a second parameter of `false`.

The second parameter in the `Encrypt` method deals with the mode of operation. If you are running Windows 2000 OS with SP2 or higher, then you can set this parameter to `true`, which will use the OAEP padding method. When set to `false`, it'll use PKCS version 1.5.

The `Encrypt` method returns an encrypted byte array. We're using the `ToBase64String` method of the `Convert` class to convert the byte array into a string for display in the text box. We also display the private/public parameters generated by the RSA algorithm in two text boxes using the `ToXmlString` method of the `RSACryptoServiceProvider` class. `ToXmlString` takes a Boolean as input, and if the value is `false`, it generates the public parameters value as an XML string; if the value is `true`, it includes the private parameters also.

Here is the code for our Decrypt button. This method just calls the Decrypt method of the RSACryptoServiceProvider object.

```
private void btnDecrypt_Click(object sender, System.EventArgs e)
{
   if (txtCipherText.Text.Trim() != "")
   {
      // Convert the input string into a byte array
      byte[] bCipherText =
          Convert.FromBase64String(txtCipherText.Text.Trim());

      // Decrypt the data and convert it back to a string
      string strValue =
         ASCIIEncoding.ASCII.GetString(objRSAProvider.Decrypt(
         bCipherText, false));

      // Display the decrypted string in a MessageBox
      MessageBox.Show(this, strValue , "Decrypted value",
      MessageBoxButtons.OK,MessageBoxIcon.Information);
   }
}
```

Now let's look at saving the public/private parameters into an XML file. We display the SaveFile common dialog box to get the desired file name from the user. Then we load the XML data into an XmlDocument object and call its Save method to save the data to disk.

```
private void btnSave_Click(object sender, System.EventArgs e)
{
   SaveFileDialog saveFileDialog1 = new SaveFileDialog();

   saveFileDialog1.Filter = "XML files (*.xml)|*.xml|All files (*.*)|*.*";
   saveFileDialog1.FilterIndex = 2;
   saveFileDialog1.RestoreDirectory = true;

   if(saveFileDialog1.ShowDialog() == DialogResult.OK)
   {
      // Write the content to an XML file
      XmlDocument xmlDoc = new XmlDocument();
      xmlDoc.LoadXml(this.txtPubParams.Text);

      // Save the document to a file
      xmlDoc.Save(saveFileDialog1.OpenFile());
   }
}
```

Figure 12-21 shows the application in action.

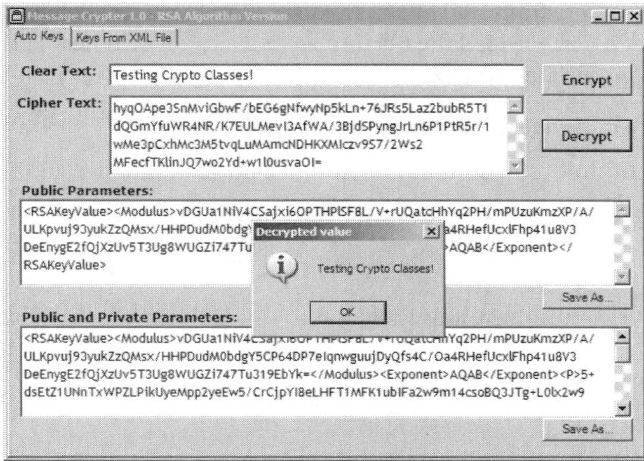

Figure 12-21. *Application displaying the clear text, encrypted cipher text, and decrypted clear text*

As you can see, the clear text, encrypted cipher text, and the decrypted clear text is shown on the screen with the public and private parameters information.

Loading the Public and Private Keys

In the previous example, we saw how to encrypt and decrypt data using the auto-generated public and private keys. We also saw how to save the keys into an XML file. However, if you want to reuse previously created or saved keys, you can do this by initializing the class with a populated `CspParameters` object. Let's see an example of this. Create a UI like the previous one, but this time we'll load the public and private keys from the XML files, as shown in Figure 12-22.

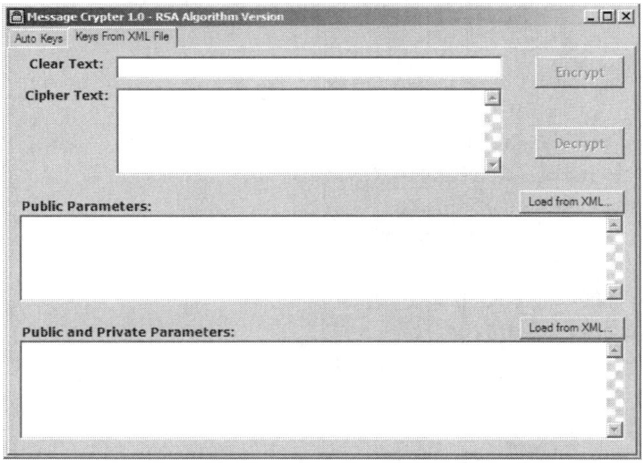

Message Crypter 1.0 - RSA Algorithm Version
Auto Keys | Keys From XML File
Clear Text: | Encrypt
Cipher Text: | Decrypt
Public Parameters: | Load from XML...
Public and Private Parameters: | Load from XML...

Figure 12-22. *UI for loading the public and private keys from XML files*

Here is the code to load the parameters from XML. First, we display an `OpenFile` dialog box to get the file name from the user. Then, we load the file into an `XmlTextReader` object and display the key information in the appropriate text box.

```
private void btnLoadPub_Click(object sender, System.EventArgs e)
{
   // Show the open file dialog
   openFileDialog1.Title = "Select the Public Parameters file";
   openFileDialog1.Filter = "XML Files (*.xml)|*.xml";

   if(openFileDialog1.ShowDialog() == DialogResult.OK)
   {
      string fileName = openFileDialog1.FileName;
      btnEncrypt1.Enabled = true;

      // Load the document
      XmlTextReader xmlReader = new XmlTextReader(fileName);
      xmlReader.WhitespaceHandling = WhitespaceHandling.None;
      xmlReader.Read();

      // Assign the public parameters to the text box
      txtPubParams1.Text = xmlReader.ReadOuterXml();
   }
}
```

Now let's look at the code behind the Encrypt button. First, we create an object of the `CspParameters` class and set the flag to use the machine store to look for the PKI keys. Then we give the key container the name `ApressRSAStore`.

```
private void btnEncrypt1_Click(object sender, System.EventArgs e)
{
   if (txtClearText1.Text.Trim() != "")
   {
      try
      {
         CspParameters cspParam = new CspParameters();
         cspParam.Flags = CspProviderFlags.UseMachineKeyStore;
         cspParam.KeyContainerName = "ApressRSAStore";
         cspParam.ProviderName = "MS Strong Cryptographic Provider";

         // CryptoAPI constant -> PROV_RSA_FULL = 1
         // This provider type supports both digital
         // signatures and data encryption, and is considered
         // general purpose. The RSA public key algorithm
         // is used for all public key operations.
         cspParam.ProviderType = 1;
```

Once we've initialized the parameters for the CSP, we create a new object of type RSACryptoServiceProvider using our CspParameters object. Then, we assign the public key by calling the FromXmlString method. After that, we perform our usual process of converting the string into a byte array and passing the byte array into the Encrypt method and converting the byte array back to a string.

```
            // Initializing the RSA Cryptography Service Provider (CSP)
            RSACryptoServiceProvider rsaProvider1 = new
                                      RSACryptoServiceProvider(cspParam);

            // Load the public parameters
            rsaProvider1.FromXmlString(txtPubParams1.Text);

            UTF8Encoding utf8 = new UTF8Encoding();
            byte[] clearText = utf8.GetBytes(txtClearText1.Text);

            // Convert encrypted text to base64
            txtCipherText1.Text = Convert.ToBase64String(
                                 rsaProvider1.Encrypt(clearText, false));
         }
         catch (Exception e)
         {
            MessageBox.Show(this, e.ToString());
         }
      }
   }
```

The decryption method is again very simple—we just create an RSA CSP object and assign the private key to it. We then decrypt the message using the Decrypt method.

```
private void btnDecrypt1_Click(object sender, System.EventArgs e)
{
   if (txtClearText1.Text.Trim() != "")
   {
      // Initialize the RSA Cryptography Service Provider (CSP)
      RSACryptoServiceProvider rsaProvider1 = new RSACryptoServiceProvider();

      // Load the private parameters
      rsaProvider1.FromXmlString(this.txtPriParams1.Text);

      // Decrypt the data received
      MessageBox.Show(this, ASCIIEncoding.ASCII.GetString(
                 rsaProvider1.Decrypt(Convert.FromBase64String(
                 txtCipherText1.Text.Trim()), false)), "Decrypted value",
                 MessageBoxButtons.OK, MessageBoxIcon.Information);
   }
}
```

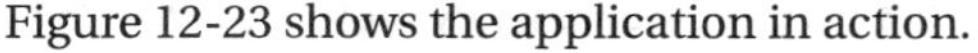

Figure 12-23 shows the application in action.

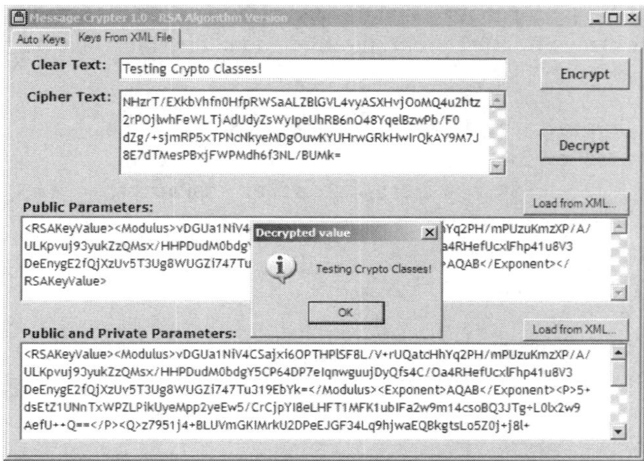

Figure 12-23. *Application getting public and private keys from XML files*

There is one limitation of the RSA algorithm that you should know—the `Encrypt` method can only encrypt up to 16 bytes if the High Encryption Pack is installed. Otherwise, it can only encrypt 5 bytes.

Reading an X509 Certificate

A certificate is like a "voucher" that contains information about the person holding the voucher, such as who authorized the certificate, its public keys, and its expiration information. Certificates are signed by a certifying authority (or CA), such as VeriSign or Thawte. The Microsoft Certificate Server also allows us to create "self-signed" certificates. However, they may not be trusted by the rest of the world, since this is not issued by a well-known CA, but they are very useful in an Intranet scenario.

Server certificates are used to identify the trustworthiness of the server, and client certificates identify a client to the server. A CA issues both client and server certificates after verifying the identity. For example, when the client is requesting a web resource, it can also send a client certificate along with the request. The server can then determine who the client is and authorize or deny them.

■ **NOTE** Thawte provides the client certificate free of charge, but VeriSign charges a fee for it.

Client certificates are usually installed on web clients such as browsers and e-mail clients. You can view all the client certificates installed in IE by clicking Tools ➤ Internet Options and selecting the Content tab in the dialog box. Click the Certificates button here. As you can see in Figure 12-24, I have two client certificates installed in IE6.

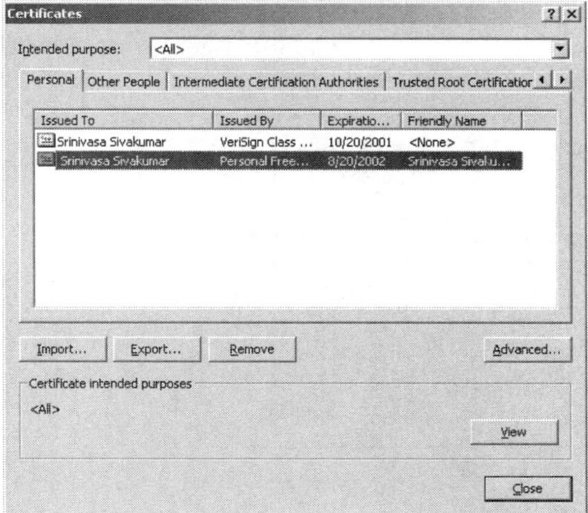

Figure 12-24. *Installed client certificates*

The Cryptography namespace also contains the child namespace X509Certificates. This contains just three classes used to represent and manage Authenticode X.509 v.3 certificates. The X509Certificate class exposes the static methods CreateFromCertFile and CreateFromSignedFile to create an instance of the certificate.

The CreateFromCertFile method reads the content of the X509 certificate from a certificate file, and the CreateFromSignedFile method reads the content of the X509 certificate from a digitally signed file. We will use the CreateFromCertFile method to read the contents of the X509 client certificate.

```
private void btnView_Click(object sender, System.EventArgs e)
{
   // Read the client certificate from the file
   // into the object variable of the type X509Certificate
   X509Certificate clientCert =
                           X509Certificate.CreateFromCertFile("test.cer");

   StringBuilder sb = new StringBuilder();

   sb.Append("Issuer Name: " + clientCert.GetIssuerName() + "\n");
   sb.Append("Public Key String: " + clientCert.GetPublicKeyString() + "\n");
   sb.Append("Key Algorithm: " + clientCert.GetKeyAlgorithm().ToString() + "\n");
   sb.Append("Serial Number: " + clientCert.GetSerialNumberString() + "\n");
   sb.Append("Effective Date: " +
            clientCert.GetEffectiveDateString().ToString() + "\n");
   sb.Append("Expiration Date: " +
            clientCert.GetExpirationDateString().ToString() + "\n");
   MessageBox.Show(this, sb.ToString());
}
```

We've declared an object of type `X509Certificate`, and we've used the `CreateFromCertFile` method to read the certificate content into the object. Then we've read the main properties of the certificate and displayed it to a message box, as shown in Figure 12-25.

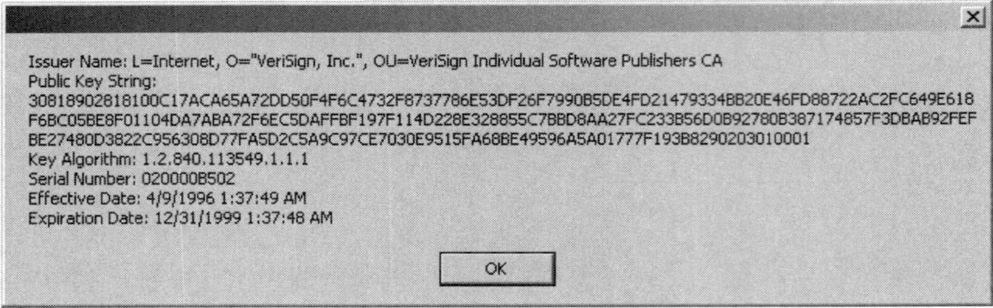

Figure 12-25. *Displaying the main properties of a certificate*

Cryptography and Network Programming

So far in this chapter, you've learned all about cryptography—now it's time to use some of the techniques in network programming. Remember the simple UDP chat utility that we wrote in Chapter 8? The UDP chat application is very simple. It takes the local and remote port numbers and the IP address and passes the information back and forth.

Here is the code before adding any cryptography algorithms. The `Send` method here gets the datagram, converts it into a byte array, and sends the data using the `Send` method of the `UdpClient` class. The `Receiver` method here also works in the same way.

```
private static void Send(string datagram)
{
   // Create UdpClient
   UdpClient sender = new UdpClient();

   // Create IPEndPoint with details of remote host
   IPEndPoint endPoint = new IPEndPoint(remoteIPAddress, remotePort);

   try
   {
      // Convert data to byte array
      byte[] bytes = Encoding.ASCII.GetBytes(datagram);

      // Send data
      sender.Send(bytes, bytes.Length, endPoint);
   }
   catch (Exception e)
   {
      Console.WriteLine(e.ToString());
   }
```

```
        finally
        {
            // Close connection
            sender.Close();
        }
    }

    public static void Receiver()
    {
        // Create a UdpClient for reading incoming data.
        UdpClient receivingUdpClient = new UdpClient(localPort);

        // IPEndPoint with remote host information
        IPEndPoint RemoteIpEndPoint = null;

        try
        {
            Console.WriteLine(
                    "-----------*******Ready for chat!!!*******-----------");

            while(true)
            {
                // Wait for datagram
                byte[] receiveBytes = receivingUdpClient.Receive(
                                                    ref RemoteIpEndPoint);

                // Convert and display data
                string returnData = Encoding.ASCII.GetString(receiveBytes);
                Console.WriteLine("-" + returnData.ToString());
            }
        }
        catch (Exception e)
        {
            Console.WriteLine(e.ToString ());
        }
    }
```

Let's use the Rijndael symmetric algorithm to send secure information between two chat clients. The `Rijndael` algorithm is a symmetric algorithm, and it is best for bulk data transfer. This is the main reason that I've chosen this algorithm. We're going to add `EncryptData` and `DecryptData` methods to this class to take care of the secure communication process. When we're sending information to the remote socket, we'll call the `EncryptData` method to encrypt the data, and then we'll pass the encrypted byte array to the other end. When we receive the encrypted byte array on the other end, we'll call the `DecryptData` method to decrypt the byte array.

As you can see, this design is very simple. To support the symmetric algorithms, we add two private class-level members that store the shared key and vector.

```
private static IPAddress remoteIPAddress;
private static int remotePort;
private static int localPort;
private static UTF8Encoding Utf8Encod;
private static string CryptoKey = "!i~6ox1i@]t2K'y$";
private static string CryptoVI =  "!~x70q{6+q1@#VI$";
```

The EncryptData method takes a string as input and returns a byte array back.

```
static byte[] EncryptData(string theDataGram)
{
   byte[] bCipherText = null;
   try
   {
```

We create a new object type of RijndaelManaged, and assign the shared key and vector. Then we create an ICryptoTransform object using the CreateEncryptor() method.

```
      // Create the Rijandael Service Provider object and assign the
      // key and vector to it
      RijndaelManaged RijndaelProvider = new RijndaelManaged();
      RijndaelProvider.Key = Utf8Encod.GetBytes(CryptoKey);
      RijndaelProvider.IV = Utf8Encod.GetBytes(CryptoVI);

      ICryptoTransform RijndaelEncrypt = RijndaelProvider.CreateEncryptor();
```

Now, we convert the datagram into a byte array using the UTF8Encoding class. Then we declare a MemoryStream object and use a CryptoStream object to perform the cryptographic transformation—you may recall that we had a fleeting look at the CryptoStream class in Chapter 2.

```
      // Convert string to byte array
      byte[] bClearText = Utf8Encod.GetBytes(theDataGram);
      MemoryStream Mstm = new MemoryStream();

      // Create Crypto Stream that transforms a stream using the encryption
      CryptoStream Cstm = new CryptoStream(Mstm, RijndaelEncrypt,
                                           CryptoStreamMode.Write);

      // Write out encrypted content into MemoryStream
      Cstm.Write(bClearText, 0, bClearText.Length);
      Ctms.FlushFinalBlock();
```

We create the byte array back from the MemoryStream and return the byte array back to the caller.

```
        // Get the output
        bCipherText = Mstm.ToArray();

        // Close the stream handlers
        Cstm.Close();
        Mstm.Close();
    }
    catch (Exception e)
    {
        Console.WriteLine(e.ToString ());
    }
    return bCipherText;
}
```

The DecryptData method, which does the decryption process, is similar to the EncryptData method. The DecryptData method takes a byte array as input and returns a string as output.

```
static string DecryptData(byte[] bCipherText)
{
    string sEncoded ="";

    try
    {
        // Create the RijndaelManaged Service Provider object and assign
        // the key and vector to it
        RijndaelManaged RijndaelProvider = new RijndaelManaged();
        RijndaelProvider.Key = Utf8Encod.GetBytes(strCryptoKey);
        RijndaelProvider.IV = Utf8Encod.GetBytes(strCryptoVI);

        ICryptoTransform RijndaelDecrypt= RijndaelProvider.CreateDecryptor();

        // Create a MemoryStream with the input
        MemoryStream Mstm = new MemoryStream(bCipherText, 0, bCipherText.Length);

        // Create Crypto Stream that transforms a stream using the decryption
        CryptoStream Cstm = new CryptoStream(Mstm, RijndaelDecrypt,
                                             CryptoStreamMode.Read);

        // Read out the result from the Crypto Stream
        StreamReader Sr = new StreamReader(Cstm);
        sEncoded = Sr.ReadToEnd();

        Sr.Close();
        Cstm.Close();
```

```
        Mstm.Close();
    }
    catch (Exception e)
    {
        Console.WriteLine(e.ToString ());
    }

    return sEncoded;
}
```

Let's call the EncryptData and DecryptData methods in the proper places in the chat application. The Send method calls the EncryptData method with the string entered by the user and sends the result via the Send method of the UdpClient. The Receiver method passes the received byte array into the DecryptData method and displays the decrypted message.

```
private static void Send(string datagram)
{
    ...
    try
    {
        // Convert string to byte array
        //byte[] bClearText = Utf8Encod.GetBytes(datagram);

        // Encrypting the data received
        byte[] bytes = EncryptData(datagram);

        // Send data
        sender.Send(bytes, bytes.Length, endPoint);
    }
    ...
}

public static void Receiver()
{
    ...
        while(true)
        {
            // Wait for datagram
            byte[] receiveBytes = receivingUdpClient.Receive(ref RemoteIpEndPoint);

            // Decrypt the incoming byte array
            string returnData = DecryptData(receiveBytes);

            Console.WriteLine("-" + returnData.ToString());
        }
    ...
}
```

We can also implement this with an asymmetric algorithm such as RSA—let's see an example of this. We'll just rewrite the `EncryptData` and `DecryptData` methods using the RSA algorithm. The rest of the implementation will remain the same.

Before writing the `EncryptData` and `DecryptData` methods, we have to store the public key and the private key in private class-level variables.

```
private static IPAddress remoteIPAddress;
private static int remotePort;
private static int localPort;
private static UTF8Encoding Utf8Encod;

private static string PubKey = "<RSAKeyValue><Modulus>sttDL3xug/BqMk13d6G5vWekmyul
/d3pz/Lpvk2Q1GNBSriatLxCRJSuOAie8g/yby624K85qJLwMMzwCru7b+kNTA2dYaK4Nk+FkZMLCVmom
iW1zns2KsT1aF9hwr32Nyje3OuJDlHqBtcOpCGbo+kJ+JC88BM1J9AkdoAa+SE=</Modulus>
<Exponent>AQAB</Exponent></RSAKeyValue>";

private static string PriKey = "<RSAKeyValue><Modulus>sttDL3xug/BqMk13d6G5vWekmyul
/d3pz/Lpvk2Q1GNBSriatLxCRJSuOAie8g/yby624K85qJLwMMzwCru7b+kNTA2dYaK4Nk+FkZMLCVmom
iW1zns2KsT1aF9hwr32Nyje3OuJDlHqBtcOpCGbo+kJ+JC88BM1J9AkdoAa+SE=</Modulus><Exponent>
AQAB</Exponent><P>3BoisxTvnh8Xtg/o2fTGtr/k8OXUOiEfKwAKzWje36v8zkTfIc4EzdZbRskJywq1N
Mo9U1EHM3DUv+Ya/KGPzQ==</P><Q>0AcCph/CdQeB2/M+q3BSlzimr9Chw9zaHk1x8MBCHdRB9c26VcSOA
mKW+G4VzjWJjI6cK8j/GQjhnRn7UbBypQ==</Q><DP>bikCjwD+gPRs6KmJOgCp6FOY4VOWYFWthNcLkQ1Y
5zfsWsyrpP649tC/dGkwZpggY6CJGwcmBIAHa1hez2yJTQ==</DP><DQ>Uzva1Xkzpvuf+89xrcq9YQArwY
DqmKGPLDyOcC2cxq6czarI+XRAyguEeFYjp2RIatLMrcA4QV4KV3+DzQWaeQ==</DQ><InverseQ>
eriVG9Kp3CQ/J9PpfMlemC7tPIs6m//LyhKD7J5zLGIzz+71C5QjVi2dRwtvjGJaexOTi+TRIv2fT
/LhWmsCDQ==</InverseQ><D>sjfHZ47OtIuf1gXY8AznfnLCO5eXrDIuo/YBsY2qredFDQaLqWIZiiq4ur
7kWoFHakAbHCGeC3p2+bmLyrYr2nm8OgjOc1NUneE8ASoKWfnbcWxW377Oeogj16frPUoAgwU1gFURdTxoz
gNLThVtNItrc3Doa5eJ+U7pRSz2edE=</D></RSAKeyValue>";
```

Here is how the `EncryptData` and `DecryptData` methods look. In the `EncryptData` method we create a new `CspParameters` object, and use the object to create a new RSA algorithm object. Next, we assign the public key from the private class member. Then, we call the `Encrypt` method of the RSA object.

```
static byte[] EncryptData(string strDataGram)
{
   CspParameters theCspParam = new CspParameters();
   theCspParam.Flags = CspProviderFlags.UseMachineKeyStore;
   theCspParam.KeyContainerName = "ApressRSAStore";

   // Initializing the RSA Cryptography Service Provider (CSP)
   RSACryptoServiceProvider theRSAProvider = new
                                      RSACryptoServiceProvider(objCspParam);

   // Set to Load the public key
   theRSAProvider.FromXmlString(PubKey);

   // Convert string to byte array
   byte[] bClearText = Utf8Encod.GetBytes(strDataGram);
```

```
    // Encrypting the data received
    byte[] bytes = theRSAProvider.Encrypt(bClearText, false);
    theRSAProvider.Clear();

    return bytes;
}
```

The DecryptData method does pretty much the same thing. It creates a new RSA object and assigns the private key from the class member. Then it calls the Decrypt method and sends the string back to the caller.

```
static string DecryptData(byte[] bCipherText)
{
    // Initializing the RSA Cryptography Service Provider (CSP)
    RSACryptoServiceProvider theRSAProvider = new RSACryptoServiceProvider();

    // Set to Load the private key
    theRSAProvider.FromXmlString(PriKey);

    // Encrypting the data received
    string strRtnData = Utf8Encod.GetString(theRSAProvider.Decrypt(bCipherText,
                                                                     false));
    theRSAProvider.Clear();

    return strRtnData;
}
```

This implementation of the EncryptData and DecryptData methods can be replaced with the previous example and the code will work fine. The only thing that we have to be careful about in this example is the size limitations of the Encrypt method—we talked about these limitations earlier.

Summary

In this chapter, we've covered lot of ground, starting with a very brief history of cryptography. We went into why we need to use cryptography, and gave a hacking example that shows how the transmitted information is visible to the whole world.

Then, we introduced the different types of cryptographic algorithms, such as symmetric algorithms, asymmetric algorithms, and hash algorithms, before looking in detail at how each of these types works. Next, we introduced the basic concepts of cryptography, such as block ciphers and stream ciphers, padding, and modes.

After the introduction to cryptography in general, we dived into the specifics of using cryptography in .NET. You learned about the System.Security.Cryptography namespace, including the cryptography class hierarchy, before walking through examples demonstrating the use of hashing, symmetric, and asymmetric algorithms in .NET. Then, we covered RSA encryption extensively, and touched on accessing X509 certificates from .NET. Finally, we saw some examples of how to use cryptography in network programming using the Rijndael and RSA algorithms.

CHAPTER 13

Authentication Protocols

Authentication has become a major issue for any application developer who expects code to run across a network or across the Internet. Making sure that users are who they say they are and verifying machine identities on demand are part of an application's security module. Developers of Windows applications should conform to the Windows-specific security procedures implemented by Microsoft, in addition to any additional security measures to be imposed by the application.

Windows 4.0 NT and Windows 2000 focus on authentication as a major issue because of the weak security implemented in earlier versions of Windows NT and the Windows 9*x* family of operating systems. Rather than invent a new authentication system from scratch, Microsoft examined the existing authentication methods and embraced them, especially the use of Kerberos with Windows 2000.

In this chapter, you'll see what the authentication protocols involved in Microsoft's networking schemes are, how they work, and how they apply to the various versions of Windows. Of course, you'll also learn how security is handled in the .NET Framework.

In this chapter, we will cover the following topics:

- NT LAN Manager (NTLM) authentication, used for Windows NT
- Kerberos authentication, used for Windows 2000
- Windows authentication
- .NET security

Authentication and Authorization

Before looking at the authentication protocols, we need to quickly define two terms:

- *Authentication* is used to determine a user's identity and what that user has access to. Any logon window provides simply authentication using a logon name and a password. This simple authentication scheme has many problems, which is why more complex authentication methods have been developed.
- *Authorization* is the determination of whether a user has access to a particular resource, both local and remote. Authorization is often tied to the concept of *trust*, where a trusted device (used by an authenticated user) is allowed access to services. Authorization always includes the concept of authentication.

NTLM

Microsoft's Windows NT LAN Manager (NTLM) authentication is a one-time password challenge/response authentication system. This type of authentication system goes back many years and has been used for many different purposes.

How Challenge/Response Authentication Works

In its simplest form, a challenge/response authentication system displays a challenge (also called a *nonce*), which is usually a number or string. A response is created based on the challenge, and once accepted, the authentication is complete. This is usually a one-time authentication, performed at the start of the session and valid until the session ends.

Early challenge/response authentication systems used manual lookups: the computer would display a challenge, and the user would look up the reply from a book or software tool (called a *password token*), sending the reply back to the computer. This process was quickly automated. Now when a client attempts to access a server resource, the server generates and sends the challenge, which the client software processes to determine the reply, based on algorithms. After the server has acknowledged that the response is correct, the client is authenticated.

Challenge/response authentication systems have a few major advantages. Since the challenge can be generated randomly every time one is needed, there is no need to store challenge and response pairs in a file or algorithm, which would be accessible to hackers or reverse-engineering attacks. With this system, reuse of a challenge and corresponding password is also extremely unlikely, thus preventing hacking using repeated codes. Also, there is no need to maintain synchronization between the client and the server. Whenever the client contacts the server, the random challenge is generated and the correct response calculated.

The primary disadvantage of the challenge/response authentication system is that the client must generate a proper response to the challenge, which means either involving the user in a lookup operation or employing an algorithm on the client. To prevent unwanted attacks, the client algorithm is usually a one-way system that does not allow generation of challenges, only responses.

Many current challenge/response authentication systems adhere to standards adopted by the American Bankers Association (the standard is called X9.9) and the U.S. Government (called FIPS 113). Both systems use the Data Encryption Standard (DES) as a one-way hash function. When the server sends the challenge, it is encrypted using DES and a secret key embedded in the hardware or software. Internal algorithms then create the password response, which is valid only one time. By publishing the standards, software developers can not only decide whether the challenge/response authentication systems are secure enough for use, but can also more easily implement them by following the standards.

NTLM Development

When Microsoft was developing its LAN Manager product (also known as LANMAN or LM), it needed an authentication system that would allow not only the (then new) Windows NT operating system, but also older PCs running DOS and Windows, to participate in client/server transactions securely. LAN Manager used a challenge/response authentication system for this reason. With the addition of a small piece of software, a client could communicate with the server in a manner much more secure than otherwise possible. NTLM was used for all NT products through Windows NT 4, but Windows 2000 also added the option of using Kerberos authentication, a more secure option than NTLM.

There are actually three versions of what we now call NTLM. Originally, there was LAN Manager, followed by the Windows NT LAN Manager (NTLM), and then NTLM version 2 (NTLMv2). LAN Manager was originally developed by IBM for the OS/2 operating system. Microsoft enhanced this protocol for Windows NT and called it NTLM. With the addition of stronger 128-bit security in Windows NT Service Pack 4, Microsoft introduced NTLMv2. Older versions of Windows can support NTLMv2 when the Directory Services Client is installed (a required update for Internet Explorer with 128-bit secure connection support). If older clients do not have NTLMv2 installed, they default to using NTLM.

A challenge/response authentication system was ideal for the early requirements of LAN Manager. Since the sharing of resources was an integral part of Microsoft's vision for Windows PCs and Windows NT servers, a way of verifying legal access to resources like printers, files, and external peripherals was necessary. Ideally, the new authentication system had to be relatively fast, require nothing more than the addition of some compatible software on the client, and be secure. With such a product, Microsoft could compete with the resource sharing and inherent security that the UNIX world offered, but within the familiar Windows environment.

Microsoft handled the network authentication by using a protocol that could be transmitted in existing Server Message Block (SMB) messages, already used for resource sharing. The client software package required contained all the complex algorithms for generating the authentication tokens, using the new protocol, and embedding that content in SMB messages.

Challenge/response authentication was necessary to prevent password sniffing on the network (wherein hackers watch for passwords in network messages and simply reuse them for their own purposes). Because challenge/response authentication systems use one-time passwords, intercepting a password would not gain a hacker any advantage. Furthermore, Microsoft made sure that all user logon passwords on the server were encrypted in an attempt to prevent reverse-engineering of the challenge and response tokens, as well as to secure the basic logon information.

Naturally, weaknesses with any challenge/response authentication system are inevitable. In Microsoft's case, the major problem with the NTLM system was not with the challenge/response authentication system itself, but with the way passwords were stored on the server.

Password Storage Concerns

The Registry is a data file maintained by Windows for information about the hardware, installed software, the user, the system security, and many other aspects of the machine. One area of the Registry is the Security Accounts Manager (SAM), which contains entries for every user allowed to access the system or to share resources. All user accounts and passwords are stored in the SAM database on Windows NT systems. With Windows 2000, workstation and local logons are managed using information retained in the SAM database, and the SAM is used exclusively if Active Directory is not in use. This means that stealing the SAM database is an easy way to obtain passwords. Using tools like L0phtCrack, freely available on the Web, passwords are easy to decrypt.

Naturally, Microsoft did its best to restrict access to the SAM and its contents, but the relatively weak encryption in Windows NT allowed hackers to access the information. Attacks on the SAM itself even became part of regular life with the Samba project, which was designed to allow non-Windows operating systems to share resources with Windows machines and vice versa. As part of the sharing from a Linux client to a Windows server, for example, the server's SAM had to be fooled into thinking it was a Windows machine at the other end and the authentication messages coming in were correct. This inevitably meant the SAM had to be compromised, and many hackers used Samba toolsets to crack Windows NT Server Registries. With Windows 2000, the password encryption system was beefed up considerably.

LAN Manager Encryption

The LAN Manager was the predecessor to NTLM, and hence worth looking at to understand the evolution of NTLM and Kerberos. The process that is performed by the LAN Manager software is easily explained in terms of hashing the user's password.

When a client attempted to access a server resource, the user's password was first converted to a 14-character string. If the password was longer than 14 characters, the extra characters were dropped; if the password was shorter than 14 characters, additional characters were added to pad the length to 14 characters. All the characters were then converted to uppercase, since case-independence was required for the LAN Manager system (DOS and early Windows systems were not case-dependent).

The client software then split the 14-character password into two 7-character strings. (Windows NT did not break the 14-character string into two, but treated the string as one entity.) Each of the two 7-character strings was then used as the key to encrypt a 64-bit constant using DES. These two encrypted strings were then concatenated into one string, which formed the encrypted password that was saved in the SAM.

When clients logged on, the passwords they typed were encrypted using this process and compared to the encrypted string in the SAM. The SAM's encrypted string was never decrypted.

As mentioned earlier, the encryption process used by LAN Manager was not as strong as most users assumed it would be. The reason is easily seen with a few calculations. Because LAN Manager used a 14-character, single-case password, there were 26^14 combinations zpossible (assuming only alphabetic characters in the password). This required 65 bits to represent. That's formidable, but the LAN Manager practice of dividing the password into two 7-character strings compromised the security. Instead of cracking a 65-bit key, a hacker needed to crack only two 32-bit keys (26^7 twice, resulting in 32 bits). While a 32-bit key is still strong, it can easily be attacked with repetitive scripts.

But cracking passwords was made even simpler for a hacker because of two factors: LAN Manager's use of concatenated strings and its lax password-length requirement. Because LAN Manager used two 7-character strings, each string could be attacked separately. If the second string could be cracked first, it could often give a clue to the first string using dictionary searches. For example, if the second string was decrypted to *tion* followed by three nulls (from the padding to 14-character strings), all dictionary words with seven letters before *tion* could be searched and tested quickly. Of course, the same applied if the first string could be cracked, leaving the second string easily tested (assuming regular dictionary words were used in the password).

The second advantage for a hacker arose because LAN Manager did not force passwords of any particular length. Most users' passwords average six or seven characters. With LAN Manager's scheme, the extra characters were padded to 14 characters with nulls, and cracking encrypted null strings is easy (which is why the second 7-character string was usually attacked before the first). So, instead of having to worry about 32-bit keys, if only half the strings were actual characters, the process of cracking the password would progress much faster.

Windows NT Encryption

LAN Manager's password encryption system was reasonably effective, but also prone to hacking. Windows NT tried to improve on the LAN Manager scheme in a number of ways by implementing the Windows logon protocol (which appeared as part of the package for Windows 9*x* client platforms). The Windows logon protocol intercepted all challenges and generated the responses automatically, using the user's password as the key for the token generation.

When a user logged on, Windows encrypted the password into a 128-bit key (which was maintained in encrypted form until the user logged off, with Windows discarding the plain text password). The Windows logon protocol worked by having a server generate a 64-bit (8 byte) challenge when a request to log on or use a resource was initiated. The client received the 64-bit challenge and used the user's 128-bit encrypted password as a key to three separate 56-bit DES encryptions of the challenge. The three 56-bit encrypted strings were then concatenated into one larger 168-bit string. Adding hyphens between the substrings resulted in a 24-byte response for the challenge.

The primary weakness of this challenge/response authentication system was the use of the encrypted passwords. If hackers could obtain the password from the Registry or through interception of network traffic containing the encrypted password, they could use that encrypted password to determine a response to a challenge. (The user's real password didn't matter, because Windows logon used the encrypted password only.) Once the encrypted password was in a hacker's control, a machine could be set up to masquerade as a valid client, and using the encrypted password, it could respond properly to a server's challenge.

A brute-force hack attack could be performed to look for the user's plain text password, but that would be much more time-consuming and less likely to succeed than with LAN Manager's challenge/response authentication scheme. A hacker had a better chance if a number of successful challenge/response messages could be intercepted, allowing analysis of the responses and potentially leading to better guesses at the plain text password.

NTLM Authentication

As security concerns increased in the 1990s, Microsoft responded by increasing security measures in each subsequent release of LAN Manager and Windows NT. Windows NT 4 provides three different authentication systems, referred to as *local*, *domain*, and *remote* by Microsoft. Both domain and remote systems use challenge/response authentication and are usually collectively treated as NTLM.

The security improvements started with the user's password itself. Instead of using only uppercase characters, Windows NT 4 supports Unicode, allowing many more characters in the password, with case-sensitivity. While the 14-character limit is still used in Windows NT 4, the extra allowable Unicode characters mean that 28 bytes (14 two-byte characters; Unicode requires 2 bytes to represent all possible characters) now made up the password string. Furthermore, Microsoft abandoned DES in favor of the commercially available Message Digest #4 (MD4), which is inherently more complex. Windows NT 4 uses MD4 and the 28-byte password to create a 128-bit encrypted password, which is used internally. This is frequently called the *NTLM hash*.

Unfortunately, because of backward-compatibility requirements, some compromises in the design of the Windows NT 4 were imposed. Instead of using only the NTLM hash, two encrypted passwords are actually used: the NTLM hash and the older LAN Manager hash. Either could be used for the challenge/response authentication process, as the client could generate responses to both challenges. Obviously, it was easier to crack the older LAN Manager hash, so hackers focused on that, instead of the harder NTLM hash. Cracking the LAN Manager hash still gave them the same access to the Windows NT 4 servers and resources.

To try to patch the security hole, Microsoft released a patch to Windows NT 4 that added encryption to the SAM entries. Called a *system key*, the encryption system is used to encrypt the SAM database, but the key must be provided every time the SAM is required. This is no problem while the machine is turned on (and the system administrator had supplied the key once), but every reboot requires the key to be retrieved. Microsoft allows the administrator to input the key each time the system reboots, but this requires a physical presence whenever the machine boots (a problem with remote systems). The patch does allow the key to be placed on a diskette and read when the system boots. However, the floppy must be available on reboot, which again is a problem for remote systems. The alternative would be to place the key in the Registry itself, allowing automatic booting and decryption of the SAM. The downside is obvious: anyone could snag a copy of the Registry and obtain the key.

Windows 2000 replaced the NTLM authentication methods with Kerberos methods, which are described in the next section.

Kerberos

NTLM and other challenge/response authentication systems work by having the client machine talk directly to the server, authenticating itself on the server. This works well in certain architectures, but it isn't very efficient when you have many different machines that want to talk to each other at intervals, without becoming overburdened by playing a role as a server. In this case, a third machine that can authenticate both machines that need to talk together is a better model, allowing many different machines to employ a single authentication server. This is the principle of key distribution centers, which are the basis of the development of Kerberos.

Kerberos authentication is used in Windows 2000, and it can be added to other operating systems. Kerberos is a key-based system, offering strong authentication capabilities. Before looking at Kerberos specifically, we'll look at key-based authentication in general and how Kerberos came to be.

How Key-Based Authentication Works

Encryption keys are a necessary part of any encryption algorithm. The problem with encryption keys is that someone or something must have them and make them available as needed (with proper authorization processes to ensure the request is valid). Static encryption keys are obviously less secure than keys that change at intervals. Changing keys frequently reduces the chances of someone obtaining a key and using it for future access. To provide dynamic keys, available on demand, the banking industry developed key distribution centers (KDCs) in the 1980s.

Key Distribution Centers

KDCs are machines that provide keys on request to any authorized user. The primary advantage of KDCs is that they can be used by any number of sites, they do not require the physical distribution of keys to many locations, and they provide constantly changing keys. Each machine has a unique master key, which it uses both as an authentication key with the KDC and as a means of encrypting temporary key information passed between the machine and the KDC, as well as to other machines that need to use the same temporary key.

As illustrated in Figure 13-1, the KDC process consists of four steps:

1. When two machines want to communicate with each other, one obtains a random, temporary encryption key from the KDC using its master key to authenticate itself, as well as to encrypt the traffic between that machine and the KDC.
2. The server sends back two temporary encryption keys: one encrypted with the master key from the originating machine and one encrypted with the master key of the other machine. These messages from the KDC containing the temporary keys are called *tickets*.
3. The machine that started the process sends the ticket with the other machine's copy of the temporary key (which is encrypted with the other machine's master key) to the other machine.
4. The receiving machine decrypts the ticket using its master key, and the two machines can then communicate using the temporary key for encryption.

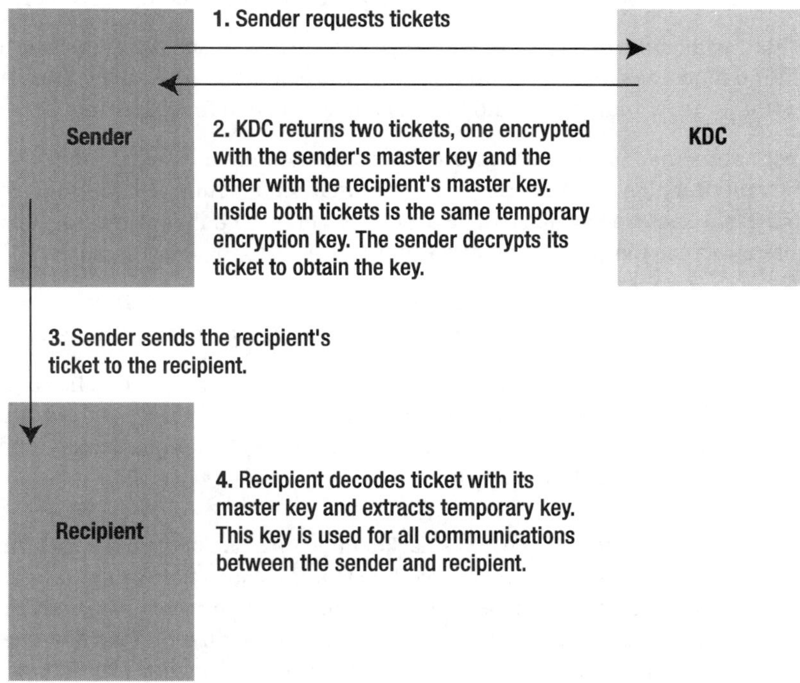

Figure 13-1. *The KDC process*

After the session terminates, the key is useless. A new, different key must be obtained from the KDC for the next session.

Because the KDC sends two tickets, one encrypted with each machine's master key, the KDC needs to maintain a master database of all the master keys. No other machine ever gets the master key of another machine.

There is one main problem with the process: the machine that starts the process has no way of knowing if the ticket for machine B really is for that machine, or whether it is for another machine masquerading as machine B. Also, there is no ability to control access on the user level to the KDC and other machines using the KDC. To solve this problem, a protocol called Needham-Schroeder was developed to incorporate a challenge/response authentication system into the KDC process.

Challenge/Response Protocol

The Needham-Schroeder protocol, which was included in the original version of Kerberos, handles challenge/response authentication, as illustrated in Figure 13-2. In this protocol, the following happens:

1. The initiating machine sends a request to the KDC, which includes its own master key (to authenticate the initiating machine), the user ID of the user initiating the process, the destination machine's identification, and a randomly generated challenge.

2. The KDC then returns the temporary key ticket for both the initiating and receiving machines, and the challenge, encrypted with the initiating machine's master key.

3. The initiating machine decrypts the message and verifies the challenge as well as the destination machine's identification (to prevent masquerading), and then forwards the destination's temporary key and the challenge nonce to that machine.

4. The destination machine uses its master key to decrypt the message from the KDC and has the temporary key for the session. The destination machine also has the initiating user's ID in the message, which can be used to generate a challenge message, encrypted with the temporary key, and sends this back to the initiating user.

5. Upon receipt, the user's software decrypts the nonce, subtracts one from it, and encrypts it again using the temporary key for retransmission to the destination.

6. Finally, the destination machine decrypts the response, checks that one has been deducted (which would not be possible without the temporary key), and assumes all is well. The user is (in theory) verified, both machines have the temporary key, and masquerading is (again, in theory) thwarted.

The theory of verification falls apart when a hacker intercepts one of the messages flying back and forth between the destination and recipient machines. With a little brute-force attack, it is possible that a hacker could decrypt the session key. By obtaining the session key, any machine could then use the same key to continue a conversation with the destination machine, even after the initiating machine terminates the session. To prevent this from occurring, timestamps were proposed in the protocols, either in addition to, or replacing, the nonce. Kerberos, originally developed at MIT, included the Needham-Schroeder protocol as well as timestamp ideas.

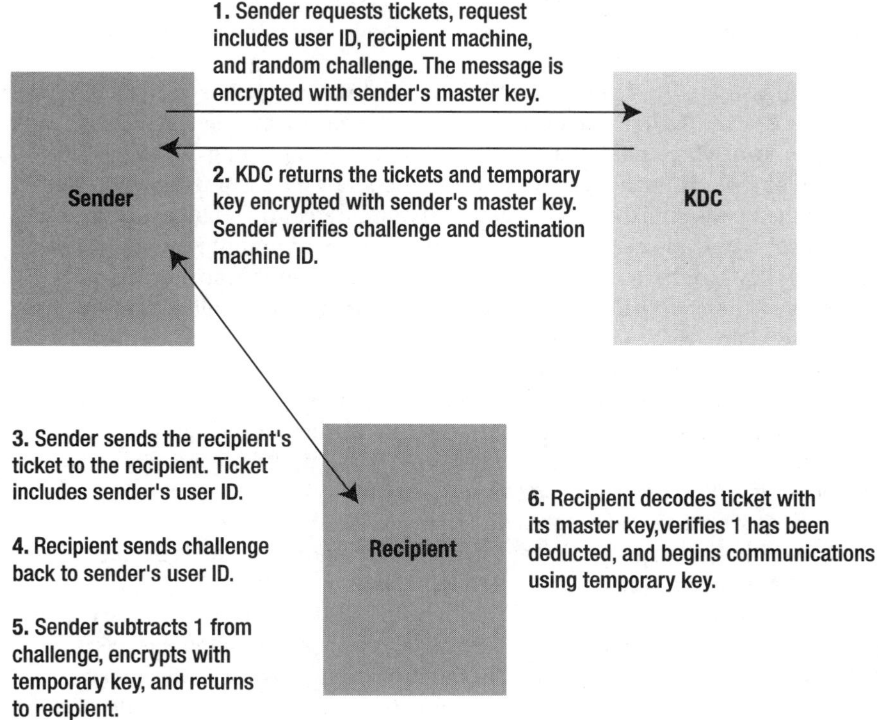

1. Sender requests tickets, request includes user ID, recipient machine, and random challenge. The message is encrypted with sender's master key.
Sender
KDC
2. KDC returns the tickets and temporary key encrypted with sender's master key. Sender verifies challenge and destination machine ID.
3. Sender sends the recipient's ticket to the recipient. Ticket includes sender's user ID.
4. Recipient sends challenge back to sender's user ID.
5. Sender subtracts 1 from challenge, encrypts with temporary key, and returns to recipient.
Recipient
6. Recipient decodes ticket with its master key,verifies 1 has been deducted, and begins communications using temporary key.

Figure 13-2. *The Needham-Schroeder protocol in the KDC process*

The Kerberos Authentication Process

Kerberos went through four iterations until it was finally released as Kerberos version 4 in 1989. The next release, Kerberos version 5, is the release used today. The Kerberos KDC employs an authentication server and a ticket-granting server in the authentication process.

Kerberos Authentication Servers and Ticket-Granting Servers

A *Kerberos authentication server* (KAS) uses a protocol similar to the Needham-Schroeder protocol, described in the previous section, to issue tickets. For a machine to be granted a ticket from a KAS, a request known as a KRB_AS_REQ (Kerberos Authentication Server Request) message is sent. This message includes the name of the initiating machine, the user name, the name of the destination machine, a nonce, and a validity time span indicating when the temporary key is to be considered valid and when it expires. The KAS generates a random temporary key and returns it in a KRB_AS_REP (Kerberos Authentication Server Reply) message, which includes the destination machine's ticket as well.

Next, the initiating machine constructs a KRB_AS_REQ message to the destination machine. This contains the encrypted ticket from the KAS, as well as the initiating user name and a timestamp. The user name and timestamp are encrypted with the temporary key. When the destination machine receives the message, it decrypts the ticket from the KAS and uses the temporary key contained therein to decrypt the user name and timestamp from the initiating machine. The user name in the KAS's ticket and the user name in the message from the initiating machine must match, and the timestamp should be recent (usually created within five minutes).

Kerberos also addresses another problem with keys: storing the master key. Master keys are maintained on the KDC and used on each machine that wants to use the KDC. This means the master key resides somewhere on the machines, vulnerable to snooping by others. The obvious solution is to obtain the master key from users when they log on or need to use Kerberos, and then lose the key as quickly as possible to prevent interception. Since prompting the user for the key every time it is needed is not good from a user's point of view, another way of handling the master key is preferable. The solution is to create a temporary key right away from the master key, and then discard the master key. The temporary key, called a *session key*, is then used for all interactions with the KDC.

To handle the session keys, another server is employed by Kerberos: the *ticket-granting server* (TGS), which accepts ticket-granting tickets. When a user logs on to a machine, the master key is used to contact the authentication server, which issues a ticket-granting ticket back, using the master key for encryption. After decrypting the reply, the master key is discarded. Then the ticket-granting ticket is used to connect to the TGS for every service the machine needs to access. Any time the user needs a new service, the temporary ticket is used with the TGS, until the user logs off, at which point the temporary ticket is invalid.

The process for these ticket-granting tickets is a variation on that for issuing KAS tickets. When the user sends the request to the KAS, the user receives back the temporary session key in a ticket-granting ticket format. To connect to the TGS, a new message called the KRB_TGS_REQ (Kerberos Ticket-Granting Server Request) is used. This contains the user name and timestamp, the ticket-granting ticket, a validity period, a nonce, and the destination name. The TGS decrypts the message, extracts the temporary key, decrypts the ticketing key with that temporary key, and checks the validity component. The TGS then creates a session key that is sent back to the initiating machine, along with a copy encrypted for the destination machine in a KRB_TGS_REP message.

If this sounds a little confusing, a walk-though may help. The Kerberos authentication process consists of the following steps:

1. The user's machine sends a request to the KAS, requesting a ticket and session key (called the *credentials*) for communicating with the Kerberos TGS.

2. The KAS examines the message and authenticates the client in its database. If the client is authenticated, the KAS generates a session key to allow communication with the TGS and sends the credentials back to the client encrypted using the client's key.

3. The client decrypts the KAS message using its master key and extracts the credentials. Then it sends a message to the TGS containing the session key from the KAS, a timestamp, and the name of the server the client wants to communicate with.

4. The TGS decrypts the client's message, validates it, and looks up the server information in its database. The TGS then creates a new message and sends that back to the client. The returned message has two parts: one for the server and one for the client, both of which contain a new ticket for the client/server communication with a new session key embedded in it.

5. The client decrypts the TGS message and extracts the session key. It then creates an authenticator message that contains the TGS-generated ticket to send to the server.

6. The server decrypts the client's authenticator message, verifies that the timestamp is recent, extracts the session key, and sends back a message to the client acknowledging the request for a session, including a timestamp. The message back to the client is encrypted with the session key.

7. The client and the server can then communicate with each other using the session key.

In this process, a single ticket is issued by the KAS upon request from a client, and that ticket is used only to communicate with the TGS. All other tickets are issued by the TGS. All tickets generated by the KAS and TGS use a unique session key. Whenever the client requires a new connection to the server, a new authenticator is required.

Kerberos 5 Enhancements

The Kerberos protocols you've seen so far do not maintain a unique key on each machine, so authentication is on the user level. This is good, because access to resources is usually on a user, not a machine, basis. It also allows users to log on from any machine and complete their tasks. The approach does have its flaws, though, especially in locations where individual PCs or workstations are assigned to single users. Local files on those machines will be specific to the machine, so there's no authentication to provide verification that the user of a particular machine is allowed to access those files. To restrict access to local resources, *preauthentication* (or *local authentication*, to use Windows NT terminology) is required.

Preauthentication was added to Kerberos version 5 to permit authentication of users or machines sending requests to a KDC, instead of relying on the KDC to authenticate the source. With preauthentication, a workstation will request the user's master key (password) before any attempt to connect with the KDC. (This is different from before, where the KDC can send a reply to a request before asking for the master key.) With preauthentication, the initial request to the KDC is slightly different, as the master key can be used to encrypt the request, which includes a timestamp. The server receives these requests and checks its internal database to see if preauthentication is required. If so, the KDC uses the master key to decrypt the request, checks the timestamp for currency, and then completes the request.

Kerberos version 5 also added two other capabilities: forwardable and proxiable tickets. A *forwardable ticket* means that a workstation can request a ticket-granting ticket tied to another network (called *realms* in Kerberos terminology). You'll see how this works with Windows 2000 domains in the next section. *Proxiable tickets* allow a workstation to request tickets valid on machines on another network. Kerberos can authenticate users on other networks by having KDC communicate with KDC using so-called *referral tickets*.

Although Kerberos version 5 has interesting capabilities, you should realize that this is still not a secure method of authenticating users and clients. The essential element of Kerberos authentication is the encryption key, which can be vulnerable to extraction by a determined hacker. Apart from direct attacks on the client to determine keys stored therein, password-guessing attacks are frequently used to try to determine the secret keys. If the key is compromised, spoof attacks are easily conducted.

Kerberos also does nothing to prevent denial-of-service (DoS) attacks. Because Kerberos hinges on timestamps for messages to be valid, a DOS attack can prevent a machine from receiving a message within the valid time span, hence invalidating the session. It is also obvious that because of the use of timestamps, all the machines participating in the authentication process must have internal clocks that are somewhat synchronized with each other and the Kerberos servers (KAS and TGS).

Windows 2000 Implementation of Kerberos

In Windows 2000, all requests for files and directories on remote machines involve tickets. When you log on to a Windows 2000 server or workstation, a ticket-granting ticket is obtained from the server, which stores all the master keys in the Active Directory.

■ **NOTE** When Windows 2000 communicates with older Windows versions, NTLM is used. Kerberos is always used for Windows 2000-to-Windows 2000 communications. Windows 2000 includes backward-compatible support for both LAN Manager and NTLM protocols, but these give up the advantages of the Kerberos protocol.

There are some differences between Kerberos and Windows 2000's implementation, although Microsoft claims complete interoperability according to the Kerberos standards. This is important to allow non-Windows machines to integrate with Windows 2000 machines. Windows 2000 treats each machine as an individual entity, storing master keys for that machine (as well as any logged-on users' master keys) on the system.

User Logon and Authentication

The way Windows 2000 institutes Kerberos in addition to the usual Windows logon is with a three-step process:

1. The Winlogon window collects the user's logon and password, which it passes to the Local Security Authority (LSA).

2. The LSA converts the password into a Kerberos master key, and then passes the user name and hashed master key to the Security Support Provider Interface (SSPI), which is described in the next section.

3. The SSPI communicates with the Kerberos servers and tries to get a ticket-granting ticket from a server using preauthenticated messages created using the user's master key. (If there is no Kerberos server available, the SSPI defaults to the NTLM protocol.)

When a user logs on to a client on a domain governed by a KDC server, as soon as the logon window has been completed, Windows 2000 performs a password hash and sends the result to a KDC. The return access token contains all the security groups the user belongs to, and it is part of the user's logon session. The access token is also inherited by any application or process the user initiates.

Authentication Between Domains

Windows 2000 allows the use of Kerberos authentication between clients and servers on different domains, both trusted and untrusted. As mentioned earlier, Kerberos supports the creation of forwardable tickets between *realms* (the Kerberos term) or *domains* (Windows terminology). Microsoft uses the term *referral tickets* instead of *forwardable tickets*, so we'll use that terminology for consistency here.

The easiest example is between trusted domains. Because the two domains are trusted, there will be an interdomain key based on the trust password. When both trusted domains have KDCs, the process for a client on one domain connecting with a server on another domain is as follows:

1. The client sends a message to its domain KDC requesting a session with a server on another domain. The KDC responds with a referral ticket for the server domain's KDC.

2. The client sends the referral ticket to the server domain KDC, encrypted with the interdomain password.

3. The server domain KDC verifies the ticket and returns a message with the server and client session tickets.

4. The server and client then communicate using the session tickets, crossing the domains.

If more than two domains are involved, such as when there's a trusted relationship with one domain that has a trust relationship with a third target domain (but which doesn't have a trust relationship with the client domain), all the domain KDCs can get involved with the referral tickets using the Windows 2000 transitive domain properties.

Windows Authentication

Microsoft supports a number of authentication methods in its Windows family of operating systems, as well as under the .NET Framework. First, we'll look at the methods that are available, and then we'll focus on SSPI, which allows access to the authentication systems available under Windows.

An Overview of Windows Authentication Methods

Most of the Windows authentication methods do not really affect network application developers, but they do factor into authenticating a user on the client launching a network application. The authentication methods include the following:

Winlogon and GINA: Winlogon, the operating system interactive logon system, is the authentication method most users are familiar with, requesting a user name and password prior to granting access to the operating system. The Winlogon service is composed of three parts: the Winlogon binary (executable), the GINA (Graphical Identification and Authentication) DLL, and zero or more network service providers. GINA is the component of the Winlogon system responsible for authentication. The default GINA DLL is called `MSGina.dll`, but it can be replaced by customized DLLs to change authentication options. GINA DLL code is available in the Platform SDK Security package, allowing additions to the authentication protocols supported by Winlogon.

Local Security Authority (LSA) authentication: The LSA package is a Windows subsystem that maintains information about all security on a system (called the Local Security Policy) as well as authenticating users logging on to the system. The LSA subsystem's functions can be used to create new GINA DLLs.

Credentials Management: The Credentials Management package provides an API that includes a Credentials Management User Interface, allowing management and receipt of usernames and passwords. This API is often used when a user's Winlogon permissions do not provide adequate permissions for an application, and an additional set of access information is requested through the application itself.

Network Provider: The Network Provider API is an operating system DLL that is a client of the WNet driver. The Network Provider API is used to allow interaction with other types of networks. The most common use is to communicate with Novell IPX/SPX networks. New network protocols can be added to a Windows system using the Network Provider API function list, creating a new API to support the new protocol. Authentication processes can be embedded in the new DLL.

Smartcard authentication: This type of authentication relies on the use of a plastic card with an embedded integrated circuit to manage physical access to a system. Obviously, card readers must be available to the operating system. These talk to the operating system through a set of DLLs (one per service card provider protocol). Some smartcard systems simply require the presence of the card to authenticate the user; others require an additional component such as a password (often dynamically generated).

Security Support Provider Interface (SSPI): The SSPI is an API that provides abstraction of authentication processes for applications. It allows access to the authentication systems available under Windows. The SSPI does not allow a new authentication system to be added, but it does provide access to existing authentication systems through a set of API functions.

The SSPI is the most versatile of the authentication systems available to developers. Because most developers who need to go beyond basic authentication tasks will most likely use the SSPI, we'll look at it in a little more detail.

Windows 2000 Security Support Provider Interface (SSPI)

The Windows 2000 SSPI is an abstraction layer that hides security implementation details from applications, services, and components. The SSPI and its security packages sit on top of the Win2000 kernel's Transport Device Interface (TDI). Within the standard installation of Windows 2000, there are four SSPI security packages: NTLMSSP, Kerberos version 5, SChannel, and Snego.

Developers can work directly with the SSPI to control security features (the SSPI is a plain-vanilla C DLL consisting of `sspi.h`, `security.dll`, and `secur32.dll`). Normally, though, developers do not use SSPI to implement security in applications, instead relying on the communication services that sit on top of SSPI (RPC, DCOM, WinSock version 2, and so on), all of which have their own security APIs. Through these communications APIs, developers can fully control the SSPI layer without writing SSPI calls directly, which is a much more convenient way to work.

However, you can work with the SSPI when necessary to allow client/server applications to use a security package feature (such as Kerberos authentication) without dealing with the underlying protocols themselves. In some cases, this will provide you with capabilities that are not part of the communication service interface itself.

The SSPI package includes three management functions:

- `EnumerateSecurity` lists all the available security packages.
- `InitSecurityInterface` returns a pointer to an SSPI dispatch table.
- `QuerySecurityPackageInfo` returns information from a particular package about its authentication method, transport, and message integrity capabilities.

When a client wants to establish a secure connection, it chooses a security package (Kerberos or NTLM in Windows 2000) and contacts the server. The server selects one of more security packages at its end and establishes the connection to the client.

In order to work with the SSPI in an application, five steps are followed:

1. Initialize the `SecBufferDesc` and `SecBuffer` structures to handle the data to be sent and received.
2. Initialize the SSPI session.
3. Create a connection using authentication.
4. Monitor the session's traffic for integrity.
5. Terminate the SSPI session.

The following sections look at each of these steps in more detail and provide an example of their use.

Initializing the SecBufferDesc and SecBuffer

The `SecBufferDesc` and `SecBuffer` structures are used to allow the application to deal with what could potentially be very large amounts of data to be sent and received.

- The `SecBuffer` structure is composed of three parts describing information sent of received: the size of the buffer in bytes (`SecBuffer.chBuffer`), an indication of the data type of information (`SecBuffer.BufferType`), and the information itself (`SecBuffer.pvBuffer`). The data types used in `SecBuffer` are listed in Table 13-1.
- The `SecBufferDesc` structure is an array of `SecBuffer` structures and contains a version number (`SecBufferDesc.ulVersion`), the number of `SecBuffer` elements in the array (`SecBufferDesc.cBuffers`), and the address of the array of `SecBuffer` (`SecBufferDesc.pBuffers`).

Table 13-1. *Data Types Used in SecBuffer*

Buffer Data Type	Description
SECBUFFER_DATA	Packet data
SECBUFFER_EMPTY	Undefined
SECBUFFER_EXTRA	Extra data
SECBUFFER_MISSING	Missing data type indicator
SECBUFFER_PKG_PARAMS	Package-specific parameters
SECBUFFER_STREAM	Security stream data
SECBUFFER_STREAM_HEADER	Security stream header
SECBUFFER_STREAM_TRAILER	Security stream trailer
SECBUFFER_TOKEN	Security token
SECBUFFER_ATTRMASK	Masks security attributes*
SECBUFFER_READONLY	Sets buffer to read-only*

**Additional data types that can be bitwise ORed with the preceding values.*

A SecBuffer element must be initialized prior to any calls to the SSPI interface, and normally you will set up both outgoing and incoming buffers. This code sits on a server and sets up three buffers for an incoming message's header, body, and trailer:

```
SecBuffer myBuffers[3];
SecBufferDesc myBufferDesc;
// Use variables for the message header, body, and tail
// called myHead, myBody, myTail
// passed as pointers and stored in strings (not shown)
myBufferDesc.ulVersion = SECBUFFER_VERSION;
myBufferDesc.cBuffers = 2;
myBufferDesc.pBuffers = myBuffers;
myBuffers[0].chBuffer = sizeof(myHead);
myBuffers[0].BufferType = SECBUFFER_DATA;
myBuffers[0].pvBuffer = myHead;
myBuffers[1].chBuffer = sizeof(myBody);
myBuffers[1].BufferType = SECBUFFER_DATA;
myBuffers[1].pvBuffer = myBody;
myBuffers[2].chBuffer = sizeof(myTail);
myBuffers[2].BufferType = SECBUFFER_DATA;
myBuffers[2].pvBuffer = myTail;
```

You could make the header and trailer of the message read-only by bitwise ORing the SECBUFFER_READONLY type:

```
myBuffers[0].BufferType = SECBUFFER_READONLY | SECBUFFER_DATA;
myBuffers[2].BufferType = SECBUFFER_READONLY | SECBUFFER_DATA;
```

The size of the buffer needed to hold data (such as a Kerberos token) must be established in order to prevent overflow.

Initializing the SSPI Session

After initializing the `SecBuffer` arrays, the SSPI interface is initialized with a call to `Init-SecurityInterface`, which returns a pointer to a dispatch table in `SecurityFunctionTable`. The dispatch table itself contains pointers to the callback functions in `Sspi.h`.

Creating a Connection Using Authentication

The third step in the process is to establish the connection using authentication. After the security package (Kerberos or NTLM) is chosen, a security context is created. The security context is an opaque data structure containing information about that connection, most important of which is the session key for encryption and timestamp information for maintaining the validity of the session. The security context is sent from the security package on the server. As you learned earlier in the chapter, the Kerberos session tickets are used in the security context, providing the session keys for the communications between the client and server.

Monitoring the Session's Traffic for Integrity

Maintaining integrity for the communications method is through the message support functions. SSPI messages use four message support functions:

- `DecryptMessage` decrypts a message using the session key.
- `EncryptMessage` encrypts a message using the session key.
- `MakeSignature` creates a secure signature using a message and security context.
- `VerifySignature` verifies a signature matches a received message.

With the buffers created for the SSPI, these functions are used to handle incoming and outgoing messages, encrypting and decrypting the contents, and creating and verifying the signatures for those messages. To send a message, the application passes the message and security context to the `MakeSignature` function. The receiver of the message uses the `Verify-Signature` function to validate the message.

Terminating the SSPI Session

Finally, terminating the SSPI closes the connection. This is done with a call (at both ends, usually) to `DeleteSecurityContext` within the security context (both Kerberos and NTLM). Both ends also have some bookkeeping to perform to free credentials and used memory.

Coding an SSPI Connection

Without delving into all the details of SSPI, we can look at both client and server ends of a sample connection. To simplify the example, only the necessary code is shown. Let's start with the client. We need to perform four tasks:

- Establish a Windows socket
- Establish an authenticated SSPI session
- Connect to the server and establish secure communications
- Send and receive secure messages from the server

We establish a Windows socket connection with the server and call the SSP authentication package:

```
WSADATA wsaData;
SOCKET myClient_Socket;
CredHandle myCred;
struct _SecHandle myCtxt;
if(WSAStartup (0x0101, &wsaData))
{
   handleError("Could not initialize the socket!");
}
if (!ConnectAuthSocket (&myClient_Socket, &myCred, &myCtxt))
{
   handleError("Authenticated server connection established!");
}
```

After a Windows socket has been established and authentication is successful, a message from the server can be handled. To do this, we need to determine the negotiated security package and the size of the signature sent from the server:

```
// These variables declared at the top of the application
#define SEC_SUCCESS(Status) ((Status) >= 0)
SecPkgContext_Sizes SecPkgContextSizes;
SecPkgContext_NegotiationInfo SecPkgNegInfo;
ULONG myMaxSignature;
ULONG mySecurityTrailer;
// Query the security package
sp = QueryContextAttributes(&myCtxt, SECPKG_ATTR_NEGOTIATION_INFO, &SecPkgNegInfo );
if (!SEC_SUCCESS(sp))
{
      handleError("QueryContextAttributes failed to initialize!");
}
else
{
     printf("Package Name: %s\n", SecPkgNegInfo.PackageInfo->Name);
}
```

```
sp = QueryContextAttributes(&myCtxt, SECPKG_ATTR_SIZES, &SecPkgContextSizes );
myMaxSignature = SecPkgContextSizes.myMaxSignature;
mySecurityTrailer = SecPkgContextSizes.mySecurityTrailer;
printf("InitializeSecurityContext result = 0x%08x\n", sp);
```

The message from the server can now be decrypted and displayed:

```
myMessage = (PCHAR) DecryptThis( Data, &myRead, &myCtxt, mySecurityTrailer);
printf ("The message is \n ->  %.*s \n", myRead, myMessage);
```

■NOTE A more complete example of server and client code for SSPI (including expansion of all the missing details from the code presented here) is available from the Microsoft MSDN site.

.NET Security

Microsoft considered security an essential component of the .NET Framework and included a complex security mechanism. For most applications, the security available in the .NET Framework is overkill; most developers will find the simpler embedded routines are all they really need.

The .NET Framework's security is composed of the following namespaces:

- The `System.Security` namespace contains the embedded security structure for .NET.
- The `System.Security.Cryptography` namespace includes three separate namespaces, providing cryptographic and authentication services.
- The `System.Security.Permissions` namespace includes classes to control access to resources.
- The `System.Security.Policy` namespace contains code groups and membership conditions used by the Common Language Runtime (CLR) to enforce security policy.
- The `System.Security.Principal` namespace includes classes representing a program's security context.

Of these namespaces, the four that are not part of `System.Security.Cryptography` are the most widely used by developers. Before we look at the use of the namespaces, though, we should see how the .NET security apparatus interacts with the Windows security features discussed earlier in this chapter.

The .NET Code Access Security Policy

When a .NET application tries to access a resource such as a file or directory, the CLR checks the security policy in place on the executing computer. Windows NT allows security policies to be implemented on a user-by-user basis (with each user's permissions and rights specified in detail as to allowed or disallowed actions) or on a machine-by-machine basis.

The .NET Framework uses a security policy called Code Access Security (CAS), which is a hierarchical extensible model, composed of *code groups*. Code groups can be set up by many criteria, such as site names, publisher names, developer names, network zone names, and so on. Each code group has a set of permissions associated with it. The allowable code group criteria are listed in Table 13-2.

Table 13-2. *.NET CAS Code Group Criteria*

Criteria	Description
Application directory	Home directory of the application
Cryptographic hash	Hash used in the encryption
Custom	Application-defined condition
File	File access
Net	Network identification for the application's home network
Software publisher	Publisher's Authenticode signature
Strong name	.NET strong name
URL	URL of the code
Web site	Website of the code
Zone	Zone of the code

.NET Resource Security

Microsoft designed the .NET Framework security to work with the existing security features of Microsoft's Windows operating systems, especially Windows 2000 and Windows NT. The CLR of .NET applications works with Windows NT's users and groups to provide controlled access to resources. Any applications written to .NET standards can specify the types of access they require, and then it is up to the operating system's security policy to decide whether to grant those permissions.

Code Access Permission Classes

For access to resources, the classes listed in Table 13-3 are involved. These classes are all derived from the `System.Security.CodeAccessPermission` base class, and they are usually called *code access permission classes.*

Table 13-3. *.NET Code Access Permission Classes*

Class	Description
`DirectoryServicesPermission`	Gives access to `System.DirectoryServices` classes
`DnsPermission`	Gives access to Domain Name System (DNS)
`EnvironmentPermission`	Gives access to environment variables
`EventLogPermission`	Gives access to the event log
`FileDialogPermission`	Gives access to files selected in the File Open dialog box
`FileIOPermission`	Gives access to files in read, write, and append modes

Class	Description
IsolatedStorageFilepermission	Gives access to virtual file systems
IsolatedStoragePermission	Gives access to storage allocated to specific users
MessageQueuePermission	Gives access to the Messaging Service
OleDbPermission	Gives access to databases using OLE DB
PerformanceCounterPermission	Gives access to performance counters
PrintingPermission	Gives access to printers
ReflectionPermission	Gives access to runtime type information
RegistryPermission	Gives access to the Registry
SecurityPermission	Gives access to execute code, and set permissions and rights
ServiceControllerPermission	Gives access to Windows services
SocketPermission	Gives access to sockets
SqlClientPermission	Gives access to SQL databases
UIPermission	Gives access to UI features (dialog boxes, the Clipboard, and so on)
WebPermission	Gives access to web connections

The `System.Security.CodeAccessPermission` base class also includes several methods that are used to implement security. These methods are listed in Table 13-4.

Table 13-4. *System.Security.CodeAccessPermission Class Methods*

Method	Description
Assert	Asserts that the code can access the resource
Copy	Creates a copy of the object
Demand	Determines whether all callers have been granted permission
Deny	Denies access to callers higher in the stack
FromXml	Reconstructs a permission object from XML code
Intersect	Creates a permission from the intersection of two other permission objects
IsSubsetOf	Determines whether one permission object is a subset of another object
PermitOnly	Restricts permissions to callers higher in the stack
RevertAll	Static, revokes all permission overrides
RevertAssert	Static, revokes each `Assert`
RevertDeny	Static, revokes each `Deny`
RevertPermitOnly	Static, revokes each `PermitOnly`
ToString	Converts the permission object to a string
ToXml	Converts the permission object to XML
Union	Creates a permission from the union of two other permission objects

The Assert, Demand, and Deny methods are used to implement runtime checking of permissions in code. To handle combinations of two permissions, you can use either the Intersect or Union methods. Here's a simple example of using these methods to allow access to the directory C:\Networking\Authentication\codetemp:

```
using System;
using System.Security;
using System.Security.Permissions;
public class FileIOPDemo
{
   public static void Main(String[] args)
   {
      FileIOPermission myPerm = new
                      FileIOPermission(FileIOPermissionAccess.AllAccess,
                           @"c:\Networking\Authentication\codetemp");
      SecurityElement mySec = myPerm.ToXml();
      Console.WriteLine(mySec.ToString());
   }
}
```

Note that you must specify an absolute path in the FileIOPermission constructor.

The FileIOPermission object is used to create an object with all access to the target directory, and the ToXml call is used to return the SecurityElement, which is converted to a string and written out to the console.

In your code, you can use the System.Security.CodeAccessPermission methods to request access to a resource. The following permissions are controlled by FileIOPermissionAccess:

- AllAccess allows full access to a file or directory.
- Append allows the append permission for a file or directory.
- NoAccess allows no access to a file or directory.
- PathDiscovery allows access to information about the path.
- Read allows read access to a file or directory.
- Write allows write access to a file or directory.

These permissions can be used as flags to a FileIOPermissionAccess variable. For example, you can write code to verify you have Read access to the file C:\Networking\Authentication\data.dat like this:

```
using System;
using System.Security;
using System.Security.Permissions;
public class FileIOPDemo2
{
   public static void Main(String[] args)
   {
      FileIOPermissionAccess myPermsAcc  = FileIOPermissionAccess.Read;
      FileIOPermission myPerm = new FileIOPermission(myPermsAcc,
                                @"c:\Networking\Authentication\data.dat ");
```

```
        try
        {
           myPerm.Demand();
        }
        catch (SecurityException)
        {
           Console.WriteLine("Sorry, no access.");
        }
    }
}
```

Code similar to this is used for the Deny and Assert methods. To deny access to a resource to prevent overwriting (or for some other reason), you can override default permissions, as in the following example, which prevents access to the file C:\Networking\Authentication\data.dat:

```
PermissionSet myPerm = new PermissionSet(PermissionState.None);
myPerm.AddPermission(new FileIOPermission(FileIOPermissionAccess.AllAccess,
                                @"c:\Networking\Authentication\data.dat ");
myPerm.Deny();
```

Deny prevents callers higher in the call stack from using the code that calls this method to access the resource specified by the current instance.

To remove the Deny permission, you can use the static RevertDeny method:

```
CodeAccessPermission.RevertDeny();
```

In your applications, you can use the System.Security.Permissions namespace with classes and objects from System.Net. For example, if you want to check access permissions to a file, the FileIOPermission class must be called for every access performed (not just the first one). Any failure of a call will result in a SecurityException being thrown.

Identity Permission Classes

A second set of classes derived from the System.Security.CodeAccessPermission base class is the *identity permission classes*. These classes involve characteristics of an application such as its digital signatures, storage location, and more. When executing, the CLR uses these characteristics to grant identity permissions. The classes involved in identity permissions are listed in Table 13-5.

Table 13-5. *.NET Identity Permission Classes*

Class	Description
PublisherIdentityPermission	Publisher's digital signature
SiteIdentityPermission	Site containing the application
StrongNameIdentityPermission	Strong name
URLIdentityPermission	Originating URL
ZoneIdentityPermission	Originating security zone

Normally, the application name, version number, and some additional information defining the local machine are enough to identify applications, but this can be insufficient for security purposes. The concept of a *strong name* was introduced to include all this basic information, as well as a public encryption key and a digital signature. Because the process of creating a strong key uses checksums, tampering with the contents of the application will be detectable. Also, the use of the private key ensures that masquerading as a particular machine is avoided.

.NET Role-Based Security

Role-based security determines whether a user executing a .NET application has a particular role and can also help determine the user's identity. All of .NET's role-based security is contained in the `PrincipalPermission` class. You can use this class by creating an object from the class and calling its `Demand` method. If users and roles don't match those contained in the object, a `SecurityException` is generated and the `Demand` method fails.

You can also perform declarative security checks by adding attributes that provide the uses and roles for the application. A failure to match the user executing the code will cause an application failure.

Client Authentication Handling

The `System.Net.IAuthenticationModule` is used to set the properties and methods for handling client authentication in .NET applications. It has two properties:

- The `System.Net.IAuthenticationModule.AuthenticationType` property is a case-insensitive string that indicates the protocol implemented by the module. These string values are reserved for use by modules implementing the indicated protocols: `Basic` for basic authentication (defined by IETF RFC 2617), `Digest` for digest authentication (defined by IETF RFC 2617), or `Kerberos` for Kerberos authentication (defined by IETF RFC 1510).

- The `IAuthenticationModule.CanPreAuthenticate` property indicates whether preauthentication is possible for the code.

The `System.Net.IAuthenticationModule` also has two methods:

- `IAuthenticationModule.Authenticate` returns an instance of the `Authorization` class that provides a response to an authentication challenge.

- `IAuthenticationModule.PreAuthenticate` returns an instance of the `Authorization` class containing client authentication information.

Anything that implements `System.Net.IAuthenticationModule` is called an authentication module. Each authentication module registered with the authentication manager is required to have a unique `System.Net.IAuthenticationModule.AuthenticationType`. An authentication module is registered with the authentication manager by calling the `System.Net.AuthenticationManager.Register` method, passing your authentication module. If the authentication manager receives an authentication request, registered authentication modules are given the opportunity to handle the authentication in their own `System.Net.IAuthenticationModule.Authenticate` method. The authentication manager searches for an authentication module by invoking the `System.Net.IAuthenticationModule.Authenticate` or `System.Net.IAuthenticationModule.PreAuthenticate` method of each registered module, in the order it was registered. Once a module returns an `Authorization` instance (which indicates it can handle the authentication) the authentication manager terminates the search.

If a client wishes to avoid waiting for the server to request authentication, it can request preauthentication information with a request using the `System.Net.IAuthenticationModule.CanPreAuthenticate` property of a registered module. If this module returns a value of `true`, the modules are given the opportunity to provide the preauthentication information.

Impersonation

One final aspect we should consider is impersonation (which is disabled by default). *Impersonation* is a useful trick when you don't want to code a lot of authentication code into a .NET application, simply letting Windows perform all the tasks for you. On the other hand, if you need to write a specific authentication table yourself, you do not need impersonation.

Impersonation is when a .NET application executes using the client's authenticated identity. Before you do a double-take and decide this is what normally happens, a quick explanation is useful. For example, when a user requesting an ASP.NET page is authenticated by IIS, IIS passes the local machine identity back to the application. In a normal configuration, the local machine identity has full access to all directories and files, leaving authorization for access to other mechanisms (such as URL authorization).

With impersonation turned on, the .NET application takes on the actual user's identity instead of the one passed back by IIS. For example, if the user `tparker` tries to access a resource, IIS will normally authenticate the user and pass back local machine as the identity to use in the .NET application. With impersonation turned on, the identity `tparker` is used instead. The advantage to this technique is that when impersonating a specific user, access control lists (ACLs) can be used to restrict access, which isn't possible with local machine, since it normally has full access.

Another way of thinking of impersonation is this: with impersonation turned off and a user properly authenticated by Internet Information Server (IIS), when a ASP.NET application tries to access a directory, Windows thinks that the local machine user is trying to access the directory and grants access on that basis. With impersonation turned on, the .NET application is treated as though it is the user, so Windows thinks the user is trying to access the resource, and the ACLs can be checked normally for permission.

■ **NOTE** The exception to using the impersonated identity is for configuration information. Even when impersonating a user, an application will use the local machine identity to read configuration files; otherwise, the application could lock up.

To turn on impersonation in ASP.NET, you add a new line to the `web.config` file using the `identity` tag:

```
<configuration>
    <system.web>
      <identity impersonate="true" />
    </system.web>
</configuration>
```

A slight twist is that you can tell ASP.NET applications to always use a specific user identity when impersonating. To do this, you need to specify the user name and password (used for authentication) on the `identity` line:

```
<configuration>
    <system.web>
      <identity impersonate="true" username="tparker" password="secret" />
    </system.web>
</configuration>
```

Why bother with impersonating a single user? The reason is simply because it can save a lot of time setting ACLs on a website for each user or group.

Summary

In this chapter, you've seen the way Windows can handle authentication of users, as well as authorization to access resources. We looked at Microsoft's LAN Manager, NTLM (Windows NT LAN Manager), and Kerberos. Each of these authentication methods can be used with .NET, although Kerberos is the preferable. We then looked at .NET resource and role-based security, and took a glimpse at several of the related modules.

The subject of authentication is a complex one. For more information, visit the Microsoft MSDN site, which has examples and explanations of these capabilities. Although they're sometimes difficult to piece together, you'll find all the components needed for .NET application coding with authentication.

Index

B

G

J

K

Q

R

U

V